A PRACTICAL TREATISE ON THE LAW, PRIVILEGES, PROCEEDINGS AND USAGE OF PARLIAMENT

A PRACTICAL TREATISE ON THE LAW, PRIVILEGES, PROCEEDINGS AND USAGE OF PARLIAMENT

Thomas Erskine May

www.General-Books.net

Publication Data:

Title: A Practical Treatise on the Law, Privileges, Proceedings and Usage of Parliament
Author: May, Thomas Erskine, 1815-1886
Publisher: London : Butterworths; [etc., etc.]
Publication date: 1851
Subjects: Great Britain. Parliament

1

A PRACTICAL TREATISE ON THE LAW, PRIVILEGES, PROCEEDINGS AND USAGE OF PARLIAMENT

THH HUillt Ifowrtrr nm!
    (H AK Li: S SH Li: i KVRK, p r I w I ii 111 11. I f.11 " N I u N S, itc. hm. im.
Tilt SBCOKD BDITION
THIS TBKATISK I WIT" Til) Mil. Ill-T Ulhl'lit
Tltr MTII'ilj I'luJ A(K TO Till. 1.(ONn rnitION
    Thk Second Eiiiticm of this Trmtise, though very cun ihtnhly t-iihirjird, is, in genfral design and oimnm'nmMit,)ntis4 ly thr snnif ils the first. For thr Inst scvfo ycnrs, tlic Work, as originally i)ul)-limh d, has Ihhmi tcsttil by c-onstnnt nfi'rence and practical use; and the prc cnl edition is the result of iu continual revision, during the whole of that)eriol. All rhnng of practice and new pn'cc-denth have been nott-d, from day to day, as they occum'il; and inf()rn ati)n has been sought, from all available sourcis, for the general improvement of the Work.

    Tlie alterations in the mole of conducting Private business have been so great, during the last few years, that the tliird book may be reganled as a new treatise upon that department of Parliamentar)' procedure, descriptive of the present practice, and embracing the most recent precedents.

    The Author has, agairij to acknowledge his deep obligations to Mr. Speaker, from whom he has derived invaluable information and assistance, which no one else could have afforded. He also desires to express his thanks to many Parliamentary and official friends, for their aid and suggestions; and he is only restrained by their number, from more particularly alluding to their kindness.

House of Commons, 29 March 1851.

PREFACE TO THE FIRST EDITION.

It is the object of the following pages to describe the various functions and proceedings of Parliament, in a form adapted, as well to purposes of reference, as to a methodical treatment of the subject. The well-known work of Ir. Hatsell abounds with Parliamentary learning, and, except where changes have arisen in the practice of later years, is deservedly regarded as an authority upon all the matters of which it treats. Other works have also appeared, upon particular branches of Parliamentary practice; or with an incidental rather than direct bearing upon all of them: but no general view of the proceedings of both Houses of Parliament, at the present time, has yet been published; and it is in the hope of supplying some part of this acknowledged deficiency, that the present Treatise has been written.

A theme so extensive has only been confined within the limits of a single volume, by excluding or rapidly passing over such points of constitutional law and history as are not essential to the explanation of proceedings in Parliament; and by preferring brief statements of the general result of precedents, to a lengthened enumeration of the precedents themselves. Copious references are given, throughout the work, to the Journals of both houses, and to Other original sources of information: but quotations have been restricted to resolutions and standing orders, to pointed authorities, and to precedents which serve to elucidate any principle or rule of practice better than a more general statement in the text.

The arrangement of the work has been designed with a view to advance from the more general to the particular and distinct proceedings of Parliament, to avoid repetition, and to prevent any confusion of separate classes of proceedings: and each subject has been treated, by itself, so as to present, first, the rules or principles; secondly, the authorities, if any be applicable; and, thirdly, the particular precedents in illustration of the practice.

As the last edition of Mr. Hatsell's work was published in 1818, the precedents of proceedings in the House of Commons have generally been selected from the Journals of the last five and twenty years, except where those of an earlier date were obviously more appropriate. But as the precedents of the House of Lords had not been collected in any previous work, no limitation has been observed in their selection.

It only remains to acknowledge the kind assistance which has been rendered by many gentlemen, who have communicated their knowledge of the practice of Parliament, in their several official de)artments, with the utmost courtesy: while the Author is under peculiar obligations to Mr. Speaker, with whose encouragement the work was undertaken, and by whose valuable suggestions it has been incalculably improved.

House of Coninions; May 2nd, 1844.

CHAPTER III.

Page. General view of the Privileges of Parliament: Power of commitment by both Houses for Breaches of Privilege. Causes of commitment cannot be inquired into by

Course of Proceedings in tlie Lords upon Private Bills sent up from tlie Commons. d?

CHAPTER XXVIII.

Page. Rules, orders, and course of proceedings in the Lords upon Private Bills brought into that House upon Petition; and proceedings of the Commons upon Private Bills brought from the Lords. Local and Personal, and Private Acts of Parliament 570

CHAPTER XXIX.

Fees payable by the parties promoting or opposing Private Bills. Taxation of costs of Parliamentary Agents, Solicitors, and others 582

APPENDIX 586 INDEX 590

ABBREVIATIONS

USED IN THE REFERENCES.

Rot. Pari. Rotuli Parliainentoruru, or Rolls of Parllaiueiit, printed by the House of Lords.

Lords' J. Lords' Journals.

Com. J. Commons' Journals.

Lords' S. O. No. 1, Sec. Lords' Standing Orders, as re-arranged and published in 1849. The references are to the new numbers.

Com. S. O. No. 1, c. Tlie Commons' published Standing Orders relating to Private Bills, 1850.

Hats. Hatsell's Precedents; edition of 1818.

Hans. Pari. Hist. Hansard's Parliamentary History.

Hans. Deb. Hansard's Parliamentary Debates. The references always distinguish the different series into which this voluminous work is dividod.

Pari. Rep. or Sess. Paper, 1849 (180), c.; refers to the Sessional Number by whicli any Parliamentary Report or Paper is distinguished.

The number preceding the reference invariably refers to the volume, and the figures which follow it denote the page, except where it is otherwise designated; as in the Standing Orders of the two Houses, which are distinguished by separate numbers.

All other works are either named at length, or the abbreviations are so partial, or so well understood, as to require no explanation.

MS. notes are occasionally given as an authority for statements in the text, where proceedings have not been otherwise rocorded.

ERRATA.

Page 131, line 16,(1784 rearf 1780. 146, 32, Soames Soanie. 168, n. 5, 1737 1707. 306, 8, 1851 1850.

383,71. 3, 1883 1833.

CONSTITUTION, POWERS, AND PRIVILEGES OF PARLIAMENT.

CHAPTER L

PRELIMINARY VIEW OF THE CONSTITUENT PARTS OF PARLIAMENT: THE CROWN, THE LORDS SPIRITUAL AND TEMPORAL, AND THE KNIGHTS, CITIZENS, AND BURGESSES; WITH INCIDENTAL REFERENCE TO THEIR ANCIENT HISTORY AND CONSTITUTION.

The present constitution of Parliament has been the introductory growth of many centuries. Its origin and early history, though obscured by the remoteness of the times and the imperfect records of a dark period in the annals of Eui'ope, have been traced back to the free councils of our Saxon ancestors. Tlie popular character of these institutions was subverted, for a time, by the Norman Conquest; but the people of England were still Saxons by birth, in language, and in spirit, and gradually recovered their ancient share in the councils of the state. Step by step the legislature has assumed its present form and character; and after many changes its constitution is now defined by

"The clear and written law, tlie deep-trod footmarks " Of ancient custom."

No historical inquiry has greater attractions than tliat which follows the progress of the British Constitution from the earliest times, and notes its successive changes and

Constituent parts of Parliament.

I. The King Queen.

development; but the immediate object of this work is to display Parliament in its present form, and to describe its various operations under existing laws and custom. For this purpose, the history of the past wdll often be adverted to; but more for the explanation of modern usage than on account of the interest of the inquiry itself. Apart from the immediate functions of Parliament, the general constitution of the British Government is not within the design of this Treatise; and however great the temptation may be to digress upon topics which are suggested by the proceedings of Parliament, such digressions will rarely be admitted. Within these bounds an outline of each of the constituent parts of Parliament, with incidental reference to their ancient history and constitution, will properly introduce the consideration of the various attributes and proceedings of the legislature.

The Imperial Parliament of the United Kingdom of Great Britain and Ireland, is composed of the King or Queen, and the three estates of the realm, viz. the Lords Spiritual, the Lords Temporal, and the Commons. These several powers collectively make laws that are binding upon the subjects of the British empire; and, as distinct members of the supreme legislature, enjoy privileges and exercise functions peculiar to each.

I. The Crown of these realms is hereditary, being subject, however, to special limitations by Parliament; and the kings or queens have ever enjoyed various prerogatives, by prescription, custom, and law, which assign to them the chief place in Parliament, and the sole executive power. But as the collective Parhament is the supreme legislature, the right of succession and the prerogatives of the Crown itself, are subject to limitations and change, by the consent and authority of the king or queen for the ' For statutory confirmation of the ancient right of females to inherit the Crown, see 1 Mar. St. 2, c. 1, and 1 Mar. St. 3, c. 1; 1 Eliz. c. 3.

time being, and the three estates of the reahn in Parha-ment assembled. To the changes that have been effected, at different times, in the legal succession to the Crown, it is needless to refer, as the Revolution of 1688 is a sufficient example. The power of Parliament over the Crown is distinctly affirmed by the statute law, and recognised as an important principle of the constitution.

AU the kings and queens since the Revolution have taken Coronatiou an oath at their coronation, by which they have " promised and sworn to govern the people of this kingdom, and the dominions thereto belonging, according to the statutes in Parliament agreed on, and the laws and customs of the same." The Act 12 13 William III. c. 2, affirms Limitations of " that the laws of England are the birthright of the people P'"' thereof; and all the kings and queens who shall ascend the throne of this realm ought to administer the government of the same according to the said laws; and all their officers and ministers ought to serve them respectively according to the same." And the statute 6 Anne, c. 7, declares it high treason for any one to maintain and affirm by writing, printing, or preaching, " that the kings or queens of this realm, by and with the authority of Parliament, are not able to make laws and statutes of sufficient force and validity to limit and bind the Crown, and the descent, limitation, inheritance, and government thereof."

Nor was this a modern principle of constitutional law established, for the first time, by the Revolution of 1688. If not admitted in its whole force, so far back as the great charter of King John, it has been affirmed by Parliament in very ancient times. In the 40th Edward III. the pope had demanded homage of that monarch for the kingdom of England and land of Ireland, and the arrears of 1,000 marks a year that had been granted by King John to 1 Will. Mary, c. 6.

Innocent III. and his successors. The king laid these demands before his Parliament, and it Is recorded that

"The prelates, dukes, counts, barons, and commons, thereupon, aftor full deliberation, answered and said with one accord, that neither the said King John, nor any other, could put himself or his kingdom, or people, in such subjection without their assent; and, as it appears by several evidences, that if this was done at all, it was done without their assent, and against his own oath on his coronation," they resolved to resist the demands of the pope with all their power."

From the words of this record it would appear, that whether the charter of King John submitted the royal prerogatives to Parliament or not, it was the opinion of the Parliament of Edward III., that even King John had been bound by the same laws which subsisted in their own time."

The same principle had been laid down by the most venerable authoritics-of the English law, before the limits of the constitution had become defined. Bracton, a judge in the reign of Henry III., declared that " the king must not be subject to any man; but to God and the law, because the law makes him king." At a later period the learned Fortescue, the lord chancellor of Henry VI., thus explained the king's prerogative to the king's son, whose banishment he shared: " A king of England cannot, at his pleasure, make any alterations in the laws of the land, for the nature of his government is not only regal but political." " He can neither make any alteration or change in the laws of the realm without the consent of the subject, nor burthen them, against their wills, with strange impositions."' Later still, during the reign of Elizabeth, who did not suffer the royal prerogative to be impaired in her 2 Rot. Pari. 290.

See also coronation oath of Edw. II. in 1307, Foedera, vol. ii. p. 36; Book of Oaths, 1689, p. 195.

Bracton, lib. 1, c. 8. De Landibus, Leg. Ang. c. 9.

time, Sir Tliomas Smyth affirmed that " the most high and absohite power of the reahn of England consisteth in the Parhament;"' and then proceeded to assign to the Crown, exactly the same place in Parliament as that acknowledged, by statute, since the Revolution.

Not to multiply authorities, enough has been said to prove that the Revolution defined, rather than limited, the constitutional prerogatives of the king, and that the Bill of Risrhts" was but a declaration of the ancient law of England.

An important principle of constitutional law was intro- profession of duced at the Revolution, by which the sovereign is bound uh! " "" ' to an adherence to the Protestant faith, and to the maintenance of the Protestant religion as established by law. He is required to swear, at his coronation, to maintain " the true profession of the Gospel, and the Protestant reformed religion established by law." By the Bill of Riglits, and the Act of Settlement,-' any person professing the popish religion, or who shall marry a papist, is incapable of inheriting or possessing the Crown, and the people are absolved from their allegiance. This exclusion is further confirmed by the second article of the Act of Union with Scotland f and, in addition to the coronation oath, every king or queen is required to make the declaration against the doctrines of the Roman Catholic Church prescribed by the 30th Charles II. st. 2, either on the throne in the House of Lords, in the presence of both Houses, at the first meeting of the ' Do rcpulilica Anglorum, book 2, c. 1, by Sir Thomas Smytli, kiit.

"Tlmt the pretended power of suspemling: or dispensing with laws, or the execution of laws, without consent of Parliament, is illegal." "That levying money for or to tlie use of the Crown, by pretence of prerogative, without grant of Parliament, for longer time or in other manner than the same is or shall be granted, is illegal." Ist, 2d, and 4th articles of the Bill of Rights.

' Coronation oath, 1 Will. Mary, sess. 1, c. 6.

1 Will. Mary, sess. 2, c. 2, s. 9. 12: 13 Will. III. c. 2, s. 2.

0 (3 Ann. c. 8.

Prerogatives in connexion with Parliament.

II. The House of Lords.

I. Lords spiritual.

first Parliament after the accession, or at the coronation, whichever shall first happen. By similar sanctions the sovereign is also bound to maintain the Protestant religion and Presbyterian church government in Scotland.

The prerogatives of the Crown, in connexion with the legislature, are of paramount importance and dignity. The le al existence of Parliament results from the exercise of royal prerogative. As the head of the church, the Crown virtually appoints all archbishops and bishops, who form one of the three estates of the realm, and, as "lords spiritual," hold the highest rank, after princes of the blood royal, in the House of Lords. All titles of honour are the gift of the Crown, and thus the " lords temporal" also, who form the remainder of the upper house, have been created by royal prerogative, and their number may be increased at pleasure. In early times the summons of peers to attend Parliament depended entirely on the royal will; but their hereditary titles have long since been held to confer a right to sit in Parliament. To a Queen's writ, also, even the House of Commons owe their election, as the representatives of the people.

To these fundamental powers are added others of scarcely less importance, which will be noticed in their proper place.

II. The Lords Spiritual and Temporal sit together and jointly constitute the House of Lords, which is the second branch of the legislature in rank and dignity. 1. The lords spiritual are the English archbishops and bishops of the United Church of England and Ireland, having seats in Parliament, and four representative bishops on the part of Ireland. Before the Conquest the lords spiritual held a prominent place in the great Saxon councils, which they retained in the councils of the Norman kings; but the rio-ht or tenure by which they have held a place in Parliament ' Actofunion,56Ann. c. 8, s. 2; 34 Ann. c. 7; Scotch Act, 5 Ann. c. 6 (for securing the Protestant religion and Preshyterian church government).

since the Conquest, has not been agreed upon by constitutional writers. In the Saxon times there is no doubt that they sat, as bishops, by virtue of their ecclesiastical office; but according to Solden, William the Conqueror, in the fourth year of his reign, first brought the bishops and abbots under the tenure by barony; and Blackstone, adopting the same view, states that " William the Conqueror thought proper to change the spiritual tenure of frank-almoign, or free alms, under which the bishops held their lands under the Saxon government, into the feudal or Norman tenure by barony; and in right of succession to those baronies, which were inalienable from their respective dignities, the bishops and abbots were allowed their seats in the House of Lords." Lord Hale was of opinion that the bishops sit by usage; and Mr. Hallam maintains that the bishops of William the Conqueror were entitled to sit in his councils by the general custom of Europe, which invited the superior ecclesiastics to such offices, and by the common law of England, which the Conquest did not overturn. It has also been suggested, that before the dissolution of the monasteries, the mitred abbots had a seat in Parliament solely by virtue of their tenures as barons; but tliat the bishops sat in a double capacity, as bishops and as barons." By the Constitutions of Clarendon, 10 Henry II., there is a legislative declaration that the bishops shall hold their lands as baronies, and attend the king's court; but it is quite clear that tlie bishops sat in Parliament in virtue of their episcopal dignities before they were thus brought under the tenure per baroniam. By subjecting their lands to the feudal services incident to the tenure j er baroniam, including the duty of attending the king's court when sum- '
Tit. of Hon. part 2, s. 20.

1 Coram, p. 156. = 2 Middle Ages, 138

Elsynge says, " ratione episcopalis dignitatis et tenurae." Htdy's Treatise on Convocations, p. 12G. See also Burn's Eccl. Law, 216 t s-'q.

moned, their prior right to sit as members of the legislature would not have been prejudiced, and if not, they would appear to have attended afterwards in both capacities. Their presence in Parliament, however, except during the Commonwealth, has been uninterrupted, and their right to sit there unquestioned; whatever nominal changes may-have been effected in the nature of their tenure.

There are two archbishops (of Canterbury and York) and twenty-four of the English bishops having seats in Parliament. By the Act 10 11 Vict. c. 108, it was enacted that the number of lords spiritual shall not be increased by the creation of the bishoprick of ISIanchester; and whenever there shall be a vacancy by the avoidance of any one of the sees of Canterbury, York, London, Durham or Winchester, or of any other see filled by the translation of a bishop already sitting, such vacancy shall be supplied by the issue of a writ of summons to the bishop elected to the same see; but if the vacancy be caused by the avoidance of any other see, such vacancy shall be supplied by the issue of a writ of summons to that bishop who shall not have previously become entitled to such writ; and no bishop elected to any see, not being one of the five sees above-named, shall be entitled to a writ of summons, unless in the order, and according to the conditions above prescribed. To the estate of lords spiritual were added four bishops on the part of Ireland, on the union of that country with Great Britain, who sit by rotation of sessions, and represent the whole episcopal body of Ireland in Parliament. Of these four lords spiritual, an archbishop of the Church in Ireland is always one.

' They were excluded by Act 16 Car. I. c. 27, and did not resume their seats, after the Restoration, in the Convention Parliament, but were restored in the next Parliament by statute 13 Car, II. c 2.

The Bishop of Sodor and Man has no seat in Parliament. The present bishop, Lord Auckland, sits as a peer amongst the barons.

' ag 40 Geo. III. c. 67 (Act of Union, art. 4); 40 Geo. III. (Irish) c. 29; 3 4 Will. 4, c. 37, s. 51, 52.

2. Tlie lords temporal are divided into dukes, mar- 2. Lords tom-quesses, earls, viscounts, and barons, whose titles are of ' ' different degrees of antiquity and honour. The title of duke, though first in rank, is by no means the most ancient Dukes. in this country. It was a feudal title of high dignity in all parts of Europe, in very early times, and among the Saxons, duces (or leaders) are frequently mentioned; but the title was first conferred after the Conquest by Edward 111., upon his son Edward the Black Prince, whom he created Duke of Cornwall." Before that time the title had often been used as synonymous with that of comes and eal-dormanp'

Marquesses were originally lords of the marches or bor- Marquesses, ders, and derived their title from the offices held by them. In the German empire, the counts or graves of those provinces which were on the frontiers had the titles of mar-chio and marggravms in Latin; of marhjraf in German, and marchese in Italian. In England similar offices and titles were anciently enjoyed without being attached to any distinct dignity in the peerage. The noblemen who governed the provinces on the borders of Wales and Scotland were called marchioncs, and claimed certain privileges by virtue of their office; but the earliest creation of marquess as a title of honour, was in the ninth year of Kichard II. Robert de Yere, Earl of Oxford, was then created larqucss of Dublin, for life, and the rank assigned to him in Parliament by right of this new dignity, was immediately after the dukes, and before the earls." In the same reign John, Earl of Somerset, was created far-quess of Dorset, but was deprived of the title by Henry IV. In the fourth year of the latter reign the Parliament prayed the king to restore this dignity, but the Earl begged to ' Seld. Tit. of lion, part t, s. 0. 29, c.

See a compurison of tlusi- titles, Kemble, Saxons, ii. p. 127, nutvs.

3 Sckl. Tit. of Hon. part 2, s. 47.

decline its acceptance, because the name was so strange in this kingdom.

Earl3. The title of Earl in England is equivalent to that of the

Koman comes or count in other countries of Europe. Amongst the Saxons there were ealdormen, to whom the civil, military, and judicial administration of shires was committed, but whose titles were official and not hereditary," although the office was frequently held by the heads of the same family in succession. That title was often used by writers indifferently with comes, on account of the similarity of character and dignity denoted by those names. A 'heu the Danes had gained ascendancy in England, the ancient Danish title of eorle, wdiich signified " noble by birth," and was also used to indicate a similar dignity, was gradually substituted for that of ealdorman. At the Norman Conquest the title of eorle or earl was in universal use, and was so high a dignity that in the earliest charters of William the Conqueror he styles himself in Latin, "Princeps Norman-norum," and in Saxon, Eorle or Earl of Normandy,"' After the Conquest the Norman name of count distinguished the noblemen who enjoyed this dignity; from whence the shires committed to their charge have ever since been called counties. ' In the course of time the original title of earl was revived, but their wives and peeresses of that rank in their own right, have always retained the French or Norman name of countesses.

Viscounts. Between the dignities of earl and baron no rank Inter- vened, in England, until the reign of Henry VI.; but in France the title of viscount, as subordinate to that of 3 Rot. Pari. 488.

West, Inquiry into the Manner of creating Peers, 3,4. Spelman, on Feuds and Tenures, p, 13. Rep. on Dignity of the Peerage, 1820, p. 17. Kemblc, Saxons, ii. p. 131-150.

3 Palgrave, Kngl. Com. 592 et seq.

Palgrave Engl. Com. 11. 118. 326, 327. Kcniblo, Saxons in England, ii. 132. Sec also 2 Ilallam, Middle Ages, p. 65, 9th edit.

Scld. Tit. Iloii. part 2, s. 2. 3 Rep. on Dignity of the Peerage, 8(5.

count, was very ancient. The great counts of that kingdom holding large territories in feudal sovereignty, appointed governors of parts of their possessions, who were called viscounts, or vicecomites. Tliese, either by feudal gift, or by usurpation, often obtained an inheritance in the districts confided to them, and transmitted the lands and dignity to their posterity. In England, the title of viscount was first conferred upon John Beaumont, Viscount Beaumont, by Henry VI., in the eighteenth year of his reign; and a place was assigned to him in Parliament, the council, and other assemblies, above all the barons. The French origin of tiiis dignity was exemplified immediately afterwards by the grant of the viscounty of Beamount, in France, to the same person, by King Henry, who then styled himself king of France and England. The rank and precedence of a viscount were more distinctly defined by patent, in the 23d of Henry VI., to be above the heirs and sons of earls, and immediately after the earls themselves.

Barons are often mentioned in the councils of the Saxon Barons. kings, and in the laws of Edward the Confessor were classed with the archbishops, bishops, and earls; but the name bore different significations, and no distinct dignity was annexed to it, as in later times. After the Conquest every dignity was attached to the possession of lands, which were held immediately of the king, subject to feudal services. The lands which were granted by William the Conqueror to his followers descended to their posterity, and those who held lands of the Crown per baroniavi, were ennobled by the dignity of baron. By the feudal system, every tenant was bound to attend the court of his immediate 8ui)erior, and hence the barons, being also tenants in capite of the king, were entitled to attend the king's court or council; but, although their obligation to attend the king's council was one of the services incident to their

SeklTil. oi" Hon. iiirt 2, s. H). " f cm. Tit. ol" Hon. i): irt 2, s. 30.

tenure, they received writs of summons from the king, when their attendance was required. At length, when the lands became subdivided, and the tenants per haroniam were consequently more numerous and poor, some of them only were summoned by writ, and thus they were gradually separated into greater and lesser barons; of whom the former continued to receive particular writs of summons from the king, and the latter a general summons only throudi the sheriffs. The feudal tenure of the baronies afterwards became unnecessary to create the dignity of a baron, and the king's writ or patent, and occasionally an Act of Parliament, or creation " in plcno Parliamento," conferred the dignity and the seat in Parliament. The condition of the lesser barons, after their sejjaration from their more powerful brethren, will be presently explained. Representative On the union of Scotland, in 1707, the Scottish peers peers of Scot- admitted, as a class, to seats in the British Parliament; but, in pursuance of the provisions of several statutes, they elect, for each Parliament, sixteen representatives from their own body. The representative peers of Scotland enjoy all the privileges of Parliament, including the right of sitting upon the trials of peers; and all peers of Scotland are peers of Great Britain, and have rank and precedency immediately after the peers of the like orders and degrees in Enoland, at the time of the union, and before all peers of Great Britain of the like orders and degrees, created since the union, and are to be tried as peers, and enjoy all privileges as peers, except the right of sitting in Parliament, or upon the trials of peers. The Scottish peerage consists exclusively of the descendants of peer's before the union, as no provision was made for any subsequent creation of Scot- 3 Selclen's Works, 713-743. West, Inquiry into tlie Manner of creating Peers, G. 14. 30,31. 38. 70, 71. 3 Rep. Dign. of Peerage, 97, c. 2 Ilallam, Middle Ages, 2G1.

Act of Union, 5 G Ann. c. 8, art. xxii. xxiii. Act of the Parliament of Scotland, 5 Ann. c. 8. G. nn. c. 23. 10: 11 Vict. c. 62.

Act of Union.

land.

tish peers by the Crown. An authentic list of the peerage was entered in the roll of peers, by order of the House of Lords, on the 12th February 1708, to which other peerages have since been added by order of that House, when claims have been established; and in order to prevent the assumption of dormant and extinct peerages, it is provided by 10 11 Victoria, c. 52, that no title standing in that roll, in right of which no vote has been given since 1800, shall be called over at an election, without an order of the House of Lords. The House of Lords, when they have disallowed any claim, may also order that such title shall not be called over at any future election. A Scotch representative peer on being created a peer of Great Britain ceases to be one of the representatives of the peerage of Scotland.

Under the Act for the legislative union with Leland, And Ireland, which came into operation in 1801, the Lish peers elect twenty-eight representatives for life from the peerage of Ireland. By that Act the power of the Queen to add to the number of Irish peers is subject to limitation. She may make promotions in the peerage at all times; but she can only create a new Irish peer as often as three of the peerages of Ireland, which were in existence at the time of the union, have become extinct. But if it should hai)pen that the number of Irish peers exclusive of those holding any peerage of the L nited Kingdom, which entitles them to an hereditary seat in the House of Lords should be reduced to one hundred; then one new Irish peerage may be created as often as one of such hundred peerages becomes extinct, or as often as an Irish peer becomes entitled, by descent or creation, to an hereditary seat in the Imperial Parliament. The object of tliat article of union was to keep up the Irish peerage to the number ' Cases of the Duke of Queoiisherry and the Marquis of Abercorn,.37 Lords' J. 59-4 b. 26 Pari. Hist. 585. 505.

39 40 Geo. IH. c. 07; 40 Gen. HI. c. 38, I.

of one hundred, exelusive of Irish peers who may be entitled by descent or creation to an hereditary seat in the House of Lords of the United Kingdom. The representative peers of Ireland are entitled to the privileges of Lords of Parliament, and all the peers of Ireland have privilege of peerage. They may be elected as members of the House of Commons for any place in Great Britain, but while sitting there they do not enjoy the privilege of peerage." These, then, are the component parts of the House of Lords, of whom all peers and lords of Parliament, whatever may be their title, have equal voice in Parliament. By a standing Order of the House of Lords, no peer is permitted to sit in the House until he is twenty-one years of age; and by the Act of union the representative peers of Scotland are required to be of full age. Lords spiritual The two cstatcs of lords spiritual and lords temporal, form one botly. thus constituted, may originally have had an equal voice in all matters deliberated upon, and had separate places for their discussion; but at a very early period they are found to constitute one assembly; and, for many centuries past, though retaining their distinct character and denominations, they have been, practically, but one estate of the realnf. Thus the Act of Uniformity, 1st Elizabeth, c. 2, was passed by the queen, the lords temporal, and the commons, althougli the whole estate of the lords spiritual dissented. The lords temporal are the hereditary peers of the realm, whose blood is ennobled, and whose dignities can only be lost by attainder, or taken away by Act of Parliament; but the bishops, not being ennobled in blood.

' See Coates v. Lord Hawarden, 7 Barn. Cr. 388.

' Fourth art. of Union.

3 Lords' S. O. No. 54. 5 Ann. c. 8. art. xxv. s. 12.

"12 Rep. 107. 12 Mod. 56. 3 Rep. Dig. Peerage, 93. In 1679, during the debates concerning Lord Danby's plea of a Royal pardon, in bar of his impeacliment, an accoramodatioq was proposed by the Court, to avoid his attainder, that he should be banished and degraded from his peerage by Act of Parliament. 2 Burnet's Own Times, 202.

are lords of Parliament only, and not peers." This dis-tinction liaving been expressly declared by the House of Lords, in 1692, must be held conclusive of the fact that bishops are not peers, although in more ancient times such a distinction appears to have been unknown. The votes of the spiritual and temporal lords are intermixed, and the joint majority of the members of both estates determine every question; but they sit apart, on separate benches, the place assigned to the lords spiritual being tlie upper part of the house, on the right hand of the throne.

The House of Lords, in the aggregate, is now composed of 455 members, who are distributed in their different classes in the following manner:

Lords Spiritual: 2 Archbishops (Canterbury and York), 24 English bishops.

4 Irish representative bishops.

Lords Temporal: 3 Dukes of the blood roj'al.

20 Dukes.

21 Marquesses. 116 Earls.

22 Viscounts. 199 Barons.

16 Representative)eers of Scotland. 28 Representative peers of Ireland.

Total 455.

in. The last estate is that of the Commons of the in. Tiie Com-realm, represented in Parliament by the knights, citizens, " " and burgesses. The date of their admission to a) iice in the legislature has been a subject of controversy among historians and constitutional writers; of whom some have ' See Lords' S. O. No. 79. " It would be resolved what privilege noblemen and peers have, betwi. xt which this difference is to be observed, tliut bishops are only lords of Parliament, hut not peers, for thpy arc not of tryal by floblilty."

Saxon Institutions.

Shire-gemot.

Witena-Kemot.

traced their claims up to tlie Saxon period, while others deny them any share In tlie government until long after the Conquest. Without entering minutely upon a subject, which, although of the deepest interest, is no longer of constitutional import, a brief statement will serve to unfold the ancient character of the House of Commons, and to render its present constitution the more intelligible.

It is agreed by many writers of learning and autliorlty, that the commons formed part of the great synods or councus before the Conquest; but how they were summoned or selected, and wliat degree of power they possessed, is a matter of doubt and obscurity. Under the Saxon kin s all the forms of local Gjovernment were un-doubtedly popular. The shire-gemot was a kind of county Parliament, over which the ealdorman, or earl of the shire, presided, with the bishop, the shire-gerlcve, or sheriff, and the assessors appointed to assist their deliberations upon points of law. A shire-gemot was held at least twice a year in every county, when the magistrates, thanes, and abbots, wuth all the clergy and landholders, were required to be present; and a variety of business was transacted; but the proceedings of these assemblies generally partook more of the character of a court of justice than of a legislative body.

That the constitution of the witena-gemot, or national council, was equally popular, cannot be affirmed with any confidence. Although the smaller proprietors of land may not have been actually disqualified by law from taking part in the proceedings; yet the distance of the council from their homes, and the absence of sufficient means or inducement to undertake a difficult and dangerous journey, must practically have prevented them from attending. It has been conjectured that they were represented by their titliing men, and the inhabitants of towns by their chief magistrates; but notwithstanding the learning and ingenuity which have been devoted to the inquiry, no system of election or political representation, projjerly so called, can be distinctly traced back to that time.

The clergy may have been virtually represented by the bishops and abbots, and the absent laity of each shire by the ealdorman, the sheriff!, and such of the rich proprietors of land as may have been able to attend the gemot. The people may thus have been held to be present at the making of laws, and their name accordingly introduced into the records. That they were actually present on some occasions, is certain; but that they had any right to attend, either by themselves or by elected representatives, may indeed be fairly conjectured, but has not yet been historically proved."

But whatever may have been the position of the people The Conquest. in the Saxon government, the Conquest, and the strictly feudal character of the Norman institutions, must have brought them completely under the subjection of their feudal superiors. From the haughty character of the Norman barons, and the helpless condition of a conquered people, it is probable that the commonalty, as a class, were not admitted to any share in the national councils until some time after the Conquest, but were bound by the acts of their feudal lords; and that the Norman councils were formed of the spiritual lords, and mainly, if not exclusively, of the tenants in chief of the Crown, who held by military service.

This inference is confirmed by the peculiar character of feudal institutions, which made the revenue of the early Norman kings independent of the people. As feudal superiors they were entitled to receive various services, fines, ' Kemble, Saxons in England, ii. 193 201.

See Sir F. Palgrave's Englisli Comnionwealtli, 314. G31. G34-G58, and Proofs, pp. ccxxix. ccclxxxv. Turner, Hist, of the Anglo-Saxons, vol. iii. p. 180. 184. Thorpe'. s Leg. Sax. i, 358. Chron. Sax. An. 1020, Preface to Lord Lyttleton's History. Ingulfus, p. 8G3.

1 Rep. Dignity of Peeriigo, 34.

and pecuniary aids from their tenants, who held under them all the lands in the kingdom. These sources of revenue were augmented by pecuniary commutations of feudal services, and by customs levied upon corporate towns, in return for commercial privileges, which were, from time to time, conceded to them. Wars were the principal causes of expense, when it was natural for kings to seek the advice of the chief barons, upon whose military services they depended. Nor had they any interest in consulting the people, from whom they had no taxes to demand, and whose personal services in war were already due to their feudal lords. In the absence of any distinct evidence, it is not, therefore, probable that the Norman kings should have summoned representatives of the people until these sources of revenue had failed, and the commonalty had become more wealthy. Knigiits of the Consistently with the feudal character of the Norman councils, the first knights of the shire are supposed to have been the lesser barons, who, though still summoned to Parliament, gradually forbore to attend, and selected some of the richest and most influential of their body to represent them. The words of the charter of King John favour this position; for it is there promised that the greater barons shall be summoned personally by letters from the king, and all other tenants in chief under the Crown, by the sheriff and bailiffs. The summons to the lesser barons being thus only general, no peculiar obligation of personal attendance was imposed; and, as their numbers increased, and their wealth was subdivided, they were naturally reluctant to incur the charge of distant journeys, and the mortification of being held in slight esteem by the o-reater barons. Tliis position receives confirmation from the ancient law of Scotland, in which the small barons and ' 1427, c. 102.

free tenants were classed together, and jointly required to send representatives. To the tenants in chief by knight's Citizens and service were added, from time to time, the representatives"

of the richer cities and boroughs; and this addition to the legislature may be regarded as the origin of the commons, as a distinct estate of the realm in Parliament.

It is not known at what time these important changes in the constitution of Parliament occurred, for no mention is made of the commons in any of the early records after the Conquest. William the Conqueror, in the fourth year of his reign, summoned, by the advice of his barons, a council of noble and wise men, learned in the law of England, and twelve were returned out of every county to show what the customs of the kingdom were;' but this assembly, although, in the opinion of Lord Hale, it was " as sufficient and effectual a Parliament as ever was held in England," bore little resemblance to a legal summons of the commonalty, as an estate of the realm.

After this period the laws and charters of "William and his immediate successoi's, constantly mention councils of bishops, abbots, barons, and the chief persons of the kingdom, but are silent as to the commons. But in the 22d year of Henry II. (a. d. 1176), Benedict Abbas relates, that about the feast of St. Paul, the king came to Northampton, and there held a great council concerning the statutes of his realm, in the presence of the bishops, earls, and barons of his dominions, and with the advice of his knights and men. This is the first chronicle which appears to include the commons in the national councils; but it would be too vague to elucidate the inquiry, even if its authority were of a higher order. And again, in the lotli of King John (a. d. 1213), a writ was directed to the sheriff of each county, " to send ibur discreet knights to ' 1 Hovelen, 34a. ' 1 Hale, Hist, of the rommoii Law, 20-2.

' See 2 Ilalliun, Mitl. Ages, 14(5.

confer with us concerning the affairs of our kingdom;" but it does not appear whether they were elected by the county, or picked, at pleasure, by the sheriff Magna Charta Two years afterwards, the great charter of King John of King John, g j j g Constitution of Parliament more clearly than any earlier record; but even there the origin of the representative system is left in obscurity. It reserves to the city of London, and to all other cities, boroughs, and towns, and to the cinque ports and other ports, all their ancient liberties and free customs. But whether the summons to Parliament which is there promised was then first instituted, or whether it was an ancient privilege confirmed and guaranteed for the future, the words of the charter do not sufficiently explain. From this time, however, may be clearly traced the existence of a Parliament similar to that which has continued to our own days.

"The main constitution of Parliament, as it now stands," saj s Blackstone, " was marked out so long ago as the seventeenth year of King John, a. d. 1215, in the great charter granted by that prince, wherein he promises to summon all archbishops,

bishops, abbots, earls, and greater barons personally, and all other tenants in chief under the Crown by the sheriff and bailiffs, to meet at a certain place, with forty days' notice, to assess aids and scutages when necessary."

Notwithstanding the distinctness of this promise, the charters of Henry III. omitted the engagement to summon the tenants in chief by the sheriff and bailiffs; and it is doubtful whether they were summoned or not, in the early part of that reign. But a writ of the 38th year (a. d. 1254) is extant, which involves the principle of representation more distinctly than any previous writ or charter. It requires the sheriff of each county " to cause to come before the king's council two good and discreet knights of his county, whom the men of the county shall have chosen for this purposey ' 2 Prynne's Register, IG. See also Palgrave's English Commonwealth, chap. IX.

in the stead of all and each of thcin, to CDn 'uk'r, akuig with the knights of other counties, what aid they will grant the king." This, however, was for a particular occasion only; and to appear before the council is not to vote aa an estate of the realm. loreovei, the practice of sununoning citizens and others before the council, for particular purposes, continued lonjr after the regular summons of members to Parliament from cities and boroughs had commenced."' Nevertheless, representation of some kind then existed, and it is interesting to observe how early the people had u share in jrranting subsidies. Another writ, in 1261, directs the sheriffs to cause knights to repair, from each county, to the king at Windsor. At length, In the 49tli Henry III. (a. D. 12G5), writs were issued to the sheriffs by. Simon de lontfort. Earl of Leicester, directing them to return two knights for each county, and two citizens or bui esses for every city and borough; and from this time may be clearly dated the recognition of the commons, as an estate of the realm in Parliament. It is true that they were not afterwards summoned without intcnnission; but there is evidence to prove that they were repeatedly assembled by Edward L, especially in the Utii, the 21st, 22d and 2; Jd years of his reign."' Passing over less prominent records of tlic participation of the commons in the government, the statute of the 2.3th Edward I., "Dc tallagio non concc-dcndo,"' must not be overlooked. It was there declared that "No tallage or aid slinll be taken or levied by us or our heirs in our realm, witliout the good will and assent of the arehbisliops, bishops, earls, barons, knights, burgesses, and otiicr freemen of the land."

' 2 Prynno's Ropistor, 23.

' For instances in tlic ui n f Edward III. and Richard II., see Hc). Dig. Peerage, A pp. I 4ii. 4o7, 408. 409. 47 I. 741. ' 2 Prynne's Register, 27.

. See Lord Lyttleton's Hist. II. 270. iv. 70, et acq.

See Table of Writs, Hep. Dig. Pecnige, 48'.). Rulhiead, Prcf. tostutuleii. The writ of the 22d Edw. I. is f. r knights only.

This statute acknowledo; es the rio-ht of the commons to tax themselves; and a few years later a general power of legislation was also recognised as inherent in them. A statute was passed in the 15th Edward II. (1322), which declares that

"The matters to be established for tbe estate of the king and of liis heirs, and for the estate of the realm and of the people, should be treated, accorded, and established in Parliament, by the king and by the assent of the prelates, earls, and barons, and the commonalty of the realm, according as had been before accustomed"

In reference to this statute Mr. Hallam justly observes, " that it not only establishes by a legislative declaration the present constitution of Parliament; but recognises it as already standing upon a custom of some length of time." It may be added, in conclusion, that during the reign of Edward III. the commons Avere regularly mentioned in the enacting part of the statutes, having been rarely mentioned there in previous reigns." Lords and Com- So far the Constituent parts of Parliament may be traced; mons originally iii n I'-n i- sat in one 3- 0 the three estates oi the realm originally sat together in chamber. chamber. When the lesser barons began to secede from personal attendance, as a body, and to send representatives, they continued to sit with the greater barons as before: but when they were joined by the citizens and burgesses, who, by reason of their order, had no claim to sit with the barons, it is natural that they should have consulted with the other representatives, although they continued to sit in the same chamber as the lords. The ancient treatise, "De modo tenendi Parliamentum," if of unquestioned authority, would be conclusive of the fact that the three estates ordinarily sat together; but that ' 1 Const. Hist. 4 n. 2 Hallam, Midd. Age?, 1 0. Hakew. 101. Cotton's Abridgment, Pref.

when any dituoiilt ami doulitliil case of ponce or war an M', each estate sat separately, by direction df the kin;. lint this work can claim no hi- her anti(juity than the rei n of Klehard II., and its authority is only useful so iiir as it may bo evidence of tradition, believed and relied on at that period. Misled by its supposed authenticity, Sir Edward Coke and Klsynge entertained no doubt of the fact as there stated; and the Ibnner alleged that he had seen a record of the 30th Henry I. (1130), of the degrees and seats of the lords and commons as one body; and that the separation took place at the desire of the commons."

The union of the two Houses is sometimes deduced from the supposed absence of a speaker of the commons in early times; but Sir Edward Coke is in error when he infers that the commons had no speaker so late as the 2Sth of Edward I. f for in the 44th of Henry HI., Peter dc lont-fort signed and sealed an answer of the l rllament to Pope Alexander, after the lords, " vice totius conimunitatis."' Nor can any decided opinion be formed from the fact of speakers of the connnons not having been mentioned in earlier times; for if they consulted apart from the lords, a speaker would have been as necessary to preside over their deliberations, as when a more complete separation ensued. The first speaker of the commons to whom that title waa expressly given was Sir T. Ilungcrford, in the 5let Edward HI.

It appears from several entries in the rolls of Parliament in the early i)art of the reign of Edwartl 111., that after the cause of summons had been declared by the king to the three estates collectively, the prelates with the clergy consulted by themselves; the carls and barons by themselves; and the commons, and sometimes even the citizens ' 13 Iloweirs St. Trials, 1130. ' 4tli Inst. 2.

' EUyngp, 1: j5. Ilakew."2U0.

-' lla. I'arl. 374. 2 llut. Vrcc. 212 n. 2 llullum. Middle Ago. U!

and burgesses, by themselves; and that they all delivered their joint answer to the king.

The inquiry, however, is of little moment, for whether the commons sat with the lords in a distinct part of the same chamber, or in separate houses as at present, it can scarcely be contended that, at any time after the admission of the citizens and burgesses, the commons intemiixed with tlie lords, in their votes, as one assembly. Their chief business was the voting of subsidies, and the bishops granted one subsidy, the lords temporal another, and the commons again, a separate subsidy for themselves. The commons could not have had a voice in the grants of the other estates; and although the authority of their name was used in the sanction of Acts of Parliament, they ordinarily appeared as petitioners. In that character it is not conceivable that they could have voted with the lords; and it is well known that down to the reign of Henry VI., no laws were actually written and enacted until the end of the Parliament. When scpa Various dates have been assigned for the formal separa- tion of the two houses, some as early as the 49th Henry III., and others so late as the 17th Edward III.; but as it is admitted that they often sat apart for deliberation, particular instances in which they met in different places, will not determine whether their separation, at those times, was temporary or permanent. When the commons deliberated apart, they sat in the chapter-house of the abbot of West- ' 111 the 4G Edw. IT I., after the Parliament had granted supplies, and the petitions of the commons had been read and answered, the knights of the shire had leave to depart, and writs for their wages and expenses were made out for them by the chancellor's order; but he commanded the citizens and burgesses to stay, who being again assembled before the prince, prelates, and lords, granted for the safe conveying their ships and goods 2 s. on every tun of wine imported or exported out of the kingdom, and 6d. in the pound on all their goods and merchandise for one year. 2 Rot. Pari. 310.

2 Rot. Pari. 5 6 Edw. III. 4 lust. 2. Elsynge, 102.

"Per Lord Ellenborough, in Burdettr. Abbot, 2 Carte's Hist. 451.

minster, and they continued their sittings in that phicc, after their final separation."

Whenever this separation may have been effected, it riicir pmnicuj produced but little practical change in the uninterrupted "",", j" " '" ' custom of Piu-liament. The causes of summons are still declared by the Cro 'n to the lords and commons assembled in one house; the two houses deliberate in separate chambers, but under one roof; they conununicatc with each other by message and conference; they agree in resolutions and in making laws, and their joint determination is submitted for the sanction of the Crown. They are separated, indeed, but in legislation they are practically one assembly, as much as if they sat in one chamber, and in the presence of each other, communicated their separate votes.

The number of members admitted to the House of Number of the Commons has varied considerably at different periods. In jitferent times, addition to those boroughs which appear from the first to have returned burgesses to Parliament, many others had that privilege conferred upon them by charter, or by statute in succeeding reigns; while some were omitted by the negligence or coituption of sheriffs, and others were discharged from what they considered a heavy burthen, the expense of maintaining their members. In the time of Edward III. 4 s. a day were allowed to a knight of the Wages of mem-shire, and 2 s. to a citizen or burgess;" and this charge was, "' in the case of poor and small communities, too gi'cat an evil to be compensated by the possible benefit of representation. In the reign of Henry VI., there were not more than.300 members of the House of Commons, being about 2o more than in the reign of Edward I, and 50 more than in the reign of Edward III. The legislature added 27 for AVales and four for the county and city of Chester, in the reign of ' Elsynge, 104. 1 Purl. Hist. ill. 2 Hot. Pari. '289. 3ol.

' 4 Inst. IG. Prynne'8 4tb Register, p. u3. 41 o.

'-27 Hon. VIII. c. 2G. 34 IIcii. VIII. c. 13.

Union of Scotland and Ireland.

Reform Acts for England and Wales.

Henry VIII.; and four for the county and city of Durham in the reign of Charles II.; while 180 new members were added by royal charter between the reigns of Henry VIII. and Charles 11."

Forty-five members were assigned to Scotland, as her proportion of members in the British Parliament, on the union of that kingdom with England; and one hundred to Ireland at the commencement of the present century, when her parliament became incorporated with that of the United Kingdom. By these successive additions the number was increased to 658, and notwithstanding the changes effected in the distribution of the elective franchise by the Reform Acts in 1832, that number continued unaltered until the disfranchisement of Sudbury in 1844.

The object of the English Reform Act, as stated in the preamble, was to correct divers abuses that had long prevailed in the choice of members; to deprive many inconsiderable places of the right of returning members; to grant such privilege to large, populous, and wealthy towns; to increase the number of knights of the shire; to extend the elective franchise to many of his Majesty's subjects who have not heretofore enjoyed the same, and to diminish the expense of elections. To effect these changes, 56 boroughs ' 25 Car. II. c. 9. Christian's Notes to Blackstone. 2 Hats. 413.

The election of representatives by the freeholders in Scotland had been recognised by the statute law so far back as the reign of James I. By Act 1425, c. 52, all freeholders were required to give personal attendance in Parliament, and not by a procurator; from which it is evident that representation was then the custom. Nor was it possible to restrain it by law, for two years afterwards it was authorised, and the constitution of the House of Commons defined. By Act 1427, c. 102, it was declared, " that the small barons and free tenants need not come to parliaments; provided that, at the head court of every sheriffdom, two or more wise men be chosen, according to the extent of the shire, who shall have power to hear, treat, and finally to determine all causes laid before Parliament; and to chuse a speaker, who shall propose all and sundry needs and causes pertaining to the commons in Parliament."

2 3 Will. IV. c. 45.

in Enf jlaiul mid ales were onliivly dl.- fnincliiscil, Jiiid 30 which liiid previously returned two members were restricted to one member; while 12 new boroughs were creuted, of which 22 were each to return two mcmbcr!, and 20 a single member. Several small boroughs in Wales were united for the purpose of contributing to return a member.

The result of these and other local armngements, which it is not necessary to describe, was as follows: The city of London having the privilige of returning four members; the Universities of Oxford and Cambridge, and 133 cities and boroughs, returning each two members; and 07 boroughs, returning each one member, jointly contributed 341 citizens and burgesses for England and Wales."

Several of the counties were divided into electoral districts or divisions, by which the number of knights of tlie shire was increased.

The county of York has two members for each of the three ridings— G 26 counties have- 4 members each– 104 7– 3. i 9—-.- IS 10,.– 1— 10 1.39

The number of members for Scotland was increased by Por Sc.-tland. tlic Scotch Reform Act ' from 45 to 03; 30 of whom arc commissioners of shires, and 23 commissioners of burirhs, representing towns, burghs, or districts of small burghs.

By the Irish Reform Act" the number of representatives And Iniami. for Ireland in the Imperial Parliament was increased from 100 to 105; 64 being for counties, 39 for cities and borouglis, and two for the University of Dublin.

' The mcmbcra for the two anircnitlcs ttre dcnonifainted " bnrgeme," and till rrprrsonuktivos of the Cinque I'uru are styled barons.

'2 Ac 3 Will. IV. c. (V. ' i. J Will. IV. c. 8t.

The following is a statement of the entire representation of the three kingdoms now composing the House of Commons:

England and Wales. 159 knights of shires. 339 citizens and buro-esses.

Total- 498

Scotland. 30 commissioners of shires. 23 commissioners of burghs.

Total- 53 Ireland.

64 knights of shires.

41 citizens and bursesses.

Total- 105

Total of the United Kingdom, 656.

Constituency The classes of persons by whom these representatives countils. are elected may be described, generally, in few words, if the legal questions connected with the franchise, which are both numerous and intricate, be avoided. To begin with the English counties. Before the 8th of Henry VI. all freeholders or suitors present at the county court had a right to vote (or, as is affirmed by some, all freemen); but by a statute passed in that year (c. 7) the right was limited to " people dwelling and resident in the same counties, whereof every one of them shall have free land or tenement to the value of 405. by the year, at the least, above all charges." By the Reform Act every person, being of full age, and not subject to any legal incapacity, who, at the time of the passing of the Act, was seised for his own life, or the life of another, or for any lives what- ever, of a 40s. freehold; or who may be seised subsequently ' Sudbury, returning two members, having been disfranchised by Act 7 8 Vict. c. 53. See Act 7 Hen. IV. c. 15.

to tlic paj5:? liig (if tlio Act, irovidcil lie lie in actual aiul bona Jide occupation; or who may conic into sucli fixcliokl estate by marriage, marriage settlement, devise, or j)romo-tion to any benefice or oflice, is still entitled to vote as a freeholder; hut any person not included in these cla."jsc. s acquiring a freehold snl)? c(iicntly to the Act, is only entitled when it sliall be " to him of the clear yearly value of not less than 10. above all rents and charges payable out of, or in rcs)cet of the same." Copyholders ha ing an estate of 1.; i year: leaseholders of land of that value whose leases were originally granted for 60 years; lease-liolders of 50., with 20 years' leases; and tenants at will occupying lands or tenements paying a rent of not less than 50. a year, had the right of voting conferred upon them by the Reform Act.

In cities and boroughs the right of votiiig tunikriy varitil nfciii. s an. i accordnig to tiie ancient custom jtrevailing in each. ith certain motlifications some t)f these ancient rights were retained by the Keform Act, as that of freemen, and other corporate qualifications; but all occupiers of houses of the clear yearly value of 10. were enfranchised by that Act, and now form the greater lart of the constituency of bortkighs,

From whatever right these various classes of nixms u. gimn. u n. claim to vote, either for counties or for cities and b roughs, it ia necessary that they shall be registered in lists prepared by the overseers of each parish. On certain days courts are held, by barristers appointed by the Lord Chief irustice of Kngland and the Scni r Judge of each Summer Circuit, to revise these lists; when claims may be made by persons omitted, and objections may be offered to any name inserted by the overseers. If an objection be sust4iined, the name is struck ofl' the list; and in ordinary cjujcs the claimant will have no right to vote at any ensuing election utdess he shall succeed, at a sub.- equcnt registnition, in establishing his claim; but on points of law there is an appeal to the Court of Common Pleas from the decisions of revising barristers; and the register is corrected in accordance with the judgment of that court.

In Scotland. The Scotch Reform Act reserved the rights of all per- sons then on the roll of freeholders of any shire, or who were entitled to be put upon it, and extended the franchise to all owners of property of the clear yearly value of 10., and to certain classes of leaseholders. In cities, towns, and burghs, the Act substituted a 10. household franchise for the system of electing members by the town councils, which had previously existed. The lists of claimants are made up, in shires by the schoolmasters of each parish, and in burghs by the town clerks; and the claims and objections are heard and determined by the sheriffs.

In Ireland. In Ireland various classes of freeholders and leaseholders were invested with the county franchise by the Reform Act, to whom were added, by the 13 14 Vict., c. 69, occupiers of land, rated for the poor rate at a net annual value of 12 Z.; and persons entitled to estates in fee, or in tall, or for life, of the rated value of 5 . And by the latter Act, in addition to the borough constituency under the Reform Act, the occupiers of lands or premises rated at 8 . are entitled to vote for cities and boroughs.

Qualification of It has not been attempted to explain, in detail, all the distinctions of the elective franchise; neither is it proposed to state all the grounds upon which persons may be disqualified from voting. Aliens, persons under 21 years of age, of unsound mind, in receipt of parochial relief, or convicted of certain offences, are incapable of voting. Many officers, also, Avho are concerned in the collection of the revenue are disqualified.

See 2 3 Will. IV. c. 45, and 0 7 Vict. c. 18.

2 2 3 Will. IV. c. G5. 3 2 3 Will. IV. c.

voters.

To be eligible as a inciuber for uny j)l: ice in Engluiul or rmimrty quali-Ircland, a person must possess the property (jualilication.",,"i' "r required by the Act 1 is: 2 ict., c. 48; vi., to be a kniixht of the shire, he must le entitled, lor his own use and benefit, to real or personal pro erty, or both together, to the amount of 600. a year; and to be a citizen or burgess, be must be entitled to one-half the amount of that qualification. Beibre the passing of that Act, a freehold proj)erty in land to the amount of GOO . had been re(piired' to qualify persons to serve as knights of shires, and 300. to enable them to sit as citizens and burgesses.

imcinbers for the Universities of Oxford and Cam1)ridge, and Trinity College, Dublin, require no such qualification; and the eldest sons or heirs apparent of peers and lords of Parliament, or of persons qualified to be knights of the shire, are by law entitled to serve, without reference to the amount of their property. In Scotland no)ropcrty qualification has ever been established, it having been contended at the passing of the Act of Queen Anne, that the estates in that country were so small that it would not be easy to find meml)ers duly qualified.

To enable jxjrsons to sit in Parliament, there are numerous oiiurr iinlifira-othcr qualificiitions besides that of projierty. Formerly it qualifkauoii!!. was necessary that the member chosen should himself be one of the bmly represented. The law, however, was constantly disregarded, and in 1774 was repealed. An alien Aliens. is disqualified to be a member of either House of l arlia-ment," The Act 2 13 Will. III., c. 2, declared that "no person born out of the kingdoms of England, Scotland, or Ireland, or the dominions thereunto belonging (although he be natundized or made a denizen, except such as are

By 9 Anne, c. 5, and 33 Geo. II. c. 20.- S.; e (t Pari. Hist. 1003, u.

1 Peck. IS). 1 Hen. V. c. I. 8 Hen. VI. c. 7. 10 Hon. VI. c. 'J. '- 3 Hon. VI. c. 1. 1 4 n. o. ni. c. M. 7 A: H Virt. c. frfl,.

born of English parents), shall be capable to be of tlie privy council, or a member of either House of Parliament." The 1st George I., stat. 2, c. 4, in order to enforce the pi'ovisions of the Act of William, required a special clause of disquahfication to be inserted in every Naturalization Act; but as no clause of this nature could bind any future Parliament, occasional exceptions have been permitted, as in the cases of Prince Leopold in 1816, and Prince Albert in 1840; and this provision of the 1st George I. has since been altogether repealed by the 7 8 Vict. c. 66, s. 2.

Minors. By the 7 8 Will. III., c. 25, s. 8, a minor was disquali- fied to be elected. Before the passing of that Act, several members were notoriously under age, yet their sitting was not objected to. On the 16th of December 1690, on the hearing of a controverted election, Mr. Trenchard was admitted by his counsel to be a minor; but, notwithstanding, upon a division he was declared to be duly elected." On the 18th of December 1667, however, the House of Lords had declared, "That according to the law of the realm, and the ancient constitution of Parliament, minors ought not to sit nor vote in Parliament."

Members By the law of Parliament a member already returned for already sitting.,.,.,.,,- i i one place is ineligible tor any other until Ins nrst seat is vacated; and hence it is the practice for a member desiring to represent some other place to accept the Chiltern Hundreds, in order to render himself eligible at the election. Mental iinbe Mental imbecility is a disqualification; and should a

"member, who was sane at the time of his election, after- wards become a lunatic, his seat may be avoided, as in the case of Grampound in 1566," but it must be proved that Peers and the malady is incurable." English peers are ineligible to the House of Commons, as having a seat in the upper 2 Hats. Prec. 9; 10 Com. J. 508. 2 12 Lords' J. 174.

3 D'Ewes, 12(5. 1 Com. J. 75. Ptogers, 57.

Mr. Alcock's case in 1811; CO Com. J. 220. 265. App. (087).

house; and Scotcli peers, as being represented there: but Irish peers, unless elected as one of the representative peers of Ireland, may sit for any place in (Jreat Britdin The P nglish, Scotch, and Irish jud;; es (with the exception of tlie Master of the Rolls in En dand) are disqualified," together with the holders of various offices, particularly ex- Offic. eluded by statutes." A large class of ofhces which incai aci-tiite the holders for Parliament are new offices, or places of profit under the Crown, created since the 25th of October 1705, as defined by the Gth of Anne, e. 7; and also new offices in Ireland under the 33d Geo. III., c, 41.

The sheriff of a county is inelipble for that county, and shcriffv an. l also for any city or borough to which his precept extends; officers but he is eligible for any other county, or for any county of a city or borough within his county, or elsewhere,)rovided the writ for the election is directed to some other returning officer, and not to himself. And no returning officer is capable of being elected for his own city or borough." liy the Scotch Reform Act (s. 36), no sheriff sul)stitute, sheriff clerk, or deputy sheriff clerk is entitled to be elected for his own shire, nor any town clerk, or depute town clerk for his own city, borough, town or district.

By the 41 Geo. III., c. 03, which arose out of Mr. rirrf y. Home Tookc's election, it is declared that " no person having been ordained to the office of priest or deacon, or being a minister of the Church of Scotland, is capable of

Act of Union.

1 Com. J. 257. 7 Geo. II. c. in. 1 2 Geo. IV. c. 44. Judge of the Admiralty Court, 3 i 4 Vict c. 00.

Ttiat nil the special disqualifications for Parliament cannot he ennmernted within the limits of this cliaptcr, will be helievoci, when it is stated that ihcy are to be colh'ct 'd fnim at loiist 1IH statutes. (See Pam hkt hy the Author, on the Consolidation of the Election Laws, IHio.)

Sec Ro); ers on Elections, 67; and General Journal Indcsei, tit. Elections, (Writs); and infra, Ch. XXII.

2 Hatj. I'rcc.:)0-.14. 4 Dougl. 87. 12:).

"9 Com. J. 72.0. (Thetford Case). Wakefield Case, Harron Austin. 20.". Rogers on Elections, 4lj-."l.

being elected;" and that if he should sit or vote, he is liable to forfeit 500 Z. for each day, to any one who may sue for the same. It is doubtful whether before the passing of this Act persons in holy orders had not been disqualified by the law of Parliament. The precedents collected upon the subject in 180P were obscure and inconclusive, and there was much difference of opinion amongst legal and parliamentary authorities as to the existing state of the law. The House of Commons refused to declare Mr. Home Tooke ineligible; and having been already elected he was excepted from the operation of the Act. The Roman-catholic clergy are also excluded by 10 Geo. IV., c. 7, s. 9. Contractors, Government contractors, being supposed to be liable to the influence of their employers, are disqualified from serving in Parliament. The Act 22 Geo. III., c. 45, declares that any person who shall, directly or indirectly, himself, or by any one in trust for him, undertake any contract with a government department, shall be incapable of being elected, or of sitting or voting during the time he shall hold such contract, or any share thereof, or any benefit or emolument arising from the same: but the Act does not affect incorporated trading companies, contracting in their corporate capacity. The penalties for violations of the Act are peculiarly severe: a contractor sitting or voting is liable to forfeit 500 Z. for every day on which he shall sit or vote, to any person who may sue for the same; and every person against whom this penalty shall be recovered, is incapable of holding any contract. The Act goes still further (s. 10), and even imposes a penalty of 500 Z. upon any person who admits a member of the House of Commons to a share of a contract. The Act 41 Geo. Ill,, s. 52, disqualifies in the same manner, and under ' See Reports of Precedents, 35 Pari. Hist. 1343. 8 Com. J. 341. 346, 1 Com. J, 27 (13 Oct. 1553). 1 Com. J. 513 (8 Feb, 1620). 2 Hats. Prec, 12.

2 35 Pari. Hist. 1402. 1414. 1542. 1544.

DISQI'AMKK ATIONS OF MKMnkHS. 'M) aimihir penalties, all persons holding contracts with any i l' the government departments In Ireland.

By the 52 George III., c. 144, whenever a member shall Himkrupn. be found and declared a bankru)t, he shall be for twelve months incapable of sitting and voting, unless the commission be superseded, or the creditors paid or satisfied to the full amount of their debts. At the expiratiun of twelve months the commissioners are required to certify the bankruptcy to the speaker, and the election of the member is void." In this Act there is no penalty fur a i)ankrupt sitting and voting, and as no official notice of his i)ank-ruptcy is required to be given to the s)eaker for twelve months, it seems that he might sit with impunity in the meantime, unless the house should take notice of his sitting, and order him to withdraw. Jt does not apj)ear that this Act would apply to the case of a Scotch sequestration, liy the Bankrupt Law Consolidation Act, 1849, s. 77, a trader, having privilege of Parliament, who shall not pay, secure, or compound a debt to the satisfaction of the creditor, or enter into a bond, with sureties, to i)ay such sum as shall be recovered, and enter an ap)earancc to the action for the recovery of such debt within one month after the service of the writ of summons, shall be deemed to have committed an act of bankruptcy from the time of the service of such summons.

A person attainted of treason or felony, being dead in pcrtioim at-law, is disqualified;' but an indictment for felony causes no '"" " disqualification until conviction; and even after conviction a new writ will nut be issued, where a writ ol" error is j end-ing, until the judgment has been affirmed."

These are the chief but not the only grounds of disqualification fur sitting in the House of Commons. Many others will be found collected in the various works ui)on ' See 85 Com. J. 3, for the form of proocoding In urli case.

4tu Inst. 47. ' Sec Itcsolution-t, 21nl Jnn. I. KO, 1 C. mi.1. III.

Ca c' of Mr.". O'Dricn. lol Com. J. 31!.

election law, where those also which have been touched upon, in this place, are more fully detailed.

To these explanations concerning the persons of whom Parliament is composed, it is not necessary to add any particulars as to the mode of election; farther than that the elections are held by the sheriffs or other returning officers, in obedience to a queen's writ out of Chancery, and are determined by the majority of registered electors.

CHAPTER 11.

POWER AND JURISDICTION OF PARLIAMENT COLLECTIVELY. RIGHTS AND POWERS OF EACH OF ITS CONSTITUENT PARTS.

Legislative authority of Parliament, collectively.

The legislative authority of Parliament extends over the United Kingdom, and all its colonies and foreign possessions; and there are no other limits to its power of making laws for the whole empire than those which are incident to all sovereign authority the willingness of the people to obey, or their power to resist. Unlike the legislatures of many other countries, it is bound by no fundamental charter or constitution; but has itself the sole constitutional right of establishing and altering the laws and government of the empire.

In the ordinary course of government. Parliament does not legislate directly for the colonies. For some, the queen in council legislates, while others have legislatures of their own, which propound laws for their internal government, subject to the approval of the queen in council; but these may afterwards be repealed or amended by statutes of the Imperial Parliament; for their legis- ' Rogers, Shepherd, Stephens, Montagu Neale, Wordswortli, c. See also Chapter XXO.

latures ami their laws are both subordiiuitc to the nui reme IX)wer of the mother country." For example, the constitution of Lower Canada was suspcn led in 1838; and a provisional government, witli legislative functions and great executive powers, was established by the Uritish Parliament. Slavery, also, was abolished by an Act of Parliament in 1833 througiiout all the British possessions, whether governed by local legislatures or not; but certain measures for carrying into effect the intentions of Parliament were left for sul)scquent enactment by the local bodies, or by the queen in council. At another time, the house of assembly of Jamaica, the most' ancient of our colonial legislatures, had neglected to pass an effectual law for the regidation of prisons, which became necessary upon the emancipation of the negroes; when Parliament inuncdiatcly interposed and passed a statute" for that purpose. The assembly were indignant at the interference of the mother country, and neglected their functions; upon which an Act' was psi ised by the Imperial Parliament, that would have suspended the constitution of Jamaica unless within a given time they had resumed them. The vast territories of British India are subject to the anomalous government of the East India Company; whose power, however, is founded upon statute, and wlio are controlled by ministers responsible to Parliament.

The power of imposing taxes upon colonies for the support of the parent state, though not now enforced, was exercised by Parliament in the case of the provinces of North America; and, as is but too well known, was the immediate occabion of the severance of that great country ' " Parliamentary legislation on any subject of excluaively internal concern to any Britisli colony podm-ssiiik a rcprt'scntative a embly, is, as a general rulf, uncnii titutional. It is a rigiit f which tjie exercise is reserved for extreme cnses, in wliicli necesnity at once creates and justifies the exctlon." Lord (ilenclg. (Pari. 1'h. I8ao (118.), j). 7.) ' 1 2 Vict. f. 07. '- 3 Viit. c 'iti.

from our own. But whatever may be urged against colonial taxation on grounds of justice or expediency, the legal right of Parliament to impose taxes upon au persons within the British dominions, is unquestionable.

There are some subjects upon which Parliament, in familiar language, is said to have no right to legislate; but the constitution has assigned no limits to its authority. Many laws may be unjust, and contrary to sound principles of government; but Parliament is not controlled in its discretion, and when it errs, its errors can only be corrected by itself. To adopt the words of Sir Edward Coke, the power of Parliament " is so transcendent and absolute, that it cannot be confined, either for causes or persons, within any bounds."

This being the authority of Parliament collectively, the laws and usage of the constitution have assigned peculiar powers, rights, and privileges to each of its branches, in connexion with their joint legislative functions. Prerogatives of It is by the act of the Crown alone that Parliament can reference to the he assembled. The only occasions on which the lords and Parliament. commons have met by their own authority, were, previously to the restoration of King Charles II., and at the Revolution in 1688. The first act of Charles the Second's reign declared the lords and commons to be the two houses of Parhament, notwithstanding the irregular manner in which they had been assembled, and all their acts were confirmed by the succeeding Parliament sunnnoned by the king; which however quahfied the confirmation of them, by declaring that " the manner of the assembling, enforced by the difficulties and exigencies which then lay upon the nation, is not to be drawn into example." In the same manner the first act of the reign of William and Mary declared the convention of lords and commons to be the two Houses of Parliament, as if they had been summoned ' 4 lust. 36.

OK I'Aiu. IA. MK. Vr. 'M) acoorclin; to the usual t'onn; and the succceclin Piu liaiikiit recorjnisetl the Icjfality of their acts.

liut although the queen may detcnnine the period for Annuni mwt-calhntr I arhaincnts, her prcroirative is rcstraincu witlnn, i., t. certain liniiti?; as she is hound ly statute' to issue writu within three years after the detcnnination of a Parliament; while the pnictice of providing money for the public service hy annual enactments, rendci's it compulsory upon her to meet Parliament every year.

The annual meeting of Parliament, now placed 1 e-yond the power of the Crown hy a system of finance rather than hy distinct enactment, had, in fact, hcen the law of England from very early times. Py the statute 4 Edw. III., c. 14, "it is accorded that Parliament shall be holden every year once, and or more often if need be."" And again in the 30 Edw. III., c. 10, it was granted " for redress of divers mischiefs and grievances which daily haj)pen a Parliament shall be holden or l)e the Parliament holden evcri year, as another tune wjis ordained by statute."

It is well known that by extending the words " if need be," to the whole sentence instead of to the last part only, to which they are obviously limited, the kings of England constantly disregarded these laws. It is impissible, however, for any words to be more distinct than those of the 3Gth Edward III., and it is j)lain from many records that they were rightly understood at the time. In the ooth Edwaixl III., the conimons petitioned the king to establish, by statute, that a Parliament should be held each year; to which the king replied: ' In i egard to a Parliament each year, there arc statutes and ordinances made, ' 10 Chaa. 11., c. 1, and 0 7 Will. Mary, c 2.

Rr-coni Comu. Statutes of the lu'ulii). ' Ibil.

By on ordinance in tiic th Kdw. III., the object of the law hud been more clearly explained; viz. " Qe le roi tiegnc I'arleincnt uue foil p an', ou deii foiz si incsticr soil." 1 Hot. I'arl. 2H6.

which should be duly maintained and kept."' So also to a similar petition in the 1st Richard II., it was answered, "So far as relates to the holding of Parliament each year, let the statutes thereupon be kept and observed; and as for the place of meeting, the king will therein do his pleasure."' And in the following year the king declared that he had summoned Parliament, because at the prayer of the lords and conmions, it had been ordained and agreed that Parliament should be held each year.

In the preamble of the Act 16 Chas. I., c. 1, it was also distinctly affirmed, thac "by the laws and statutes of this realm. Parliaments ought to be holden at least once every year for the redress of grievances, but the appointment of the time and place of the holding thereof hath always belonged, as it ought, to his majesty and his royal progenitors."" Yet by the 16th Chas. II., c. 1, a recognition of these ancient laws was withheld: for the Act of Charles I. was repealed as " derogatory of his majesty's just rights and prerogative;" and the statutes of Edward III. were incorrectly construed to signify no more than that "Parliaments are to be held very often." All these statutes, however, were repealed, by implication, by this Act, and also by the 6 7 Will. Mar., c. 2, which declares and enacts " that from henceforth Parliament shall be holden once in three years, at the least." Summons. The Parliament is summoned by the queen's writ or letter issued out of Chancery, by advice of the privy council. By the 7 8 Will. III., c. 25, it is required that there shall be forty days between the teste and the return of the writ of summons; but since the union with ' 2 Rot. Pari. 335. 3 lb. 23. lb. 32.

"Act for preventing of inconvenience happening from long intermission of Parliaments."

Forty flays were assigned for the period of the summons by the great charter of King John, in which are these words: " Faciemus summoneri. ad certura diem, scilicet ad terminum quadraginta dieiim ad minus, et ad certum locum."

Sootlaml, it has hccn the liivarialtle custom to extend this period to titty day.-," 8ik-h lieinj; the peritml Jis. i; iied in the case of the first Pnrlliiinent of Great Britain after the Union. The writ of summons has always named tlie day and phioe of meitiuir, without which the reiuisiti(in to meet would be imperfect and nu xatory.

The demise of the Crown is the only contiiipjency upon D. mii."of the which Parliament is re(uirel to meet without sunuuons in the usual torm. By the (5 Anne, c. 7, on the demise of the Crown, Parliament, if sitting, is iuunediately to proceed to act, and if separated by adjournment or proro-g-ation, is immediately to meet and sit. In pui suance of this Act, Parliament has three times met on Sunday." By the 37 Geo. III., c. 127, in case of the demise of the Crown after the dissolution or exi)iration of a Parliament, and before the day appointed by the writs of summons for assemblinir a new Parliament, the last precedinf Parliament is iuunediately to convene and sit at Westminster, and be a Parliament for six months, subject in the meantime to proro;

ation or dissolution. In the event of another demise of the Crown during this interval of six months, before the dissolution of the Parliament thus revived, or before the meeting of a new Parliament, it is to convene again and sit immediately, as before, and to be a Parliament for six months from the date of such demise, subject, in the same manner, to be prorogued or dissolved. If the demise of the Crown should occur on the day appointed by the writs of summons for the assembling of a new Parliament, or after that day and before it has met and sat, the new Parliament is immediately to convene, and sit, and be a Parliament fur six months, as in the preceding cases.

' See 22 Art. of Uoioo, fith Anne. c. 8. 2 Hnu. 2 0.

Qu en Amu-, 18 Com. J. 3; fieorgc II., 28 ib. thil), 03. M, fjc. rnn III, 75 111. f2, 80. For other orca ioii,. c 20 ib. eoO (George I.), W ib. M'J (George l.), Jn ib. 490 OViuiiim IV.) moiis.

42 MEETING OF PARLIAMENT.

Causes of 9UU1- As the queen appoints the time and place of meeting, so also at the commencement of every session she declares to both houses the causes of summons, by a speech delivered to them in the House of Lords by herself in person, or by commissioners appointed by her. Until she has done this, neither house can proceed with any business; but the causes of summons as declared from the throne, do not bind Parliament to consider them alone, nor to proceed at once to the consideration of any of them. After the speech, any business may be commenced; and both houses," in order to assert their right to act without reference to any authority but their own, invariably read a bill a first time, pro forma, before they take the speech into consideration. Other business may also be done at the same time. In the commons new writs are issued for places which have become vacant during a recess; returns are ordered, and even addresses are presented on matters unconnected with the speech. In 1840 a question of privilege, arising out of the action of Stockdale against the printers of the house, was entertained before any notice was taken of her majesty's speech.

On two occasions during the illness of George IIL, the name and authority of the Crown were used for the purpose of opening the Parliament, when the sovereign was personally incapable of exercising his constitutional functions. On the first occasion Parliament had been prorogued till the 20th November 1788, then to meet for the dispatch of business. When Parliament assembled on that day, the king was under the care of his physicians, and unable to open Parliament, and declare the causes of summons. Both houses, however, proceeded to consider the measures necessary for a regency, and on the 3d February 1789, Parliament was opened by a commission, to

' This is done in the lords in comijliauce with a standing order (No. 8), and in the commons by usage.

wliioh the, Mvat fseni Imd been nthxed hy the Inrd rhan-ccllor, without the authority of the kin Apiin in IHIO Pnrujiment stood prorogued till tlje Ist November, and met at a time when the king was incapable of issuing a commission. His illness continued, and on the l."th. January, without any personal exercise of authority by the king, Parliament was formally opened, and the causes of summons declared in virtue of a commission imdcr the great seal, and " in his majesty's name."

It may here be incidentally remarked, that the Crown has also an important privilege in regard to the deliberations of both houses. The speaker of the lords is the lord high chancellor or lord keeper of the great seal, an ofhcer more closely connected with the Crown than any other in the state; and even the speaker of the commons, though elected by them, is submitted to the approv: d of the Crown.

Parliament, it has been seen, can only commence its rron ition 1 i-i 1 '.111 ' 1 "" " Ijoiiru- dcliberations at the tune appointed by the queen; neither, j. m can it continue them any longer than she pleases. She may prorogue Parliament by having her command signified, in her presence, lv the lord chancellor or spiaker f the House of Lords to both Houses; or by writ under the great seal," or by commission. The effect of a prorogation is at once to suspend all business until Parliament shall be summoned again. Not only are the sittings of Parliament at an end, i)ni all proceedings cnding at the time are quashed, except impeachments by the commons, and writs of error and appeals before the House of Lords. Lvery bill nmst be renewed after a prort)gation," na if it had never been introduced, though the prorogation be for no more than a day. William III. jiroiogued Parliament ' But parlianieot is aevcr prorogued by writ afl r its flrst racvuiig.

Ity 1 (ieo. IV. c. 101, an Indian divorce bill in vxcrpti-d from till rule, in certain ca is. And l)y the 11 i'J Vict., c. DS, clccliun couiuiilt ca arc nut di olvcd by a prorogutiun.

from the 21st of October 1689, to the 23d, in order to renew the Bill of Rights, concerning which a difference had arisen between the two houses that was fatal to its progress. As it is a rule that a bill of the same substance cannot be passed in either house twice in the same session, a prorogation has been resorted to, in other cases, to enable a second bill to be brought in.

When Parliament stands prorogued to a certain day, her majesty is empowered by Act 37 Geo. III., c. 127, to issue a proclamation, giving notice of her royal intention that Parliament shall meet and be holden for the dispatch of business on any other day, not less than fourteen days distant; and Parliament then stands prorogued to that day, notwithstanding the previous prorogation."" And by other Acts, whenever the Crown shall cause the supplementary militia to be raised and enrolled, or drawn out and embodied, either in England or Scotland, when Parliament stands prorogued or adjourned for more than fourteen days, the queen is required to issue a proclamation for the meeting of Parliament within fourteen days. Adjournment. Adjournment is solely in the power of each house respectively. It has not been unusual, indeed, for the pleasure of the Crown to be signified in person, by message, commission, or proclamation, that both houses should adjourn, and in some cases such adjournments have scarcely differed from prorogations." But although no instance has occurred in which either house has refused to adjourn, the communication might be disregarded. Business has frequently been transacted after the king's desire has been made known, and the question for adjournment has after-

See Chap. X, ' Parliament was assembled by proclamation, pursuant to this Act, in September 1799. 54 Com. J. 745; 55 lb. 3. 3 42 Geo. III. c. 90, s. 147, and c. 91, s. 142. 9 Com. J. 158.

wards been put, In the onllnary manner, and dcternunetl after debate, amendment, and division."

Under these circumstances it is surprising that so many instances of this practice should have occurred in comparatively modern times. Hotli lutn. ses adjourn at their own discretion, and daily exercise their ri dit. Any interference on the part of the Crown is therefore impolitic, OS it may chance to meet with opposition; and unnecessary, as the ministers need only assign a cause for adjournment, when each house would adjourn of its own accord. The last occasion on which the pleasure of the Crown was siji nified, was on the 1st larch 1814," and it is probable that the practice will never be resorted to a ' ain.

A power of interfering with adjournments in certain cases has been conceded to the Crown by statute. The 39 40 Geo. III., c. 14, enacts that when both houses of Parliament stand adjourned for more than fourteen days, the queen may issue a proclamation, with the advice of the privy council, declaring that the Parliament shall meet on a day not less than fourteen days from the proclamation; and the houses of Parliament then stand adjourned to the day and place declared in the proclamation; and all the orders which may have been made by either house, and appointed for the original day of meeting, or any subsequent day, stand appointed ftr the day named in the proclamation.

The queen may also put an end to the existence of Par- nimoiuuoo. liament by a dissolution. She is not, however, entirely free to define the duration of a Parliament, for luidor the statute 1 Geo. I., c. 38, commonly known as the isoptennial Act, it ceases to exist after seven years from the day on which, by the writ of summons, it was ap K)inted to meet. But before the Triennial Act, 6th of William Mary, c 2, ' 2 Hau. ni(, 317. 1 Tom J. 807, W)e, 800. 10 lb. (MM; 17 lb. 0, 27. cc. 40 I. rii ' J. 747 00 Com. I.: V2.

there was no constitutional limit to the continuance of a Parliament but the will of the Crown.

Parliament is usually dissolved by proclamation under the great seal, after having been proi'ogued to a certain day. This proclamation is issued by the queen with the advice of the privy council, and announces that the queen has given order to the lord chancellor of Great Britain and the lord chancellor of Ireland to issue out writs in due form, and according to law, for calling a new Parliament, and that the writs are to be returnable on a certain day.

Since the dissolution of the 28th March 1681, by Charles II., the sovereign had not dissolved the Parliament in person until the 10th June 1818, when it was dissolved by the prince regent in person. Parliament has not since been dissolved in that form, but proceedings not very dissimilar have occurred in recent times. On the 22d April 1831, the king having come down to prorogue Parliament, said, ' I have come to meet you for the purpose of proroguing Parliament, with a view to its immediate dissolution;" and Parliament was dissolved by proclamation on the following day. And on the 23d July 1847, the queen, in proroguing Parliament, announced her intention immediately to dissolve it, and it was accordingly dissolved by proclamation on the same day, and the writs were dispatched by that evening's post.

In addition to these several powers of calling a Parliament, appointing its meeting, directing the commencement of its proceedings, determining them from time to time by prorogation, and finally of dissolving it altogether, the Crown has other parliamentary powers, which will hereafter be noticed in treating of the functions of the two houses.

73 Com. J. 427. gg j,, jy 3 102 Com. J. 960; 103 lb. 3.

Peers of the realm enjoy ri lits uiul exercise runctionh ii'tiii. t iiinli. ill five distinct clmnicters: Fiiist, tlity possess, individiiullv, ' """'"

"' ' rciiliii.

titles of honour which avc them rank and precedence; secondly, they are, individually, hereditary coun elk)rs of the Crown; thinlly, they are, collectively, to cther with the lords spiritual, when not assemblrd in Parlininrr. t, the permanent council of the Crown; fourthly, they are, 'itl-lectivcly, together with the lords spiritual, when a scndded in Parliament, a court of judicature; and lastly, they are, conjointly with the h)rds spiritual and the counnons, in Parliament assembled, the legislative asscmhly of the kingdom, by Avhosc advice, consent and authority, with the sanction of the C'rown, all laws are made."

The most distinguishing characteristic of the birds is Jn. li. ntur. f their judicature, of which they exercise several kinds. They have a judicature in the trial of peers; and another in claims of peerage and otticcs ol honour, under references from the Crown, but not otherwise." Since the union with Scotland, they have also bad a judicature for controverted elections of the sixteen rcprcsontative jieers of Scotland; and since the union with Ireland all questions touching the rotation or election of lords spiritual or temponil of Irelan l, are to be decided by the House of Lords. Hut, in addition to these special cai es, they have a gcnend judicature as a supreme court of ajipcal from other courts of justice. This high judicial oftice has een retained by them a. the ancient consilium retis, which, assisted by the judges, and with the assent of the king, administered justice in the early periods of English luw. Their appellate jurisdiction '

See 1 lu'p. Dig. of Proragp, 14.

Sec Knolly'9 raso, V2 St. Tr. 1107-1207. 1 T. or. l Rayni. I(. S Ik."iol. Cartli. 207. 2 I, ord Campb. Lives of Cli. Juot. 14S. Lord Cunipb. Spcpclu, 3S6.

' Act. of the rnrl. of Scotland, 6 Ann. c. 8. (Ann. e. 23. 10 X II Vict c."j2. 4th Art. of Union.

Hair's Jurisdiction of the House of Lords, c. 14. Harrington on Ihc Sututm, 244.

would also appear to have received statutory confirmation from the 14 Edw. III., c. 5, a. d. 1340. In the 17th century they assumed a jurisdiction, in many points, which has since been abandoned. They claimed an original jurisdiction in civil causes, which was resisted by the commons, and has not been enforced for the last century and a half. They claimed an original jurisdiction over crimes without impeachment by the commons, but that claim was also abandoned." Their claim to an appellant jurisdiction over causes in equity, on petition to themselves without reference from the Crown, has been exercised since the reign of Charles I.; and in spite of the resistance of the commons in 1675, they have since been left in undisputed possession of it. They have, at the present time, a jurisdiction over causes brought, on writs of error, from the courts of law, originally derived from the Crown, and confirmed by statute," and to hear appeals from courts of equity on petition; but appeals in ecclesiastical, maritime, or prize causes, and colonial appeals, both at law and in equity, are determined not by them, but by the privy council. The powers which are incident to them, as a court of record, will claim attention in other places.

A valuable part of the ancient constitution of the co7i-silium regis has never been withdrawn from the lords, viz. the assistance of the judges, the master of the rolls, the attorney and solicitor-general, and the queen's learned counsel, being Serjeants, who are still summoned to attend the House of Lords by writs from the Crown, and for whom places are assigned on the woolsacks. But the opinion of the judges alone is now desired on points of law on which the lords wish to be informed.

' See 5 Howell, St. Tr. 711. 4 Pari. Hist. 431. 443. 3 Hats. Prec. 336.

2 8 Com. J. 38. 3 See q Howell, St. Tr. 1121.

27 Eliz. c. 8. See also Intr. to Sugd. Law of R. Prop. 2.

Hargrave's Preface to Hale's Jurisdiction of the Lords.

31 Hen. VIII. c. 10, s. 8. Lords' S. O, Nos. 4. 5. 6. 4tli Inst. 4.

In passing Act.- of attaiiulcr aiul oi' pains anil pcnalticm, imih-aehmmiu. the judiaiturc of the entire Parliament is cxercisetl; ami there is another hi h parliamentary jmlicatnrc in wliieh huth houscj alj o have a share. In impcachment. s the eom-uions, a; the j reat representative in(pu'. t of the nation, first find the erime, and tlun, as prosecntors, support their charge before the lords; while the lords exercising at once the functions of a high court (f justice and of: i jury, try anil adjudicate tlie charge preferred.

Im eachnicnt hy the conuuons is a proceeding of great importance, Involving the exercise of the highest judilal j)o vers by Parliament; and though in modern times it h; is rarely been resorted to, in fi)rmer perlotls of our hitory it was of frequent occurrence. The earliest recorded instance of impeachment by the commons at the bar of the House of Lords, was in the reign of Kdward III. (1370), Before that time the lords appear to have tried both peers and commoners for great public offences, but not ujk)n complaints addressed to them by the commons. During the next four reigns, csises of regular imjh'achmcnt wore frequent; but no instances occurred in the reigns of Kdward IV., Henry VII., Henry III., IMward-1., Queen Mary, or Queen Elizabeth.

"Tlie institution iiaii fullni into ijisuir,"" f. nys Mr. llnllnm, " partly from tlie loss of that control which the coiiuiions hnd obtainod under Uichard II., and the Lancastrian kin x, an! partly from the preference the Tudor jirinces had given to Idils of attainder or of pains and pennltien, when they wislied to turn the arm of Parliament against an obnoxious subject."'

Prosecutions also in the Star Chamber, during that time, were perj)etually resorted to by the Crown for the punishment of state oftenders. In the reign of James I., the practice of impeachment was revived, and was used with great energy by the commons, both as an instrmnent of popular)ower and for the furthenincc of public justice.

1 Conrt. Hint, n-', K

Between the year 1620, when Sir Giles Mompesson and Lord Bacon were impeached, and the revolution in 1688, there were about 40 cases of impeachment. In the reigns of William III., Queen Anne, and George I., there were 15; and in the reign of George II. none but that of Lord Lovat, in 1746, for high treason. The last memorable cases are those of Warren Hastings, in 1788, and Lord Melville, in 1805.

A description of the proceedings of both houses, in cases of impeachment, is reserved for a later part of this treatise. The Commons: The most important power vested in any branch of the ' tino-s ii H es legislature is the right of imposing taxes upon the people, and of voting money for the exigencies of the public service. It has been already noticed that the exercise of this right by the commons, is practically a law for the annual meeting of Parliament for redress of grievances; and it may also be said to give to the commons the chief authority in the state. In all countries the public purse is one of the main instruments of political power; but, with the complicated relations of finance and public credit in England, the power of giving or withholding the supplies at pleasure, is one of absolute supremacy. The mode in whicli the commons exercise their right, and the proceedings of Parliament generally in matters of supply, will be more conveniently explained in the second book. Riefht of deter- Another important power peculiar to the commons is tions." that of determining all matters touching the election of their own members. This right has been regularly claimed and exercised since the reign of Queen Elizabeth, and probably in earlier times, although such matters had been ordinarily determined in chancery. Their exclusive right to determine the legality of returns, and the conduct of returning officers in making them, was fully recognised in the case of Barnadiston v. Soame, by the Court of Exchequer ' See Chap. XXIII. " See Chap. XXI.

Clmmber in 1(571," by tlio lloiit e of Lonls in 1689," and altjo by tlie courts, in the cases of Onslow in KIHO," and in Pridcaiix r. Morris in 1702. Tlicir juri liclit n in determining the riizht of eh'etion was further at-knowk-dije! by statute 7 Will. III., c, 7; but in rej ard to tlie rij hts of electors, a nicnionible contest arose between the lords and commons in 1704. Ashby, a burgess of Aylesbury, brought an action at common law: i; ainst 'ihiam White and others, the returning uflieers of that boruugh, for having refused to permit him to give his vote at an elettinn. A verdict was obtained by him, but it was moved in the Court of Queen's Bench, in arreat of judgment, " tiiat this action did luit lie;" and in opposition to the opinion of L(rtl Chief. Justice Holt, judgment was entered iur the defendant; but was afterwards reversed by the House of Lords upon a writ of error. Upon this the commons declared that " the determination of the right of election of mendjers to serve in Parliament is the proper business of the House of Commons, which they would always be very jealous of, and this jurisdiction of theirs is uncontested; that they exercise a great power in that matter, for they oblige the ofli 'er to alter his return according to their judgment; and that they cannot judge of the right of election without determining the right of the electors; and if electors were at liberty to prosecute suits touching their right ol" giving voices in other courts, there might be ditfcrent voices in other court, which woidd make confusion, and be dishonourable to the House of Commons; and that therefore such an action was a breach of privdege." In addition to the onlinary exercise of their jurisdiction, the commons relied upon the Act 7 Will. HI., c. 7, by which it had been declared that " the last determination of the House of Commons concerning the right of clecti tnft is to be pursued." On the other ' J How, II, St. Tr. H; J. ' II. 11)!. '-2 Vent.: 7. 5 I v W.

i Sulk.",.". I I. niw. MJ. 7. Mod. la. K liand, it was objected that " there Is a great diffei'ence between the right of the electors and the right of the elected: the one is a temporary right to a place in Parliament pro hdc vice; the other is a freehold or a franchise. Who has a right to sit in the House of Commons may be properly cognizable there; but who has a right to choose, is a matter originally established, even before there is a Parliament. A man has a right to his freehold by the common law, and the law having annexed his right of voting to his freehold, it is of the nature of his freehold, and must depend upon it. The same law that gives him his right must defend it for him, and any other power that will pretend to take away his right of voting, may as well pretend to take away the freehold upon which it depends." These extracts from the report of a lords' committee, 27th March 1704, upon the conferences and other proceedings in the case of Ashby and White, give an epitome of the main arguments upon which each party in the contest relied.

Encouraged by the decision of the House of Lords, five other burgesses of Ayles-bury, now familiarly known as " the Aylesbury men," commenced actions against the constables of their borough, and were committed to Newgate by the House of Commons for a contempt of their jurisdiction. They endeavoured to obtain their discharge on writs of habeas corpus, but did not succeed. The commons declared their counsel, agents, and solicitors guilty of a breach of privilege, and committed them also. Res-olutions condemning these proceedings were passed by the lords conferences were held, and addresses presented to the queen. At length the queen prorogued Parliament, and thus put an end to the contest, and to the imprisonment of the Aylesbury men and their counsel. The plaintiffs, no longer impeded by the interposition of privilege, and sup- ' See all the proceedings collected, in App. to 3d vol. of Hatsell's Precedents. The whole of this report, together with another of the 13th Marcii, inav he read with iateiest.

ported by tlic jiuli incnt of the House of Lords, il)taliud verdicts and exooution afjainst the returning ofhcera.

The question which was ajjitated at that time has never since arisen. The commons liave continued to exercise (what was not denied tt them by the House of Lords) the sole riiiht of determininlT whether electoi 8 have had the right to vote, while incjuiring into the conflicting claims of candidates for seats in Parliament; and specific modes for trying the right of election by the house have been prescribed by statutes, and its determination declared to be "final and conclusive in all subsequent elections, and to all intents and purposes whatsoever."'

So complete is the jurisdiction of the commons in matters of election, that, although all writs arc issued out of chancery, every vacancy after a general election is su)plied by their authority. The speaker is empowered to issue wan-ants to the clerk of the crown to make out new writs; and when it has been determined that a return should be amended, the clerk of the crown is ordered to attend the house, and amend it accordingly. During the sitting of the house, vacancies are siq) rud by warrants issued by the speaker, by order of the house; and during a recess, after a prorogation or adjournment, he is requireil to issue warrants, in certain cases, withniit an order."

Iut, notwithstanding their extensive jurisdiction in re- K puui.-n of gard to elec-tions, the conunons luive no control over the cli; ibility of candidates, except in the administration of the laws which define their qualifiaitions. luhii Wilkes was ex elled, in 17(54, for Ining the author of a seditious libel. In the next Parliament ('-id February 1701)) he was again expelled for another libel; a new writ was ordered for the county of isIiddlesex, which he represented, and he was re-elected without a contest; upon w Inch it was resolved, ' n (iw. IV. c. 2 J,."4. ' 24 (, c. III. c s. '2, c. M.:2 Ciih). 111, c. 144 8m kim Chap. X. X 11.

54 EXPULSION OF MEMBERS.

on the 17 th of February, " that, having been in this session of Parliament expelled this house, he was and is incapable of being elected a member to serve in this present Parliament." The election was declared void, but Mr. Wilkes was again elected, and his election was once more declared void, and another writ issued. A new expedient was now tried: Mr. Luttrell, then a member, accepted the Chiltern Hundreds, and stood against Mr. Wilkes at the election; and, being defeated, petitioned the house against the return of his opponent. The house resolved that, although a majority of the electors had voted for Mr. Wilkes, Mr. Luttrell ought to have been returned, and they amended the return accordingly. Against this proceeding the electors of jsIiddlesex presented a petition, w'ithout effect, as the house declared that Mr. Luttrell was duly elected. The whole of these proceedings Avere, at the time, severely condemned by public opinion, and proved by unanswerable-arii-uincnts' to be illegal; and on the 3d. of May 1782, the resolution of the 17th of February 1769, was ordered to be expunged from the journals, as " subversive of the rights of the whole body of electors of this kingdom.""

Expulsion and perpetual disability had been part of the many punishments inflicted upon Arthur Hall, in 1580; and on the 27th May 1641, Mr. Taylor, a member, Avas expelled, and adjudged to be for ever incapable of being a member of the house. During the Long Parliament incapacity for serving in the Parliament then assembled, was frequently part of the sentence of expulsion. In 1711, Mr. liobert Walpole, on being re-elected after his expulsion, was declared incapable of serving in the present Parliament, having been expelled for an offence."' But all these cases can only be regarded as cxam)les of an excess of its jurisdiction by the commons; for one house of Parliament cannot create a ' Sec jailicularly the speech of Mr. Wedderlmru, 1 Cavendibli Deb. 332. = 38 Com. J. 977. 2 lb. 158, ' 17 lb. 128.

disability unknow n to the l:. On the 27th April 1641, Mr. Hollis, a member, was suspended the house during the session; a sentence of a more modified character, and one in which the rights of electors were no more infringed, than if the house had exercised its unquestionable power of imprisonment.

CHAPTER III.

GENERAL VIEW OF THE PRIVILEGES OF PARLIAMENT: POWER OF COMMITMENT BY BOTH HOUSES FOR BREACHES OF PRIVILEGE. CAUSES OF COMMITMENT CANNOT BE IN-

QUIRED INTO BY COURTS OF LAW: NOR THE PRISONERS

"' ' " i II. IWH1WIM. IMUII. I.

BE ADMITTED TO BAIL. ACTS CONSTRUED AS BREACHES OF PRIVI-LEGE. DIFFERENT PUNISHMENTS INFLICTED BY THE TWO HOUSES.

Both houses of Parliament enjoy various privileges in Privileges en-their collective capacity, as constituent parts of the High "iaw' and custom Court of Parliament; which are necessary for the sujuiort " Pariianient ' J 1 i and by statute.

of their authority, and for the proper exercise of the functions entrusted to them by the constitution. Other privileges, again, are enjoyed by individual members; which protect their persons and secure their independence and dignity.

Some privileges rest solely upon the law and custom of Parliament, while others have been defined by statute. Upon these grounds alone, all privileges whatever are founded. The lords have ever enjoyed them, simply because "they have place and voice in Parliament;"' but a practice has obtained with the commons, that would appear
' 2 Com. J. 128. See also other cases, 8 Com. J. 289; 9 lb. 105; 10 lb. 84G.- Ilakew. 82.

to submit their privileges to the royal favour. At the commencement of every Parliament since the 6th of Henry VIII., it has been the custom for the speaker.

Speaker's " In the name, and on behalf of the commons, to lay claim, pelitiou. r, y humble petition, to their ancient and undoubted' rights and privileges; particularly that their persona, their estates, and servants might be free from arrests and all molestations; that they may enjoy liberty of speech in all their debates; may have access to her majesty's royal person whenever occasion shall require; and that all their proceedings may receive from her majesty the most favourable construction."

To which the Lord Chancellor replies, that

"Her majesty most readily conjinm all the rights and privileges which have ever been granted to or conferred upon the commons, by her majesty or any of her royal predecessors."

The influence of the Crown in regard to the privileges of the commons is further acknowledged by the report of the speaker to the house, " that their privileges have been confirmed in as full and ample a manner as they have been heretofore granted or allowed by her majesty or any of her ro-al predecessors."

This custom probably originated in the ancient practice of confirming laws in Parliament, that w ere already in force, by petitions from the commons, to which the assent of the king was given with the advice and consent of the lords. In Atwyll's case, 17 Edward IV., the petition of the commons to the king states that their "liberties and franchises your highness to your lieges, called by your authority royal to this your High Court of Parliament, for the shires, cities, burghs, and five ports of this realm, by your authority royal, at commencement of this Parliament, graciously have ratified and confirmed to us, your ' See the memorable protestation of the commons, in answer to James I., who took offence at the words used by the speaker in praying for their privileges as " their antient and undoubted right and inheritance." 5 Pari. Hist. 512; 2 Proceedings and Deljatcs of the Commons, 1620-1, 359.

73 Lords' J. 571; 80 lb. 8. 103 Com. J. 7, said commons, now assembled by your said royal commandment in this your said present Parliament."

But whatever may have been the origin and cause of this custom, and however great the concession to the Crown may appear, the privileges of the commons are nevertheless independent of the Crown, and are enjoyed irrespectively of their petition. Some have been confirmed by statute, and are, therefore, beyond the control either of the Crown or of any other power but Parliament; while others, having been limited or even abolished by statute, cannot be granted by the Crown.

Every privilege will be separately treated, beginning with such as are enjoyed by each house collectively, and proceeding thence to such as attach to individual members; but, before these are explained, two of the points enumerated in the speaker's petition may be disposed of, as being matters of courtesy rather than privilege. The first of these is "freedom of access to her majesty;" and the second " that their proceedings may receive a favourable construction."

1. The first request for freedom of access to the sove- Freedom of 3CCCSS tor tllg reign is recorded in the 28th Henry VIII.; " but," says commous. Elsynge, "it appeareth plainly they ever enjoyed this, even when the kings were absent from Parliament;" and in the "times of Richard II., Henry IV., and downwards, the commons, with the speaker, were ever admitted to the king's presence in Parliament to deliver their answers; and oftentimes, under Richard II., Henry IV., and Henry VI., they did propound matters to the king, which were not given them in charge to treat of." The privilege of access is not enjoyed by individual members of the House of Commons, but only by the house at large, with their speaker; and the only occasion on which it is exercised is when an address is presented to her majesty by the ' 6 Rot. Pari. 191. Elsynge, 17o, 170. whole house. Without this privilege it is undeniable that the queen might refuse to receive such an address presented in that manner; and that so far as tlie attendance of the whole house in person may give effect to an address, it is a valuable privilege. But addresses of the house may be communicated by any members who have access to her majesty as privy councillors; and thus the same constitutional effect may be produced, without the exercise of the privilege of the house.

The only right claimed and exercised by individual members, in availing themselves of the privilege of access to her majesty, is that of accompanying the speaker with addresses, and entering the presence of royalty, in their ordinaiy attire. Such a practice is, perhaps, scarcely worthy of notice, but it is probably founded upon the concession to the House of Commons, of a free access to the throne, which may be supposed to entitle them, as members, to dispense with the forms and ceremonies of the court.

Free access for I ar different is the privilege enjoyed by the House of Peers. Not only is that house, as a body, entitled to free access to the throne, but each peer, as one of the hereditary counsellors of the Crown, is individually privileged to have an audience of her majesty.

Favourable 2. That all the proceedings of the commons may receive construction of r., o i the commons' irom her majesty the most favourable construction, is proceedings. conducive to that cordial co-operation of the several branches of the legislature which is essential to order and good government; but it cannot be classed among the privileges of Parliament. It is not a constitutional right, but a personal courtesy; and if not observed, the proceedings of tlie house are guarded against any interference, on the part of the Crown, not authorized by the laws and constitution of the country. The occasions for this courtesy are also limited; as by the law and custom of Par- ' See also Cliap. XVII., On Addresse?. luiinent the queen cannot take notice of anything said or clone in the house, but by the report of the house itself."

Each house, as a constituent part of Parliament, exer- Privileges of cises its own privileges inclepcndently of the otlicr. They lectivuly. are enjoyed, however, not by any separate right peculiar to each; but solely by virtue of the law and custom of Parliament. There are rights or powers peculiar to each, as explained in the last chapter; but all privileges, properly so called, appertain equally to both houses. These are declared and expounded by each house; and breaches of privilege are adjudged and censured by each; but still it is the law of Parliament that is thus administered.

The law of Parliament is thus defined by two eminent Law and cus-authorities: " As every court of justice hath laws and j. " customs for its direction, some the civil and canon, some the common law, others their own peculiar laws and customs, so the high court of Parliament hath also its own peculiar law, called the lex et consuetudo Parlia-mentir' This law of Parliament is admitted to be part of the unwritten law of the land, and as such is only to be collected, according to the words of Sir Edward Coke, " out of the rolls of Parliament and other records, and by precedents and continued experience;" to wliich it is added, that "whatever matter arises concerning either house of Parliament, ought to be discussed and adjudged in that house to which it relates, and not elsewhere."'

Hence it follows that whatever the Parliament has constantly declared to be a privilege. Is the sole evidence of its being part of the ancient law of Parliament. " The only method," says Blackstone, "of proving that this or that maxim is a rule of the common law, is by showing that it hath always been the custom to observe it;" and " it is laid down as a general rule that the decisions of courts of ' 4 Inst. 15. See also infra. Chap. IV., On Fiuedom of Speech. ' 4 lust. 1.3. 1 ni. Conim. 10:5. 4 Inst. ir.

GO BUEACIIES OF PnivILEGE.

justice are the evidence of what is common law."' The same rule is strictly applicable to matters of privilege, and to the expounding of the unwritten law of Parliament. New privileges But although either house may expound the law of created. Parliament, and vindicate its own privileges, it is agreed that no new privilege can he created. In 1704, the lords communicated a resolution to the commons at a conference, "That neither house of Parliament have power, by any vote or declaration, to create to themselves new privileges, not warranted by the known laws and customs of Parliament;" which was assented to by the commons.

In treating of the privileges of individual members, it will be shown, that in the earlier periods of parliamentary history, the commons did not always vindicate their privileges by their own direct authority; but resorted to the king, to special statutes, to writs of privilege, and even to the House of Lords, to assist them in protecting their members. It will be seen in what manner they gradually assumed their just position as an independent part of the legislature, and at lengtli established the present mode of administering the law of Parliament. Breach of privi- Both houscs DOW act upon precisely the same grounds ovtiie hiU"' ' In matters of privilege. They declare what cases, by the ourt of Par- jj y jjjj custom of Parliament, are breaches of privile2: e; liament. ' i ' and punish the offenders by censure or commitment, in the same manner as courts of justice punish for contempt. Their modes of punishment may occasionally differ, in some respects, in consequence of the different powers of the two houscs; but the principle upon which the offence is determined, and the dignity of Parliament vindicated, is the same in both houses. Commitment. The right to commit for contempt, though universally acknowledged to belong equally to both houses, is often 1 Comm. G8. 71. 14 Com. J. 555. i, (jo.

8 Grey's Debates, 232.

regarded with jealousy when exercised by the commons. This has arisen partly from the powers of judicature in-lierent in the lords, which have endowed that house with the character of a high court of justice; and partly from the more active political spirit of the lower house. But the acts of the House of Lords, in its legislative capacity, onght not to be confounded with its judicature; nor should the political composition of the House of Commons be a ground for limiting its authority. The particular acts of l)oth hovises should, undoubtedly, be watched with vigilance when they appear to be capricious or unjust; but it is unreasonable to cavil at privileges, in general, which have been long established by law and custom, and which are essential to the dignity and power of Parliament.

The power of the House of Lords to commit for con- By tiie Lords. tempt was questioned in the cases of the Earl of Shaftesbury," in 1675, and of tlower, in 1779; but was admitted without hesitation by the Court of King's Bench.

The power of commitment by the commons is estab- By tiie Com-lished upon the ground and evidence of immemorial usage. It was admitted, most distinctly, by the lords, at the conference between the two houses, in the case of Ashby and White, in 1704," and it has been repeatedly recognised by the courts of law: viz. by 1 of the judges, in the case of the Aylesbury Ien; by the Court of King's Bench, in Murray's case;" by the Court of Common Pleas, in Crosby's case; by the Court of Exchequer, in the case of Oliver (1771); by the Court of King's Bench, in Burdett's case, in 1811;" in the case of Mr. Hobhouse, in 1819;"

' G Howell, St. Tr. 12G9, et seq. 8 Durnf. Ea=t, 314.

Mr. Wynn states that nearly 1,000 instances of its exercise have occurred since 1547, tiie period at wiiicli the Journals commence (Aryuiueiif, p. 7); and numerous cases have occurred since the publication of Mr. Wynn's treatise.

17 Lords' J. 714. 2 Lord Raym. lloo; 3 Wils. 20o.

1 Wils. 299 (1751). 7 3 Wils. 203 (1771). lb.

9 14 E: ist, 1. '" 2 Chit. R."p. 207; Barn. He Aid. 420.

mons.

in the case of the Sheriff of Midtllcsex, in 1840;' and lastly, by the Conrt of Exchequer Chamber, in Howard's case, in 1846. The power is also virtually admitted by the statute 1 James I., c. 13, s. 3, which provides that nothing therein shall " extend to the diminishing of any punishment to be hereafter, by censure in Parliament, inflicted upon any person," c.

Authority and The right of Commitment being thus admitted, it be- ofti! erstn cxe-comcs an important question to determine, what authority ciitinii orders of j protection are acquired by officers of eitlier house in either liousc., r i executing the orders of their respective courts.

Any resistance to the serjeant-at-arms, or his officers, or others acting in execution of the orders of the house, has always been treated as a contempt by both houses, and the parties, in numerous instances, have suffered punishment accordingly. y, j, g The lords will not suffer any persons, whether officers of the house or others, to be molested for executing their orders," or the orders of a committee," and will protect them from actions.

On the 28th November 1768, the house being informed that an action had been commenced against Mr. Ilesse, a justice of tlie peace for Westminster, who had acted under the immediate orders of the house in suppressing a riot at the doors of the house, in Palace-yard, Biggs, the plaintiff, and Aylett, his attorney, were ordered to attend. On the 1st December, Biggs was attached, but afterwards discharged out of custody, with a reprimand, upon his signing a release to Mr. Hesse. Aylett was sent to Newgate, whence he was discharged on the 9th December, on his petition expressing contrition for his offence."'

On the 26th June 1788, Aldern, a constable, complained ' 1 Adolphu9 Elli?, 273.
Printed Papers, 2d Report, 1845 (30.5), (307); 1847 (39).
13 Lords' J. 104; 1,5 lb. 5G.5; 21 lb. 190; 38 lb. 640; 45 lb. 340. GIO.
13 Lords' J. 412. " 32 lb. 187. 107.
that in pursuance of an order of the house he had refused Mr. Hyde admittance to AVestnihister Hall during the trial of Warren Hastings, for which he had been indicted for an assault, and put to much expense. ISIr. Hyde was ordered to attend, and committed for his offence. On the 30th June he was discharged, with a reprimand, on submitting himself to the house."

The last case of the kind was that commonly known as "the umbrella case." On the 26th March 1827, complaint was made that John Bell had served F. Plass, a doorkeeper, when attending his duty in the house, with process from the Westminster Court of Requests, first to appear, and afterwards to pay a debt and costs awarded against him by that court, for the loss of anj imbrella which had been left with the doorkeeper during a debate. Bell and the clerks of the Court of Requests were summoned: the former was admonished; and the latter, not being aware of the nature of the complaint, were directed to withdraw.

In the case of Ferrers, in 1543, the commons committed Oommons. the sheriffs of London to the Tower, for having resisted their serjeant-at-arms, w4th his mace, in freeing a member who had been imprisoned in the Compter.

In 1681, after a dissolution of Parliament, an action Avas brought against Topham, the serjeant-at-arms attending the commons, for executing the orders of the house in arresting certain persons. Topham pleaded to the jurisdiction of the couit, but his plea was overruled, and judgment was given a2; ainst him. The house declared this to be a breach of privilege, and committed Sir F. Pemberton and Sir T. Jones, who had been the judges in the case, to the custody of the serjeant-at-arms. This case will be referred to again for another purpose, but here it is adduced as a precedent of the manner in which officers have been supported by the house in the execution of its orders.

In 1771, the House of Commons had ordered a person ' 38 Lords' J. 219, 250, 261. ' 59 lb. 199. 20G.
to be tiikcn into custody, who was arrested by a messenger by virtue of the speaker's warrant. The messenger was charged with an assault, and brought before the lord mayor and two aldermen, at the Mansion house, who set tlie prisoner at liberty and committed the messenger of the house for an assault." For this obstruction to the orders of the house, Mr. Alderman Oliver and the lord mayor (Brass Crosby) were

committed to the Tower. Assistance of It Cannot, Indeed, be supposed that when the house has tu'civi power. Qj. jg- j q Serjeant to execute a warrant, it will not sustain his authority, and punish those who resist him. But a question still arises concerning the authority with which he is invested by law, when executing a warrant properly made out by order of the house; and the assistance he is entitled to demand from the civil power. Both houses have always considered every branch of the civil government as bound to assist, when required, in executing their warrants and orders; and have repeatedly required such assistance.

In 1640, all mayors, justices,: c. in England and Ireland were ordered, l)y the commons, to aid in the apprehension of Sir G. llatcliffe."' In 1660, the scrjeant was expressly empowered

"to break open a house n case of resistance, and to call to his assistance the slieriff of Middlesex, and all other officers, as he shall see cause; and who are required to assist him accordingly."

And on the 23d October 1690, the lords authorised the black rod to break open the doors of any house, in the presence of a constable, and there search for and seize Lord Keveton."

On the 24th January 1670, the House of Commons ordered a warrant to be issued for apprehending several persons, who had resisted the deputy scrjeant, and resolved,

"That the high sheriff of the county of Gloucester, and other officers concerned, are to be required by warrant from the speaker, to be aiding and assisting: in the execution of such warrant."' ' 33 Com. J. 263; and Report of Committee, 1771. ' lb. 285. 28!).

See other Cases, 1) Com. J. 341. f)87; 13 lb. 820. 2 Com. J. 29.

' 8 Com. J. 222. 14 Lords' J."530. ") Com. J. 1!)3.

And again, on the 5th April 1679, it was ordered,

"That the speaker do issue out. his warrant, requiring all sheriffs, bailiffs, constables, and all otiier his majesty's officers and subjects, to be aiding and assisting to the serjeant-at-arms attending tiiis house." '

The Lords also have frequently required the assistance of the civil power in a similar manner."

And at the present time, by every speaker's warrant to the serjeant-at-arms for taking a person into custody, " all mayors, sheriffs, under-sheriffs, bailiffs, constables, head-boroughs and officers of the house are required to be aiding and assisting in the execution thereof."

Before the year 1810, however, no case arose in which the legal consequences of a speaker's warrant and the powers and duties of the serjeant-at-arms in the execution of it, were distinctly explained and recognised by a legal tribunal, as well as by the judgment of Parliament, in punishing resistance.

In the case of Sir Francis Burdett, in 1810, a doubt Break incf open arose relative to the power of the serjeant-at-arms to '" ' '"

break into the dwelling-house of a person, against whom a speaker's warrant had been issued. The serjeant-at-arms having, in execution of a warrant, been resisted and turned out of Sir Francis Burdett's private dwelling-house by force, required the opinion of the attorney-general, "whether he would be justified in breaking open the outer or any inner door of the i rivate dwelling-house of Sir F. Burdett, or of any other person in which there is reasonable cause to suspect he is concealed, for the purpose of apprehending liini; and whether he might take to his assistance a sufficient civil or military force for that purpose, such force acting under the direction of a civil magistrate; and whether such proceedings would be justifiable during the night as well as in the day-time."

The opinion of the attorney-general is so important, as pointing out the legal authority of the serjcant, and cau- ' 8 Com. J. 586; See also 2 lb. 371; 9 lb. 363.

' 21st December 1078,13 Lords' J. 429; 21st ami 23d OctoberlgOO, 14 lb. 527. 530; 21st INlay 1747, 27 lb. 118. 05 Com. J. 204.

tioning him as to the mode of exerting it, that it may be inserted nearly at lengtli:

"No instance is stated to nie, and I presume that none is to be found in which tlie outer door of a house has been broken open under the speaker's warrant, for the purpose of ajiprehending the person against whom such warrant issued, then being therein. I must, therefore, form my opinion altogether ujion cases which have arisen upon the execution of writs or warrants issuing from other courts, and which seem to fall within the same principle.

"I tind it laid down in Semayne's case, 5 Co. 91, that where the king is a party, the sheriflp may break open the defendant's house, either to arrest him or to do other execution of the king's process; if otherwise, he cannot enter. So if the defendant be in the house of another man, the sheriff may do the same; but he cannot break into the house of the defendant in the execution of any process at the suit of an individual. This distinction proceeds, as I apprehend, upon the greater importance of enforcing the process of the Crown for the public benefit, than that of individuals for the support of their private rights. Reasoning from hence, I should think that the speaker's warrant, which had issued to apprehend a man under sentence of commitment for a breach of the privileges of the House of Commons, might be executed in the same manner with criminal i)rocess in the name of the king, inasmuch as th se privileges were given to the House of Commons for the benefit of the public only; and the public are interested in the due support of them. If the act had been done, and I were asked whether it could be defended, I should say that it could; but where it is previously known that the execution of the warrant will be resisted by force, and if death should ensue in such a conflict, the officer who executes tlie warrant would stand justified, or not, as the breaking of the house may be held lawful or unlawful: I feel myself obliged to bring this under his notice, leaving liim to judge for himself whether he will venture to act upon my opinion, which has no direct authority in point to support it, but rests upon reasoning from other cases, which appear to me to fall within the same principle. Should the officer resolve to break into the house, if it be found necessary, he must be careful, first, to signify the cause of his coming, and make request to open the doors, and not use any force until it appears that those within will not comply; and he should be assured that the party whom he seeks to apprehend is within the house. For the purpose of executing the warrant, he may take with him a sufficient force of such description as the nature of the case renders necessary. If he has reason to apprehend a degree of resistance, which can only be repelled by a military force, he may take such force with him; but in this case it will be prudent to take with him also a civil magistrate.

"I do not think it advisable to execute the warrant in the night.

"The officer should understand, that when Sir Francis Burdutt has once been arrested, if he afterwards eftects his escape or is rescued, his own house or the house of any other person into which he retreats, may be broken for the purpose of re-taking him. "V. GibBS."

In consequence of this opinion the serjeant-at-arms forced an entrance into Sir F. Burdett's house, down the area, and conveyed liis prisoner to the Tower, with the assistance of a military force. Sir F. Burdett subsequently Burdett r. Ab- broufjht actions against the speaker and the serjeant-at-arms '

T J 1 Biinlett V. Col- in the Coui't of King's Bench. The house dn-ected the man.

attorney-general to defend them. The causes were both tried, and verdicts were obtained for the defendants.

With respect to the authority of the serjeant-at-arms to break open the outer door of Sir F. Burdett's house. Lord

Ellenborough said,

"Upon autliorities the most unquestionable this point has been settled, that where an injury to the public has been committed, in the shape of an insult to any of the courts of justice, on which process of contempt is issued, the officer charged with the execution of such process may break open doors, if necessary, in order to execute it; and it cannot be contended that the houses of legislature are less strongly armed in point of protection and remedy against contempts towards them, than the courts of justice are."

Thus confirming the opinion of the attorney-general, upon which the serjeant had acted. This judgment was afterwards affirmed, on a writ of error, by the Exchequer Chamber, and ultimately by the House of Lords."

But although the serjeant-at-arms may force an en- Howardr. Gos-trance, he is not authorised to remain in the house if the igt"Action party be from home, in order to await his return. Mr. Howard, a solicitor, brought an action of trespass against certain officers of the House of Commons, who, in execut- ' G5 Com. J. 264. ' 14 East, 157.

3 4 Taunt. 401. 5 Dow. 1G5.

ing a speaker's warrant for his apprehension, had stayed several hours in his house. The trial caine on before Lord Dennian, in the sittings at "Westminster after Michael-mas term, 1842, when it appeared in evidence that the messengers had remained for several hours in the house awaiting the return of Howard, after they knew that he was from home.

The attorney-general, who appeared for the defendants, admitted that, although they had a right to enter Howard's house, and to be in his house for a reasonable time to search for him, yet that they had no right to stay there until he returned; and Lord Denman directed the jury to say what just and reasonable compensation the officers should make for their trespass, which their warrant from the House of Commons did not authorise. A verdict was consequently given for the plaintiff on the second count, with 100. damages. The verdict proceeded entirely upon the ground of the defendants having exceeded their authority, and without any reference to the jurisdiction of the House of Commons. But if the officer should not exceed his authority he will be protected by the courts, even if the warrant should not be technically formal, according to the rules by which the warrants of inferior courts are tested. Howard r. G09- Li 1843, Mr. Howard commenced another action of 2(1 Action. trespass against Sir W. Gosset, the serjeant-at-arms, and the Court of Queen's Bench gave judgment for the plaintiff, on the ground that the warrant was technically informal, and did not justify the acts of the Serjeant. This judgment, however, was reversed by the Court of Exchequer Chamber, which thus stated the difference of the opinion of that court and of the Queen's Bench: " They construe the warrant as they would that of a magistrate; we construe it as a writ from a superior court; the authorities relied upon by them relate to the warrants

' Carrington Marsliman, 382. Adol. Ellis, 209.

and couiiuitments of magistrates; they do not apply to the writs and mandates of superior courts, still less to those of either branch of the High Court of Parliament."
" Writs issued by a superior court, not appearing to be out of the scope of their jurisdiction, are valid of themselves, without any further allegation, a7id a protection to all officers and others in their aid, acting under them; and that although on the face of them they be irregular, as a capias against a peeress (Countess of Rutland's case, 6 Coke's Rep. 54 a), or void in form, as a capias ad respondendum not returnable the next term (Parsons v. Loyd, 3 Wilson, 341); for the officers ought not to examine the judicial act of the court, whose servants they are, nor exercise their judgment touching the validity of the process in point of law, but are bound to execute it, and are therefore protected by it '

The power of commitment, with all the authority which Causes of com- 1.,,,. 1 T 1 T 1 mitnient cannot can be given by law, bemg thus established, it becomes be inquired into the key-stone of parliamentary privilege. Either house yj courts o may adjudge that any act is a breach of privilege and contempt; and if the warrant recite that the person to be arrested has been guilty of a breach of privilege, the courts of law cannot inquire into the grounds of the judgment; but must leave him to suffer the punishment awarded by the High Court of Parliament, by which he stands committed.

The Habeas Corpus Act is binding upon all persons Habeas Corpus, whatever who have prisoners in their custody, and it is therefore competent for the judges to have before them persons committed by the Houses of Parliament for contempt. There have been cases, indeed, in which writs of habeas corpus have been resisted: as in 1675, when the House of Commons directed the lieutenant of the Tower to make no return to any writ of habeas corpus relating to persons imprisoned by its order f and in 1704, when similar ' Shortiiand writer's notes, 1847 (39),). 16G. 168.- 31 Car. II. c. 2. y (jo j. r directions were given to the serjeant at-arms." But tlicse orders arose from the contests raging between the two houses; the first in regard to the judicature of the lords, and the second concerning the jurisdiction of the commons in matters of election; and it has since been the invariable practice for the serjeant-at arms and others, by order of the house, to make returns to writs of habeas corpus.

rrisoners can- But although the return is made according to law, the parties who stand committed for contempt cannot be admitted to ball by the courts of law. It had been so adjudged by the courts, during the Commonwealth, in the cases of Captain

Streater" and Sir Robert Pye."' The same opinion was expressed in Sheridan's case, by many of the first lawyers in the House of Commons, shortly after the passing of the Habeas Corpus Act f and it has been confirmed by resolutions of the House of Commons and by numerous subsequent decisions of the courts of law; of which the following are some of the most remarkable.

Earlofshaftes- In 1675 Lord Shaftesbury, who had been committed by the House of Lords for a contempt, was brought before the Court of King's Bench, but remanded. In that case Lord Chief Justice Kainsford said,

"He is in execution of the judgment given by tbe lords for contempt; and therefore if he should be bailed, he would be delivered out of execution." And again, "This court has no jurisdiction of the cause, and therefore the form of the return is not considerable."

' 14 Com. J. og5.

95 Com. J. 25. Hans. Deb., 24 Jan. 1840, 51 N. S. 550.

By order of the House of Commons, 23d June 1647, the seijeant and keepers of persons are directed to make returns to writs of habeas corpus, with the causes of detention; but the Judges are not to proceed to bail or discliarge the prisoners without notice to the House. 5 Com. J. 221. See also 2 lb. 9G0.

5 Howell, St. Tr. 365. Styles. 415. 5 Howell, St. Tr. 948.

e A. D. 1680; 4 Hans. Pari. Hist. 1262.

7 9 Com. J. 356, 357; 12 lb. 174; 14 lb. 565. 599.

6 Howell, St. Tr. 1269. 1 Freem. 153. 1 Mod. 144. 3 Keble, 792.

In the case of the Queen v. Paty," objections had been Paty'ucaee. taken to the form of the warrant, but JMr. Justice Gould said, "if this had been a return of a commitment by an inferior court, it had been nauglit, because it did not set out a sufficient cause of commitment; but this return being of a commitment by the House of Commons, which is superior to this court, it is not reversible for formp And Mr. Justice Powys, relying upon the analogy of commitments by the House of Commons and by the superior courts, said, "The House of Commons is a great court, and all things done by them are to be intended to have been rite acta, and the matter need not be so specially recited in their warrants, by the same reason as we commit people by a rule of court of two lines; and such commitments are held good, because it is to be Intended that we understand what we do." And in the record of this case it is expressed that he was remitted to custody, "quod cognitio causai captionls et detentlonis pr dicti Johannis Paty non pertinet ad curiam."

In 1751 Mr. Murray was committed to Newgate by the Murray's case. commons for a contempt, and was brought up to the Court of King's Bench by a habeas corpus. The court refused to admit him to ball, Wright, J., saying,

"It need not apjiear to us what the contempt was for; if it did appear, we could not judge thereof; the House of Commons is superior to this court in this particular. This court cannot admit to bail a person committed for a contempt in any other court in Westminster Hall."

In Brass Crosby's case, in 1771, De Grey, C. J., said, Brass Crosby's case.

""When the House of Commons adjudge anything to be a contempt or a breach of privilege, their adjudication is a conviction, and their commitment in consequence an execution; and no court can discharge or bail a person that is in execution by the judgment of any other court." And again, "Courts of justice have no cognisance of the acts of the Houses of Parliament, because they belong ' ad aliud examen.""

2 Lord Raymond, 1109. Salk. 503.

= 1 Wil8.200. 3 ly Howell, St. Tr. 1137. 3 Wils. Itttj. 203.

Flower's case. Again, in the case of Flower, who had been committed by the House of Lords for a libel on tlie Bisliop of Llan-dallj the prisoner applied in vain to the King's Bench to be admitted to bail, and Lord Kenyon, adopting the same view as other judges before him, said,

"We were bound to grant tliis habeas corpus; but having seen the return to it, we are bound to remand the defendant to prison, because the sul)ject belongs to 'aliud examen.""

Hoiiiiouse's In the case of Mr. Ilobhouse, Lord Chief Justice Abbott case., said,

"Tlie power of commitment for contempt is incident to every court of justice, and more especially it belongs to the High Court of Parliament; and therefore it is incompetent for this court to question the privileges of the House of Commons, on a commitment for an offence which they have adjudged to be a contempt of those privileges." And again, "We cannot inquire into the form of the commitment, even supposing it to be open to objection on the ground of informality."

Sh. riffof Mid- TJie last case that occurred was that of the sheriff of Middlesex, in 1840, who had been committed for executing a judgment of the Court of Queen's Bench against the printers of the House of Commons. In obedience to an order of the house," the serjeant made a return to the writ, that he had taken and detained the sheriff by virtue of a warrant under the hand of the speaker, which warrant was as follows:

"Whereas the House of Commons have this day resolved that W. Evans, esq. and J. Wheelton, esq sheriff of Middlesex, having been guilty of a contempt and breach of the privileges of this liouse, be committed to the custody of tlie serjeant-at-arms attending this house; these are tlierefore to require you to take into your custody the bodies of the said W. Eviins and J. Wheelton, and them safely to keej) during the pleasure of this house; for which this shall be your sufficient warrant."

It was argued that, under the 56 Geo. HI., c. 100, s. 3, the judges could examine into the truth of the facts set forth in the return, by affidavit or by affirmation; that 8 Dnrnf. East, 314. 2 (hit. Rcii. 207.3 Barn. Aid. 420.

95 Com. J. 2o.

the return was bad because it did not state the facts on which the contempt arose; and that the warrant did not show a sufficient jurisdiction in those who issued it. No one appeared in support of the return, but the judges were unanimously of opinion that the return was good, and that they could not inquire into the nature of the contempt," although it was notorious that the sheriff had been committed for executing a judgment of that court.

From these cases it may now be considered as established beyond all question, that the cause of commitments by either house of Parliament, for breaches of privilege and contempt, cannot be inquired into by courts of law, but that their " adjudication is a conviction, and their commitment, in consequence, an execution." Nor, indeed, could any other rule be adopted consistently with the independence of either house of Parliament. It has been seen that no greater power is claimed by Parliament than is readily conceded by the courts to one another; and another recent example may be added. On the 18th November 1845, Mr. William Cobbett was brought before the Court of Common Pleas by the keeper of the Queen's Prison, in obedience to a writ of habeas corpus. It appeared that the prisoner was detained under a writ of attachment which had been issued against him by the Court of Chancery, for a contempt of that court, in not having paid certain costs. Upon which the court said, that "if Mr. Cobbett had any complaint to make against the legality of the detainer (and the court were far from saying that he might not have a just ground for such a complaint), he ought to apply to the Court of Chancery. This court had no right and no power to interfere with the proceedings of a court of co-ordinate jurisdiction, and therefore Ir. Cobbett must be remanded to his former custody."' ' 11 Adol. Ellis, 273. ' See also in re V. Dimes, 17 Jiimuiry 1850, 14 Jurist, 198.

Not necessary to express any cause of commitment.

Persons sent for in custody.

One qiialificiition of this doctrine, however, must not be omitted. Mlcu it appears, upon the return of the writ, simply that the party has been committed for a contemi)t and breach of privilege, it has been universally admitted that it is incomjjetent for the courts to inquire further into the nature of the contempt; but if the causes of commitment were stated on the warrant, and appeared to be beyond the jurisdiction of the house, it is probable that their sufficiency would be examined. Lord EUenborough, in his judgment in Burdett v. Abbot, drew the distinction between such cases in the following manner:

"If a commitment appeared to be for a contempt of the House of Commons generally, I would, neither in the case of that court nor of any other of the superior courts, inquire further; but if it did not profess to commit for a contempt, but for some matter ap-poarinf; on the return, which could by no reasonable intendment be considered as a contempt of the court committing, but a ground of commitment palpably and evidently arbitrary, unjust and contrary to every principle of positive law or natural justice; I say, that in the case of such a commitment (if it ever should occur, but which I cannot possibly anticipate as ever likely to occur), we must look at it and act upon it as justice may require, from whatever court it may profess to have proceeded."

And in this opinion Lord Denman appears to have acquiesced, in the case of the sheriff of Middlesex. The same principle may be collected from the judgment of the Exchequer Chamber, in Gosset v. Howard, where it is said " it is presumed, with respect to such writs as are actually issued by superior courts, that they are duly issued, and in a case in which they have jurisdiction, unless the contrary appear mi the face of them

But it is not necessary that any cause of commitment should appear upon the warrant, nor that the prisoner should have been adjudged guilty of contempt. It has been a very ancient practice in both houses, to send for per- ' 14 East, 1.

sons in custody to answer charges of contempt;' and in the lords, to order them to be attached and brought before the house to answer complaints of breaches of privilege, contempts, and other offences. This practice is analogous to writs of attachment upon mesne process in the superior courts, and is unquestionably legal.

In the judgment of the Court of Exchequer Chamber, in the case of Gosset v. Howard, already alluded to, it was stated that

"Writs of attachment from superior courts do not state the previous steps of a charge of contemjit, the rule of the court that tliey slioukl issue, or the nature of the contempt." " It ai)pears, indeed, that if a writ of a superior court expressed no cause at all, it wouhl be legal, and the defendant not bailable, according to what Lord Coke says in the Brewers' case, 1 Roll. R. 134. It was a mistake to assert, as was done at the bar, that an adjudication of a contempt was a necessary part of every committal for a contempt, and that an attachment would be invalid without it. It is not so in the superior courts of common law, as has been stated, nor in the Court of Chancery, as Lord Lyndliurst has lately decided, after an inquiry into precedents." Ex parte Van Sandan, 1 Phillips' Rep., 605.) In earlier times it was not the custom to prepare a formal Arrests wiih- ' out warrant, warrant for executing the orders of the House of Commons; but the serjeant arrested persons with the mace, without any written authority; and at the present day he takes strangers into custody who intrude themselves into the house, or otherwise misconduct tliemselves, in virtue of the general orders of the house, and without any specific instructions.

' 2 Lords' J. 201 (26th Nov. 1597); 2 lb. 256 (17th Dec. 1601); 2 Tb. 296; and for several other cases, see Calendar to Lords'Journ. (1509-1642), p. 117 et seq., and 257 et seq. 11 Lords' J. 252, c. 1 Cora. J. 175. 680 (9th March 1623); 1 lb. 886 (22d April 1628); 9 Ih. 351 (2d June 1675); 17 lb. 493 (12th March 1713); 21 lb. 705 (30th March 1731); 23 Ih. 146. 451, 452 (1738-9); 35 lb. 323 (27th April 1775); 80 lb. 445 (20th May 1825); 82 lb. 561 (14th June 1827); 95 lb. 30 (4th Feb. 1840).

' See precedents collected In App. to 2d Rep. on Printed Papers, 1845 (397), p. 104.

Bainbri-ge's case, 29th Feb. 1575. 1 Com. J. 109. 1 Hats. 92. 2d Rep. Printed Papers, 1845, p. vl.

' 85 Com. J. 461; 86 lb. 323; 88 lb. 246.

The lords attach and conunit persons by order, without any warrant. The order of the house Is signed hy the clerk-assistant of the Parliaments, and is the authority under which the officers of the house and others execute their duty. Breaches of AVilful disobedicncc to orders, within its jurisdiction, is a tiued. ' contempt of any court, and disobedience to the orders and rules of Parliament, in the exercise of its constitutional functions, is treated as a breach of privilege. Insults and obstructions, also, offered to a court at large, or to any of its members, are contempts; and in like manner, by the law of Parliament, are breaches of privilege. It would be in vain to attempt an enimieration of every act which might be construed into a contempt, because the orders of every court must necessarily vary with the circumstances of each case; but certain principles may be collected from the Journals, which will serve as general declarations of the law of Parliament.

Brcaclies of privilege may be divided into, 1. Disobedience to general orders or rules of either house; 2. Disobedience to particular orders; 3. Indignities offered to the character or proceedings of Parliament; 4. Assaults or interference with members in discharge of their duty, or reflections upon their character and conduct in Parliament. Disobedience of 1. Disobedience to any of the orders or rules which are aud rules. madc for the convenience or efficiency of the proceedings of the house, is a breach of privilege, the punishment of which would be left to the house, by those who are most jealous of parliamentary privilege. But if such orders should appear to clash with the common or statute law of the country, their validity is liable to question, as will be shown In a separate chapter upon the jurisdiction of the courts in matters of privilege.

' Cliapter VI.

debates. Lords.

PUBLICATION OF DEBATES. 77

As examples of general ordci's, the violation of which would be regarded as breaches of privilege, the following may be sufficient.

The publication of the debates of either house has been Puwicntion of repeatedly declared to be a breach of privilege, and especially fjilse and perverted reports of them; and no doubt can exist that if either house desire to withhold their proceedings from the public, it is within the strictest limits of their jurisdiction to do so, and to punish any violation of their orders. The lords have a stfinding order, of the 27th February 1698, by which it is declared,

"That it is a breach of the privilege of this house, for any person whatsoever to print, or publish in print, anything relating to the proceedings of the house without the leave of this house."' In 1801, Allan Macleod, a prisoner in Newgate, con- Cases. victed for a misdemeanor, was fined 100., and committed to Newgate for six months after the expiration of his sentence, for publishing certain paragraphs purporting to be a proceeding of the house, which had been ordered to be expunged from the Journal, and the debate thereupon. He was also ordered to be kept in safe custody until he should pay the fine." And John Higginbottom, for vending and publishing these paragraphs, was fined 6 5. 8 d., and committed to Newgate for six months, and until he should pay the fine. He afterwards presented a petition to be liberated, was brought to the bar, reprimanded and discharged.

In the same year, H. Brown and T. Glassington were committed to the custody of the black rod, for printing and publishing in the Morning Herald some paragraphs purporting to be an account of what passed in debate, but which the house declared to be a scandalous misrepresentation.

' Lords' S. O. No. 22. = 4:3 Lords'J. 105. = II). U). 115.225.230.

43 Lords' J. fiy).

Commons. On the 13th July 1641, it was ordered by the commons,

"That no member shall either give a copy or publish in print anything that he shall speak here, without leave of the house.""

And on the 22d,

"That all the members of the house are enjoined to deliver out no copy or notes of anything that is brought into the house, propounded or agitated in the house."

On the 28th March 1642 it was resolved,

"That what person soever shall print (or) sell any act or passages of this house, under the name of a diurnal or otherwise, without the imrticular license of this house, shall be reputed a high contemner and breaker of the privilege of Parliament, and so punished accordingly."

The commons have also ordered at different times,

"That no news-letter writers do, in their letters or other papers that they disperse, presume to intermeddle with the debates or any other proceedings of this house."" " That no printer or publisher of any printed newspapers do presume to insert in any such papers any debates or any other proceedings of this house, or of any committee thereof." " That it is an indignity to and a breach of the privilege of this house, for any person to presume to give, in written or printed newspapers, any account or minute of the debates or other proceedings. That, upon discovery of the authors, printers, or publishers of any such news iaper, this house will proceed against the offenders with the utmost severity."

Other orders also to the same effect, though not verbally the same, have been repeated at different times." These orders, however, have long since fallen into disuse: debates are daily cited in Parliament from printed reports galleries have been constructed for the accommodation of reporters ' 2 Com. J. 209. This proceeding arose out of the printing of a speech of Lord Digby.

2 Com. J. 220. 3 2 lb. 501.

Orders, 22d Dec. 1694. 11th Feb. 1695. 18th Jan. 1697. 3d Jan. 1703. 23d Jan. 1722. 11 Com. J. 193; 11 lb. 439; 12 lb. 48; 14 lb. 270; 20 lb. 99.

20 Com. J. 99. b 26 Feb. 1728; 21 Com. J. 238.

7 13th April 1738. lotb April 1753. 3d March 1762. 23 Com. J. 148. 26 lb. 754; 29 lb. 207.

committees have been appointed to provide increased facilities for reporting, and complaints have been repeatedly made, in both houses, that the reports of debate? have sometimes not been sufficiently full. If any wilful misrepresentation of the debates should arise, or if on any particular occasion it should be thought necessary to enforce the restriction, there can be no question but that the house is still justified in punishing the offender, whether he be a member of the house, or a stranger admitted to its debates." But as orders prohibiting the publication of debates are still retained upon the Journals, the formal proceedings of the house, in case of any misrepresentation of its debates, are somewhat anomalous. The ground of complaint is, that a speech has been incorrectly reported; but the motion for the punishment of the printer assumes that the publication of the debate at all is a breach of privilege."' The principle, however, by which both houses are governed, is now sufficiently acknowledged. So long as the debates are correctly and faithfully reported, the privilege which prohibits their publication is waived; but when they are reported maldjide, the publishers of newspapers are liable to censure.

It is declared to be a breach of privilege for a member or any other person to publish the evidence taken before a select committee, until it has been reported to the house; ' and the publisher of a newspaper has been committed for this offence by the House of Commons.

There are various other orders and rules connected with parliamentary proceedings; for example, to prevent the forgery of signatures to a petition; for the protection of ' 74 Com. J. 537. See also Cliap. YII.

2 See debate on Mr. Christie's motion, 12th Feb. 1844. 72 Hans. Deb. 3d Series, 580. Debate, 1st May 1849. 104 Hans. Deb. 3d Series, 1054.

3 92 Com. J. 282.

87 Com. J. 3G0. See also Report on Postal Communication witli France, 1850 (381). " 4 Com. J. 800.

Disobedience to piirticular orders.

Libels upon tlie house.

Avitncsscs;' for scciirlnu true evidence before the house or committees;" for the correct jmbucation of the votes;' and for many other purposes which will appear in different parts of this work. A wilful violation of any of these orders or rules, or general misconduct in reference to the proceedings of Parliament, will be censured or punished, at the pleasure of the house whose orders are concerned."

2. Particular orders are of various kinds: as for the attendance of persons before the house or committees; the production of papers or records;" for enforcing answers to questions put by the house or by committees;' and, in short, for compelling persons to do, or not to do, any acts that are within the jurisdiction of the house. If orders be made beyond its jurisdiction, the house, as already shown, may punish the parties who refuse compliance with or obstruct the execution of them; but the enforcement of them may become a matter liable to question before the courts of law.

3. Indignities offered to the character or proceedings of Parliament, by libellous reflections, have always been resented and punislied as breaches of privilege. Some of the offenders have escaped with a reprimand; others have been committed to the custody of the black rod, or the serjeant-at-arms; while many have been confined in the Tower and in Newgate; and in the lords, fine, imprisonment, and the pillory have been adjudged. Prosecutions at law have also been ordered against the parties. The ' 22 Com. J. 146. Sessional orders. j, 4 Lords' J. 705; 37 Ib.613; 38 lb. 338.649. Lords' J., 12tli April 1850 (Mr. Nash); 13th August 1850 (Liverpool Corporation Waterworks).

5 91 Com. J. 338.

90 Com. J.564. 575. 19th April 1849; 104 Hans. Deb., 3d Series, 452.

' 88 Com. J. 218; 90 lb. 504.

See 4 Lords' J. 247, where Ilarwood and Drinkwater were committed to the Fleet, and pilloried, for disobedience to an order for quieting the possessions of Lord Lindsey; and 6 II). 493.

34 Lords' J. 3.30. 11 Com. J. 774; 23 lb. 546; 26 11). 9. 304; 34 lb. 4G4; 44 Ih. 463.

cases are so numerous that only a few of the most remarkable need be given.

The following extract from the report of a committee of Lords. the lords, 18th May 1716, will serve to show the practice of that house:

"That wliere offences have been committed against the honour and dignity of the house in general, or any member thereof, the house have proceeded, botli by way of fine and corporal punishment upon such offenders; but in other cases the attorney-general has been ordered to prosecute the offenders according to law; and the committee, on perusal of the several orders directing prosecutions by the attorney-general, do not find that, at any time, addresses have been made to the king for such prosecutions."'

Very severe punishments were formerly awarded by the lords in cases of libel, as fine, imprisonment, and pillory; but in modern times commitment with or without fine, has been the ordinary punishment. On the loth December 1756, George King was fined 50 Z. and committed to Newgate for six months, for publishing "a spurious and forged printed paper, dispensed and publicly sold as his majesty's speech to both houses of parliament.""' In 1798 Messrs. Lambert and Perry were fined 501. each, and committed to Newgate for three months, for a newspai)er paragraph higlily reflecting on the honour of the house."

In the commons, William Thrower Avas committed to Procedonts in the custody of the serjeant, in 1559, for a contempt in "'"'"""-words against the dignity of the house." In 1580 Mr. Arthur Hall, a member, was imprisoned, Jinerl and expelled, for having printed and published a libel containing " matter of infamy of sundry good particular members of the house, and of the whole state of the house in general, and also of the power and authority of the house." " In 1628 Henry Alcyn was committed to the custody of the ' 20 Lords' J. 362.

2 4 lb. G15; i, lb. 241. 244; 20 lb. ng.3; 22 lb. 3. W, 3. 4.

22 lb.: J51. 307. 380. " 2!) Lords'. T. 10, ami I."'; Pari. Hist. 770.

41 Lords' J. 506. " 1 Com. T. 00. ' S. o infra,. 02.

1 Com. J. 126; D'Ewos, 201-20 1.

Serjeant for a libel on the last Parliamentj In 1640 the Archdeacon of Bath was committed for abusing the last Parliament. In 1701 Thomas Colepepper was committed for reflections upon the last House of Commons; and the attorney-general was directed to prosecute him. The house also resolved, shortly after the last case, " that to print or publish any books or libels reflecting upon the proceedings of the House of Commons, or any member thereof, for or relating to his service therein, is a high violation of the rights and privileges of the House of Commons." In 1805 Peter Stuart was committed for printing, in his paper, libellous reflections on the character and conduct of the house. In 1810 Sir F. Burdett, a member, was sent to the Tower for publishing " a libellous and scandalous paper reflecting upon the just rights and privileges of the house.""' In 1819 INIr. Hobhouse, having acknowledged himself the author of a pamphlet, was committed to Newgate. The house had previously declared his pamphlet to be "a scandalous libel, containing matter calculated to inflame the people into acts of violence against the legislature, and against this house in particular; and that it is a high contempt of the privileges, and of the constitutional authority of this house."' On the 26th February complaint was made of certain expressions in a speech of Mr. O'Connell, a member, at a public meeting, as containing a charge of foul perjury against members of the house, in the discharge of their judicial duties in election committees. Mr. O'Connell was heard in his place, and avowed that he had used the expressions complained of. He was declared guilty of a breach of privilege, and, by order of the house, was reprimanded in his place, by the speaker.

' 1 Com. J. 925. 2 2 lb. 63. 13 lb. 735.

lb. 767. 5 65 lb. 113. 65 ii, 252.

' 75 lb. 57. Many other cases are cited in the Appendix to the Second Report on Sir F. Burdett, in 1810.

93 Com. J. 307. 312. 316. 41 flans. Deb., 3d Series, 99. 207.

The power of the house to commit the authors of libels was questioned before the Court of King's Bench, in 1811, by Sir F. Burdett, but was admitted by all the judges of that court, without a single expression of doubt.

On the 21st May 1790 a general resolution was passed by the commons:

"That it is against the law and usage of Parliament, and a high breach of the privilege of this house, to write or publish, or cause to be written or published, any scandalous and libellous reflection on the honour and justice of this house, in any of the impeachments or prosecutions in which it is engaged,"

4. Interference with, or reflections upon members, have Assaults, in- .-in suits, or libels always been resented as indignities to the house itself. upoa members.

In the Lords this ofience has been visited with peculiar Lords, severity, of which numerous instances are to be found in the earlier volumes of their Journals. Of these only a few of the most remarkable need be particularly mentioned.

On the 22d March 1623, Thomas Morley was fined 1,000., sent to the pillory, and imprisoned in the Fleet, for a libel on the lord keeper."' On the 9th July 1663, Alexander Fitton was fined 500 ., and committed to the King's Bench, f(; r a libel on Lord Gerard of Brandon, and ordered to find sureties for his behaviour during life; and others who had been privy to signing and publishing the libel, were imprisoned in the Fleet, and ordered to find security for their good behaviour during life. On the 18th December 1667, William Carr, for dispersing scandalous and seditious printed papers against the same nobleman, was fined 1,000 ., sentenced to stand thrice in the pillory, to be imprisoned in the Fleet, and the papers to be burned by the hand of the hangman."' On the 8th March 1688, W. Downing was committed to the Gatehouse '

Burdett v. Abbot, 14 East, 1. 4.5 Com. J. 508.

3 3 Lords' J. 842. 851; 4 lb. 131; 5 lb. 24.

3 lb. 27G. Ml lb. 554. 12 lb. 174.

Commons.

Assaulting or obstructing members.

and fined loOZ., for printing a paper reflecting on the Lord Grey of AVark."

In later times parties have been attached for libels on peers, as in 1722, for printing libels concerning Lord Strafford," and Lord Kinnoul;' and fined and committed, as in the case of Flower, in 1779, for a libel on the Bishop of Llandaff.

In 1776 Eichard Cooksey was attached for sending an insulting letter to the Earl of Coventry, and afterwards reprimanded, and ordered " to be continued in custody until he find security for his good behaviour."

In the commons, on the 12th April 1733, it was resolved and declared, nem. con.,

"That the assaulting, insuhing, or menacing any member of this house, in his coming to or going from the house, or upon the account of his behaviour in Parliament, is an high infringement of the privilege of this house, a most outrageous and dangerous violation of the rights of Parliament, and an high crime and misdemeanor." And again, on the 1st June 1780, "That it is a gross breach of the privilege of this house for any person to obstruct and insult the members of this house in the coming to or going from the house, and to endeavour to compel members by force to declare themselves in favour of or against any proposition then depending or expected to be brought before tlie house."'

And in numerous instances, as well before as after these resolutions, persons assaulting, challenging, threatening, or otherwise molesting members on account of their conduct in Parliament, have been committed or otherwise punished by the house.

On the 22d June 1781, complaint was made that Sir J. Wrottesley had received a challenge for his conduct as a member of the Worcester election committee; and Swift, the person complained of, was committed to the custody 14 Lords' J. 144. 22 lb. 129. 3 lb. 149.

42 lb. 181. 5 0 lb.314. Hl. e 22 Com. J. 115.

37 lb. 902. 8 li lb. 405; 16 lb. 562, c.

of the serjeant-at-arms. On the 13th April 1809, Sir Charles Hamilton complained that he had been arrested, and otherwise insulted by Daniel Butler, a sheriflts officer; and Butler was committed to Newgate for his offence."

On the 11th July 1824, the speaker, having received information that a member had been assaulted in the lobby, ordered the serjeant-at-arms to take the person into custody, and doubts being entertained of his sanity, he was ordered to stand committed to the custody of the serjeant.

In 1827, complaint was made of three letters which had been sent to Mr. Secretary Peel, taking notice of his speeches, and threatening to contradict them from the gallery of the house. The letters were delivered in and read, and the writer, H. C. Jennings, was ordered to attend. He acknowledged that the letters were written by him, and he was declared guilty of a breach of privilege, but was suffered to escape with a reprimand from the speaker.

Libels upon members have also been constantly punished. l-'"els on mem-In 1680, A. Yarington and R. Groome were committed for a libel against a member."' In 1689, Christopher Smelt was committed for spreading a false and scandalous report of Peter Rich, a member. ' In 1696, John Rye was committed for having caused a libel, reflecting on a member, to be printed and delivered at the door. In 1704, James Mellot was committed for false and scandak)us reflections upon two members." In 1733, Wilham Noble was committed for asserting that a member received a pension for his voting in Parliament." In 1774, H. S. Woodfall was committed for publishing a letter, reflecting on the character of the speaker."" In 1821, the author of a paragraph in the John Bull newspaper, containing a false and scan-diuous libel on a member, was committed to Newgate."

38 Com. J. 5:3.5. 537. = 64 lb. 210. 213. ' 79 lb. 483.

82 lb. 3U5. 399. 9 lb. 054. (J5(i. 10 lb. 244.

Ml lb. 05(5. 14 lb. 505. 23 lb. 245.

"' 34 lb. 450, " 70 lb. 335.

Misreprcsea-tatiou.

Offering bribes to members.

Persons committed liy the speaker.

In 18.32, Messrs. Kidson Wright, solicitors, were admonished for having adth'cssed to the committee on the Sunderland Dock Bill a letter, reflecting on the conduct of members of the committee, copies of which were circulated in printed handbills.

On the 1st jsIarch 1824, IVIr. Abercromby made a complaint to the house that the lord chancellor in his court had used offensive expressions with reference to Avhat had been said by himself in debate; but on division the matter was not allowed to proceed any further.

Other cases, too numerous to mention, have occurred, in some of which the parties have been committed or reprimanded; and in others the house has considered that the remarks did not justify any proceedings against the authors or publishers.

On some occasions the house has also directed prosecutions against persons who have published libels reflecting upon members, in the same manner as if the publications had affected the house collectively."

Of a similar character with libels, is wilful misrepresentation of the proceedings of members.

On the 22d April 1699, it was resolved,

"That the publishing the names of the members of this bouse, and reflecting upon them, and misreiiresenting their proceedings in Parliament, is a breach of the privilege of this house, and destructive of the freedom of Parliament."

To offer a bribe, in order to influence a member in the proceedings of the house, has been treated as a breach of privilege," being an insult not only to the member himself, but to the house.

"When the speaker is accompanied by the mace, he has power to order persons into custody for disrespect, or other ' 87 Com. J. 278. 294. jq Hans. Deb. N. S. 571.

See the head of Privileges in the General Journ. Ind. 1547-1713, and Complaints in the other Journal Indexes.

13 Com. J. 230; 14 lb. 37. 12 lb. 6G1.

11 lb. 274, 275; 14 lb. 474; 17 lb. 493, 494.

breaches of privilege committed in his presence, without any previous order of the house. Mr. Speaker Onslow ordered a man into custody who pressed upon him in Westminster Hall;' and a case Is mentioned by D'Ewes in which a member seized upon an unruly page and brought him to the speaker, by whom he was committed prisoner to the Serjeant." In 1675, Sir Edward Seymour, the speaker, seized Mr. Serjeant Pemberton, and delivered him into the custody of a messenger; but in that case Pemberton had already been in custody, and had escaped from the serjeant-at-arms.

In all these classes of offences, both houses will commit inquiry into al- ,.,., 1-111 le otl breaches or otherwise punish, in the manner described; but not of privilege, without due inquiry into the alleged offence.

By a standing order of the lords of 11th January 1699, Lords. it is ordered,

"That in case of complaint by any lord of tliis house of a breach of privilege, wherein any person shall be taken into custody for the future; if the house, upon examination of the matter complained of, shall judge the same to be no breach of privilege, the lord who made the complaint shall pay the fees and expenses of the person so taken into custody; and that no person shall be taken into custody upon complaint of a breach of privilege, but upon oath made at tlie bar of this house."

This order was explained, on the 3d June 1720, "to be understood only of breaches of privilege committed in Great Britain; but that oath made by affidavit, in writing, of a breach of privilege committed in Ireland, may be sufficient ground to take into custody the person thereby proved to have been guilty of such breach of privilege, though no oatli be made thereof, at tlie bar of this house."

Before the year 1845, it had been customaiy for the House of Lords, when inquiring into any alleged breach of privilege, to conduct such inquiries with closed doors; but, in later cases, strangers have not been ordered to withdraw."

' 2 Hats. 241 n. D'Ewes, 629.

3 9 Cora. J. 351. 353. See also 1 Com. J. 157. 210. 972. Lords' S. O. No. 81. " lb. No. 82.

Lord Hawarden's case, 31 Jan. 1828. 59 Hans. Deb. 09. The Umbrella case, 20 March 1827. 58 Hans. Deb. 35.

Coiuiiioiis. lu the commons it was resolved, 31st January 1694,

"That no persons shall be taken into custody, upon complaint of any breach of privilege of this house, before the matter be first examined;" but it was at the same time resolved and declared, " that the said order is not to extend to any breach of privilege upon the person of anv member of this house."'

Again, on the 3d January 1701, it was resolved.

Committee of " That no person be taken into custody of the serjeant-at-arms, privileges. upon any complaint of a breach of privilege, until the matter of si ch complaint shall have been examined by the committee of privih ges, and reported to the house, and tliat the same be a standing order of the house."

It is no longer the practice to refer such matters to the committee of privileges, although that committee is still nominally appointed. The appointment, at the commencement of each session, of the committee of privileges was discontinued in 1833, but has since been revived, pro forma, although no members have been nominated; except for a special purpose, in 1847. It is the present practice, when a complaint is made, to order the party complained of to attend the house; and on his appearance at the bar, he is examined and dealt with, according as the explanations of his conduct are satisfactory or otherwise; or as the contrition expressed by him for his offence conciliates the displeasure of the house. If there be any special circumstances arising out of a complaint of a breach of privilege, it is usual to appoint a select committee to inquire into them, and the house suspends its judgment until their report has been presented. Complaints of AVhen a complaint is made of a newspaper, the newspaper must be produced, in order that the paragraphs complained of may be read. On the 30th May 1848, a member complained of the report of his speech on the previous day, in a newspaper, and was proceeding to ' 11 Com. J. 219. = 13 lb. fi48.

' 93 lb. 8; 104 lb. 24. 104 lb. 24. 103 lb. 139.

ucwspapers.

address the house, when he was stopped l)y the speaker, as he had no copy of the newspaper on which to found his comphiint. The member who makes the complaint must also be prepared with the names of the printer or publisher, if he intend to follow up his complaint with a motion.

In order to discourage frivolous complaints, a resolution, similar to the standing order of the lords, was agreed to, on the 11th February 1768:

"That in case of any complaint of a breach of privilege hereafter to be made by any member of this house, if the house shall adjudge that there is no ground for such complaint, the house will order satisfaction to the person comjilained of, for his costs and expenses incurred by reason of such complaint;" and this was ordered to be made a standing oifder.

Either house will punish in one session offences that have offences in a been committed in another. On the 4th and 14th April 1707, it was resolved, by the commons, nem. con.,

"That when any person ordered to be taken into the custody of the serjeant-at-arms, shall either abscond from justice, or having been in custody shall refuse to pay the just fees, that in either of those cases the order for commitment shall be renewed at the beginning of the next session of Parliament, and that this be declared to be a standing order of the house."'" In 1751, Mr. Murray, who had been imprisoned In Newgate until the close of the session, for a libel, was, on the next meeting of Parliament, again ordered to be committed; but he had absconded, in the meantime, to escape a second imprisonment."

It also appears, that a breach of privilege committed against one Parliament may be punished by another; and libels against former Parliaments have often been punished." In the debate on the privilege of Sir R. Howard, in 1625, ' See Hans. Deb. 30th i Jay 1848; and Debate, 1st May 1841) (Mr. J. O'Connell;. 31 Com. J. OO'i.

' 21 Lords' J. 18!). 17 Com. J.-203; '20 lb. o4!);-li lb.-210.

1.5 Com. J. 376. 38(5.-2; jjj 3 3 1 lb. 925; 2 lb. 03; 13 lb. 735.

Mr. Scklen said, "It is clear that breach of privilege in one Parliament may be punished in another succeeding," Differences in In all the cases that have been noticed as breaches of hi'nirutijytiie pi'ivilege, both houses have agreed in their adjudication; lor. u and by tiie j j jj ggyeral iniiiortant particulars, there is a difference in couinions.

their modes of punishment. The lords claim to be a court of record, and, as such, not only to imprison, but to impose fines. They also imprison for a fixed time, and order security to be given for good conduct; and their customary form of commitment is by attachment-' The commons, on the other hand, commit for no specified period, and of late years, have not imposed fines.

There can be no question but that the House of Lords, in its judicial capacity, is a court of record; but, according to Lord Kenyon, " when exercising a legislative capacity, it is not a court of record," However this may be, instances

Fines. too numerous to mention have occurred, in which the lords have sentenced parties to pay fines: many have already been noticed in the present chapter, as well as cases in which they have ordered security to be given for good conduct, even during the whole life of the parties. The following is a standing order of the lords, of the 3d April 1624:

"Whereas this high court of the Upper House of Parliament do often find cause in their judicature to impose fines, amongst other punishments, upon offenders, for the good example of justice, and to deter others from like offences; it is ordered and declared, that at the least once before the end of every session, the committees for the orders of the house and privileges of the lords of Parliament, do acquaint the lords with all the fines that have been laid tliat session, that thereupon their lordships may use that power which they justly have, to take off or mitigate such fines, either wholly or in part, according to the measure of penitence or ability in the offenders, or suffer all to stand, as in equity their lordships shall think fit.""

' 1 Hats. Piec. 184. Lords' Minutes, 22d July and 13th Aug. 1850.

= Flower's case, 1779. 8 Dumf. East, 314.

"3 Lords' J. 276; 11 lb. 554; 12 lb. 174; 14 lb. 144; 30 lb. 493 (Report of Precedents); 42 lb. 181; 43 lb. 60. 105, 11 Lords' J. 554; 39 lb. 331. Lords' S. O. No. 98.

The lords have power to commit offenders to prison for a S2)ecified term, even beyond the duration of the session;' and thus on the 13th August 1850, being within two days of the prorogation, certain prisoners were committed for a fortnight."' If no thne were mentioned and tlie commitment were general, it has been said that the prisoners could not be discharged on habeas corpus even after a prorogation; but in the case of Lord Shaftesbury, a doubt was expressed by one of the judges whether the imprisonment, which was for an uncertain time, would be concluded by the session; and another said, that if the session had been determined, the prisoner ought to have been discharged. The latter opinion derives confirmation from the following precedent. On the 14th January 1744, the serjeant-at-arms acquainted the house that he had kept a prisoner in his custody, " until he was discharred of course hy the j rorogation of Parliament, without his having made his submission;" whereupon the offender was ordered to be re-attached.

Whether the House of Commons be, in law, a court of whether House record it would be difficult to determine; for this claim was a court of re-formerly maintained, but has latterly been virtually abandoned, although never distinctly renounced. In Fitzherbert's case, in 1592, the house resolved " that this house being a court of record, would take no notice of any matter of fact at all in the said case, but only of matter of record;" and the record of Fitzherbert's execution was accordingly sent to the house by the lord keeper." In the debate on Floydc's case, in 1621, Sir Edward Coke said, "no question but this is a house of record, and that it hath power of judicature in some cases;" and exclaimed, "I wish his tongue ' 43 Lords'J. 105. ' Lords' Minutes, 1.3th August 1850.

Lord Denuuui's judgment in Stockdale v. Hansard, p. 147.

Howell, St. Tr. 1200. 1 Mod. Rep. 144.

26 Lords' J. 420. " UEwes, 502. ' 1 Com. J. G04.

cord.

may cleave to his mouth that f-aith that this house is no court of record." And in 1604 the apology of the commons contains these words: " Wc avouch also that our house is a court of record, and ever so esteemed." In Jones v. Kandallj' Loi'd Mansfield said the House of Commons was not a court of record.

It may be argued that if the commons, as a branch of the High Court of Parliament, be not a court of record in adjudging breaches of privilege, the judicature of the lords is not sufficient alone to constitute that house a court of record in their legislative capacity; for though they have various kinds of judicature, the commons also have parallel kinds of judicature. The lords have a judicature for their privileges, and for the election of representative jdcers of Scotland; the commons have, in like manner, a judicature for their privileges, and in the election of members. It is true that the lords have other judicial functions which the commons do not possess; but so far as each house is acting within its own peculiar jurisdiction, the one would appear to be a court of record as well as the other: and when does the legislative character cease and the judicial character begin in either house? In their dehberations they are both legislative, but when their privileges are infringed, their judicature is called into action. If this view of the question be allowed, both houses, in mattei's of privilege, are equally courts of record; and the lords have no further claim to that character than the commons, except when they are sitting as a court of appeal, in trials of peers, in hearing claims of peerage, or in cases of impeachment. Fines. Acting as a court of record, the commons formerly imposed fines and imprisoned offenders for a time certain.

In 1575, Smalley, a member's servant, who had fraudulently procured himself to be arrested, in order to be discharged of a debt and execution, was committed to the '

1 Hats. 233. 1 Cowp. 17. y g also Chapters VII. XV.

Tower for a month, and until he should pay to AV. Ilewctt the sum of 100."

Again, in 1580, Mr. Arthur Hall, a member, aviio liad offended the house by a libel, was ordered to be committed to the Tower, and to remain in tlie said prison for six montlts, and so much longer as until himself should tcillingli make retractation of the said book, to the satisfaction of the house; and it was resolved that a fine should be assessed by this house, to the queen's majesty's use, of 500 marks, and that he should be expelled. There are also a few other cases in the earlier journals, in which offenders were committed by the house for a time certain; and in which prisoners have been admitted to bail.

In 1586 Bland, a currier, was fined 20. for having used contumacious expressions against the House of Commons."

In Floyde's case, in 1G21, the commons clearly exceeded Floyde's case, their jurisdiction. That person had spoken offensive words concerning the daughter of James L, and her husband, the elector palatine. In this he may have been guilty of a libel, but certainly not of any breach of parliamentary privilege. Yet the commons took cognizance of the offence, and sentenced Floyde to pay a fine of 1,000., to stand twice in the pillory, and to ride backwards on a horse, with the horse's tail in his hand. ' Upon this judgment beinggiacn, first the king, and then the lords interfered, not on account of the severity of the punishment, nor because it was thought to exceed the power of the house; but I ecause the offence was altogether beyond the jurisdiction of the commons. The commons perceived their error, and lefl the offender to be dealt with by the lords; but at the same time they guarded 1 Com. J. 112,113. 1 lb. 125, 12G.

3 1 lb. 2G9.333. G30. G5-j; 7 lb. 531. 501; 9 lb. 543. G87. 737.

1 lb. G21; 2 lb. 80G; 9 lb. 9G. 21(); 10 lb. 84; 12 lb. 255, 25G; 13 II). 318, c.

D'Ewes, J. 3GG. 1 Com. J. G()9. 1 Ilnns. Pari. Hist. 1250.

their own rights by an ambiguous protestation that their proceedings against Floyde " should not be drawn or used as a precedent to the enlarging or diminishing the lawful rights and privileges of either house, but that the rights and privileges of both houses should remain in the selfsame state and plight as before."

But if the commons exceeded their jurisdiction in this case, the lords equally disregarded the limits of their own, and proceeded to still more disgraceful severities. Floyde was charged by the attorney-general before the lords, and received sentence that he should be incapable of bearing arms as a gentleman; that he should be ever held an infamous person, and his testimony not to be taken in any court or cause; that he should ride twice to the pilloiy with his face to the horse's tail, holding the tail in his hand; that he should be branded with the letter K on his foi'e-head, be whipped at the cart's tail, be fined 5,000. to the king, and be imprisoned in Newgate for life.

The last case of a fine by the commons occurred in 1666, when a fine of 1,000. was imposed upon Thomas White, who had absconded after he had been ordered into the custody of the serjeant-at-arms."

The modern practice of the commons is to commit persons to the custody of the serjeant-at-arms, to Newgate, or to the Tower, during the pleasure of the house; and to keep offenders there until they present petitions praying for their release, and expressing contrition for their offences; or until, upon motion made in the house, it is resolved that they shall be discharged. It is then usual for the parties to be brought to the bar, and after an admonition or reprimand from the speaker, to be discharged on payment of their fees. But, under peculiar circumstances, their attend- 1 1 Com. J. 619.

' 3 Lords' J. 134. See also " Proceedings and Debates of the Commons," 1020, 1621 (Oxford), and 1 Hans. Pari. Hist. 12.!.9. 8Coni. J. Ono.

ance at the bar and the admonition or reprimand' liave been dispensed with.

It cannot fail to be remarked that this condition of the rayment of payment of fees still partakes of the character of a fine. The payment of the money forms part of the punishment, and is compulsory; nor could any limit be imposed upon the amount fixed by order of the house. Payment has been occasionally remitted under special circumstances" as, for example, on account of the poverty of the parties;" and in one case, because the prisoner was labouring under mental delusion.

No period of imprisonment is named by the commons. Imprisonment . by tlio commons and the prisoners committed by them, if not sooner dis- conchuied by charged by the house, are immediately released from their P' s confinement on a prorogation, whether they have paid the fees or not. If they were held longer in custody, there is little doubt but that they would be discharged by the courts upon a writ of habeas corpus. Lord Denman, in his judgment in the case of Stockdale v. Hansard, said,

"However flagrant the contempt, the House of Commons can only commit till the close of the existing session. Their privilege to commit is not better known than this limitation of it. Though the party should deserve the severest penalties, yet, his offence being committed the daj- before the prorogation, if the house ordered his imprisonment but for a week, every court in Westminster Hall, and every judge of all the courts, would be bound to discharge him by habeas corpus."" It was formerly the practice to make prisoners receive the judgment of the house, kneeling at the bar. In both houses, however, the practice has long since been discontinued; althou"; h the entries in the Lords' Journals still ' 75 Com. J. 4G7. ' 80 lb. 333; 90 lb. 532; 101 lb. 7G8.

3 58 lb. 221; 80 lb. 470; 83 lb. 199; 90 lb. 532. 74 lb. 192. 85 lb. 465.

But this law never extended to an adjournment, even when it was in tlie nature of a prorogation. See 10 Com. J. 537.

' Judgment in Stockdale i'. Hansard, 1839 (283), p. 142.

assume that the prisoners are " on then- knees " at the bar."

On the 16th INIarch 1772, it was resolved by the commons, nem. con.,

"That when any person shall from henceforth be brought to the bar of this house to receive any judgment of this house, or to be discharged from the custody of the serjeant-at-arms attending this house, or from any imprisonment inflicted by order of the house, such person shall receive such judgment, or the order of the house for his discharge, standing at the bar, unless it shall be otherwise directed, in the order of the house made for that purpose;" and ordered to be made a standing order.

The discontinuance of this practice arose from tlie refusal of Mr. Murray to kneel when brought up to the bar of the House of Commons on the 4th of February 1750. For this refusal he was declared " guilty of a high and most dangerous contempt of the authority and privilege of this house;" was committed close prisoner to Newgate, and not allowed the use of pen, ink and paper. It appears that there had previously been only one other instance of such a refusal to kneel.

CHAPTEE IV.

PRIVILEGE OF FREEDOM OF SPEECH CONFIRMED BY THE ANCIENT LAW OF PARLIAMENT AND BY STATUTE '. ITS NATURE AND LIMITS.

Necessity of FREEDOM of spccch is a privilege essential to every free freedom of-ii-i t n speech. council or legislature. It is so necessary for the making of laws, that if it had never been expressly confirmed, it must still have been acknowledged as inseparable from Parliament, and inherent in its constitution. Its principle was well stated by the commons, at a conference on the 11th of ' 77 Lords' J. 737, c. 2 33 Coin. J. 594.

3 14 H; ins. Pari. Hist. 894. 1 Walpole's Memoirs of George II., p. 13.

Report of Precedents. 20 Com. J. 48.

December 1667: "No man can doubt," they said, "but whatever is once enacted is hawt'ul; but nothing can come into an Act of Parliament, but it must be first affirmed or propounded by somebody; so that if the Act can wrong nobody, no more can the first propounding. The members must be as free as the houses: an Act of Parliament cannot disturb the state; therefore the debate that tends to it cannot; for it must be propounded and debated before it can be enacted."'

But this important privilege has not been left to depend Confirmed by upon abstract principles, nor even upon the ancient law and ment. custom of Parliament, but has been recognised and confirmed as part of the law of the land.

According to Elsynge, the " commons did oftentimes, under Edward III., discuss and debate amongst themselves many things concerning the king's prerogative, and agreed upon petitions for laws to be made directly against his prerogative, as may appear by divers of the said j)etitions; yet they were never interrupted in their consultations, nor received check for the same, as may appear also by the answers to the said petitions."- In the 20th of liichard II., however, a case occurred iiaxey'scase. in which this ancient privilege was first violated, though afterwards confirmed, llaxey, a member of the commons, having displeased the king, by oftering a bill for reducing the excessive charge of the royal household, was condemned in Parliament as a traitor. But on the accession of Henry IV., Ilaxey exhibited a petition to the king in

Parliament, to reverse tliat judgment, as being " against the law and custom which had been before in Parliament;" and the judgment was reversed and annulled accordingly by the king, witli the advice and assent of all the lords spiritual and temporal. This was unquestionably an acknowledgment of the privilege by the highest judicial ' 12 Lords' J. 1G6. Elsynge, 177.

3 1 Hon. IV.; 3 Rot. Pari. 430.

authority the king and tlie House of Lords; and in the same year the commons took up the case of Haxey, and in a petition to the king affirmed "that he had been condemned against the law and course of Parliament, and in annihilation of the customs of the commons;" and prayed that the judgment might be reversed, "as well for the furtherance of justice as for the saving of the liberties of the commons." To this the king also assented, with the advice and assent of the lords spiritual and temporal; and thus the whole legislature agreed that the judgment against Haxey, in derogation of the privileges of Parliament, " should be annulled and held to be of no force or effect."

Young's case. In the 33d Henry VI., Thomas Young, a member, presented a petition, complaining that he had been imprisoned 'for matters by him showed in the house." The commons transmitted his petition to the lords, and the king " willed that the lords of his council do and provide for the said suppliant, as in their discretion shall be thought convenient and reasonable."

Stiode's case. Again, in the 4th Henry VIII. (1512), Mr. Strode, a member of the House of Commons, was prosecuted in the Stannary Court, for having proposed certain bills to regulate the tinners in Cornwall, and was fined and imjiri-soned in consequence. Upon which an Act was passed, which, after stating that Strode had agreed with others of the commons in putting forth bills " the which here in this High Court of Parliament, should and ought to be communed and treated of," declared the proceedings of the Stannary Court to be void, and further enacted,

"That all suits, condemnations, executions, fines, amerciaments, punishments, c. put or had, or hereafter to be put or had, upon ' " Si bien en accompllsseinent de droit, come pur salvation des libertes dc lez ditz communes." 3 Rot. Pari. 434.

5 Rot. Pari. 337. 4 p.,. j j- g- j jj g

"4 Hen. VIII. c. 8.

the said Richard (Strode), and to every other of the person or persons tliat now be of tlie present Parliament, or that of any Parliament thereafter shall be, for any bill, speaking, reasoning', or declaring of any matter or matters concerning the Parliament, to be communed and treated of, be utterly void and of none effect."

As the proceedings which had ah'eady taken place against Strode were declared to be void, it is evident that freedom of speech was then admitted to be a privilege of Parliament, and was not, at that time, first enacted. The words of the statute also leave no doubt that it was intended to have a general operation in future, and to protect all members, of either house, from any question on account of their speeches or votes in Parliament.

Thirty years afterwards the petition of the commons to Petition of the the king, at the commencement of the Parliament, appears commons. for the first time to have included tliis privilege amongst those prayed for of the king. The first occasion on which such a petition is recorded, was in the 33d Henry VI. (1541), when it was made by Thomas Moyle, speaker."

But although the petitions for freedom of speech had not been previously made in that form, there is a remarkable petition of the commons, and answer of the king, in the 2d Henry IV., relating to this privilege. Tiie commons prayed the king not to take notice of any reports that might be made to him of their proceedings; to which the king replied, that it was his wish that the commons should deliberate and treat of all matters amongst themselves, in order to bring them to the best conclusion, according to their wisdom, for the welfare and honour of himself and all his realm; and that he would hear no person, nor give him any credit, before such matters were brouglit before the king, by the advice and assent of all the commons, according to tlie purport of their petition."

The independent right of free discussion in Parliament was further confirmed by the same king, in the ninth year ' Elsynrc, 176. 23 j f pjj, r of his reign, who, in a disagreement between tlie houses concerning the grant of subsidies, declared, by the advice and consent of the lords,

"That it sliall be lawful for the lords to debate together in tliis present Parliament, and in every other for time to come, in the king's absence, concerning the condition of the kingdom, and the remedies necessary for it. And in like manner it shall be lawful for the commons, on their part, to debate together concerning the said condition and remedies; provided always, that neither the lords on their part, nor the ccmmous on their part, do make any report to our lord the king of any grant granted by the commons, and agreed to by the lords, nor of the communications of the said grant, before the said lords and commons are of one accord and agreement in the said matter." i Interpretation But notwithstanding the repeated recognition of this e privi ege. pj-jyjiggg jq crown and the commons were not always agreed upon its limits. In reply to the usual petition of the speaker. Sir Edward Coke, in 1593, the lord keeper said, "Liberty of speech is granted you, but you must know what privilege you have; not to speak every one Avhat he listeth, or what cometh in his brain to utter; but your privilege is, 'aye or 'no. "'
In 1621, the commons, in their protestation, defined their privilege more consistently with its present limits. They affirmed, " that every member hath freedom from all impeachment, imprisonment, or molestation, other than by censure of the house itself, for or concerning any bill, speaking, reasoning, or declaring of any matter or matters touching the Parliament or Parliament business."

Violations of It is necdless to recount how frequently this privilege was formerly violated by the power of the Crown. The Act of the 4th of Henry VIII. extended no further than to protect members from being questioned, in other courts, for their proceedings in Parhament; but its principle should equally have saved them from the displeasure of the Crown. The cases of Mr. Strickland, in 1571,"' of ' 3 Rot. Pari. Gil. 2 1 Pad. Hist. 862.

1 Hats. 79. D'Ewes, IGG. 4 Pari. Hist. 153.

the privilege.

Mr. Cope, Mr. Wentworth, and others, in 1586," and of Sir Edwyn Sandys, in 1621," will serve to remind the reader how imperfectly members were once protected against the unconstitutional exercise of prerogative.

The last occasion on which the privilege of freedom of Sir J. Elliot speech was directly impeached, was in the celebrated case of Sir John Elliot, Denzil Mollis, and Benjamin Valentine, against whom a judgment was obtained in the King's Bench, in the 5th Charles I., for their conduct in Parliament. On the 8th July 1641, the House of Commons declared all the proceedings in the King's Bench to be against the law and privilege of Parliament. The prosecution of those members was, indeed, one of the illegal acts which hastened the fate of Charles I. It was strongly condemned in the petition of right, and after the restoration it was not forgotten by the Parliament.

The judgment had been given against the privilege of Parliament, upon the false assumption that the Act of the 4th Henry VIII. had been simply a private statute, for the relief of Strode, and had no general operation; and in order to condemn this construction of the plain words of the statute, the commons resolved, on the 12th November 1667, "That the Act of Parliament in 4th Henry VIII., commonly intituled, An Act concerning Richard Strode," is a general laic, extending to indemnify all and every the members of both houses of Parliament, in all Parliaments, for and touching any bills, speaking, reasoning, or declaring of any matter or matters in and concerning the Parliament, to be communed and treated of; and is a declaratory law of the ancient and necessary rights and privileges of Parliament."'" And on a subsequent day, they also resolved, "That the judgment givep, 5 Car., against Sir John Elliot, Denzil Ilollis, and Benjamin Valentine, in the King's Bench, was an illegal judgment, and against ' D'Ewes, 410. " 1 Com. J. mi, 1 Plats. 13C, 137.

"2 Cora. J. 203. 3 St. Tr. 23. J-33o. 9 Cora. J. 19.

by statute.

102 FREEDOM OF SPEECH.

the freedom antl privilege of Parliament." A conference was afterwards demanded wuth the lords and their lord-Bhijjs agreed to the resolutions of the commons; and, finally, upon a writ of error, the judgment of the Court of King's Bench was reversed by the House of Lords, on 15th April 1668. Its recognition This would have been a sufficient recognition, by law, of the privilege of freedom of speech; but a further and last confirmation was reserved for the Revolution of 1688. By the 9th article of the Bill of Rights it was declared, " that the freedom of speech, and debates or proceedings in Parliament, ought not to be impeached or questioned in any court or place out of Parliament."

But, although by the ancient custom of Parliament, as well as by the law, a member may not be questioned out of Parliament, he is liable to censure and punishment by the house itself of which he is a member. The cases in which members have been called to account and punished for offensive words spoken before the house, are too numerous to mention. Some have been admonished, others inipi isoned, and in the commons some have even been expelled. Less severity has been shown in modern times, ill the censure of intemperate speeches. The members who offend against propriety are called to order, and generally satisfy the house with an explanation or apology." Privilege does Taking care not to say anything disrespectful to the pubi hed' house, a member may state whatever he thinks fit in debate, 8)eeche9. howcvcr offensive it may be to the feelings, or injurious to the character of individuals, and he is protected by his privilege from any action for libel, as well as from any other question or molestation. And here it may be noticed that ' 9 Com. J. 25. 12 Lords' J. 166. 12 lb. 223.

1 Will. Mary, sess. 2, c. 2.

4 Lords' J. 475. 5 lb. 77. Sir R. Canue, 1G80; 9 Com. J. G42. Mr. Mauley, 1006; 11 Com. J. 581.

Mr. Shepherd, 1 Com. J. 521. ' See Chapter XI. on DiibATES.

the rule by which all published reports of debates are ignored by Parliament is an auxiliary to the privilege of freedom of speech. What is said in Parliament is supposed to be unknown elsewhere, and cannot be noticed without a breach of privilege. But if a member should proceed to publish his speech, his printed statement will be regarded as a separate publication, unconnected with any proceedings in Parliament. This construction of the law cannot be complained of by the Houses of Parliament, as, by their rules and orders, the publication of a debate is forbidden; and it is therefore impossible to protect, by privilege, an irregular act, which is itself declared to be a breach of jirivilege.

This view of the law has been established by two remarkable cases.

In 1795 an information was filed against Lord Abingdon Lord Abing-for a libel. His lordship had accused his attorney of improper conduct in his profession, in a speech delivered in the House of Lords, which he afterwards had printed in several newspapers at his own expense. His lordship pleaded his own case in the Court of King's Bench, and contended that he had a right to print what he had, by the law of Parliament, a right to speak. But Lord Kenyon said,

"That a member of Parliament had certainly a right to publish his speech, but that speech should not be made a vehicle of slander against any individual; if it was, it was a libel." The court gave judgment, that his lordship should be imprisoned for three months, pay a fine of 100 Z., and find security for his good behaviour."

In 1813 a much stronger case occurred. Mr. Creevey, Mr. Creevcy's a member of the House of Commons, had made a charge against an individual in the house, and incorrect reports of his speech having appeared in several newspapers, Mr. C. sent a correct report to the editor of the Liverpool paper, 1 Esp. N. p. C. 228.

with a request that he loouldjmblish it in his newspaper. Upon ail information filed against him, the jury found the defendant guilty of libel, and the King's Bench refused an application for a new trial, Lord EUenborough saying,

"A member of that house has spoken what he thought material, and wliat he was at liberty to speak, in his character as a member of that house. So far he is privileged; but he has not stopped there; but, unauthorized by the house, has chosen to publish an account of that sjieech, in what he has pleased to call a corrected form; and in that publication has thrown out reflections injurious to the character of an individual."'

Mr. Creevey, who had been fined 100 ., complained to the house of the proceedings of the King's Bench, but the house refused to admit that they were a breach of privilege."

The privilege which protects debates, extends also to reports and other proceedings in Parliament. In the case Rex V. Wright, of Rex V. Wright, Mr. Home Tooke applied for a criminal information against a bookseller, for publishing the copy of a report made by a committee of the House of Commons, which appeared to imply a charge of high treason against Mr. Tooke, after he had been tried for that crime and acquitted. The rule, however, was discharged by the court, partly because the report did not appear to bear the meaning imputed to it, and partly because the court would not regard a proceeding of either House of Parliament as a libel. Publication of- 7 3 4 Vict., c. 9, which was passed in conse-pariiaraentary qucnce of the decision of the Court of Queen's Bench in paj)er9.

tlic memorable case of Stockdale v. Hansard, it was enacted that i)roceedings, criminal or civil, against persons for the publication of papers printed by order of either House of

Parliament, shall be immediately stayed, on the production of a certificate, verified by affidavit, to the eff'ect that such ' 1 M. S. 278. = 68 Com. J. 604. Hans. Deb., 25th June 1813.

8 Term Reports, 293.

publication is by order of either House of Parliament. Proceedings are also to be stayed, if commenced on account of the publication of a copy of a Parliamentary paper, upon the verification of the correctness of such copy. And in)roceedings commenced for printing any extract from or abstract of a Parliamentary report or paper, the defendant may give the rei)ort in evidence under the general issue, and prove that his own extract or abstract was published honci Jide and without malice; and if such shall be the opinion of the jury, a verdict of Not guilty will be entered."

CHAPTER V.

FREEDOM FROM ARREST OR MOLESTATION: ITS ANTIQUITY; LIMITS AND MODE OF ENFORCEMENT. PRIVILEGE OF NOT BEING IMPLEADED IN CFV IL ACTIONS: OF NOT BEING LIABLE TO BE SUMMONED BY SUBP-CENA OR TO SERVE ON JURIES. COMMITMENT OF MEMBERS BY COURTS OF JUSTICE. PRIVILEGE OF WITNESSES AND OTHERS IN ATTENDANCE ON PARLIAaieNT.

The privilege of freedom from arrest or molestation is Antiquity of of great antiquity, and dates probably from the first exist- ' " ' ence of parliaments or national councils in England. By some writers its recognition by the law has been traced so far back as the time of Ethelbert, at the end of the sixth century, in whose laws it is said, "If the king call his people to him i, e. in the witena-gemot), and any one does an injury to one of them, let him pay a finc."' Blackstone has shown that it existed in the reign of Edward the Confessor, in whose laws we find this precept, " ad synodos ' 3 4 Vict. c. 9, s. 3.

' Wilkins' Leges Anglo-Sax. p. 2. '2 Hall. Middle Ages, 231. 2 Kciublc, Saxons in England, 33.

vcnicutlbus, sivc summoniti siut, sivc per se quid agendum liabuerint, sit suinma pax:" and so too in the old Gothic constitutions, " extenditur haec pax et securitas ad qua-tuordecim dies, convocato regni senatu." In later times there are various precedents explanatory of the nature and extent of this privilege, and of the mode in which it was sustained. From these it will be seen that not only are the persons of members of both Houses of Parliament free from arrest on mesne process or in execution, but that formerly the same immunity was enjoyed in regard to their servants and their property. The privilege was strained still further, and even claimed to protect members and their servants from all civil actions or suits, during the time over which privilege was supposed to extend. The privilege of freedom from arrest has also been construed to discharge members and their servants from all liability to answer subpoenas in other courts and to serve on juries; and in some cases to relieve them from commitments by courts of justice. Privileges Tlicsc various immunities have undergone considerable change and restriction, and being now defined, for the most part, with tolerable certainty, they wiu be best understood by considering them in the following order: 1, Privilege of members and their servants from arrest and distress, and the mode of enforcing it. 2. Their protection from being impleaded in civil actions. 3. Their liability to be summoned by subpoena or to serve on juries. 4. Their privilege in regard to commitments by legal tribunals, 5. Privilege of witnesses and others in attendance on Parliament. It may, however, be stated at once, that although many cases that will be given apply equally to members and to their servants, according to the privilege existing in those times, the latter have, at present, no privilege whatever. These cases, though at variance with modern usage, could not be 1 Coram. 1G5. Steirnh. de Jure Goth.

omitted consistently with a perfect view of tlic privilege of freedom from arrest and molestation.

So far back as the 19th of Edward I., in answer to a Freedom from n n 1 n 1 T arrest and dis-)etition of the master of the iemple, for leave to distrain tress of goods, for the rent of a house held of him by the Bishop of St. David's, the king said, "It does not seem fit that the king should grant that they who are of his council should be distrained in time of Parliament." From this precedent Sir Edward Coke infers that at that time a member of Parliament had privilege, not only for his servants, but for his horses or other goods distrainable. The privilege was also acknoavledged very distinctly by the Crown in the case of the Prior of Malton, in the 9th Edward 11.

The freedom, both of the lords c and commons, and their Chedder's case, servants, from all assaults or molestation, when coming to Parliament, remaining there, and returning thence, was distinctly recognised in the case of Richard Cheddcr, a member, by statute 5 Henry IV., c. 6, and again by another statute of the 11th Henry VI., c. 11. In the 5th Henry IV., the commons, in a petition to the king, alleged that according to the custom of the realm, the lords, knights, citizens, and burgesses were entitled to this privilege; and this was admitted by the king; who instead of agreeing to the proposition of the commons, that treble damages should be paid by parties violating their privilege, answered that there was already a sufficient remedy." Hence this privilege appears distinctly, not to have been created by statute, but to have been confirmed as the ancient law and custom of Parliament and of the realm. Much later, viz., in the 17th Edward IV., the commons affirmed, in Atwyll's case, that Atw ll's case, the privilege had existed, " whereof tyme that mannys mynde is not the contrarie j'" thus placing it on the ground ' 1 Hot. Pari. Gl. 4th Inst. 24 E. M Flats. 12.

3 Hot. Pari. Wl. ' U lb. I'Jl.

of prescription, and not on the authority of statutes then in force. Thorpe's case. The only exception to the recognition of this privilege was in the extraordinary case of Thorpe, the speaker of the commons, who was imprisoned, in 1452, under execution from the Court of Exchequer, at the suit of the Duke of York. The judges delivered their opinion to the lords, " that if any person that is a member of this High Court of Parliament be arrested in such cases as be not for treason or felony, or surety of the peace, or for a condemnation had before the Parliament, it is used that all such persons should be released of such arrests, and make- an attorney, so that they may have their freedom and liberty, freely to attend upon the Parliament." As Thorpe was in execution for a civil action, that had been brought during an adjournment, he was obviously entitled to his release, according to the opinion of the judges; yet it is entered on the rolls of Parliament, that after having "heard this answer and declaration, it was thoroughly agreed, assented, and concluded, by the lords spiritual and temporal, that the said Thomas, according to the law, should still remain in prison, the privilege of Parliament, or that the said Thomas was speaker of the Parliament, notwithstanding."' Yet even here it is worthy of notice, that the privilege of Parliament was admitted, but adjudged to be overruled by the law. The whole case, however, has been regarded as irregular and " begotten by the iniquity of the times."' Down to 1543, although the privilege had been recognised by statute, by declarations of both houses, by the frequent assent of the klng, and by the opinions of the judges," the commons did not deliver their members 5 Rot. Pari. 239. " 1 Com. J. 546.

Larke's case, "Le Roi, par advis des seigneurs espirituelx et temporelx, et a les especiales requestes des communes." 4 Rot. Pari. 357. Atwyll's case, 6 Rot. Pari. 191.

Larke's case, 4 Rot. Pari. 357. Parr's case, 5 Rot. Pari. 111. Hyde's case, G Rot. Pari. 160. Thorpe's case, 5 Rot. Pari. 239.

out of custody by their own authority; but when the members were in execution, in order to save the rights of the plaintiff, they obtained special statutes to authorise the Lord Chancellor to issue writs for their release;' and when confined on mesne process only, they were delivered by a writ of privilege issued by the Lord Chancellor." And in the singular case of Mr. Speaker Thorpe, already mentioned, the commons even submitted the vindication of their privilege to the House of Peers, as well as to tlie king."

At length, with sudden energy, the commons, for the Case of George first time, vindicated the privilege of Parliament, and acted independently of any other power. In 1543, G eorge Ferrers, a member, was arrested in London, by a process out of the King's Bench, at the suit of one White, as surety for the debt of another. The house, on hearing of his arrest, ordered the serjeant to go to the Compter and demand his delivery. The serjeant was resisted by the city officers, who were protected by the sheriffs, and he was obliged to retui'n without the prisoner. The liouse then rose in a body, and laid their case before the lords, " who, judging tlie contempt to be very great, referred tlie punishment thereof to the order of tlie commons' house." The commons ordered the serjeant to repair to the sheriffs, and to require the delivery of Ferrers, without any writ or warrant. The lord chancellor had offered them a writ of privilege, but they refused It, " being of a clear opinion, that all commandments and other acts proceeding from the neathcr house were to be done and executed by their serjeant without w rit, only by shew of his mace, which was his warrant." The sheriffs, in the meantime, were alarmed, and surrendered the prisoner; but the serjeant, by order of the house required their attendance at the bar, together with the clerks of the Compter, and White, the plaintiff; ' Cases of Larke, Clerk, Hyde, and Atwyll, 4 Rot. Pari 357; 5 lb. 374; G lb. 160. 191.

Sadcliffe's case, 1 Hats. 51. 32 Hen. VI., 5 Rot. Tarl. 23!).

and on their appearance, they were all committed for their contempt.

Tlie king, on hearing of these proceedings, called before him the lord chancellor, the judges, the speaker, and some of the gravest persons of the lower house, and addressed them. Having commended the wisdom of the commons in maintaining the privileges of their house, and stated that even their cooks were free from arrest, he is reported to have used these remarkable words:

"And further, we be informed by our judges, that we at no time stand so highly in our estate royal, as in the time of Parliament; wherein we as head, and you as members, are conjoined and knit together into one body politick, so as whatsoever oifence or injury during that time, is offered to the meanest member of the house, is to be judged as done against our person and the whole court of Parliament; which prerogative of the court is so great (as our learned counsel informeth us), that all acts and processes coming out of any other inferior courts, must for the time cease, and give place to the highest."

When the king had concluded his address, "Sir Edward Montagu, the lord chief justice, very gravely declared his opinion, confirming by divers reasons all that the king had said, which was assented unto by all the residue, none speaking to the contrary."

As this case rests upon the authority of Holinshed," and not upon parliamentary records, its accuracy has sometimes been doubted: but the positions there maintained are so conformable with the law of Parliament, as since asserted; the circumstances are so minutely stated, and were of so notorious a character, that there can be little ground for distrusting the general correctness of the account. Its probability is confirmed by the fact that Ferrers was a servant of the king, and the proceedings of the commons on his behalf, were therefore the more likely to be accept-aljle to the king, and to be sanctioned by his councillors and the House of Lords.

' 3 Holinshed, 824. i Hats. 57.

The practice of releasing members by a writ of privilege was still continued, notwithstanding the com'se pursued in the case of Ferrers, but henceforward no such writ was suffered to be obtained without a warrant, previously signed by the speaker. Thirty years later, Smalley, the servant of Smalley'scase. a member being under arrest, " was ordered to be brought hither to-morrow by the Serjeant, and so set at liberty by warrant of the mace, and not by writ." Again, in Fitzherbert's 1592, in the case of Fitzherbert, a member, who had been outlawed and taken in execution, the house, after many discussions as to his title to privilege, and concerning the manner in which he should be delivered, were at length acquainted that the lord keeper thought it best, " in regard to the ancient liberties and privileges of the house, that a serjeant-at-arms be sent by order of the house for Mr. Fitzherbert, by which he may be brought hither without peril of being further arrested by the way, and the state of the matter then considered of and examined into. ' In this case, however, the house determined that the member should not have privilege; " first, because he was taken in execution before the return of the indenture of his election; secondly, because he had been outlawed at the queen's suit, and was now taken in execution for her majesty's debt; thirdly, in regard that he was so taken by the sheriff, neither sedente Parliamento, nor eundo, nor redeundo."

This case was scarcely settled, when Mr. Neale, a mem- Neale's case, ber, complained that he had been an ested upon an execution; that he had paid the money, but out of regard to the liberties and privileges of the house, he thought it his duty to acquaint them with it. Upon which the house committed to the Tower the person at whose suit the execution was obtained, and the officer who executed it.

' 27tli Feb. 1375, 1 Com. J. 108. ' 1 Hats. 107. D'Ewcs, 482.014. D'Ewes, 518.

Three days afterwards the prisoners were reprimanded and discharged.

The principal cases in the lords, up to this period, show an uncertainty in their practice similar to that of the commons; privileged persons being sometimes released immediately, and sometimes by writs of privilege. On the 1st December, 1585, they ordered to be enlarged and set at liberty James Diggs, servant to the Archbishop of Canterbury, " by virtue of the privilege of this coart:" and again in the same year, a servant of Lord Leicester, and in 1597, the servants of Lord Chandois and the Archbishop of Canterbury." In the two last cases the officers who had arrested the prisoners were committed by the house. Later still, in November 1601, they adopted the precedent of Ferrers. William Hogan, like Ferrers, a servant of the queen, was imprisoned in execution; and the lords debated whether he should be discharged by a warrant from the lords to the lord keeper, to grant a writ in the queen's name for bringing up Hogan, or by immediate direction and order of the house, without any writ; and at length it was agreed that he should be brought up by order from the house. By virtue of their order, he was brought up and discharged on giving a bond for the payment of his debt; and the under-sheriff was committed to the Fleet for having arrested him. Yet, soon afterwards, in Yaughan's case, the lords resorted to the old method of discharging a prisoner by an order to the lord keeper for a writ of privilege; after having first committed the keeper of Newgate for refusing to obey their order to bring up his prisoner.

These cases have been cited not only as illustrative of the ancient claims of privilege, but also as throwing light, incidentally, upon the general law and privilege of Par- ' D'Ewes, 518. 520. 2 Lords' J. 66.

= 2 Lords' J. 93. " lb, 201. 205.

lb. 230. D'Ewes,603. 2 Lords' J. 238. 240. D'Ewes, 607.

liament. But it is now time to pass to the modifications of the ancient privilege which have since been effected by statute; and to the modern practice of Parliament in protecting members from arrest.

In 1603, the case of Sir Thomas Shirley occasioned a sir T. Shirley's more distinct recognition of the privilege by statute and an improvement in the law. Sir Thomas had been imprisoned in the Fleet, on execution, before the meeting of Parliament, and the commons first tried to bring him into the house by habeas corpus, and then sent their serjeant to demand his release. The Avarden refused to give up his prisoner, and was committed to the Tower for his contempt. Many proposals were made for releasing their member, but as none were free from objection, the house endeavoured to coerce the warden, and committed him to the prison called " Little Ease," in the Tower. At length the warden, either overcome by his durance, or commanded by the king, delivered up the prisoner, and was discharged, after a reprimand. So far the privileges of the house were satisfied, but there was still a legal diflsculty to be overcome, that had been common to all cases in which members were in execution, viz. that the warden was liable to an action of escape, and the creditor had lost his right to an execution." In former cases a remedy had been provided by a special Act, and the same expedient was now adopted; but in order to provide for future cases of a similar kind, a general Act was also passed.

The Act 1 James I., c. 13, after stating " that doubts had statutes reiat-been made, if any person, being arrested in execution, and from arrest '" by privilege of Parliament set at liberty, whether the party at whose suit such execution was pursued, be for ever barred and disabled to sue forth a new writ of execution in that case;" proceeded to enact, that after such time as the privilege of that session in which privilege is granted, shall ' 1 Com. J. 155 et seq. 5 Pari. Hist. 113, c. 1 Hats. 157. See 1 Com. J, 173. 195; and Collection of Precedents, 10 lb. 401.

cease, parties may sue forth and execute a new writ; and that no sheriff, c. from whose arrest or custody persons shall be delivered by privilege, shall be chargeable with any action. Lastly, the Act provided that nothing therein should " extend to the diminishing of any punishment to be hereafter by censure in Parliament inflicted upon any person who shall hereafter make or procure to be made any such arrest." Three points are here distinctly recognised; viz. 1, the privilege of freedom from arrest; 2, the right of either house of Parliament to set a privileged person at liberty; and 3, the right to punish those who make or procure arrests: while two other points were for the first time established; viz. that the officer should not be liable to an action of escape, and that the debt should not be satisfied.

But although the privilege of either house of Parliament was admitted to entitle a prisoner to his release, the manner of releasing him was still indefinite; and for some time it continued to be the practice, where privileged persons had been imprisoned in execution, to issue warrants for a writ of privilege or a writ of habeas corpus. In 1625, however, the commons declared, "that the house hath power, when they see cause, to send the serjeant immediately to deliver a prisoner;" and in some cases during the 17th century peers and members arrested in execution were released without any writ of privilege or habeas corpus, as Lord Baltinglasse in 1641," Lord Rich in 1646, and Sir Robert Holt in 1677. '

During the same period also, when the property of peers ' 2 Lords' J. 270. 296. 299. 302. 588; 3 lb. 30. 1 Hats. 1C7, 168.

"1 Com. J. 820.

' Mr. Hatsell states, that " since the end of Elizabeth's reign we have not actually met with any instance where a person entitled to privilege, if in custody in execution, hath been delivered by any other mode than by virtue of a writ of privilege, or by a writ of habeas corpus." (Vol. i. p. 167). But this statement had reference to the period from the accession of James I. to 1028; and, unless it be understood with this limitation, it is calculated to mislead.

4 Lords' J. Gra. 8 Lords'J. G35. G.3). 9 Com. J. 411.

or of their servants was distrained, the lords were accustomed to interfere by their direct authority, as in 1628, in the case of a ship belonging to the Earl of Warwick;

and in 1648, in regard to the tenants of Lord Montague. But privilege did not attach to property held by a peer as a trustee only. In cases of arrest on mesne process, the practice of releasing the prisoners directly by a warrant, or by sending the black rod or serjeant, in the name of the house, to demand them, was continually adopted.

At length, in the year 1700, an Act was passed," which while it retailed the privilege of freedom from arrest with more distinctness than the 1st James I., made the goods of privileged persons liable to distress infinite and sequestration, between a dissolution or prorogation and the next meeting of Parliament, and during adjournments for more than fourteen days. In suits against the king's immediate debtors, execution against members was permitted even during the sitting of Parliament, and the privilege of freedom from arrest in such suits was not reserved to servants. Again by the 2 3 Anne, c. 18, executions for penalties, forfeitures, c. against privileged persons, being employed in the revenue or any office of trust, were not to be stayed by privilege. Freedom from arrest, however, was still maintained for the members of both houses, in such cases, but not for their servants.

By the 10th Geo. III., c. 50, a very important limitation Servants' privi-of the freedom of arrest was effected. Down to that time tinued? ' the servants of members had been entitled to all the privileges of their masters, except as regards the limitations effected by the two last statutes; but by the 3d section of the 10th Geo. III., the privilege of members to be free from arrest upon all suits, authorised by the Act, was expressly reserved; while no such reservation was intro- 3 Lords' J. 776, 777. 2 jq o ds' J. 611.

3 12 lb. 194. 390; 14 lb. 36. 78; 16 lb. 294; 22 lb. 412.

liassett's case, 1 Com. J. 807.

4 Lords' J. 654; 8 lb. 577. 601. Boteler's case, 17 Com. J. 6.

12 13 Will. III. c. 3, afterwards extended by 11 Geo. II. c. 24.

tluced in reference to their servants. And thus, without any distinct abrogation of the privilege, it was, in fact, put an end to, as executions were not to be stayed in their favour, and their freedom from arrest was not reserved. Members how By these several statutes the freedom of members from released at pre- j j, j, gg ms bccome a legal right rather than a parliamentary privilege. The arrest of a member has been held, therefore, to be irregular ab initio, and he may be discharged immediately upon motion in the court from which the process issued.

For the same reason, writs of jjrivilege have been discontinued. In 1707, a few years after the passing of the 12th 13th Will. III., the Serjeant was sent with the mace to the warden of the Fleet, who readily paid obedience to the orders of the house, and discharged Mr. Asgill, a member then in execution. Peers, peeresses, and members are now discharged directly by order or waitant, and the parties who cause the arrest are liable to censure and punishment, as in the case of the baroness Le Cale in 1811; ' and Viscount Hawarden in 1828.

In 1807, Mr. Mills had been arrested on mesne process, and was afterwards elected. The house determined that he was entitled to privilege, and ordered him to be discharged out of the custody of the marshal of the King's Bench. In 1819 Mr. Christie Burton had been elected for Beverley, but being in custody on execution, and also on mesne process, was unable to attend his service in Parliament. The house determined that he was entitled to privilege, and ordered him to be discharged out of the custody of the warden of the Fleet." An action was brought against the warden by the assignees of a creditor of Mr. Burton, for his escape, who were declared guilty of a breach of privilege, and ordered to attend the house;

Colonel Pitt's case, 2 Strange, 985. K. B. Cases, temp. Hard. 28. 2 15 Com. J. 471. 3 48 Lords' J. 60. 63.

"60 lb. 34 (and Rep. of Precedents, 28). 62 lb. 654.

6 74 lb. 44. 7 75 Com. J. 286.

but having acknowledged their offence by petition, they were not subjected to any punishment.

It now only remains to inquire what is the duration of Duration of ,.,, privilege. the privilege of freedom from arrest; and it is singular that this important point has never been expressly defined by Parliament. The person of a peer (by the privilege of peerage) "is for ever sacred and inviolable." This immunity rests upon ancient custom, and is recognised by the Acts 12 13 Will. III., c. 3, and 2 3 Anne, c. 18. It would seem to have been an ancient feudal privilege of the barons, the law assuming that there would always be upon the demesnes of their baronies sufficient to distrain for the satisfaction of any debt. Peeresses are entitled to Peeresses, the same privilege as peers, whether they be peeresses by birth, by creation, or by marriage; but if a peeress by marriage should afterwards intermarry with a commoner, she forfeits her privilege." It is also ordered and declared by the lords that privilege of Parliament shall not be allowed to minor peers, noblewomen, or widows of peers (saving their right of peerage)."

And by the 23d article of the Act of Union with Scot- Representative land (5 Anne, c. 8) the sixteen representative peers are " ' allowed all the privileges of the peers of the Parliament of Great Britain; and all other peers and peeresses of Scotland, though not chosen, enjoy the same privileges." In the same manner, by the Act of Union with Ireland, the peers and peeresses of Ireland are entitled to the same privileges as the peers and peeresses of Great Britain.

With regard to members of the House of Commons, " the time of privilege " has been repeatedly mentioned in statutes, but never explained.

1 Bl. Comm. 165. " 1 West. Inq. 27.

' Countess of Rutland's case, 6 Co. 52.

Co. Litt. 166. 4 Bacon's Abridg. 229. Lords' S. O. No. 78. 11 Lords'J. 298; 15 lb. 241. Lords' S. 0. No. 78. See also 12 Lords' J. 714; 13 lb. 67. 79, 80. 659. 3 Strange, 990.

Autiiorities as It is Stated by Blackstone, and others, and is the general to the dura-tion.,,. o o t f l of privilege. opinion, that the privilege of freedom Iroiu arrest remains Avith a member of the House of Commons, "for forty days after every prorogation, and forty days before the next appointed meeting;" but the learned commentator cites the case of the Earl of Athol v. the Earl of Derby, which hardly supports so distinct a conclusion. It appears from the report of that case, that the lords claim privilege for twenty days only before and after each session; and the report adds, " but it is said, the commons never assented to this, but claim forty days after and before each session." In another report of the same case, it is also said, that " they claim forty days;" and in another report, "that the commons claimed forty days, which ought not to be allowed." But that the commons have claimed so long a duration of this immunity, there are no precedents to show. By the original law of Parliament, privilege extended to the protection of members and their servants, "eundo, morando et exinde redeundo:" but Parliament has never yet determined what time shall be considered convenient for this purpose; and Prynne expresses an opinion, that no such definite extent of privilege is claimable by the law of Parliament. There has, however, been a general belief and tradition (founded, probably, upon the ancient law and custom, by which writs of summons for a Parliament were always issued at least forty days before its appointed meeting), that privilege extended to forty days; and several Acts of the Irish Parliament have defined that time as the duration of privilege in Ireland. Parliamentary precedents alone will not be found to establish this extent of privilege in England, but it has been allowed by the courts of law, on the ground of usage and universal opinion. And by reason of frequent prorogations the enjoyment of this privilege is never liable to interruption.

' 2 Levinz, 72. 2 j Q ia."a. Cas. 221.

' Bid. 29. 4 Prynne, Reg. 1216.

See 3 Edw. LV. c. 1, Ir, 6 Anne, c. 3, Ir. 1 Geo. II. c. 8, s. 2, Ir.

On the 6th December 1555, a case occurred, which has Piedall's case, been rehecl upon as a declaration of Parhament concerning the duration, of privilege, but to which no importance can be attached. The commons sent a message to the lords, to complain that their privilege was broken, by reason of Gabriel Pledall, a member, having been bound in a recognizance in the Star Chamber, to appear before the council, within twelve days after the end of the Parliament, which was about to be dissolved. A message was afterwards received for six members to confer with the lords, who went, and reported, on their return, " that the chief justices, master of the rolls, and Serjeants, do clearly affinn that the recognizance is no breach of the privilege." From this case Prynne infers, that the commons "have not twelve, much less twenty or forty days, after the Parliament ended:" but no such inference can be supported; for it does not appear whether the oj inion of the judges related to the recognizance itself, or to the duration of the privilege after the dissolution. The case is not mentioned in the Lords' Journal; the lords were not said to have pronounced this opinion, but only the judges; and there was no acquiescence on the part of the commons, for the Parliament was dissolved two days afterwards.

In the case of Mr. Marten, in 1586, who had been ar- Mr. Marten's rested twenty days before the meeting of Parliament, the question was put, whether the house would limit any time for privilege. The house answered a convenient time; but they determined that the twenty days were within a convenient time, and that Mr. Marten should, therefore, be discharged.

Twenty days, therefore, have been allowed, which would exclude any inference from Piedall's case.

On the 14th December 1621, the lords resolved that Resoiutious in . p o n-I th houses.

their servants were free from arrest "lor twenty days before and after every session; in which time the lords may ' 1 Com. J. 46. 2 D'Ewes, 410. 1 Hats. 100.

conveuiently go home to their houses, in the most remote l)arts of this kingdom."' And again, on the 28th May 1624, they adopted a similar resolution." On the 27th January 1628, they added, that this freedom should " begin with the date of the writ of summons, in the beginning of every Parliament, and continue twenty days before and after every session of Parliament." On the 24th April 1640, it was ' said in the House of Commons, and not contradicted, that members had privilege for sixteen days exclusive, and fifteen days inclusive, before the begiiming and ending of every Parliament;" and in a case of privilege considered on that day, it is entered, " the contempt of his arrest to be declined, because it was not committed within time of privilege; viz., within sixteen days before the beginning of the Parliament, or so many days after."'" And on the 17th January 1689, the lords declared that the freedom of their servants should begin twenty days before the return of the writ of summons, and continue twenty days before and after every session.

A confirmation of the claim of forty days, however, has been indirectly found in the several Acts of Parliament relating to the privilege of franking letters (now abolished by statute), in which the power of franking was given to members for forty days before any summons, and forty days after any prorogation. Mr. Dun On the 7th September 1847, Mr. Duncombe was released combe's case., i i r i-i from arrest by a judge s order in vuiue of his privilege.

He had been elected member for Finsbuiy on the 28th of July, and on the 2d September was taken in execution on a ca. sa. The writs for the new Parliament were returnable on the 21st Sei)tember; but Parliament was prorogued by writ to the 12th October. The arrest had taken place forty days after the dissolution, and twenty days before the 21st September, the day first appointed for the meeting of Parliament. It was contended in support of ' 3 Lords' J. 195. 3 lords' J. 417.

" 4 Lords' J. 13. 1 Hats. 41 h. 2 Corn. J. 10. Lords' S. O. No. 65. For a history of tbi privilege, see Report, IGth April 1735.

the arrest, 1st, that twenty days was a sufficient thne; and, 2dly, supposing a longer period to be allowed, that the period should be reckoned to the 12tli October, which would leave the member forty days for coming to Parliament. Mr. Justice Williams, however, was satisfied that the privilege extended to forty days, and that the period must be reckoned to the 21st September only. On a motion for rescinding the judge's order, the Chief Baron, in delivering the judgment of the court, at once determined that the period must be reckoned to the 21st September, as the day on which the vrits were returnable; and after citing the authorities as to the duration of privilege, concluded in these words: " We think that the conclusion to be drawn from all that is to be found in the books on the subject is this: That whether the rule was originally for a convenient time, or for a time certain, the period of forty days before and after the meeting of Parliament has, for about two centuries, at least, been considered either a convenient time, or the actual time to be allowed. Such has been the usage, the universally prevailing opinion on the subject; and such, we think, is the law."' It has been determined by the courts of law, that the After dissolu-privilege, even after a dissolution, is still enjoyed for a " convenient and reasonable time for returning home. What this convenient time may be has never been determined; but the general claim of exemption from arrest, eundo et recleundo, extends as well to dissolutions as to prorogations, as no distinction is made between them.

These cases apply to arrests made after the privilege has Members in ex-accrued; but the effect of the election of a person already i election. in execution, still remains to be considered. In Thorpe's case the judges excepted from privilege the case of "a con demnation had before the Parliament;" but their opinion has not been sustained by the judgment of Parliament.

' 1 Welshy, H. G. 430.

Colonel Pitt's case, 1 Strange, D85. Baruardo v. Mordauut, 1 Lord Ken. 2b.

Persons iiiicler iirrest becoming peers.

Members not admitted as bail.

Not to be impleaded.

Case of Bogo de Clare.

Unless a member has incurred some legal disability, or has subjected himself to processes more stringent than those which result from civil actions, it has been held that his service in Parliament is paramount to all other claims. Thus in 1677, Sir Kobert Holt was discharged, although he had been " taken in execution out of privilege of Parliament;" and, not to mention intermediate cases, or any which are of doubtful authority, Mr. Christie Burton obtained his release in 1819, although he had been in the custody of the warden of the Fleet before his election.

A person succeeding to a peerage while under arrest Is entitled to his discharge in virtue of his privilege. On the 1st January 1849 Lord Harley, having succeeded, by the death of his father, to the Earldom of Oxford, applied to a judge in chambers (Mr. Baron Piatt), for his discharge from the Queen's Prison. It was submitted that he was not entitled to privilege until he had taken his seat as a peer; but this position could not be supported by any authorities, and the earl was ordered to be discharged. It has been decided by the lords that a peer is entitled to privilege when he has not qualified himself to sit, by taking the oaths."

As a consequence of the immunity of a member of Parliament, it has been held that he cannot be admitted as bail; for not being liable to the ordinary processes of the court, by reason of his privilege, he cannot be proceeded against in the event of the recognizances being forfeited.

2. The earliest case in which the privilege of not being impleaded appears to be recorded, is that of Bogo de Clare, in the 18th Edward I. (1290)." A complaint was made that 9 Com. J. 411.

See Reports of Precedents, 10 Com, J, 401. 62 Com. J. 642. 633, 654. 2 Hats. 37. 3 74 Com. J. 44; 75 lb. 230. M'Cabe v. Lord Harley.

Lords' J. 24th Feb. 1691; 13th May 1720.

Duncan v. Hill (1 Dowling Ryland's Rep. 126); Graham v. Sturt, (4 Taunton's Rep. 249); Burton v. Athurton, 2 Marsh, 232; and case of Mr. Feargus O'Connor, who offered himself as bail for Ernest Jones, the Chartist, 11th June 1848, at Bow-street. i Uyt. Pari. 17.

the prior of the Holy Trinity in London, by procurement of Bogo cle Clare, had cited the Earl of Cornwall, in Westminster Hau, in Parliament time, to appear before the Lord Archbishop of Canterbury. Both of them were sent for, to answer before the king, and having appeared, and submitted themselves, were sent to the Tower. Bogo de Clare afterwards came and paid a fine of two thousand marks to the king. This case has been cited by Sir E. Coke, Elsynge, and others, as a claim of Parliamentary privilege; but has latterly been held to have arisen out of the service of a citation in a privileged place; although the words " in Parliament time," would suggest an opposite conclusion.

In tlie 8th Edward II., writs of supersedeas were issued to the justices of assize, to prevent actions from being maintained against members in their absence, by reason of their inability to defend their rights while in attendance upon the Parliament. This privilege appears to have fallen into disuse, for in the 12th Edward IV., it was disallowed in the case of Walsh, a servant of the Earl of Cases of Walsh Essex. That person pleaded a king's writ, in which his right not to be impleaded was affirmed; but the lords, with the advice of the judges, determined, that there " was no custom, but that members and their servants might be impleaded; " and they disallowed the writ, and ordered Walsh to plead. In the same year a similar decision was given in the case of Cosyn." Yet, while this was held to be the law in England, the privilege thus disallowed had been confirmed not long before, by a statute in the Parliament of Ireland. A few years later, the commons, in Atwyll's case, claimed it as a prescriptive privilege, that they " should not be impleaded in any action personal,"

1 Burdett v. Abbot.

2 1 Hats. Prec. 7, 8. " Ne per eorum absentiam, dum sic in dicto Parlia-mento steterint, exhceiedacionem aliquam sustineaut, aliqualiter vel incur-rant." And again, " presertini cum absentes jura sua dc-fendere nequeant ut presentes."

' 1 Hats. 41, 42. lb. 43. 3 Edw. IV. c. I.

and their claim seems to have been admitted both by the king and by the House of Lords.

One of the most marked cases of later times, in which the privilege was enforced, was on the 21st February 1588; when the House of Commons, being informed that several members had writs of nisi prius brought against them, to be tried at the assizes, a motion was made " that writs of supersedeas might be awarded in these cases, in respect of the privilege of this house, due and appertaining to the members of the same." Upon which it was resolved, " that those of this house which shall have occasion to require such benefit of privilege in that behalf, may repair unto Mr. Speaker, to declare unto him the state of their cases; and that he, upon his discretion, if the case shall so require, may direct the warrant of this house to the lord chancellor of England, for the awarding of such writs accordingly."'- Suits stayed by At the beginning of the reign of James I., another practice was adojited. Instead of resorting to writs of supersedeas, the speaker was ordered to stay suits by a letter to the judges; and sometimes by a warrant to the party also; and the parties and their attorneys who commenced the actions were brought, by the serjeant, to the bar of the house. Applications for the stay of suits, at length, became so frequent and troublesome, that it was ordered, where any member of the house hath cause of privilege, to stay any trial, a letter shall issue, under Mr. Speaker's hand, for stay thereof, without further motion in the house." This power of staying suits appears to have been generally acquiesced in by the courts; but in the case of Hodges and Moore, in 1626, the court of King's Bench refused to obey the speaker's letter, and was about to return a sharp answer, when the Parliament was dis- ' Atwyll's case,17 Edw. IV.; 6 Rot. Pari. 191.

D'Ewes, 43G. ' 1 Com. J. 286.381. 421, c.

1 Com. J. 804. 5 lb. 304. 1G20; 1 Com. J. 525.

solved. In numerous instances, however, members agreed to waive their privilege; and upon the petitions of the parties, suits were occasionally allowed to proceed.

The privilege insisted upon in this manner, continued Limitations of until the end of the seventeenth century, when it under- statute. went a considerable limitation by statute. The 12th 13th Will, III., c. 3, enacted, that any persons might commence and prosecute actions against any peer, or member of Parliament, or their servants, or others entitled to privilege, in the courts at Westminster, and the duchy court of Lancaster, immediately after a dissolution or prorogation, until the next meeting of Parliament, and during any adjournment for more than 14 days; and that during such times, the court might give judgment and award execution. Processes and bills against members were authorised, during the same intervals, to be had or exhibited, and to be enforced by distress infinite or sequestration; and actions, c. against the king's immediate debtors were not to be stayed, at any time, by privilege of Parliament. The privilege was thus limited in its operation; but it was still acknowledged, especially by the third section, which provided that where actions were stayed by privileo-e, the plaintiffs should be at liberty to proceed to judo-ment and execution upon the rising of Parliament.

Soon afterwards, it was enacted, by the 2d 3d Anne, c. 18, that no action, suit, process, proceeding, judgment, or execution, against privileged persons, employed in the revenue, or any office of public trust, for any forfeiture, penalty, c., should be stayed or delayed by or under colour or pretence of privilege of Parliament. The Act of William III. had extended only to the principal courts of law and equity; but by the 11th Geo. II., c. 24, all actions in relation to real and personal property, were allowed to be ' Prynne's 4th Register, 810. 1 Com. J. 8G1. 1 Hats. 184,185.

1 Com. J. 378. 421. 595, c.; 10 lb. 280. 300. 596; 11 lb. 557, c.

commenced and prosecuted in the recess and during adjournments of more than fourteen days, in aiiy court of record, c. Still more important limitations of the privilege were effected by the Act 10 Geo. III., c. 50. The preamble of that Act states, that the previous laws were insufficient to obviate the inconveniences arising from the delay of suits by reason of privilege of Parliament; and it is therefore enacted that,

"Any person may at any time commence and prosecute any action or suit in any court of record, or court of equity, or of admiralty; and in all causes, matrimonial and testamentary, against any peer or lord of Parliament of Great Britain, oragainstanyof the knights, citizens, or burgesses, c. for the time being, or against any of their menial, or any other servants, or any other person entitled to the privilege of Parliament; and no such action, suit, or any other process or proceeding thereupon, shall at any time be impeached, stayed, or delayed, by or under any colour or pretence of any privilege of Parliament."

' Sect. 2. But nothing in this Act shall extend to subject tle person of any of the knights, citizens, and burgesses for the time being, to be arrested or imjirisoned upon any such suit or proceeding."

Stringent modes of enforcing the processes of the courts were enacted by this Act, and still further facilities were given to plaintiffs by the 45th Geo. III., c. 124, and the 47th Geo. III., sess. 2, c. 40. Under these Acts members of Parliament may be coerced by every legal process, except the attachment of their bodies. Subpoenas and 3. The claim to resist subpoenas was founded upon the same principle as other personal privileges, viz., the paramount right of Parliament to the attendance and service of its members. Yet it does not appear to have been maintained in early times. In 1554, a complaint was made by the lords that Mr. Beamond, a member of the commons, had caused a subpoena to be served upon the Earl of Huntington; to which the commons returned an answer, " that juries.

' The 4th article of the Act of Union extends all privileges of English peers to the peers of Ireland.

they take this writ to be no breach of privilege."' Yet, in 1557, on a complaint being made that Mr. T. Eyms, a member of the commons, had been served with a subpoena, two members w ere sent to the chancellor, to require that the process might be revoked." And again, in the case of Richard Cook, in 1584, three members were sent to the Court of Chancery, to signify to the chancellor and master of the rolls that, by the ancient liberties of this house, the members of the same are privileged from being served with subpoenas, "and to desire that they will allow the like privileges for other members of this house, to be signified to them in writing under Mr. Speaker's hand." But the chancellor replied, that " he thought the house had no such liberty of privilege for subpoenas." A committee was then appointed to search for precedents, but made no report." Immediately afterwards, the house punished a person who had served a member with a subpoena. Various other cases subsequently occurred in which the parties who had served subpoenas upon members of both houses were committed, or otherwise punished for their contempt. But, of late years, so far from withholding the attendance of members as witnesses in courts of justice, the commons have frequently granted leave of absence to their members on the express ground that they have been summoned as witnesses and have even admitted the same excuse for defaulters at calls of the house." But although this claim of privilege is not now enforced as regards other courts, one house will not permit its members to be summoned by the other without a message desiring his attendance, nor without the consent of the member whose attendance is 1 Cora. J. 34. " lb. 48. 1 Pari. Hist. 630.

3 D'Ewes, 347. 1 Hats. 96, 97. " 1 Hats. 97.

1 Hats. Prec. 169.175. 3 Lords' J. 630. 1 Com. J. 203.205. 211.368. 1040, c.; 9 lb. 339.

6 56 Com. J. 122; 68 lb. 218. 243. 292; 71 lb. 110; 82 lb. 306. 379. See also Hans. Deb. 1st March 1844 (Earl of Devon).

7 48 lb. 318.

required. And it may be doubtful whether the house would not protect a member served with a subpoena from the legal consequences of non attendance in a court of justice, if permission had not been previously granted by the house for liis attendance. Members sum- As the withdrawal of a witness may affect the adminlstra- monedasjurors. of justice, the privilege has very properly been waived; but the service of members upon juries not being absolutely necessary, their more imni' diate duties in Parliament are held to supersede the obligation of attendance in other courts. The privilege is of great antiquity; the tenure per haroniam having conferred an exemption from serving on juries, not only upon those summoned to Parliament, but also upon all tenants jjer haroniam.""

The first complaint of a member being summoned on a jury appears to have been made on the 22d November 1597, in the case of Sir J. Tracy. In that case the Serjeant was immediately sent with the mace to call Sir J. Tracy to his attendance in the house, who shortly returned accordingly, Another case occurred in 1607, in which it was ordered that two members, retained as jurors by the sheriff, should be spared their attendance, and the serjeant-at-arms was sent with his mace to deliver the pleasure of the house to the secondary of the King's Bench, the court then sitting. On the 15th May 1628, it was determined that Sir W. Alford should have privilege not to serve; and a letter was ordered " to be written by Mr, Speaker to the judges, that he be not amerced for his not appearance." The last occasion on which a complaint was made of a member having been summoned as a juryman was in 1826, when the house agreed that he should have privilege; and, upon the report of the committee of privileges, resolved, nem. con., that it is " amongst the most ancient and un- ' 78 Com. J. 132. 2 1 West. Inq. 28.

D'Ewes, 5G0. 1 Hats. 112. M Com. J. 369. lb. 898.

doubted privileges of Parliament, that no member shall be withdrawn from his attendance on his duty in Parliament to attend on any other court."" To this It may be added, that in the last clause of the Act of 1825, for consolidating the laws relative to jurors and juries, there Is an express reservation that nothing shall " abridge or affect any privilege of Parliament." This privilege is not ordinarily claimed by members when Parliament is not sitting; but it may be presumed that such a claim would be allowed " eundo morando et redeundo," i. e. for 40 days before the meeting of Parliament, and 40 days after each prorogation.

4. The privilege of freedom from arrest has always been Criminal com-limited to civil causes, and has not been allowed to interfere with the administration of criminal justice. In Larke's case, in 1429, the privilege was claimed, " except for treason, felony, or breach of the peace;" and in Thorpe's case, the judges made exceptions to such cases as be "for treason, or felony, or surety of the peace." The privilege was thus explained by a resolution of the lords, 18th April 1626: " That the privilege of this house is, that no peer of Parliament, sitting the Parliament, is to be Imprisoned or restrained, without sentence or order of the house, unless it be for treason or felony, or for refusing to give surety of the peace;" and again, by a resolution of the commons, 20th May 1675, "that by the laws and usage of Parliament, privilege of Parliament belongs to every member of the House of Commons, in all cases except treason, felony, and breach of the peace."

It was stated by the commons, at a conference on the 17 th August 1641:

"1. That no privilege is allowable in case of peace betwixt private men, much more in case of the peace of the kingdom. 2. That privilege cannot be pleaded against an indictment for any thing done out of Parliament, because all indictments are ' contra pacem domini regis. 3. Privilege of Parliament is granted in regard of

"81 Cora. J. 82. 87. = 6 Geo. 4, c. 50.

3 4 Rot. Pari. 357. 5 lb. 239. 3 Lords' J. 562.

tlie service of the Commonwealth, and is not to be used to the danger of the Commonwealth. 4. That all privilege of Parliament is in the power of Parliament, and is a restraint to the proceedings of other inferior courts, but is no restraint to the proceedings of Parliament, and, therefore, seeing it may, without injustice, be denied, this being the case of the Commonwealth, they conceive it ought not to be granted." '

On the 14th April 1697, it was resolved, " that no member of this house has any privilege in case of breach of the peace, or forcible entries, or forcible detainers."

On the 1st December 1763, it was resolved, by both houses,

"that privilege of Parliament does not extend to the case of writing and publishing seditious libels, nor ought to be allowed to obstruct the ordinary course of laws in the speedy and effectual prosecution of so heinous and dangerous an offence."

"Since that time," said the committee of privileges, in 1831, " it has been considered as established generally, that privilege is not claimable for any indictable offence." Case of These being the general declarations of the law of Par- liament, one case will be sufficient to show how little protection is practically afforded by privilege, in criminal offences. In 1815, Lord Cochrane, a member, having been indicted and convicted of a conspiracy, was committed by the Court of King's Bench to the King's Bench Prison. Lord Cochrane escaped, and was arrested by the marshal, whilst he was sitting on the privy councillors' bench, in the House of Commons, on the right hand of the chair, at which time there was no member present, prayers not having been read. The case was referred to the committee of privileges, who reported that it was " entirely of a novel nature, and that the privileges of Parliament did not appear to have been violated, so as to call for the interposition of the house by any proceedings against the marshal of the King's Bench."

' 2 Com. J. 2G1. 4 Lords' J. 369. " 11 Com, J. 784. 29 lb. 689. Sess. Paper, 1831 (114). See also case of Lord Oliphaut, in 1709. 19 Lords' J. 31. 34; and 26 lb. 492 (Gaming-houses). Sess. Paper, 1814-15 (239).

Thus the house will not allow even the sanctuary of its Causes of mitment to communicated.

walls to protect a member from the process of criminal law. '"

But in all cases in which members are arrested on criminal charges, the house must be informed of the cause for which they are detained from their service in Parliament.

The various Acts which have suspended for a time the Habeas Corpus Act, have contained provisions to the effect that no member of Parliament shall be imprisoned, during the sitting of Parliament, until the matter of which he stands suspected, shall he first communicated to the house of which he shall be a member, and the consent of the said house obtained for his commitment.

But in cases not affected by these Acts, it has been usual to communicate the cause of commitment, after the arrest, as in the case of Lord George Gordon, for high treason in 1784, and Mr. Smith O'Brien in 1848, and whenever members have been in custody in order to be tried by naval or military courts martial.

The same distinction between civil and criminal processes has been observed in the case of bankrupts. By the Bankrupt Law Consolidation Act, 1849, s. 66, it is enacted that "if any trader having privilege of Parliament sliall commit any act of bankruptcy, he may be dealt with under the Act in like manner as any other trader; but such person shall not be subject to be arrested or imprisoned during the term of such privilege, except in cases made felonies and misdemeanors by this Act."

Another description of offence, partaking of a criminal Commitment character, is a contempt of a court of justice; and it was contempt. for some time doubtful how far privilege would extend to the protection of a member committed for a contempt.

' See 17 Geo. II, c. 6. 45 Geo. III. c. 4, s. 2. 57 Geo. III. c. 3, s. 4. 57 Geo. III. c. 55, 3. 4. 3 Geo. IV. c. 2, s. 4.

37 Com. J. 903. 103 lb. 808.

37 lb. 57. 39 lb. 479. 51 lb. 139. 557. 58 lb. 597. 67 lb. 246, c. 47 Lords' J. 349 (Lord Gambier); and see case of Lord Torringtoii, 14 lb. 521, 523. 525. 527. ' 12 13 Vict. c. 106.

Case of On the 30th June 1572, a complaint was made to the

Lord Cromwell, j. Henry Lord Cromwell, that his person had been attached by the slieriff of Norfolk, by a writ of attachment from the Court of Chancery, for not obeying an injunction of that court, "contrary to the ancient privileges and immunities, time out of mind, unto the lords of Parliament and peers of this realm, in such cases used and allowed." The lords, after examining this case in the presence of the judges and others of the queen's learned counsel, agreed that " the attachment did not appear to be warranted by the common law or custom of the realm, or by any statute law, or by precedents of the Court of Chancery," and they ordered Lord Cromwell to be discharged of the attachment. They were, however, very cautious in giving a general opinion, and declared that if at any future time cause should be shown that by the queen's prerogative, or by common law or custom, or by any statute or precedents, the persons of lords of Parliament are attachable, the order in this case should not affect their decision in judging according to the cause shown." Prynne, in reference to til is case, lays it down that the persons of peers would only be attachable in cases of breach of the peace and contempts with force, when there would be a fine to the king," This precedent was adopted and confirmed by the lords on the 10th February 1628. It had been referred to the committee of privileges to inquire " whether a serjeant-at-arms may arrest the person of a peer (out of privilege of Parliament) upon a contempt of a decree in the Chancery." The committee reported that no case of attachment had occurred befere that of Lord Cromwell, and that "the lords of Parliament ought to enjoy their ancient and due privileges, and their persons to be free from such attachments, with the same proviso as in the case of Lord Cromwell;" to which the lords generally assented. But on the 22d October 1667, a report of the committee of privileges, ' 1 Lords'. J. 727. ' 4tb Res. 792. 4 lq Js' J. 27.

containing the same proviso, was confirmed by the house, leaving out the proviso.

In 1605, in the case of Mr. Brereton, who had been Mr. Brereton. committed by the Court of King's Bench for a contempt, the commons brought up their member by a writ of habeas corpus, and received him in the house. The case of Sir W. Bampfield, in 1614, throws very little light upon the matter, as after he had been brought in by writ of habeas corpus, the speaker desired to know the pleasure of the house, but no resolution or order appears to have been afterwards agreed to." On the 8th February 1620 a complaint was made, in the commons, that two of the members' pages had been punished for misbehaviour in the Court of King's Bench. It was stated, however, that the judges had sent one of the offenders to be punished by the house, and would send the other when he could be found; " and yet, but for respect for this house, they would have indicted them for stroke in face of the court; and many for less offences have lost their hands."'

On the 9th February 1625 the Lord Vaux claimed his Lord Vaux. privilege for stay of the proceedings in an information against him in the Star Chamber; and it was granted; and shortly afterwards, in the case of the Earl of Arundel, Earl of Arun-the lords' committee maintained that " though a lord, at ' the suit of the king, be sued in the Star Chamber for a contempt, yet the suit is to be stayed by privilege of Parliament in parliament time." But on the 8th June 1757, it was " ordered and declared by the lords, that no peer or lord of Parliament hath privilege of peerage, or of Parliament, against being compelled, by process of the courts of Westminster Hall, to pay obedience to a writ of habeas corpus directed to him;" and that this be a standing order." And it was decided, in the case of Earl Ferrers, ' 12 Lords' J. 122. M Com. J. 2G9. lb. 466.

1 Com. J. 513. 5 3 Lords' J. 496.

3 Lords' J. 558 (Report of Preeedeuts) 562, c. 29 lb. 181, that an attachment may be granted if a peer refuses obedience to the writ In more recent cases members committed by courts for contempt have failed in obtaining their release by virtue of privilege. Mr. Long Wei- In 1831, Mr. Long Wellesley, a member, having con-lesley. fessed in the Court of Chancery that he had taken his infant daughter, a ward in chancery, out of the jurisdiction of the court. Lord Brougharr C. at once committed him for contempt, saying,

"It is no violation of the privil- ges of Parliament if the members of Parliament have violated the rights and privileges of this court, which ia of as high a dominion, and as undisputed a jurisdiction, as the High Court of Parliament itself; it is no breach of, but a compliance with, their privileges, that a member of either house of Parliament, breaking the rules of this court, and breaking the law of the land by a contempt committed against this court, should stand committed for that contempt."

Mr. Wellesley applied to the House of Commons, and claimed his privilege. His case was referred to the committee of privileges, who reported, "That his claim to be discharged from imprisonment, by reason of privilege of Parliament, ought not to be admitted." Mr. Lcchmere The last casc was that of Mr. Lechmere Charlton, in 1837. That member had been committed by the lord chancellor, for a contempt in writing a letter to one of the masters in chancery, " containing matter scandalous with respect to him, and an attempt improperly to influence his decision." Mr. Charlton complained to the speaker of his commitment, and his letters were referred to a com- ' 1 Burr. 631. It is said in Bacon's Abridgment (vol. 6, p. 546), "Also peers of the realm are punishable by attachment for contempts in many instances: as for rescuing a person arrested by due course of law j for proceeding in a cause against the king's writ of prohibition; for disobeying other writs wherein the king's prerogative or the liberty of the subject are nearly concerned; and for other contempts which are of an enormous nature." 2 Hawk. P. C, c. 22, s. 33. 1 Burr. G34.

' ' But the courts will not grant an attachment against a peer or member of Parliament for non-payment of money according to award." 7 Term Re., 171.546. 86 Com. J. 701.

Charlton.

mlttee of privileges. As the lord chancellor's order did not set forth the obnoxious letter, the committee directed it to be produced, as they considered,

"That although the lord chancellor had the power to declare what he deemed to be a contempt of the High Court of Chancery, it was necessary that the House of Commons, as the sole and exclusive judge of its own privileges, should be informed of the particulars of the contempt before they could decide whether the contempt was of such a character as would justify the imjirison-ment of a member."

After inquiring fully into the nature of the contempt, the committee reported, that Mr. Charlton's claim to be discharged from imprisonment ought not to be admitted.

Before these last cases, the ordinary process for contempts against persons having privilege of Parliament or of peerage, had not been that of attachment of the person, but that of sequestration of the whole property, as in the case of the Countess of Shaftesbury. In 1829, an order for the commitment of Lord Roscommon, for contempt, had been made by the lord chancellor, but was never executed, nor even taken out of the registrar's office. Nor must it be omitted that, so late as 1832, an Act was passed, by which contempts of the ecclesiastical courts," in face of the court, or any other contempt towards such court, or the process thereof, are directed to be signified to the lord chancellor, who is to issue a writ de contumace capiendo, for taking into custody persons charged with such contempt," in case such person "shall not be a peer, lord of Parliament, or member of the House of Commons." It must not, therefore, be understood, that either house has waived its right to interfere when members are committed for contempt. Each case is open to consideration, when it arises; and although reluctance would undoubtedly be felt in obstructing the process of 92 Com. J. 3 et seq. 1 Pari. Rep. 1837, No. 45. 2 Peere Williams, 110. 2 3 Will. IV., c. 93.

I'rivilege of witnesses and otliers.

rreedoiu from arrest.

other courts, privilege would still be allowed, if the circumstances of the case appeared to justify it.

As yet the personal privilege of members, and the ancient privilege of their servants, have alone been noticed. These were founded upon the necessity of enabling members freely to attend to their duties in Parliament. Upon the same-ground, a similar privilege of freedom from arrest and molestation is attached to all witnesses summoned to attend before either house of Parliament, or before parliamentary committees, and to others in personal attendance upon the business of Parliament, in coming, staying, and returning. In the early Journals there are numerous orders that all persons attending in obedience to the orders of the house, and of committees, shall have the privilege or protection of the house. A few precedents wiu serve to explain the nature and extent of this privilege.

Instances of protections given by the lords to witnesses and to parties, while their causes or bills were depending, appear very frequently on the Journals of that house.

In 1640, Sir Pierce Crosbie, sworn as a witness in Lord Straflford's cause, being threatened with arrest, was allowed privilege, " to protect him during the time that this house examine him;" and many similar protections have been granted in later times.

In 1641, it was ordered that Sir T. Lake, who had a cause depending, should " have liberty to pass in and out unto the house, and to his counsel, solicitor, and attorney, for and during so long time only as his cause shall be before their lordships in agitation;'" and many similar orders have been made in the case of other parties, who have had causes depending, or bius before the house.

' 1 Com. J. 505. 2 lb. 107. 9 lb. 62. 13 lb. 521, c.

= 4 Lords' J. 143, 144. 25 lb. G25, 27 lb. 19.

4 lb. 2()2.

' 4 lb. 203. 289. 330. 477. 5 lb. 47G.

"5 lb. 5(53. 574. 053. 080. 27 lb. 538. 28 lb. 512,

On the 12th May 1624, the master and others of the felt-makers were ordered, by the commons, to be enlarged from the custody of the warden of the Fleet, for the prosecution of a bill then depending, "till the same be determined by both houses." On the 24th May 1626, it was ordered, " that J. Bryers shall be sent for to testify, and to have privilege for coming, staying, and returning."' In the same manner, privilege was extended to persons who had bills depending, on the 22d and 29th January 1628, on the 3d May 1701, and the 11th May 1758. On the 23d January 1640, certain persons having petitions before the grand committee on Irish affairs, Avere ordered " to have liberty to come and go freely to prosecute their petition, without molestation, arrest, or restraint; and that there be a stay of committing any waste upon the lands mentioned in the petition, during the dependency of the business here."" Numerous instances have occurred, in which witnesses, who have been arrested on their way to or from Parliament, or during their attendance there, have been discharged out of custody; ' and the same protection is extended, not only to parties, but to their counsel and agents, in prosecuting any business in Parliament. On the 2d May 1678, Mr. J. Gardener, solicitor in the cause concerning Lyndsey Level, who had been arrested as he was coming to attend on the house, was discharged from his arrest. On the 9th April 1742, complaint was made, that Mr. Gilbert Douglas, a solicitor for several bills depending in the House of Commons, had been arrested as he was attending the house, and he was immediately ordered to be discharged from his arrest."

In the same way, solicitors for bills depending in the 1 Com. J. 702. 2 ib 863 ' lb. 921. 924. 13 In. 512. 28 lb. 244. " 2 16. 72.

5 8 lb. 525. 9 lb 20. 366. 472. 12 lb. 364. Glo. 66 lb. 226. 232. 90 lb. 521. 9 lb. 472. ' 24 lb. 170.

Protection of witnesses and otliera from suits and molestation.

house, were discharged from arrest, on the 30th April 1753; on the 12th February and the 22d March 1756.

On the 29th March 1756, Mr. Aubrej, who had an estate bill depending in the House of Commons, presented a petition, in which he stated that he apprehended an arrest, and it was ordered " that the protection of the house be allowed to him during the dependence of his bill in this house." The last case that need be mentioned is that of Mr. Petrie, in 1793. That gentleman was a petitioner in a controverted election, and claimed to sit for the borough of Cricklade. Having received the usual notice to attend, by himself, his counsel, or agents, he had attended the sittings of the election committee as a party in the cause; and although he had a professional agent, he had himself assisted his counsel, and furnished them with instructions before the committee. He was arrested before the committee had closed their inquiries; and on the 20th March the house, after receiving a report of precedents, ordered, nem. con., that he should be discharged out of the custody of the sheriff of Middlesex.

"Witnesses, petitioners, and others being thus free from arrest, while in attendance on Parliament, are further protected, by privilege, from the consequences of any statements which they may have made before either house; and any molestation, threats, or legal pi'oceedings against them will be treated by the house as a breach of privilege.

On the 23d November 1696,

"A complaint being made that Sir George Meggott had prosecuted at law several persons for what they testified, the last session, at the committee of privileges and elections," it was referred to that committee to examine the matter of the complaint. It appeared from their report, 4th December, that Sir G. Meggott,

"Having thought himself injured by their evidence, did think ' 26 Com. J. 797.

'" 21 lb. 447. 537. 48 lb. 426.

3 27 lb. 548.

he might lawfully have done himself right by an action, but as soon as he was better advised, he desisted, and suffered himself to be non-suited, and had paid them their costs."

Notwithstanding his submission, however, the house agreed with the committee in a resolution, that he had been guilty of a breach of privilege, and committed him to the custody of the serjeant-at-arms.

On the 27th November 1696, a petition was presented from T. Kemp and other hackney coachmen, complaining that an action had been brought against them by! Mr. Gee, for libel, on account of a petition which had been presented to the house from them in the last session. From the report of the committee of privileges, to whom the matter was referred, 9th February 1696, it appeared that Mr. Gee had desisted from his action when he understood it was taken notice of by the house, and offered to release the same. The house agreed with the committee in a resolution, that Mr. Gee, " for prosecuting at law the hackney coachmen for petitioning this house, is guilty of a high misdemeanor and breach of privilege," and committed him to the custody of the serjeant-at-arms.

On the 8th April 1697, the lords attached T. Stone, for striking and giving opprobrious language to a witness, below the bar, who had been summoned to attend a committee, and directed the attorney-general to prosecute him for his offence. On the 5th March 1710, on the report from a committee that John Hare, a soldier, was afraid of giving evidence, the conunons resolved, " that this house wiu proceed with the utmost severity against any person that shall threaten, or any way injure, or send away, the said J. Hare, or any other person that shall give evidence to any committee of this house."

On the 9th February 1715, a complaint was made that C. Medlycot, esq., had been abused and insulted, "in ' 11 Com. J. 591. 613. lb. 599. lb. 699.

16 Lords' J. 144. = jq Com. J. 535.

respect to the evidence by him given " before a committee. Mr. Tovey, the person complained of, was resolved to be guilty of a breach of privilege, and was committed to the custody of the serjeant-at-arms.

On the 28th February 1728, it was reported to the house by a committee appointed to inquire into the state of the gaols, that Sir W. Rich, a prisoner in the Fleet, had been misused by the warden of the Fleet, in consequence of evidence given by the Ibrmer to the committee. The house declared, nem. con., that the warden was guilty of contempt, and committed him to the custody of the serjeant-at-arms.

On the 10th May 1733, complaint was made that Jeremiah Dunbar, esq., had been censured by the House of Representatives of Massachusetts Bay, for evidence given by him before a committee on a Bill, upon which the house resolved, nem. con., " that the presuming to call any person to account, or to pass a censure upon him for evidence given by such person before this house, or any committee thereof, is an audacious proceeding, and a high violation of the privileges of this house."

On the 12th March 1819, the house being informed that Mr. Goold, who had given his evidence at the bar, had been insulted and threatened, in consequence of such evidence, resolved, nem. con., that,

"T. W. Grady having used insulting language to a witness attending this house, and having threatened him with personal violence on account of evidence already given by him, and which lie may hereafter be called upon to give at the bar of the house, has been guilty of a high contempt, c.," and committed him to the custody of the serjeant-at-arms."

On the 2d July 1845, Mr. Jasper Parrott complained to the house, by petition, that an action had been commenced against him in respect of evidence which he had given before a committee. On the 3d July a copy of the dccla- ' 18 Com. J. 371. 2 21 lb. 247. 22 ib. 146.

' 74 lb. 223. 100 lb. 672.

ration was delivered in by Mr. Parrott's agent, and the plaintiff and his solicitors were ordered to attend on a future day. On the 7th July they all attended, and having disclaimed any intention of violating the privileges of the house, and having declared that the action would be discontinued, they were severally discharged from further attendance, although the commencement of the action was declared to be a breach of privilege. It is worthy of remark, that the plaintiflf's solicitor stated, in a petition to the house, that the declaration had been framed upon the assumption that a witness would not be protected, by privilege, in respect of any evidence which was wilfully and maliciously false, any more than the powers of the superior courts at Westminster would be exerted to protect any witness from an indictment for perjury. The house, however, did not recognise any such analogy, but resolved to protect the witness from all proceedings against him in respect of the evidence given by him before a committee.

In the same year a similar case occurred in the House of Lords. Peter Taite Harbin had brought an action by John Harlow, his attorney, against Thomas Baker, for false and malicious language uttered before the House of Lords in giving evidence before a committee. The plaintiff and his attorney were summoned to the bar, and on their refusal to state that the action should not be proceeded with, were both declared guilty of a breach of privilege, and committed. On the following day the prisoners submitted themselves to the house by petition, and stated that the action had been withdrawn, upon which they were brought to the bar, reprimanded by the lord chancellor, and discharged."

The privilege of protection from all molestation in respect Protection to of what they have stated professionally, is also extended to ' 100 Com. J. G80. u, (597 gj Hans. Deb. 1436.

"82 Hans. Deb., new series, 431 (14 July 1845). See also the protest in the Lords' Journal, and Debates. lb. 494.

Mr. Fonblanque.

Statements to Parliament not actionable.

But are admissible in evidence.

counsel. On the 21st March 1826, complaint was made that an insulting letter had been written by John Lee Wharton to Mr. Fonblanque, Q. C, in relation to a speech made by him at the bar of the House of Lords on the 22nd Iarch. Wharton attended, according to order, and on making a proper submission and apology, was discharged from further attendance.

And apart from the protection afforded by privilege, it appears that statements made to Parliament in the course of its proceedings, are not actionable at law.

In Lake v. Kiug, which was an action upon the case for printing a false and scandalous petition to the committee of Parliament for grievances, it was agreed by the court " that the exhibiting the petition to a committee of Parliament was lawful, and that no action lies for it, although the matter contained in the petition was false and scandalous, because it is in a summary course of justice, and before those who have power to examine whether it be true or false. But the question was, whether the printing and publishing of it in the manner alleged by the defendant in his plea; " viz., by delivering printed copies to the members of the committee, " according to custom used by others in that behalf, and approved of by the members of the said committee," was justifiable or not. After this case had depended twelve terms, judgment was given in Hilary Term, 19 20 Charles II., for the defendant, by Hale, C. J. upon the ground " that it was the order and course of proceedings in Parliament to print and deliver copies, whereof they ought to take judicial notice."

In Rex. V. Merceron there was an indictment against a magistrate of the county of Middlesex for misconduct in his office, in having corruptly and improperly granted licences to public-houses which were his own property.

1 Saunders' Reports, 131 b. 1 Lev. 240. 2 Keb. 361. 383. 462. 496. 659. 801. See also 2 Inst. 228, as to evidence before n jury being privileged.

JURISDICTION OF COURTS. 143 In the course of the evidence for the prosecution it was proposed to prove what had been said by the defendant in the course of his examination before a committee of the House of Commons, appointed for the purpose of inquiring into the police of the metropohs. The defendant had been compelled to appear before this committee, and had, upon examination, delivered in a list of certain public-houses, with the names of the owners, c.

On the part of the defendant it was objected, that since this statement had been made under a compulsory process from the House of Commons, and under the pain of incurring punishment as for a contempt of that house, the declarations were not voluntary, and could not be admitted for the purpose of criminating the defendant; but Abbott, C, J., was of opinion that the evidence was admissible.

CHAPTER VI.

JURISDICTION OF COURTS OF LAW IN MATTERS OF PRIVILEGE.

The precise jurisdiction of courts of law in matters of Difficulty of privilege, is one of the most difficult questions of consti- ' question. tutional law that has ever arisen. Upon this point the precedents of Parliament are contradictory, the opinions and decisions of judges have differed, and the most learned and experienced men of the present day are not agreed. It would, therefore, be presumptuous to define the jurisdiction of the courts, or the bounds of Parliamentary privilege; but it may not be useless to explain the principles involved in the question; to cite the chief authorities, and to advert to some of the leading cases that have occurred.

' 2 Starkie's Nisi Prius Cases, 366.

Principles It lias been shown already, that each house of Par- liament claims to be the sole and exclusive judge of its own privileges, and that the courts have repeatedly acknowledged the right of both houses to declare what is a breach of privilege, and to commit the parties offending, as for a contempt. But, although the courts will neither interfere with Parliament in its punishment of offenders, nor assume the general right of declaring and limiting the privileges of Parliament, they are bound to administer the law of the land, and to adjudicate when breaches of that law are complained of. The jurisdiction of Parliament and the jurisdiction of the courts are thus liable to be brought into conflict. The House of Lords, or the House of Commons, may declare a particular act to have been justified by their order, and to be in accordance with the law of Parliament; while the courts may acknowledge no right to exist in one house, to supersede by its sole authority the laws which have been made by the assent, or which exist with the acquiescence, of all the branches of the legislature. It is true, that, in a general sense, the law of Parliament is the law of the land; but if one law should appear to clash with the other, how are they to be reconciled? Is the declaration of one component part of Parliament to be conclusive as to the law; or are the legality of the declaration, and the jurisdiction of the house, to be measured by the general law of the land? In these questions are comprised all the difficulties attendant upon the conflicting jurisdictions of Parliament and of the courts of law.

It is contended, on the one hand, that in determinino-matters of privilege, the courts are to act ministerially rather than judicially, and to adjudicate in accordance with the law of Parliament as declared by either house; while, on the other, it is maintained that although the declaration of either house of Parliament in matters of privilege within its own immediate jurisdiction may not be questioned; its orders and authority cannot extend beyond its jurisdiction, and influence the decision of the courts in the trial of causes legally brought before them. From these opposite views it naturally follows that, in declaring its privileges, Parliament may assume to enlarge its own jurisdiction, and that the courts may have occasion to question and confine its limits.

The claim of each house of Parliament to be the sole and exclusive judge of its own privileges has always been asserted in Parliament upon the principles and with the limitations which were stated in the third chapter of this book, and is the basis of the law of Parliament. This claim has been questioned in the courts of law; but before the particular cases are cited, it will be advisable to take a general view of the legal authorities which are favourable or adverse to the claim, in its fullest extent, as asserted by Parliament.

The earliest authority on which reliance is usually placed. Authorities in in support of the claim, is the well-known answer of the exclusive jvris- iudo-es in Thorpe's case. diction of Par-

J f I liament.

In the 31st Henry VI., on the lords putting a case to the judges, whether Thomas Thorpe, the speaker of the commons, then imprisoned upon judgment in the Court of Exchequer, at the suit of the Duke of York, " should be delivered from prison by virtue of the privilege of Parliament or not," the Chief Justice Fortescue, in the name Tiiorpe's case. of all the justices, answered,

"That they ought not to answer to that question, for it hath not been used aforetyme, that the justices should in anywise determine the privilege of this High Court of Parliament; for it is so high and so mighty in its nature, that it may make law, and that that is law it may make no law; and the determination and knowledge of that privilege belongeth to the lords of the Parliament, and not to the justices."

In regard to this case it must be observed that no legal question had come before the judges for trial in their 5 Rot. Pari. 240. See also Lord Ellenborough's observations upon this case, 14 East, 29.

Sir E. Coke.

Lord Clarendon.

Lord C. J. North.

judicial capacity; but that, as assistants of the House of Lords, their opinion was desired upon a point of privilege wliich was clearly within the immediate jurisdiction of Parliament, and was awaiting its determination. Under these circumstances it was natural that the judges should be reluctant to press their own opinions, and desirous of leavinjr the matter to the decision of the lords. That part of their answer which alleges that Parliament can make and unmake laws, as a leason why the judges should not determine questions of privilege, can only apply to the entire Parliament, and not to either house separately, nor even to both combined: and, consequently, it has no bearing upon the jurisdiction of Parliament except in a legislative sense.

The principle of this answer was adopted and confinned by Sir Edward Coke, who lays it down that " whatever matter arises concerning either house of Parliament, ought to be discussed and adjudged in that house to which it relates, and not elsewhere;" and again, that "judges ought not to give any opinion of a matter of privilege, because it is not to be decided by the common laws, but secundum leges et consuetudinem Parliavienti; and so the judges, in divers Parliaments, have confessed."'-

These general declarations were explained and qualified by Lord Clarendon, who in his History of the Rebellion thus defines the jurisdiction of the commons: ' They are the only judges of their own privileges; that is upon the breach of those privileges which the law hath declared to be their own, and what punishment is to be inflicted upon such breach. But there can be no privilege of which the law doth not take notice, and which is not pleadable by and at law." ' In the case of Barnardiston v. Soames, in 1674, Lord

Chief Justice North said,

"I can see no other way to avoid consequences derogatory to the honour of the Parliament but to reject the action, and all ' 4th Inst. 15. 2 jj,

Clarendon's Ilist. of the Rebellion, vol. ii. book 4, p. 195,8vo. edit. Oxf.

others that shall relate either to the proceedings or privilege of Parliament, as our predecessors have done. For if we should admit general remedies iu matters relating to the Parliament, we must set bounds how far they shall go, which is a dangerous province; for if we err, privilege of Parliament will be invaded, which we ought not in any way to endamage." ' But in the same argument he alleged " that actions may be brought for giving Parliament protections wrongfully; actions may be brought against the clerk of the Parliament, serjeant-at-arms, and speaker, for aught I know, for executing their offices amiss, with averments of malice and damage; and then must judges and juries determine what they ought to do by their officers. This is in effect prescribing rules to the Parliament for them to act by."

In the case of Paty, one of the Aylesbury men, brought Mr. Justice up by habeas corpus, Mr. Justice Powell thus defined the ' jurisdiction of the courts in matters of privilege:

"This court may judge of privilege, but not contrary to the judgment of the House of Commons." Again, "This court judges of privilege only incidentally; for when an action is brought in this court, it must be given one way or other." " The Court of Parliament is a superior court; and though the King's Bench have a power to prevent excesses of jurisdiction in courts, yet they cannot prevent such excesses in Parliament, because that is a superior court, and a prohibition was never moved for to the Parliament."' In several other cases which related solely to commitments by either house of Parliament, very decided opinions have been expressed by the judges in favour of privilege and adverse to the jurisdiction of the courts of law; but most of these may be taken to apply more especially to the undoubted right of commitment for contempt, rather than to general matters of law in which privilege may be concerned.

In the case of Brass Crosby, IVIr. Justice Blackstone Mr. Justice went so far as to affirm that " it is our duty to presume the ' ckstone. orders of that house (of commons), and their execution, to be according to law;" and in Kex v. Wright, Lord Kenyon Lord Kenyon. said, "This is a proceeding by one branch of the legislature, and therefore we cannot inquire into it;" but he added, 6 Howell, St. Tr. 1110. "lb. ' 2 Lord Raym. 1105.

See supra, p. 69.

Hawkins.

Lord C. B. Jomyu.

Authorities in support of the jurisdiction of courts in matters of privilege.

Sir O. Bridg-raan.

Lord C. J. Willes.

"I do not say that cases may not be put in which we would inquire whether the House of Commons were justified in any particular measure."

It is laid down by Hawkins that

"There can be no doubt but that the highest regard is to be paid to all the proceetiingsof either of those houses; and that wherever the contrary does not plainly and expressly appear, it shall be presumed that they act within their jurisdiction, and agreeably to the usages of Parliament, and the rules of law and justice.""

And Lord Chief Baron Comyn, following the opinion of

Sir Edward Coke, affirms that

"All matters moved concerning the peers and commons in Parliament, ought to be determined according to the usage and customs of Parliament, and not by the law of any inferior court."

These authorities are sufficient, for the present purpose, to show the general confirmation of the exclusive jurisdiction of Parliament in matters of privilege: but even here the parliamentary claim is occasionally modified and limited, as in the opinions of Lord Clarendon, Chief Justice North, and Lord Kenyon. In other cases the jurisdiction of courts of law has been more extensively urged, and the privileges of Parliament proportionately limited. In Benyon v. Evelyn, the lord chief justice, Sir Orlando Bridgman, came to the conclusion,

"That resolutions or resolves of either house of Parliament, singly, in the absence of parties concerned, are not so concludent upon courts of law, but that we may, nay (with due respect, nevertheless, had to their resolves and resolutions,) we must, give our judgment according as we upon our oath conceive the law to be, though our opinions fall out to be contrary to those resolutions or votes of either house."'

On another occasion Lord Chief Justice Willes said,

"I declare for myself, that I will never be bound by any determination of the House of Commons, against bringing an action at common law for a false or double return; and a party may proceed in Westminster Hall, notwithstanding any order of the house,"" ' 2 Pleas of the Crown, c. 15, s. 73. Benyon v. Evelyn, Bridgman, 324.

Digest " Parliament" (G. 1.) Wynne v. Middleton, 1 Wils. 128.

Lord Mansfield, in arguing for the exclusive right of the Lord Mansfield, commons to decide upon elections, said,

"That, in his opinion, declarations of the law by either House of Parliament were always attended with bad effects: he had constantly oioposed them whenever he had an opportunity; and, in his judicial capacity, thought himself bound never to pay the least regard to them; " " but he made a wide distinction between general declarations of law, and the particular decision which might be made by either house, in their judicial capacity, on a case coming regularly before them, and properly the subject of their jurisdiction."'

At another time the same great authority declared that ' a resolution of the House of Commons, ordering a judgment to be given in a particular manner, would not be binding in the courts of Westminster Hau." And in L d Eileu-Burdett V. Abbot, Lord Ellenborough said, " the question boro gh-in all cases would be, whether the House of

Commons were a court of competent jurisdiction for the purpose of issuing a warrant to do the act."

Passing now to the most recent judicial opinions, the cases of Stockdale v. Hansard and Howard v. Gosset present themselves. An outline of all the proceedings in these cases (the most important that had arisen since that of Ashby and White), will be presently attempted; but, for the present, the expositions of the judges, in reference to the general jurisdiction of the courts, will be necessary to close this summary of authorities.

In giving judgment in that case on the 31st May 1839, stockdale u. Lord Denman used these words: ""

"But having convinced myself that the mere order of the house will not justify an act otherwise illegal, and that the simple declaration that that order is made in exercise of a privilege, does not prove the privilege; it is no longer optional with me to decline or accept the office of deciding whether this privilege exist in law. If it does, the defendant's prayer must be granted, and judgment awarded in his favour: or, if it does not, the plaintiff, under whatever disadvantage he may appear before us, has a right to obtain 16 Hansard, Pari. Hist. 653. ' 24 lb. 517. 14 East, 128.

at our hands, as an English subject, the establishment of his lawful rights, and the means of enforcing them."' In the same trial Mr. Justice Littledale argued, "It is said the House of Commons is the sole judge of its own privileges; and so I admit, as far as proceedings in the house, and some other thinf:? s, are concerned; but I do not think it follows that they have a power to declare what their privileges are, so as to preclude inquiry whether what they declare are part of their pri-vileo-es. The attorney-general admits that they are not entitled to create new privileges; but they declare this (the publication of papers) to be their privilege. But how are we to know that this is part of their privileges without inquiring into it, when no such privilege was ever declared before? We must therefore be enabled to determine whether it be part of their privileges or not.""

To this argument, however, it is an obvious answer that assuming the house to be the judge of its own privileges, it is its province to determine whether a privilege be new or not, from an examination of the Journals and other authorities. The learned judge said further,

"I think that the mere statement that the act complained of was done by the authority of the House of Commons is not of itself, without more, sufficient to call at once for the judgment of the court for the defendant."

Mr. Justice Patteson thus expressed his opinion:

"If the orders (of the House of Commons) be illegal, and not merely erroneous, upon no principle known to the laws of this country can those who carry them into eft'ect justify under them. A servant cannot shelter himself under the illegal orders of his master, nor could an officer under the illegal orders of a magistrate, until the legislature interposed and enabled him to do so. The mere circumstance, therefore, that the act complained of was done under the order and authority of the House of Commons, cannot of itself excuse the act, if it be in its nature illegal; and it is necessary, in answer to an action for the commission of such illegal act, to show, not only the authority under which it was done, but the power and right of the House of Commons to give such authority."

And upon the question of jurisdiction he laid it down,

"That every court in which an action is brought upon a subject matter generally, and prima facie within its jurisdiction, and in ' Proceedings, printed by tlie commons, 1839 (283), p. 155.

- lb. pp. 161, 162. 3 lb. p. 162. 4 lb. p. 169.

which by the course of the proceedings in that action the powers and privileges and jurisdiction of another court come into question, must of necessity determine as to the extent of those powers, privileges, and jurisdiction; and the decisions of that court, whose powers, privileges, and jurisdiction are so brought into question as to their extent, are authorities; and, if I may so say, evidences in law upon the subject, but not conclusive." ' In conclusion, Mr. Justice Coleridge thus summed up his view of the duties of a court of law:

"The cause is before us; Ave are sworn to decide it according to our notions of the law; we do not briug it here; and being here, a necessity is laid upon us to deliver judgment; that judgment we can receive at the dictation of nu power; we may decide the cause erroneously, but we cannot be guilty of any contempt in deciding it according to our consciences."

In the case of Howard v. Gosset Mr. Justice Coleridge Howard v. again expressed his opinion as to the powers of a court of-'-law in matters of privilege:

"It is enough to say that the law is supreme over the House of Commons, and over the Crown itself. If the limits of the law be passed by either, for most satisfactory reasons, they are indeed themselves irresponsible, but the law will require a strict account of the acts of all persons and their agents; and these, according to the nature of the illegality, will be answerable civilly or criminally."

With these conflicting opinions as to the limits of judgments ad-parliamentary privilege, and the jurisdiction of courts of of' rivoe' """ law, if either House of Parliament insist upon precluding other courts from inquiring into matters which are held to be within its own jurisdiction, the proper mode of effecting that object, is the next point to be determined. If the courts were willing to adopt the resolutions of the house as their guide, the course would be clear. The authority and adjudication of the house would be pleaded, and the courts, acting ministerially, would at once give effect to

Proceedings, printed by the commons, 1839 (283), p. 174. 2 lb. p. 188.

Arguments and judgment, as printed by tiie House of Commons, 1845 (305), p. 105.

them. But if the courts regard a question of privilege as any otlier point of law, and assume to define the jurisdiction of the house, in what manner, and at what point, can their adverse judgments be prevented, overruled, or resisted? The several modes that have been attempted will appear from the following cases; but it must be premised that when a privilege of the commons is disputed, that house labours under a peculiar embarrassment. If the courts admit the privilege, their decisions are liable to be reversed by the House of Lords; and thus, contrary to the law of Parliament, one house would be constituted a judge of the privileges claimed by the other. And if the privilege be denied by the courts, the house has no other remedy, in the ordinary course of law, but an ultimate appeal to the House of Lords. It is difficult to determine which alternative is the least satisfactory the denial of a privilege by the lords on a writ of error, or an application to them for redress, when the authority of the house has been discredited by an inferior tribunal. With these perplexities before them, it is not surprising that the commons should frequently have viewed all legal proceedings in derogation of their authority, as a breach of privilege and contempt. They have restrained suitors and their counsel by prohibition and punishment, they have imprisoned the judges, they have coerced the sheriff; but stiu the law has taken its course.

Having opened the principles of the controversy respecting parliamentary jurisdiction, it is time to proceed with a narrative of the most important cases in which the privileges of Parliament have been called in question. Case of Sir W. Sir William Williams, speaker of the House of Commons in the reigns of Charles II. and James II., had printed and published, by order of the house, a paper well known in the histories of that time as Dangerfield's Narrative. This paper contained reflections upon tlie Duke of York, afterwards James II., and an information for libel was filed against the speaker, by the attorney-general, in 1684. He pleaded to the jurisdiction of the court, that as the paper had been signed by him, as speaker, by order of the House of Commons, the Court of King's Bench had no jurisdiction over the matter. On demurrer, this plea was overruled, and a plea in bar was afterwards made, but withdrawn; his plea, that the order of the house was a justification, was set aside by the court, without argument, as " an idle and insignificant plea," and he was fined 10,000 1. Two thousand pounds of this fine were remitted by the king, but the rest he was obliged to pay. The commons were indignant at this contempt of their authority, and declared the judgment to be an illegal judgment, and against the freedom of Parliament. It was also included in the general condemnation, by the bill of rights, of " prosecutions in the Court of King's Bench for matters and causes cognisable only in Parliament."" Three bills were brought in, in 1689, in 1690, and in 1695, to reverse this judgment; but they all miscarried, chiefly, it is understood, because it was proposed to indemnify the speaker out of the estate of Sir Robert Sawyer, who had filed the information, as attorney-general.

The next important case is that of Jay v. Topham In Jayv. Topliam. 1689. After a dissolution of Parliament, an action Avas brought in the Court of King's Bench against John Toijham, esq., serjeant-at-arms, for executing the orders of the house in arresting certain persons. Mr. Topham pleaded to the jurisdiction of the court the said orders; but his plea was overruled, and judgment given against him. The house declared this judgment to be a breach of privilege, and committed Sir F. Pemberton and Sir T. Jones, who had been the judges in the cause, to the custody of the serjeant-at-arms."

They had protested, in their examination, that they had ' 12lli July 1689, 10 Com. J. 215. ggg jq Com. J. 146. 177.

3 2 Shower, 471. 13 Howell, St. Tr. 1370. Wynn's Argument. 10 Com. J. 177. 205. 4 10 Com. J. 227.

Ashby and White, c.

not questioned the legality of the orders of the house, but had overruled, on technical grounds, the plea to the jurisdiction. They averred also, that if there had been a plea in bar, the defendant would have been entitled to a judgment. Assuming the truth of their statements, it has been generally acknowledged that these proceedings against the judges were liable to great objection. Lord Ellen-borough said, that it was surprising "how a judge should have been questioned, and committed to prison by the House of Commons, for having given a judgment, which no other judge who ever sat in his place could have differed from." And Lord Denman, in Stockdale v. Hansard, said that this judgment was righteous, and that the judges "vindicated their conduct by unanswerable reasoning;" and again, in Howard v. Gosset, he called the commitment of these judges "a flagrant abuse of privilege." But, on the other hand. Lord Campbell has pointed out that there had been a plea in bar, which had been overruled, as stated in the petition of Topham to the House of Commons, and that the authority of that house had, in fact, been questioned by the judges."

The remarkable cases of Ashby and White, and the Aylesbury men, in 1704, are next worthy of a passing notice. They have been already alluded to in the second chapter, with reference to the right of determining elections; but they must again be brought forward, to point out the course adopted by the commons to stay actions derogatory to their privileges. Enraged by a judgment of the House of Lords, which held, that electors had a right to bring actions against returning officers touching their right of voting, the commons declared that such an action was a breach of privilege; and, "That whoever 1 12 Howell, St. Tr. 829. 831.

Shorthand writer's notes, 1839 (283), 149. 10 Com. J. 104.

" Shorthand writer's notes of argument in Stockdale v. Hansard, 76. 2 Lives of the Ch. Justices, 67. 2 Nelson's Abridg. 1248. See p. 50.

shall presume to commence any action, and all attorneys, solicitors, counsellors, and serjeants-at-law, soliciting, prosecuting, or pleading in any case, are guilty of a high breach of the privileges of this house." In spite of this declaration, five burgesses of Aylesbury, commonly known as " the Aylesbury men," commenced actions against the constables of their borough, for not allowing their votes. The House of Commons obtained copies of the declarations, and resolved, that the parties were " guilty of commencing and prosecuting actions," " contrary to the declaration, in high contempt of the jurisdiction, and in breacii of the known privileges of this house." For which offence, the parties and their attorney were committed to Newgate. Thence they endeavoured to obtain their release by writs of habeas corpus, but without success; and the counsel who had pleaded for the prisoners, on the return of the writs, were committed to the custody of the serjeant-at-arms. The lords took part with the Aylesbury men against the commons; and after a tumultuous session, occupied with addresses, conferences, and resolutions upon privilege, the queen prorogued the Parliament.

On this occasion, the commons, consistently with ancient usage,"' endeavoured to stop the actions at their commencement, and thus to prevent the courts from giving any judgment. But although this course of proceeding may chance to be effectual, an action cannot be legally obstructed, if the parties be determined to proceed with it. Their counsel may be prevented from pleading, but others would be immediately instructed to appear before the court; and it must not be forgotten, that during a recess, neither house could interfere with the parties or their counsel, and that judgment mlo; ht be obtained and executed before the meetinoj of Parlia-ment. This mode of preventing actions, however, is so natural, that it has since been resorted to; but the principle '14 Com. J. 444. ' lb. 445. lb. 552. ' See mipra, 123.

has not been uniformly asserted, and it is difficult to determine whether commencing such actions, in future, will be regarded as a breach of privilege or not. Burdett V. When Sir Francis Burdett brought actions against the ijewt 'colman. Speaker and the serjeant-at-arms, in 1810, for taking him to the Tower in obedience to the orders of the House of Commons, they were directed to plead, and the attorney-general received instructions to defend them. A committee at the same time reported a resolution " that the bringing these actions for acts done in obedience to the orders of the house is a breach of privilege," but it was not adopted by the house. The actions proceeded in the regular course, and the Court of King's Bench sustained and vindicated the authority of the house. The judgment of that court was afterwards affirmed, on a writ of error, by the Exchequer Chamber, and ultimately by the House of Lords."

Within the last few years a series of cases have arisen, in which the authority of the House of Commons, and the acts of its officers, have been questioned. They have caused so much controversy, and have been so fully debated and canvassed, that nothing is needed but a succinct statement of the proceedings, and a commentary upon the present position of parliamentary privilege and jurisdiction. Printcdpapers; Messrs. Hansard, the printers of the House of Commons, Hansard. ' printed, by order of that house, the reports of the inspectors of prisons, in one of which a book published by John Joseph Stockdale was described in a manner which he conceived to be libellous. He brouii'ht an action aj ainst Messrs. Hansard, during the recess in 1836, who pleaded the general issue, and proved the order of the house to print the report. This order, however, was held to be no defence to the action; but Stockdale had a verdict against him upon a plea of justification, as the jury considered the description of the work in question to be accurate. On that occasion ' G5 Com. J. 355. M4 East, 1. 34-,.401. 5 Dow, 1G5.

Lord Chief Justice Denman, who tried the cause, made a declaration adverse to the privileges of the house, which Messrs. Hansard had set up as part of their defence. In his direction to the jury, his lordship said " that the fact of the House of Commons having directed Messrs. Hansard to publish all their parliamentary reports is no justification for them, or for any bookseller who publishes a parliamentary report containing a libel against any man." In consequence of these proceedings, a committee was appointed, on the meeting of Parliament in 1837, to examine precedents, and to ascertain the law and practice of Parliament in reference to the publication of papers printed by order of the house. The result of these inquiries was the passing of the following resolutions by the house:

"That the power of publishing such of its reports, votes, and jiroceedings as it shall deem necessary or conducive to tlie public interests, is an essential incident to the constitutional functions of Parliament, more especially of this house, as the representative portion of it.

"That by the law and privilege of Parliament, this house has the sole and exclusive jurisdiction to determine upon the existence and extent of its privileges; and that the institution or prosecution of any action, suit, or other proceeding, for the purpose of bringing them into discussion or decision before any court or tribunal elsewhere than in Parliament, is a high breach of such privilege, and renders all parties concerned therein amenable to its just displeasure, and to the punishment consequent thereon.

"That for any court or tribunal to assume to decide upon matters of privilege inconsistent with the determination of either house of Parliament thereon, is contrary to the law of Parliament, and is a breach and contempt of the privileges of Parliament."
'

Nothing could have been more comprehensive than these resolutions; they asserted the privilege, and denounced the parties, the counsel, and the courts who should presume to question it; yet Stockdale immediately commenced another action, and the house, instead of acting upon its resolutions, directed Messrs. Hansard to plead, and the attorney-general to defend them.

' 92 Com, J. 418.

In the former case Messrs. Hansard had obtained judgment upon a plea which would have availed them equally if they had printed the report upon their own account, like any other bookseller; but in the second action the privileges and order of the house were alone relied upon in their defence, and the Court of Queen's Bench unanimously decided against them.

Damages paid. Still the House of Commons was reluctant to act upon its own resolutions, and instead of punishing the plaintiff, and his legal advisers, " under the special circumstances of the case," it ordered the damages and costs to be paid. The resolutions, however, were not rescinded, and it was then determined that, in case of future actions, Messrs. Hansard should not plead at all, and that the parties should suffer for their contempt of the resolutions and authority of the house. Another action was brought by the same person, and for the publication of the same report. Messrs. Hansard did not plead, the judgment went against them by default, and the damages were assessed by a jury in the Sheriff's Court at 600. The sheriffs of Middlesex levied for that amount, but having been served with copies of the resolutions of the house, they were anxious to delay paying the money to Stockdale as long as possible, in order to avoid its threatened displeasure.

Commitment of At the Opening of the session of Parliament in 1840 the tli6 sheriffs money was still in their hands. The House of Commons at once entered on the consideration of these proceedings, which had been carried on in spite of its resolutions, and in the first place committed Stockdale to the custody of the serjeant-at-arms. The sheriffs were desired to refund the money, and, on their refusal, were also committed. Mr. Howard, the solicitor of Mr. Stockdale, was suffered to escape with a reprimand. The sheriffs retained possession of the money until an attachment was issued from the Queen's Bench, when they paid it over to Stockdale.

' 11 Adolphus Ellis, 25.3.

Stockdale, while in prison, commenced a fourth action by the same solicitor, and with him was committed to Newgate for the offence; and Messrs. Hansard were again ordered not to plead. Once more judgment was entered up against them, and a writ of inquiry of damages issued.

Mr. France, the under-sheriff, upon whom the execution of this writ devolved, having been served with the resolutions of the commons, expressed by petition his anxiety to pay obedience to them, and sought the protection of the house. He then obtained leave to show cause before the Court of Queen's Bench, on the fourth day of Easter term, why the writ of inquiry should not be executed.

Meanwhile the imprisonment of the plaintiff and his attorney did not prevent the prosecution of further actions. Mr. Howard's son, and his clerk, Mr. Pearce, having been concerned in conducting such actions, were committed for the contempt; and Messrs. Hansard, as before, were instructed not to plead. At length, as there appeared to be Act for the no probability of these vexatious actions being discon- papersf " tinned, a bill was introduced into the commons, by which proceedings, criminal or civil, against persons for publication of papers printed by order of either house of Parliament, are to be stayed by the courts, upon delivery of a certificate and affidavit that such publication is by order of either house of Parliament. This bill was agreed to by the lords and received the royal assent. It has removed one ground for disputing the authority of Parliament, but has left the general question of privilege and jurisdiction in the same uncertain state as before.

In executing the speaker's warrant for taking Mr. Howard?. Gos-Howard into custody, the officers employed by the serjeant-at-arms for that purpose had remained some time in his house during his absence, for which he brought an action ' The action of Harlow v. Hansard was stayed 14th July 1845, by Mr. Jiistice Wightrnan in chambers, on the production of the speaker's certificate. 2 3 4 Vict. c. 9.

of trespass against them. As it was possible that tley might have exceeded their authority, and as the right of the house to commit was not directly brought into question, the defendants were, in this case, permitted to appear and defend the action; although a clause for staying further proceedings in the action was contained in the bill which was pending, at that time, in the House of Lords, where it was afterwards omitted.

This action, after some delay, proceeded to trial. On the 15th June 1842, the serjeant-at-arms informed the house that he had received a subpoena to attend the trial on the part of the defendants; and leave was given to him to attend and give evidence. At the same time the clerk of the journals who had received a subpoena, had leave to attend and give evidence, and to produce the Journal of the house. The cause was tried before Lord Denman, in the sittings after Michaelmas term, 1842, when Parliament was not sitting, and a verdict was given for the plaintiff, with 100. damages. This verdict, however, did not proceed upon any question of the jurisdiction of the house; but simply on the ground that the officers had exceeded their authority, by remaining in the plaintiff's house, after they were aware of his absence from home. The attorney-general, who appeared in their defence, admitted that they were not justified in their conduct; and the case can scarcely be cited as one of privilege.

Howard's But Other actions were afterwards commenced by Mr.

second action. Howard against Sir William Gosset and other officers of the house, for taking him into custody, and conveying him to Newgate, in obedience to orders of the house and the speaker's warrants. The house gave all the defendants leave to appear and defend the actions, and directed the attorney-general to defend thera. The only action that ' 95 Com. J. 236. Hans. Deb. 31st March 1840.

2 97 Com. J. 378, jj Adolphus Ellis, 273.

98 Com. J. 59. = i. jj, j. j3.,, j j j j rch 1843.

came on for trial was that against the Serjeant himself; but three other actions were commenced against the officers of the house, in one of which the damages were laid at 100,000.

The second action of Howard v. Gosset, came on for trial on the 15th November 1844; and the circumstances in which it originated, and the results to which it led, may be briefly described. Mr. Howard, having expressed his regret for commencing Stockdale's third action against Messrs. Hansard, had been reprimanded by the speaker and discharged; when he immediately commenced a fourth action. He was then ordered to attend the house forthwith, but it appeared from the evidence of the messengers, that he was wilfully evading the service of the order and could not be found. The house, instead of resolving that he was in contempt, adopted the precedent of 31st March 1771, and, according to ancient custom, ordered that he should be sent for in the custody of the serjeant-at-arms, and that Mr. Speaker should issue his warrant accordingly. The warrant was in the follovvino; form:

"Whereas the House of Commons have this day ordered that Form of war-Thomas Burton Howard be sent for, in the custody of the serjeant- '"' " at-arms attending this house: these are therefore to require you to take into your custody the body of the said Thomas Burton Howard," c. c.

Howard was taken into custody on this warrant and brought to the bar; and it was for this arrest that the action of trespass was brought. Pleas were put in justifying the acts of the serjeant, under the authority of the warrant, to which there were special demurrers, denying their sufficiency in law.

In the argument it was contended, not only that the Arguments and warrant was informal, but that the house had exceeded its '"' jurisdiction in sending for a person in custody, Vv'ithout having previously adjudged him guilty of a contempt. The house might have sent for him, it was urged, and when he did not appear, have declared him in contempt, and com- ' 21 Com. J. 705. 95 lb, 30.

mitted him for his offence; but they had no right to bring him in custody, and thus imprison him upon a charge, instead of on conviction. This doctrine, however, was not supported by the court; but judgment was given for the plaintiff on other grounds. The three judges whose opinion was for the plaintiff, each differed as to the grounds of the judgment. Mr. Justice Wightman thought the warrant technically bad, because in the mandatory part it merely directed the serjeant to take the plaintiff into custody, whereas in the recital it appeared that he was to be sent for in custody. Mr. Justice Coleridge differed upon this point, and thought the mandatory part was to be read with the recital, and thus made consistent. His main objection to the warrant was, that it did not express the cause for which the plaintiff was to be sent for. From this opinion, again. Lord Denman expressed his dissent; but thought the warrant otherwise bad. On the other hand, Mr. Justice Williams was of opinion that there should be judgment for the defendant. The grounds upon which the judgment was pronounced were so far technical, that the judges considered that no question of privilege was involved in their decision; and " that the form of the warrants issued by Mr. Speaker by order of the house may be questioned and adjudged to be bad, without impugning the authority of the house, or in any way disputing its privileges." From this doctrine a committee of the commons entirely dissented. " They could not admit the right of any court of law to decide on the propriety of those forms of warrants which the house, through its highest officer, has thought proper to adopt on any particular occasion. If the highest court of law has this right, it is impossible to deny it to the lowest." The committee in considering the course to be adopted by the house in consequence of this judgment, thus expressed the difficulties of their situation;

"They are not insensible to the public evil which might result from the adoption by the House of Commons of decisive measures ' 2d Rep. on Printed Papers, 1845 (397), p. vi.

for resisting the execution of a judgment of a court of law. They are not without apprehension that such measures may hereafter become inevitable; but they entertain a strong conviction that it would be inexpedient for the house needlessly to precipitate such a crisis; and they think that every other legitimate mode of asserting and defending its privileges should be exhausted before it resorts to the exercise of that power which it possesses, of preventing, by its own authority, the further progress of an action in which judgment has been obtained."

The house concurred in the opinion of the committee. Writ of error. and ordered that a writ of error be brought upon the judgment of the Court of Queen's Bench. In the meantime, in order to avoid " submitting to abide by the judgment of the court of error, in the event of its being adverse," the Serjeant was not authorised to give bail, and execution was levied on his goods. Judgment was given by the Court of Exchequer Chamber, on the writ of error, on the 2d February 1847, when the judgment of the court below was reversed by the unanimous opinion of all the judges of whom the court was composed. They found " that the privileges involved in this case are not in the least doubtful, and the warrant of the speaker, is, in our opinion, valid, so as to be a protection to the officer of the house."

Thus far the course adopted by the house led, for the Present posi-present, to a fortunate termination of their contests with the leo". ' courts of law; but if the judgment had been adverse to their privileges, they would have been involved in still greater embarrassments. It is to be hoped that further contests may be very remote; but it must be acknowledged that the present position of privilege is, in the highest degree, unsatisfactory. Assertions of privilege are made in Parliament, and denied in the courts; the officers who execute the orders of Parliament are liable to vexatious actions, and if verdicts are obtained against them, the damages and costs are paid by the Treasury. The parties who bring such actions, instead of being prevented from 100 Com. J. 642. See also Hans. Deb. 30th May and 26th June 1845. " 100 Com. J. 562.

Shorthand writer's notes, 1847 (39), p. 164. See also supra,), 151.

statute.

164 REMEDY BY STATUTE.

proceecling with them by some legal process acknowledged by the courts, can only be coerced by an unpopular exercise of privilege, which does not stay the actions. If Parliament were to act strictly upon its own declarations, it would be forced to commit not only the parties, but their counsel and their attorneys, the judges, and the sheriffs; and so great would be the injustice of punishing the public officers of justice for administering the law according to their consciences and oaths, that Parliament would shrink from so violent an exertion of privilege. And again, tlie intermediate course adopted in the case of Stockdale v. Hansard, of coercing the sheriff for executing the judgment of the court, and allowing the judges wlio gave the obnoxious judgment to pass without censure, is inconsistent in principle, and betrays hesitation on the part of the house distrust of its own autliority, or fear of public opinion. Remedy by A remedy has already been applied to actions connected with the printing of parliamentary papers; and a well-considered statute, founded upon the same principle, is the only mode by which collisions between Parliament and the courts of law can be prevented for the future. The proper time for proposing such a measure is when no contest is pending; and when its provisions may be calmly examined, without reference to a particular privilege, or a particular judgment of the courts. It is not desired that Parliament should, on the one hand, surrender any privilege that is essential to its dignity, and to the proj er exercise of its authority; nor on the other, that its privileges should be enlarged. But some mode of enforcing them should be authorised by law, analogous to an injunction issued by a court of equity to restrain parties from proceeding with an action at common law, and even with a private Bill in Parliament; and such a prohibition should be made binding, not only upon the parties, but upon the courts.

' Hartlepool Junction Railway Bill, 1848. See 100 Hans. Deb. 3(1 Series, 78.3. North Staffordshire Railway 6111,1850.

INTRODUCTORY REMARKS. MEETING OF A NEW PARLIAMENT. ELEC-TION AND ROYAL APPROBATION OF THE SPEAKER OF THE COMMONS, OATHS. QUEEN's SPEECH AND addresses IN ANSWER. PLACES OF PEERS AND MEMBERS OF THE HOUSE OF COMMONS. ATTENDANCE ON THE SER-VICE OF PARLIAMENT. OFFICE OF SPEAKER IN BOTH HOUSES. PRINCIPAL OFFICERS. JOURNALS. ADMISSION OF STRANGERS. PROROGATION.

The proceedings of Parliament are regulated chiefly by introductory ancient usage, or by the settled practice of modern times, apart from distinct orders and rules: but usage has frequently been declared and explained by both houses, and new rules have been established by positive orders and resolutions. Ancient usage, when not otherwise declared, Ancient usage, is collected from the Journals, from history and early treatises, and from the continued experience of practised members. Modern practice is often undefined in any Modern prac-written form; it is not recorded in the Journals; it is not to be traced in the published debates; nor is it known in any certain manner but by personal experience, and by the daily practice of Parliament in conducting its various descriptions of business.

Numerous orders and resolutions for regulating the proceedings of Parliament are to be found in the Journals

Standing orders.

Sessional orders.

Orders and resolutions.

of both houses, which may be divided into, 1, standing orders; 2, sessional orders; and 3, orders or resolutions undetermined in regard to their permanence.

1. Both houses have agreed, at various times, to standing orders, for tlie permanent guidance and order of their proceedings; which, if not vacated or rescinded, endure from one Parliament to another, and are of equal force in all. They occasionally fall into desuetude, and are regarded as practically obsolete; but, by the law and custom of Parliament, they are binding upon the proceedings of the house by which they were agreed to, as continual bye-laws, until their operation is concluded by another vote of the house upon the same matter.

In the house of Lords particular attention is paid to the making and recording of standing orders. No motion may be granted for making a standing order, or for dispensing with one the same day it is made, nor before the house has been summoned to consider it;' and every standing order, wlien agreed to, is added to the " Roll of Standing Orders," which is carefully preserved and published from time to time. In the House of Commons, however, no such care is taken. When an order or resolution has been agreed to and ordered to be made a standing order, it appears in that form in the Journals; but there is no authorised collection of the standing orders, except in relation to private bills.

2. At the commencement of each session both houses agree to certain orders and resolutions, which, from being constantly renewed from year to year, are evidently not intended to endure beyond the existing session. They are few in number, and have but a partial effect upon the business of Parliament.

3. The operation of orders or resolutions of either house, of which the duration is undetermined, is not settled upon any certain principle. By the custom of Parliament they ' Lords' S. O. No. 39.

would be concluded by a prorogation; but many of them are practically observed and held good in succeeding sessions, and by different Parliaments, without any formal renewal or repetition. In such cases, it is presumed that the house regards its former orders as declaratory of its practice; and that without relying upon their absolute validity, it agrees to adhere to their observance as part of the settled practice of Parliament.

In addition to these several descriptions of internal statutes and authority, by which the proceedings of both houses are P sative. regulated, they are governed, in some few particulars, by statutes and by royal prerogative.

The proceedings of Parliament will now be followed in pian of the se the order which appears the best adapted for rendering "' them intelligible, without repetition, and apart from any presumption of previous knowledge on the part of the reader. For which purpose, it is proposed, in this chapter, to present an outline of the general forms of procedure, in reference to the meeting, sittings, adjournment, and prorogation of Parliament; and, in future chapters, to proceed to the explanation of the various modes of conducting parliamentary business, with as close an attention to methodical arrangement as the diversity of the subjects will allow. Where the practice of the two houses differs, the variation will appear in the description of each separate proceeding; but wherever there is no difference, one account of a rule or form of proceeding, without more particular explanation, must be understood as applicable equally to both houses of Parliament.

On the day appointed by royal proclamation for the Meeting of a first meeting of a new Parliament for despatch of business, ment. the members of both houses assemble in their respective chambers. In the House of Lords, the lord chancellor acquaints the house, " that her Majesty not thinking it fit to be personally present here this day,, had been pleased to cause a commission to be issued under the great seal, in

Commons attend in the House of Peei's.

Proceedings in the lords.

order to the opening and liolding of this Parhament." The lords commissioners being in their robes, and seated on a form between the throne and the woolsack, then command the o: entleman usher of the black rod to let the commons know "the lords commissioners desire their immediate attendance in this house to hear the commission read."

Meanwhile, the clerk of the Crown in Chancery has delivered to the clerk of the House of Commons a book, containing the names of the members returned to serve in the Parliament; after which, on receiving the message from the black rod, the commons go up to the House of Peers. The lord chancellor there addresses the members of both houses, and acquaints them that her Majesty has been pleased " to cause letters patent to be issued, under her great seal, constituting us, and other lords therein men-ticjned, her commissioners, to do all things in her Majesty's name, on her part necessary to be performed in this Parliament," c. These letters patent are next read at length by the clerk; after which the lord chancellor again addresses both houses, and acquaints them

"that her Majesty will, as soon as the members of both houses shall 1)6 sworn, declare the causes of her calling this Parliament; and it being necessary a speaker of the House of Commons should be first chosen, tliat you, gentlemen of the House oj Commons, repair to the jilace where you are to sit, and there proceed to the appointment of some proper person to be your speaker; and that you present such person whom you shall so choose here, to-morrow (at an hour stated), for her Majesty's royal approbation."'

The commons immediately withdraw, and return to their own house, while the House of Lords is adjourned during pleasure, to unrobe. On that house being resumed, the prayers, Avith which the business of each day is commenced, 1 The forms here described have been in use, with little variation, since the 12th Anne (1713). Before that time the sovereign usually came down on tlie iirst day of the new parliament; and on one occasion Queen Anne came down three times, viz. to open parliament, to Hpprove the speaker, and to declare the causes of summons in a speech from the throne, (1737), 15 Com. J. 393. 17 lb. 472.

are read for the first time, by a bisho)," or if no bishop be Prayers, present, by any peer in holy orders, or if there be none present, then by any peer who may be in the house. The lord chancellor then takes the oaths, and takes and subscribes the oath of abjuration. The certificate of the clerk of the Crown of the return of the sixteen representative peers of Scotland is next read, after which the lords who are present take the oaths required by law," and subscribe the roll of the lords spiritual and temporal.

At tliis time, also, peers are introduced who have received introduction of writs of summons, or who have been newly created by letters patent, and they present their writs or patents to the lord chancellor kneeling on one knee. They are introduced in their robes, between two other peers of their own dignity, also in their robes, and are preceded by the gentleman usher of the black rod, (or in his absence by the yeoman usher), by Garter king of arms (or in his absence by Clarenceux king of arms, or any other herald oflsciating for Garter king of arms), and by the earl marshal and lord great chamberlain. It is not necessary, however, that the two last officers should be present. Being thus introduced, peers are conducted to their seats, according to their dignity.

When a new representative peer of Ireland has been elected, the clerk of the Crown in Ireland attends with the writs and returns with his certificate annexed, which certificate is read and entered on the Journal."'

A bishop is introduced by two other bishops, and con- And bishops, ducted to his seat amongst the spiritual lords; but without the formalities observed in the case of the temporal peers. The representative bishops of Ireland are not introduced by ' Usually the junior bishop, i. e. the bishop last admitted to the house.

2 73 Lords' J. 568. 26 lb. 138. 157.

"Tliese are the oatli of tidelity, the oath of supremacy, the oatli of abjuration, or the oath to be taken by Roman-catholics under 10 Geo. 4, c. 1; which are inserted at length in the Ajipendix.

73 Lords' J. 5(ia. ' lb 575.

Peers by descent.

By special limitations in remainder.

Election of a speaker by the commons.

other bisliops, but take the oaths, subscribe the roll, and proceed to their seats without any particular ceremony.

With regard to peers by descent, or by special limitation in remainder, there are the following standing orders:

"That all peers of this realm by descent, being of the age of one and twenty years, have right to come and sit in the House of Peers without any introduction.

"That no such peers ought to pay any fee or fees to anyherauld upon their first coming into the House of Peers.

"That no such peers may or shall be introduced into the House of Peers by any herauld, or with any ceremony, though they shall desire the same."

"That every peer of this realm claiming by virtue of a special limitation in remainder, and not claiming by descent, shall be introduced."

The commons, in the meantime, proceed to the election of their speaker. A member, addressing himself to the clerk, (who, standing up, points to him, and then sits down), proposes to the house some other member then present, and moves that he " do take the chair of this house as speaker," which motion is seconded by another member. If no other member be proposed as speaker, the motion is ordinarily supported by an influential member (generally the leader of the House of Commons), and the member proposed is called by the house to the chair. He now stands up in his place and expresses his sense of the honour proposed to be conferred upon him, and submits himself to the house; the house again unanimously call him to the chair, when his proposer and seconder take him out of his place and conduct him to the chair. But if another member be proposed, a similar motion is made and seconded in regard to him, and both the candidates address themselves to the house. A debate ensues in relation to the claims of each candidate, in which the clerk continues to act the part of speaker, standing up and pointing to the

Lords' S. O. No. 55. 96 Com. J. 4G3.

See p. 199.

members as they rise to speak, and then sltthig down. When this debate is closed, the clerk puts the question that the member first proposed " do take the chair of this house as speaker," and if the house divide, he directs one party to go into one lobby, and the other into the other lobby, and appoints two tellers for each. If the majority be in favour of the member first proposed, he is at once conducted to the chair; but if otherwise, a similar question is put in relation to the other, which being resolved in the affirmative, that member is conducted to the chair by his proposer and seconder.

The speaker elect, on being conducted to the chair. Speaker elect ,,, T, r l i l returns thanks.

stands on the upper step and "expresses his grateiul thanks,"""" or "humble acknowl-edgments:" or "truesense of the high honour the house had been pleased to confer upon him;'" and then takes his seat. The mace, which The mace.

up to tliis time has been under the table, is now laid upon the table, where it is always placed during the sitting of the house, with the speaker in the chair. Mr. Speaker elect is then congratulated by some leading member, and the house adjourns.

The house meets on the following day, and Mr. Speaker Royal appro-elect takes the chair and awaits the arrival of the black speaker elect. rod from the lords com-missioners. When that officer has delivered his message, Mr. Speaker elect, with the house, goes up to the House of Peers and acquaints the lords commissi oners,

"that in obedience to her Majesty's commands her Majesty's faithful commons, in the exercise of their undoubted right and privilege, have proceeded to the election of a speaker, and as the object of their choice he now presents himself at your bar, and submits himself with all humility to her Majesty's gracious approbation."

' Election of imr. Shaw Lefevre, 94 Com. J. 274. It had previously been the custom to appoint one teller only for each party. See Chap. XII., Divisions. 2 90 Com. J. 5, 3 9(3 i, j 4Q5. qo lb. 7. 94 lb. 274.

In reply, the lord cliancellor assures him of her Majesty's sense of his sufficiency, and " that her Majesty most fully approves and confirms him as the speaker."

Lays diiim to When the speaker has been approved, he lays claim, if Uie'commons. 0 half of the commons, " by humble petition to her

Majesty, to all their ancient and undoubted rights and privileges," which being confirmed, the speaker, with the commons, retires from the bar of the House of Lords.

Speaker elected The Speaker thus elected and approved continues in that

Pariiament ' officc during the whole Parliament, unless in the meantime he resigns or is removed by death. In the event of a

Vacancy during vacancy during the session, similar forms are observed in the session. j g election and approval of a speaker; except that instead of her Majesty's desire being signified by the lord chancellor in the House of Lords, a minister of the crown in the commons acquaints the house that her Majesty ' gives leave to the house to proceed forthwith to the choice of a new speaker;""

and when the speaker has been chosen, the same minister acquaints the house that it is her Majesty's pleasure that the house should present their speaker to-morrow (at an hour stated) in the House of Peers for her Majesty's royal approbation. Mr. Speaker elect puts the question for adjournment, and when the house adjourns, he leaves the house, without the mace before him. On the following day the royal approbation is given Avith the same forms as at the meeting of a new Parliament, except that the claim of privileges is omitted.

' 73 Lords' J. 571; 80 Tb. 8. It was formerly customary for the speaker elect to declare that he felt the difficulties of liis high and arduous office, and that, " if it should he her Majesty's pleasure to disapprove of this choice, her Majesty's faithful commons will at once select some other member of their liouse better qualified to fill the station than himself."

94 Com. J. 274. For probably the earliest instance of proceedings on the death of a speaker, see 1 Com. J. 116. 1 Pari. Hist. 811.

3 71 Lords' J. 308. 11 Com. J. 272. 94 lb. 274.

The ceremony of receiving the royal permission to elect Exceptions to a speaker, and the royal approbation of him when elected, has been constantly observed, except on three occasions, when from peculiar circumstances it could not be followed.

1. Previous to the Restoration in 1660, Sir Harbottle Grimston was called to the chair without any authority from Charles II., who had not yet been formally recognised by the Convention Parliament. 2. On the meeting of the Convention Parliament on the 22d January 1688, James II. had fled, and the Prince of Orange had not yet been declared king; when the commons chose Mr. Henry Powle as speaker by their own authority. 3. Mr. Speaker Cornwall died on the 2d January 1789, at which time George HI. was mentally incapable of attending to any public duties; and on the 5th the house proceeded to the choice of another speaker, who immediately took his seat and performed all the duties of his office.

The only instance of the royal approbation being re- Royal approba-fused was in the case of Sir Edward Seymour in 1678."' Sir John Popham, indeed, had been chosen speaker in 1450, but his excuse being admitted by the king, another was chosen by the commons in his place; and Sir Edward Seymour, who knew that it had been determined to take advantage of his excuse, purposely avoided making any, so as not to give the king an opportunity of treating him in the same manner as his predecessor had been treated in a former reign.

The speaker, on returning from the lords, reports to Oatlis, c. in the house his approval by her Majesty, and her confirma- """ commons. tion of their privileges, and " repeats his most respectful acknowledgments to the house for the high honour they have done him." He then puts the house in mind that the first thing to be done is to take and subscribe the oaths ' 8 Com. J. 1. 2 10 lb. 9. 44 lb. 4.5.

"Pari. Hist. 1092. 1 lb. 385.

See also the case John Cheyne, 1st Hen. IV., 1399, who excused himself on account ofillness, after he had been appointed by the king; 3 Rot. Pari. 424.

required by law; and himself first, alone, standing upon the upper step of the chair, takes the oaths of allegiance and supremacy, and takes and subscribes the oath of abjuration; and also delivers to the clerk of the house a statement of his qualification, and makes and subscribes a declaration that he is duly qualified; in which ceremonies he is followed by the other members who are present. The house adjourns at four o'clock, for a reason that will be presently explained, and niuets early on the following day, when the daily prayers are read for the first time by ISIr. Speaker's chaplain." The members continue to take the oaths on that and the succeeding day, after which the greater part are sworn, and qualified to sit and vote.

But, before any further proceedings of the session are described, it may be well to advert more particularly to the laws and practice relating to oaths, and the qualification and identity of members. Refusal to take Where members have refused to take the oaths of allegiance and supremacy, they have been adjudged by the house to be disqualified by the statutes from sitting, and new writs have been issued in their room. Soon after the Revolution of 1688, Sir H. Mounson and Lord Fanshaw refused to take the oaths, and were discharged from being members of the house; and on the 9th of January following, Mr. Cholmly, who said he could not yet take the oaths, was committed to the Tower for his contempt. But the most remarkable ' The " out-door oaths," formerly taken by members of both houses before the lord steward, were abolished by 1 2 Will. 4, c. 9.

In case of the accidental absence of the chaplain. Mr. Speaker would read prayers, as was done once by Mr. Speaker Abercromby and twice by his successor. Chaplains or ministers were first appointed " to pray with the house daily," during the Long Parliament. 3 Com. J. 365. 7 lb. 366. 424. 595. Before that time prayers had been read by the clerk, and sometimes by the speaker. On the 23d March 1G03 prayers " were read by the clerk of the house (to whose place that service anciently appertains), and one other special prayer fitly conceived for that time and purpose was read by Mr. Speaker; which was voluntary, and not of duty or necessity, though heretofore of late time tlie like liath been done by other speakers." 1 Com. J. 150.

3 10 Com. J. 131. 5 Pari. Hist. 254. 10 Com. J. 328.

precedent is that of Mr. O'Connell, who had been returned for the county of Clare, in May 1829, before the passing of the Roman Catholic Relief Act. On the oaths being tendered to him by the clerk, he refused to take the oath of supremacy, and claimed to take the new oath contained in the Roman Catholic Relief Act, which had been substituted for the other oaths, as regards Roman Catholic members to be returned after the passing of the Act. Mr. O'Connell was afterwards heard upon his claim; but the house resolved that he was not entitled to sit or vote, unless he took the oath of supremacy. Mr. O'Connell persisted in his refusal to take that oath, and a new writ was issued for the county of Clare. Every member Roman Catho-returned since the passing of that Act, being a Roman Catholic, is entitled to take the Roman Catholic oath instead of the oaths of fidelity, supremacy, and abjuration. On the 13th May 1844, a member having embraced the Roman Catholic religion since his election, and after he had taken the usual oaths, took and subscribed the oath required to be taken by Roman Catholics.

The only legal obstacle to the admission of a Jew to sit Jews, and vote in Parliament arises from the words, " upon the true faith of a Christian," at the end of the oath of abjuration. These words were omitted from the oath when taken by a Jew, in certain cases, by the 10 Geo. I., c. 4; and again, by the 13 Geo. II., c. 7, for the naturalising foreign Protestants; and lastly, on admission to municipal offices, by the 8 9 Vict. c. 52; but as regards the Parliamentary oaths, there is no statute which can be construed so as to justify the omission of these words. In 1850, Baron Lionel Nathan de Rothschild, who during the two previous sessions had been one of the members for the city of London, but had not taken the oaths and his seat, was admitted to be sworn on the Old Testament, being the form most ' 84 Com. J. 303.311. 314. 325. 99 lb. 291. S. e also Votes, 5 Feb. 1851.

binding on his conscience Having taken the oaths of allegiance and supremacy, he proceeded to take the oath of abjuration, but omitted the concluding words, " on the true faith of a Christian," "as not binding on his conscience;" whereupon he was directed to withdraw. After debate, the house resolved that he was " not entitled to vote in this house, or to sit in this house during any debate, until he shall take the oath of abjuration, in the form appointed by law." No new writ, ho: v'ever, was issued, as it appeared that the statutes by which the oath of abjuration was appointed to be taken, did not attach the penalty of disability to the refusal to take that oath, but solely to the offence of sitting and voting without having taken it. Declarations by Quakers, Moravians, Separatists, and others, who have ers, c. conscientious objection to an oath, are now permitted to make affirmations to the same effect. In 1693 John Arch-dale, a Quaker, having declined to take the oaths " in regard to a principle of his religion," a new writ was Issued in his room."' But subsequently to that case, several statutes permitting Quakers to make affirmations instead of oaths were passed; and upon a general construction of these statutes, in 1833, Mr. Pease, a Quaker, was admitted to sit and vote upon making affirmation to the effect of the oaths directed to be taken at the table." In the same year an Act was passed to allow Quakers and Moravians to make affirmation In all cases where an oath is or shall be required. Acts have also been passed giving the same privilege to persons who have ceased to be Quakers and Moravians,"' and to ' Votes and Hans. Deb. 29tli July. See 1 2 Viet. c. 105. 2 Votes and Hans. Deb. 30tli July. lb. 5th August.

M3 Will III. C.6. 6Anne, c.7. 6 Geo. III. c. 53. Debates."ioth July and 5th August. See also liepurt of the Committee on Oaths of Members, 1850 (268).

12 Com. J. 386. 388.

6 Anne, c. 23. 1 Geo. I. st.2, c. 6 and c.13. 8Geo. I. c.6. 22 Geo. I I. e. 46. ' 88 Com. J. 41. See also report on his case, 1833 (6).

3 4 Will. 4, c. 49. M 2 Vict. c. 77.

Separatists;' and several members of these dlfferent religious denominations have since made affirmations instead of oaths.

By the 30th Chas. IL, stat. 2, and the 13th Will. III., Omission to 1. 1 T 1!, T 1 take the oaths.

C. D, severe penalties and disabilities are incurred by any Penalties.

member of either house, who shall sit and vote without having taken the oaths at the table; but when they neglect to take them from haste, accident, or inadvertence, it is usual to pass Acts of indemnity, to relieve them from the consequences of their neglect. In the commons, however, it is necessary to move a new writ immediately the omission is discovered, as the member is disabled from sitting and voting, and a new writ is required to be issued in pursuance of the 30th Chas. II., st. 2, s. 8

But although a member may not sit and vote until he Members en-has taken the oaths, he is entitled to all the other privileges il l before " of a member, and is otherwise regarded, both by the house y sworn. and by the laws, as qualified to serve, until some other disqualification has been shown to exist. Thus in 1715 it was resolved, " that Sir Joseph Jekyll was capable of being chosen of a committee of secrecy, though he had not been sworn at the clerk's table."

In 1849 Baron Lionel Nathan de Rothschild had been a member for tvv o sessions without having taken the oaths; when he accepted the Chlltern Hundreds. On the 27th June a new writ was issued for the city of London, and he was again returned, and continued to be a member without taking the oaths. It is usual for members who have not yet taken the oaths to sit below the bar; and care must be taken that they do not, inadvertently, take a seat within the bar, by which they would render themselves liable to the penalties and disqualifications imposed by the statutes.

' 3 4 Will. 4, c. 82.

90 Com. J. 5; 92 lb. 490. 495; 93 lb. 7; 98 lb. 3; 103 lb. 7. 566.

3 45 Geo. III. c. 5. 66 Geo. III. c. 48, c. (private).

60 Com. J. 148; 67 lb. 280; 60 lb. 144; 71 lb. 42; 86 lb. 35.3.

5 2 Hats. 98 Ji.

On tlie 18th May 1849, when notice was taken that strangers were

Certificate of Clerk of the Crown.

Time for taking the oaths.

Doubts have arisen as to the period at which a person elected to serve as a member is entitled to take the oaths and his seat. At the beginning of a Parliament, the Ee-turn Book received from the clerk of the Crown is sufficient evidence of the return of a member, and the oaths are at once administered. If a member be elected after a general election, the clerk of the Crown sends to the clerk of the house a certificate of the return of the indenture into the Crown Office; and it is usual to require the member to produce a memorandum from a clerk in the Public Business Office that this certificate has been received before the clerk of the house will administer the oaths. The neglect of this rule in 1848 gave rise to doubts as to the validity of the oaths taken by a member. Mr. Hawes was elected for Kinsale on the 11th March; on the 15th l)e was sworn at the table; but his return was not received by the clerk of the Crown until the 18th; and it was questioned whether the oaths which he had taken before the receipt of the return had been duly taken. A committee was appointed to inquire into the matter, who reported, "That although the return of the indenture to the Crown Office has always been required by the house as the best evidence of a member's title to be sworn, yet that the absence of that proof cannot affect the validity of the election, nor the right of a person duly elected to be held a membe of the house." The committee at the same time recommended a strict adherence to the practice of requiring the production of the usual certificate.

The time for taking the oaths by both houses was limited.

present, Baron Rothschild was sitting below the bar, and retained his scat there during the exclusion of strangers, in virtue of his return to the house, although he had not taken the oaths and his seat.

' 1848, Sess. No. 256.

' It was stated in evidence, that in July 1846 Lord Alfred Paget, being returned for Lichfield, brought up the return himself, which he took with him and produced at the table of the house; and after he had been sworn the return was fent to thj Crown Office. Questions, 87-89.

by the Acts 30 Chas. II. 13 Will. III., to the hours between nine and four; but by an Act 6 7 Vict., c. 6, the lords are now enabled to take the oaths until five o'clock in the afternoon. The same Acts order the oaths to be taken, in both houses, at the table in the middle of the house, with the house sitting, and the speaker " in his place," or " in the chair." This provision causes the ordinary meeting of the House of Commons to be fixed for a quarter before four o'clock in the afternoon, excejdt on Wednesday, when the house sits from twelve till six o'clock by virtue of the Sessional Orders. The appearance of a member to be sworn, before four o'clock, immediately supersedes any other business."

By the Qualification Act of 1838, every member of the Declaration of House of Commons (not being the eldest son of a peer, ' " ' ' " peeress," or bishop, being a lord of Parliament, ' or otherwise exempted from the provisions of the Act), before he shall sit or vote, after the choice of a speaker, is required to deliver at the table of the house a statement of his property qualification, and at the same time, to make and subscribe a declaration that, to the best of his belief, he is duly qualified. If he shall make a false declaration, or deliver an untrue statement, he will be guilty of a misdemeanor. This declaration is made at the time of taking the oaths; and an omission to comply with the requirements of the Act will avoid the election. " At the beginning 2 Hats. 90. Votes 8th August 1850 (Mr. W. Williams). 105 Com. J. 629. " 2 Hats. 62 w.

' On the 29th May 1848 the speaker called the attention of the house to the fact, that Mr. Vernon Harcourt, the eldest son of the late Archbishop of York, bad given in his qualification as the eldest son of a peer of parliament, a qualification by which he had sat in parliament for 40 years; but it appeared that under the Act of Parliament the death of his father had invalidated this qualification, and Mr. Harcourt was permitted to give in the particulars of his property qualification. 99 Hans. Deb., 3d Series, 67. See also 2 Bacon's Abridgment, 429 n, as to bishop's eldest son.

See supra, p. 31, and Appendix. The proper forms are to be obtained at the " Public Business Office."

1 2 Vict. c. 48, s. 6-8. 18 Com. J. 129. 21 lb. 754.

N 2-I- queen's speech.

New members sworn after ge neral election.

Members seated on petition.

of a Parliament every member also subscribes the Rolls in the custody of the clerk of the house.

Members returned after the general election, take the oaths in the same manner, before four o'clock; and " in compliance with an ancient order and custom," explained by a resolution of the 23d February 1688, "they are introduced to the table between two members, making their obeisances as they go up, that they may be the better known to the house;" but this practice is not observed in regard to members who come in upon petition, for they are supposed to have been returned at the general election. Another difference of form is to be remarked, in reference to new members and to members seated on petition, when coming to be sworn. The former not being on the original roll of returns, must bring with them, as already stated, a certificate of their return from the clerk of the Crown; but the latter having become members by the adjudication of an election committee, the clerk of the Crown amends the return by order of the house, and their names are consequently upon the roll as if they had been originally returned.

In the event of the demise of the Crown, all the members of both houses again take the oaths. Queen's speecii. To proceed with the business of the session. When the greater part of the members of both houses are sworn, the causes of summons are declared by her Majesty in person, or by commission. This proceeding is, in fact, the true commencement of the session; and in every session but the first of a Parliament, as there is no election of a speaker, nor any general swearing of members, the session is opened at once by the Queen's speech, without any preliminary proceedings in either house."

Demise of the Crown.

' 10 Com. J. 34. 2 2 Hats. 85 n. 6 Anne, c. 7.

In the commons prayers are said before the Queen's speech, but in the lords usually not until their second meeting, later in the afternoon.

When the Queen meets Parhament in person, she pro- The Queen pre-ceeds in state to the House of Lords, where, " seated on ' ' the throne, adorned with her Crown and regal ornaments, and attended by her officers of state," (all the lords being in their robes, and standing until her Majesty desires them to be seated,) she commands the gentleman usher of the black rod, through the lord great chamberlain, to let the commons know, " it is her Majesty's pleasure they attend her immediately, in this house." The usher of the black rod goes at once to the door of the House of Commons, which he strikes three times with his rod; and on being admitted, he advances up the middle of the house towards the table, making three obeisances to the chair, and says, ' Mr. Speaker, the Queen commands this honourable house to attend her Majesty immediately in the House of Peers." He then withdraws, still making obeisances; nor does he turn his back upon the house until he has reached the bar. The speaker, with the house, immediately goes up to the bar of the House of Peers; upon which the Queen reads her speech to both houses of Parliament, which is delivered into her hands by the lord chancellor, kneeling upon one knee.

When her Majesty is not personally present, the causes By commission. of summons are declared by the lords commissioners. The gentleman usher of the black rod is sent, in the same manner, to the commons, and acquaints the speaker that the lords commissioners desire the immediate attendance of this honourable house in the House of Peers, to hear the commission read: and when Mr. Speaker and the house have reached the bar of the House of Peers, the lord chancellor reads the royal speech to both houses.

When the speech has been delivered, either by her Majesty in person, or by commission, the House of Lords is adjourned during pleasure. The commons separate for an hour or two, without any formal adjournment; and if any members desire to be sworn on that day, it is usual for the house to reassemble before four o'clock.

Report of When the houses are resumed in the afternoon, the main business is for the lord chancellor in the lords, and the speaker in the commons, to report her Majesty's speech. In the former house the speech is read first by the lord chancellor and then by the clerk, and in the latter by the speaker, who states that for greater accuracy he had

Bill read pro obtained a copy. But before this is done it is the practice in both houses to read some bill a first time pro forma, in order to assert their right of deliberatino; without reference to the immediate causes of summons.

This practice in the lords is enjoined by a standing order." In the commons the same form is observed by ancient custom only. There is an entry in the Journal of the 22d March 1603,

"That the first day of every sitting, in every Parliament, some one bill, and no more, receiveth a first reading for form sake."

And this practice has continued till the present time. By the lords' standing order it would appear necessary that this form should be observed immediately after the oaths have been taken; but in the commons the bill is only required to be read before the report of the Queen's speech, and other business is constantly entered upon before the reading of the bill, as the issue of new writs, the consideration of matters of privilege, the presentation of papers, and the usual sessional orders and resolutions. Address. When the royal speech has been read, an address in answer to it is moved in both houses. Two members in each house are selected by the Administration for moving and seconding the address, and they appear in their places in uniform or full dress for that purpose. The address is an answer, paragraph by paragraph, to the Queen's speech. Amendments may be made to any part of it, and when the question for an address, whether amended or not, has been ' Lords' S. O. No. 8. j q j j q y supra, p. 42.

' 95 Cora. J. 3. 96 lb. 407.

agreed to, a select committee is appointed " to prepare " or " draw up " an address. Upon the report being received from this committee, amendments may still be made to the address before it is agreed to: and after it has been finally agreed to, it is ordered to be presented to her Majesty. When the speech has been delivered by the Queen in person, and she remains in town, the address is presented by the whole house; but when it has been read by the lords commissioners, or if the Queen be in the country, the address of the upper house is presented " by the lords with white staves;" and the address of the commons by " such members of the house as are of her Majesty's most honourable privy council." When the address is to be presented Presented by by the whole house, the " lords with white staves " in the Houle!" one house, and the privy councillors in the other, are ordered " humbly to know her Majesty's pleasure when she will be attended " with the address. Each house meets when it is understood that this ceremony wiu take place, and after her Majesty's pleasure has been reported, proceeds separately to the palace. For this purpose care must be taken to make a house at the proper time: 1st, because it has been ordered that the address shall be presented by the whole house; and 2dly, because the house, properly constituted, has to receive her Majesty's pleasure, which can only be communicated to the house at large. From a neglect of this precaution her Majesty was kept waiting by the commons for upwards of half an hour on the 6 th February 1845. If before the presentation of the address, by the whole house, any circumstance should be communicated which would make it inconvenient for her Majesty to receive the house, the address is presented by the " lords with white staves " and privy councillors, as was done on the 3d February 1844. The proceedings upon ' Of tlie royal household.

' 74 Lords' J. 10. 9G Com. J. 11; 101 lb. 10. 99 Com. J. 12.

House of Lords.

184 PLACES OF PEERS.

addresses need not be pursued any further, as they will be described more fully in a separate chapter. Duces ill the In the upper house " The lords are to sit in the same order as is prescribed by the Act of Parliament, except that the lord chancellor sitteth on the woolsack as speaker to the house."' But this order is not usually observed with any strictness. The bishops always sit together in the upper part of the hojse, on the right hand of the throne; but the lords temporal are too much distributed by their offices, by political divisions, and by the part they take in debate, to be able to sit according to their rank and precedence. The members of the administration sit on the front bench on the right hand of the woolsack, adjoining the bishops: and the peers who usually vote with them, occupy the other benches on that side of the house. The peers in opposition are ranged on the opposite side of the house; while many who desire to maintain a political neutrality, sit upon the cross benches which are placed between the table and the bar. The standing order, however, is occasionally enforced.

On the 20th January 1740, the Roll of Standing Orders was read, and the lords present took their due places; and again on the 1st February 1771.

On the 10th February 1740, "it was insisted that the lords should take their due places, and the Act 31 Hen. VIII., ' for placing of the lords," being read, it was moved that the house be called over, but this motion was negatived;" and on the 4th December 1741, " it was insisted on that the lords should take their due places.""

' Chapter XVII, 2 Lords' S. O. No. 1, 31 Hen. VIII., c. 10. By this statute the precedence of princes of the blood royal, and of the bishops, peers, and liigh officers of state is defined. See also 1 Will. Mary, c. 21, s. 2; 5 Ann. c. 8; 10 Ann. c. 4.

25 Lords' J. S72. 33 lb. 47.

25 lb. 593. 26 lb. 0.

On the 22d January 1740, it was agreed by the house that the end of the lowest cross bench, next the bishops' bench, is the place of the junior baron.

If the eldest son of a peer be summoned to Parliament Ancient by the style of an ancient barony held by his father, he takes precedence amongst the peers according to the antiquity of his barony; whereas if he be created, by patent, a baron by a new style or title he ranks as junior baron.

In the commons no places are particularly allotted to Places in the . n l r l l xi, commous.

members; but it is the custom for the front bench on the right hand of the chair to be appropriated for the members of the Administration, which is called the treasury or privy councillors' bench. The front bench on the opposite side is also usually reserved for the leading members of the opposition, who have served in high offices of state; but other members occasionally sit there, especially when they have any motion to offer to the house. And on the opening of a new Parliament, the members for the city of London claim the privilege of sitting on the treasury or privy councillors' bench. It is understood that members who have received the thanks of the house in their places, are entitled, by courtesy, to keep the same places during the Parliament; and it is not uncommon for old members who are constantly in the habit of attending in one place, to be allowed to occupy it without disturbance.

All other members who enjoy no place by courtesy. Secured at upon any of these grounds, can only secure a place for the P ' "-debate by being present at prayers. On the back of each seat there is a bronze plate, in which a member may put 25 Lords' J. 575.

' See case of Baron Mowbray, eldest son of Duke of Norfolk, 32 Clias. II., summoued by writ, and sat as premier baron. West, Inq. 49, and Lord Stanley, 77 Lords' J. 18.

' In 1628 a question was raised whether the nieuibers for the city of London were "knights;" but there appears to have been no decision. 1 Com. J. 894.

2 Huts. 94.

a card with his name, if he be at prayers; but by a standing order of the 6th April 1835, "No member's name may be affixed to any seat in the house before the hour of prayers."' Places secured at prayers, may be kept the whole evening, unless there be a division, or unless the members attend the speaker to the House of Lords, vhen there is a commission for giving the royal assent to bills. Disputes sometimes arise when members leave their seats for a short time, and on returning, find them occupied by others. On the 14th April 1842, Mr. Speaker thus explained the rule of the house upon this point:

"A member having been present at prayers, and having put a card at the back of his seat, is entitled to it for the whole night, unless a division should intervene. But should a member who had not been present at prayers, leave his seat, there is no rule of the house which gives him a claim to return to it; but by courtesy it is usual to permit a member to secure it, in his absence, by a book, glove, or hat."

Service of Par- Every member of the Parliament is under a constitu-lamen. tlonal obligation to attend the service of the house to which he belongs. A member of the upper house has the privilege of serving by proxy, by virtue of a royal license which authorises him to be personally absent, and to appoint another lord of Parliament as his proxy. But in the House of Commons the personal service of every member is required. By the 5 Rich. II., c. 4, "If any person summoned to Parliament do absent himself, and come not at the said summons (except he may reasonably and honestly excuse himself to our lord the king), he shall be amerced, or otherwise punished according as of old times hath been used to be done within the said realm, in the said case." And by an Act, 6 Hen. VIII., c. 16, it was declared that no member should absent himself " without the license of

Cards, with the words " at prayers " printed on them, are always put upon the table for the convenience of members.

90 Com. J. 202. See also 22 lb. 40G. 414. ' See Chapter XII.

the speaker and commons, which license was ordered to be entered of record in the book of the clerk of the Parliament, appointed for the Commons' House." The penalty upon a member for absence was the forfeiture of his wages; and although that penalty is no longer applicable, the legislative declaration of the duty of a member remains upon the statute-book. In 1554, informations were filed in the Court of Queen's Bench against several members who had seceded from Parliament, of whom six submitted to fines.

On ordinary occasions, however, the attendance of mem- Attendance of l r- T n f 1 members.

bers upon their service m Parliament is not enforced by any regulation; but when any special business is about to be undertaken, means are taken to secure their presence.

In the upper house, the most common mode of obtaining Lords sum- , moned.

a larger attendance than usual, is to order the lords to be summoned; upon which a notice is sent to each lord to acquaint him " that all the lords are summoned to attend the service of the house " on a particular day. No notice is taken of the absence of lords who do not appear, but the name of every lord who is present during the sitting of the house, is taken down each day by the clerk of the house and entered in the Journal.

When any urgent business is deemed to require the at- Call of the tendance of the lords, it has been usual to order the house to be called over; and this order has sometimes been enforced by fines and imprisonment upon absent lords.

On some occasions the lord chancellor has addressed letters to all the peers, desiring their attendance, as on the 1 1 Hans. Pari. Hist. 625.

16 Lords' J. 16. 26. 31, 40, c. All the cases in which this order has been enforced, and the various modes of enforcement, are collected in the 53d volume of the Lords' Journals, (p. 356, et seq.) There is an order on the Roll of Standing Orders (No. 41), which may be regarded as obsolete; viz., "It is to be observed, that the first or second day the house be called, and notice to be taken of such lords as either have not sent their" proxies, or are excused by his Majesty for some time."

illness of George the Third, 1st November 1810." Tlie most important occasion on which the house was called over in modern times, was in 1820, when the bill for the degradation of Queen Caroline was pending. The house then resolved,

"That no lord do absent himself on pain of incurring a fine of 100. for each day's absence, pendinir the three first days of such proceedings, and of 50 1, for each subsequent day's absence from the same; and in default of payment, of being taken into custody. That no excuses be admitted, save disability from age, being 70 and upwards, or from sickness, or of being abroad, or out of Great Britain on public service, or on account of the death of a parent, wife, or child. That every peer absenting himself from age or sickness do address a letter to the lord chancellor, stating, upon his honour, that he is so disabled; and that the lord chancellor do write a letter to the several peers and prelates with these resolutions."

Order in whicli The lords were accordingly called over by the clerk on caued!" ' " cach day during the pendency of that bill, beginning, according to ancient custom, with the junior baron. The custom of beginning with the junior baron applies to every occasion upon which the whole house is called over for any purpose, within the house, or for the purpose of proceeding to Westminster Hall, or upon any public solemnity. But when the house appoints a Select Committee, the lords appointed to serve upon it are named in the order of their rank, beginning with the highest; and in the same manner, when a committee is sent to a conference with the commons, the lord highest in rank is called first, and the other lords follow in the order of their rank. Call of the When the House of Commons is ordered to be called

House 01 Com- j-g xsusx to name a day which will enable the members to attend from all parts of the country. The interval between the order and the call has varied from one day to six weeks." If it be really intended to enforce the call, ' 18 Hans. Deb. 1. 53 Lords' J. 364.

= 87 Com. J. 311. 77 lb. 101.

mons.

not less than a week or ten days should intervene between the order and the day named for the call. The order for the house to be called over is always accompanied by a resolution, " that such members as shall not then attend, be sent for, in custody of the serjeant-at-arms." And it was formerly the custom to desire Mr. Speaker to write to all the sheriffs to summon the members to attend. On the day appointed for the call, the order of the day is read and proceeded with, postponed, or discharged, at the pleasure of the house. If proceeded with, the names are called over Order in wliich from the Return Book, according to the counties, which are "ailed! ' arranged alphabetically. The members for a county are called first, and then the members for every city or borough within that county. The counties in England and Wales are called first, and those of Scotland and Ireland in their order. This point is mentioned, because it makes a material difference in the time at which a member is required to be in his place.

The names of members who do not answer when called when Members are taken down by the clerk of the house, and are afterwards called over again. If they appear in their places at this time, or in the course of the evening, it is usual to excuse them for their previous default; but if they do not appear, and no excuse is offered for them, they are ordered to attend on a future day. It is also customary to excuse them if they attend on that day, or if a reasonable excuse be then offered; as, that they were detained by their own illness, or by the illness or death of near relations; by public service, or by being abroad. If a member should not attend, and no excuse is offered, he is liable to be committed to the custody of the serjeant-at-arms, and to the payment of the fees incident to that commitment. But, instead of committing the defaulters, the house sometimes ' 12 Com. J. 552 J 16 lb. 565; 17 lb. 184, c. go ib. 147. 3 84 Ib. 106. " 80 Ib. 130. 80 Ib. 130.

e 80 Ib. 130. 7 91 Ib. 278. 80 Ib 150. 153. 157.

Leave of absence.

Obligation to attend committees.

names another day for their attendance, or orders then' names to be taken down." In earlier times it was customary for the house to inflict fines upon defaulters, as well as other punishment.

On the 3d March, 1801, when a call of the house was deferred for a fortnight, it was ordered, " that no member do presume to go out of town without leave of the house." And, in the absence of any specific orders to that effect, members are presumed to be in attendance upon their service in Parliament. When they desire to remain in the country, they should apply to the house for " leave of absence," for which sufficient reasons must be given; as, that they are about to attend the assizes, or to go circuits, ' or that they desire to be absent on account of urgent public or private business," the illness or death of near relations, or their own ill-health. Upon these and other grounds, leave of absence is generally given, but has been occasionally refused."

Attendance upon the service of Parliament includes the obligation to fulfil all the duties imposed upon members by the orders and regulations of the house. And unless leave of absence has been obtained, a member cannot excuse himself from serving upon committees to which he may be appointed, or for not attending them, where his attendance is made compulsory by the orders of the house. In 1846 Mr. W. S. O'Brien declined serving as a selected member of a railway committee, and the Committee of Selection, not being satisfied with his excuses, nominated him to a committee, in the usual manner. He did not attend the committee, and his absence being reported to the house, he ' 91 Com. J. 278, 90 lb. 132.

1 lb. 300. 862; 2 lb. 294; 9 lb. 75, c. 56 lb. 103.

90 lb. 129. 91 lb. 89. 86 lb. 130.

89 lb. 190. s 92 lb. 314.

' 75 lb. 338; 82 lb. 376; 86 lb. 863.

"See Debates on the absence of Lord Gardner from a private bill committee, 24th and 26th June 1845. 81 Hans. Deb., 3rd Series, 1104.1190.

was ordered to attend the committee on the following day. Being again absent, and his absence being reported to the house, he attended in his place, and stated that he adhered to his determination not to attend the committee; upon which he was declared guilty of a contempt, and committed to the custody of the serjeant-at-arms.

The lords usually meet, for despatch of legislative busi- Time of meet-ness, at five o'clock in the afternoon, and the commons at ' a quarter before four.

To facilitate the attendance of members without inter- Obstructions in ruption, both houses order, at the commencement of each ' ' " ' session,

"That the commissioners of the police of the metropolis do take care that, during the session of Parliament, the passages through the streets leading to this house be kept free and open, and that no obstruction be permitted to hinder the passage of the lords (or members) to and from this house; and that no disorder be allowed in Westminster Hall, or in the passages leading to this house, during the sitting of Parliament; and that there be no annoj'ance therein or thereabouts; and that the gentleman usher of the black rod (or the serjeant-at-arms) attending this house do communicate this order to the commissioners aforesaid."

The upper house may proceed with business if only three Quorum in lords be present; but the commons require as many as commons forty, including the speaker, to enable them to sit. This rule, however, which appears to have been first established in 1640," is only one of usage, and might be altered at pleasure. In 1833, it was determined that the house should sit from twelve o'clock till three, for private business and petitions; when it was resolved, that in the morning sittings, the house should transact business with only twenty members. Immediately after prayers each day, the speaker nouse counted, counts the house, and, if forty members be not present, he waits until four o'clock, when he again counts; and, if ' 101 Com. J.566. 582. 603; and Special Rep. of Committee of Selection, 24th April 1846. lb. 555.

' 5th Jan. 1640, 2 Com. J. 63. From an entry, 20th April 1607, it would appear that sixty was not then a sufficient number; 1 Com. J. 364.

88 Com. J. 95.

Coramission makes a bouse.

House counted out- the proper number have not arrived before he has ceased counting, he adjourns tlie house, without a question first put, until the following day. If the house met at an earlier hour, the speaker, without a prior resolution of the house, could not adjourn the house for want of forty members, but business would be suspended until the proper number were present; and at four o'clock he would adjourn the house. The only exception to this rule is when a message is received from the Queen or the lords commissioners, for the attendance of the commons in the House of Lords. This proceeding often occurs in the course of a session, for the purpose of giving the royal assent to bills, from time to time; and is held to constitute the house, as duly sitting, without the usual number of members.

After the house has been made, if notice be taken by a member that forty members are not present, the speaker immediately tells the house; and, when it is before four o'clock, business is suspended until the proper number come into their places; but if after four o'clock, the speaker at once adjourns the house until the following day. When it appears, on the report of a division, after four o'clock, that forty members are not present, the house is adjourned immediately; but when the house is in committee, and forty members are discovered to be wanting, either upon a division, or upon notice being taken of the fact, the chairman reports the circumstance; when the speaker again tells the house, and, if forty members be not then present, he adjourns the house forthwith. In the meantime, while the house is being counted, the doors continue open, and members can enter during the whole time occupied by the counting. When these accidents happen on Saturday, the speaker adjourns the house until Monday. Saturday ' The importance attached to the hour of four is said to arise from the provisions of tlie Acts which require the oaths to be taken between the hours of nine in tlie morning and four in the afternoon. 2 Hats. 00.

78 Com. J. 8.

not being an ordinary day of meeting, it is usual, at an early hour on Friday, to resolve that the house, on rising, do adjourn till Monday next, lest the speaker should be obliged, by the want of members, to adjourn the house till Adjournment

Saturday. Except from these causes, the house can only be adjourned by Mr. Speaker, upon question put and resolved in the affirmative.

The sitting of the house is sometimes suspended and Sittings sus-afterwards re-sumed without any formal adjournment. The speaker retires from the house, the mace being left upon the table, and returns at a later hour, when the business proceeds, in the accustomed manner, without counting the house. When this occurs there is no entry in the Journal of the circumstance, as technically tlie house has continued sitting.

If the suspension of the sitting be desired when a committee of the whole house is sitting, the chairman may be directed to report progress; when the mace is put upon the table; the members disperse, and the report is not brought up by the chairman until the speaker returns to the house at a later hour. But when the house meets in the morning and adjourns to a later hour on the same day, the house is again counted at its second meetino;.

On the 15th September 1646 both houses adjourned to House adjourns mark their sense of the loss of the Earl of Essex; and on a cdnn"bust ' recent melancholy occasion an adjournment was agreed to " ' by the commons, nem. con., as a suitable mode of expressing the grief of the house on hearing of the death of its most distinguished member, Sir Robert Peel.

The duties of the lord speaker of the upper house, and of Speaker of the ,1 1 i? ii-n-J.! House of Lords.

the speaker oi the commons, will appear in the various proceedings of both houses, as they are explained in different parts of this work;" but a general view of the office is necessary, in this place, for understanding the forms of parliamentary procedure.

9 Com. J. 560. 2 4 Com. J. 670.

=" 3d July 18.30. loo Com. J. 484. ' See Index, tit. " Speaker."

His duty to attend.

Not necessarily a peer.

By a standing order of the lords It is declared to be the duty of the lord chancellor, or the lord keeper of the great seal of England, ordinarily to attend as speaker; but if he be absent, or if there be none authorised under the great seal to supply that place in the House of Peers, the lords may choose their own speaker during that vacancy. It is singular that the president of this deliberative

Great seal in commission.

Deputy speakers.

Speaker pro tempore.

body is not necessarily a member. It has even happened that the lord keeper has officiated, for years, as speaker, without having been raised to the peerage; and on the 22d November 1830, Mr. Brougham sat on the woolsack as speaker, being at that time lord chancellor, although his patent of creation as a peer had not yet been made out. The woolsack, indeed, is not strictly within the house, for the lords may not speak from that part of the chamber, and if they sit there during a division, their votes are not reckoned.

When the great seal is in commission, it is usual for the Crown to appoint (if he be a peer) the chief justice of the Court of Queen's Bench, or Common Pleas, the chief baron of the Exchequer, or the Master of the Rolls, to be lord speaker; and at all times there are deputy speakers appointed by commission to officiate as speaker, during the absence of the lord chancellor or lord keeper. When the lord chancellor and all the deputy speakers are absent at the same time, the lords elect a speaker)ro tempore; but he gives place immediately to any of the lords

Lords' S. O. No. 3. And see observations as to the obligation of the lord chancellor to attend, 23 August 1831, and 20th June 1834 j 6 Hans. Deb., 3d Series, 453; 7 lb. 646-662; 24 lb. 597. 600. 604.

"When Sir Robert Henley was keeper of the great seal, and presided in the House of Lords as lord keeper, he could not enter into debate as a chancellor, being a peer, does, and therefore when there was an appeal from his judgments in the Court of Chancery, and the law lords then in the house moved to reverse his judgments the lord keeper could not state the grounds of his opinions given in judgment, and support his decisions." Lord Eldon's Anecdote Book, 1 Twiss, Life, 319. 5 Lord Campb. Lives of Chancellors, 188. 3 63 Lords'.!. 114.

commissioners, on their arrival in the house; who, in their turn, give place to each other according to their precedence, and all at last to the lord chancellor.

The duties of the oflsce are thus generally defined by the Duties of speaker in tlie standing orders: lords.

"The lord chancellor, when he speaks to the house, is always to speak uncovered, and is not to adjourn the house, or to do anything else as mouth of the house, without the consent of the lords first had, except the ordinary thing about bills, which are of course, wherein the lords may likewise overrule; as, for preferring one bill before another, and such like: and in case of difference among the lords, it is to be put to the question; and if the lord chancellor will speak to anything particularly, he is to go to his own place as a peer."'

The position of the speaker of the House of Lords His anomalous is somewhat anomalous; for though he is the president of a deliberative assembly, he is invested with no more authority than any other member; and if not himself a member, his office is limited to the putting of questions, and other formal proceedings. Upon points of order, the speaker, if a peer, may address the house; but as his opinion is liable to be questioned, like that of any other peer, he does not often exercise his right.

The duties of the speaker of the House of Commons Speaiser of tiie commons.

are as various as they are important. He presides over the deliberations of the house, and enforces the observance of all rules for preserving order in its proceedings; he puts all questions, and declares the determination of the house. As " mouth of the house," he communicates its resolutions to others, conveys its thanks, and expresses its censure, its reprimands, or its admonitions. He issues warrants to execute the orders of the house for the commitment of offenders, for the issue of writs, for the attendance of witnesses, for the bringing up prisoners in custody, and, in short, for giving effect to all orders which require the

Lords' S. O. No. 2. But if lord chancellor, he goes, by virtue of liis office, to the left of the chamber above all dukes not being of the blood royal. 31 Hen. VIII. c. 10, s. 4.

His rank.

When absent.

Office of speaker in the two houses.

sanction of a legal form. He is, in fact, the representative of the house itself, in its powers, its proceedings, and its dignity. When he enters or leaves the house, the mace is borne before him by the serjeant-at-arms; when he is In the chair, it is laid upon the table; and at all other times, when the mace is not in the house, it remains with the speaker, and accompanies him upon all state occasions.

In rank, the speaker takes precedence of all commoners, both by ancient custom and by legislative declaration. The Act 1 Will. Mary, c. 21, enacts, that the lords commissioners for the great seal " not being peers, shall have and take place next after the peers of this realm, and the speaker of the House of Commons."' In the absence of the speaker, there is no provision for supplying his place by a deputy speaker or speaker pro tempore, as in the upper house; and when he is unavoidably absent, no business can be done, but the clerk acquaints the house with the cause of his absence, and puts the question for adjournment. It seems that some doubts were formerly entertained whether the house could be adjourned in this manner, otherwise than from day to day, but many precedents show that there Is no limitation as to the period of adjournment in such cases.

When the speaker has been so ill as to be unable to attend for a considerable time. It has been necessary to elect another speaker, with the usual formalities of the permission of the Crown, and the royal approval. On the recovery of the speaker, the latter resigns or " falls sick," and the former is re-elected, with a repetition of the same ceremonies.

The difference in the constitution of the office of speaker in the two houses has an important influence upon the

See also 2 Hats. Free. 249 n. 83 Com. J. 547.

3 1 Com. J. 353; 25 lb. 532; 39 lb. 841; 44 lb. 45. 9 Com. J. 4G3. 476; 11 lb. 271, 272. For instances during the Commonwealth, see 7 Com. J. 482, 483. 612. 811.

power of each house in regard to its own sittings. In tlie upper house the speaker may leave the woolsack, but his place is immediately supplied by another speaker, and the proceedings of the house are not suspended. Thus, on the 22d April 1831, when the king was approaching to prorogue parliament, the lord chancellor suddenly left the woolsack to attend his Majesty, upon which Lord Shaftesbury was appointed speaker, pro tempore, and the debate, which had been interrupted for a time, proceeded until his Majesty entered the house. But in the commons no business can be transacted unless the speaker be in the chair, and the only question that can be put in his absence is for the adjournment of the house. This general description of the office of speaker in both houses leads to a brief notice of the principal officers whose duties are immediately connected with the proceedings of Parliament.

The assistants of the House of Lords are the judges of Assistants of tlig lords.

the Courts of Queen's Bench and Common Pleas, and such barons of the exchequer as are of the degree of the coif, the master of the rolls, the attorney and solicitor-general, and the queen's Serjeants. They are summoned at the beginning of every Parliament by writs under the great seal, to be " personally present in Parliament, with us and with others of our council to treat and give advice." " They were present in the ancient consilium regis, either as members of that high court, or as assistants, and their presence has been uninterruped until this day. The judges, as assistants of the lords, held a more important place in Parliament, in ancient times, than that which is now assigned to them, having had a voice of suffrage as weu as a voice of advice. When the petitions of the commons, and the answers of the king were drawn up into the form of 63 Lords' J. 511; 80 lb. 10. Hans. Deb., 22d April 1831. See supra, p. 194. In

1826, Sir J. Leach, M. R., and in 1835, Sir L. Shadwell, V. C, though not peers, were made Lord Speakers, when the Great Seal was la commission. Macq. 30 n.

' Hale, Hist, of H. of Lords. Litro. to Sugd. Law of R. P. 2.

statutes, after the session, the judges, if not regarded as legislators themselves, were at least concerned in the most important part of legislation. They were also occasionally made joint committees with the lords of parliament, a jjractice which continued until the latter end of the reign of

Queen Elizabeth. Their attendance was formerly enforced on all occasions, but they are now summoned by a special order when their advice is required. Their place is on the woolsacks, and they

"are not to be covered until the lords give tliem leave, whicli they ordinarily signify by the lord chancellor; and they being then appointed to attend the house, are not to s eak or deliver any opinion until it be required, and they be admitted so to do by the major part of the house, in case of difference."

Attendants. The masters in ordinary in chancery also attend in the

House of Lords as attendants, and are usually employed In carrying bills and messages to the House of Commons. They are not summoned by writ, but one of them attends each day, by rotation." Like the assistants, they also sit upon the woolsacks, but are never covered."'

Chief officers of The chief officers of the upper house are the clerk of the Parliaments (whose office is executed by the first and second clerks assistant), the gentleman and yeoman usher of the black rod, and the serjeant-at-arms. The clerks assistant and the reading clerk attend at the table, and take minutes of all the proceedings, orders, and judgments

Lords' Minutes of the housc. Thesc are published daily as the " Minutes of the Proceedings," and they are printed, in a corrected and enlarged form, as the Lords' Journals, after being examined " by the sub-committees for privileges and perusal of the Journal Book."

' 1 Lords' J. 586.606, 26th Jan., 20th March 1563. West, Inq. 48.

2 Lords' S. O. No. 4. 3 See Chapters XVI. and XVIIL

Macq. 66, s Lords' S. O. No. 5.

6 " 23d May 1678. Ordered that, for the future, the said lords' sub-committees are hereby empowered to meet after every session for examining of so much of tlie Journal Book as shall be left unexamined at the time of the ending of such session, without any furtiier order." Lords' S. O. No. 58.

The gentleman usher of the black rod is appointed by Black rod. letters patent from the Crown, and he, or his deputy, the yeoman usher, is sent to desire the attendance of the commons in the House of Peers when the royal assent is given to bills by the Queen or the lords commissioners, and on other occasions. He executes orders for the commitment of parties guilty of breaches of privilege and contempt, and assists at the introduction of peers, and other ceremonies.

The serjeant-at-arms is also appointed by the Crown. Serjeaut-at-He attends the lord chancellor with the mace, and executes the orders of the house for the attachment of delinquents, when they are in the country. He is, however, the officer of the lord chancellor rather than of the house.

The chief officers of the House of Commons are, the Chief officers of clerk of the house, the first and second clerks assistant, and the serjeant-at-arms. The clerk of the house is appointed Clerk of the by the Crown for life, by letters patent, in which he is styled " under clerk of the Parliaments, to attend upon the commons." He is sworn before the lord chancellor, on entering upon his office, "to make true entries, remembrances, and journals of the things done and passed in the House of Commons;" he signs all orders of the house, endorses the bills, and reads whatever is required to be read in the house. He has the custody of all records or other documents," and is responsible for the regulation of all matters connected with the business of the house, in the several official departments under his control. The clerks assistant sit at the table of the house, on the left hand of the clerk.

The short entries of the proceedings of the house, which votes and ivo-are made by the clerks at the table, are printed and dis- journals!

' 2 Hats. 255. London Gazette, 1st October 1850. See also 3 Com. J. 54. 57.

= 1 Com. J. 30G; 6 lb. 542; 17 lb. 724, c.

tributed every day, and are entitled, the " Votes and Proceedings." From these the Journal is afterwards prepared, in which the entries are made at greater length, and with the forms more distinctly pointed out. These records are confined to the votes and proceedings of the house, without any reference to the debates. The earlier volumes of the Journals contain short notes of speeches, which the clerk had made, without the authority of the house; but all the later volumes record nothing but the res gestcb. It was formerly the practice for a committee " to survey the Clerk's Book every Saturday,"- and to be entnisted with a certain discretion in revising the entries; but now the votes are prepared on the responsibility of the clerk; and after "being first perused by Mr. Speaker," are printed for the use of members, and for general circulation. But no person may print them, who is not authorised by the speaker. Lords' A few words may here be interposed in regard to the

Journals.

legal character of the Journals of the two houses. The Journals of the House of Lords' have always been held to be public records. They were formerly "recorded every day on rolls of parchment," and in 1621 it was ordered that the Journals of the House of Commons " shall be reviewed and recorded on rolls of parchment." But this practice has long since been discontinued by the lords, and does not appear to have been adopted by the commons." All persons may have access to the commons' Journals, in the same manner as to the Journals of the other house.

1 Com. J. 885; 2 lb. 12. 42. For a history of the early Journals, see 24Coni. J. 2G2.

2 1 Com. J. G73. 3 iij (37(3 (333 j 2 lb. 42.

Sess. order since 1G80. 9 Com. J. 043.

Befi)re the commencement of the Lords' Journals the proceedings of Tarlianient were recorded in the Rolls of Parliament, A. D. 1278-1G03,; Edward I. to 19 Henry VII. The Lords' Journals commence in lo09, 1 lJenry VIII.

2 Oxford Debates, 22. 1 Com. J. 608. 3 Hats. 37.

The Journals of the House of Commons however, arc Commons' not regarded as records, although their claim to that character is upheld by weighty considerations.

Sir Edward Coke speaks of " the book of the clerk of the House of Commons, which is a record, as it is affirmed by Act of Parliament, in anno 6 Hen. VIIL, c. 16."

This is the statute already alluded to, which prohibits the departure of any member of the House of Commons " except he have license," c.; " and the same license be entered of record in the book of the clerk of the Parliament appointed or to be appointed for the commons' house." This entry was obviously intended to be a legal record, to be given in evidence in any claim for wages; from the payment of which the counties, cities, and boroughs were discharged in case of the unauthorised departure of their members. The Clerk's Book and the Journals were unquestionably the same, and the latter are still prepared from the former. A license was granted by a vote of the house, and necessarily formed part of its ordinary proceedings, which were entered at the same time and by the same person, in the Clerk's Book; and the words of the statute raise no inference that the entry of a license was distinguishable, in law, from the other entries in the same book. This statute was urged by the commons in 1606, at a conference with the lords, as evidence in support of their claim to be a court of record, to which the lords took no distinct objection, though they answered that " in all points they were not satisfied."

' The Journals of the Commons commence in 1547, 1 Edw., VI.; and, with the exception of a short period during the reign of Elizabeth, are complete to the present time.

Jones V. Randall, Cowp. 17. Per Lord JMansfield: " Formerly a doubt was entertained whether the minutes of the House of Commons were admissible, because it is not a court of record; but the Journals of the House of Lords Lave always been admitted, even iu criminal cases." 1 Starkie on Ev. 109. 2 Fhil. Amos, 591.

"4th lust. 23. "" 1 Com. J. 1G8. 349.

Given in evi The Only point of importance in reference to the question, is that of the legal effect of the Journals as evidence in a court of law, and no difference is then perceptible in respect to the Journals of either house. An unstamped copy of the minutes of the reversal of a judgment in the House of Lords, as entered in the Journals, is evidence of the reversal, like the record of a judgment in another court. The Journals of that house would also be evidence of a proceeding in Parliament having taken place, as that an address had been presented to the king, and his answer; and in certain cases they might be admitted as evidence of other facts, as in the cause just cited, that there had been differences between the king of England and the king of Spain. But, undoubtedly, a resolution of the House of Lords, affirming a particvilar fact, would not be admitted as evidence of the fact itself, although the Journals would be evidence of such a resolution having been agreed to.

In the same manner, a copy of the Journals of the House of Commons has constantly been admitted as evidence of a proceeding in that house;" but a resolution would not be evidence of a fact. Thus, upon the indictment of Titus Oates for perjury, a resolution of the House of Commons, alleging the existence of a Popish plot, was rejected as evidence of that fact; and although that trial must be held of doubtful authority, and the reasons assigned for the rejection of the evidence were not sound, yet upon general principles the determination of this matter was right. As evidence, therefore, the Journals of the two houses stand upon the same grounds; they are good evidence of proceedings in Parhament, but are not conclusive of facts alleged by either house, unless they be within their imme- ' Jones V. Randall, Cowp. 17.

Francklin's case, 17 Howell, St. Tr. 635, G36.

3 Doug. 593. Cowp. 17. Str. 126. See also Bruyeres v. Ilalcomb, 6 Nev. M. (K. B.) 149. 3 Adol, Ell. 381.

R. V. Oates, 10 Howell, St. Tr. 1105-1107.

diate jurisdiction. Thus a resolution might be agreed to by either house, that certain parties had been guilty of bribery; but in a prosecution for that offence, such a resolution would not be admitted as evidence of the fact, although in both cases it may have been founded upon evidence taken upon oath. But the reversal of a judgment by the lords, and the proceedings of the commons upon a controverted election, would be equally proved by their respective Journals. In the same manner, a resolution of either house as entered in the Journals, that a party had been guilty of a breach of privilege, would be conclusive evidence of the fact that the party had been adjudged by the house to be guilty of such offence. And indeed, upon all other points, except, perhaps, when the House of Lords is sitting in its judicial capacity, the Journals of the two houses cannot be viewed as differing in character. Every vote of either house upon a bill is of equal force: in legislation their jurisdiction is identically the same; they are equally constituent parts of the High Court of Parliament, and whatever is done in either house is, in law, a proceeding in Parliament, and an act of that high court at large. There are bills also of a strictly judicial character, in which the commons have equal voice with the lords. Acts of attainder, of pains and penalties, of grace or pardon, and of divorce a vinculo matrimonii require the sanction of the commons to become law. The endorsement of these bills by the clerk of the house is evidence of their agreement, by whom an entry is made at the same time in the Journal Book, to record the same proceeding. To use the words of Sir Edward Coke, ' the lords in their house have power of judicature, and the commons in their house have power of judicature, and both houses together have power of judicature." Their legislative and judicial functions are sometimes merged; at one sitting they constantly exercise both functions ' 4th Inst. 23.

cated 204 JOURNALS GIVEN IN EVIDENCE.

separately, and their proceedings upon both are entered by their sworn officers in the same form and in the same page of one book. If the judicature of the lords be held to constitute them a court of record, and their Journals a public record; the judicature of the commons in Parliament, it may be argued, would constitute them equally a court of record, and would also give to their Journals the same character as a public record. How autl. enti- When the Journals of the House of Lords are required as evidence, a party may have a copy or extract, authenticated by the signature of the assistant clerk of the Parhaments, which it may be as well that he should be able to prove on oath, by having been personally present when the copy was signed by that officer; and in some cases the lords have allowed an officer of their house to attend a trial with the original Journal. In the commons it is usual for an officer of the house to attend with the printed Journal, when a cause is tried in London; but when it is tried at the assizes, or at a distance, a party may either obtain from the Journal Office a copy of the entries required, without the signature of any officer, and swear himself that it is a true copy;

or, with the permission of the speaker or the house, he may secure the attendance of an officer with the printed Journal; or with extracts which he certifies to be true copies; or, if necessary, with the original manuscript Journal Book. The printed Journals were formerly not admitted by the courts as evidence; but by Act 8 9 Vict., c. 113, s. 3, it is enacted that all copies of the Journals of either House of Parliament purporting to be printed by the printers to either House of Parliament, or by any or either of them, shall be admitted as evidence thereof by all courts, judges, justices, and others, without ' Lords' Minutes, 13th and 15th February 1844. 2 99 Com. J. 1-28; 100 lb. 114.

See Lord Melville's case, 29 Howell, St. Tr. G83. R. v. Lord G. Gordon, 2 Doug. 593.

arms.

SERJEANT-AT-ARMS. 205 any proof being given that such copies were so printed. This Act, however, does not extend to Scotland.

This notice with regard to the Journals has necessarily interrupted the account of the chief officers of the House of Commons, to which it is now time to return.

The serjeant-at-arms is the last officer immediately con- Serjeant-at-nected with the proceedings of the house, to whom reference need be made. He is appointed by the Crown, under a warrant from the lord chamberlain, and by patent under the great seal, "to attend upon her Majesty's person when there is no Parliament; and, at the time of every Parliament, to attend upon the speaker of the House of Commons." But after his appointment he is the servant of the house, and may be removed for misconduct. On the 2d June 1675, the house committed Sir James Norfolke to the Tower, for " betraying his trust," and addressed the Crown to appoint another serjeant-at-arms " in his stead." His duties are, to attend the speaker with the mace on entering and leaving the house, or going to the House of Lords, or attending her Majesty with addresses; to keep clear the gangway at the bar and below it; to take strangers into custody who are irregularly admitted into the house, or who misconduct themselves; to give orders to the doorkeepers and other officers under him, for the locking of all doors upon a division; to introduce peers or judges attending within the bar, and messengers from the lords; to attend the sheriffs of London at the bar, on presenting petitions; to bring to the bar, with the mace, prisoners to be reprimanded by the house, or persons in custody to be examined as witnesses. For the better execution of these duties he has a chair close to the bar of the house, and is assisted by a deputy serjeant. Out of the house he is entrusted with the execution of all warrants for the commitment of persons ordered into cus- ' Officers and usages of the hnusc, MS. 1805. 9 Com. J. 351.

Admission of strangers.

Lords.

Commons.

tody by the house; and for removing them to the Tower or Newgate, or retaining them in his own custody. He maintains order in the lobby and passages of the house, and gives notice to all committees when the house is going to prayers. He has the appointment and supervision of various officers in his department; and, as housekeeper of the house, has charge of all its committee rooms and other buildings, during the sitting of Parliament.

By the ancient custom of Parliament, and by orders of both houses, strangers are not to be admitted while the houses are sitting.

It is ordered by the lords,

"That for the future no person shall be in any part of the house during the sitting of the house, except lords of Parliament and peers of the United Kingdom, not being members of the House of Commons, and heirs apparent of such peers or of peeresses of the United Kingdom in their own right, and such other persons as attend this house as assistants."'

Strangers, however, are regularly admitted below the bar, and in the galleries; but the standing order may, at any time, be suspended.

By the standing orders of the commons, the serjeant-at-arms is directed,

"From time to time to take into his custody any stranger or strangers that he shall see, or who may be reported to him to be in any part of the house or gallery appropriated to the members of this house, and also any stranger who, having been admitted into any other part of the house or gallery, shall misconduct himself, or shall not withdraw when strangers are directed to withdraw, while the house, or any committee of the whole house, is sitting; and that no person, so taken into custody, be discharged out of custody without the special order of the house;" and it is also ordered, ' That no member of this house do presume to bring any stranger into any part of the house or gallery appropriated to the members of this house, while the house, or a committee of the whole house, is sitting.

' Lords' S. O. No. 12.

2 Orders 5th Feb. 1845, made Standing Orders; and see 15 Com. J. 527, from wliich it appears that members had been prevented from sitting by the pressure of strangers.

The exclusion of strangers can at any time be enforced without an order of the house; for, on a member taking notice of their presence, the speaker is obhged, by ancient usage, to order them to withdraw without putting a question; 1 and, upon divisions of the house, the speaker orders them to withdraw immediately, and the messengers, under the orders of the serjeant, see that they are excluded. They are present upon sufferance, and upon no other ground has their presence ever been recognised.

The only other matters connected with the meeting and sitting of the two houses, which will not be more particularly described elsewhere, are the forms observed on the prorogation of Parliament. Some of these, also, will be adverted to again; but a general description of the ceremony of prorogation will bring this chapter to a close.

If, after a dissolution, the new Parliament be prorogued Parliament . 1 T 1-I n 1 proionjued I)e- to any lurtner day than was appomted tor its meeting by fore its first the writ of summons, it is prorogued by writ directed to both the houses. On the day first appointed for the meeting of Parliament, the commons proceed directly to the door of the House of Lords, without going into tlieir own house, or expecting any message from the lords. They are admitted by the usher of the black rod to the bar, and stand there uncovered, while the lords remain sitting and covered. The lord chancellor then declares that a writ has been issued under the great seal for proroguing the Parliament; " which he doth standing up uncovered, in respect he speaks to the lords as well as to the commons:" and, after the writ is read, the Parliament stands prorogued by virtue of the writ, without further formality.

' 77 Hans. Deb., 31 Series, 138 (Mr. Speaker's explanation of the rule;). On the 18th imay 1849 a member took notice tliat strangers were present, who were ordered to withdraw. The doors were accordingly closed for upwards of two hours, and no report of the debates during that time appeared iu the newspapers. Strangers were re-admitted without any order of the speaker.

Lords' S. O. No. 7. 59 Lords' J. 3. 82 Com. J. 4. 2 Hats. 328.

meetint.

After its first But the form is different in the prorogation of Parlia- ineetiiig. meeting. If her Majesty attend in person to prorogue Parhament at the end of the session, the same ceremonies are observed as at the opening of Parliament: the attendance of the commons in the House of Peers is commanded; and on their arrival at the bar, the speaker addresses her Majesty, on presenting the supply bills, and adverts to the most important measures that have occupied the attention of Parliament during the session. The royal assent is then given to the bills which are awaiting that sanction, and her Majesty reads her speech to both Houses of Parliament; after which, the lord chancellor, having received directions from her Majesty for that purpose, addresses both houses in this manner, "My lords and gentlemen, it is her Majesty's royal will and pleasure that this Parliament be prorogued to" a certain day, " to be then here holden; and this Parliament is accordingly prorogued," c. When her Majesty is not present at the end of the session. Parliament is prorogued by a commission under the great seal, directed to certain peers, who, by virtue of their commission, prorogue the Parliament. The attendance of the commons is desired in the House of Peers; and, on their coming, with their speaker, the lord chancellor states to both houses, that her Majesty, not thinking fit to be personally present, has caused a commission to be issued under the great seal, for giving the royal assent to bills. The commission is then read, and the speaker, loithout any speech, delivers the money bills to the clerk assistant of the House of Lords, who comes to the bar to receive them. The royal assent is signified to the bills in the usual manner; after which the lord chancellor, in pursuance of her Majesty's commands, reads the royal speech to both houses. The commission for proroguing the Parliament is next read by the ' See Chajiter XXL, Supply. = See Chapter XVIIL clerk, and the lord chancellor, by virtue of that commission, prorogues the Parliament accordingly. On further prorogations the Queen never attends personally; and, the speaker being in the country, the commons are represented at the bar of the House of Lords by their clerk assistant, or second clerk assistant;' the commission is read, and the lord chancellor prorogues the Parliament in the usual manner. Public notice of such prorogations is also given by proclamation in the Gazette, in which, if it be intended that Parliament shall sit " for dispatch of business," it is stated that it will "sit for the dispatch of divers urgent and important affairs."

CHAPTER VIIL

MOTIONS AND QUESTIONS. NOTICES OF MOTIONS. QUESTIONS MOVED AND SECONDED. MOTIONS W ITHDRAWN. QUESTIONS SUPERSEDED BY ADJOURNMENT; OR BY READ-DJG THE ORDERS OF THE DAY. PREVIOUS

QUESTIONS. NEW QUESTIONS SUBSTITUTED BY AMENDMENT. COMPLI-CATED QUESTIONS. QUESTIONS PUT.

Every matter is determined in both houses, upon ques- Questions a tions put by the speaker, and resolved in the affirmative proceeding, or negative, as the case may be. As a question must thus form part of every proceeding, it is of the first importance that good rules should prevail for stating the question clearly, and for enabling the house to decide upon it.

The speaker formerly attended. The earliest instance of the clerk attending was in 1672 (9 Com. J. 244); and of the clerk assistant, in 1700 (15 lb. 199).

' Hatsell states that there should be forty days' notice of a meeting of parliament for dispatch of business (vol. ii. 330); but although this is the ordinary custom, it cannot conveniently be observed on all occasions. A new parliament was prorogued by writ from lltli to 18th November 1S47, and the proclamution appeared on the SOth October.

Notices of mo' tions.

However simple such rules may be, the complexity of many questions, and the variety of opinions entertained by members, must often make it difficult to apply them. Very few general rules have been entered in the Journals of either house; but the practice of Parliament has established certain forms of procedure, which numerous precedents rarely fail to make intelligible.

Every member is entitled to propose a question, which is called " moving the house," or, more commonly, " making a motion." But in order to give the house due notice of his intention, and to secure an opportunity of being heard, it is customary to state the form of his motion on a previous day, and to have it entered in the Order Book or Notice

House of Lords. Paper. In the House of Lords, the pressure of business is not so great as to require any strict rules in regard to notices; but in order to apportion the public business according to the convenience of the house, it is usual for

House of Com- the House of Commons to set apart certain days for considering the "orders of the day," (or matters which the house have already agreed to consider on a particular day), and to reserve other days for original motions. For several years it has been the practice to agree to the following sessional resolutions, viz.:

"That in the present session of Parliament, all orders of the day set down in the Order Book for Mondays, Wednesdays, and Fridays, shall be disposed of before the house will proceed upon any motions of which notices shall have been given.

"That the house do meet every Wednesday, at twelve o'clock at noon, for private business, petitions, orders of the day, and notices of motions, and do continue to sit until six o'clock, unless previously adjourned.

"That when such business has been disposed of, or at six o'clock precisely, notwithstanding there may be business under discussion, Mr. Speaker do adjourn the house, without putting any question.

"That whenever the house shall be in committee on Wednesday, at six o'clock, the chairman do immediately report progress, and Mr. Speaker do resume the chair, and adjourn the house, without putting any question.

Orders of the day.

Sittings on Wednesday.

"That the business under discussion, and any business not disposed of at the time of such adjournment, do stand as orders of the day, for the next day on whicli the house shall sit."

Subject to this regulation, it was formerly the practice Restriction in to allow members to give notices for any day, however '" " " distant; but by another sessional resolution, it is now provided,

"That no notice shall be given beyond the period which shall include the four days next following on which notices are entitled to precedence, due allowance being made for any intervening adjournment of the house, and the period being in that case so far extended as to include four notice days falling during the sitting of the house."

The Order Book cannot, therefore, be occupied in advance, with notices, for a longer period than a fortnight, when the house is sitting without interruption. On Monday a member may give notice for the Thursday week following, and on Tuesday for that day fortnight. No allowance is made for an intended adjournment, until the house has actually agreed upon it. Thus, for example, if it be intended to move the Easter adjournment on a Thursday until the Monday week following, a member cannot on the Tuesday preceding such adjournment give notice for a later day than that day fortnight; but immediately the house has agreed, at its rising, to adjourn for the holidays, notices may be given for the four next notice nights during the sitting of the house after the adjournment. Notices may be given for days on which orders of the day are allowed precedence, as well as for notice days; but as the orders usually occupy the greater part of the night, notices of importance are rarely given for such days, unless it has been agreed that the orders shall be postponed.

It is also resolved,

"That the orders of the day be disposed of in the order in which Precedence of they stand upon the paper, the right being reserved to her Majesty's ministers of placing government orders at the head of ' Motion on foreign policy, 24th June 1850.

the list, in the rotation in which they are to be taken on the daj-s on which government bills have precedence."' Orders of the " That at the time fixed for the commencement of public busi- ay rea. ness, on days on which orders have precedence of notices of motions, and after the notices of motions have been disposed of on all other days, Mr. Speaker do direct the clerk at the table to read the orders of the day without any question being put."

So soon as an order of the day has been read, the business to which it relates is to be immediately proceeded with, and the speaker, therefore, will not permit any question to be put to a minister or other member, unless it relate to such order of the day. And when the order for resuming an adjourned debate on the second reading of a bill has been read, and the question again proposed, the speaker has not permitted petitions to be presented relating to such bill, as the adjoui' ued debate is then, in fact, resumed. Notices, how When a member desires to give notice of a motion, he should first examine the Order Book, or the printed lists of notices and orders of the day for the ensuing week, which are printed with the Votes every Saturday morning. When he has fixed upon the most convenient day, he should be present at the meeting of the house; and immediately after prayers, when the house has been made, he may enter his name on the Notice Paper, which is placed upon the table. Each name upon this paper is numbered; and when the speaker calls on the notices, at about half-past four o'clock, the clerk puts the numbers into a glass, and draws them out one by one. As each number is drawn, the name of the member to which it is attached in the Notice Paper is called. Each member in his turn, then rises and reads the notice he is desirous of giving, and afterwards takes it to the table, and delivers it, fairly given.

' The origin of Government nights may probably be traced to the following order, 15th November 1670: That Mondays and Fridays be appointed for the only sitting of committees to whom public bills are committed; and that no private committee do sit on the said days." 9 Com. J. 164. See also 1 lb. 523.640 (Committee of Grievances, 1621).

= 27th Feb. 1849; Dublin Consolidation Waterworks Bill, written out, and with the day named, to the second clerk assistant, who enters It in the Order Book; but only one notice may be given by a member until the other names upon the list have been called over. It is not necessary that the notice should comprise all the Avords of the intended motion; but if the subject only be stated in the first instance, the question, precisely as it is intended to be proposed, should be given in the day before that on which it stands in the Order Book, so that it shall be printed at length in the Votes of the following morning. But it is not necessary to give notice of the express terms of resolutions intended to be proposed in committee of the whole house. Should a member desire to change the day, after he has given his notice, he must repeat it for a more distant day, since it has been declared irregular to fix an earlier day than that originally proposed in the house.- One member may give notice for another not present at the time, by putting his name upon the list, and answering for him when his name is called at the ballot.

No positive rule has been laid down as to the time which must elapse between the notice and the motion; but the interval is generally extended in proportion to the importance of the subject. Notices of motions for leave to bring in bills of trifling interest, or for other matters to which no opposition is threatened, are constantly given the night before that on which they are intended to be submitted to the house; and there is a separate notice paper for unopposed returns, for which no ballot is taken, and motions entered upon it may be brought forward whenever a convenient opportunity arises. For the purpose of gaining precedence, the more usual mode and time for giving notices, are those already described; yet it is competent for a member to give a notice at a later hour, ' Navigation laws, 15th May 1848. ' Mirror of Parliament, 1835, p. 275. 3 Hansard's Debates, ittu April 1843.

Motions without notice.

Questions of privilege, c.

Leave to make motions.

provided he docs not interrupt the course of business, as set down in the Order Book.

An unopposed motion can be brought on by consent of the house, without any previous notice; but if any member should object it cannot be pressed. Questions of privilege, also, and other matters suddenly arising, may be considered without previous notice; and the former take precedence, not only of other motions, but of all orders of the day. But in order to entitle a question of privilege to precedence, it must refer to some matter which has recently arisen, and of which no notice has, therefore, been given, and which directly concerns the piivileges of the house. It is usual to give precedence, as a matter of courtesy, to a motion for a vote of thanks; but care should be taken as to the proper time for claiming priority, lest all the motions should become entitled to the same privilege. On the 12th February 1844, the orders of the day had precedence; and after the speaker had put the question for reading the first order of the day, and the house had agreed to it. Sir Robert Peel rose to move the thanks of the house to Sir Charles Napier, on account of the military operations in Sinde. It was then necessary to read each order of the day in succession, and defer it; and after the vote of thanks had been agreed to, the notices of motions following that of Sir Robert Peel were called on in preference to the orders of the day, which had been deferred expressly for the vote of thanks. This could not be avoided, as all the orders of the day had been disposed of, and the notices of motion called on, which it was necessary to go through before the house could revert to the orders of the day. This consequence would have been avoided, if Sir R. Peel had risen before any order of the day had been read.

Entries are occasionally found in the Journals of leave ' 12th May 1848, interference of a peer with the election for Stamford; 98 Hans. Deb. N. S. 931. 22a May 1848, Sligo election compromise, 98 Hans. Deb. N. S. 1236. = E. cj. 24th April 1849.

being given to make a motion. In these cases, it appears, that all the orders of the day had been previously disposed of; and that the house allowed members to bring on motions which they had not entitled themselves to make, according to the ordinary regulations. But as unopposed motions only can be made without previous notice, they are now offered with the general assent of the house, and without any formal leave being given.

As motions for which notices have been given need not be actually made when the time arrives, the Order Book is sometimes used for the expression of opinions not intended to be ultimately proposed for adoption. This is a deviation from the true object of the Order Book; but it is not a practical evil of much importance, nor is there, perhaps, any remedy for it: but in resorting to this practice, members Notices ex-must be careful, lest they give offence to the house by unbecoming expressions; for the notice maj, for such a cause, be expunged from the Notice Paper."- If a notice of motion be dropped, by the adjournment of the Dropped house, before it has been disposed of, it is usually renewed 'i' '-and j)ut down in the Notice Paper for some other day. If, however, it contain no matter that is debateable, a member is permitted to make the motion on the next sitting day, when the notices of motions are read; otherwise it will be put off until all the other notices for the day have been disposed of, when it will probably be too late for the member to bring on his motion.

When a member is at liberty to make a motion, he may inlotions made. speak in its favour, before he actually proposes it; but a speech is only allowed upon the understanding, 1st, that he speaks to the question; and, 2dly, that he concludes by 75 Com. J. 155,156; 85 lb. 107; 86 lb. 857. There was an order of the house, 25th November 1095, that no new motion be made after one o'clock. This probably occasioned the practice of giving leave to make motions, although the order has long since been inapplicable to modem usage and regulations. See also 1 Com. J. 45.

' 90 Com. J. 435. = 99 Hans. Deb., 3d Series, 1290.

Questions moved and seconded.

Motions not seconded.

Proposed by tlie spealier.

When debate arises.

Motions by leave withdrawn.

Questions superseded.

proposing Ills motion formally. In the upper house, any lord may submit a motion for the decision of their lordships without a seconder; but in the commons, after the motion has been made, it must be seconded by another member; otherwise it is immediately dropped, and all further debate should, be discontinued, as no question is before the house. When a motion is not seconded, no entry appears in the Votes, as the house is not put in possession of it, and res gestae only are entered.

In the lords, when a motion has been made, a question is proposed " that that motion be agreed to;" but in the commons, when the motion has been seconded, it merges in the question, which is then proposed by the speaker to the house, and read by him; after which the house are said to be in possession of the question, and must dispose of it in one way or another, before they can proceed with any other business. At this stage of the proceeding the debate upon the question arises in both houses. If the entire question be objected to, it is opposed in debate; but no amendment or form of motion is necessary for its negation; for when the debate is at an end, the speaker puts the question, and it is resolved simply in the affirmative or negative. The precise mode in which the determination of the house is expressed and collected, will be explained hereafter.

It may happen, however, that it is desired by members to avoid any distinct expression of opinion; in which case it is competent for the majority of the house to evade the question in various ways; but the member who proposed Jt, can only withdraw it by leave of the house, granted without any negative voice.

The modes of evading or superseding a question are, 1, by adjournment of the house; 2, by motion " that the

But see Debates, 8th February 1844. See infra, p. 224, and Chapter XII.

orders of the day be read;" 3, by moving the previous question; and 4, by amendment.

1. In the midst of the debate upon a question, any By adjoum-member may move " that this house do noic adjourn," "' " " not by way of amendment to the original question, but as a distinct question, which interrupt- and supersedes that already under consideration. If this second question be resolved in the affirmative, the original question is superseded; the house must immediately adjourn, and all the business for that day is at an end. The motion for adjournment, in order to supersede a question, must be simply that the l ouse do now adjourn; it is not allowable to move that the house do adjourn to any future time specified; nor to move an amendment to that effect, to the question of adjournment. The house may also be suddenly adjourned by notice being taken that 40 members ai'e not present, and an adjournment caused

in that manner, has the eflfect of superseding a question in the same way as a formal question to adjourn, when put and carried. In either case the original question is so entirely superseded, that if it has not yet been proposed to the house by the speaker, it is not even entered in the Votes, as the house was not fully in possession of the question before the adjournment.

If a motion for adjournment be negatived, it may not Motions for be proposed again without some intermediate proceeding; iio ise ncf the and, in order to avoid any infringement of this rule, it is debate, a common practice for those who desire to avoid a decision upon the original question, on that day, to move alternately that " this house do now adjourn," and " that the debate be now adjourned." The latter motion, if carried, merely defers the decision of the house, while the former, as already explained, supersedes the question altogether: yet members who only desire to enforce the continuance of the debate on another day, often vote ' 2 Hats. 113-115, for an adjournment of the house, which, if carried, would supersede the question which they are prepared to support. This distinction should always be borne in mind, lest a result should follow that is widely different from that anticipated. Suppose a question to be opposed by a majority, and that the minority are anxious for an adjournment of the debate; but that on the failure of a question proposed by them to that effect, they vote for an adjournment of the house: the majority have only to vote with them and carry the adjournment, when the obnoxious question is disposed of at once, and its supporters have themselves contributed to its defeat. By reading the 2. On a day upou which motions have precedence, a or ers o e motion, " that the orders of the day be now read," is also permitted to interrupt the debate upon a question; and, if put by the speaker and carried in the affirmative, the house must proceed with the orders of the day immediately, and the original question is thus superseded. A motion for reading a particular order of the day, however, will not be permitted to interrupt a debate; and, when the house are actually engaged upon one of the orders of the day, a motion for reading the orders of the day is not admissible, as the house are already doing that which the motion, if carried, would oblige them to do. Previous ques- 3. The previous question is an ingenious method of avoiding a vote upon any question that has been proposed, but its technical name does little to elucidate its operation. When there is no debate, or after a debate is closed, the speaker puts the question, as a matter of course, without any direction from the house; but, by a motion for the previous question, this act of the speaker may be intercepted and forbidden. The words of this motion are, " that this question be now put;" and those who wish to avoid the ' An instance of this occurred on the 23d March 1818, on a motion relative to the game laws; 97 Hans. Deb.; 3d Series, 963.

putting of the original question, vote against the previous (or second) question; and, if it be resolved in the negative, the speaker is prevented from putting the original question, as the house have refused to allow it to be put. It may, however, be brought forward again on another day, as the negation of the previous question merely binds the speaker not to put the main question at that time. If the previous question be put, and resolved in the aflsrmative, no words can be added to or taken from the main question by amendment; nor is any further debate allowed, or motion for adjournment, before the question is put, as the house have resolved that the question be now put, and it must accordingly be put at once to the vote. In reference to this proceeding, it may be remarked, that according to the strict rule of debate, each member should speak directly to the question before the house; and, supposing this to be observed, the debate upon the previous question would be hmited to the propriety of putting the question noiv, or at a future time; but, practically, the main question is discussed throughout. If the rule were not evaded in this manner, the main question would be altogether excluded from discussion, merely because another question had been interposed; although, by affirming the previous question, the house would have agreed that the main question was a proper one to have been offered for their decision.

The last two questions, viz. for reading the orders of the day, and the previous question, may both be superseded by a motion for adjournment; for the latter may be made at any time (except, as already stated, when the previous question has been resolved in the affirmative), and must always be determined before other business can be proceeded with. The debate upon the previous question may also be adjourned; as there is no rule or practice which assigns a limit to a debate, even when the nature of the question would ' 2 Hats. 122 n. Lex Pari. 292.

seem to require a present determination. But when a motion has been made for reading the orders of the day, in order to supersede a question, the house will not afterwards entertain a motion for the previous question; as the former motion was itself in the nature of a previous question. By amend 4. The general practice in regard to amendments will be explained in the next chapter; but here such amendments only need be mentioned as are Intended to evade an expression of opinion upon the main question, by entirely altering its meaning and object. This may be effected by moving the omission of all the words of the question, after the word " that" at the beginning, and by the substitution of other words of a different import. If this amendment be agreed to by the house, it is clear that no opinion is expressed directly upon tlie main question, because it is determined that the original words " shall not stand part of the question;" and the sense of the house is afterwards taken directly upon the substituted words, or practically ujjon a new question. There are many precedents of this mode of dealing with a question; but the best known in parliamentary history are those relating to Mr. Pitt's administration, and the peace of Amiens, in 1802. On the 7th May 1802, a motion was made in the commons for an address, " expressing the thanks of this house to his Majesty for having been pleased to remove the Eight Hon. W. Pitt from his councils;" upon which an amendment was proposed and carried, which left out all the words after the first, and substituted others in direct opposition to them. Not only was the sense of the original question entirely altered by this amendment, but a new question was substituted, in which the whole policy of Mr. Pitt was commended. Immediately afterwards an address was moved in both Houses of Parliament, condemning the 24 Com. J. 650; 30 lb. 70; 52 lb. 203. Protection of Life (Ireland) Bill, 30th March 1846. Navigation Laws, 29th May 1848. ' 57 Com. J. 419. 36 Hans. Pari. Hist. 598-654.

treaty of Amiens, in a long statement of facts and arguments. In each house an amendment was moved and carried, by which all the declamation in the proposed address was omitted, and a new address resolved upon, by which Parliament was made to justify the treaty.

This practice has often been objected to as unfair, and never with greater force than on these occasions. It is natural for one party, commencing an attack upon another, to be discomfited by its recoil upon themselves, and to express their vexation at such a result; but the weaker party must always anticipate defeat in one form or another. If no amendment be moved, the majority can negative the question itself, and affirm another in opposition to the opinions of the minority. On the very occasion already mentioned, of the 7th May 1802, after the address of thanks for the removal of Mr. Pitt had been defeated by an amendment, a distinct question was proposed and carried by the victorious party, "That the Eight Hon. W. Pitt has rendered great and important services to his country, and especially deserves the gratitude of this house." Thus, if no amendment had been moved, the position of Mr. Pitt's opponents would have been but little improved, as the majority could have affirmed or denied whatever they pleased. It is in debate alone that a minority can hope to compete with a majority: the forms of the house can ultimately assist neither party; but, so far as they offer any intermediate advantage, the minority have the greatest protection in forms, while the majority are ' met by obstructions to the exercise of their will.

These are the four modes by wlilch a question may be Questions intentionally avoided or superseded; but a question is also " ' ""P '-liable to casual interruption and postponement from other causes; as, by a matter of privilege, words of heat between members in debate, a question of order, a message from ' 57 Com. J. 450. 43 Lords' J. G03.30 Hans. Pari. Hist. 686.

By reading Acts, papers, c.

Candles.

Complicated questiouo.

the other house or a motion for reading an Act of Parliament, an entry in the Journal, or other public document. The rule, by which such documents are permitted to be read, though not absolutely without recognition in modern times, is so far restrained by more recent regulations with regard to motions and orders of the day, that it is almost obsolete, and a member would scarcely be permitted to avail himself of it except for the purpose of reading some document strictly relevant to the question under discussion. These proceedings, however, may obstruct and delay the decision of a question, but do not alter its position before the house; for, directly they are disposed of, the debate is resumed at the point at which it was interrupted. In the House of Commons, another interruption was sometimes caused by moving that candles be brought in; but, by a standing order of the 6th February 1717, it was ordered,

"That when the house, or any committee of the whole house, shall be sitting, and daylight be shut in, the serjeant-at-arms attending this house do take care that candles be brought in, without any particular order for that jjurpose."' If a question be complicated, the house may order it to be divided, so that each part may be determined separately." A right has been claimed, in both houses, for an individual member to insist upon the division of a complicated question; but it has not been recognised, nor can it be reasonable to allow it, because, 1st, the house might not think the question complicated; and, 2dly, the member objecting to its complexity, may move its separation by amendments. It is probable that this claim arose out of the ancient custom by which the framing of a question was entrusted to the speaker, who prepared it during the debate. The member who had introduced the matter to the notice of the house would then very naturally have objected to a question which did not express his own opinion only, but ' 8 Com. J. 718.

2 lb. 43; 32 lb. 710.

included also the opinions of others. At that time also the subtle practice of amendments was less perfectly understood. But, as the house can order a question to be divided, it may be moved for that purpose, and it is difficult to state an objection to such a proceeding, although the ordinary practice has been to resort to amendments, instead of attempting the dissection of a question in another form. On the 29th January 1722, a protest was entered on the Journals of the lords, in which it was alleged " to be contrary to the nature and course of proceedings in Parliament, that a complicated question, consisting of matters of a different consideration, should be put, especially if objected to, that lords may not be deprived of the liberty of giving their judgments on the said different matters, as they think fit.""

When all preliminary debates and objections to a ques- Question put, tion are disposed of, the question must next be put, which is done in the following manner. The speaker, if necessary, takes a written or printed copy of the question, and states or reads it to the house, at length, beginning with " The question is, that." This form of putting the question is always observed, and precedes (or is supposed to precede) every vote of the house, however insignificant, except in cases where a vote is a formal direction, in virtue of previous orders; as where private bills having been read a second time, are referred to the Committee of Selection.

In the lords, when the question has been put, the ' 2Com. J. 43; 32 lb. 710; 33 lb. 89; 34 lb. 330; 35 lb. 217 (a question divided into five).

2 22 Lords' J. 73. See also 24 lb. 460, 407. 4 Timberland's Debates of tlie Lords, 392.

' " Order, that nothing pass by order of the house without a question, and that no order be without a question affirmative and negative." (1014.) 1 Com. J. 404. " Resolved, that wjien a general vote of the house concurreth in a motion propounded by the speaker witliout uny contradiction, there needeth no question." (1021.) lb. 030.

speaker says, "As many as are of that opinion say content," " and " as many as are of a contrary opinion say not content;' " and the respective parties exclaim " content " or " not content," according to their opinions. In the commons, the speaker takes the sense of the house by desiring that " as many as are of that opinion say aye,"" and " as many as are of the contrary opinion say ' no."" On account of these forms, the two parties are distinguished in the lords as "contents" and "not contents," and in the commons as the " ayes " and " noes." When each party have exclaimed according to their opinion, the speaker endeavours to judge, from the loudness and general character of the opposing exclamations, which party have the majority. As his judgment is not final, he expresses his opinion thus: " I think the (' contents' or) ' ayes' have it;" or, "I think the (not contents' or) ' noes' have it." If the house acquiesce in this decision, the question is said to be "resolved in the aflfirmative" or " negative," according to the supposed majority on either side; but if the party thus declared to be the minority, dispute the fact, they say " no; the ' contents' (or not contents ') the ' ayes' (or ' noes ') have it:" and the actual numbers must be counted, by means of what is called a division. Questions The question is stated distinctly by the speaker; but, in case it should not be heard, it will be stated acfain.

On the 15th April 1825, notice was taken that several members had not heard the question put, and the speaker desired any such members to signify the same; which being done, the question was again stated to them, and they declared themselves with the noes.

The form of putting the question and taking the vote was very similar in the Roman senate. The consul who presided there was accustomed to say, "Qui licec sentitis in hanc partem; qui alia omnia, in earn partem, ite, qua sentitis." Plinii Epistolse, lib-viii. ep. 14.

' See Chapter XII. 80 Com. J. 307.

again stated.

It must be well understood by members that their Voices on the opinion is to be collected from their voices in the house, " ' "' and not by a division; and if their voices and their votes should be at variance, the former will be held more binding than the latter.

On the report of the Holy rood Park Bill, August 10th, 1843, a member called out with the noes, " the noes have it," and thus forced that party to a division, although he was about to vote with the " ayes," and went out into the lobby with them. On his return, and before the numbers were declared by the tellers, Mr. Brotherton addressed the speaker, sitting and covered (the doors being closed), and claimed that the member's vote should be reckoned with the noes. The speaker put it to the member, whether he had said, " the noes have it; " to which he replied that he had, but without any intention of voting with the noes. The speaker, however, would not admit of his excuse, but ordered that his vote should be counted with the " noes," as he had declared himself with them in the house.

It would seem, however, that by the ancient rules of the house, a member was at liberty to change his opinion upon a question.

1st May 1G06, "A question moved, whether a man saying yea, may afterwards sit and change his opinion.

' A precedent remembered in 39 Eliz., of Mr. Morris, attorney of the Court of Wards, by Mr. Speaker, that changed his opinion.

"Misliked somewhat, it should be so; yet said that a man might change his opinion."

There is no entry of this proceeding in the Votes; but Mr. Brotherton, at the time, kindly supplied the precedent.

1 Com. J. 303.

Object and principle of an amendment.

Varions modes of amendment.

AMENDMENTS TO QUESTIONS; AND AMENDMENTS TO PROPOSED AMENDMENTS.

The object of an amendment is to effect such an alteration in a question as v ill enable certain members to vote in favour of it, who, without such alteration, must either have voted against it, or have abstained from voting. Without the power of amending a question, an assembly would have no means of expressing their opinions with consistency: they must either affirm a whole question, to parts of which they entertain objections, or negative a whole question, to parts of which they assent. In both cases a contradiction would ensue, if they afterwards expressed their true judgment in another form. In the first case supposed, they must deny what they had before affirmed; and in the second, they must affirm what they had before denied. Even if the last decision were binding, both opinions would have been voted, and probably entered in their minutes, and the contradiction would be manifest. The confusion which must arise from any irregularity in the mode of putting amendments, is often exemplified at public meetings, where fixed principles and rules are not observed; and it would be well for persons in the habit of presiding at meetings of any description, to make themselves familiar with the rules of Parliament, in regard to questions and amendments; which have been tested by long experience, and are found as simple and efficient in practice, as they are logical in principle.

An amendment may be made to a question, 1, by leaving out certain words; 2, by leaving out certain words in order to insert or add others; 3, by inserting or adding certain words. The proper time for moving an amend- ment is after a question has been proposed by the speaker, and before it has been put. Any member may then rise

Amendments 1 X-ii J. i J. i' without notice.

and propose an amendment, without havmg given notice or it; nor is another member, who may have given notice of an amendment, entitled to precedence on that account. The order and form in which the points arising out of amendments are determined, are as follow: 1. When the proposed amendment is, to leave out cer- To leave out tain words, the speaker first states the question, but instead of putting it, he adds, Since which it has been proposed, by way of amendment, to leave out the words," proposed to be omitted. He then puts the question, "That the words proposed to be left out stand part of the question." If that question be resolved in the affirmative, it shows that the house prefer the original question to the amendment, and the question, as first proposed, is put by the speaker. If, however, the question " That the words stand part of the question," be negatived, the question is put, with the omission of those words; unless another amendment be then moved, for the addition of other words.

2. "When the proposed amendment is to leave out certain To leave out words in order to insert or add others, the proceeding com- insert'or add mences in the same manner as the last. If the house re- '-solve " That the words proposed to be left out stand part of the question," the original question is put; but if they resolve that such words shall not stand part of the question, by negativing that proposition when put; the next question proposed is, that the words proposed to be substituted be inserted or added instead thereof. This latter question being resolved in the affirmative, the main question, so amended, is put. It is sometimes erroneously supposed that a member who is adverse both to the original ' See 84 Hans. Deb., N. S., 641, 5th March 184G (Andover Union), where it was so ruled by Mr. Speaker.

To insert or add words.

Restrictions in proposing amendments.

question and to the proposed amendment, would express an opinion favorable to the question, by voting " that the words proposed to be left out stand part of the question." By such a vote, however, he merely declares his opinion to be adverse to the amendment. After the amendment has been disposed of, the question itself remains to be put, upon which each member may declare himself as distinctly as if no amendment whatever had been proposed. If, however, he be equally opposed to the question and to the amendment, it is quite competent for him to vote with the noes on both.

3. In the case of an amendment to insert or add words, the proceeding is more simple. The question is merely put, that the proposed words "be there inserted" or ' added." If it be carried, the words are inserted or added accordingly, and the main question, so amended, is put; and if negatived, the question is put as it originally stood unless it be proposed to insert or add other words.

Several amendments may be moved to the same question, but subject to these restrictions: 1. No amendment can be made in the first part of a question, after the latter part has been amended, or has been proposed to be amended, if a question has been put upon such proposed amendment. But if an amendment to insert or add words to a question be witlidraicn, by leave of the house, the fact of that amendment having been proposed will not preclude the proposal of another amendment, affecting an earlier part of the question, so long as it does not extend farther back than the last words upon which the house have already expressed an opinion: for the withdrawal of the first amendment, leaves the question in precisely the same condition as if no amendment had been proposed. Each separate amendment must be put in the order in which, if agreed to, it would stand in the amended question;2 but

So ruled (privately) by Mr. Speaker, 19th Feb. 1845. 2 Hats. 12.3.

should a member, being in possession of the house, move an amendment, another member may propose to amend an earlier part of the question, and his amendment, though proposed the last, will be put first to the vote. 2. When the house have agreed that certain words shall stand part of a question, it is irregular to propose any amendment to those words; as the decision of the house has already been pronounced in their favour. But this rule would not exclude an addition to the words, if proposed at the proper time. 3. In the same manner, when the house have agreed to add or insert words in a question, their decision may not be disturbed by any amendment of those words.

But when a member desires to move an amendment to a part of the question proposed to be omitted by another amendment, or to alter words proposed to be inserted, it is sometimes arranged that only the first part of the original amendment shall be formally proposed, in the first instance, so as not to preclude the consideration of the second amendment. The convenience of the house may also be consulted, in some cases, by the withdrawal of an amendment, and the substitution of another, the same in substance as the first, but omitting certain words to which objections are entertained. Another proceeding Amendments to may also be resorted to, by which an amendment is inter- "" ' cepted, as it were, before it is offered to the house, in its original form, by moving to amend the first proposed amendment. This can be done when the original amendment proposed is, to leave out or to insert or add certain words: or when certain words have been left out of a question, and it is then proposed to insert or add other words instead thereof. In such cases an amendment may be proposed to the proposed amendment, and the questions ' See debate on Address, Ist Feb. 1849, 102 Hans. Deb., N. S., 117; Mr. Disraeli and Mr. Grattan.

See Mr. Duncombe's amendment (Education), 22d April 1847. 91 Hans. Deb., 3d Series, 1236. = See case of Duke of York, 04 Com. J. 131.

put by the speaker thereupon, deal with the first amendment as if it were a distinct question, and with the second as if it were an ordinary amendment.

A short example will make this complicated proceeding more intelligible. To avoid a difficult illustration, (of which there are many in the Journals,") let the simple question be, "That this bill be nuiv read a second time;" and let an amendment be proposed, by leaving out the word "now," and adding " this day six months;" let the question that the word "now" stand part of the question, be negatived, and the question for adding " this day six months " be proposed. An amendment may then be proposed thereto, by leaving out " months," and adding " weeks," or by leaving out " six months," and adding " week," " fortnight," c., or by leaving out " six," and inserting " two," " three," or "four." The question will then be put, "That the words proposed to be left out stand part of the said proposed amendment." If that be affirmed, the question for adding " this day six months," is put; and if carried, the main question, so amended, is put, viz. " That this bill be read a second time this day six months." But if it be resolved, that "six months" shall not stand part of the proposed amendment, a question is put that " week" or " fortnight," c. be added; and if that be agreed to, the first amendment, so amended, is put, viz. that the words " this day week" be added to the original question. That being agreed to, the main question, so amended, is put, viz. " That this bill be read a second time this day week." Several amendments may be moved, in succession, to a proposed amendment subject to the same rules as amendments to questions.

It must be observed, tliat no motion to amend a proposed amendment can be entertained, until the amendment has, for the time, assumed the place of the original ques- ' See Com. Gen. Journ, Indexes, 1774-1837, lit. Amendments. 101 Com. J. 865, tion, and become, as it were, a substantive question itself; otherwise there would be three points under consideration at once, viz. the question, the proposed amendment, and the amendment of that amendment. But when the question for adopting the words of an amendment is put forward distinctly, and apart from the original question, no confusion arises from moving amendments to it, before its ultimate adoption is proposed.

' It appears, from a curious letter of the younger Pliny (Plinii Epistolae, lib. viii. ep. 14), that the Roman senate were perplexed in tlie mode of disentangling a question that involved three different propositions. It was doubtful whether the consul, Afranius Dexter, had died by his own hand, or by that of a domestic; and if by the latter, whether at his own request, or criminally; and the senate had to decide on the fate of his freedmen. One senator proposed that the freedmen ought not to be punished at all; another, that they should be banished; and a third, that they should suffer death. As these judgments differed so much, it was urged that they must be put to the question distinctly, and that those who were in favour of each of the three opinions should sit separately, in order to prevent two parties, each differing with the other, from joining against the third. On the other hand, it was contended that those who would put to death, and those who would banish, ought jointly to be compared with the number who voted for acquittal, and afterwards among themselves. Tlie first opinion prevailed, and it was agreed that each question should be put separately. It happened, however, that the senator who had proposed death, at last joined the party in favour of banishment, in order to prevent the acquittal of the freedmen, which would have been the result of separating the senate into three distinct parties. The mode of proceeding adopted by the senate was clearly inconsistent with a determination by the majority of an assembly; being calculated to leave the decision to a minority of the members then present, if the majority were not agreed. The only correct mode of ascertaining the will of a majority, is to put but one question at a time, and to have that resolved in tlie affirmative or negative by the whole body. The combinations of different parties against a third cannot be avoided (which after all was proved in the senate); and the only method of obtaining the ultimate judgment of a majority, and reconciling different opinions, is by amending the proposed question until a majority of all the parties agree to affirm or deny it as it is ultimately put to the vote. (I am indebted to the late Mr. Hickman for a reference to Pliny's letter, accompanied by a very animated translation, which I regret is too long to be inserted.) The following is another example of the mode of determining a question without amendment, which involved a distinct contradiction. During the rivalry between Porapey and Cassar it was proposed in the senate, either that they should both give up, or both retain their troops. It is stated by Plutarch, that " Curio, with the assistance of Antonius and Piso, prevailed so far as to have it put to tlie regular vote. Accordingly he

Amendments moved before previous question.

After previous question proposed.

It may sometimes happen, that an amendment clashes with the proposal of the previous question; in which case the priority of either would depend upon the period at which the conflict arises. If the members who are about to offer these conflicting motions could previously arrange, with each other, the intended order of proceeding, it would generally be most convenient to move the amendment first; because it is manifestly reasonable to consider, in the first place, what the question shall be, if put at all; and, secondly, whether the question shall be put or not. Unless this course were adopted, an amendment, which might alter the question so as to remove objections to its being put, could not be proposed; for if the previous question were resolved in the affirmative, it must be put immediately by the speaker, as it stands; and if in the negative, the question would no longer be open to consideration. But if the amendment has been first proposed, it must be withdrawn or otherwise disj)osed of, before a motion for the previous question can be admitted.

If, on the other hand, the previous question has been first proposed by the speaker, no amendment can be received until the previous question is withdrawn. If the members who moved and seconded the previous question, agree, by leave of the house, to withdraw it, the amendment may be proposed, but not otherwise. If they refuse to withdraw it, the previous question must be put and determined. If, however, the house should generally concur in the amendments which were precluded from being put, they would permit a new and distinct question to be afterwards pro- proposed tliat tliose senators should move off to one side who were in favour of Cajsar alone laying down his arms and Ponipeius remaining in command; and the majority went over to that side. Again, upon his proposing that all who were of opinion that both should lay down their arms, and that neither should hold a command, only twenty-two were in favour of Pompeius, and all the rest were on the side of Curio." Plutarch, Life of Pompey, by Professor Long, p. 80. ' 36 Com. J. 825.

posed, embodying the spirit of those amendments, upon which a separate vote might be taken.

In the commons, every amendment must be proposed and seconded in the same manner as an original motion; and if no seconder can be found, the amendment is not proposed by the speaker, but drops, as a matter of course, and no entry appears of it in the Votes.

CHAPTER X.

THE SAME QUESTION OR BILL MAY NOT BE TWICE OFFERED m A SESSION.

It is a rule, in both houses, not to permit any question Object of the or bill to be offered, which is substantially the same as one on which their judgment has already been expressed in the current session. This is necessary, in order to avoid contradictory decisions, to prevent surprises, and to afford proper opportunities for determining the several questions as they arise. If the same question could be proposed again and again, a session would have no end, or only one question could be determined; and it would be resolved first in the affirmative, and then in the negative, according to the accidents to which all voting is liable.

But, however wise the general principle of this rule may Exceptions-be, if it were too strictly applied, the discretion of Parliament would be confined, and its votes be subject to irrevocable error. A vote may therefore be rescinded, and Votes re-an order of the house discharged, notwithstanding a rule urged (April 2d, 1604,) " That a question being once made, and carried in the affirmative or negative, cannot be questioned again, but must stand as a judgment of the house." ' ' 1 Com. J. 306. 434. 89 lb. 69. = 1 lb. 162.

Technically, indeed, the rescinding of a vote is the matter of a new question; the form being to read the resolution of the house, and to move that it be rescinded; and thus the same question which had been resolved in the affirmative is not again offered, although its effect is annulled. The same result is produced when a resolution has been agreed to, and a motion for bringing in a bill thereupon is afterwards negatived, as in the proposed reduction of the malt duty, in 1833."

To rescind a negative vote, except in the diflferent stages of bills, is a proceeding of greater difficulty, because the same question would have to be offered again. The only means, therefore, by which a negative vote can be revoked, is by proposing another question similar in its general purport to that which had been rejected, but with sufficient variance to constitute a new question; and the house would determine whether it were substantially the same question or not. Evasions of the A mere alteration of the words of a question, without any substantial change in its object, will not be sufficient to evade this rule. On the 7th July 1840, Mr. Speaker called attention to a motion for a bill to relieve dissenters from the payment of church rates, before he proposed the question from the chair. Its form and words were different from those of a previous motion, but its object was substantially the same, and the house agreed that it was irregular, and ought not to be proposed from the chair. But, when a motion for leave to bring in a bill has been rejected, it is competent to move for a committee of the whole house to consider the laws relating to the subject to which that bill referred; and this expedient is often used to evade the orders of the house.

It is also possible in other ways so far to vary the character of a motion as to withdraw it from the operation ' 88 Com. J. 317. 329. =" 95 lb, 495. Mirror of Pari. 1840, p. 4387.

of the rule; thus, in the session of 1845, no less than five distinct motions were made upon the subject of opening letters at the post-office, under warrants from the secretary of state. They all varied in form and in matter, so far as to place them beyond the restriction; but in purpose they were the same, and the debates raised upon them embraced the same matters. But the rule cannot be evaded by renewing in the form of an amendment a motion which has been already disposed of. On the 18th July 1844, an amendment was proposed to a question, by leaving out all the words after " that," in order to add, "Thomas Sllngsby Duncombc, esq., be added to the committee of secrecy on the post-office;" but Mr. Speaker stated, that on the 2d July a motion had been made, 'Hhat Mr. Duncombe be one other member of the said committee;" that the question had been negatived; " and that he considered it was contrary to the usage and practice of the house that a question which had passed in the negative should be again proposed in the same session." The amendment was consequently withdrawn."

The rule, however, does not apply to cases in which a Rfotions witu-motion has been by leave of the house withdrawn; for such repeated. a motion has not been submitted to the judgment of the house, and may, therefore, be repeated.

It will now be necessary to anticipate, in some measure, the proceedings upon bills, which are reserved for future explanation; but it is desirable to understand, at one view, the precise effect of a decision or vote, whatever may be the nature of the question.

In passing bills, a greater freedom is admitted in pro- Rule as a)i)lied posing questions, as the object of different stages is to afford the opportunity of reconsideration; and an entire bill may be regarded as one question, which is not decided ' 100 Com. J. 42. 54. 185. 199. 214. 2 76 Hans. Deh., N. S., 1021, 18th July 1844.

Se;' motion on railway bills withdrawn l(5tli, and renewed 23d May 1845. 80 Hans. Deb., N. S., 432, 798. Chapter XVIII.

to bills.

until it has passed. Upon this principle it is laid down by Hatsell, and is constantly exemi)lified, " that in every stage of a bill, every part of the bill is open to amendment, either for insertion or omission, whether the same amendment has been, in a former stage, accepted or rejected." ' The same clauses or amendments may be decided in one manner by the committee, in a second by the house on the report, and in a third on the third reading; and yet the inconsistencey of the several decisions will not be manifest when the bill has passed. One precedent only need be mentioned.

On the 8th August 1836, a clause was, after divisions, added on the report of the Pensions Duties Bill, to exempt the pension of the Duke of Marlborough from the provisions of that bill." On the third reading an amendment was proposed, by leaving out this clause, and the question that it should stand part of the bill was, on division, passed in the negative. Bills once When bills have ultimately passed, or have been rejected, jected. rules of both houses are positive, that they shall not be introduced again; but the practice is not strictly in accordance with them. The principle is thus stated by the lords, 17th May 1606:

"That when a bill hath been brought into the house, and rejected, another bill of the same argument and matter may not be renewed and begun again in the same house in the same session where the former bill was begun; but if a bill begun in one of the houses, and there allowed and passed, be disliked and refused in the other, a new bill of the same matter may be drawn and begun again in that house whereunto it was sent; and if, a bill being begun in either of the houses, and committed, it be thought by the committees that the matter may better proceed by a new bill, it is likewise liolden agreeable to order, in such case, to draw a new bill, and to bring it into the house."

It was also declared, in a protest, signed by seven lords, 23d February 1691, in reference to the Poll Bill, in which ' 2 Hats. 135. 91 Com. J. 762. lb. 817.

2 Lords' J. 435.

a proviso contained the substance of a bill which had dropped in the same session; " that a bill having been dropped, from a disagreement between the two houses, ought not, by the known and constant methods of proceedings, to be brought in again in the same session." The lords, nevertheless, agreed to tliat bill, but with a special entry, that " to prevent any ill consequences from such a precedent for the future, they have thought fit to declare solemnly, and to enter upon their books, for a record to all posterity, that they will not hereafter admit, upon any occasion whatsoever, of a proceeding so contrary to the rules and methods of Parliament."

In the commons it was agreed for a rule, 1st June 1610, that " no bill of the same substance be brought in the same session."'

A common practice, however, has since grown up, with Lords' Journals the sanction of both houses, by which these rules are par- tially disregarded. When a bill has passed the commons, and the further consideration of the amendments made by the committee, is deferred by the lords for a period beyond the probable duration of the session, it is usual, if the lords' amendments are acceptable, for the commons to appoint a committee to inspect the lords' Journals; and, on their report, to order another bill to be brought in. This bill often has precisely the same title, but its provisions are so far altered as to conform to the amendments made in the lords. With these alterations it is returned to the lords, received by them without any objection, and passed as if it were an original bill. Such a bill is not identically the same"as that which preceded it; but it is impossible to deny that it is " of the same argument and matter," and "of the same substance." This proceeding is very frequently resorted to, when the lords' committees find it necessary to insert clauses imposing rates, tolls, or 15 Lords' J. 90. lb. 1 Com. J. 434.

other charges, upon the people. The House of Lords cannot agree to such clauses without mfringing upon the privileges of the commons, and the bill is therefore dropped; but the commons, by bringing in another bill, and adopting the clauses to which, in themselves, they do not object, avoid any clashing of privileges, and the bill is ultimately agreed to by both houses.

Bills laid aside. A proceeding somewhat similar may arise when a bill is returned from the lords to the commons, with amendments which the latter cannot, consistently with their own privileges, entertain. In that case, the proper course, if the commons be willing to adopt the amendments, is to order the bill to be laid aside, and another to be brought in.

A third proceeding resembles the two last in principle, but differs from both in form. When the lords pass a bill and send it down to the commons, with clauses that trench upon the privileges of the latter, it is usual for the commons to lay the bill aside, and to order another precisely similar to be brought in, which, having passed through all its stages, they send up to the lords exactly in the same manner as if the bill had originated in the commons.

Lords search If a bill has been postponed or laid aside in the commons Votes"'" the lords sometimes appoint a committee to search the Votes and Proceedings of the commons, and may, if they think fit, introduce another bill, and send it to the commons.

Prorogation, to But in all the preceding cases the disagreement of the two houses is only partial and formal, and there is no difference in regard to the entire bill. If the second or third reading of a bill sent from one house to the other be deferred for three or six months, or if it be rejected, there is no regular way of reviving it in the same session; and, so imperative has that regulation been esteemed, that in 1707, Parliament was actually prorogued for a week, in ' See further Chapter XXI.

2 91 Com. J. 777. 810; 103 lb. 888. 100 lb. 664. Deodands Abolition Bill, 1845. 3 75 Loi.(jg. j qq. 77 j, q renew bills.

order to admit the revival of a bill which had been rejected by the lords.

The rule in regard to bills already passed has been construed with equal strictness; and, in 1721, a prorogation for two days was resorted to, in order to enable Acts relating to the South Sea Company to be passed, contradictory to clauses contained in another Act of the same session. On the latter occasion, the commons presented an address to the king, recommending a resort to the expedient of a prorogation, "as the ancient usage and established rules of Parliament make it impracticable" otherwise to prepare the bills. These rules, however, have not been invariably observed."

In order to avoid the embarrassment arising from the Clauses in Acts. irregularity of dealing with a statute passed in the same session, it had, for many years, been the practice to add a clause to every bill, enacting, "that this Act may be amended or repealed by any Act to be passed in this session of Paruament." But by 13 14 Vict., c. 21, " every Act may be altered, amended, or repealed in the same session of Parliament, any law or usage to the contrary notwithstanding;" and the usual clause will therefore be omitted from all Acts passed after the session of 1850.

' 19 Com. J. 639. 18 lb. 121. 334, 4th May 1772.

Manner of In the House of Lords, a peer addresses his speech " to speaking. g. xq lords in general." In the commons, a member addresses the speaker, and it is irregular for him to direct his speech to the house, or to any party on either side of the house. A member is not permitted to read his speech; but may refresh his memory by a reference to notes. In both houses, proper respect is paid to the assembly, by every member who speaks rising in his place, and standing uncovered. The only exception to this rule is in cases of sickness or infirmity, when the indulgence of a seat is frequently allowed, at the suggestion of a member, and with the general acquiescence of the house." In the commons, also, during a division, with closed doors, it is the practice for members to speak sitting and covered. But this practice is confined to questions of order referred to the decision of the speaker, and does not apply to distinct motions proposed for the adoption of the house. On the 10th July 1844, after the numbers had been reported by the tellers, but before they had been declared by the speaker, motions were made for disallowing the votes of certain members on the ground of personal interest, and ' Lords' S. O. No. 17.

"1 Com. J. 494. 83 Hans. Deb., N. S., 1169, 19th Feb. 1846, Interference of peers at elections. But it seems to have been permitted in the Lords 26th June 1845. 81 Hans. Deb., N. S., 1190. See also 1 Com. J. 272.

3 A member may speak from the galleries appropriated to members; but the practice is inconvenient, and not often resorted to.

"Lord Wynford, 64 Lords' J. 167. Mr. Wynn, 9th March 1843. 67 Hans. Deb., N. a., 658; and 9th July 1844 (Sudbury Disfranchisement). 76 lb. 542.

as the doors were still closed, the member who made the first motion was proceeding to speak sitting and covered; but the speaker desired him to rise in his place, and the debate proceeded in the same way as if the doors had been opened.

It has been said, when treating of questions, that the Timeofspeak-proper time for a debate is after a question has been pro- " " posed by the speaker, and before it has been put; and it is then that members generally address the house or the speaker and commence the debate. But there are occasions upon which, from irresolution, or the belief that others are about to speak, members permit the speaker to put the question before they rise in their places. They are, however, entitled to be heard even after the voice has been given in the affirmative; but if it has also been given in the negative, they have lost their opportunity; the question is fully put, and nothing remains but the vote. It is explained in the standing orders of the lords, "that when a question hath been entirely put, by " the speaker, no lord is to speak against the question before voting;" and a question being entirely put, implies that the voices have also been given.

On one occasion, in the commons (27th January 1789,) the debate Avas re-opened, after the question had been declared by the speaker to have been resolved in the affirmative: for a member had risen to speak before the question had been put, but had been unobserved by the speaker; and it was admitted that he had a right to be heard, although the question had been disposed of before his offer to speak had attracted attention.

From the limited authority of the speaker of the House Who may of Lords, in directing the proceedings of the house, and 1,.,. In tlie lords.

in maintaining order, the right of a peer to address their lordships depends solely upon the will of the house. When two rise at the same time, unless one immediately gives ' Lords' S. O. No. 22. 2 Hats. 102 n.

In the commons.

way, the house call upon one to speak; and if each be supported by a party, there is no alternative but a division. Thus, on the 3d February 1775, the Earl of Dartmouth and the Marquis of Rockingham both rising to speak, it was resolved, upon question, that the former "shall now be heard." So again on the 28th May 1846, in a debate on the Corn Bill, the Earl of Eglintoun, Lord Beaumont, and the Earl of Essex rose together. The Duke of Richmond moved that Lord Eglintoun be heard; but the Lord

Chancellor then rose and moved that Lord Essex be heard, and having immediately put the question, declared that the contents had it. His decision was demurred to, but Lord Essex proceeded with his speech.

In the commons, the member who, on rising in his place, is first observed by the speaker, is called upon to speak; but his right to be firet heard depends, in reality, upon the fact of his having been the first to rise, and not upon his being first in the speaker's eye. It is impossible for the speaker to embrace all parts of the house in his view at the same moment, and it may sometimes be obvious to the house that he has overlooked a member who had the best claim to be heard. When this occurs, it is not unusual for members to call out the name of the member Avho, in their opinion, is entitled to be heard; and, when the general voice of the house appears to give him the preference, the member called upon by the speaker usually gives way. If the dispute should not be settled in this manner, a question might be proposed, "which member was first up;" or, " which member should be heard;" or, " that a particular member be heard." But this mode of proceeding is very rarely adopted, and should be avoided, except in extreme cases, more especially as a member is often called upon to speak, not because he was up the first, but because the house desire to hear him. It is the 34 Lords' J. 30G.

members rise.

DEBATE. 243 speaker's duty to watch the members as they rise to speak; and, from his position in the house, he is better able to distinguish those who have priority than the house itself, and the decision should be left with him. In the commons, not less than twenty members have been known to rise at once, and order can only be maintained by acquiescence in the call of the speaker.

It occasionally happens that two members rise at the When two same time, and on one of them being called upon by the speaker, the house are desirous of hearing the other. If the latter be a minister of the Crown, or have any other claim to precedence, the former rarely persists in speaking, but yields at once to the desire of the house. If, however, they should both be men of equal eminence, or supported by their respective parties; and if neither will give way, no alternative remains but a question that one of them ' be now heard," or " do now speak." This question arose between Mr. Pitt and ISIr. Fox on the 20th February 1784 and more recently between Sir R. Peel and Sir F. Burdett." On the 9th July 1850, Mr. Locke being called upon by Mr. Speaker to proceed with a motion, of which he had given notice, and several members objecting on account of the lateness of the hour, and Mr. Forbes Mackenzie rising in his place to speak upon the question that certain petitions do lie upon the table, and objection having been made to his proceeding, motion made and question, " that Mr. Mackenzie do now speak," put and negatived; and Mr. Locke proceeded with his motion. In a debate upon a bill, the priority of a member might be determined in another way, as on the 6th June 1604, it was agreed for a rule, "that if two stand up to speak to a bill, he against the bill (being known by demand or otherwise) to be first heard;" but it is doubtful whether this rule would not now be treated as obsolete.

' 39 Com. J. 943. 2 86 lb. 617.

s 105 lb. 509. 112 Hans. Deb. 3d Series, 1190. M Com. J. 232.

Must speak to the question.

When no question is before the house.

When a member is in possession of the house (as it is called), he has not obtained a right to speak generally; but is only entitled to be heard upon the question then under discussion, or upon a question or amendment intended to be proposed by himself," or upon a point of order. Whenever he wanders from it, he is liable to be interrupted by cries of " question," and in the commons, if the topics he has introduced are clearly irrelevant, the speaker acquaints him that he must speak to the question. The relevancy of an argument is not always perceptible, and the impatience and weariness of members after a long debate, often cause vociferous interruptions of " question," which do not signify, that the member who is speaking is out of order, so much as that the house are not disposed to listen to him. These cries are disorderly, and, when practicable, are repressed by cries of " order " from the house and the speaker; but nevertheless, when not mistimed, they often have the intended eifect, and discourage a continuance of the debate. When they are immoderate and riotous, they not only disgrace the proceedings of the house, but frequently defeat the object they are intended to attain, by causing an adjournment of the debate.

Considerable laxity had, until recently, prevailed in allowing irrelevant speeches upon questions of adjournment, which were regarded as exceptions to the general rule: but since the commencement of the session of 1849 a stricter practice has been enforced, and Mr. Speaker has called upon members to confine their observations upon such motions to the question properly before the house, viz., whether the house should adjourn or not.

It is a rule that should always be strictly observed, that no member may speak except when there is a question already before the house, or the member is about to'con- ' 69 Hans. Deb. N. S. 507.

2 See Debates, 23d and 2Gth June, and 24th and 2oth August 1848.

3 jtli Feb. and 22d Feb. 1840.

elude with a motion or amendment. The only exceptions which are admitted, are, 1, in putting questions to particular ministers or other members of the house; and, 2, in explaining personal matters. But in either of these cases the indulgence given to a particular member will not justify a debate.

1. By the practice of both houses, questions are fre- Qupstions to ,1,,., ii n other members.

quently put to mmisters of the Crown concernmg any measure pending in Parliament, or other public event; and to particular members who have charge of a bill, or who have given notices of motions, or are otherwise con-cerned in some business before the house; but such questions should be limited, as far as possible, to matters immediately connected with the business of Parliament, and should be put in a manner which does not involve argument or inference. On the 13th December 1847, a member was proceeding to put a question relating to the affairs of Switzerland, but the speaker interposed and explained to him that his question involved an opinion and argument." In the same manner an answer should be confined to the points contained in the question, with such explanation only as will render the answer intelligible. In the lords the rule is properly the same as in the commons; but is not observed with equal strictness, and is occasionally disregarded altogether. On the 14th December 1847, Lord Stanley prefaced certain questions concerning Lord Minto and the affairs of Italy, with a long speech, in which various opinions wxre expressed and arguments urged, and he was answered by Lord Lansdowne in the same manner.

2. In regard to the explanation of personal matters, the Personal expla-house is usually indulgent. General arguments ought not to be used by the member who is permitted to speak, without any question being before the house; bu t if his object be clearly confined to the removal ofany impression

See Speaker's ruling, 22d Feb. 1849; 102 Hans. Deb. 3a Series, 1100. ' Hans. Deb. 13 Dec. 1847. ' n, Y i Dec. 1847.

concerning his own conduct or words, he is generally per- mitted to proceed without interruptionj This indulgence, however, should be granted with caution; for unless wisely-used it is apt to lead to irregular debates.

On the 19th April 1849, after the speaker had directed the clerk to read the orders of the day, Lord Castlereagh rose to speak upon a matter in which he stated himself to be personally concerned, and claimed the indulgence of the house. The speaker interposed, and explained that his lordship was out of order, and that the house must proceed to the order of the day. Lord C, however, again claimed the indulgence of the house and proceeded with his explanation, after which Lord John Kussell spoke in reply. Mr. Disraeli then rose, and was proceeding to address the house, when Lord J. Russell stated that he should claim a right to reply to him, and the speaker rising, pointed out in strong terms the extreme inconvenience of departing from the rules of the house, upon which all further debate was arrested, and the house proceeded to the order of the day. To speak once It IS a rule strictly to be observed in both houses, that " no member shall speak twice to the same question, except, 1st, to explain some part of his speech which has been misunderstood; 2dly, in certain cases, to reply at the end of a debate; and 3dly, in committee.

1. It is an ancient order of the House of Lords that.

To explain. " No man is to speak twice to a bill at one time of reading it, or to any other proposition, unless it be to explain hijiiself in some material part of his speech; but no new matter, and that not without the leave of the house first obtained. That if any lord stand up and desire to speak again, or to exjdain himself, the lord keeper is to demand of the house first whether the lord shall be permitted to speak or not; and that none may speak again to the same matter, though upon new reason arising out of the same; and that none may speak again to explain himself, unless his former speech be mistaken, and he hath leave given to explain himself; and if the cause require much debate, then the house to be put into committee."'

See Hans Deb. 19th April 1849. 3 Lords' J. 590. Lords' S. O. No. 21.

In the commons the privilege of explanation is allowed without actual leave from the house; but when a member rises to explain, and afterwards adverts to matters not strictly necessary for that purpose, or endeavours to strengthen by new arguments his former position, which he alleges to have been misunderstood, he is called to order by the house or by the speaker, and is desired by the latter to confine himself to simple explanation. But here, again, a greater latitude is permitted in cases of personal explanation, where a member's character or conduct has been impugned in debate.

2. A reply is only allowed by courtesy to the member Reply. who has proposed a distinct question to the house. It is not conceded to a member who has moved any

order of the day, as that a bill be read a second time; nor to the mover of an instruction to a committee of the whole house; nor to the mover of any amendment. Under these circumstances, it is not uncommon for a member to move an order of the day or second a motion without remark, and to reserve his speech for a later period in the debate. In some cases, however, the indulgence of the house is extended so far as to allow a reply on questions which do not come within the ordinary rules of courtesy."' 3. In a committee of the whole house, the restriction In committee. upon speaking more than once is altogether removed, as will be more fully explained in speaking of the proceedings of committees.

The adjournment of a debate does not enable a member New question. to speak again upon a question, when the discussion is renewed on another day, however distant;" but directly a new question has been proposed, as " that this house do ' See Debates, 15th June 1846 (Sir R. Peel and Mr. Disraeli). See Debates, 1st March 1844 (Mr. T. Dunconibe's amendment). 3 Chapter XIII. Com. J. 245.

now adjourn," " that the debate be adjourned," " the previous question," or an amendment, members are at liberty to speak again; as the rule applies strictly to the prevention of more than one speech to each separate question proposed. Upon the same grounds a member who has ah-eady spoken, may rise and speak again upon a point of order or privilege. Order in debate. For preserving decency and order in debate various rules have been laid down, which, in the lords, are enforced by the house itself, and in the commons by the speaker in the first instance, and, if necessary, by the house. The violation of these rules any member may notice, either by a cry of "order," or by rising in his place, and, in the lords, addressing the house, and in the commons the speaker. The former mode of calling attention to a departure from order is, perhaps, not strictly regular, and sometimes interrupts a member, and causes disturbance; but it is often joractlsed with good eifect; it puts the member who is irregular in his conduct upon his guard, arouses the attention of the house and the speaker, and prevents a speech to order, a reply, and perhaps angry discussion. When a member speaks to order, he should simply direct attention to the point complained of, and submit it to the decision of the house or the speaker. He may move, also, that the words of a member, which he conceives to be disorderly, may be taken down; which the house will direct to be done where it appears necessary, provided the objection be taken immediately.

The rules for the conduct of debates divide themselves into two parts, viz.: I., such as are to be observed by members addressing the house; and, II., those which regard the behaviour of members listenino; to the debate.

Words taken down.

' fi5 Hans. Deb. N. S. 826.

66 Com. J. 391; 68 lb. 322; 93 lb. 307. 312, 313. 2 Hats. Prec. 2G9. See also ivfia, p. 259.

Referring to prior debates.

ORDER IN DEBATE. 249 I. (1). A member, while speaking to a question, may not Rules formem- 111-1111 speaking.

allude to debates upon a question already decided by the house in the same session; (2), nor speak against, or reflect upon, any determination of the house, unless he intends to conclude with a motion for rescinding it; (3), nor allude to debates in the other house of Parliament; (4), nor use the Queen's name irreverently, or to influence the debate; (5), nor speak offensive and insidting words against the character or proceedings of either house; (6), nor against particular parties or members of the house in which he is speaking.

A few words will suffice to explain the object and application of each of these rules.

(1). It is a wholesome restraint upon members, to prevent them from reviving a debate already concluded; for otherwise a debate might be interminable; and there would be little use in preventing the same question or bill from being offered twice in the same session, if, without being offered, its merits might be discussed again and again. The rule, however, is not always strictly enforced; peculiar circumstances may seem to justify a member in alluding to a past debate, or to entitle him to indulgence, and the house and the speaker will judge in each case how far the rule may fairly be relaxed. On the 30th August 1841, for instance, an objection was taken that a member was referring to a preceding debate, and that it was contrary to one of the rules of the house. The speaker said " that rule applied in all cases; but where a member had a personal complaint to make, it was usual to grant him the indulgence of making it."' And again, on the 7th March 1850, he said, "The house is always willing to extend its indulgence when an honorable member wishes to clear up any misrepresentation

See Hans. Deb. 28th Feb. 1845 (wliere Mr. Roche had come from Ireland on purpose to asii Mr. Roebuck a question, but was stopped by Mr, Speaker).

2 69 Hans. Deb. N. S. p. 48G. See albo (io Hans. Deb. N. S. p. G4'i, '2Gth Julv 1842.

of his character; but that indulgence ought to be strictly limited to such misrepresentations, and ought not to extend to any observations other than by way of correction." But he may not read any portion of a speech made in the same session from a printed newspaper. This rule, indeed, applies to all debates whatsoever; but of late years it has been relaxed by general acquiescence, in favour of speeches delivered in former sessions. It is also irregular to read extracts from newspapers, or other documents referring to debates in the house. Rrflcctingupon (2). The objections to the practice of referring to past liouse!"' " debates apply with greater force to reflections upon votes of the house; for these not only revive discussion upon questions already decided, but are also uncourteous to the house, and irregular in principle, inasmuch as the member is himself included in, and bound by, a vote agreed to by a majority." It is very desirable that this rule should be observed, but its enforcement is a matter of considerable difficulty, as principles are always open to argument, although they may have been affirmed or denied by the house. Allusions to de- (3). The rule that allusions to debates in the other house bates in the. n i, c, n, other house. f rc out ot order IS convenient tor preventmg iruitless arguments between members of two distinct bodies who are unable to reply to each other, and for guarding against recrimination and offensive language in the absence of the party assailed; but it is mainly founded upon the understanding that the debates of the other house are not known, and that the house can take no notice of them. Thus when, in 1641, Lord Peterborough complained of words spoken concerning him by Mr. Tate, a member of the commons, "their lordships were of opinion that this house 7th March 1850 (Mr. Campbell and Mr. B. Osborne), 109

Hans. Deb. 3d Scries, 462. See also 30th March 1846 (Sir J. Graham and Mr. Shaw), 85 Hans. Deb. 3d Series, 300.

' Hans. Deb. itth Feb. 1846 (Mr. Ferrand).) jiats. 234 n.

covild not take any cognizance of wliat is spoken or done in the House of Commons, unless it be by themselves, in a parliamentary way, made known to this house."' The daily publication of debates in Parliament offers a strong temptation to disregard this rule. The same questions are discussed by persons belonging to the same parties in both houses, and speeches are constantly referred to by members which this rule would exclude from their notice." The rule has been so frequently enforced that most members in both houses have learned a dexterous mode of evading it by transparent ambiguities of speech; and although there are few orders more important than this for the conduct of debate, and for observing courtesy between the two houses, none, perhaps, are more generally transgressed. An ingenious orator may break through any rules, in spirit, and yet observe them to the letter.

The rule applies to debates only, and not to reports of Allusions to committees of the other house. On the 9th June 1848, objection was taken that a member was quoting from a report made to the House of Lords, which had not been communicated to the commons; but the speaker decided that the member was not out of order.

(4). An irreverent use of her Majesty's name would be Queen's name rebuked by any subject out of Parliament; and it is only consistent with decency that no member of the legislature should be permitted openly to insult the Queen, in the presence of her Parliament. Members have not only been called to order on this account, but have been reprimanded.

' 4 Lords' J. 582.

See Lords' Debates, 3d April 1845 (Lord Ashburton); Commons' Debates, 4th April 1845 (Lord J. Russell), on the Ashburton Treaty. See also Commons' Debates (Mr. Ffrench), 21st and 23d July 1845; and Lords' Debates, (Lord Brougham), 22d and 24th July 1845, on the Irish Great Western Railway Bill; and Lords' Debates, 27th June 1848 (Earl Grey), as examples of the inconvenience arising from any violation of this rule.

3 Hans. Deb. 9th June 1848.

a debate.

252 queen's name used.

or committed to the custody of the serjeant, and even sent to the Tower." To influnnce The Irregular use of the Queen's name to influence a decision of the house is unconstitutional in principle, and inconsistent with the independence of Parliament. Where the Crown has a distinct interest in a measure, there is an authorized mode of communicating her Majesty's recommendation or consent, through one of her ministers; ' but her Majesty cannot be supposed to have a private opinion apart from that of her responsible advisers; and any attempt to use her name in debate, to influence the judgment of Parliament, would be immediately checked and censured.

On the 12th November 1640, it was moved that some course might be taken for preventing the inconvenience of his Majesty being informed of anything that is in agitation in this house before it is determined. In the remonstrance of the lords and commons to Charles I., 16th December 1641, it was declared,

"That it is their ancient and undoubted right and privilege tliat your majesty ought not to take notice of any matter in agitation or debate in either of the houses of Parliament, but by their information or agreement; and that your Majesty ought not to propound any condition, provision, or limitation, to any bill or act in debate or preparation in either house of Parliament, or to manifest or declare your consent or dissent, approbation or dislike, of the same, before it be presented to your majesty in due course of Parliament."'

On the 17th December 1783, the commons resolved, "That it is now necessary to declare, that to report any opinion or pretended opinion of his majesty, upon any bill or other proceeding depending in either house of Parliament, with a view to influence the votes of the members, is a high crime and misdemeanor, derogatory to the honour of the Crown, a breach of the fundamental privileges of Parliament, and subversive of the constitution of this country."

1 Com. J. 51; 15 lb. 70; 18 lb. 49. D'Ewes, 41. 244. 2 See Cliapter XVII. ' 1 Com. J. 697. " 2 lb. 27.

The rule, however, must not be construed so as to Expiiumtions exclude a statement of facts, by a minister, in which tlic Queen's name may be concerned. In the debate on the Foreign Loans Bill, 24th February 1729, Sir R. Walpolc stated that he was " provoked to declare what he knew, what he had the king's leave to declare, and what would effectually silence the debate." Upon which his statement was called for, and he declared that a subscription of 400,000. was being raised in England for the service of the emperor. When he sat down, Mr. Wortley Montagu complained that the minister had introduced the name of the king to " overbear their debates;" but he replied, that as a privy councillor he was sworn to keep the king's council secret, and that he had therefore asked his majesty's permission to state what he knew; but which, without his leave, he could not have divulged. And thus the matter appears to have ended, without any opinion being expressed by the speaker or by the house.

On the 9th May 1843 Sir Robert Peel said, "On the part of Her Majesty I am authorized to repeat the declaration made by King Wilham," in a speech from the throne, in reference to the legislative union between Great Britain and Ireland. On the 19th, Mr. Blewitt objected to these expressions; but the speaker, after noticing the irregularity of adverting to former debates, expressed his own opinion,

"That there was nothing inconsistent with the practice of the house in using the name of the sovereign in the manner in which the right hon. baronet had used it. It was quite true tliat it wouhl be highly out of order to use the name of the sovereign in that house so as to endeavour to influence its decision, or that of any of its members, upon any question under its consideration; but he apprehended that no expression which had fallen from the right hon. gentleman could be supposed to bear such a construction."

7 Chandler's Debates, 6. G4.

of the rule.

Words against Parliament, or either house.

Aud Lord John Russell explained, that " the declaration of the sovereign was made by the right hon. baronet's advice, because any personal act or declaration of the sovereign ought not to be introduced into that place;" to which Sir R. Peel added,

" that he had merely confirmed, on the part of Her Majesty, by the advice of the government, the declaration made by the former sovereign."

(5). It is obviously unbecoming to permit offensive expressions against the character and conduct of Parliament to be used without rebuke; for they are not only a contempt of that high court, but are calculated to degrade the legislature in the estimation of the people. If directed against the other house, and passed over without censure, they would appear to implicate one house in discourtesy to the other; if against the house in which the words are spoken, it would be impossible to overlook the disrespect of one of its own members. Words of this objectionable character are never spoken but in anger; and when caued to order, the member must see the error into which he has been misled, and retract or explain his words, and make a satisfactory apology. Should he fail to satisfy the house in this manner, he will be punished by a reprimand, or by commitment." It is most important that the use of such words shoidd be immediately reproved, in order to avoid complaints and dissension between the two houses.

In 1614 Dr. Richard Neile, Bishop of Lincoln, uttered some words which gave offence to the commons, and they complained of them in a message to the lords, to which they received an answer, that the bishoj)

"Had made solemn protestation, upon his salvation, that he had not spoke anything with any evil intention to that house, which he doth with all his heart duly respect aud highly esteem, expressing with many tears his sorrow that his words were so misconceived, ' 69 Hans. Deb, N. S. 24. 574.

9 Com. J. 147.760; 10 lb. 512; 11 lb. 580.

and strained further than he ever meant, whicli submissive and ingenuous behaving of himsejf had satisfied tlie lords; and tlieir lordships assure the commons that if thej had conceived the lord bishop's words to have been spoken, or meant, to cast any aspersion of sedition or undutifulness upon that house, their lordshijjs would forthwith have proceeded to the censuring and punishing thereof with all severity."

Their lordships added, that hereafter no member of their house ought to be called in question, when there is no other ground thereof but puljlic and common fame only.

In 1701 a complaint was made by the commons of expressions used by Lord Haversham, at a free conference, and numerous communications ensued, which were terminated by a prorogation.

On the 14th December 1641, exception was taken to Excei)tion, 1 1 T 1 T-i 1 11 taken to words, words used by Lord irierpomt; he was commanded to withdraw, and committed to the custody of the gentleman usher.

On the 20th May 1642, the Lord Herbert of Cherbury, having used offensive words in debate, was commanded to withdraw, and committed to the custody of the gentleman usher; but on the following day was released upon his submission.

On the 14th March 1770, exception was taken to certain words used in debate by the Earl of Chatham; and the house resolved, " that nothing had appeared to this house to justify his assertion."

Disrespectful or abusive mention of a statute would Against a sta-seem to be partly open to the same objections as improper language applied to the Parliament itself; for it imputes discredit to the legislature which passed it, and has a tendency to bring the law into contempt. INIore license, however, is allowed in speaking of a statute, than is consistent 2 Lords' J. 713. See also 4 Lords' J. 582. 1 Com. J. 496. 499, c. 2 Hats. 73.

2 13 Com. J. 629. 634. 637. 639.

3 4 Lords' J. 475. 5 lb. 77. 32 lb. 476.

Personal allusions.

Against members.

In the lords.

with this view of its clanger; and though intemperate language should always be re-pressed, it must be admitted, that the frequent necessity of repealing laws justifies their condemnation in debate; and the severity of the terms in which they are condemned can only be regarded as an argument for their re)eal.

(6). In order to guard against all appearance of personality in debate, it is a rule that no member shall refer to another in debate by name. In the upper house, every lord is alluded to by the rank he enjoys; as the " noble marquis," or the " right reverend prelate;" and in the commons, each member is distinguished by the office he holds, by the place he represents, or by other designations; as " the noble lord the secretary for foreign affairs," the " honourable" or " right honourable gentleman the member for York," or the " honourable and learned member who has just sat down." The use of temj erate and decorous language is never more desirable than when a member is canvassing the opinions and conduct of his opponents in debate. The warmth of his own feelings is likely to betray him into hasty and unguarded expressions, which the excitement of his adversaries will exaggerate; and he cannot be too careful in restraining himself within those bounds which Parliament has wisely established. The imputation of bad motives, or motives different from those acknowledged; misrepresenting the language of another, or accusing him, in his turn, of misrepresentation; charging him with falsehood or deceit; or contemptuous and insulting language of any kind; all these are unparliamentary, and call for prompt interference.

The rules of the House of Lords upon this point are very distinctly laid down in their standing orders, 13th

June 1626:

"To prevent misunderstanding-, and for avoiding of offensive speeches, when matters are debating, either in the house, or at committees, it is for honour sake thought lit, and so ordered, that all personal, sharp, or taxing speeches be forborne; and whosoever answereth another man's speech, shall apply his answer to the matter, without wrong to the person; and as nothing offensive is to be spoken, so nothing is to be ill taken, if the party that speiiks it shall presently make a fair exposition, or clear denial of the words that might bear any ill construction; and if any offence be given in that kind, as the house itself will be very sensible thereof, so it will sharply censure the offender, and give the party offended a fit reparation and a full satisfaction."'

On the 10th December 1766, notice was taken of some Words of heat, words that had passed between the Duke of Richmond and the Earl of Chatham; upon which they were required Lords. by the house to declare, upon their honour, "that they would not pursue any further resentment."

The lords are also prompt in their interference to prevent quarrels in debate between their members, and extend their jurisdiction over them even further, by ordering

"That if any lord shall conceive himself to have received any affront or injury from any other member, either in the Parliament house, or at any committee, or in any of the rooms belonging to the Lords' House of Parliament, he shall appeal to the lords in Parliament for his reparation, which if he shall not do, but occasion or entertain quarrels, declining the justice of the house, then the lord that shall be found therein delinquent shall undergo the severe censure of the House of Parliament.""

Sometimes the lords have extended this principle to the prevention of quarrels which have arisen out of the house. On the 6th November 1780, the lords being informed that the Earl of Pomfret had sent a challenge to the Duke of Grafton, upon a matter unconnected with the debates or proceedings of Parliament, declared the earl "guilty of a high contempt of this house," and committed him to the Tower.

The House of Commons will insist upon all offensive Commons. words being withdrawn, and upon an ample apology being made, which shall satisfy both the house and the member to whom offence has been given. If the apology be refused, '
Lords' S. O. No. 19. See also 12 Lords' J. 31; Mirror of Parlt. 1833, p. 2855. 2 31 Lords' J. 448.

3 IG lb. 378; Earl Rivers and Earl of Peterborow, 8th Feb. 1G98. Lords' S. O. No. 16. ' 3G Lords' J. 191.

6 78 Com. J. 224; 9G lb. 40.

or if the offended member decline to express his satisfaction, the house take immediate measures for preventing the quarrel from being pursued further, by committing both the members to the custody of the serjeant; whence they are not released until they have submitted themselves to the house, and given assurance that they will not engage in hostile proceedings.

In 1770 words of heat having arisen between Mr. Fox and Mr. Wedderburn, the former rose to leave the house, upon which the speaker ordered the serjeant to close all the doors so that neither Mr. Fox nor Mr. Wedderburn should go out till they had promised the house that no farther notice should be taken of what had happened. Challenges. The commons will also interfere to prevent quarrels between members, arising from personal misunderstanding in a select committee, as in the case of Sir Frederick Trench and Mr. Eigby Wason, on the 10th June 1836. One of those gentlemen, on refusing to assure the house that he would not accept a challenge sent from abroad, was placed in custody; and the other, by whom the challenge was expected to be sent, was also ordered to be taken; nor were either of them released until they had given the house satisfactory assurances of their quarrel being at an end.

The sending a challenge by one member to another, in consequence of Avords spoken by him in his place in parliament, is a breach of privilege, and will be dealt with accordingly, unless a full and ample apology be offered to the house. But it does not appear that the speaker or the house would interfere to prevent a quarrel from being proceeded with where it had arisen from a private misunderstanding, and not from words spoken in debate, or in any proceedings 89 Com. J. 9. II; 91 lb. 484, 485; 92 lb. 270.

' MS. Officers and Usages of the House of Commons, 1805, p. 138.

3 91 Com. J. 464. 468.

Case of Rlr. Roebuck and Mr. Somers, 16th June 1845; 100 Com. J. 589.

of the house, or of a committee." In such cases, if any interference should be deemed necessary, information wovdd probably be given to the police. But in 1701, Mr. Mason, a member, had sent a challenge to Mr. Molyneux, a merchant, and the house required his assurance that the matter should go no fiirther.

Whenever any objectionable words have been used by a words taken member in debate, notice should be immediately taken of "' the words objected to, in order that they may be taken down correctly by the clerk, if directed to do so by the speaker, in compliance with the general wish of the house. The commons have agreed, "that when any member had spoke between, no words which had passed before could be taken notice of, so as to be written down in order to a censure." The same principle would seem to apply, if the member had afterwards been permitted to continue his speech without interruption; and this appears to be the rule in the lords, where the words are required to be taken down instanter?

II. The rules to be observed by members present in the Rules to be ob-houseduring a debate are: (1), to keep their places; (2), to ' errnot s"eak-enter and leave the house with decorum; (3), not to cross " the house irregularly; (4), not to read books, newspapers, or letters; (5), to maintain silence; (6), not to hiss or interrupt. ' (1). "The lords in the upper house are to keep their dignity and 7 j g jj j. order in sitting, as much as may be, and are not to move out places, of their places without just cause, to the hindrance of others that Toj-ds sit near them, and the disorder of the house; but when they must cross the house, they are to make obeisance to the cloth of estate."

In the commons, also, the members should keep their Commons.

Private memorandum, 22d Feb. 1849. 13 Com. J. 444. 3 2 Hats. 272 n.

2 Hats. 269 n. See also 69 Hans. Deb. N. S. 566. 93 Com. J. 307. 312, 313; but see 13 Cora. J. 123.

48 Hans. Deb. 321, 17th June 1839 (Beer Bill).

Another rule, " that no member do take tobacco," is unworthy of a place in the text. See 11 Com. J. 137. " Lords' S. O. No. 16.

Entering the bouse.

Lords.

Commons.

Crossing before members speaking.

Lords,

Commons.

places, and not walk about the house, or stand at the bar, or in the passages.

On the 10th February 1698, it was ordered,

"That every member of this house, when he comes into the house, do take his place, and not stand in the passage as he comes in or goes out, or sit or stand in any of the passages to the seats, or in the passage behind the chair, or elsewhere that is not a proper place." ' If after a call to " order," members who are standing at the bar or elsewhere do not disperse, the speaker orders them to take their places, when it becomes the duty of the serjeant-at-arms to clear the gangway, and to enforce the order of the speaker, by desiring those members who still obstruct the passage, immediately to take their places. If they refuse or neglect to comply, or oppose the serjeant in the execution of his duty, he may at once report their names to Mr. Speaker.

(2). " Every lord that shall enter the house, is to give and receive salutations from the rest, and not to sit down in his place, unless he hath made an obeisance to the cloth of estate."

Members of the commons who enter or leave the house during a debate must be uncovered, and should make an obeisance to the chair while passing to or from their places.

(3). In the lords it has been seen that care should be taken in the manner of crossing the house, and it is especially irregular to pass in front of a peer who is addressing their lordships. In the commons, members are not to cross between the chair and a member who is speaking, nor between the chair and the table, nor between the chair and the mace, when the mace is taken off the table by the serjeant. When they cross the house or otherwise leave their places, they should make obeisance to the chair.

12 Com. J. 496; 19 lb. 425. " Lords' S. 0. No. 15.

3 See 8 Com. J. 264.

This rule, however, is not observed when a member is speaking from the tliird or any higher bench from the floor.

(4). They are not to read books, newspapers, or letters in their places. This rule, however, must now be understood with some limitations; for although it is still regarded as irregular to read newspapers, any books and letters may be referred to by members preparing to speak, but ought not to be read for amusement, nor for business unconnected with the debate.

(5). Silence is required to be observed in both houses. Silence.

In the lords it is ordered,

"That if any lord have occasion to speak with another lord in Lords, this house, while the house is sitting, they are to go together below the bar, or else the speaker is to stop the business in agitation."

In the commons all members should be silent, or should Commons, converse only in a whisper. Whenever the conversation is so loud as to make it difficult to hear the debate, the speaker exerts his authority to restore silence by repeated cries of " order." On the 5th May 1641, it was resolved

"That if any man shall whisper or stir out of his place to the disturbance of the house at any message or business of importance, Mr. Speaker is ordered to present his name to the house for the house to proceed against him as they shall think fit,"

(6). They should not disturb a member who is speaking Hissing or in- by hissing, exclamations," or other interruption. The fol- ' ' " '""

lowing is the declaration of this rule by the House of

Commons, 22d January 1693:

"To the end that all the debates in this house should be grave and orderly, as becomes so great an assembly, and tliat all interruptions should be prevented, be it ordered and declared, that no member of this house do presume to make any noise or disturbance whilst any member shall be orderly debating, or whilst any bill, order, or other matter shall be in reading or oi ening; and in case of such noise or disturbance, that Mr. Speaker do call upon the member, bj' name, making such disturbance; and that every such person shall incur the displeasure and censure of the house."'' ' 4 Com. J. 51. 2 Lords' S. O. No. 20. 2 Com. J. 135.

1 Com. J. 473. " Motion against hissing to the interruption and liin-drance of the speech of any man in the house, well approved of." 1604. 1 Com. J. 935.

13 Lords' J. 387 (E. of Clarendon and M. of Winchester, 28th November 1678). 6 11 Co,, J g(j gg, jji o 1 n, jr o.

This rule is too often disregarded. In the House of Commons the most disorderly noises are sometimes made, which, from the fulness of the house, and the general uproar maintained when 500 or 600 members are impatiently waiting for a division, it is scarcely possible to repress.

"Hear, hear." "Without any such noises, however, there are words of interruption which, if used in moderation, are not unparliamentary; but when frequent and loud, they cause serious disorder. The cry of " question " has already been noticed, and its improper use condemned. Another is that of " hear, hear," which has been sanctioned by long parliamentary usage in both houses. It is generally intended to denote appro-bation of the sentiments expressed, and, in that form, is a flattering encouragement to the member who is speaking; it is not uttered till the end of a sentence, and offers no interruption to the speech. But the same words may be used for very different purposes, and pronounced with various intonations. Instead of implying approbation, they may distinctly express dissent, derision, or contempt; and if exclaimed with a loud voice and before the completion of a sentence, no mode of interruption can be more distracting or offensive to the member who is speaking. Whenever exclamations of this kind are obviously intended to interrupt a speech, the speaker calls to " order," and if persisted in, would be obliged to name the disorderly members, and leave them to be censured by the house.

Interruptions Indecent interruptions of the debate or proceedings in a committee of the whole house, are regarded in the same light as similar disorders while the house is sitting.

On the 27th February 1810, the committee on the expedition to the Scheldt reported that a member had misbehaved himself during the sitting of the committee, making use of profane oaths and disturbing their proceedings. Mr. Fuller, the member complained of, was heard to excuse himself; in doing which he gave greater offence, by repeat- ' 1 Com. J.-isQ; 2 lb. 135.

ing and persisting in his disorderly conduct; upon which Mr. Speaker called upon him by name, and he was ordered to withdraw. It was immediately ordered, nem. con., that for his oifensive words and disorderly conduct, he be taken into the custody of the serjeant." The offence for which he was ultimately committed may appear to have been his disorderly conduct before the house; but there can be no doubt, that if, without giving fresh offence, he had failed in excusing himself for his misconduct in the committee, the house would have inflicted some punishment, either by commitment or reprimand. This member further aggravated his offence by breaking from the serjeant, and returning into the house in a very violent and disorderly manner, whence he was removed by the serjeant and his messengers."

In the enforcement of all these rules for maintaining Authority of order, the speaker of the House of Lords has no more " ' ' f 1 Lords.

authority than any other peer, except m so far as his own personal weight, and the dignity of his office, may give effect to his opinions, and secure the concurrence of the house. The result of his imperfect powers is, that a peer who is disorderly is called to order by another of an opposite party, and that an irregular argument is liable to ensue, in which each speaker imputes disorder to the last, and recrimination takes the place of orderly debate. There is no impartial authority to whom an appeal can be made, and the debate upon a question of order generally ends with satisfaction to neither party, and without any decision upon the matter to which exception had been taken.

In so large and active an assembly as the House of Com- commons, mons, it is absolutely necessary that the speaker should be invested with authority to repress disorder, and to give effect, promptly and decisively, to the rules and orders of the house. The ultimate authority upon all points is the 65 Com. J. 134. 136.

house itself; but the speaker Is the executive officer, by whom its rules are generally enforced. In ordinary cases an Infringement of the usage or orders of the house is obvious, and Is immediately checked by the speaker; in other cases his attention Is directed to a point of order, when he at once gives his decision, and calls upon the member who Is at fault, to conform to the rule as explained from the chair. But doubtful cases may arise, upon which the rules of the house are indistinct or obsolete, or do not apply directly to the point at issue; and then, the speaker, being left without specific directions, refers the matter to the judgment of the house. On the 27th April 1604, it was "agreed for a rule, that if any doubt arise upon the bill, the speaker is to explain, but not to sway the house with argument or dispute;" and in all doubtful matters this course Is adopted by the speaker. Speaker always Whenever the speaker rises to speak in the course of a debate, he should be heard In silence, and the member who Is speaking should Immediately sit down. It was agreed for a rule on the 21st June 1604, "That when Mr. Speaker desires to speak, he ought to be heard without interruption, if the house be silent, and not in dispute;"" but this is an imperfect explanation of the present practice, for the rising of the speaker Is the signal for immediate silence, and for the cessation of all dispute; and members who do not maintain silence, or who attempt to address the speaker, are called to order by the majority of the house, with loud cries of " order " and " chair." Members to It Is a rule In both houses, that when the conduct of a their conduct is i ember Is under consideration, he is to withdraw during under debate, the debate. The practice is to permit him to learn the charge against him, and after being heard In his place, for him to withdraw from the house. The precise time at which he should Avithdraw is determined by the nature of ' 1 Com. J. 187. 2 lb. 244.

the charge. Wlien it Is founded upon reports, petitions, or other documents, or words spoken and taken down, which sufficiently explain the charge, it is usual to have them read and for the member to withdraw before any question is proposed; as in the cases of Lord Coningesby, in 1720; of Sir R Burdett in 1810;= of Sir T. Troubridge, in 1833; 3 of Mr. O'Conneu, in 1836, and of Mr. S. O'Brien in 1846; but if the charge be contained in the question itself, the member is heard in his place, and withdraws after the question has been proposed; as in the cases of Mr. Secretary Canning, in 1808; and of Lord Brudenell, in 1836."' If the member should neglect or refuse to withdraw at the proper time, the house would order him to withdraw. Thus, in the lords. Lord Pierpoint, in 1641, and Lord Herbert of Cherbury, in 1642, were commanded to withdraw; and in the commons, in 1715, it was ordered upon question and division, " that Sir W. Wyndham do now withdraw."'"

On the 17th May 1849, petitions were presented com- Petitions plaining of the conduct of three members, as railway directors. Memb rs." The members were permitted to explain and defend their conduct, but did not afterwards withdraw. It being contrary to the standing orders of the house to make a motion or to enter upon a debate on the presentation of a petition, the conduct of the members could scarcely be regarded as under the consideration of the house at that time, and as soon as the members were heard, the petitions were ordered to lie upon the table, without further debate. One of the members withdrew, but returned almost immediately to his seat.

On the 28th April 1846, the house had resolved that Members in Mr. W. S. O'Brien, a member, had been guilty of a con- tempt. tempt; but the debate upon the consequent motion for his 21 Lords' J. 450. "" 65 Com. J. 224. ' 88 lb. 470.

91 lb. 42. 5 J 01 lb. 582. G3 lb. 149.

7 91 lb. 319. 8 4 Lords' J 476. ' 5 lb. 77. ' 18 Com. J. 49.

commitment was adjourned until a future day: upon which Mr. O'Brien immedi- ately entered the house and proceeded to his place. Mr. Speaker, however, acquainted hira that it would be advisable for him to withdraw until after the debate concerning him had been concluded. The reason for this Intimation was, that the member had been already declared to be in contempt, although his punishment was not yet determined upon. On the 30th, a request was made through a member, that he should be heard in his place; but this was regarded as clearly irregular, and he was not permitted to be heard. Adjournment A motion for adjourning the debate may be offered at any period of the discussion; and in the lords, whether seconded or not, must be disposed of before the debate can proceed. In the commons, if it be not seconded, it drops like any other motion, and the debate is continued as if no such motion had been made; but if seconded, it must either be withdrawn or negatived, before the debate upon the question can be resumed. The speaker, however, will not allow a member to move the adjournment, if he have already spoken in the debate, lest under cover of a new question, he should advert to topics connected with the debate itself; but if the adjournment be moved by any other member, he may then speak to that question. It has been explained in a previous chapter, in what manner it is customary to alternate motions for the adjournment of the house, and for the adjournment of the debate; and repeated motions to that effect in opposition to the general desire of the house, cannot be restrained unless the house should alter their rules with reference to such motions.

1 85 Hans. Deb. 3d Series, 1198. 2 lb. 1291.

3 l9t May 1846 (Lord G. Bentinck), "Siqmi, p. 217.

See Mr. Speaker's Ev. before Committee on Public Business, 1848.

In the House of Lords every lord who desires to vote, Members not and holds proxies for other lords, must be present in the question put! house when the question is put. And in the commons no member is permitted to vote unless he was in the house when the question was put.

On the 16th March 1821 Mr. Speaker called the atten- Precedents, tion of the house to his having caused a member to vote in a division, who was not within the doors of the house when the question was put; and the house resolved, nem. con., "That the said member had no right to vote, and ought not to have been compelled to vote on that occasion."' Another case occurred on the 27th February 1824, when, after a division, and before the numbers were reported by the tellers, it was discovered that a member had come into the house after the question was put; he was called to the table, and upon the question being put to him by Mr. Speaker, he declared himself for the noes; he was then let out of the house by the Serjeant, and his name was not reckoned by the tellers for the noes, with whom he had voted.

On the 3d May 1819, after the numbers had been reported by the tellers, notice was taken that several members had come into the house after the question was put. Mr. Speaker desired any members who were not in the house when the question was put, to signify the same; and ' 76 Com. J. 172.

- 79 lb. 106. This case is entered so ambiguously in the Journal, that it might appear as if the member had been let out into the lobby, in order to vote with the " noes," who had gone forth; but such was not the fact, nor would such a proceeding have been consistent with the rules of the house.

certain members having stated that they were not in the house, their names were struck off from the yeas and from the noes respectively; and the numbers, so altered, were reported by Mr. Speaker to the house.

On the 2d June 1825, the noes on a division were directed to go forth, and certain members refusing to retire from the lobby, the other members in the house were desired again to take their places, and the members were called in from the lobby. The speaker then asked one of the six members who had refused to retire, where he was when the question was put, and he replied that he had been in the lobby; upon which he was informed by Mr. Speaker that he could not be permitted to vote, and the serjeant was ordered to open the outer door of the lobby, that the six members might be enabled to withdraw."

On the 14th June 1836 the house was informed by a member who had voted with the majority on a former day, that he was not in the house when the question was put, and had therefore no right to vote on that occasion; and it was resolved that his vote should be disallowed.

These precedents show that at whatever time it may be discovered that members were not present when the question was put, whether during the division, before the numbers are reported, or after they are declared, or even several days after the votes were given, such votes are disallowed. And in the lords a similar rule prevails." In order to prevent the accidental absence of members at so critical a time, precautions are taken to secure their attendance, and to prevent their escape between the putting of the question and the division. House cleared Before a division can take place, the house must be of strangers. cleared of strangers in the galleries, below the bar, and in the lobby. This occupies a considerable time when there are many strangers, but scarcely a minute when the gal- 74 Com. J. 393. qq jf, 433 3 gj jj

G5 Lords' J. 481 (Local Jurisdiction Bill, 1833).

leries are not full. When it is known that a division is about to ensue, the speaker, directly the debate is closed, and without putting the question, gives the order that ' strangers must withdraw,"' and at the same instant the doorkeepers shout " Clear the gallery!" and ring a bell which communicates with every part of the building. This " division bell" is heard in the libraries, the refreshment rooms, the waiting rooms, and wherever members are likely to be dispersed, and gives notice that a division is at hand. Those who wish to vote, hasten to the house immediately, and while the messengers are engaged in excluding strangers, they have time to reach their places. Directly the strangers have withdrawn, the usher of the black rod in the lords, and the serjeant-at-arms in the commons, and the doorkeepers and messengers under their orders, close and lock all the doors leading into the house and the adjoining lobbies simultaneously. Those members who arrive after the doors are shut, cannot gain admittance, and those who are within the house must remain there and vote. On the 31st March 1848, a member having been found in the house who had not voted on either side, he was brought to the table, and was informed by Mr. Speaker that he must vote, whereupon the question was stated to him, and he declared that he voted with the ayes." In the upper house, lords who desire to avoid voting may withdraw to the woolsacks, where they are not strictly within the house, and are not therefore counted in the division. By shutting all the doors at once, care is taken, in the commons, to prevent members from gaining the lobby, and yet being shut out of the house; but it may occasionally happen that a member with difficulty squeezes himself through the outer door of the lobby, and the next instant the serjeant shuts the door of the house. The In the Irish Parliament strangers were permitted to be present during a division. See 1 Sir J. Barrington, Personal Sketches, 195.

Election Recognizances Bill, 103 Com. J. 40G.

Question sometimes twice put.

Divisions on Wednesday.

Votes upon an amendment.

member would then find himself enclosed between the two locked doors, and unable to vote; in which case the doorkeeper will open the outer door of the lobby, and permit him to withdraw.

When all the doors are thus closed, the speaker puts the question, and the contents and not-contents, or the ayes and noes respectively, declare themselves. When a division is not expected, the speaker is obliged to put the question twice, because when his decision has been disputed after the first putting of the question, the strangers must withdraw before the question can be decided by a division; and in the meantime members who were not present when the question was put, gain admittance to the house. None of these could vote unless the question were put a second time, and it is therefore the practice to put the question after the doors are closed, whether it has been already put or not, in order that the whole house may have notice of a division, and be able to decide upon the question when put by the speaker. But after the question has been once put no member is permitted to speak.

It may sometimes happen on a Wednesday morning sitting that the division on a question, which has been put by the speaker, must be postponed until a future day. At six o'clock the speaker is bound to adjourn the house," and cannot therefore proceed with the division. But if the division should have commenced before six o'clock, the speaker will allow it to proceed, as, by the rules of the house, the doors must remain closed until after the numbers have been reported.

A member who has not voted upon an amendment is nevertheless entitled to vote upon the main question, when subsequently put, and for that purpose has a right to be admitted to the house so soon as the numbers have been declared after the first division. On the 28th May 1845 some members complained that they had been denied
' See supra, p. 224, 241. 2 See supra, p. 210.

"This occurred 13th May 1846.

admittance to the house between a division upon an amendment, and another upon the main question. The speaker stated that they had been improperly exeludedj and that proper directions should be given to prevent the recurrence of such an accident.

A similar complaint was made on the 13th March 1849, and the speaker again stated that the doors should have been opened after the first division, for the admission of members."

A division is effected in the lords by the not-contents Division in the remaining within the bar, and the contents ffoinc: below the bar. The lord speaker appoints two lords, being of the same degree, as tellers one from each party by whom the numbers are counted. The not-contents remainino- in the house are first counted, and then the contents who are below the bar. After the not-contents have been told, the lord chancellor or lord speaker gives his voice like the other lords on being required by the tellers, but he does not leave the woolsack to vote. When all the lords then present have been told, they resume their places, and if proxies are called, the clerk at the table calls over the names of those lords who hold proxies, who, rising uncovered in their places," declare whether those for whom they are proxies are "content" or "not-content." The total number of lords present and of the proxies are then declared, and the question is decided by the joint majority of both classes of votes.

In case of an equality of voices and proxies combined, "Wiien voices the not-contents have it, and the question is declared to ll, '" " have been resolved in the negative. When this occurs it is always entered in the journal " Then, according to the ancient rule of the law," ' or " the ancient rule in the like cases, ' semper prcesumitur pro negante c." The effect of this rule is altered when the house is sittino- judi-

M. S. note, 28tli May 1845.

' lb. isth March 1849 (Church Rates division). lords' S. O. No. 25.

lb. 33 Lords' J. 519. j Loads' J. 107, 1G8.

cially, as the question is then put " for reversing, and not for affirming;" ' and consequently if the numbers be equal, the house refuse to reverse the judgment, and an order is made that the judgment of the court below be affirmed. Law lords. As a general rule, none but " law lords," i. e., peers who have held high judicial offices, vote in judicial cases, or Votes of otiier Otherwise interfere with the decisions of the house. All cases'" " peers, however, are entitled to vote, if they think fit, and the right has been exercised in some very remarkable cases. In 1685, in the case of Howard v. the Duke of Norfolk, a decree of the Lord Keeper Guildford was reversed, after an angry debate, by a house attended by eighteen bishops and sixty-seven temporal peers.""'
In Reeve v. Long, in 1694, the judgment of the court below was reversed by all the lords, without a division. In 1697, the cause of Bertie v. Falkland, was debated like any other question, and the lay lords entered protests. The case of Ashby v. White, in 1704, having been made a party question, and a subject of contest between the two

houses, the judgment of the Court of Queen's Bench was reversed on a division, by fifty against sixteen. In the Douglas peerage case, in 1769, some lay lords took part in the debates and proceedings, and entered a protest, but abstained from voting. In Alexander v. Montgomery, in 1773, the lay lords voted, and the numbers being equal (four and four), the judgment was affirmed. In 1775, judgment was given in Hill v. St. John, in the presence of lay lords, and with their authority, but without any division, In the case of the Bishop of London v. Fytche, in 1783, the bishops voted as well as several lay lords, and the judgment was reversed, by nine-

Lords' S. O. No. 126.

14 Lords' J. 30. Select Chancery cases. 3 Lord Campb. Lives of Chancellors, 485, 486.

16 Lords' J. 446. Sugden, Law of Real Prop., Introduction. 16 Lords' J. 230. 236, 7. 240, 1. 247, 8. 17 lb. 369.

32 lb. 264. 16 Pari. Hist. 518. Cavendish Deb. 618. 7 33 Lords'J. 519. Sugden, Law of R. P. Intr. 21.

teen to eighteen. In the writ of error of Queen v. O'Connell, in 184-4, a discussion arose, in which some of the lay lords seemed inclined to exercise their right, but abstained from voting."

The following are standing orders in regard to voting, when no formal division takes place:

"That after a question is put, and the house hath voted there Lords to keep upon, no lord is to depart out of his place, unless upon a divi t'" """ I'liiccs sion of the house, until the house have entered on some other "' business."

"In voting, the lowest, after the question is put by the lord Manner of chancellor, begins first, and every lord in his turn rises, uncovered, voting in tiie and only says content or non-content.""

The practice in the commons, until 1836, was to send inthecom-one party forth into the lobby, the other remaining in the house. Two tellers for each party then counted the numbers and reported them. In 1836 it was thought advisable to adopt some mode of recording the names of members who voted, and for this purpose several contrivances were proposed: but by that adopted and now in operation, there are two lobbies, one at each side of the house, and, on a division, the house is entirely cleared; one party being sent into each of the lobbies. The speaker, in Tellers. the first place, directs the ayes to go into one lobby, and the noes into the other, and then appoints two tellers for each party; of whom one for the ayes and another for the noes are associated, to check each other in the telling. If two tellers cannot be found for one of the parties, no division is allowed to take place.

On the 4th June 1829, a member was appointed one of the tellers for the yeas; but no other member remaining in the house to be a teller for the yeas, the noes, who had gone forth, returned into the house, and Mr. Speaker declared that the noes had it. In another case, 14th August 1835, ' 36 Lords' J. 687. 2 Brown's Pari. Cases, 211. 5 Lord Camph. Clmn-cellors, 5-23. 2 11 Clar. Fin. 1.05, 421.

Lords' S. O. No. 24. lb. No. 23. 84 Com. J. 379.

the yeas were directed to go forth, and a member was appointed a teller; but no member going forth, nor any-other member appearing to be a second teller for the yeas, Mr. Speaker declared the noes had it;' and several cases, of the same kind, have occurred more recently."" Proposed It would, indeed, be unreasonable to allow a division, upon divisions, when, without Counting the majority, the minority obviously consists of one member only, opposed to the whole house; and it would be worthy of consideration whether a rule could not be established, by which no division should be allowed, unless a certain number of members declared themselves with the minority, besides the tellers. An unnecessary division is a great evil; it occupies much time, and causes considerable inconvenience to the members; while the more unequal the parties, the longer is the time consumed in the division, and the more irksome the process of dividing to the majority. The speaker can rarely doubt which party is the minority, when the number is obviously small; and if that party nevertheless, disputed his decision, he might desire them to stand up, before the division, and no time would be lost in counting them. Occasions for enforcing this rule would not occur very often; but, whenever the speaker had reason to believe, or any member took notice, that the ayes or the noes were less than the prescribed number, it would be a fair and simple mode of avoiding a division."" Such a restriction upon the right of dividing, would most facilitate the progress of public business, in cases where a very small party oppose themselves to a bill, or 90 Com. J. 550.

"" 97 lb. 183. 354; 98 lb. 605. 23d May 1850,105 Com. J. 364.

' A practice analogous to that proposed, is already sanctioned in regard to divisions in committees of the whole house. (See p. 277). And in the American House of Representatives there is a rule very similar to the suggestion contained in the text; viz., "No division and count of the house shall be in order, but upon motion seconded by at least one-fifth of a quornni of the members." Standing Orders and Rules, No. 4. See also the Author's Pamphlet on Public Business in Parliament, 1849, 2d edit. p. 29, 30.

DIVISIONS. 275 insist upon an acljournraent. Frequent divisions must then arise, in which hundreds, perhaps, retire into one lobby, and units into the other; and, time being thus lost, the weaker party succeed at last, by reason of the unwieldy force of the majority.

When there are two tellers for each party, the division Form. f , 1,11 1 1 division in tlie proceeds, and the house is cleared. commons.

Two clerks are then stationed at each of the entrances to the house, holding lists of the members, in alphabetical order, printed upon large sheets of thick pasteboard, so as to avoid the trouble and delay of turning over pages. While the members are passing into the house again, the clerks place a mark against each of their names, and the tellers count the nvimber.

When both parties have returned into the house, the tellers on either side come up to the table and report the numbers; and, if they agree, the speaker also declares them, and states the determination of the house. If the two tellers should differ as to the numbers on the side told by them, or if any mistake be discovered, there appears to be no alternative but a second division, unless the tellers agree as to the mistake, when the numbers will be correctly reported by the speaker. If a mistake be subsequently discovered, it will be ordered to be corrected in the Journal.

If the numbers should happen to be equal, the speaker Casting- voice (and in committee the chairman), who otherwise never votes, must give the casting voice. In the performance of this duty, he is at liberty to vote like any other member, according to his conscience, without assigning a reason; but, in order to avoid the least imputation upon his impartiality, it is usual for him, when practicable, to 33 Com. J. 212. jq3 j iq2.

On the 19th February 1847 notice was taken that the number of the noes reported by the tellers on a previous day did not correspond with the printed lists; and tlie tellers for the noes being present, stated tliut the number had been reported by them by mistake. The clerk was ordered to correct the number in the Journal. 102 Com. J. 131.

vote in such a manner as will not make the decision of the house final, and to explain his reasons, which are entered in the Journals. Precedents. On the 8th April 1805, in the proceedings against Lord

Melville, prior to his impeachment, the numbers were equal upon the previous question, and the speaker gave his casting vote in favour of the previous question, on the ground that " the original question was now fit to be submitted to the judgment of the House."

On the 14 th June 1821, the speaker declared himself with the yeas, on a question for reading the amendments made by a committee to a bill a second time, " upon the ground of affording a further opportunity to the house of expressing an opinion upon the bill."

Upon the second reading of a bill, 1st May 1828, the numbers being equal, Mr. Speaker stated, " that as the bill had been entertained by the house, although they were now undecided as to whether it should proceed or not, he considered that he should best discharge his duty by leaving the bill open to further consideration, and therefore gave his vote with the yeas." The speaker acted upon the same principle on the third reading of a bill, 23d June 1837; and a similar course has generally been taken at other stages in the progress of bills. A case, however, occurred on the 2d April 1821, in which the speaker voted with the noes on the second reading of a bill, and so threw it out, without assigning any reason for his vote.

The principle by which the speaker is usually guided in giving his casting voice, has been carried even further than in the case of bills.

On the 26th May 1826, within a few days of the end of the session, a resolution was proposed in reference to the practice of the house in cases of bribery at elections. The previous question was moved, and, on a division, the 60 Com. J. 202. 7 n,, 439. 3 gg j. 292.

92 lb. 496. 95 lb. 536; 96 lb. 344; 98 lb. 163.

76 lb. 229.

numbers being equal, "Mr. Speaker said, tbat it being now his duty to give his vote, and considering the proposed resolution as merely declaratory of what are the powers and what is the duty of the house, and that any inaccuracy in the wording of the resolution might be amended, when in the new Parliament it must be re-voted, he should give his vote with the yeas."'

And on the 19th May 1846, on a question for referring a petition, complaining of bribery at Bridport, to a committee of inquiry, the numbers being equal, Mr. Speaker said, "That as the house had no better means of forming a judgment upon the question than the election committee, who had already declined to entertain it, and as it would still be open to any elector of the borough, under the provisions of the Act 5 6 Vict. c. 2, to present a petition to the house, praying that a committee, having power to examine upon oath, might be appointed to in-vestigate the subject of bribery and compromise, he therefore declared himself with the noes.""

On the 25th May 1841, on a motion for an address to the Crown in behalf of pohtical offender, Mr. Speaker declared himself with the noes, as " the vote, if carried, would interfere with the prerogative of the Crown."

After the division, the sheets of pasteboard on which Publication of the names of members are marked are examined by the division clerks, and sent off to the printer, who prints the marked names in their order; and the division lists are delivered on the following morning, together with the Votes and Proceedings of the house. This plan of recording the names of members, on a division, has been quite successful; they are taken down with great accuracy, and very little delay is occasioned by the process.

In committees of the whole house, it is the rule, that Divisions in divisions are to be taken by the members of each party ' o '" "'-crossing over to the opposite side of the house, unless five ' 81 Com. J 387. ' 101 lb. 731. ' 96 lb. 344.

members require that the names shall be noted in the usual manner; but the custom of publishing the names has become so popular and general, that no practical difference exists in the mode of taking divisions in committee. If less than five members should happen to object to a question, and were not assisted by any of the opposite party, they could not have their names recorded; but an inconsiderable minority are generally the most anxious for the publication of their votes; and if more than five in number, they could insist upon it. A division in committee cannot be taken unless there be two tellers for each side, as in the house itself." Proxies. In the lords, it has been seen, that not only those peers who are present may vote in a division, but, on certain questions, absent peers are entitled to vote by proxy, and their votes are numbered with the rest; the joint majority of votes and proxies being decisive of the question. The following rules and restrictions are incident to the right of voting by proxy:

Nolordtohave " No lord of this house shall be capable of receiving above two above two. proxies, nor more to be numbered in any cause voted. All proxies from a spiritual lord shall be made to a spiritual lord, and from a temporal lord to a temporal lord." Proxies vaca " If peer having leave of the king to be absent from Par- ted upon lords' liament, gives his proxy, and afterwards sits again in the house, his coming and sitting again in Parliament doth determine that proxy." New proxies. " If a peer having leave to be absent, makes his proxy and re- turns, he cannot make a new proxy without new leave."

Proxies not to " That proxies may be used in preliminaries to private causes, ne iis-ed in judi-,.,,,= cial cases. "" " '" givmg judgment.""

Though by bill. " That no proxy for the future shall be made use of in any judicial cause in this house, although the proceedings be by way of 15th June 1848 (Borough Elections Bill). 23d May 1850 (Wood used in shipbuildin-z), 105 Com. J. 364.

Lords' S. O. No. 26. See also 51 Lords' J. 192. Proxies were originally made to strangers. 5 Rot. Pari. 350. Hakewell, 29.

See Report of Precedents, when King George IIL was incapacitated from granting such leave. 48 Lords' J. 21. 48. Lords' S. O. No. 27. lb. No. 28. lb. o. 29.

bill."" And this rule is extended to the trial of controverted elections of the representative peers of Scotland,"

"That a lord having a proxy and voting on the question ought Lords to vote to give a vote for that proxy in case proxies be called for."' furtlieir proxies

"That the proxy of no lord shall be entered the same day on j, question which he has been present in the house, and that no proxy entered proxies when in the book after three of the clock, shall be made use of the same to be entered, day in any question, and that the clerks give an account thereof to the house."

It is also a rule that no proxy can be used in a com- in committee, mittee of the whole house.

The most usual practice is for lords to hold the proxies Peers and tiicir of other lords of the same political opinions, and for the vote alike!! votes of botli to be declared for the same side of a question. This is the true intent of a proxy; but it occasionally happens, that a lord has been privately requested by another lord, whose proxy he holds, to vote for him on the opposite side; in which case, it is understood to be regular to admit their conflicting votes in that manner. But it is said, that this variation from the ordinary rule is permitted upon the supposition, that between the time of voting and of declaring the vote of the proxy, a lord may be supposed to have altered his own opinion; for the form of the proxy would appear to delegate to the lord who holds it, the absolute right of decision for the absent lord, without any reference to the opinions of the latter, expressed after the signature of that instrument.

A practice, similar in effect to that of voting by proxy, Pairs. has for many years been resorted to in the House of j the com-Commons. It has been shown, that no member can vote " " " unless he be present when the question is put; and no sanction has ever been given, by the house, to any custom partaking of the character of delegation. But a system of negative proxies, known by the name of ' pairs," enables a member to absent himself, and to agree with another member that he also shall be absent at the same ' Lords' S. O. No. 30. 3L Lords' J. 33; 41 lb. 24

Lords' S. O. No. 31. " lb. No. 32.

time. By this mutual agreement, a vote is neutralized on each side of a question, and the relative numbers on the division are precisely the same as if both members were present. The division of the house into distinct political parties facilitates this arrangement, and members pair with each other, not only upon particular questions, or for one sitting of the house, but for several weeks, or even months, at a time. There can be no parliamentary recognition of this practice, although it has never been expressly condemned," and it is therefore conducted privately by individual members, or arranged by the gentlemen who are entrusted, by the two great parties, with the office of collecting their respective forces on a division. The system has been found so convenient, that it is also practised in the lords. Protest. In addition to the power of expressing assent or dissent by a vote, peers may record their opinion, and the grounds of it, by a "protest," which is entered in the Journals, together with the names of all the peers who concur in it.

On the 27th February 1721, it was ordered.

When to be en- " That such lords as shall make protestation, or enter their dis- " " sents to any votes of this house, as they have a right to do without asking leave of the house, either with or without their reasons, shall cause their protestation or dissents to be entered into the clerk's book, the next sitting day of this house, before the hour of two o'clock, otherwise the same shall not be entered; and shall sign the same before the rising of the house the same day."

When a protest has been drawn up by any peer, other lords may either subscribe it without remark, if they assent to all the reasons assigned in it; or they may signify the particular reasons which have induced them to ' On the 6tb March 1743 a motion was made, " that no member of this house do presume to make any agreement with another member to absent themselves from any service of this hou.-e, or any committee tliereof; and that this house will proceed with the utmost severity against all such members as shall offend therein; " but it was negatived, on division. 24 Cora. J. 602.

Lords' S. O. No. 33 as to dissents injudicial cases, see Macq- 28, 29.

PERSONAL INTEREST. 281 attach their signatures. But by the usage of the House of Lords, the privilege of entering a protest is restricted to those lords who were present when the question to which they desire to express their dissent was put; and in conformity Avith this rule, a peer cannot protest by proxy. Any protest or reasons, if considered by the house to be unbecoming, or otherwise irregular, may be ordered to be expunged.

In 1796, a general resolution was proposed in the lords. Personal ia-" That no peers shall vote who are interested in a ques-tion;" but it was not adopted."' It is presumed, however, that such a resolution was deemed unnecessary; and that it was held, that the personal honour of a peer will prevent him from forwarding his own pecuniary intei'ests by his votes in Parliament. By standing order. No. 178, lords are " exempted from serving on the committee on any private bill wherein they shall have any interest."

In the commons, it is a distinct rule, that no member Commona. who has a direct pecuniary interest in a question shall be allowed to vote upon it; but in order to operate as a disqualification, this interest must be immediate and personal, and not merely of a general or remote description.

On the 17th July 1811, the rule was thus explained by Mr. Speaker Abbot: "This interest must be a direct pecuniary interest, and separately belonging to the persons whose votes were questioned, and not in common with the rest of his Majesty's subjects, or on a matter of state policy." This opinion was given upon a motion for disallowing the votes of the bank directors upon the Gold Coin Bill, which was afterwards negatived without a division.

No instance is to be found in the Journals in which the Questions of vote of a member has been disallowed upon questions of ' Protests with reasons date from 1G41. 2 Lord Clarendon, Hist. Reb. B. 4, p. 407.

See 87 Hans. Deb., N. S. p. 1137; protest against Corn Importation Bill, where certain peers who had not been present signed the protest.

3 43 Lords' J. 82. " 40 Lords' J. 640. 650. " 20 Hans. Deb. 1001.

public policy. On the 1st June 1797, however, Mr. Manning submitted to the speaker whether he might vote, consistently Avith the rules of the house, upon the proposition of Mr. Pitt, for granting compensation to the subscribers to the Loyalty Loan, he being himself a subscriber. The speaker explained generally the rule of the house, and Ir. Manning declined to vote. After the division, the votes of two other members were objected to as being subscribers, but one stated that he had parted with his subscription, and the other that he had determined not to derive any advantage to himself; upon which questions for disallowing their votes were severally negatived.

On the 3d June 1824, a division took place on a "Bill for repealing so much of an Act 6 Geo. I., as restrains any other corporations than those in the Act named, and any societies or partnerships, from effecting marine insurances, and lending money on bottomry." An objection was made to the numbers declared by the tellers, that certain members who voted with the ayes were personally interested in the passing of the bill, as being concerned in the Alliance Insurance Company; but it was decided that they were not so interested as to preclude their voting for the repeal of a Public Act.

On the 10th July 1844, on the question for hearing counsel against a bill for suspending certain actions for penalties under the gaming laws, objections were taken to the votes of members who were defendants; but one stated that it was not his intention to take advantage of the provisions of the bill, and plead the same in bar of such action; and the other that he had not been served with any process. Motions for disallowing their votes were withdrawn."

On the 11th July 1844, the vote of a member upon the second reading of a public bill relating to railways, was '.33 Hans. Pail. Hist. 791. 52 Com. J. 632. 79 ji,. 455. 99 lb. 486.

objected to upon the ground that he had a direct pecuniary-interest as a proprietor of railroad shares, but a motion for disallowing his vote was withdrawn.

On the 20th May 1825, notice was taken that a member Private Bills, who had voted with the yeas on the report of the Leith Docks Bill, had a direct pecuniary interest in passing the bill. He was heard in his place; and having allowed that he had a direct pecuniary interest in passing the bill; that on that account he had not voted in the committee on the bill; and that he had voted, in this instance, through inadvertence, his vote was ordered to be disallowed."

In some cases, also, members who have been subscribers to undertakings, have voted in favour of bills before the house, for carrying them into effect; and when they have admitted that they were subscribers, their votes have been disallowed.

But it is not sufficient to be interested in a rival undertaking. On the 22d February 1825, a member voted against a bill for establishino: the London and Westminster Oil Gas Company, and notice was taken that he was a proprietor in the Imperial Gas Light and Coke Company, and thereby had a pecuniary interest in opposing the bill. A motion was made that his vote be disallowed, but after he had been heard in his place, it was withdrawn."

On the 16th June 1846, objection was taken to the vote of a member who had voted with the noes, on the ground that he was a director and shareholder in the Caledonian Railway Company, and had a direct pecuniary interest in the rejection of the Glasgow, Dumfries, and Carlisle Kail-way Bill. Whereupon he stated, that the sole direct interest that he had in the Caledonian Railway was being the holder of twenty shares, to qualify him to be a director in that undertaking; and that he voted against the ' 99 Com. J. 491. ' 80 lb. 443.

3 80 lb. 110, 91 lb. 271. " 80 lb. 110.

Glasgow, Dumfries, and Carlisle Railway, conceiving it to be in direct competition with the Caledonian Railway, as decided by the legislature in the last session. A question for disallowing his vote, on the ground of direct pecuniary interest, was negatived.

On the second reading; of the Birmingham and Gloucester Railway Bill, 15th May 1845, objection was taken to one of the tellers for the noes, as being a landholder upon the line whose property would be injured. A motion for disallowing his vote was withdrawn.

If any doubt should be entertained by the house whether a vote should be disallowed or not, the member whose vote is under consideration should withdraw immediately after he has been heard in his place, and before the question is proposed." In Committees. The principle of the rule which disqualifies an interested member from voting, must always have been intended to apply as well to committees as to the house itself; but it is undeniable that a contrary practice had very generally obtained in committees upon private bills, although it was not brought directly under the notice of the house before 1844. In the case of the Leith Docks Bill, noticed above, it may be observed that the member stated he had abstained from voting in the committee on the bill, on account of his pecuniary interest. Some years later the intention of the house may be clearly collected from the following case. On the 20th March 1843, the chairman of ways and means having stated to the house that he had a personal interest in the Lancaster Lunatic Asylum Bill, the house instructed the committee of selection to refer the bill to the chairman of the standing orders committee, instead of the chairman of ways and raeans. At length, on the 21st June 1844, the ISIiddle Level Drainage Bill Committee instructed their chairman to report that a member "had received an intima-101 Com. J. 873. 100 lb. 436.

3 80 Com. J. 110: 91 lb. 271. i 98 lb. 129.

tion that he ought not to vote on questions arising thereon, by reason of his interest in the said bill;" and desired the decision of the house upon the following question: " Whether a member of the House of Commons, having property within the limits of an improvement bill, which property may be affected by the passing of the bill, has such an interest as, in the judgment of the house, disqualifies him as a member of the house, and the representative of general local interests, from voting on all questions affecting the preamble or clauses of the said bill." On the 27th June, three different propositions were submitted to the consideration of the house, in answer to the question suggested by the committee, which, after a debate, were all ultimately withdrawn; when the house agreed to an instruction to the committee, " that the rule of this house relating to the vote, upon any question in the house, of a member having an interest in the matter upon which the vote is given, applies likewise to any vote of a member so interested, in a committee." A selected member, on a committee on a private bill or group of bills, will be discharged from any further attendance, if it be discovered that he has a direct pecuniary interest in the bills, or one of them.

Upon the same principle that every member should be offer of money, free from any pecuniary interest in the votes he may give, it was resolved, on the 2d May 1695,

"That the offer of any money, or other advantage, to any member of Parliament, for the promoting of any matter whatsoever, depending, or to be transacted, in Parliament, is a high crime and misdemeanor, and tends to the subversion of the English constitution."

And, more recently, it has been declared contrary to the law and usage of Parliament, for any member to be engaged in the management of private bills for pecuniary reward.

' 101 Com. J. 904 J 104 lb. 357. 11 lb. 331, and supra, p. 86. ' 85 lb. 107.

Counsel. And, upon the same grounds, it was ordered, on the 6th

November 1666,

"That such members of this house as are of the long robe shall not be of counsel on either side, in any bill depending in the Lords' House, before such bill shall come down from the Lords' House to this house." '

CHAPTER XIII.

Mode of appointment.

Chairman of lords' committees.

COMMITTEES OF THE WHOLE HOUSE: GENERAL RULES OF PROCEEDING: CHAIRMAN; MOTIONS AND DEBATE: HOUSE RESUMED.

A COMMITTEE of the whole house is, in fact, the house itself, presided over by a chairman, instead of by the speaker. It is appointed in the lords by an order " that the house be put into a committee," which is followed by an adjournment of the house dui'ing pleasure. In the commons it is appointed by a resolution, "That this house will resolve itself into a committee of the whole house;" after which a question is put by the speaker, viz.: " That I do now leave the chair;" and when that is agreed to, the speaker leaves the chair immediately, the mace is removed from the table, and placed under it, and the committee commences its sittino;.

The chair is taken, in the lords, by the chairman of committees, who is appointed at the commencement of each session, by virtue of the standing orders of that house," by which it is ordered that he

"Do take the chair in all committees of the whole house, and in all committees upon private bills, unless where it shall have been otherwise directed by this house."'
' 8 Com. J. 646. See case of Mr. Roebuck (18th July 1842), 97 lb. 499; and of Mr. C. Buller (4tli May 184G), 101 lb. 6:27. In both these cases the bill had already passed the House of Commons.

' Lords' S. O. No. 8. lb. No. 44; ami 42 Lords' J. 636.

"That when the house is in a committee of the whole house, if the chairman of committees, or any lord appointed by the house in his place, shall be absent (unless by leave of the committee), the house be resumed."

In pursuance of these orders, in the absence of the chairman of committees, the committee cannot proceed to business; but the house is resumed, and a chairman is appointed by the house.

In the commons the chair is generally taken by the ciiainnan of ,. n ' n 1 Ti' committees in chairman ot the committee or ways and means, it a tiie commons, difference should arise in the committee concerning the election of a chairman, it must be determined by the house itself, and not by the committee. The speaker resumes the chair at once, and puts a question, "That a particular member do take the chair of the committee;" which being agreed to, the mace is again removed from the table, and the committee proceeds to business under the chairman appointed by the house.

The proceedings are conducted in the same manner as Conduct of bn-when the house is sitting. In the lords a peer addresses himself to their lordships, as at other times; in the commons, a member addresses the chairman, who performs in committee all the duties which dcaolve upon the sjjeaker in the house. He calls upon members as they rise to speak, puts the questions, maintains order, and gives the casting vote in case of an equality of voices.

On the 28th June 1848, in committee on the Koman Casting voice Catholic Relief Bill, the numbers in a division were equal, and the chairman gave his casting voice. It Avas stated, in debate, that no such case was recollected, and doubts were expressed as to the regularity of the proceeding; but it was clearly consistent with the rules of the house. As regards select committees the rule has been declared by the house;" It was otherwise before the 3d July 1848, when S. 0. No. 44 was amended. See Lords' J. and Debates, 22d June 1848.

' lcom. J.6oo;9 Ib.38G; 13Ib.7D4;21 lb. 255; 6J lb. 30, c., 3 Grey's Debates, 301.

= Lords' S. O. Nos.42, 43. 91 Com. J. 214; and sec infra, p. 303.

Matters committed.

Instructions and amendments on going into committee.

When tliere are several amendments.

Motion not seconded in committee.

and there can be no principle at variance with the practice which was adopted on tliis occasion.

A committee can only consider those matters which have been committed to them by the house. If it be desirable that other matters should also be considered, an instruction is given by the house to empower the committee to entertain them. An instruction should always be moved distinctly after the order of the day has been read, and not as an amendment to the question for the speaker leaving the chair.

Except in the case of the committees of supply, and ways and means, all motions for instructions, and amendments to the question for Mr. Speaker leaving the chair, must be moved before the first sitting of the committee. By a sessional resolution,

"When a bill or other matter (except supply or ways and means) has been partly considered in committee, and the chairman has been directed to report progress, and ask leave to sit again, and the house shall have ordered that the committee shall sit again on a particular day, the speaker shall, when the order for the committee has been read, forthwith leave the chair, without putting any question, and the house shall thereupon resolve itself into such committee."'

When there are several amendments to be proposed to the question that the speaker " do now leave the chair," for the house to resolve itself into committee, if the first amendment be negatived by the house affirming that the words proposed to be left out shall stand part of the question, no other amendment can be ofliered; but if the amendment be carried, the question for the speaker to leave the chair must be again proposed, and another amendment may be offered."' It is an understood rule that a motion in committee need not be seconded, which is observed inj practice, although it has never been distinctly declared, and its ' See Hans. Deb. 28tli June 1848.

104 Com. J. 22.

See Voti'8, 8th April 1850 (Committee of Supply), p. 238.

See also Chapter XVIII.

propriety is sometimes questioned. It derived confirmation from the former practice of appointing one teller only for each side on a division in committee; and, although two tellers are now appointed, without whom no division in the lobbies is allowed to proceed, a question is still put from the chair on the motion of one member.

A motion for the previous question is not admitted in Previous ques-committee; since the committee being only authorised to consider the matters which have been referred to them by the house, the consideration of such matters should be preferred to a motion which is offered for the purpose of excluding them from a decision. Motions, however, having the same practical effect, have sometimes been allowed in committees on bills.

On the 3d November 1675, it was declared to be an Questions of ancient order of the house, " that when there comes a question between the greater and lesser sum, or the longer or shorter time, the least sum and longest time ouoht first to be put to the question." This rule has more immediate reference to the committees of supply, and ways and means, but is also observed in other committees.

The main difference between the proceedings of a com- Members may mittee and those of the house is, that in the former a tbanon'ce member is entitled to speak more than once, in order that the details of a question or bill may have the most minute examination; or, as it is expressed in the standing orders of the lords, ' to have more freedom of speech, and that arguments maybe used pro et contra. These facilities for speaking are not often abused so as to protract the debates; but are rather calculated, in ordinary cases, to discourage long speeches, and to introduce a more free and conversational mode of debating. When a member may not speak more than once, he cannot omit any argument that he is prepared to offer, as he will not have another oppor- ' See Chapter XVIIL, on Bills. 9 Com. J. 367.

3 Lords' S. O., No. 42.

tunlty of urging it; but when he is at liberty to speak again, he may confine himself to one point at a time. To speak stand- Members must speak standing and uncovered, as when '"- the house is sitting, although it appears that, in earlier times, they were permitted to speak either sitting or standing:

On the 7th November 1601, in a committee on the subsidy or supply, Sir Walter Ealeigh was interrupted by Sir E. Hobby, who said, "We cannot hear you; speak out; you should speak standing, that so the house might the better hear you. ' To this Raleigh replied, " that being a committee, he might either speak sitting or standing." Mr. Secretary Cecil rose next, and said, "Because it Is an argument of more reverence,

I chuse to speak standing." ' Houee re It was ordered and declared by the lords, 10 June 1714, sunied. n i

"That when the house shall be put into a committee of the whole house, the house be not resumed without the unanimous consent of the committee, unless upon a question put by the lord who sha, ll be in the chair of such committee."

Chairman I the commons. If any doubt should arise as to a point leaves the chair. q order or Other proceeding, which the committee cannot Commons. i i i i i agree upon, or which may appear beyond their province to decide, the chairman should be directed to leave the chair, report progress, and ask leave to sit again. Thus, on the 2d March 1836, a debate having concluded In committee, the chairman stated, that before he put the question, he wished to have the opinion of the committee as to the manner in which the committee should be divided, in case of a division; and it being the opinion of the committee, that that matter ought to be decided by the house, the chalraian left the chair; and Mr. Speaker having resumed the chair, the chairman reported that a point of order had arisen in the committee, with respect to the manner in which the committee should be divided, upon which the committee wished to be instructed by the house. The house proceeded to consider this point, and Mr.

' 1 Hane. Pari, Hist. 91G. Lords' S. O., No. 44.

Speaker having been requested to give his opinion, stated it to the house; after which the house again resolved itself into the committee, the question was immediately put, and the committee divided in the manner pointed out by the speaker.

If any public business should arise in which the house Speaker re- . surnes thecliair is concerned, the speaker resumes the chair at once, with- in certain cases. out any report from the committee; as if the usher of the black rod should summon the house to attend her Majesty or the lords commissioners in the House of Peers, or if the time be come for holding a conference with the lords.

So, also, if any sudden disorder should occur by which the honour and dignity of the house are affected, the urgency of such a circumstance would justify the speaker in resuming the chair immediately, without awaiting the ordinary forms.

On the 10th May 1675 a serious disturbance arose in a grand committee, in which bloodshed was threatened; when it is related that " the speaker, very opportunely and prudently rising from his seat near the bar, in a resolute and slow pace, made his three respects through the crowd, and took the chair." The mace having been forcibly laid upon the table, all the disorder ceased, and the gentlemen went to their places. The speaker being sat, spoke to this purpose, "That to bring the house into order again, he took the chair, though not according to order." No other entry appears in the Journal than that "Mr. Speaker resumed the chair;" but the same rejdort adds, that though " some gentlemen excepted against his coming into the chair, the doing it was generally approved, as the only expedient to suppress the disorder."

The speaker certainly acted with judgment on that occasion, and a more recent case would seem to prove that he was clearly not out of order.

91 Com. J. 104. 67 lb. 431.

1 lb. 8: J7. 3 Grey's Del). 1-29.

Forty members required.

Cannot adjourn.

Lords.

Commons.

On the 2 7 til February 1810, a member who, for disorderly conduct, had been ordered into custody, returned into the house, during the sitting of a committee, in a very violent and disorderly manner; upon which Mr. Speaker resumed the chair, and ordered the Serjeant to do his duty. When the member had been removed by the serjeant, the house again resolved itself into the committee.

The house has also been resumed on account of words of heat or disputes between members."

A committee of the whole house, in the commons, like the house itself, cannot proceed with business, unless forty members be present; but it has no power of adjournment, as, according to the present rules, the sitting of the house itself would be concluded by such adjournment. When notice, therefore, is taken that forty members are not present, the chairman counts the committee, and if less than that number be present, he leaves the chair, and Mr. Speaker resumes the chair, and tells the house. If forty members be then present, the house again resolves itself into the committee; but if not, the speaker adjourns the house, without a question first put, in the same manner as when forty members are not present during the sitting of the house. So, also, if it appear on a division in committee, that forty members are not present, the chairman leaves the chair, and the speaker tells the house in the same manner."

A committee of the whole house has no power either to adjourn its own sittings or to adjourn a debate to a future sitting; but if a debate be not concluded, or if all the matters referred be not considered; in the lords, the house is resumed, and the chairman moves "that the house be again put into committee" on a future day; and in the commons, the chairman is directed to " report progress, and ask leave to sit again." It is the practice, therefore, 65 Com. J. 134. 91 lb. G59,. C.

10 lb. 806; H lb. 480; 43 lb. 467. 85 lb. GO, c.

for members, who desire an adjournment, to move that the " chairman do report progress," in order to put an end to the proceedings of the committee on that day; as this motion, in committee, is analogous to that frequently made at other times, for adjourning the debate. A motion " That the chairman do now leave the chair" would, if carried, prevent a report from being made, and would supersede the business of a committee; as an adjournment of the house supersedes a question.

But although a committee of the whole house cannot sitting sus-adjourn, its sitting has been suspended for a certain time. ' " On the 11th August 1848 the house met at twelve o'clock, and shortly afterwards resolved itself into the committee of supply. At three o'clock the committee was still sitting, when the chairman left the chair, without any question first put, and resumed it at five o'clock. In the course of the evening some observations were made upon the subject. It seemed to be admitted that there was no precedent for this proceeding; but that there was no more irregularity in it than in the common practice, at morning sittings, of the speaker leaving the chair, and resuming it at five o'clock, without any question.

If none of the interruptions and delays to which com- Report, mittees ai'c liable should occur, the chairman is directed to report the resolutions or other proceedings to the house. Sometimes he is instructed to move for leave to bring in bills, or to inform the house of matters connected with the inquiries or deliberations of the committee.

When a committee have agreed to resolutions, they are Report of reso-twice read on the report, before they are agreed to by the house; and may be amended, disagreed to, postponed, or recommitted to the committee. The first reading is a formal proceeding, and it is upon and after the second reading that amendments are ordinarily proposed. On reporting a ' 101 Hans. Dcl., 3d Scr., 90, U

Grand committees.

Committee of privileges.

Entry of pro-ceedinjjs in the Journals.

resolution from a coinniittce of tlie whole house, an amendment, proposed to the question for reading the resolution a second time, takes precedence of a proposed amendment to the resolution itself."

In the commons, the principal proceedings in committees of the whole house are in reference to bills, and the voting of supply, and ways and means; of which a description will be found in the chapters relating to these matters.

Since 1832 the annual appointment of the ancient Grand Committees for Religion, for Grievances, for Courts of Justice, and for Trade, has been discontinued. They had long since fallen into disuse, and served only to mark the ample jurisdiction of the commons in Parliament. When they were accustomed to sit, they were, in fact, committees of the whole house, like the modern committee of supply; and until 1641 little difference is to be detected in their constitution and proceedings.

The ancient committee of privileges is also analogous to a grand committee, consisting of certain members specially nominated, of all knights of shires, gentlemen of the long robe, and merchants in the house; and " all who come are to have voices." This committee is still appointed at the commencement of each session; but it is not nominated or appointed to sit, unless there be some special matter to be referred to it, as was the case in 1847."

In the House of Lords, the proceedings of committees do not appear upon the Journals; nor in the commons were they entered until, on the 23d February 1829, the speaker submitted to the house that arrangements shoidd be made to effect that object, to which the house assented." Since that time the proceedings in committee have been recorded.

' Maynooth College (Consolidated Fund) Report, 28th April 1845. 100 Com. J. 351.

See Chapters XVIII. and XXI. a l Com. J. 873.

1 Com. J. 220. 822. 1042, c.; 2 lb. 1.53. 202. 321, c. Lfx Pari. 339. Scobell, 38.

' 103 Com. J. 139 (West Gloucester election), 84 lb, 78.

and are a valuable addition to the means of comprehending the forms of parliamentary procedure. It may be added, that in a committee of the whole house it is customary for the clerk assistant to officiate as clerk.

CHAPTER XIV.

APPOINTMENT, CONSTITUTION, POWERS, AND PROCEEDINGS OF SELECT COMMITTEES IN BOTH HOUSES.

A SELECT committee is composed of certain members General pro-

VillcG 01 L S6l(ip appointed by the house to consider or inquire into any committee, matters, and to report their opinions, for the information of the house. Like a committee of the whole liouse, a select committee are restrained from considering matters not specially referred to them by the house. When it is thought necessary to extend their inquiries beyond the order of reference, a special instruction from the house gives them authority for that purpose; or if it be deemed advisable to restrict their inquiries further than was originally intended, an instruction may be given by the house, prescribing the limits of their powers. Inquiry by evidence is the most general object of a select committee; but committees may be appointed for any other purpose in which they can assist the house, and petitions, bills, and other documents are constantly referred to them for consideration.

It is a common practice to refer to a committee the reports Reports and of previous committees and other printed reports and papers. 1'" " Such a reference is usually intended to direct the particular attention of the committee to documents relating to the subject of their inquiry, or to explain or enlarge the original ' 91 Com. J. 422. 687. ' 75 lb. 259; 90 lb. 522.

terms of the reference. It has been questioned' whether such documents can be considered and cited in the report of a committee, unless they have been expressly referred by the house; but it would seem that if they be relevant to the subject of inquiry, the only question for the committee to determine would be, whether they should be received in evidence or not. If a document should have been laid upon the table of the house, but not printed, it would not be accessible to the committee without an order of the house; but if printed by order of the house, or laid upon the table in a printed form, the general power to send for papers and records would entitle a committee to avail itself of all the information contained in it. Appointment in In the Housc of Lords there are no special rules in t '6 o' regard to the appointment and constitution of select com- mittees. The house resolve, that a select committee be appointed; after which it is ordered that certain lords then nominated shall be appointed a committee to inquire into the matters referred, and to report to the house. Their lordships, or any three of them, (or a greater number, if necessary), are ordered to meet at a certain time in the Prince's Lodgings, near the House of Peers, and to adjourn as they please. Sittings and The Order of sitting on the lords' committees, and other proceedings. matters, are thus defined by the standing orders:

"If they be a select committee, they usually meet in one of the rooms adjoyning to the upper house, as the lords like; any of the lords of the committee speak to the rest uncovered, but may sit still if he please; the committees are to be attended by such judges or learned councel as are appointed; they are not to sit there or be covered, unless it be out of favour for infirmity; some judge sometimes hath a stool set behind, but never covers, and the rest never sit or cover. The Lord Chief Justice Popham did often attend committees; and though he were chief justice, privy councillor, and infirm, yet would he very hardly ever be perswaded to sit down, saying it was his duty to stand and attend, and desired the lords to keep those forms which were their due.""

Ceylon Committee, 1849. = Lords' S. O., No. 45.

The House of Lords do not give select commlttecfl any Witnesses, how special authority to send for witnesses or documentary evidence; but parties are ordinarily served with a notice from the clerk attending the committee, that their attendance is requested on a certain day, to be sworn at the bar of the house, in order to be afterwards examined before the committee. Where a positive order is thought necessary to enforce the attendance of a witness, or the production of documents, it emanates from the house itself.

In order to ensure fairness and efficiency in the consti- Appointment, , T n 1, 1,1 constitution, tution and proceedings oi select committees, and to make and practice iu their conduct open to observation, the House of Commons commons. have laid down the following regulations: 1. "That no select committee shall, without previous leave Number of obtained of the house, consist of more than fifteen members; that '" 2mber9. such leave shall not be mo-ved for without notice; and that in the case of members proposed to be added or substituted after the first appointment of the committee, the notice shall include the names of the members proposed to be added or substituted."' 2. " That it be recommended to every member moving for the Attendance, appointment of a select committee, to ascertain previously whether each member proposed to be named by him on such committee will give his attendance tliereupon."

3. " That every member intending to propose a select committee, Notice of shall, one day next before the nomination of such committee, place " C9. on the notices the names of the members intended to be proposed by him to be members of such committee."

4. " That lists be affixed in some conspicuous place in the com- List of raem-mittee clerks' office, and in the lobby of the house, of all members ' " serving on each select committee."

5. " That to every question asked of a witness under examination Questions to in the proceedings of any select committee, there be prefixed in witnesses. the minutes of the evidence the name of the member asking such question."

G. "That the names of the members present each day on the Minutes of pro-sitting of any select committee be entered on the minutes of evi- ceedings. dence, or on the minutes of tlie proceedings of the committee (as the case may be), and reported to the house on the report of such committee."' !)I Com. J. 30; 02 lb. 8. ' 93 lb. 221.

Divisions. 7. " That in the event of any division taking place in any select committee, the question j roposed, the name of the proposer, and the respective voles tliereupon of each member present, be entered on the minutes of the proceedings of the committee (as the case may be), and reported to the house on the report of such committee."

Appointnieutof In Compliance with the first of these resolutions, a select mera ers. committee is usually confined to fifteen members, but if from any special circumstances a larger number should be thought necessary, the house will allow it. In special cases, the house have also thought fit to appoint certain committees by ballot; ' or to name two members, and to appoint the rest of the committee by ballot; or to choose twenty-one names by ballot, and to permit each of two members nominated by the house to strike off four from that number." Members have also been nominated to serve on a committee, to examine witnesses, without the power of voting.

Members added Members are frequently added to committees, and other ihc large. jjjgjj jjgj. g originally nominated are discharged from further attendance.

Quorum. Whatever may be the number of a committee, it is not probable that all could attend, and the house order in each case what number shall be a quorum. If no quorum were named, it would be necessary for all the members of the committee to attend. Three are generally a quorum in committees of the upper house, and in the commons the usual number is five; but three are sometimes allowed, and occasionally seven, or any other number which tlie house may please to direct. In two cases where the investigations of committees partook of a judicial character, the house named a quorum of five, but at the same time ordered the committee to report the absence of any member on two consecutive days.

A committee cannot proceed to business without a 92 Com. J. 91; 103 lb. 114; 10-1 lb. 54. 80. 74 lb. Gt, c.

3 88 lb. 144. 467, c. 88 lb. IGO. 475.

91 lb. 42. 6 90 lb. 457. 504.

quorum, but must wait until the proper number of members have come into the room. And on the 27th March 1849 it was resolved,

"That if, at any time during the sitting of a select committee of this house, the quorum of members fixed by the house shall not be present, the clerk of the committee shall call the attention of the chairman to the fact, who shall thereupon suspend the proceedings of the committee until a quorum be present, or adjourn the committee to some future day.""

As the object of select committees is usually to take Evidence, evidence, the House of Commons, when necessary, give them "leave to send for persons, papers, and records." By virtue of this authority, any witness may be summoned by an order, signed by the chairman, and he must bring all documents which he is informed will be required for the use of the committee. Any neglect or disobedience of a summons will be reported to the house, and the offender will be treated in the same manner as if he had been guilty of a similar contempt to the house itself. This general notice of the power of committees in respect to witnesses will suffice in this place, as the proceedings of Parliament iu regard to the summoning, examination, and punishment of witnesses will appear more at length in the next cliapter."' In 1849 the Fisheries (Ireland) Committee was appointed, with power to send for papers and records only, but examined witnesses who voluntarily tendered their evidence. This arrangement was made in order to save the expense of witnesses summoned in the usual manner; and placed the committee in the same position, in regard to the examination of witnesses, as a committee on a private Bill.

When a select committee of the House of Lords are Presence of taking the examination of witnesses, strangers are rarely allowed to be present; but in the commons the presence of strangers is generally permitted. Their exclusion, how- ' 104 Com. J. 178. 2 See infra, p. 30G.

5 104 Com. J. lo.

All lords may come, but liot vote.

Presence of members.

Precedents.

Charges against tlie Duke of Buckingham.

ever, may be ordered at any time, and continued as long as the conmiittee may think fit. When they are deliberating, it is the invariable practice to exclude all strangers, in order that the committee may be exposed to no interruption or restraint.

All the lords are entitled to attend the select committees of that house, subject to the following regulations:

"Here it is to be observed, that at any committee of our owr, any member of our bouse, though not of the committee, is not excluded from coming in and speaking, but he must not vote: as also he shall give place to all that are of the committee, though of lower degree, and shall sit behind them, and observe the same order for sitting at a conference with the commons."

Members of the House of Commons have claimed the right of being present as well during the deliberations of a committee as while the witnesses are examined; and although, if requested to retire, they would rarely make any objection, and on the grounds of constant practice and courtesy to the committee, they ought immediately to retire when the committee are about to deliberate; yet it does not appear that the committee, in case of their refusal, would have any power to order them to withdraw.

On the 24th April 1626, Mr. Glanvyle, from the select committee on the charges against the Duke of Buckingham, stated that exceptions were taken by some members of the house against the examinations being kept private, without admitting some other members thereof, and desired the direction of the house. It is evident from this statement that the committee had exercised a power of excluding members; and though it is said in the Journal that much dispute arose upon the general question, " whether the members of the house, not of a select committee, may come to the select committee," no general rule was laid down; but in that particular case the house ordered,

"That no member of the house shall be present at the debate, ' Lords' S. 0., No. 40.

disposition, or penning of the business by the select committee; but onl v to be present at the examination, and that without interposition." '

An odinlon somewhat more definite may be collected Eastindiajudi, cature.

from the proceedings of the India Judicature Committee, in 1782. In that case the committee were about to Mr. Banvell. deliberate upon the refusal of Mr. Barwell to ausw er certain questions, and on the room being cleared, he insisted upon his privilege, as a member of the house, of being present during the debate. The committee observed, that Mr. Barwell being the party concerned in that debate, they thought he had no right to be present. Mr. Barwell still persisted in his right, and two members attended the speaker, and returned witli his opinion, that Mr. Barwell had no right to insist upon being present during the debate; upon which Mr. Barwell withdrew. Here the ground taken by the committee for his exclusion was, that he was concerned in the debate, and not simply that, as a member, he had no right to be present at their deliberations. The house soon afterwards ordered,

"That when any matter sball arise on which the said committee wish to debate, it shall be at their discretion to require every person, not being a member of the committee, to withdraw."

The inference from this order must be, that the committee would not otherwise have been authorized to exclude a member of the house.

When committees were appointed to examine the phy- King's physi-sicians of King George III., in 1810 and 1811, the house also ordered, "That no member of this house, but such as are members of the committee, be there present."

On the 29th June 18-42 the committee on election pro- Eleetion proceedings reported that they had unanimously resolved, that nfttee! ' it was desirable that no person should be present except the witness under examination; " but that the committee, havino; reason to believe that the rio; ht of members to be Irish Poor

Committee, 1849.

present at their proceedings will be insisted on, had directed the chairman to call the attention of the house to the subject." The exclusion proposed in this case extended not only to the deliberations of the committee, but also to the examination of witnesses, and was not sanctioned by the house.

And on the 23d February 1849, in the case of the Irish Poor Committee, the speaker stated, that although it had been the practice for members, not being members of the committee, to withdraw while the committee were deliberating or dividing; yet if members persisted in remaining, the committee have no power to exclude them, unless by application to the house. Generalresults. Until some more positive rule shall be laid down upon this matter by the house itself, the result of all these precedents appears to be, that members cannot be excluded from a committee room by the authority of the committee; and that if there should be a desire on the part of the committee, that members should not be present at their deliberations, when there is reason to apprehend opposition, they should apply to the house for orders similar to those already noticed.

But secret committees are sometimes appointed, whose inquiries are conducted throughout with closed doors; and it is the invariable practice for all members, not on the committee, to be excluded from the room throughout the whole of its proceedings.

When members attend the sittings of a committee, they assume a privilege similar to that exercised in the house, and sit or stand without being uncovered. Divisions. Every question is determined in a select committee in

Secret commit tees.

' 97 Com. J. 4.38. 2 102 Hans. Deb., 3d Ser., 1183.

.03 Lords' J. 115. 02 Com. J. 26, c.

For a discussion as to the peculiarities of a secret committee, see debates upon the Budget and Navy Estimates, 22d Feb. 1848. 96 Hans. Deb., 3d Ser., 987. 105G.

the same manner as in the house to which it belongs.

In the lords' committees, the chairman votes like any other peer; and if the numbers on a division be equal, the question is negatived, in accordance with the ancient ride of the House of Lords, " semper prcesumiter pro negante.

In the commons, the practice is similar to that observed in divisions of the house itself.

On the 25th March 1836 the house were informed that Casting voice of Cliairman. the chairman of a select committee had first claimed the privilege to vote as a member of the committee, and afterwards, when the voices were equal, of giving a casting vote as chairman; and that such practice had, of late years, prevailed in some select committees: upon which the house declared, "That, according to the established rules of Parliament, the chairman of a select committee can only vote when there is an equality of voices."

But in committees on private Bills a different practice Committees on . private Bills, has been introduced, as it is ordered,

"That all questions shall be decided by a majoritj' of voices, includiny the voice of the chairman; and whenever the voices are equal, the chairman shall have a second or casting vote."

This deviation from the ordinary rule of voting in select committees was rendered necessary by the peculiar constitution of group committees, consisting of five members only. When one member was absent, a difficulty arose in determining a question without some new regulation; for otherwise two members could have decided every question, although the chairman agreed with the remaining member.

A select committee may adjourn its sittings from time to Adjournment time, and occasionally a power is also given by the house to adjourn from place to place. But without special leave no committee of the commons may sit during the sitting of the house, nor after any adjournment for a longer period ' 91 Com. J. 214. This misconception of the usage of parliament may have arisen from the peculiar practice of election committees, as regulated by Act of Parliament.

' S. O. 99. ' 89 Com. J. 419; 101 lb. 152; 105 lb. 215, c.

of committees.

Prayers.

Printed minutes of evidence.

than till the next dcay. By a sessional order of the commons, it is ordered,

"That the serjeant-at-arms attending this house do, from time to time, when tlie house is going to prayers, give notice thereof to all committees; and that all proceedings of committees in a morning, after such notice, be declared to be null and void."

In order to avoid any interruption to urgent business before committees, leave is frequently obtained, on the meeting of the house, for a committee to sit till five o'clock; and on Friday night leave is given, when necessary, to a committee to sit on Saturday, notwithstanding the adjournment of the house.

The evidence of the witnesses examined before a select committee is taken down in short-hand, and printed daily for the use of the members of the committee. A copy of his own examination is also sent to each witness for his revision, with an instruction that he can only make verbal corrections, as corrections in substance must be effected by re-examination. The corrected copy should be returned without delay to the committee clerk. In the lords the printed evidence is not circulated to the members of the committee until the corrections have been approved by the chairman; but in the commons the corrections are made after the circulation of the proofs.

On the 20th July 1849 an instruction was given to a select committee to re-examine a witness " touching his former evidence," as it appeared that he had corrected his evidence more extensively than the rules of the house permitted, and his corrections had consequently not been reported by the committee.

In 1849 a committee of the House of Lords' reported that the alterations made by some of the witnesses were so unusual, that they had ordered the alterations and corrections to be marked, and printed in the margin.

' 104 Com. J. 525.

Audit of Railway Accounts (North Wales Railway).

Neither the members nor the witnesses to whom these Not to be pub- . lished before copies are entrusted, are at hberty to piibhsh any portion report. of them, until they have been reported to the house. On the 21st April 1837, it was resolved by the commons,

"That according to the undoubted privileges of this house, and for the due protection of the public interest, the evidence taken by any select committee of this house, and documents presented to such committee, and which have not been reported to the house, ought not to be published by any member of such committee, nor by any other person." '

Any publication of the report of a committee before it has been presented to the house, is treated as a breach of privilege. On the 31st May 1832 complaint was made of the publication of a draft report of a committee, in a Dublin newspaper: the proprietor admitted that he had sent the copy, and stated that he was willing to take the responsibility upon himself; but must decline to give information which might implicate any other person. He was accordingly declared guilty of a breach of privilege, and committed to the custody of the serjeant.

In 1850, a draft report of the Committee on Postal Communication with France was published in two newspapers, while it was under consideration. The committee vainly endeavoured to trace the parties from Avhom the copy had been originally obtained; but recommended improved regulations for the printing, distribution, and custody of such documents.

It is the general custom to withhold the evidence until To report from the inquiry has been completed, and the report is ready to be presented; but, whenever an intermediate publication of the evidence, or more than one report may be thought necessary, the house will grant leave, on the application of the chairman, for the committee to " report from time to time," or to "report minutes of evidence" only, from time to time."

' 92 Com. J. 282. 87 lb. 360. Rep. p. vi., Sess. ISr O (381).

74 Lords' J. 80, c. 92 Com. J. 18. 107, c.

Reports of Committees.

When the evidence has not been reported by a committee, it has sometimes been ordered to be laid before the house. It is usual, however, to present the report, evidence, and appendix together, which are ordered to lie upon the table and to be printed. Any motion may be founded upon a report; as that it be re-committed; or taken into consideration on a future day; or communicated to the lords at a conference." In 1851, the house, instead of ordering the evidence taken before a committee to be printed, referred it " to the secretary of state for the colonies, for the consideration of Her Majesty's government."

CHAPTER XV.

How sum-rconed by the lords.

WITNESSES: MODES OF SUMMONS AND EXAMINATION: ADMINISTRA-TION OF OATHS: EXPENSES.

All witnesses who are summoned to give evidence before the House of Lords, or any of the lords' committees, are ordered to attend at the bar on a certain day, to be sworn, and they are served with the order of the house, signed by the assistant clerk of the Parliaments. And if a witness be in the custody of a keeper of a prison, the keeper is ordered to bring him up in custody, in the same manner. If the house have reason to believe that a witness is purposely keeping out of the way, to avoid being served with the order, it has been usual to direct that the service of the order at his house shall be deemed good service. If, after such service of the order, the witness should not attend, he is ordered to be taken into custody; but the execution of this order is sometimes stayed for a certain time. If the officers of the house do not succeed in taking the witness into custody, by virtue of this order.

' 88 Com. J. 671; 105 lb. 637 c. 3 86 lb. 167. " 91 lb. 9. 66 Lords' J. 295. 358. 2 76 1b. 213; 88 lb. 583.

105 lb. 661, (Ceylon Committee.) 7 66 lb. 400. 8 66 lb. 358.

the last step taken is to address the Crown to issue a proclamation, with a reward for his apprehension.

When the evidence of peers, peeresses, or lords of Par- Poors, c. how 11111 II 1 1 sumiiioned.

Lament has been required, the lord chancellor has been ordered to write letters to them, desiring their attendance to be examined as witnesses; but they ordinarily attend and give evidence without any such form.

When the attendance of a witness is desired, to be Witnesses sum- ,1,1 TT r r iiimied bv the exammed at the bar by the House or Commons, or a com- commons. mittee of the whole house, he is simply ordered to attend at a stated time; and the order, signed by the clerk of the house, is served upon him personally, if in or near London, and if at a distance, it is forwarded to him by the serjeant-at-arms, by post, or, in special cases, by a messenger. If he should be in the custody of the keeper of any prison, the speaker is ordered to issue his warrant, which is personally served upon the keeper by a messenger of the house, and by which he is directed to bring the witness in his custody to be examined." If the order for the attendance of a witness be disobeyed, he is ordered to be sent for in custody of the serjeant-at-arms, and Mr. Speaker is ordered to issue his warrant accordingly. ' Any person, also, who aids or abets a witness in keeping out of the way, is liable to a similar punishment." When the Serjeant has succeeded in apprehending such persons, they are generally sent to Newgate for their offence.

If a witness should be in custody by order of the other house, his attendance is secured by a message, desiring that he may attend in the custody of the black rod, or the serjeant-at-arms, as the case may be, to be examined.

All witnesses intended to be examined before an election By election committee, are summoned, before the appointment of the ' 75 Lords'J. 441, 442. lb. 144. ' 78 Com. J. 240. 91 lb. 338.

MOCom. J.476. 82 lb. 464. 86 lb. 795. 99 lb. 89. 5 95 Com. J. 58. See also as to the form of the warrant, supra, p. 161, (Howard v. Gosset). go Qq j j 330. 7 90 ib. 343, 344.

8 11 Ib. 296. 305. 15 Ib. 376. J9 Ib. 461, 462. 21 Ib. 356.926.

By select committees.

On private bills.

Witnesses absconding.

Attendance of members, how required.

committee, by a speaker's warrant, on the application of the parties. Tlie speaker issues his warrant without any-special order of the house in each case, under a general order, given when the petition is presented, "That Mr. Speaker do issue his warrant for such persons, papers, and records as shall be thought necessary by the several parties, on the hearing of the matter of the said petition." Disobedience to a speaker's warrant, issued by virtue of this general order, has always been punished in the same manner as disobedience to a special order of the house. After the appointment of an election committee, the witnesses are summoned by orders of the committee, signed by the chairman.

The attendance of a witness to be examined before a select committee, is ordinarily secured by an order signed by the chairman, by direction of the committee; but if a party should neglect to appear when summoned in this manner, his conduct is reported to the house, and an order is immediately made for his attendance. If, in the meantime, he should appear before the committee, it is usual to discharge the order for his attendance:" but if he still neglect to appear, he is dealt with as in the other cases already described. The attendance of a witness before a committee on a private bill, is generally secured by the promoters and opponents themselves, without any order or other process; but if a witness should decline to attend at the instance of the parties, his attendance is enforced by an order of the house."'

When witnesses have absconded, and cannot be taken into custody by the serjeant-at-arms, addresses have been presented to the Crown for the issue of proclamations, with rewards for their apprehension.

If the evidence of a member be desired by the house, or a committee of the whole house, he is ordered to attend in his place on a certain day. But when the attendance '

82 Com. J. 351. Ml 12 Vict. c. 98, s. 83. ' 91 lb. 352.

98 lb. 152, 288, c. 104 lb. 386, c. 75 j,,. 419. 32 lb. 345.

61 lb. 386. 64 lb. 17. 65 lb. 21, 30, c.

of a member is required before a select committee, it is the custom to request him to come, and not to address a summons to him in the ordinary form. The proper course to be adopted by committees, in reference to members, has been thus laid down by two resolutions of the commons, of the 16th March 1688:

"That if any member of the house refuse, upon being sent to, to come to give evidence or information as a witness to a committee, the committee ought to acquaint the house therewith, and not summon such member to attend the committee."

"That if any information come before any committee that chargeth any member of the house, the committee ought only to direct that the house be acquainted with the matter of such information, without proceeding further thereupon."'

There has been no instance of a member persisting in a reftisal to give evidence before a committee, but members have been ordered by the house to attend select committees."

In 1731, Sir Archibald Grant, a member, was committed to the custody of the serjeant-at-arms, " in order to his forthcoming to abide the orders of the house," and was afterwards ordered to be brought before a committee, from time to time, in the custody of the serjeant."

On the 28th June 1842, a committee reported that a member had declined complying with their request for his attendance." A motion was made for ordering him to attend the committee, and give evidence; but the member having at last expressed his willingness to attend, the motion was withdrawn.

If the attendance of a peer should be desired, to give Attendance of evidence before the house, or any committee of the House other house, of Commons, a message is sent "to the lords, to request that their lordships will give leave to the peer in question to attend, in order to his being examined" before the house, or a committee, as the case may be, and stating the ' 10 Com, J. 51. 19 lb. 403. 21 lb. 851, 852. "!)7 lb. 438. 97 lb. 438. 453. 458. Sec also Report of Precedents, ib. 449.

matters in relation to which his attendance is required. If the peer should be in his place when this message is received, and he consents, leave is immediately given for him to be examined, if he think fit. If not present, a message is returned on a future day, when the peer has, in his place, consented to go. Exactly the same form is observed by the lords, when they desire the attendance of a member of the House of Commons. A message is also sent requiring the attendance of a member to be examined, when the lords are sitting on the trial of an impeachment f but if the lords be sitting as a court of criminal judicature on the trial of a peer, they will order the attendance of a member of the House of Commons without a message. Whenever the attendance of a member of the other house is desired by a committee, it is advisable to give him private intimation, and to learn that he is willing to attend, before a formal message is sent to request his attendance. But these formalities, though occasionally adopted," are not usual or necessary in the case of private bills where the attendance of witnesses is voluntary." If a member should be in custody when leave has been given ' The jealousy of the House of Lords of the attendance of its members in the House of Commons, is shown by the following standing orders; which, tliough not immediately applicable to them as witnesses, may be noticed in passing.

25th November 1696. " Tliat no lord of this house sliall go into the House of Commons whilst the house, or any committee of the wliole house, is sitting there, without tlie leave of this house first had." Lords' S. O., No. 62.

20th January 1673. "The lords conceive that it may deeply intrench into the privileges of this house, for any lord of this house to answer an accusation in the House of Commons, either in person or by sending his answer in writing, or by his councel there. Upon serious consideration had whereof, and perusal of the said precedents in this house, it is ordered, that for the future no lord shall either go down to the House of Commons, or send his answer in writing, or appear by councel to answer any accusation there, upon penaltie of being committed to the black rod, or to the Tower, during the pleasure of this house." Lords' S. O. No. 61.

12 Lords' J. 84; 16 lb. 33. 747. 3 Hats. Prec. 21 n.

Liverpool Docks Bill (Lord Harrowby), 103 Com. J. 438.

3 Hats. 21. See supra, p. 308.

him to attend the House of Lords, the serjeant-at-arms is ordered to permit him to attend, in his custody.

The same ceremony is maintained between the two Officers of houses in requesting the attendance of officers connected with their respective establishments; but when leave is given them to attend, the words " if they think fit," which are used in the case of members, are omitted in the answer."-'

Whether a peer who is not a lord of Parliament may be Peers, not being ordered to attend in the same form as a commoner, is a ' ' ' matter upon which the two houses have not agreed.

On the 3d May 1779, the Earl of Balcarras, of the peerage of Scotland, was ordered to attend the house."' On the 5th June 1806, the House of Commons ordered the attendance of Lord Teignmouth, of the peerage of Ireland, and he attended accordingly; but the House of Lords, at a conference, took exception to the mode of summons, and stated, "That it doth not appear that there is any other precedent but that of the Earl of Balcarras in 1779, in which either house of Parliament, desiring information of a peer of the realm, has required his attendance for that purpose, by an order of such house." To this, however, the commons replied, that Lord Teign-moqth " is not a lord of Parliament, nor hath the right and privilege of sitting in the House of Lords, nor is entitled to any of the privileges thereupon depending." The House of Lords continued to maintain the privilege of peerage as apart from the privilege of Parliament, and resolved, "Tliat it is the undoubted privilege of all the peers of the United Kingdom of Great Britain and Ireland, except such as may have waived their privilege of peerage by becoming members of the commons' house of Parliament, to decline, if they so think fit, to attend the 11 Com. J. 296. 305. 15 lb. 3 76. (Mr. W. S. O'Brien), 101 lb. 603.

' 83 Com. J. 278; 91 lb. 75; 103 lb. 658.

= 37 Com. J. 366. 61 lb. 374.

House of Commons, for the purpose of giving information upon inquiries instituted by the said house, and that the said house has no right to enforce such attendance; and that it is the incumbent duty of this house to maintain and uphold such the privilege of all the peers aforesaid, and to protect them against any attempt to enforce their attendance on the House of Commons, contrary to such pri-vilefre."' But this resolution was not communicated to the Commons. Mode of exa These being the various modes of securing the attendance mination. witnesses to give evidence before either house of Parlia- ment, the mode of examination is next to be considered. In Lords. the House of Lords, every witness is sworn at the bar, whether he is about to be examined by the house, by a committee of the whole house, or by a select committee. But lords of Parliament, and peers not being lords of Parliament, and peeresses, are sworn at the table of the house. The lords formerly claimed the privilege of being examined upon honour, instead of upon oath. On the 22nd May 1732, the committee of privileges reported that the lords should be examined in all courts upon protestation of honour only, and not upon the common oath; and in an earlier instance the house had declared a master in chancery guilty of a breach of privilege for having refused to receive a protestation of honour by Lord Plymouth; but this supposed privilege has long since been abandoned, and peers are everywhere examined upon oath, even in the House of Lords itself. When examined at the bar, if counsel be engaged in the inquiry, the witnesses are examined by them, and by any lord who may desire to put questions. When counsel are not engaged, the witnesses are examined by the lords generally. A lord of Parliament is examined ' 45 Lords' J. 812. ggg 2 Hats. App. 9.

3 38 Lords'J. 68,69. Lords' Minutes, U July 1845.

24 Lords' J. 136. s j, jg in his place, and peers not being lords of Parliament, and peeresses, have chairs placed for them at the table.

In select committees, witnesses are placed in a witness- Committees, box to be examined; but members of the House of Commons are allowed a seat near the table, where they sit uncovered.

False evidence before the lords, being upon oath, renders Oaths. a witness liable to the penalties bf wilful and corrupt perjury; and prevarication, or other misconduct of a witness, is also punished as a contempt."

By the laws of England, the power of administering oaths has been considered essential to the discovery of truth; it has been entrusted to small-debt courts, and to every justice of the peace; but is not enjoyed by ihe House of Commons, the grand inquest of the nation. From what anomalous cause, and at what period, this power, which must have been originally inherent in the High Court of Parliament, was retained by one branch of it and severed from the other, cannot be satisfactorily established; but, even while the commons were contending most strenuously for their claim to be a court of record, they did not advance any pretension to the right of administering oaths. The two houses, in the course of centuries, have appropriated to themselves different kinds of judicature, but the one has exercised the right of administering oaths without question, while the other, except during the Commonwealth, has never yet asserted it.

During the 17th century the commons were evidently Expedients of alive to the importance of this right, and anxious to exercise it; but, for reasons not explained, they admitted, by various acts, that the right was not inherent in them; and ' 25 Lords' J. 303. See also ib. 100, where the judges of the Court of Justiciary in Scotland had chairs set for them at the bar, to be examined. 38 Lords' J. 69.

"48 Lords'J, 371, c.

' See 6 Com. J. 214. 451; 7 Ib. 55. 287. 484, c. See also 2 Ib. 455, resorted to various expedients in order to supply the defect in their own authority.

1. They selected some of their own members, who were justices of the peace for Middlesex, to administer oaths in their magisterial capacity; a practice manifestly irregular, if not illegal, since justices may only administer oaths in investigating matters within their own jurisdiction, as limited by law.

2. They sent witnesses to be examined by one of the judges."

3. They sought to aid their own inquiries by having their witnesses sworn at the bar of the House of Lords, and by examining witnesses on oath before joint committees of both houses f in neither of which expedients were they supported by the lords.

To examine in All these methods of obtaining the sanction of an oath to evidence taken at their instance, were so many distinct admissions of their own want of authority; but in the 18th century a practice of a different character arose, which appeared to assume a right of delegating to others, a power which they had not claimed to exercise themselves. On the 27th January 1715, they empowered justices of the peace for

Middlesex to examine witnesses in the most solemn manner before a committee of secrecy; and the same practice was resorted to in other cases."

On the 12th January 1720 a committee was appointed to inquire into the affairs of the South Sea Company, and the witnesses were ordered to be examined before them in the most solemn manner, without any mention of the persons by whom they were to be sworn. Between this time and 1757, several similar instances occurred; but from that year the most important inquiries have been the most solemn manner.

2 Hats. Free. 151, et seq. 2 9 Com. J. 521; 10 lb. 682.

' 10 11). 415. 417. 8 lb. 325. 327. 2 lb. 502; 8 lb. 647. 655.

18 Com. J. 353. 18 lb. 596; 19 lb. 301. 19 lb. 403 3 21 lb. 851, 852. 2 Hats. 151-157.

conducted, without any attempt to revive so anomalous and questionable a practice.

As the penalties of perjury do not attach to false testi- False evidence mony before the House of Commons, the only mode by vileoe! "' which it can be discouraged, is by treating it as a breach of privilege. To give notice of this fact, and to secure respect to the authority of the house in its inquiries, two resolutions are ao; reed to at the beginning of each session: 1. " That if it shall appear that anyperson hath been tampering with any witness, in respect of his evidence to be given to this house, or any committee thereof, or directly or indirectly hath endeavoured to deter or hinder any person from appearing or giving evidence, the same is declared to be a high crime and misdemeanor; and this house will proceed with the utmost severity against such offender."

2. "That if it shall appear that any person hath given false evidence in any case before this house, or any committee thereof, this house will proceed with the utmost severity against such offender."

The house have rarely failed to act up to the spirit of these resolutions with strictness and severity, and the Journals abound with cases in which witnesses have been punished by commitment to the Serjeant at-arms, and to Newgate, for prevaricating, or giving false testimony, or suppressing the truth; for refusing to answer questions, or to produce documents in their possession.

Evidence is taken before election committees under the Election com-sanction of an oath, by Act of Parliament; and false evidence is not only liable to punishment as a breach of privilege, but also to the penalties of perjury.

But, while the house punishes misconduct with severity, Protection to it is careful to protect witnesses from the eifects of their evidence given by order of the house.

On the 26t. h May 1818, the speaker called the attention Short-hand writers.

' See the lieadings, "Committees," " Complaints," " House," " Elections," and " Witnesses," in the three last General Journal Indexes. DO Com. J. 504,520.564.; 103 lb. 258.

See Chapter XXII., on Elections.

of the house to the case of the King v. Merceron," in which the short-hand writer of the house was examined without previous leave, and it was resolved, nem. con.,

"That all witnesses examined before this house, or any committee thereof, are entitled to the protection of this house, in respect of anything that may be said by them in their evidence;" and, "That no clerk or officer of this house, or short-hand writer employed to take minutes of evidence before this hcnise, or any committee thereof, do give evid nce elsewhere, in respect of any proceedings or examination had at the bar, or before any committee of this house, without the special leave of the house."

These resolutions state distinctly that no officer of the house, or short-hand writer, shall attend without the special leave of the house; but during the recess it has been the constant practice for the speaker to grant such leave, on the application of the parties to a suit. Examined at When a witness is examined by the House of Com- mons, or by a committee of the whole house, he attends at the bar, which is then kept down. If the witness be not in custody, the mace remains upon the table; when according to the strict rule of the house, the speaker should put all the questions to the witness, and members should only suggest to him the questions which they desire to be put; but, for the sake of avoiding the repetition of each question, members are usually permitted to address their questions directly to the witness. When a witness is in the custody of the serjeant-at-arms, or is brought from any prison in custody, it is the usual, but not the constant practice, for the serjeant to stand with the mace at the bar. When the mace is on the Serjeant's shoulder, the speaker has the sole management; and no member may speak, or even suggest questions to the chair. In such cases, therefore, the questions to be 2 Starkie, N. P. Cases, 366.

73 Cora. J. 389. See also supra, p. 138.142.

3 2 Hats. Prec. 140; but see 2 Com. J. 26. See I Com. J. 536.

See 2 Hats. 140.

proposed should either be put in writing, by individual members, or settled upon motions in the house, and given to Mr. Speaker before the prisoner is brought to the bar. If a question be objected to, or if any difference should arise in regard to the examination of a witness, he is ordered to withdraw, before a motion is made, or the matter is considered.

Members of the house are always examined in their Members, places; and peers, lords of Parliament, the judges, and ment c ' ' ' the lord mayor of London, have chairs placed for them within the bar, and are introduced by the serjeant-at-arms. Peers sit down covered, but rise and answer all questions uncovered. The judges and the lord mayor are told by the speaker that there are chairs to repose themselves upon; which is understood, however, to signify that they may only rest with their hands upon the chair backs.

When a peer is examined before a select committee it is the practice to offer him a chair at the table, next to the chairman; where he may sit and answer his questions covered.

When a witness is summoned at the instance of a party, Expenses of his expenses are defrayed by him; but when summoned for ' nesses. any public inquiry, to be examined by the house or a committee, his expenses are paid by the Treasury, under orders signed by the assistant clerk of the Parliaments, the clerk of the House of Commons, or by chairmen of committees in either house. In order to check the expenses of witnesses examined before committees, the House of Commons have adopted certain regulations, by which the following parti-cijars are annexed, in a tabular form, to the printed proceedings of every committee: 1. The name of the witness; 2. His profession or condition; 3. By what member the ' See 2 Hats. 142 and 7i.

2 Agreed that members ought not to be brought to the bar unless they are accused of any crime;" 10 Com. J. 46.

' 2 Hats. 149; where all these forms are minutely described.

motion was made for his attendance; 4. The date of his arrival; 5. The date of his discharge; 6. Total number of days in London; 7. Number of days under examination, or acting specially under the orders of the committee; 8. Expenses of journey to London and back; 9. Expenses in London; 10. Total expenses allowed to each witness, and to all collectively. No witness residing in or near London is allowed any expenses, except under some special circumstances of service to the committee. Every witness should report himself to the committee clerk on his arrival in London, or he will not be allowed his expenses for residence, prior to the day of making such report.

The lords have sometimes appointed a select committee to inquire into the expenses that should be allowed to witnesses, and have received their report in detail before the items were agreed to.

CHAPTER XVL

COMMUNICATIONS BETWEEN THE LORDS AND COMMONS. MESSAGES AND CONFERENCES; JOINT COMMITTEES, AND COMMITTEES COMMU-NICATING WITH EACH OTHER.

Different modes of communication.

The two houses of Parliament have frequent occasion to communicate with each other, not only in regard to bills which require the assent of both houses, but with reference to other matters connected with the proceedings of Parliament. There are four modes of communication; viz. 1. By message; 2. By conference; 3. By joint committees of lords and commons; and, 4. By select committees of both houses communicating with each other. These will each be considered in their order.

' See Report, 1840, No. 555.

62 Lords' J. 910.

1. A message is the most simple and frequent mode of Messages. communication; it is daily resorted to for sending bills from one house to another; for requesting the attendance of witnesses, for the interchange of reports and other documents, and for communicating all matters of an ordinary description, which occur in the course of parliamentary proceedings. It is also the commencement of the more important modes of intercourse, by means of conferences and joint committees. The main difference between the From tiie lords modes of sending messages by either house is, that the mong, lords ordinarily send messages by the masters in chancery, their attendants; and on special occasions by their assistants, the judges: while the commons always send a deputation of their own members. The ancient practice is thus defined by a standing order of the House of Lords:

"Here it is to be noted, that we never send to the lower house by any members of our own, but either by some of the learned councel, masters of the chancery, or such like which attend us, and in weighty causes some of the judges; but the lower house never send unto us any but of their own body."'

The weighty matters here spoken of were generally bills By the judges, relating to the Crown or royal family, which, until 1847, were sent to the commons by two judges; but when the judges were on circuit, or for other causes were not in attendance, such bills were sent by one judge and one master in chancery.

It often happened, prior to 1847, that two masters in chan- By masters in eery were not in attendance when the lords desired to send others! a message; in which case, they sent one master in chancery and the clerk assistant of the Parliaments. But whenever this deviation from the ordinary practice occurred, the lords acquainted the commons that, from the absence of one of their usual messengers, and from the urgency of the case, or in consideration of the late period of the session, they had

Lords' S. O., No. 49. 80 Com. J. 573. 86 lb. 514. 805. 86 lb. 713.

been induced to send the message by the clerk assistant, and by one of their usual messengers On other occasions no master in chancery has been in attendance; when the lords have sent messages by their clerk assistant, and additional clerk assistant or reading-clerk, with similar explanations of the cause of sending the messages in an unusual manner." But whenever the commons received a message brought by any officers not being assistants or attendants of the House of Lords, they always agreed to a resolution, "That this house doth acquiesce in the reasons assigned by the lords," c., " trusting that the same will not be drawn into precedent for the future." inlessages from The Commons send messages to the lords by one of their the commons to n i i the lords, own members (generally the chairman of the committee oi ways and means, or a member who has had charge of a bill), who, until 1847, was required to be accompanied by at least seven others. Eight was formerly the common number which formed a quorum of a select committee, and was probably, for this reason, adopted as the number for carrying a message to the House of Lords.

Much inconvenience had been sustained by requiring so many messengers to communicate the most ordinary matters; more especially as each bill formed the subject of a distinct message, accompanied by all the customary formalities; and, at length, on the 12th July 1847, the lords communicated the following resolutions, at a conference:

"1st. That the lords are willing to receive from the commons in one message, all commons' bills when first brought up to this house; all lords' bills returned from the House of Commons without any amendment made thereto, and all commons' bills returned therefrom with the lords' amendments thereto agreed to, without any amendment; a list of such bills, with a statement of the assent of the commons thereto, being brought by the messengers from the House of Commons, and delivered together with the bills so brought up.

Com. J. 727. 90 lb. 650. 72 lb. 5. 85 lb. 652.

See also Chapter XVIII. on Bills,

"2d. That whereas, by custom heretofore, all messages from the House of Commons to the House of Lords have been attended by eight members of the House of Commons; and whereas the attendance of so many may occasionally be inconvenient to the members of the said house, the lords desire to communicate to the commons their willingness to receive such messages when brought up "by Jive members only."' In return for this concession the commons resolved,

"That the commons should be willing to receive messages from the lords brought by one master in chancery instead of two masters, as heretofore."

And without any express resolution they have since received a message by one judge, instead of two, bringing the agreement of the lords to a bill relating to the royal family.

The form of receiving the messengers from the commons, Messensers by the House of Lords, is appointed by a standing order' mon's how ' of the latter house. In general conformity with this stand- received. ing order, when the messengers from the commons are announced by the usher of the black rod, they are directed to be called in, and the Lord Speaker goes down to meet them at the bar." The usher then advances with the messengers, who make three bows, which are returned by the Lord Speaker. The messengers deliver the message to the Lord Speaker, who returns with it to the woolsack; and when they have retired (again bowing thrice), he reads it to the house. If an answer be required, they are again called in, and the Lord Speaker sitting on the woolsack receives them covered; but returns their bows by raising his hat, and communicates the answer, or states that their lordships will send an answer by messengers of their own.

The messenger from the lords proceeds to the House of Messengers Commons, and if that house be then engaged in business Jot reiewel" ' 102 Com. J. 861. 2 lb. 868.

= Duke of Cambridge's Annuity Bill, 1850. 105 lb. 661. " Lords' S. O. No. 48.

' If the lord chancellor be sitting as speaker, he takes the purse with him, which he places upon the bar.

Answers to messages.

Business interrupted.

General character of a conference.

which will not admit of immediate interruption, he takes a seat below the bar until he can be received. It is usual, however, to admit him when the member then addressing the house has resumed his seat. For this purpose the serjeant-at-arms goes up to the table, making three obeisances, and acquaints the speaker that there is a " message from the lords;" alter which he retires to the bar. The speaker then acquaints the house that there is a message from the lords, and puts a question, that the messenger be now called in; which being agreed to, as a matter of course, he directs the serjeant to call in the messenger. The Serjeant again advances to the table, and takes the mace, with which he introduces the messenger, and walks up to the table of the house on his right hand. They both make three obeisances in coming up the house, and, on reaching the table, the master reads the message; and, when there are bills, delivers them to the clerk of the house. The Serjeant retires with him to the bar (both making obeisances), and then returns and replaces the mace upon the table.

When answers are required to be made to messages, they are returned either by the same messenger, who is again called in for that purpose; or the messenger is acquainted that the house will send an answer by messengers of their own.

The business of the house by which a message is sent is not interrupted while their messengers are proceeding to the other house: but the house by which a message is received, usually take an early opportunity of discontinuing the business under discussion, so as not to detain the messenger.

2. A conference is a mode of communicating important matters by one house of Parliament to the other, more formal and ceremonious than a message, and better calculated to explain opinions and reconcile differences. By a conference both houses are brought into direct intercourse with each other, by deputations of their own members; and so entirely are they supposed to be engaged in it, that while the managers are at the conference, the deliberations of both houses are suspended.

Either house may demand a conference upon matters Subjects for a confcrbiicc which, by the visage of Parliament, are allowed to be proper occasions for such a proceeding: as, for example, 1. To communicate resolutions or addresses to which the concurrence of the other house is desired." 2. Concerning the privileges of Parliament. " 3. In relation to the course of proceeding in Parliament. 4. To require statements of facts on which bills have been passed by the other house." 5. Concerning matters affecting the public peace or security. 6. To offer reasons for disagreeing to amendments made by one house, to bills passed by the other.

On all these and other similar matters it is regular to When to be de-demand a conference; but as the object of communications of this nature is, to maintain a good understanding and co-operation between the houses, it is not proper to use them for interfering with and anticipating the proceedings of one another, before the fitting time. Thus, while a bill is pending in the other house, it is irregular to demand a conference concerning it; and although this rule was not formerly observed with much strictness, it was distinctly declared by the House of Commons, in 1575, to be " according to its ancient rights and privileges, that conference is to be required by that court which, at the time of the conference demanded, shall be possessed of the bill, and not of any other court." The convenience and propriety of this rule is so obvious that it has now, for a long course of years, been invariably observed, with regard not only to bills, but also to resolutions that have been communicated. For instance, if the commons have communicated a resolution to the lords, they must 88 Com. J. 488. 2 9 lb. 344.

3 89 lb. 220. 90 lb. 656. 102 lb. 861. 87 lb. 421.

19 lb. 6.30. 1 lb. 114.

Purpose to be stated.

Heasons offered.

wait until some answer has been returned, and not demand another conference upon the same subject. When the lords are prepared with their answer, it is their turn to demand another conference.

In demanding a conference, the purpose for which it is desired should be explained, lest it should be on a subject not fitting for a conference; as concerning a bill in possession of the house of whom the conference is demanded, or any other interference with the independent proceedings of the other house; in which case a conference might properly be declined." The causes of demanding a conference need not, however, be stated with minute distinctness. It has been held sufficient to specify that they were " upon a matter of high importance and concern, respecting the due administration of justice;" "' "upon a subject of the highest importance to the prosperity of the British possessions in India;" " upon a matter deeply connected with the interests of his Majesty's West India colonies;'" and "upon a matter essential to the stability of the empire, and to the peace, security, and happiness of all classes of his Majesty's subjects." None of these expressions pointed out the precise purpose of the conference, but they described its general object, in each case, so far as to show that it was a proper ground for holding a conference.

The occasions upon which conferences are most frequently demanded are to offer reasons for disagreeing to-amendments to bills; when the course of proceeding is as follows: When any amendment made by the other house is disagreed to, a committee is appointed to draw up reasons for such disagreement, to be offered at a conference; and when the reasons prepared by the committee are reported to the house and agreed to, a message is sent to desire the conference. It is the peculiar privilege of the lords to ' See 2 Com. J, 581. 9 lb. 555. 3 88 lb. 488 (E. I. C. Charter). 89 lb. 232 (Union with Ireland).

' 85 lb. 473 (Sir J. Barrington). 81 lb. 116 (Slaves).

name both the time and place of meeting, whether the Time and place conference be desired by themselves or by the commons;' and when they agree to a conference, they at the same time appoint when and where it shall be held. Both houses communicate to each other their agreement to a conference by messages in the ordinary manner.

Each house appoints managers to represent it at the Managers ap-conference, and it is " an ancient rule, that the number of the commons named for a conference are always double to those of the lords." It is not, howevei-, the modern practice to specify the number of the managers for either house. The managers for the house which desires the conference are the members of the committee who drew up the reasons, to whom others are generally added; and on the part of the other house they are usually selected from those members who have taken an active part in the discussions on the bill, if present; or otherwise any members are named who happen to be in their places.

The duty of the managers is confined to the delivery Dutyofmana-and receipt of the resolutions to be communicated, or the bills to be returned, with reasons for disagreeing to amendments. They are not at liberty to speak, either to enforce the resolutions or reasons communicated, or to oflfer objections to them. One of their number reads the resolutions or reasons, and afterwards delivers a paper on which they are written, which is received by one of the managers for the other house. When the conference is over, the managers return to their respective houses and report their proceedings.

In order to make the subsequent proceedings upon a Conferences in bill perfectly intelligible, let it be supposed that a bill sent up from the commons has been amended by the lords and returned; that the commons disagree to their amendments, draw up reasons, and desire a conference; that the ' 1 Com. J. 154; and see this claim as stated by the Lords, 9 Com. J. 348. = 1 lb. 154. ' See also Chapter XVIII. 367, 368.

conference is held, and the bill and reasons are in possession of the House of Lords. If the lords shovdd be satisfied with the reasons oifered, they do not desire another conference, but send a message to acquaint the commons that they do not insist upon their amendments. But if they insist upon the whole or part of their amendments, they desire another conference, and communicate the reasons of their perseverance. If the commons should be still dissatisfied with these reasons, and persist in their disagreement to the lords' amendments, they were formerly precluded, by the usage of Parliament, from desiring a third conference; and unless they allowed the bill to drop, laid it aside, or deferred the consideration of the reasons and amendments, they desired a free conference. This practice, however, has been departed from on one special occasion. In 1836, after two conferences upon the Municipal Corporations Bill, a free conference was held, according to ancient usage; but the disagreement between the two houses continued, and the consideration of the lords' amendments and reasons was postponed for three months. In the following session another bill was brought in, to which various amendments were made by the lords, to which the commons disagreed. The results of the free conference, however, had been so unsatisfactory, that the usage of Parliament was departed from, and four- ordinary conferences were successively held, which so far accommodated the differences between the two houses that the bill ultimately received the royal assent. Free confer A free conference differs materially from the ordinary conference; for, instead of the duties of the managers being confined to the formal communication of reasons, they are at liberty to urge their own arguments, offer and combat objections, and, in short, to attempt, by personal persuasion, to effect an agreement between the houses, ' 91 Com. J. 783. ")2 lb. 466. 31-2.580. 646.

ence.

which the written reasons had failed in producing. If a free conference should prove as unsuccessful as the former, the disagreement is almost hopeless; but if the house in possession of the bill should at length be prepared to make concessions, in the hope of an ultimate agreement, it is competent to desire another free conference upon the same subject; or if any question of privilege or other new matter should arise, an ordinary conference may be demanded.

It only remains to notice the manner in which confer- Forms of hoid-ences are held. When the time appointed has arrived, business is suspended in both houses, the names of the managers are called over, and they leave their places, and repair to the chamber in which they are to meet. The commons, who come first to the conference, enter the room uncovered, and remain standing the whole time. The lords have their hats on till they come just within the bar of the place of conference, when they take them off, and walk uncovered to their seats; they then seat themselves, and remain sitting and covered during the conference. The lord who receives or delivers the paper on which the resolutions or reasons are written, stands up uncovered while the paper is being transferred from one manager to the other; but while reading it, he sits covered. When the conference is over, the lords rise from their seats, take off their hats, and walk uncovered from the place of conference. The lords who speak at a free conference, do so standing and uncovered.

The lords have the following standing orders in regard to the manner of holding conferences:

"The place of our meeting with the lower house upon conference is usually the Painted Chamber," where they are commonly before we come, and expect our leisure. We are to come thither ' 4 Hats. Prec, 42-45. 52. 4 lb. 28 n.

After the fire, in 1834, the Painted Chamber was fitted up and occupied as the temporary House of Lords, until tlie completiou of the present house.

Commons not to be covered.

None to speak at a conference but those of the committee.

No stranger to be at a conference or committee.

Joint committees of lords and commons.

in a whole body, and not some lords scattering before the rest, which both takes from the gravity of the lords, and besides may hinder the lords from taking their proper places. We are to sit there, and be covered;. but they are at no committee or conference ever either to be covered, or sit down in our presence, unless it be some infirm person, and tliat by connivance in a corner out of sight, to sit, but not to be covered."'

"None are to speak at a conference with the lower house but those that be of the committee; and when anything from such conference is reported, all the lords of that committee are to stand up."

"No man is to enter at any committee or conference (unless it be such as are commanded to attend), but such as are members of the house, or the heir apparent of a lord who has a right to succeed such lord, or the eldest son of any peer who has a right to sit and vote in this house, upon pain of being punished severely, and with example to others."' 3. There have been several Instances of the appointment of joint committees of the tvro houses;" but during the last century and a half no such committee has been appointed. A rule similar to that adopted in regard to conferences, that the number on the part of the commons should be double that of the lords, obtained in the constitution of joint committees; and was inconsistent with any practical union of the members of the two houses, in deliberation and voting. The principal advantages of a joint committee were that the witnesses were sworn at the bar of the House of Lords, and that one inquiry, common to both houses, could be conducted preparatory to any decision of Parliament. But the power possessed by the commons of outvoting the lords their right to meet their lordships without the respectful ceremonies observed at a conference, and their share in the privilege of taking the evidence of sworn witnesses, naturally rendered a joint committee distasteful to the House of Lords, by whom no power or facilities were gained in return.

' Lords' S. O. No. 50. lb. No. 51.

3 lb. No. 52 J see also 1 Com. J. 1.56. 3 Hats. Prec. 38, et seq.

The last was appointed im April 1695, 11 Com. J. 314.

2 lb. 602; 5 lb. 647. 655.

4. A modification of the practice of appointing joint Select commit- t fy-, t. nil tee8 communi- committees, may be eirected by puttnig committees of both eating with houses in communication with each other. In 1794, the ' c' ther. commons had communicated to the lords certain papers which had been laid before them by the king, in relation to corresponding societies, together with a report of a committee of secrecy; and on the 22d May 1794, the lords sent a message, to acquaint the commons that they had referred the jjapers to a committee of secrecy, and had " given power to the said committee to receive any communication which may be made to them, from time to time, by the committee of secrecy, appointed by the House of Commons;" ' to which the commons replied, that they had given power to their committee of secrecy to communicate, from time to time, with the committee of secrecy appointed by the lords." And similar proceedings were adopted, upon the inquiry into the state of

Ireland, in 1801, which was conducted by secret committees of the lords and commons communicating with each other.

1 49 Com. J. 619. lb. 620. 66 lb. 287. 291.

Queen present The Queen is always supposed to be present In the 111 ar lamen. jjjgj Court of Parliament, by the same constitutional principle which recognises her presence in other courts: but she can only take part in its proceedings by means which are acknowledged to be consistent with the Parliamentary prerogatives of the Crown, and the entire freedom of the debates and proceedings of Parliament. She may be present in the House of Lords, at any time, during the deliberations of that house, where the cloth of estate is; but she may not be concerned in any of its proceedings, except when she comes in state for the exercise of her prerogatives. In earlier times the sovereign was habitually present in the House of Lords, as being his council, whose advice and assistance he personally desired. King Henry VI., in the ninth year of his reign, declared, with the advice and consent of the lords, "That it shall be lawful for the lords to debate together in this present parliament, and in every other, for time to come, in the king's absence, concerning the condition of the kingdom, and the remedies necessary for it." Whence it appears that, at that time, it was customary for the king to be present at the deliberations of the lords, even if his presence was not essential to their proceedings. When he ceased to take a personal part in their deliberations, it was still customary for the sovereign ' See Hale, Jurisd. of Lords, c. 1. Fortescue, c. 8 (by Amos), with note B.; and 2 Inst. 18G. 3 Rut. Pari. 611.

to attend the debates as a spectator. Charles II.," and his successors, James II., William III., and Queen Anne, were very frequently present; but this questionable practice, which might be used to overawe that assembly, and influence their debates," has wisely been discontinued since the accession of George I. And, according to the practice of modern times, the Queen is never personally present in Parliament, except on its opening and prorogation; and occasionally for the purpose of giving the royal assent to bills during a session.

The various constitutional forms by which the Crown communicates with Parliament, and by which Parliament communicates with the Crown, will now be noticed in succession, according to their relative importance and solemnity.

The most important modes by which the Crown com- Commanica-municates with the Parliament, are exemplified on those crown, in per-occasions when her Majesty is present, in person or by """"

"""' L J mission.

commission, in the House of Lords, to open or prorogue Parliament, and when a royal speech is delivered to both houses. In giving the royal assent to bills in person or by commission, the communication of the Crown with the Parliament is of an equally solemn character." On these occasions the whole Parliament is assembled in one chamber, and the Crown is in immediate and direct communication with the three estates of the realm.

The mode of communication next in importance is by a By message under the sign man ual.

' 12 Lords J. 318. "Charles II. being sat, he told them it was a privilege he claimed from his ancestors to be present at their deliberations; that, therefore, they should not for his coming interrupt their debates, but proceed, and be covered." Andrew Marvell's Letters, p. 405. Nor was Charles II. an inattentive observer; for on the 26th January 1670 he reprimands the lords for their " very great disorders, both at the hearing of causes and in debates amongst themselves." 12 Lords' J. 413.

' See 2 Macaulay's Hist. 35.

3 2 Hats. Prec. 371 n.; Cliltty on Prerogatives, 74. The last occasion appears to have been the attendance of Queen Anne, on the 9th and 12th January 1710, during the debates upon the war ith Spain.

63 Lorilb' J. 885, See Chapter XVIII. p. 370.

written message under the royal sign manual, to either house singly," or to both houses separately. The message is brought by a member of the house, being a minister of the Crown, or one of the royal household, in the official uniform. In the House of Lords the peer who is charged with the message, acquaints the house that he has a message under the royal sign manual, which her Majesty had commanded him to deliver to their lordships. And the lord chancellor then reads the message at length, which is afterwards read again by the clerk. In the House of Commons the member who is charged with the message appears at the bar, where he informs the speaker that he has a message from her Majesty to this house, signed by herself; which he takes to the table, and presents to the House- The message is delivered to the speaker, who reads it at length, while all the members of the house are uncovered.

Subjects of such The subjects of such messages are usually commu-messages. i. it i. i nications in regard to important public events which require the attention of Parliament; the prerogatives or property of the Crown; provision for the royal family; and various matters in which the Executive seeks for pecuniary aid from Parliament. They may be regarded, in short, as additions to the royal speech, at the commencement of the Session, submitting other matters to the deliberation of Parliament, besides the causes of summons previously declared. Should be com- This analogy between a royal speech and a message both houses." Under the sign manual, is supported by several circumstances common to both. A speech is delivered to both houses, and every message under the sign manual should also be sent, if practicable, to both houses; but when they ' 86 Com. J, 488. qq Lg ds' J. 958. 89 Com. J. 575.

3 66 Lords' J. 958. 40 Lords' J. 86. 44 lb. 74. 82 Com. J. IIL 85 Com. J. 466; 89 lb. 189. 579.

43 Lords' J. 566 j 86 Com. J. 719; 105 Com. J. 539, 18th July 1850 (Duke of Cambridge); 82 Lords'J. 368, 22d July 1850. ' 42 Lords' J. 361; 82 Com. J. 529.

are accompanied by original papers, they have occasionally been sent to one house only. The more pro wr and regular course is to deliver them on the same day, and a departure from this rule has been a subject of complaint; but from the casual circumstance of both houses not sitting on the same day, or other accidents, it has frequently happened that messages have been delivered on different days.

In the royal speech, the demand for supplies is ad- On matters of dressed exclusively to the commons, but it still forms part of the speech to both houses; and in the same manner, messages for pecuniary aid are usually sent to both houses; but the form differs so far as to acknowledge the peculiar right of the commons in voting money, while it seeks no more than the concurrence of the lords."

The lords have taken exceptions to any message for supplies being sent exclusively to the commons," and for upwards of a century it has been the custom, with few exceptions, to send such messages to both houses; v rhich is consistent with their constitutional relations, in matters of supply.

Another form of communication from the Crown to Verbal mes-either house of Parliament, is in the nature of a verbal message, delivered, by command, by a minister of the Crown to the house of which he is a member. This communication is used whenever a member of either house is arrested for any crime at the suit of the Crown; as the Members im-privileges of Parliament require that the house should P" '" be informed of the cause for which their member is im- ' 2 Hats. 366 n.

' 66 Lords'J. 958; 89 Com. J. 575; 82 Lords' J. 368; 105 Com. J. 539.

' 73 Lords' J. 28; 96 Com. J. 29 (Lord Keane).

25th June 1713; 28th February 1739. 2 Hats. 366 n.

A recent exception was the message in regard to the provision for her Majesty Queen Adelaide, on the 14th April 1831, which was presented to the commons alone; 86 Com. J. 488.

See Lords' and Commons' Gen. Journ. Indexes, tit- " Messages."

queen's pleasure signified.

Military courts martial.

Naval courts martial.

Arrest in Ireland.

Queen's pleasure signified.

prisoned, and detained from his service in Parliament. Thus, in 1780, Lord North informed the House of Commons that he was commanded by his Majesty to acquaint the house, that his Majesty had caused Lord George Gordon, a member of the house, to be apprehended, and committed for high treason. And at the same time Lord North presented, by command, the proclamation that had been issued, in reference to the riots in which Lord George Gordon had been implicated.

In the same manner, when members have been placed under arrest, in order to be tried by military courts martial, the secretary-at-war, or some other minister of the Crown, being a privy-councillor, informs the house that he had been commanded to acquaint them of the arrest of their member, and its cause.

Communications of the latter description are made when members have been placed under arrest, to be tried by naval courts martial; but in these cases they are not in the form of a royal message, but are communications from the lord high admiral or the lords commissioners of the Admi-ralty, by whom the warrants are issued for taking the members into custody; and copies of the warrants are, at the same time, laid before the house.

In 1848, the arrest of a member in Ireland, on a charge of treason, was communicated to the house by a letter from the lord lieutenant, addressed to the speaker.

The other modes of communicating with Parliament are by the royal " pleasure," " recommendation," or " consent," beincr signified.

The Queen's pleasure is signified at the commencement of each Parliament, by the lord chancellor, that the commons should elect a speaker; and when a vacancy in the ' 37 Com. J. 903. 58 lb. 597; 59 lb. 33; 70 lb. 70.

3 62 Com. J. 145; 64 lb. 214; 67 lb. 246. See also supra, p. 131. 103 lb. 888; 8th August 1848 (Mr. VV. S. O'Brien).

office of speaker occurs in the middle of a Parliament, a communication of the same nature is made by a minister in the house. Her Majesty's pleasure is also signified for the attendance of the commons in the House of Peers; in regard to the times at which she appoints to be attended with addresses; and concerning matters personally affecting the interests of the royal family."- At the end of a session, also, the royal pleasure is signified, by the lord chancellor, that Parliament should be prorogued. Under this head may likewise be included the approbation of the speaker elect, signified by the lord chancellor.

The royal recommendation is signified to the commons by Royal recom- , n, T n n,-, rneudation or a mmister oi the brown, on motions tor receivmg petitions, consent. for the introduction of bills, or on the offer of other motions involving any grant of money not included in the annual estimates, whether such grant is to be made in the committee of supply, or any other committee; or which would have the effect of releasing or compounding any sum of money owing to the Crown. The royal consent is given to motions for bills, or amendments to bills, or to bills in any of their stages, which concern the royal prerogatives, the hereditary revenues, or personal property or interests of the Crown or duchy of Cornwall. The mode of communicating the recommendation and consent is the same; but the former is given at the very commencement of a proceeding, and must precede all grants of money; while the latter may be given at any time during the progress of a bill, in which the consent of the Crown is required.

On the 1st July 1844, on the third reading of the St. Consent of the Asaph and Bangor Dioceses Bill, in the House of Lords, it heldt" ' was stated by the Duke of Wellington, that her Majesty's ministers had not been instructed to signify the consent of ' See supra, p. 172. 2 gg Com. J. 460.

' See Chapter XXI. on Supply, p. 411.

75 Com. J. 152. 167; 89 lb. 52. See also Cliapter XXI. p. 412. 5 77 lb. 408; 86 lb. 485. 560; 91 lb. 648; 105 lb. 492.

queen's consent signified.

Crown places its interests at the disposal of Parliament.

Constitutional character of these commu-Dications.

the Crown to the bill, and that the royal prerogative was aifected by it. The lord chancellor then desired to be instructed by the house whether he was at liberty to put the question, until her Majesty's royal consent had been given; upon which a committee was appointed to search for precedents, whether the lord speaker can, according to the usage of this house, put the question "that this bill do pass?" until the consent of her Majesty is given." This committee reported that there were no precedents; but that the bill belonged to that class to which it had been the usage to give the consent of the Crown before passing the house; and that it had been the custom to receive such consent at various stages. The consent of the Crown was still with-held, and the bill was consequently withdrawn.

Another form of communication, similar in principle to the last, is when the Crown " places its interests at the disposal of Parliament," which is signified in the same manner, by a minister of the Crown.

These several forms of communication are recognised as constitutional declarations of the Crown, suggested by the advice of its responsible ministers, by whom they are announced to Parliament, in compliance with established usage. They cannot be misconstrued into any interference with the proceedings of Parliament, as some of them are rendered necessary by resolutions of the House of Commons, and all are founded upon parliamentary usage, which both houses have agreed to observe. This usage is not binding upon Parliament; but if, without the consent of the Crown, previously signified. Parliament should dispose of the interests or affect the prerogative of the Crown, the Crown could still protect itself, in a constitutional manner, by the refusal of the royal assent to the bill. And it is one ' 76 Hans. Deb., 3d Ser., 122. ' 2d Rep., ib. 422.

1st Rep., ib. 294.

Ib. 591.

88 Com. J. 381; 90 Ib. 447. 91 Ib. 427.

of the advantages of this usage, that it obviates the necessity of resorting to the exercise of tliat prerogative.

Having enumerated all the accustomed forms in which How acknow-the royal will is made known to Parliament, it may now be shown, in the same order, in what manner they are severally acknowledged by each house.

The forms observed on the meeting and prorogation of Addresses in-r T 11 1' 1-111 answer to writ-

Parliament, and the proceedmgs connected with the ad- ten messages.

dress in answer to the royal speech, were described in the seventh chapter, and the royal assent to bills will be treated of hereafter. Messages under the royal sign manual are generally acknowledged by addresses in both houses, which are presented from one house by the " lords with white staves," and from the other by privy councillors, in the same manner as addresses in answer to royal speeches, when Parliament has been opened by commission.

In the commons, however, it is not always necessary to Exceptions in T,,, 111. tbe commons.

reply to these messages by address; as a prompt provision, made by that house, is itself a sufficient acknowledgment of royal communications for pecuniary aid. The House of Lords invariably present an address, in order to declare their willingness to concur in the measures which may be adopted by the other house; ' but the bills consequent upon messages relating to grants, are presented by the speaker of the commons, and are substantial answers to the demands of the Crown. The rule, therefore, in the commons, appears to be, to answer, by address, all written messages which relate to important public events, or matters connected with the prerogatives, interests, or property of the Crown;" or which call for general legislative measures ' but, in regard to messages relating exclusively to pecuniary aids of whatever kind, to consider them in a committee of the whole house, on a future day, when provision is made accordingly.

Supra, pp. 167. 182. 207. Infra, p. 370. See supra, p. 183.

63 Lords' J. 892. 82 Com. J. 114. Sr lb. 466; 89 Ih. 578. 7 65 Com. J. 214. 86 lb. 488. 491; 105 lb. 539. 544.

To verbal messages.

On royal pleasure, c. being signified.

Addresses.

Joint addresses.

When the house are informed, by command of the Crown, of the arrest of a member to be tilled by a military court martial, they immediately resolve upon an address of thanks to her Majesty, " for her tender regard to the privileges of this house." And in all cases in which the arrest of a member for a criminal offence is communicated, an address of thanks is voted in answer." But as the arrest of a member to be tried by a naval court martial does not proceed immediately ii'om the Crown, and the communication is only made from the lords of the Admiralty, no address is necessary in answer to this indirect form of message.

The matters upon which the royal pleasure is usually signified need no address in answer, as immediate com-pliance is given by the house; and the recommendation and consent of the Crown, as already explained, are only signified as introductory to proceedings in Parliament, or essential to their progress.

These being the several forms of acknowledging communications proceeding from the Crown, it now becomes necessary to describe those which originate with Parlia-ment. It is by addresses that the resolutions of Parliament are ordinarily communicated to the Crown. These are sometimes in answer to royal speeches or messages, but are more frequently in regard to other matters, upon which either house is desirous of making known its opinions to the Crown.

Addresses are sometimes agreed upon by both houses, and jointly presented to the Crown, but are more generally confined to each house singly. TVlien some event of unusual importance makes it desirable to present a joint address, the lords or commons, as the case may be, agree to a form of address; and having left a blank for the insertion of the title of the other house, communicate it at a conference, and desire their concurrence. The blank is ' 70 Com. J. 70.

37 lb. 903.

3 87 lb. 421. 89 lb. 233.

there filled up, and a message Is returned, acquainting the house with their concur-rence, and that the blank has been filled up. Such addresses are presented either by both houses in a bodj, or by two peers and fi ur members of the House of Commons; and they have been presented also by committees of both houses; ' by a joint commit-tee of lords and commons," and by the lord chancellor and the speaker of the House of Commons; but the lords always learn her Majesty's pleasure, and communicate to the commons, by message, the time at which she has appointed to be attended.

The addresses in answer to the royal speech at the com- separate ad-mencement of the session are formally prepared by a com- '"' sses. mittee, upon whose repoi't they are agreed to, after having been twice read; but at other times no formal address is prepared, and the resolution for the address is alone presented. They are ordered to be presented by the whole house; by the lords with white staves, or pi'ivy councillors;'- and, in some peculiar cases, by members specially nominated.

The subjects upon which addresses are presented are Their subjects. too varied to admit of enumeration. They have comprised every matter of foreign " or domestic policy;'" the administration of justice;" the confidence of Parliament in the ministers of the Crown; ' the expression of congratulation or condolence (which are agreed to nem. con.); ' and, in short, representations upon all points connected with the government and welfare of the country. But they ought not to be presented in relation to any bill depending in either house of Parliament. '

When a joint address is to be presented by both houses. Mode of presenting.

Joint addresses.

Separate addresses.

Dress of peers and members.

Answers to addresses.

the lord chancellor and the House of Lords, and the speaker and the House of Commons, proceed in state to the palace at the time appointed. The speaker's state coach, and the carriages of the members of the House of Commons, are entitled, by privilege or custom, to approach the palace through the central Mall in St. James's Park. Whether this distinction be enjoyed as part of their privilege of freedom of access to her Majesty, or by virtue of any other right or custom, it is peculiar to the commons, who always take this route, while the lords advance by the ordinary carriage-road.

On reaching the palace, the two houses assemble in a chamber adjoining the throne-room, and when her Majesty is prepared to receive them, the doors are thrown open, and the lord chancellor and the speaker advance side by side, followed by the members of the two houses respectively, and are conducted towards the throne by the lord chamberlain. The lord chancellor reads the address, to which her Majesty returns an answer, and both houses retire from the royal presence.

When addresses are presented separately, by"either house, the forms observed are similar to those described, except that addresses of the commons are then read by their speaker. Each house proceeds by its accustomed route to the palace, and is admitted with similar ceremonies. In presenting the address, the mover and seconder are always on the left hand of the speaker.

It is customary for all the lords, without exception, who attend her Majesty, to be in full dress; but several members of the commons always assert their privilege of freedom of access to the throne, by accompanying the speaker in their ordinary attire.

When addresses have been presented by the whole house, the lord chancellor in one house, and the speaker ' The speaker is always on the left hand of the chancellor. ' They are not permitted to enter the royal presence witli sticks or umbrellas. See 2 Hats. Prec, 390 n.

in the other, reports tlie answer of her Majesty; but when they have been presented by privy councillors only, the answer is reported by one of those who have had the honour of attending her Majesty, or by one of the royal household.

Another mode of communication with the Crown, less Resolutions. jj,,,,.-,,, 11 communicated, direct and lormai than an address, has been occasionally adopted;

when resolutions of the house, and resolutions and evidence taken before a committee ' have been ordered to be laid before the sovereign. In such cases the resolutions have been presented in the same manner as addresses, and answers have sometimes been returned.

It is to the reigning sovereign or regent alone that Messages to the n 1 1 T T royal family.

addresses are presented by I arliament; but messages are frequently sent by both houses to members of the royal family, to congratulate them upon their nuptials, or other auspicious events;" or to condole with them on family bereavements. Resolutions have also been ordered to be laid before members of the royal family. Certain members are always nominated by the house to attend those illustrious personages with the messages or resolutions; one of whom afterwards acquaints the house (in the lords, in his place or at the table, and, in the commons, at the bar) with the answers which were returned.

Communications are also made to both houses by mem- Communica-bers of the royal family, which are either delivered by l i fa iiy members in their places, or are conveyed to the house by letters addressed to the speaker.

37 Com. J. 330. 39 lb. 884. 40 lb. 1157. 60 lb. 206. 67 lb. 462. 78 lb. 316, c. = 90 lb. 534.

3 72 Lords' J. 53. 73 Com. J. 424. 95 lb. 88.

40 Lords' J. 584. 74 lb. 6.

5 53 Lords' J. 367. 75 Com. J. 480. 105 lb. 508.

53 Lords' J. 369; 72 lb. 53. 95 Com. J. 95; 105 lb. 539. Hans. Deb., N. S., vol. 52, p. 343; lb., 18th July 1850.

' 58Com. J. 211. 75 lb. 288.

64 Com. J. 86. 68 lb. 253. 69 lb. 324. 433.

General nature of a bill.

Ancient mode of enacting laws.

PROCEEDINGS OF PARLIAMENT IN PASSING PUBLIC BILLS: THEIR SEVERAL STAGES IN BOTH HOUSES. ROYAL ASSENT.

It has been explained in what manner each separate question is determined in Parliament; and the proceedings upon bills will require less explanation, if it be borne in mind that all the rules in relation to questions and amendments are applicable to the passing of bills. If bills were not a more convenient form of legislation, both houses might enact laws by agreeing to a series of resolutions, proposed without concert or combination, provided the royal assent were afterwards given. In the earlier periods of the constitution of Parliament, all bills were, in fact, prepared and agreed to in the form of petitions from the commons, which were entered on the Rolls of Parliament, with the king's answer subjoined; and at the end of each Parliament the judges drew up these Imperfect records into the form of a statute, which was entered on the Statute Rolls. This practice was incompatible with the full concurrence of the legislature, and matters were often found in the Statute Rolls that the Parliament had not petitioned for or assented to. Indeed, so far was this principle of independent legislation occasionally carried, that in the 13th and 21st of Richard II., commissions were appointed for the express purpose of completing the legislative measures which had not been determined during the sitting of Parliament. These usurpations of legislative power ' Rot. Pari, passim.

2 3 Rot. Pari. 25G (13 Ric. II). 3 lb. 368 (21 Ric. II). Stat. 21 Ric. II. c. 16.

were met with remonstrances in particular instances," and at length in the 2nd Hen. V., the commons prayed that no additions or diminutions should in future be made, nor alteration of terms which should change the true intent of their petitions, without their assent; for they stated that they had ever been " as well assenters as petitioners." The king, in reply, granted, " that henceforth nothing should be enacted to the petitions of the commons contrary to their asking, whereby they shoidd be bound without their assent; saving always to our liege lord his real prerogative to grant and deny what him lust, of their petitions and askings aforesaid.""

No distinct consequences appear to have immediately followed this remarkable petition; and, so long as laws were enacted in the form of petitions, to any portions of which the king might give or withhold his assent, and attach conditions or qualifications of his own, the assent of the entire Parliament was rather constructive than literal: and the Statute Rolls, however impartially drawn up, were imperfect records of the legislative determinations of Parliament. But petitions fi'om the commons, Origin of mo-which were originally the foundation of all laws, were ultimately superseded; and in the reign of Henry VI. bills began to be introduced in either house in the form of complete statutes, which were passed in a manner approaching that of modern times, and received the distinct assent of the king, in the form in Avhich they had been agreed to by both houses of Parhament. It is true that Henry VI. and Edward IV. occasionally added new provisions to statutes, without consulting Parliament; but the constitutional 3 Rot. Pari. 102 (5 Rlc. II. No. 23). 3 Rot. Pari. 141 (6 Ric. II. No. XXX.) 3 Rot. Pari. 418 (1 Hen. IV.) Hale's Hist. Common Law, 14. Reeve's Hist, of tlie English Law. Pref. to Cotton's Abridgment. Ruff-head's Statutes, Preface.

4 Rot. Pari. 22, No. X.

Riiffhcad's Statutes, Preface. Cotton's Abridgment, Preface.

form of legislating by bill and statute, agreed to in Parliament, undoubtedly had its origin and its sanction in the reign of Henry VI.

Similarity of Before the present method of passing bills in Parliament ho'uses ' '" " entered upon, it may be premised, that the practice of the lords and commons is so similar in regard to the several stages of bills, and the proceedings connected with them, that, except where variations are distinctly pointed out, the proceedings of one house are equally descriptive of the proceedings of the other.

AViicre bills As a general rule, bills may originate in either house; originate. j exclusive right of the commons to grant supplies, and to impose and appropriate all charges upon the people, renders it necessary to introduce by far the greater pro-

Toor law bills, portion of bills into that house. Bills relating to the relief and management of the poor, for example, involve almost necessarily, some charge upon the people, and generally originate with the commons. Two bills only relating to the poor have been sent to the commons by the lords during the present century. The first. In 1801, was laid aside nem. con., when IVIr. Speaker called attention to it; the second, in 1831, was received but not proceeded with, the first reading being postponed for three months. But amendments involving the principle of a charge upon the people have frequently been made to such bills by the lords, which, on account of the extreme difiiculty of separating them from other legislative provisions to which there was no objection, have been assented to by the commons. Such amendments, however, ought not to interfere with regard to the amount of the tax, the mode of levying or collecting it, the persons who shall pay or receive it, the ' See 8 Com. J. 311. 602. 56 lb. 88. gg n,. 734.

"Poor Laws (England) Bill, 1834. Irish Poor Relief Bill, 1838. Poor Relief (Ireland) Bill, 1st June 1847; 92 Hans. Deb,, 3d Series, 1299. Poor Relief (Ireland) Bill, 27lli July 1849; 107 Ilaus. Deb., 3d Series, 1043, manner of its appropriation, or the persons who shall have the control and management of it. In any of these cases the commons may insist upon their privileges, and it is only by waiving them in particular instances, and under special circumstances, that such amendments have ever been admitted. On the other hand, the lords claim that bills for the restitution of honours and in blood should commence with them; and they are presented to that house by her Majesty's command." A bill for a general pardon is an exception to General pardon, the usual mode of passing bills; it begins with the Crown, and is read once only in each house, after which it receives the royal assent in the ordinary form.

Bills are divided into the two classes, of public and Public and pri-private bills; of which the former are introduced directly by members of the house, while the latter are founded upon the petitions of parties interested. As the distinct character of private bills, and the proceedings of Parliament in relation to them, will form the subject of the Third Book, the present chapter is strictly confined to the passing of bills of a public nature. The greater part of these proceedings apply equally to both classes of bills; but the progress of private bills is governed by so many peculiar regulations and standing orders, in both houses, that an entire separation of the two classes can alone make the progress of either intelligible.

In the House of Lords, any peer is at liberty to present Public bills a bill and to have it laid upon the table; but in the com- P-' ' j ' " ' " ' mons, a member must obtain permission from the house. Ordered in the before he can bring in a bill. Having given notice, he must move " that leave be given to bring in a bill," and add the proper title of his proposed measure. It is usual, in making this motion, to explain the object of the bill, and to give reasons for its introduction; but unless the motion be opposed, this is not the proper time for any lengthened ' Maxwell's Restitution Bill, 1848, 103 Com, J. 341. " 25 Com. J. 400 1747.

Preliminaries.

Bills originating in committee.

debate upon its merits. When an important measure is oifered by a member, tliis opportunity is frequently taken for a laboured exposition of its character and objects; but where the proposed bill is not of an imj)ortant character, debate should be avoided at this stage, unless it be expected that the motion will be negatived, and' that no future occasion will arise for discussion. If the motion be agreed to, the bill is ordered to be prepared and brought in by the mover and seconder, to whom other members are occasionally added." Instructions are sometimes given to these gentlemen to make provision in the bill for matters not included in the original motion and order of leave.

Bills are not always introduced in this manner by members, upon motion; but proceedings preparatoiy to the bringing in of bills first occupy the attention of the house. Sometimes a resolution is agreed to by the house, and a biu immediately ordered, as in the Bribery and Treating Bill, in 1831; at other times, resolutions of the house in a former session are read, and bills ordered thereupon." It is very common, also, to read parts of speeches from the throne. Queen's messages, Acts of Parliament, entries in the Journal, reports of committees, or other documents in possession of the house, before the motion is made for leave to bring in a bill. But the most frequent preliminary to the introduction of bills is the report of resolutions from a committee of the whole house. The chairman is sometimes instructed by the committee to move for leave to bring in a bill or bills, and sometimes the resolutions are simply reported, and after being agreed to by the house, a bill is ordered thereupon.

Many classes of bills are required to originate in a committee of the whole house; and if, by mistake, this form has been omitted, all subsequent proceedings are vitiated.

91 Com. J. 613. 632, c. 91 lb. 716; 105 lb. 337. 3 86 lb. 821. 82 lb. 442.

See Gen. Journ. Index, tit. " Bills" (1820-1837), p. 296.

and must be commenced again. By two standing orders of the 9th November 1703, and the 30th April 1772, it is ordered,

"That no bill relating to religion or trade, or the alteration of Relating to the laws coucerninof relisrion or trade, be brought into this house, religion aud . trade, until the proposition shall have been first considered in a committee of the whole house, and agreed unto by the house."'

By another standing order of the 29th March 1707, it was resolved,

"That this house will not proceed upon any petition, motion, Public Money, or bill, for granting any money, or for releasing or compounding any sum of money owing to the Crown, but in a committee of the whole house."

By a resolution, 18th February 1667,

"If any motion be made in the house for any public aid, or Charge upon charge upon the people, the consideration and debate thereof ought the subject, not presently to be entered upon; but adjourned till such further day as the house shall think fit to appoint; and then it ought to be referred to the committee of the whole house; and their ojiinions to be reported thereupon, before any resolution or vote of the house do pass therein."

The standing order concerning religion has usually been Construction of , J 1 J. T-J. 'i 1 1 X rules; as to re- construed as applying to religion m its spiritual relations ii-iou. its doctrines, profession or observances; but not to the temporalities or government of the church, or other legal incidents of religion. The distinction, however, between spiritual and temporal matters is often so nice, that a correct and uniform application of the rule is not always observable in the precedents which are to be found in the Journals. The Eoman-catholic Relief Bills in 1825, 1829, and 1848, were brought in upon resolutions of committees; and bills for removing civil disabilities of the Jews; ' for the relief of Dissenters; for amending the Acts relating to the Roman Catholic College of Maynooth;' and for altering 14 Com. J. 211; 33 lb. 678. 714.

2 15 Com. J. 367; 16 lb. 405. 3 g n, 52.

80 lb. 144; 84 lb. 116; 103 lb. 22. There were, however, exceptions to this practice in 1846 and 1847; 101 Com. J. 59; 102 lb. 88.

88 Com. J. 287; 89 lb, 222; 91 lb. 418; 103 lb. 124. But in 1841 it was otherwise; 96 Com. J. 35. 68 Com. J. 451, 100 lb. 193.

the oaths of members have originated in committe. On the 6th June 1816, the standing order was held to apply to a bill for the punishment of persons disturbing congregations in a Roman Catholic chapel, or assaulting any Koman Catholic clergyman while officiating therein. On the other hand, the Church Temporalities, Ireland, Bill, of 1833, which may be said to have reconstituted the church government in that country, Avas not, on that account, required to originate in a committee. So also the Tithe Commutation Bills, and the bills for carrying into effect the recommendations of the ecclesiastical commissioners, in regard to the revenues of the Church of England, have all been introduced upon motion, without any previous resolution of a committee." In 1848 a bill relating to Roman Catholic charities was brought in without a committee, as it concerned revenues or temporalities, and not religion. And in 1851 the Ecclesiastical Titles Assumption Bill was held, after full consideration, not to come within the standing order.

The standing order regarding trade has been held to apply not only to trade generally, but also to any particular trade, if directly affected by a bill." On this account, bills to regulate the sale of beer, and of bread, have been required to originate in a committee; and, in 1840, the Copyright of Designs Bill was withdrawn, as affecting the trade of calico printers and others, and in subsequent sessions was brought in upon resolution from a committee. Yet bills relating to the copyright of books have been suffered to proceed without a previous committee. On an objection being taken, 19th February 1840, that a copyright bill related to trade, the speaker held that it did not directly interfere with trade, in any sense in which that 104 Com. J. 74. 71 43 34 jj j g p j j, gj, jqjo.

3 88 Com. J. 35. 91 lb. 17; 93 lb. 377; 94 lb. 29, c.

102 lb. 22. Mirror of Pari. 1840, pp. 1108, 1109.

' 88 Com. J. G73. 103 lb. 747. f 95 lb. 170. 97 lb. 83.

term is used In the standing orders. And on the 6th February 1844, the speaker decided that a bill to regulate the employment of children in factories did not come within the meaning of the standing order. It has been held that the standing order relates to the trade of a British colony, as well as to the trade of the United Kingdom. The Australian Colonies Government Bill, 1849, contained clauses relating to the trade and commerce, and altering the customs' duties of those colonies, and the bill was withdrawn, and another bill presented with those clauses printed in italics.

No grant of public money is ever attempted to be made Grants ofpabiic in a bill, without the prior resolution of a committee; but bills are often introduced, in which it becomes incidentally necessary to authorise the application of money to particular purposes. In order to accomplish this object without any violation of the standing order, the money clause is originally inserted in the bill in italics; a committee of the whole house is appointed to consider of authorising the advance of money; and on their report being made and agreed to by the house, an instruction is given to the committee on the bill to make provision accordingly. When the main object of a biu

Is the grant of money, it is invariably brought In upon the resolution of a committee, in the first Instance.

The house are as strict in proceedings for levying a tax. Tax upon the as they are in granting money, and it is the practice, '"" ' ' without any exception, for au bills that directly impose a charge upon the people, to originate In a committee of the whole house; but this rule has not been held to apply to bills authorising the levy or application of rates for local purposes, by local officers or bodies representing the ratepayers. In 1833, notice was taken that the Church Tem-

Mirror of Pari, 1840, p. 1110.

72 Hans. Deb., Sd Series, 286. (Clauses 28, 29). 104 Com. J. 424.

"Metropolis Police Bill, 84 Com. J. 233. Highway Rates Bill, 94 lb. 363. Poor Relief (Ireland) Bill, 93 lb. 90. Prisons (Scotland) Bill, 94 lb. 22. Coal Trade (Port of London) Bills, 86 lb. 658.

poralities Bill (which proposed to levy " an annual tax " instead of first fruits) should have originated in a committee. Before the house decided upon this point, a select committee was appointed to examine precedents, and on receiving their report the order for reading the bill a second time was discharged, and the bill withdrawn.

Preparing bills. In preparing bills, care must be taken that they do not contain provisions not authorised by the order of leave, that their titles correspond with the order of leave," and that they are prepared in proper form; for, if it should appear, during the progress of a bill, that these rules have not been observed, the house wnll order it to be withdrawn. A clause, for instance, relating to the qualification of members, was held to be unauthorised in a bill for regu-

Bianks or lating the expenses at elections. All dates, and the Italics, amount of salaries, tolls, rates, or other charges, were formerly required to be left blank; but the more convenient practice of printing such matters in italics is now adopted." Technically the words so printed are still treated as blanks, and are afterwards inserted in committee as if they had not been previously printed in the bill; but in the meantime, they indicate the intentions of the framers of the bill, and otherwise render the context intelligible and consistent.

Bills presented. Unless a bill be founded upon the resolution of a committee of the whole house for a charge upon the people, it may be presented on the same day, and during the same sitting, as that in which it was ordei'cd; but some other votes are generally allowed to be passed before it is offered. A member who is about to present a bill, should take his draft of it to the Public Bills Office, where it will be prepared in a proper form for presentation; and, when he has it ready, he should watch his opportunity for presenting it. By an order of the 10th December 1692, it ' Pari. Paper, No. 8G of 1833. io2 Com. J. 832; 103 lb. 522. 3 80 Com. J. 329; 82 lb. 32.3. 339; 84 lb. 261; 92 lb. 254. 90 lb. 411. 5 100 lb. 252.

is desired, " that every member presenting any bill (or petition) to this house, do go from his place down to the bar of the house, and bring the same up from thence to the table: " and in accordance with this rule, the member appears at the bar, when the speaker calls upon him by name. He answers, "A bill. Sir;" and the speaker desires him to " bring it up;" upon which he carries it to the table and delivers it to the clerk of the house, who reads the title aloud; when the bill is said to have been " received by the house." After a bill has been received in either house, a question is put, "That this bill be now First reading. read the first time," which is rarely ol jected to, either in the lords or commons; and in the commons can only be opposed by a division. Since the 5th Feb, 1849 the commons have adopted a sessional resolution:

"That-svlien any bill shall be presented by a member in pursuance of an order of this house, or shall be brought from the lords, the questions, ' That this bill be now read a first time;' and That this bill be printed," shall be decided without amendment or debate.".

When the bill has been read a first time, the question Second reading next put in the commons is, "That this bill be read a second time;" the second reading, how ever, is not taken at that time, but a future day is named, on which the bill is ordered to be read a second time. The bill is then ordered to be printed, in order that its contents may be published and distributed to every member, before the second reading. Every public bill is printed, except ordinary supply bills, which merely embody the votes of the committees of supply and ways and means, and the annual mutiny bills, which are the same, with very few exceptions, year after year. In the lords the questions for the printing and second reading of a bill on a future day are ' 10 Cora. J. 740. 2 ggg 1 jjj 223.

3 Lords'S. O. No. 34. 17 Com. J. 9. 88 11). G14. 104 Com. J. 22.

rarely put, but are entered in the minutes, upon an intimation from the peer Yho has charge of the bill. Reading bills. It need scarccly be said that the bill is not actually read at length; but it was formerly the practice for the clerk, on the first reading, to read to the house, first, the title and then the bill itself; after which the speaker read the title, and opened' to the house the effect and substance of the bill, either from memory, or by reading his breviate, which was filed to the bill; and sometimes he even read the bill itself. So tedious a practice is rendered unnecessary by the circulation of printed copies of the bill; and Breviates of the analysis of the several clauses, which is now prefixed ' "' ' to the bill, supplies the place of the ancient breviate. The practice of affixing a breviate or brief to every bill prevailed during the greater part of the I7th century. On the 2d May 1651, it was ordered,

"That no Act ought to be presented to this house without a brief thereof be given to Mr. Speaker; and that Mr. Sjieaker ought not to open any bill, nor to command the same to be read, unless a brief thereof be first delivered unto him; and that the said order be, from henceforth duly and exactly observed accordingly." And this had been the practice at that time for many years, for on the 3d March 1G06, it was " ordered, on Mr. Speaker's motion, that every committee, when they proceed to the amendment of any bill committed to them, should also amend the brief annexed, and make it agree with the bill."

By a standing order of the House of Lords it is ordered,

"That the name of the lord who moves the second reading of any public bill shall be entered on the Journals of this house."

"That the name of the lord presenting a public bill to this house, and of the lord who shall give notice to the clerk assistant that he intends to move the second reading of any public bill brought up from the commons, shall be printed in the minutes of proceedings of this house, in connexion with the same."

Second reading. The day having been appointed for the second reading, ' 1 Com. J. 380. 45G.

Order and course of passing Bills in Parliament, 4to, 1641. 1 Com. J. 208. G Com. J. 570. 1 lb. 347.

Lords' S. O. No. 34.

the bill stands in the Order Book, amongst the other orders of the day, and is called on in its proper turn, when that day arrives. This is r- garded as the most important stage through which the bill is required to pass; for its whole principle is then at issue, and is affirmed or denied by a vote of the house. The member who has charge of the bill moves, "That the bill be now read a second time;" and usually takes this opportunity of enlarging upon its merits. It is sometimes agreed to defer the discussion of the principle until a later stage of the bill; but the practice is irregular and objectionable. As the house have already ordered that the bul shall be read a second time, and the second reading stands as an order of the day, the motion for now reading the bill a second time need not be seconded, and the same rule applies to other similar stages. The opponents of the bill may simply vote against this question, and so defeat the second reading on that day; but this course is rarely adopted, because it must still be decided on what other day it shall be read a second time, or whether it shall be read at all. The ordinary practice, therefore, is to move an Amendments amendment to the question, by leaving out the word secont read- "" "now," and adding "three months," "six months," or " any other term beyond the probable duration of the session. The postponement of a bill, in this manner, is regarded as the most courteous method of dismissing the bill from any further consideration, and is resorted to in every other stage of the proceedings, except on the question for the passing of the bill. Another reason for using this form of amendment is, that the house have already ordered that the bill shall be read a second time, and the amendment, instead of reversing that order, merely appoints a more distant day for the second reading.

It is also competent to a member to move as an amend- ' 88 Com. J. 309. A A ment to the question, a resolution declaratory of some principle adverse to that of the Bill, provided it be strictly relevant. The practice, however, is objectionable, as such a resolution rarely amounts to more than a negation of the principle of the bill; and a vote against the second reading would, therefore, express the member's opinion with sufficient distinctness. Nor does the resolution, if agreed to, interfere with the progress of the bill. Where the objection is of a more limited and peculiar character, the most regular mode of taking a vote upon" it is by moving an instruction to the committee, at a later stage.

Bills rejected. Instances of rejecting bills altogether were formerly not uncommon, but are now comparatively rare: two cases only appearing in the Journals of the commons for upwards of half a century; but in the lords the practice has been more general." In more ancient times, bills were treated with even greater ignominy. On the 23d January, in the 5th Elizabeth, a bill was rejected and ordered to be torn; so, also, on the 17tli March 1620, Sir Edward Coke moved " to have the bill torn in the house;" and it is entered, that the bill was accordingly "rejected and torn, without one negative." There is no restriction in regard to the time at which motions for rejecting bills shall be made; but, if the house think fit, such rejection may be voted on the first, second, or third readings, or any other stage of the bill. It has been thought better, however, to notice the practice in this place, in connexion with the postponement of bills, in order to save repetition when the other stages are under consideration.

Counsel. The second reading is the stage at which counsel are more usually heard, whenever the house have agreed that a public bill is of so peculiar a character as to justify the hearing of parties whose interests are directly afiected by ' Bank Charter Bill, 1844, 99 Com. J. 39G. ggg infra, p. 356.

3 37 Com. J. 444; 80 lb. 425.

See Gen. Indexes to Lords' J. tit. " Bills."

1 Com. J. 252. 262. 311. 1 lb. 63. 1 lb. 560.

it It is a general principle of legislation, that a public bill being of national interest, should be debated in Parliament upon the grounds of public expediency; and that the arguments on either side should be restricted to members of the house, while peculiar interests are represented by the petitions of the parties concerned. Questions of public policy can only be discussed by members; but where protection is sought for the rights and interests of public bodies, or others, it has not been unusual to permit the parties to represent their claims by counsel. Counsel have also been heard at various other stages of bills, as well as on the second reading.

When a bill has been read a second time, a question is Committees on put, " that this bill be committed," which is rarely opposed, and on being agreed to, a day is named for the committee. On the order of the day being read for the committee, it is Lords, moved in the lords, that the house be now put into committee on the bill; to which an amendment may be moved, that the. house be put into committee on a future day, beyond the probable duration of the session. When the Commons. order of the day is read in the commons, for the house to resolve itself into a committee on the bill, the speaker puts a question, "That I do now leave the chair," to which the proper amendment is, to leave out all the words after " that," in order to add, " this house will on this day three months," or ' six months," resolve itself into the said committee," c. If attention were not paid to this form of amendment, the absurdity might arise of ordering Mr. Speaker to " leave the chair this day six months." But instructions to before the house resolves itself into committee, an instruc- " i"""' ' 88 Com. J. 501; 90 It. 587, c. Municipal Corporations Bill (lords), 1833. Canada Government Bill (commons), 1838, Mr. Roebuck. Jamaica Bill, the commons, "isd and 23d April, and 7th June 1839; and lords, 28th June. For explanations of the principle upon which Parliament have permitted counsel to be heard against public bills, and precedents cited, see Lords' Debate on Australian Colonies Biil, 10th June 1850, 111 Haas. Deb., 3d Series, 943.

See Com. Gen. Journ. Indexes, tit. " Counsel."

Lords' S. O. No. 34.

to be moved.

tion may be given to the committee empowering them to make provision fur certain matters which they could not otherwise entertain, as being foreign to the title of the bill. An instruction cannot order a committee to make any provision; but merely instructs them " that they have power" to make it. If the proposed provision be within the title, it cannot be the subject of an instruction, which would be nugatory, as the committee would already have the power which it is the object of the instruction to confer. Nor can an instruction be given to make any provision, if it be of such a nature that it ought to have been first considered in a committee of the whole house; for in that When and how casc the rules of the house would be evaded. The most proper and convenient time for moving an instruction is, after the order of the day for the committee on the bill has been read, when it should be a distinct motion; for if it be moved as an amendment to the question for the speaker leaving the chair, and be agreed to, it interferes with the determination of the house upon that question, which is not the object of the amendment, nor the desire of its mover.

A distinct resolution is sometimes moved as an amendment to the question for the speaker leaving the chair, which, if agreed to, may have the same ultimate effect as an instruction, by declaring the opinion of the house, to which effect can afterwards be given in proper form. Such a resolution may thus be moved when an instruction would be irregular; for if it comprise matters which must be first considered in a committee of the whole house, effect is given to the resolution of the house, by considering the matter in committee, and afterwards giving the required ' See supra, p. 346 et seq.

Warwick Borough Bill, 5th March 1834, 80 Com. J. 91. Established Church Bill, 8th July 1836, 91 lb. 639. Poor Relief (Ireland) Bill, 9th May 1837, 92 lb. 358. Freemen's Admission Bill, 10th May 1837, 92 lb. 364. Colleges (Ireland) Bill, 23d June 1845, 100 lb. 621. Election Recogaizances Bill, 15th March 1848, 103 lb.330.

3 Sugar Duties Bill, 14th March 1845 (Mr. Hawes).

Resolutions in the nature of instructions.

instruction to the committee on the bill. The form of an instruction is such as to preclude the house from complying with these preliminary formalities, as it takes immediate effect, and it would therefore be irregular, as already explained, under circumstances in which a resolution is not inconsistent with the rules of the house. The Committee on the bill, however, would not be bound to take notice of such a resolution, unless it were followed by an instruction.

All such motions, however, if in the form of amendments. Before first must be made before the first sitting of the committee, for committee. by a resolution of the 5tli February 1849, since made a sessional resolution, if the bill have already been partly considered, the speaker will forthwith leave the chair, when the order for the committee has been read. When a distinct instruction is to be given, after the first sitting of the committee, it is done before the order of the day is read."

If the house agree to the question for the speaker leaving the chair, the mace is removed from the table, and the committee begin the consideration of the bill. As its principle has been affirmed at the second reading, the details of the bill are to be examined in committee, clause by clause, and line by line, and every blank filled up; for which purpose the permission to speak more than once, oifers great facilities."

The chairman, on taking the chair, puts a question. Proceedings in rrii 1 1 Ml 1 1 f ' I'll. committee.

"That this bill be read a first time; which being agreed to, he puts another, viz. that it "be read a second time, paragraph by paragraph." When that also is affirmed, the preamble is ordered to be postponed, and the chairman proceeds to call out each clause in succession, together with the short marginal note, stating the nature of each clause. If no amendment be offered to any part of a clause, he puts the question, "That this clause stand part of the bill," and proceeds to tlie next; but when an amendment is proposed, he states the line in which the alteration ' 105 Com. J, 635.- See supra, p. 289.

Aiiic! idiiieiit9, wlien to be oft'cred.

Blanks filled up.

AVliat amend-iiients admissible.

Title of the Bill not to be amended.

is to be made, and puts the question in the ordinary form. Members who are desirous of offering amendments in committee, should watch carefully the progress of the bill, and propose them at the proper time; for if the committee have passed on to another clause, or even amended a later line in the clause than that proposed to be amended, amendments cannot be made in an earlier part of the bill. When a clause has been amended, the question put from the chair is, "That this clause, as amended, stand part of the bill."

The blanks are filled up as they occur; and if it be proposed to fill them up with different words, a distinct motion is made upon each proposal, instead of moving an amendment upon that first suggested. The chairman puts the question upon each motion separately, and in the order in which they were made, unless the later motion be for a smaller sum, or a longer time; in which cases, it should be put first. This rule, indeed, is more peculiarly api)li-cable to the committees of supply and ways and means; but has generally been observed in committees upon bills, and other committees of the whole house.

Every description of amendment may be made in committee; whole clauses and schedules are added, or omitted, or substituted one for another, provided that, in the commons, they be within the title; and verbal alterations are made in every part, whether in the preamble, the clauses, or the schedules But in the commons, the title of the bill may not be amended, as that is reserved for the house, after all the amendments have been made to the bill in its several stages; nor should any amendment be admitted which is in the nature of a previous question. If it be convenient, clauses may be postponed and considered afterwards out of their order, but must not have been previously ' 88Com. J. 61?!

But see proceedings in committee on Reform Bill; 87 Com. J. 133. 141. 16r, 173, questions and amendments concerning Amersham, Helston, Gateshead, and South Shields.

amended. The committee may also divide one clause into two; or decide that the first part of a clause, or the first part of a clause with a schedule, shall be considered as an entire clause. Wlien instructions have been given by the no use for that purpose, the committee may receive clauses or make provision in the bills committed to them, which they could not otherwise have considered, as being extraneous to the titles. In compliance with instructions, also, they may make two bills into one, or divide one bill into two or more; or examine witnesses and hear counsel. When all the clauses and schedules have been agreed to, the preamble, wliich had been postponed, is considered, and, if necessary, is amended so as to conform to amendments made in the bill; and the chairman puts the question, "That this be the preamble of the bill," which he reads to the committee.

The house is not supposed to be informed of any of the Proceedings of proceedings of the committee until the bill has been re- kn 'antir " ported, and any discussion of the clauses, with the speaker reported. in the chair, is consequently irregular. For this reason, on a motion for postponing the further sitting of the committee on the Scotch Poor Law Bill, on the 17th July 1845, on the ground of certain alterations which had been made in committee, Mr. Speaker stopped the discussion of the merits of those alterations.

If the committee cannot go through the whole bill at Report of one sitting in the lords, the chairman leaves the chair, Progress. and moves that the house be put into committee on a future day; and in the commons, the committee instruct the chairman to report progress, and ask leave to sit again. When the bill has been thoroughly considered, the Report of the chairman puts a question, "That I do report this bill with ' the amendments to the house;" which being agreed to, the sitting of the committee is concluded, and Mr. Speaker 89 Com. J. 409; 87 lb. 80; 86 lb, 728. ' See supra, 356. 3 See Com. Gen. Journ. Index (1820-1837), p. 003.

resumes his chair; upon which the chairman approaches the steps of the speaker's chair, and reports from the committee that " they had gone through the bill, and had made amendments," or " several amendments thereunto." If no amendments have been made, he reports " that they had gone through the bill, and directed him to report the same, without amendment." In the lords the bill is at once reported if there be no amendments; but there is a standing order, 28th June 1715, which declares "that no report be received from any committee of the whole house, the same day such committee goes through the bill, when any amendments are made to such bill." Proceedings od On the 5th February 1849, and afterwards at the commencement of each session, the commons have resolved:

"That at the close of the proceedings of a conniiittee of the whole house on a bill, the chairman shall report the bill forthwith to the house, and when amendments siiall have been made thereto, the same shall be received without debate, and a timg appointed for taking the same into consideration."

When the report has been received, if no amendments have been made, the bill is usually ordered to be read a third time on a future day. If amendments have been made by the committee, the report is a formal proceeding, and the bill, as amended, is ordered to be taken into consideration on a future day. In the lords no bill may be read a third time on the same day on which it is reported from the committee, unless the standing orders be suspended for that purpose; " but in the commons, bills reported from a committee without amendments, have frequently been read a third time on the same day, especially at the end of a session. Bills reprinted.-At this Stage also it is customary to reprint the bill, if several amendments have been made; for no verbal explanation of numerous amendments can possibly make the amended bill intelligible, and the practice of both houses is to rely more upon a reprint of the bill, than upon any ' Lords' S. O. No. 36, 37. Lords' S. O. No. 37.

' " 90 Com. J. 337; 105 Ih. 372.

proceedings in the house, on the report of very numerous or important amendments.

When the bill as amended by the committee is con- Clauses added, sidered, the house may not only agree or disagree to the mentsmade. amendments, but may make fresh amendments and add new clauses, whether they be within the title or not; but the practice of adding clauses at this time is inconvenient, and should be avoided as far as possible. The amendments of the committee are considered first; clauses may then be offered; after which amendments may be made to other parts of the bill. When a member offers a clause on the consideration of the bill as amended, he moves, 1st, "That it be brought up;" 2d, "That it be read a first time;" 3d, "That it be read a second time;" 4th, "That it be made part of the bill." Amendments also may be proposed to clauses offered in this manner, and if agreed to by the house, the last question put by the speaker is, "That this clause, as amended, be made part of the bill." Clauses containing rates, penalties, or other blanks, must also pass through a committee before they are added to the bill.

It often becomes necessary to recommit a bill to a com- Bills recom-mittee of the whole house, and occasionally to a select committee, before it is read a third time; and a recommitment of the bill is always advisable when numerous amendments are to be proposed.

A bill may be recommitted: 1. Without limitation, in which case the entire bill is again considered in committee, and reported with " other" or " further" amendments. 2. On amendments being proposed on the consideration of the bill as amended, the bill may be recommitted with respect to those amendments only." 3. On clauses being offered, the bill may be recommitted with respect to these clauses. 4. The bill may be recommitted, and an instruc- ' 99 Com. J. G3. 83 lb. 533. 92 lb. 413, niitted.

Again recommitted.

Comitiitted to select committees.

Discontinuance of ingrussment.

tion given to the committee, that they have power to make some particular or additional provision.

A bill may be recommitted as often as the house think fit. It is not uncommon for bills to be again recommitted once or twice," and there are cases in which a bill has been six and even seven times through a committee of the whole house, in consequence of repeated recommitments. The proceedings on the report of a recommitted bill are similar to those already explained; the report is received at once, and the bill, as amended, is ordered to be taken into consideration on a future day.

Notwithstanding the facilities for discussion afforded by a committee of the whole house, the details of a bill may often be considered more conveniently by a select committee. Indeed, according to the ancient practice, all ordinary bills were committed to select committees, and none but the most important were reserved for the consideration of a committee of the whole house. Every public bill, however, is now considered in committee of the whole house, whether it be also committed to a select committee or not. When it has not been determined until after the second reading, to commit a bill to a select committee, the order, or order of the day, as the case may be, for the committee of the whole house, is read and discharged, and the bill is committed to a select committee. It had not been the custom until recently, to empower such a committee to send for persons, papers, and records; and when it was deemed necessary to take evidence, another committee was appointed to consider the subject-matter of the bill, consisting of the same members as the committee on the bill. This inconvenient and useless practice, however, may now be considered as obsolete; and all necessary powers will be given to the committee on the bill."

The ancient system of ingrossing all bills upon parch- 89 Com. J. 127.

= G5 lb. 384. 396. 420; G9 lb. 420. 444. 460.

83 lb. 354; 89 lb. 286. 104 1b. 253.348. 402.

ment after the report, was discontinued in 1849, when both houses agreed to the following arrangements:

"That in lieu of being ingrossed, every bill shall be printed fair immediately after it shall have been passed in the house in which it originated, and that such fair printed bill shall be sent to the other house, as the bill so passed, and shall be dealt with by that house, and its officers, in the same manner in which engrossed bills are now dealt with.

"That when such bill shall have jjassed both houses of parliament it shall be fair printed by the Queen's printer, who shall furnish a fair print thereof on vellum to the House of Lords, before the royal assent, and likewise a duplicate of such fair print, also on vellum.

"That one of such fair prints of each bill shall be duly authenticated by the clerk of the parliaments, or other proper officer of the House of Lords, as the bill to which both houses have agreed.

"That the royal assent shall be indorsed in the usual form on such fair print so authenticated, which shall be deposited in the Record Tower, in lieu of the present ingrossment.

"That the copies promulgated in the first instance by the Queen's printer, shall be impressions from the same form as the deposited copy.

" That the master of the rolls shall, upon being duly authorized in that behalf, receive in lieu of the copies of public general acts as now inrolled, the hereinbefore-mentioned duplicate fair print of each public general bill, to be held for the same purposes, and subject to the same conditions for and upon which the inrolled acts are now received and held by him.

"That it is expedient, with a view to economy, convenience, and dispatch, and to the diminution of the chance of errors, that one printer should print the public general bills for both houses; and that inasmuch as the Queen's printer is by virtue of his office bound to print the acts, it would be advisable for the attainment of the before-mentioned objects, that the Queen's printer should be employed by both houses to print the public general bills."'

These resolutions were confined to public bills during the session of 1849; but on July 27th they were extended in future sessions to local, personal, and private bills, except as to the printing of such bills by one printer for both houses. By the adoption of this system, the old form of ' 104 Com. J. 51. ' lb. 578. 620.

question " that this bill be ingrossed," which always followed after the report, or further consideration of report, is dispensed with.

Third reading. On the third reading, the judgment of the house is expressed upon the entire bill, as it stands after all the amendments introduced in committee and at other stages. When the bill has been read a third time clauses and schedules may be added, and amendments may still be made by the house to any part of the bill before it is passed; but it is advisable to resort to this practice as rarely as possible, as the proper time for offering clauses and amendments is in committee, when the speaker is not in the chair. An ordinary clause, offered at this stage, is read three times; but if it have any blanks, it must be read twice, and committed to a committee of the whole house, and reported; after which it is read a third time, and added to the bill'

Time of pro- caution may here be useful to members, in reference posing new. g manner of proposing clauses, that whether they be offered on the consideration of the bill, as amended, or on the third reading, they should be offered before any amendments are made to the bill. This rule is observed, because the addition of a new clause may render it necessary to introduce amendments in other parts of the bill; and all the clauses should, therefore, have been under consideration before amendments are admitted.

Bill passed. Occasionally, a bill is read a third time, and "further proceedings thereon " are adjourned to a future day; but the general practice is to follow up the third reading with the question, "That this bill do pass." This question has sometimes passed in the negative, after all the preceding stages of the bill have been agreed to; " but it is not usual to divide upon it.

' Before the discontinuance of iugrossments clauses were added to bills on the third reading " by way of rider."

"" 76 Com. J. 413; 80 lb. G17; 89 lb. 4J7.

In the lords, the orighial title of a bill is amended at Title of the Mil. any stage at which amendments are admissible, when alterations in the body of the bill have rendered any change in the title necessary. But in the commons, the original title is not amended during the progress of the bill, unless the house agree to divide one bill into two, or combine two into one; and the last question to be determined is, "That this be the title of the bill," which is accordingly read by the speaker. Amendments may then be offered to the title, which are generally such as render the title conformable with amendments which may have been made to the bill since its first introduction. It may be as well to recall to mind in this place, that the standing order of the commons, 17th November 1797, requiring the duration of a temporary law to be expressed both in the title and in a clause at the end of the bill, was rescinded on the 24th July 1849, when the following standing order was substituted:

"That the precise duration of (very temporary law be expressed in a distinct clause at the end of the bill."-

The next step is to communicate the bill to the other Communicated from lords commons.

house. It has been already stated elsewhere, that the lords ""

usually send down their bills to the commons by a master in chancery; and that if they concern the Crown or royal family, they should be sent by one of the judges. When the bill has originated in the lords, " a message is ordered to be sent to the House of Commons to carry down the said bill, and desire their concurrence." If the bill has been sent up from the commons, and has been agreed to, the lords return the bill with a message " to acquaint them, that the lords have agreed to the said bill without any amendment;" or, ' that the lords have agreed to the same with some amendments, to which their lordships desire their concurrence."

If a bill or clause be carried to the other house by mistake. Bills sent by mistake. 104 Com. J. 581. 104 lb. 558.

' See su2)rfi, p. 321. 74 Lords' J. 382.

From commons to lords.

Amendments agreed to or amended.

or if any other error be discovered, a message is sent to have the bill returned, or the clause expunged, or the error otherwise rectified.

The commons send up bills to the lords by a member (generally the chairman of the committee of ways and means, or the member who has had charge of the bill), who, as in other messages, is accompanied to the bar of the House of Lords by not less than four members; and when a bill is popular, perhaps by a considerable number. The member who has charge of the bill delivers it to the lord speaker of the House of Lords, who comes to the bar to receive it. The form of message, mutatis mutandis, is similar to that used by the House of Lords.

If one house agree to a bill passed by the other without any amendment, no further discussion or question can arise upon it; but the bill is ready to be put into the commission for receiving the royal assent. If a bill be returned from one house to another with amendments, these amendments must either be agreed to by the house which had first passed the bill, or the other house must waive their amendments; otherwise the bill will be lost. Sometimes one house agrees to the amendments with amendments to 1 Com. J. 132; 75 lb. 447; 78 lb. 317; 80 lb. 512; 91 lb. 639. 758; 92 lb. 572. 609. Lunatic Asylums' Bill; 100 lb. 804. Poor Employment (Ireland) Bill; 101 lb. 1277.

' In sending bills from the commons to the lords, it was formerly the custom to wait until several had passed, when they were carried up together, and delivered at the bar of the lords in the following order: 1. Lords' bills; 2. Commons' bills amended by the lords; 3. Public bills in order, according to their imjiortance; and, 4. Private bills, in such order as the speaker ajipointed. It was then usual for 30 or 40 members to accompany ihe member who had charge of the bills. On the 17th March 1588, a private bill was sent up with only four or five members, and the lords took exception to the smallness of the number, and said, " that they had cause to doubt that it passed not with a general consent of the house, because it passed not graced with a greater number, and left it to the consideration of the house to send it back in such sort as it was fit." D'Ewes, 447. Order and Course of Passing Bills in Parliament, 4to. 1641. See also supra, p. 320.

which the other house agrees. Occasionally, this interchange of amendments is carried even farther, and one house agrees to amendments with amendments, to which the other house agrees with amendments, to which, also, the first house, in its turn, agrees. But it is a rule, that Conseqnentiul . 1 1 1 ameudmeiits.

neither house may, at this time, leave out or otherwise amend anything which they have already passed themselves; unless such amendment be immediately consequent upon amendments of the other house, which have been agreed to, and are necessary for carrying them into effect. These several agreements and amendments are communicated by one house to the other with appropriate messages.

When it is determined to disagree to amendments made wiien amend-by the other house, one of three courses may be adopted: ao-reed to. 1. The bill may be laid aside. 2. The consideration of the amendments may be put off for three or six months, or to any time beyond the probable duration of the session. 3. A conference may be desired with the other house. The Conferences. two first modes of proceeding are only resorted to when the privileges of the house are infringed by the bill, or when the ultimate agreement of the two houses is hopeless; the latter is preferred whenever there is a reasonable prospect of mutual agreement and compromise. The practice of Parliament in regard to conferences has been fully explained elsewhere, and it would be unnecessary and irksome to describe, at length, every variety of procedure which may arise in the settlement of amendments to bills by conference." It will be sufficient to state generally that when a bill has been returned by either house to the other, with amendments which are disagreed to, a conference is desired 90 Com. J. 575. 105 lb. 631. Supra, p. 322, c.

All the minute details of practice may be traced by referring to the head "Conferences," in the three last Commons'Generaljournal Indexes; but more particularly by following the proceedings upon the Municipal Corporations Bill in 1836, to which ample references will be found in the Index to the Journal of that year, and at p. 413 of the General Index 1820-1837.

Free conference.

Conference, by whom desired.

by the house which disagrees to the amendment, to acquaint the other with the reasons for such disagreement; in order, to use the words of Hatsell,

"That after considering those reasons, the house may be induced, either not to insist upon their amendments, or may, in their turn, assign such arguments for having made them, as may prevail upon the other house to agree to them." " If the house which amend the bill are not satisfied and convinced by the reasons urged for disagreeing to the amendments, but persevere in insisting upon their amendments, the form is to desire another conference; at which, in their turn, they state their arguments in favour of the amendments, and the reasons why they cannot depart from them; and if after such second conference the other house resolve to insist upon disagreeing to the amendments, they ought then to demand a ' free conference," at which the arguments on both sides may be more amply and freely discussed. If this measure should prove ineffectual, and if, after several free conferences, neither house can be induced to depart from the point they originally insisted upon, nothing further can be done, and the bill must be lost."'

An interesting occasion, on which all these proceedings were successively adopted, occurred in 1836. A free conference was then held upon the amendments made by the lords to a bill for amending the Act for regulating Municipal Corporations. No free conference had previously been held since the year 1702; nor has any subsequent case arisen.

It will only be necessary to add, that it is irregular to demand a conference with the house which is in possession of a bill; which rule was thus affirmed by the commons,

13th March 1575: " That by the ancient liberties and privileges of this house, conference is to be required by that court which, at the time of the conference demanded,
shall be possessed of the bill, and not of any other court."" As the conference is desired
by that house which is in possession of the bill, the bill which is the subject of the
conference is always delivered by the managers, with the reasons and amendments, to
the house with whom the conference was desired.

4 Hats. 49.

2 1 Com. J. 114,

The official record of the assent of one house to bills indorspments passed, or
amendments made by the other, is by indorse- " '"" " ment of the bill in old Norman
French. Thus, when a bill is passed by the commons, the clerk of the house writes
upon the top of it, "Soif. bailie mix seigneursr When the lords make amendments,
it is returned with an indorsement, signed by the clerk assistant of the Parliaments, "
ceste Mile avesque des amendmens les seignieurs sont assentus." When it is sent back
with these amendments agreed to, the clerk of the House of Commons writes, 'A ces
amendmens les communes sont assentus;" and bills are communicated by the lords to
the commons with similar indorsements, mntatis mutandis. When amendments are
dis' agreed to, such disagreement is not indorsed upon the bill, but forms the subject
of a message to demand a conference.

When bills have been finally agreed to by both houses, jal Assent. they only await
the royal assent to give them, as Lord Hale says, " the complement and perfection of
a law: " and from that sanction they cannot legally be withheld. For this purpose they
remain in the custody of the clerk of the enrolments, in the House of Lords, except
money bills, which are returned to the commons before the royal assent is given;
and when several have accumulated, or when the royal assent is required to be given
without delay to any bill, the lord chancellor has notice that a commission is wanted.
The clerk of the enrolments then prepares two copies of the titles of all the bills, each
title being upon a separate piece of paper. One of these copies is for the clerk of
the Crown to insert in the commission, and the other for her Majesty's inspection,
before she signs the commission. When the Queen comes in person to give her royal
assent, the clerk assistant of the Parliaments waits ' In his absence the clerk assistant
is authorised to indorse hills. Jurisd. of Lords, c. 2.

See 2 Hats 339. 13 Lords' J. 756. 3 Lord Caniiibe; rs Live of the Chancellors, 354.
2 Burnet's Own Time, 274.

Session is not concluded by royal assent.

upon her Majesty in the robing room before she enters the house, reads a list of the
bills, and receives her commands upon them.

It was formerly a matter of doubt whether a session was not concluded by the
royal assent being signified to a bill. So far back as 1554 the House of Commons
declared against this construction of law," and yet in 1625 it Avas thought necessary
to pass an Act to declare that the session should not be determined by the royal assent
being given to that and certain other Acts; and again, in 1670, a clause to the same
effect was inserted in an Act; but for the last centiuy and a half, without any express
enactment, the law has become defined by usage, and the royal assent is now given to
every bill shortly after it has been agreed to by both houses, without any interruption

of the session. By commission. During the progress of a session, the royal assent is generally given by a commission issued under the great seal for that purpose. The first instance in which the royal assent appears to have been given by commission, was in the 33d of Henry VIII., although proceedings very similar had occurred in the 23d and 25th years of the reign of that king. The lord chancellor produced two Acts agreed to by the lords and commons; one for the attainder of the queen and her accomplices, and the other for proceeding against lunatics in cases of treason; each Act being signed by the king, and the royal assent being signified by a commission under the great seal, signed by the king, and annexed to both the Acts." To prevent any doubts as to the legality of this mode of assenting to an Act, the two following clauses were put into the Act for the attainder of the queen:

"Be it declared by authority of this present Parliament, that the king's royal assent, by his letters patent under his great seal ' Mr. Birch's Ev. No. 413, of 1843. 2 1 Com. J. 38.

1 Car, I., c. 7. 22 23 Car. II., c. 1, s. 9.

33 Hen. VIII., c. 21. Stat, of the Realm, vol. 1. p. lxxiii.

1 Lords' J. 198.

Originofgiving royal assent by commission.

and assigned with his hand, and declared and notified in his absence to the lords spiritual and temporal, and to the commons, assembled together in the high house, is and ever was of as good strength and force as though the king's person had been there personally present, and had assented openly and publickly to the same. And be it also enacted, that this royal assent, and all other royal assents hereafter to be so given by the kings of this realm, and notified as is aforesaid, shall be taken and reputed good and effectual to all intents and purposes, without doubt or ambiguity; any custom or use to the contrary notwithstanding." ' In strict compliance with the words of this statute, the Form of com-comraission is always " by the Queen herself signed with her own hand," and attested by the clerk of the Crown in chancery. Towards the latter end of the reign of George IV., it became painful to him to sign any instrument with his own hand, and he was enabled, by statute, to appoint one or more person or persons, with full power and authority to each of them to affix, in his Majesty's presence, and by his Majesty's command given by word of mouth, his Majesty's royal signature, by means of a stamp to be prepared for that purpose; and the commission for giving the royal assent to bills on the 17th June 1830, bears the stamp of the king, attested according to the provisions of that Act.

On the 5th February 1811, the Regency Bill received Regency Bill, the royal assent by commission under peculiar circum- ' stances. The king was incapable of exercising any personal authority; but the great seal was nevertheless affixed to a commission for giving the royal assent to that bill. When the commons had been summoned to the bar of the House of Lords by the lords commissioners, the lord chancellor said, "My lords and gentlemen, by the commands, and by virtue of the powers and authority to us given by the said commission, we do declare and notify his Majesty's royal assent to the Act in the said commission mentioned.

' Stat, of the Realm, vol. 1, p. lxxiv. '11 Geo. 4, c. 23.

62 Lords' J. 732.

Form of royal assent by commission.

Royal assent refused.

and the clerks are required to pass the same in the usual form and words;" after which the royal assent was signified by the clerk in the usual words, "Le roy le veulv

The form in which the royal assent is signified by commission is as follows:

Three or more of the lords commissioners, seated on a form between the throne and the woolsack in the House of Lords, command the usher of the black rod to signify to the commons that their attendance is desired in the house of peers to hear the commission read, upon which the commons with the speaker immediately come to the bar. The commission is then read at length, and the titles of the bills being afterwards read by the clerk of the Crown, the royal assent to each is signified by the clerk of the Parliaments in Norman French; and is so entered in the Lords' Journal. A money bill is carried up and presented by the speaker, and receives the royal assent before all other bills. The assent is pronounced in the words, "La reyne remercie ses hons siijets, accepte leur benevolence, et ainsi le veult."' For a public bill the form of expression is, "Xa reyne le veult; " for a private bill, "Soit fait comme il est desire;" upon a petition demanding a right, whether public or private, "Soit droit fait comme il est desire." In an act of grace or pardon which has the royal assent before it is agreed to by the two houses, the ancient form of assent was, "Les prelats, seigneurs, et communes, en ce present parliament assemblees, au nom de touts vos aiitres sujets, remercient tres humhlement vostre majeste, et prient a Dieu vous donner en sante bonne vie et longue;" but according to more modern practice the royal assent has been signified in the usual form, as to a public bill." The form of words used to express a denial of the royal assent would be, "La reyne ' 48 Lords'J. 70. 18 Hans. Deb. 1124. See also Debates, 27th Feb. 1804 (Commons); 1st and 9th March 1804 (Lords). 1 Twiss, Life of Eldon, 2d edit., 416. 418. = D'Ewes. Journ. 35.

20 Lords' J."J46; 27 Ih.

s'avisera." ' The necessity of refusing the royal assent is removed by the strict observance of the constitutional principle, that the Crown has no will but that of its ministers; who only continue to serve in that capacity so long as they retain the confidence of Parliament. This power was last exercised in 1707, when Queen Anne refused her assent to a bill for settling the militia in Scotland.

During the Commonwealth the lord protector gave his Use of the Nor-assent to bills in English; but on the Restoration, the old '" " French. form of words was reverted to, and only one attempt has since been made to abolish it. In 1706, the lords passed a bill " for abolishing the use of the French tongue in all proceedings in Parliament and courts of justice." This bill dropped in the House of Commons; and although an Act passed in 1731 for conducting all proceedings in courts of justice in English, no alteration was made in the old forms used in Parliament. Until the latter part of the reign of Edward HI., all parliamentary proceedings were conducted in French, and the use of English was exceedingly rare until the reign of Henry VI. All the statutes were then enrolled in French or Latin, but the royal assent was occasionally given in English. Since the reign of Henry VIL., all other proceedings have been in the Eno-lish language, but the old form of royal assent has been retained.

The royal assent is rarely given in person, except at the Given by tiie close of a session, when the Queen attends to prorogue the n "' '" Parliament, and then she signifies her assent to such bills as may have passed since the last commission was issued; but bills for making provision for the honour and dignity of the Crown, such as the bills for settling the civil lists, have generally been assented to by the Sovereign in person, ' 1 Lords' J. 102; 13 lb. 394, (with reasons); 18 lb. 506. 18 lb. 506. See Pref. to Statutes of tlie Realm, for a liistory of the progress of the Englisli language in parliamentary proceedings.

lisrossinent rolls.

Commencement of Act.

immediately after they have passed both houses. When her Majesty gives her royal assent to bills in person, the clerk of the Crown reads the titles, and the clerk assistant of the Parliaments makes an obeisance to the throne, and then signifies her Majesty's assent in the manner already described. A gentle inclination, indicative of assent, is given by her Majesty, who has, however, already given her commands to the clerk assistant, as shown above.

AMien Acts are thus passed, the original ingrossment rolls (or, since 1849, the authenticated prints) are preserved in the House of Lords, and all public and local and personal Acts, and nearly all private Acts, are printed by the Queen's printer, and printed copies are referred to as evidence in courts of law. The original rolls or prints may also be seen, when necessary, and copies taken, on the payment of certain fees.

All Acts of Parliament, of which the commencement was not specifically enacted, were formerly held, in law, to take effect from the first day of the session; but the clerk or clerk assistant of the Parliaments is now required by Act 33 Geo. III., c. 13, to indorse, in English, on every Act of Parliament, immediately after the title, the day, month, and year, when the same shall have passed and received the royal assent, which indorsement is to be a part of the Act, and to be the date of its commencement, when no other commencement is provided in the Act itself.

See Civil List Bills, 75 Com. J. 258; 86 lb. 517; 93 lb. 227. On the 2(of Argust 1831, the speaker, after a short speech in relation to the bill for supporting the royal dignity of her Majesty Queen Adelaide, delivered it to the clerk, when it received the royal assent in the usual form; but the Queen, attended by one of the ladies of her bedchamber, and her maids of honour, was present, and sat in a chair placed on a platform raised for that jiurposc between the archbishops' bench and the bishops' door, and after the royal assent was pronounced, her majesty stood np, and made three curtesies, one to the king, one to the lords, and one to the comnious. 63 Lords' J. 885, and Index to tliat volume, p. 1157.

' Sec p. 370.

The forms commonly observed by both houses, iu the Forms not bind-passing of bills, having been explained, it must be under- gressot'ball'! stood that they are not absolutely binding. They are founded upon long parliamentary usage, indeed; but either house may vary its own peculiar forms, without question elsewhere, and without affecting the validity of any Act which has received, in proper form, the ultimate sanction of the thi'ee branches of the legislature. If an informality be discovered during the progress of a bill, the house In which it originated wiu either order the bill to be withdrawn, or will annul the informal proceeding itself, and all subsequent proceedings; but if irregularities escape detection until the bill has passed, no subsequent notice can be taken of them, as it is the business of each house to enforce compliance with its own orders and practice.

In the ordinary progress of a bill, the proceedings either Bills passed follow from day to day, or some days are allowed to intervene p!(jmou"' between each stage subsequent to the first reading; yet when any pressing emergency arises, bills are frequently passed through all their stages in the same day, and even by both houses. This unusual expedition is commonly called " a sus)ension of the standing orders," and in the lords is at variance with a distinct order, which prohibits the passing of a bill through more than one stage in a day; but there are no orders to be found in the Journals of the commons which forbid the passing of public bills in this manner; and it is nothing more than an occasional departure from the usage of Parliament. From the urgent necessity of such cases, the bills so passed are often of great importance in themselves, and may require more deliberation than bills passed with the ordinary intervals. On this ground the practice may appear objectionable, but it must be recollected that no bill can pass rapidly without the general, if not unanimous, concurrence of the house. One stage may follow another with unaccustomed rapidity, but ' 58 Com. J. 645, 046; 103 lb. 770. Lords' S. O. No. 37.

they are all as much open to discussion as at other times; and a small minority could protract the proceedings for an indefinite period, Tnfornialitics But, though a departure from the usage of Parliament, illen'rotboui during the progress of a bill, will not vitiate a statute; houses. informalities in the final agreement of both houses have been treated as if they Avould affect its validity. No decision of a court of law upon this question has ever been obtained; but doubts have arisen there, and in two recent cases Paruament has thought it advisable to correct, by law, irregularities of this description. It has already been explained that when one house has made amendments to a bill passed by the other, it nmst return the bill with the amendments, for the agreement of that house which first passed it. Without such a proceeding, the assent of both houses could not be complete; for, however trivial the amendments may be, the judgment of one house only would be given upon them, and the entire bill, as amended and ready to become law, would not have received the formal concurrence of both houses. If, therefore, a bill should receive the royal assent, without the amendments made by one house having been communicated to the other and agreed to, serious doubts naturally arise concerning the effect of this omission; since the assent of the Queen, lords, and commons is essential to the validity of an Act. 1. Will the royal assent cure all prior irregularities, in the same way as the passing of a bill in the lords would jn-eclude inquiry as to informalities in any previous stage? 2. Is the indorsement on the bill, recording the assent of Queen, lords, and commons, conclusive evidence of that fact? or, 3. May the Journals of either house be permitted to contradict it? Pylkinston's The first case in which a diflsculty arose, was in the 33d Henry VI. In the session commencing 29th April 1450, the commons had passed a bill requiring John Pylking-ton to appear, on a charge of rape, " liy the feast of case, 33 IJeii. G. Pentecost then next ensuing." ' It does not appear distinctly whether the bill was even brought into the commons before that day in the year 1450; but it certainly was not agreed to by the lords until afterwards. By the law of Parliament then subsisting, the date of an Act was reckoned from the beginning of a session; and the lords, to avoid this construction, altered the date to " the feast of Pentecost, which will be in the year of our Lord 1451;" but did not return the bill, so amended, to the commons. Pylkington appeared before the Exchequer Chamber, to impeach the validity of this Act, "because the lords had granted a longer day than was granted by the commons, in which case the commons ought to have had the bill back." Chief Justice Fortescue held the Act to be valid, as it had been certified by the king's writ to have been confirmed by Parhament; but Chief Baron Illingworth and Mr. Justice Markham were of opinion, that if the amendment made the bill vary in effect from that which was sent up from the commons, the Act would be invalid. No decision ii recorded in the Year Book; and the evidence respecting the dates was too imperfect to justify more than hypothetical opinions. Fortescue, C. J., concluded the case by sayino-,

"This is an Act of Farliament, and we will be well advise 1 before we annul any Act made in Parliament; and, peradventuie, the matter ought to wait until the next Parliament, then we cnn be certified by them of the certainty of the matter; but, notwithstanding, we will be advised what shall be done."

In 1829, a bill "to amend the law relating to the em- Factories Bill, ployment of children in factories," passed the commons, and was agreed to by the lords, with an amendment; but instead of being returned to the commons, it was, by mistake, included in a commission, and received the royal assent. The amendment was afterwards agreed to by the commons; but, in order to remove all doubts, an Act ' ' Year Books, 33 Heii. VI. Pari. Rep. No. 413, of 1843. ' 10 Ceo. IV. c. 63, was passed to declare that the Act "shall be valid and effectual to all intents and purposes, as if the amendment made by the lords had been agreed to by the commons before the said Act received the royal assent." Spiioolniastcis' lu 18 43, the Schoolmasters' Widows' Fund (Scotland)

Widows'Fuiiil-r,., 1, '11 1

Uill. Bill was returned to the commons with amendments; but, before these were agreed to, the bill was removed from the table, without authority from the house, and carried up to the lords with other bills. The proper indorsement, viz. " A ces amendemens les communes soiit assentus' was not upon this bill; yet the omission was not observed, and the bill received the royal assent on the 9th May. After an examination of precedents, this Act was made valid by a new enactment.

Imperfect in It is a curious fact, in connexion with an informality of dorsement. i i i p p i-n i this character on the race oi a bill, that a commission expressly recites that the bills "have been agreed to by the lords spiritual and temporal, and the commons, and indorsed by them as hath been accustomed." The informality in this case would therefore appear to have been greater than in that of 1829; because, in the former, the indorsements were complete, and as they are without date, it would not appear, except from the Journals, that the amendment had been agreed to after the royal assent had been given; but in the latter, the agreement of the commons would be wanting on the face of the record.

In case of any accidental omission in the indorsement, the bill should be returned to the house whence it was received; as, on the 8th March 1580, 23 Ehz., when a schedule was returned to the commons and the indorsement amended there; because

" Soit bailie aux seigneurs " had been omitted, and the lords had therefore no warrant to proceed.- ' 6 k 7 Vict. c. Ixxvi. riocal and personal).

2 D'Ewes, 303. 1 Com. J. 132. Order and Course of Passing Bills in Parliament, 4to. 1641.

Having noticed the effect of informalities in the consent informalities in of both houses to a bill, the last point that requires any observation is the consequence of a defect or informality in the commission or royal assent. On the 27th January 1546, when King Henry VIII. was on his death-bed, the lord chancellor brought down a commission under the sign manual, and sealed with the great seal, addressed to himself and other lords, for giving the royal assent to the bill for the attainder of the Duke of Norfolk, which had been Duke of Nor-passed with indecent haste through both houses. Early the next mornino: the king died, and the duke was saved from the scaffold, but was imprisoned in the Tower during the whole reign of Edward VI. On the accession of Queen Mary, he took his seat in the House of Lords, was appointed to be one of the triers of petitions; and also, by patent, on the 17 th August, to be lord high steward for the trial of the Duke of Northumberland.

The political causes which restored him to fiwour will Declared void, account for the impunity he enjoyed, notwithstanding his attainder; but in the next session the Act of Attainder was declared by statute,

"To have been void and of none effect," because there were no words in the commission " whereby it may appere that the saide late king did himself give his royall assent to the saide bill; and for that allso the saide comissyon was not signed with his hignes hande, but with his starajje putt thereunto in the nether parte of the writing of the said commissyon, and not in the upper parte of the said commissyon, as his hignes was accustomed to doo; nor that it appereth of any recorde that the saide commissyoners did give his royall consent to the bill aforesaide; therefore all that was done by virtue of the said commissyon was clerelie voyde in the lawe, and made not the same bill to take effecte, or to be an Acte of Parlyament," but it " remayneth in verie dede as no Acte of Parlyament, but as a bill onelie exhibited in the saide Parlyament, and onelie assented unto hy the said lordes and cornons, and not bv the saide late king."

VI Mary, No. 27; Introduction to Statutes of Uec. Com. p. 75.

The same Act declared,

"That the lawe of this realrne is and allwaies hath byn, that the royall assent or consent of the king or kings of this realme to any Acte of Parlyament ought to be given in his own royall presence, being personallie in the higher howse of Parlyament, or by his letters patents under his great seale, assigned with his hande, and declared and notified in his absence to the lords spiritual and temporal, and the comons, assembled together in the higher house, according to a statute made in the 33d j-ere of the reigne of the saide late King Henry VIII."

Transposition In 1821 the titles of two local Acts had been, by mistake, transposed in the indorsement when the bills received the royal assent. Each Act, consequently, had been passed with the title belonging to the other; and the mistake was corrected by Act of Parliament."

Royal assent In 1844 there were two Eastern Counties Railway Bills given by mis-.-,. - i i i i in- i take. in r arliament. One had passed through ail its stages, and the other was still pending in the House of Lords, when on the 10th May the royal assent was given, by mistake, to the latter instead of to the former. On the discovery of the error an Act was passed by which it was enacted that when the former Act sliall have received the royal assent it shall be as valid and effectual from the 10th May, as if it had been properly inserted in the commission, and had received the royal assent on that day; and that the other bill shall be in the same state as if its title had not been inserted in the commission, and shall not be deemed to have received the royal assent.

' 1 2 Geo. IV. c. xcv. (local and personal). 7 Vict. c. xlx. (lucal and personal).

The various communications between the several branches The people of the legislature which have been describee! in the last three vitii Pariia-chapters, lead to the consideration of petitions, by which the J" " " i'" '" people are brought into communication with the Parliament.

The right of petitioning the Crown and Parliament for redress of grievances is acknowledo; ed as a fundamental principle of the constitution; and has been uninterruptedly exercised from very early times. Before the constitution Ancient mode of Parliament had assumed its present form, and while its pititioniug. judicial and legislative functions were ill-defined, petitions were presented to the Crown and to the great councils of the realm, for the redress of those grievances which were beyond the jurisdiction of the common law. There are petitions in the Tower of the date of Edward I., before From Edw. i. which time it is conjectured that the parties aggrieved came personally before the council, or preferred their complaints in the country, before inquests composed of officers of the Crown.

Assuming that the separation of the lords and commons had been effected in the reign of Henry III.," these petitions appear to have been addressed to the lords alone; but, taking the later period, of the 17th Edward HI., for the separation of the two houses, they must have been addressed to the whole body then constituting the High ' " Nulli negabimus, aut differemus rectum vel justitiam." Magna Chaita of King John, c. 29. See Bill of Rights, Art. 5, 1 2 Will. Mary, sess. 2, c. 2. See supra, p. 24.

Receivers and triers of petitions.

Receivers and triers still appointed.

Reign of Hen. IV.

Court of Parliament. Be tins as it may, it is certain that, from the reign of Edward I., until the last year of the reign of Richard 11. no petitions have been found which were addressed exclusively to the commons.

During this period the petitions were, with few exceptions, for the redress of private wrongs; and the mode of receiving and trying them was judicial rather than legislative. Receivers and triers of petitions were appointed, and proclamation was made, inviting all people to resort to the receivers. These were ordinarily the clerks of the chancery, and afterwards the masters in chancery (and still later some of the judges), who, sitting in some public place accessible to the people, received their complaints, and transmitted them to the auditors or triers. The triers were committees of prelates, peers, and judges, who had power to call to their aid the lord chancellor, the lord treasurer, and the serjeants-at-law. By them the petitions were examined; and in some cases the petitioners were left to their remedy before the ordinary courts; in others, their petitions were transmitted to the chancellor or to the judges on circuit; and if the common law offered no redress, their case was submitted to the High Court of Parliament.- The functions of receivers and triers of petitions have long since given way to the immediate authority of Parliament at large; but their appointment at the opening of every Parliament has been continued by the House of Lords without interruption. They are still constituted as in ancient times, and their appointment and jurisdiction are expressed in Norman French.

In the reign of Henry IV., petitions began to be addressed, in considerable numbers, to the House of Commons. The courts of equity had, in the meantime.

3 Rot. Pari. 448. " See Elsynge, chap. 8; Coke, 4th Inst. 11, 3 Tliere are receivers and triers for Great Britain and Ireland; and others for Gascony and the lands and countries beyond the sea, and the isles. No spiritual lords are now appointed triers. 7.3 Lords' J. 579. 80 lb. 13.

relieved Parliament of much of its remedial jurisdiction; and the petitions were now more in the nature of petitions Petitions to the for private bills, than for equitable remedies for private wrongs. Of this character were many of the earliest Origin of pri- petitions; and the orders of Parliament upon them can only be regarded as special statutes, of private or local application. As the limits of judicature and legislation became defined, the petitions applied more distinctly for legislative remedies, and were preferred to Parliament through the commons; but the functions of Parliament, in passing private bills, have always retained the mixed judicial and legislative character of ancient times.

Proceeding to later times, petitions continued to be Change of sys-received in the lords by triers and receivers of petitions, or by committees whose office was of a similar character; and in the commons, they were referred to the committee of grievances, and to other committees specially appointed for the examination and report of petitions; but since the Commonwealth, it appears to have been the practice of both houses to consider petitions in the first instance, and only to refer the examination of them, in particular cases, to committees. In early times all petitions prayed for the redress of some specific grievance, but after the revolution of 1688 the present practice of petitioning in respect of all measures of public pohcy was gradually introduced.

From this summary of ancient customs, it is now time to pass to the existing practice in regard to petitions, which it will be convenient to consider under thi-ee divisions; viz. 1. The form of petitions; 2. The character and substance of petitions; 3. Their presentation to Parliament.

See 1 Pari. Writs, 160; 2 lb. 156. 3 Rot. Pari. 448. Coke, 4th Inst. 11.21.24. Elsynge, c. 8. Hale, Jurisd. of the Lords, chap. 6-13. Com. Par). Report, 1883 (g g); especially the learned evidence of Sir F. Palgrave.

2 I Com. J. 582 J 2 lb. 49. 61; 3 lb. 649; 4 lb. 228; 7 lb. 287.

3 11 Lords' J. 9. 57. 184; 14 lb. 23. 12 Cora. J. 83.

See 13 Chas. II. c. 5; 10 Com. J. 88; 13 lb. 287; 13 lb. 518 (Kentish petition, 1701); 18 lb. 425. 429. 430. 431 (Septennial Bill). 2 Hallam, Const. Hist. 435 n.

Form of petitions.

Remonstrances.

Signatures, isfc.

1. Petitions to the House of Lords should be superscribed, "To the right honourable the lords spiritual and temporal in Parliament assembled;" and to the House of Commons, "To the honourable the commons (or knights, citizens, and burgesses) of the United Kingdom of Great Britain and Ireland in Parliament assembled." A general designation of the parties to the petition should follow; and if there be one petitioner only, his name, after this manner: " The humble petition of here insert the name or other designation, sheweth." The general allegations of the petition are concluded by what is called the " prayer," in which the particular object of the petitioner is expressed. To the whole petition are generally added these words of form, "And your petitioners, as in duty bound, will ever pray;" to which are appended the signatures or marks of the parties.

Without a prayer, a document will not be taken as a petition; and a paper, assuming the style of a remonstrance, will not be received. The rule upon this subject has thus been laid down in the commons: On the 10th August 1843, a member oifered a remonstrance. Mr. Speaker said,

"That the custom was this, that whenever remonstrances were presented to the house, coujjled with a prayer, they were received as petitions; but when they were oft'ered without a prayer, the rule was to refuse them." He added, "That there was a standing order, requiring that the prayer of every petition should be stated by the member presenting it; " from which it is obvious that a prayer is essential to constitute a petition."'

The petition should be written upon parchment or paper, for a printed or lithographed petition will not be received; and at least one signature should be upon the same sheet or skin upon which the petition is written. It must be in ' A petition intended for the last Parliament will not be received. See Mir. of Par. 1831, vol. 3, p. 2199. " 7 Com. J. 427; 98 lb. 457. 461.

= Co Hans. Deb. N. S. p. 1225.1227. See also 67 Com. J. 398; 74 lb. 391; and infra, p. 389, 390. " 48 Com. J. 738; 68 lb. 624. 648; 72 lb. 128. 156.

62 Com. J. 155; 72 lb. 128. 144; 77 lb. 127. 66 Hans. Deb., N. S., 1032. 100 Com. J.,335. If petitions are presented without any signaluns to the sheet on which they are written, they are not noticed in Xh(Votes.

the English language, or accompanied with a translation which the member who presents it states to be correct; it must be free from interlineations or erasures;' it must be signed; ' it must have original signatures or marks, and not copies from the original," nor signatures of agents on behalf of others, except in case of incapacity by sickness; and it must not have letters, affidavits, or other documents annexed. The signatures must be written upon the petition itself, and not pasted vipon, or otherwise transferred to it. Petitions of corporations aggregate should be under their common seal. To these rules another may be added, that if the chairman of a public meeting signs a petition on behalf of those assembled, it is only received as the petition of the individual, and is so entered on the Journals, because the signature of one party for others cannot be recognised.""

It may be a useful caution to state that any forgery or Forgery or fraud in the preparation of petitions, or in the signatures attached, or the being privy to, or cognizant of, such forgery or fraud, will be punished as a breach of privilege. By a resolution of the House of Commons, 2d June 1774, it was declared,

"That it is highly unwarrantable, and a breach of the privilege of this house, for any person to set the name of any other person to any petition to be presented to this house.""

And there have been frequent instances in which such irregularities have been discovered and punished by both houses."' 76 Com. J. 173. 76 lb. 173. 189; 100 lb. 560.

3 82 lb. 262; 86 lb. 748. 85 lb. 541; 91 lb. 325. 91 lb. 576.

8 9 Com. J. 369.433; 10 lb. 285; 34 lb. 800; 82 lb. 118. See also Rep. of Pub. Petitions Committee, 26th June 1848.

9 104 lb. 283(Sp. Rep. of Petns. Committee).

o 10 lb. 285. 1' 34 lb. 800.

'2 80 lb. 445; 82 lb. 561. 582; 84 lb. 187; 89 lb. 92; 98 lb. 523. 528. Epworth Petition, 1843. 98 Com. J. 523. 528. Cheltenham Petition, 2d March 1846. Lords'Journals and Debates, 22d July and 13th. Vngust 185!).

Character and substance of petitions.

2. The language of a petition should be respectful and temperate, and free from offensive imputations upon the character or conduct of Parliament, or the courts of justice, or other tribunal or constituted authority. On the 28th March 1848, a petition having been brought up and read, objection was taken to a paragraph praying for the abolition of the House of Lords, on the ground that it prayed for a fundamental alteration of the institutions of the country; but the objection, after debate, was not pressed, and the petition, being otherwise temperately expressed, was ordered to lie upon the table. A petition may not allude to debates in either house of Parliament, nor to intended motions. On the 31st March 1848, notice was taken that in a petition which had been printed with the votes, reference was made " to what passed in a debate in this house, in violation of the rules and practice of the house; and the orders, that such petition do lie upon the table, and be printed, were read and discharged, and the petition, as printed in the appendix to the votes, was ordered to be cancelled. A petition to the commons, praying directly or indirectly for an advance of public money; for compounding any debts due to the Crown; or for remission of duties payable by any person, will only be received if recommended by the Crown. Petitions distinctly praying for compensation for losses are viewed under this category and are constantly refused; ' but in many instances petitions have been received which prayed

See Hans. Deb., 29th May 1848 (Lord G. Bentinck), Petition on the Navigation Laws.

' 82 Com. J. 589; 84 lb. 273. s q h,. iqs.

7G lb. 92. 5 7g lb 431. gj n, ggg 103 lb. 384. 97 Hans. Deb. 3d Series, 1055.

' 77 Com. J. 150; 82 lb. 604; 91 lb. GIG; 103 lb. G33. 105 lb. 100, 19lh Feb. 1851 (Window Tax).

8 85 Cora. J. 107. s 103 lb. 406.

'" 90 lb. 42. 487. 507; 92 lb. 74. Votes, 19th March 1850.

"75 lb. 107. See also p. 203, 325, 326. ' 81 lb.353.

'3 87 lb. 571; 90 lb. 487, c. cc.

that provision should be made for the compensation of petitioners, for losses contingent upon the passing of bills pending in Parliament. Nor will the commons receive petitions complaining of elections, or returns which are in the nature of election petitions under the Act, but in respect to which the proper forms have not been observed."-

On the 18th June 1849 a petition was offered from Petition from W. S. O'Brien and others, attainted of treason, praying tainted. to be heard by counsel against the Transportation for Treason (Ireland) Bill. It was objected that no petition could be received from persons civilly dead; but the house, after debate, agreed, under the peculiar and exceptional circumstances of the case, to receive the petition. The petitioners' sentence of death had been commuted to transportation; they had denied the legal power of the Lord Lieutenant to transport them, and the bill against which they had petitioned was introduced in order to remove doubts upon the question which they had raised. It was, in fact, a bill to declare the legality of a sentence which they maintained to be contrary to law. Before the introduction of the bill a petition from W. S. O'Brien, upon the subject of his sentence, had been already received by the house.

3. Petitions are to be presented by a member of the Presentation house to which they are addressed. But petitions from ' ' " ' the corporation of Lon Ion are presented to the House of Commons, by the sheriffs, at the bar,"' (being introduced by the serjeant, with the mace,) or by one sheriff only, if the other be a member of the house" or unavoidably absent Petitions from the corporation of Dublin may ' 90 Com. J. 136; 92 lb. 469.

82 lb. 317. 4.36; 86 lb. 195. 786. See also Chapter XXII. ' See 106 Hans. Deb., 3d Series, p. 389.

92 Com. J. 120.

MS. Officers and Usages of tlie House of Commons, p. 46.

90 Com. J. r,06. 7 75 n, ojn.

Transmission by post.

To be read by members.

Lords.

be presented in the same manner, by their lord mayor. If the lord mayor should be a member he must present the petition, in his place as a member, and not at the bar. If the sheriffs (or lord mayor of Dublin, not being a member) have more than one petition to present, they are directed to withdraw when the first has been received, and are again called in to present the other.

To facilitate the presentation of petitions, they may be transmitted through the Post-office, to members of either house, free of postage, provided they be sent without covers, or in covers open at the sides, and do not exceed 32 oz. in weight. " If a member desire to have a petition from himself presented to the house, he should entrust it to some other member, as he will not be permitted to present it himself.

In both houses it is the duty of members to read petitions which are sent to them, before they are offered to the house, and to see that no flagrant violation of any of these rules is apparent on the face of them. Up to this point the practice of the lords and commons is similar; but the forms observed in presenting petitions differ so much, that it wiu be necessary to describe them separately. It was ordered by the lords, 30tli

May 1685, "That any lord who presents a petition, shall open it before it be read." At the same time the lord may comment upon the petition, and upon the general matters to which it refers; and there is no rule or order of the house that Imiits the duration of the debate, on receiving a petition.

68 Com. J. 209. 212. 219.

On the Ist July 1850 a petition from the corporation of Dublin was presented by the lord mayor in his place as a member (wearing his robes). The officers of the corporation, in their robes, were allowed seats below the bar; but having brought the mace into tlie house, they were desired by the serjeant to remove it; M. S. note.

' MS. Officers and Usages of the House of Commons, p. 46.

34 Vict. c. 96, s. 41.

So ruled by Mr. Speaker 30th April 1846 (Sir J. Graham), and 9th July 1850 (Mr. F. O'Connor).

14 Lords'J. 22.

When the petition has been laid upon the table, an entiy of that fact is made in the lords' minutes, and appears afterwards in the Journals, with the prayer of the petition, amidst the other proceedings of the house; but the nature of its contents is rarely to be collected from the entry; and in very few cases indeed have petitions been printed at length in the Journals, unless they related to proceedings partaking of a judicial character." If no debate, therefore, arises on the presentation of a petition, there remains no public record of its substance, nor statement of the parties by whom it was signed. The Journals are not published for some months after each session, and are accessible to a very small number of persons. But few petitions are addressed to the House of Lords; and while, on the one hand, no inconvenience arises from the licence of debate on presenting them, so on the other hand the necessity for any general system of classification and publicity is little felt.

It is to the representatives of the people that petitions Petitions to the are chiefly addressed, and to them they are sent in such ' ' numbers, that it is absolutely necessary to impose some restrictions upon the discussion of their merits. Until very recently, the practice of presenting petitions had been generally similar to that of the House of Lords; but the number had so much increased, and the business of the house was liable to so many interrputions and delays, from the debates which arose on receiving petitions, that after vain attempts to reconcile the opposing claims of petitions and of legislation, upon the time of the house, ' the following standing orders have been adopted:

"That every member ottering to present a petition to the petitions to be house, not being a petition for a private bill, or relating to a opened by members.

' 74 Lords' J. 236.

In the five years ending 1831, 24,492 public petitions were presented to the House of Commons; in the five years ending 1843, 94,292; and in the five years ending 1848, 60,501.

For tlie two sessions, 1833 and 1834, morning sittings from 12 to 3 were devoted to petitions and private bills, but they were not found to be efl'ectual.

l Iay be read by the clerk.

In some cases printed with the Votes.

Urgent cases discussed.

rivate bill before tlie house, do confine himself to a statement of the parties from whom it comes, of the number of signatures attached to it, and of the material allegations contained in it, and to the reading of the prayer of such petition."

"That every such)etition, not containing matter in breach of the privileges of this house, and which, according to the rules or usual practice of this house, can be received, be brought to the table by the direction of the speaker, who shall not allow any debate, or any member to speak upon or in relation to such petition, but it may be read by the clerk at the table if required."

"That if such petition relate to any matter or subject which the member presenting it is desirous of bringing before the house, and if such member shall state it to be his intention to make a motion thereupon, such member may give notice that he will make a motion on some subsequent day, ' that the petition be printed witli the Votes.""

This motion for printing a petition with the votes is usually permitted to be made at the time of presenting public petitions. It is not a matter of right, but is open to debate and objection like any other motion. On the 15th April 1845, it was objected, that a motion intended to be made by a member was not such as could be properly founded upon a petition proposed to be printed; and the motion for printing it was withdrawn.

"That in the case of such petition complaining of some present personal grievance, for whicli there may be an urgent necessity for providing an immediate remedy, the matter contained in such petition may be brought into discussion on the presentation thereof."

On the 14th June 1844, it was ruled by Mr. Speaker, that a petition of parties complaining of their letters having been detained and opened by the Post-office, and praying for inquiry, was not of that urgency that entitled it to ' See Debates llth April 1845, when objection was taken that a member was evading this order by reading more than was regular.

' On the llth April 1845 a debate arose on the presentation of a petition from the Dublin Protestant Operative Association, but it related to matters of order, which, of course, may be debated at any time.

Southampton writ, 1st June 1842. 97 Com. J. 329. 03 Hans. Deb. 3d Ser., 1057. 79 Hans. Deb., 3d Series, 086.

immediate discussion, especially as notice of its presentation had been given on the previous day, which proved that the matter was such as admitted of delay. But on the 24th June 1844, a similar petition, of which no previous notice had been given, was permitted to open a debate. In the latter case, however, the complaint was, that " letters are secretly detained and opened; " and thus a " present personal grievance " was alleged, while in the former case a past grievance only had been complained of. '

"That all other petitions, after they shall have been ordered All petitions to lie on the table, be referred to the committee on public petitions ' "-"""; ' .- coiiimiittee tor Without any question being put." classification.

"That, subject to the above regulations, petitions against May oppose any resolution or bill imposing a tax or duty for the current ser- taxes tor tlie vice of the year, be henceforth received, and the usage under yg r. which the house has refused to entertain such petitions be discontinued."

An attentive perusal of these orders will show that the Debates upon restriction on debate does not extend to any urgent cases. It must always be borne in mind that the discussion of a petition is not, in itself, introductory to legislative measures; and that every resolution or bill must commence with a distinct motion, in proposing which a member is at liberty to enforce the claims of all petitioners who have submitted their cases to the house.

It has been seen that, in certain cases, petitions may be Printing peti-printed and distributed with the Votes; but the general practice is, for all public petitions to be referred to the " Committee on Public Petitions," under whose directions they are classified, analysed, and, when necessary, printed at length. The reports of this committee are printed three times a week, and point out, under classified heads, not only the name of each petition, but the number of signatures, the general object of every petition, and the 75 Hans. Deb., 3d Ser., 894. lb. 12G4.

3 97 Com. J. 191. And see also 88 lb. 10. 95; 94 lb. 16. 88 lb. 95.

total number of petitions and signatures in reference to each subject; and whenever the peculiar arguments and facts, or general importance of a petition, require it, it is printed at full length in the Appendix, where it is accessible to the public at the cheapest rate of purchase. In some cases petitions have been ordered to be printed with the signatures attached thereto, and in others for the use of members only. Time and mode A few words may now be offered in reference to the petitions. time and mode of presenting petitions in the House of

Commons. It was resolved, 20th March 1833, "That every member presenting a petition to the house, do affix his name at the beginning thereof;" and it is always printed with the petition, in the reports of the committee. The time for receiving petitions is at the conclusion of the private business, and members who are desirous of obtaining precedence in presenting the petitions entrusted to them, should attend at the table of the house at half-past three; or, when the house meets at an unusual hour, at a quarter of an hour before the time appointed for Ballot. ivir. Speaker taking the chair." The members then pre- sent ballot for precedence, and their names are entered on a list, and are afterwards called by the speaker in their order. When petitions relate to any motion or bill set down for consideration, a member may present them before the debate commences, at any time during the sitting of the house. In the case of a bill, they should be offered immediately after the order of the day has been read, and before any question has been proposed.

98 Com. J, 396; 101 lb. 142. 100 lb. 538. 648; 101 lb. 1021. ' lb. 190. " 91 lb. 2G. See supra, p. 212.

Parliament, in the exercise of its various functions, is Returns by invested with the power of ordering all documents to be address" laid before it which are necessary for its information. Each house enjoys this authority separately, but not in all. cases independently of the Crown. The ordinary accounts relating to trade, finance, and general or local matters, are ordered directly, and are returned in obedience to the order of the house whence it was issued; but returns of matters connected with the exercise of royal prerogative, are obtained by means of addresses to the Crown.

The distinction between these two classes of returns should always be borne in mind; as, on the one hand, it is irregular to order directly that which should be sought for by address; and, on the other, it is a compromise of the authority of Parliament to resort to the Crown for information which it can obtain by its own order. The application of the principle is not always clear: but as a general rule, it may be stated that all public departments connected with the collection or management of the revenue, or which are under the control of the Treasury, may be reached by a direct order from either house of Parliament; but that public officers and departments subject to her Majesty's secretaries of state are to receive their orders from the Crown.

Thus returns from the Commissioners of Customs and of Inland Revenue, the Post-office, the Board of Trade, and the Treasury, are obtained by order. Th se include every

When addresses have been answered.

Orders discharged.

Returns not made.

account that can be rendered of the revenue and expenditure of the country; of commerce and navigation; of salaries and pensions; of general statistics; and of facts connected with the administration of all the revenue departments. Addresses are presented for treaties with foreign powers, for despatches to and from the governors of colonies, and for returns connected with the civil government, and the administration of justice.

When an address for papers has been answered by the Crown, the parties who are to make them appear to be within the immediate reach of an order of the house; as orders of the House of Commons for addresses have been read, and certain persons who had not made the return required, have been ordered to make the returns to the house forthwith.

When it is discovered that an address has been ordered for papers which should properly have been presented to the house by order, it is usual, when no answer has been reported, to discharge the order for the address, and to order the papers to be laid before the house." In the same manner, when a return has been ordered, for which an address ought to have been moved, the order is discharged, and an address is presented instead.

If parties neglect to make returns in reasonable time, they are ordered to make them forthwith. If they continue to withhold them, they are ordered to attend at the bar of the house; and unless they satisfactorily explain the causes of their neglect, and comply with the order of the house, they will be censured or punished according to the circumstances of the case. A person has been reprimanded by the lords for having made a return to an order, which he was not reriuired or authorised to make, and for framing it in a form calculated to mislead the house. ' 90 Com. J. 413. G50.

lb. 366; 104 lb. 623, c.

90 lb. 575. 81 Lords' J. 134.

92 lb. 580.

75 lb. 404. 89 lb. 386.

82 Lords' J. 89.

When Parliament is prorogued before a return is pre- Effect of a presented, the ordinary practice is to renew the order in ' ' the ensuing session, as if no order had previously been given. This practice arises from the general effect of a prorogation, in putting an end to every proceeding pending in Parliament; and unquestionably an order for returns loses its effect at a prorogation; yet returns are frequently presented by virtue of addresses in a preceding session, without any renewal of the address, and occasionally in compliance with an order of a former session. Orders have also been made which assume that an order has force from one session to another. For example, returns have been ordered "to be prepared, in order to be laid before the house in the next session;" and orders of a former session have been read, and the papers ordered to be laid before the house. And the order for an address made by a former Parliament has been read, and the house being informed that certain persons had not made the return, they were ordered forthwith to make a return to the house.

Besides the modes of obtaining papers by order and by Papers pre-address, both houses of Parliament are constantly put in mand, and by possession of documents by command of Her Majesty, and ' in compliance with Acts of Parliament.

When papers are presented by ministers who are mem- Forms observed bers of the house, they are brought up by them and laid upon the table. But numerous papers are presented to both houses by other official persons. In the lords, if the paper relate to judicial proceedings, the person, is called to the bar, sworn, and examined respecting it; if it be an ordinary paper, he is called in, delivers the paper at the bar, and is directed to withdraw. In the commons the person, by direction of the speaker, is introduced at the bar by the serjeant with the mace, delivers the paper to the 98 Com. J. 428; 103 lb. 570. 775; 104 lb. 239. 284, c.

"99 lb. 301; 103 lb. 131; 104 lb. 35. 8S. 133, c.

3 78 1b. 472; 80 lb. G31. 78 lb. 72. 90 lb. 413.

in presenting papers.

Papers presented.

Printing committee in the commons.

Unprinted papers.

Distribution of pajiers. Lords.

clerk of the house, and is directed by the speaker to withdraw. If he have papers from more than one department to present, he is again introduced, and presents them separately, with the same formalities.

When accounts and papers are presented, they are ordered to lie upon the table; and, when necessary, are printed or referred to committees, or abstracts are ordered to be made and printed. In the commons, a select committee is appointed at the commencement of each session, " to assist Mr. S)eaker in all matters which relate to the printing executed by order of the house; and for the purpose of selecting and arranging for printing, returns and papers presented in pursuance of motions made by members." To this committee all papers are referred, and it is the usual practice for the house not to order papers to be printed until they have been examined by the committee. No distinct reference or report is made; but when papers are laid upon the table, they are, from time to time, submitted to the committee or the speaker, by whom it is determined whether orders shall be made for printing them in their present form, or for preparing abstracts.

If not considered worthy of being printed, or if the members who moved for them do not virge the printing, they are open to the inspection of members in an unprinted form. The papers of past sessions are deposited in the custody of the clerk of the Journals, and those of the current session are placed in the library, for the convenience of members, and returned, at the end of the session, to the clerk of the Journals. In some cases papers of a local or private character have been ordered to be printed at the expense of the parties, if they think fit. In other cases they have been ordered to be returned to a public department."

All papers printed by order of the lords are, by courtesy, distributed gratuitously to members of the House of Com- 101 Com. J. 990.

lb. 880.

mons who apply foi' them; and also to other persons, on application, with orders from peers. But the commons have Commons, adopted the principle of sale, as the best mode of distribution to the public. Each member receives a copy of every paper printed by the house, but is not entitled to more, without obtaining an order from the speaker. The chairman of a committee, the member who has brought in a bill, and others, may obtain a greater number of copies for special purposes; but no general distribution can be obtained, except by purchase. The rule is not strictly enforced, as regards bills and estimates before the house, which may generally be obtained by members, on application at the Vote-office; but more than one copy of reports and papers is not delivered without authority from the speaker.

The Vote-office is charged with the delivery of printed Delivery to papers to members of the house; and those who wish to vote-office. receive them regularly should take care to leave their addresses, in order that all papers may be forwarded to them, either during the session, or in the recess. Papers in which any libellous matter is detected by the printing committee, are occasionally ordered to be printed " for the use of members only," and the distribution of these is confined to members, and delivered by the Vote-office alone. The papers ordered to be printed generally, are accessible to the public in the several " offices for the sale of parliamentary papers," established under the management of the printers of the house, and the control of the speaker. They are sold at a halfpenny per sheet, a price sufficient to raise them above the quality of waste paper; and moderate enough to secure the distribution of them to all persons who may be interested in their contents.

To facilitate the distribution of parliamentary papers. Transmission they are entitled to be sent through the Post-office, to all ' ' See Reports of Printed Papers Committee, 1835 (61. 392). 90 Com. J. 544.

places in the United Kingdom, at a rate of postage not exceeding Id. for every four ounces in weight, whether prepaid or not, provided they be sent without a cover, or with a cover open at the sides, and without any writing or marks upon them. The members of both houses are also entitled, during a session, to send, free of postage, all Acts of Parliament, bills, minutes, and votes, by writing their names upon covers provided for that purpose in the Vote-office, and in the office for the sale of parliamentary papers in the House of Commons. Arransenientof By these various regulations, the papers laid before Par-Japira? " ""' liament are effectually published and distributed. In both houses they are systematically arranged in volumes, at the end of each session, with contents and indexes, to secure a uniform classification, and convenient reference. General indexes have also been published, by means of which the papers that have been printed during many years may readily be discovered. Each paper is distinguished by a sessional number at the foot of the page, and by the date at which the order for printing is made, except in cases where papers are presented by command of her Majesty, in a printed form. Tiieir statistical The Collected papers of the two houses contain an extraordinary amount of information in all departments of legislative inquiry; in law, history, the privileges of Parliament, negotiations with foreign powers, and every variety of statistics. The statistical returns have been moved for at diffisrent times, for particular objects, and do not present so regular and complete a series as could be desired. Sometimes a return has been presented for several years in succession, when the series is interrupted, and 3 4 Vict. c. 96.

There is a General Index to the Lords' Papers from 1801 to 1845; and to the Commons' Papers there is one from 1801 to 1832 inclusive; another from 1832 to 1844, and another from 1844 to 1850.

commences again at a later period. At other times, the returns for succeeding years, though similar in object, are not moved for or prepared in a uniform manner. One return, for example, is found to include the United Kingdom, while another extends to Great Britain only; one shows the gross, another the net revenue; one dates from the 1st January, another from the 5th April; one calculates the value of exports by the official rate of valuation, another by the declared or real value. By discrepancies of this nature, the statistical importance of parliamentary papers has been very much impaired.

To secure a more complete and uniform collection of Tables of re-statistics, the statistical department of the Board of Trade "" ' was established some years since. Accounts of the revenue, commerce, and navigation of the country, are there collected from every department, and annually laid before Parliament. The tables prepared by this department have greatly improved the statistics of the last twenty years; and, in the commons, other parliamentary papers have recently been moved for, and prepared with considerable care.

The causes of imperfection in the statistical accounts Improvement have been: 1. The irregular manner in which they have returns.

been moved for, without any settled plan or principle; 2. The imperfect mode of preparing the orders; 3. The want of proper forms and instructions addressed to those who are to prepare the returns; 4. The absence of control and superintendence in editing the returns before they were printed. With a view to improve the character of parliamentary returns, a plan was proposed by the printing committee in 1841, and has since been partly carried into effect; the gradual operation of which cannot fail to be attended with benefit. The committee suggested: 1. " That every member be recommended, before he gives notice of a motion for a return, to consult the librarian of the House of Commons."

' Pari. Paper, 1841 (181).

Orders for returns.

Blank forms.

Abstracts.

2. "That after the order for a return has been made by the House, the librarian do)repare, when necessary, a form, to be submitted to Mr. Speaker for his approval; and that such form shall be forwarded with the order in the usual manner."

3. " That before any return which has been presented to the house shall be ordered to be printed, it shall be inspected by the librarian, and approved by Mr. Speaker."

By attending to the first of these suggestions, a member will generally obtain assistance in framing a motion for returns. Documents of a similar character can be consulted, and their merits or defects in form and matter, will serve as guides to further investigation. The pre-jparation of the order, also, frequently requires a practical acquaintance with the forms and character of parliamentary accounts, in order to secure the information desired.

The object in preparing blank forms to accompany the orders of the house, is to ensure complete and uniform answers from the parties to whom they are addressed. An order of considerable length, and containing various queries, has often been forwarded to a great number of persons in all parts of the country. Each person is thus left to his own interpretation of the order, and is at liberty to return his answers in whatever forai he pleases. When all the answers are afterwards collected, they are found to be so different both in form and matter, that they are almost useless for purposes of comparison, and cannot be reduced, with the greatest pains, into a consistent and uniform return. A blank form, with columns properly headed, interprets the order, and obtains the answers in such a shape, that if properly given, they are ready for printing; and if not, any imperfection can be readily detected.

When this precaution has been neglected, an attempt is still made, by means of abstracts, to improve the form in which returns are originally presented. They are compressed into the best form of which they will admit, and when practicable, general results are deduced from them, in illustration of the purposes of the order.

In England, as in many other countries of Europe, the Feudal origin of origin of taxation may be referred to the feudal aids and taxation. ' " services due from the tenants of the Crown to their feudal superior. Before the growth of commerce, the royal revenue could only be derived from land; and after the Conquest the entire soil of England was placed under the feudal sovereignty of the Conqueror. The greater portion was held by military service, and the councils of William being composed of the tenants-in-chief of the Crown, granted and confirmed, as a Parliament, the aids and services to which the king, as their feudal superior, was entitled. This connexion between feudal rights and legislative taxation is singularly illustrated by the Charter of William the Conqueror," which declared that all freehold tenants by military service should " hold their lands and possessions free from all unjust exactions, and from all tallage, so that nothing be exacted or taken from them except their free service, which had been given and conceded to him for ever, of hereditary right, by the common council of

See supra, J), n. 1 Fcedera, 1. (Record Coram, ed.)

"Liberi homines." See explanations of this term, Rep. on Dignity of the Peerage, p. 31.

Tallage was raised upon the demesne lands of the Crown, upon the burglis and towns of the realm, and upon escheats and wardships. 1 Madox. Hist, of the Exchequer, 694.

his realm." In the words of this charter two remarkable points may be observed; the first, that the claims of the Crown upon those classes who formed its councils were confined to feudal aids and services; and secondly, that even these had been freely given by the common council of the realm or Parliament.

At the same time the Crown was entitled to other sources of revenue from classes who did not hold lands by military service, and who had no place in the national councils, either personally or by representation. But the various claims of the Crown gradually became less determined, and required repeated assessments, for which purpose the council or Parliament was convened. And by the Great Charter of King John, the archbishops, bishops, abbots, earls, greater barons, and all other tenants-in-chief of the Crovn were to be summoned with forty days notice to assess aids and scutages, which the king bound himself not to impose otherwise than by the common council of his realm. The strictly feudal nature of these impositions was exemplified by the reservations which were made in favour of the king's right to aids for the ransom of his person, on making his eldest son a knight, and on the marriage of his eldest daughter. But the practice first noticed in this charter, of summoning the tenants-iii-chief of the Crown through the sheriffs and bailiffs, led to the princijile of representation, as was shown in the first chapter of this work, and had an important influence upon the revenue of future kings. Growth of the After the property in land had undergone many chauq-es commons right. J o of supply. and subdivisions, and the commonalty had grown in num- bers and wealth, the taxation became less feudal in its character. On the one hand, the tenants of the Crown had contrived to defraud their superior of many of his ' For a full explanation of tlu; nature of these feudal sources of revenue, see Madox, chapters 15 and 16. See also suprfi, p. 17. Supra, p. 18 et seq.

lawful clues; and, on the other, the kings had been improvident; and while tlieir feudal revenues were diminished in amount, and confused in title, their necessities were continually increasing. The commons, in the meantime, had assumed their place as an estate of the realm in Parliament, and represented wealthy communities. These changes are marked by the well-known statute, De tallagio non concedendo, in the 25 th Edward L, by which it was declared, "That no tallage or aid shall be taken or levied without the goodwill and assent of the archbishops, bishops, earls, barons, knigjds, burgesses, and other freemen of the land."' The popular voice being thus admitted in matters of taxation, the laity were henceforth taxed by the votes of their representatives in Parliament. The lords spiritual and the lords temporal voted separate subsidies for themselves; and from the reign of Edward I. the clergy, as a body, granted subsidies, either as a national council of the clergy in connexion with the Parliament, or, at a later period, in convocation, until the surrender or disuse of their right in the reign of Charles 11.

At length, when the commons had increased in political influence, and the subsidies voted by them had become the principal source of national revenue, they gradually Commous'right assumed their present position in regard to taxation and grants. supply, and included the lords as well as themselves in 1 Edward I. inserted in every bishop's writ of summons a clause (called the prsemunientes clause), commanding him to bring the dean or prior and chapter of his cathedral church, the arclideacons, and tlie clergy of his diocese, to parliament; thus making the bishop, as it were, an ecclesiastical sheriff, to whom the king's general precept was directed. To this mandate the archbishop objected, as he assumed to himself the sole right of assembling the clergy; but a compromise was effected by the continuance of the prsemunientes clause, whereby the clergy were summoned to parliament, while the archbishops summoned the clergy of their respective provinces to assemble at the same time as the parliament. Hence the origin of convocations, and of their time of meeting. See the Parliamentary Original and Rights of the Lower House of Convocation, by Bishop Atterbury, p. 7, 4to. 1702. They are still summoned to meit at the same time as tiie parliament, but since 1717 have not transacted any business.

Taxes by prerogative.

Uecof ition of tlie exclusive riji'lit of tlie commons.

Lecfal effect of grants.

tlicir grants. So far back as 1407, it was stated by King Henry IV., in the ordinance called " The Indempnity of the Lords and Commons," that grants were " granted by the commons, and assented to by the lords." That this was not a new concession to the commons is evident from the words that follow, viz, "That the reports of all grants agreed to by the lords and commons should be made in manner and form as hath hitherto been accustomed; that is to say, by the mouth of the speaker of the House of Commons for the time being."'

Concurrently with parliamentary taxation, other imposts were formerly levied by roy. al prerogative without the consent of Parliament, but none of these survived the Revolution of 1688."" Since that time the revenue of the Crown has been entirely dependent upon Parliament, and is derived either from annual grants for specific public services, or from payments already secured and appropriated by Acts of Parliament, and which are commonly known as charges upon the Consolidated Fund.

In modern times, her Majesty's speech at the commencement of each session recognizes the peculiar privilege of the commons to grant all supplies; the preamble of every Act of Supply distinctly confirms it; and the form in which the royal assent is given is a further confirmation of their right.

A grant from the commons is not efltectual, in law, without the ultimate assent of the Queen and of the House of Lords. It is tlie practice, however, to allow the issue of public money, the apjtlication of which has been sanctioned by the House of Commons, before it has been appropriated to specific services, by the Appropriation Act, which is reserved until the end of the Session. This power is necessary for the pul lic service, and faith is reposed in the authority of Parliament being ultimately obtained; but 3 Kot. Pari. Gil.

Bill of Ri-lits, Art. 4.

it Is liable to be viewed with jealousy, if the ministers liave not the confidence of Parliament.

In order to make the grants of the commons available, Effect given to and to anticipate the legal sanction of an Appropriation Act, coinmons before clauses are inserted in the Acts passed at an earlier period! ", j' ' ' r '" " ' of the session, for the application of money out of the Consolidated Fund, and for raising money by exchequer bills, for the service of the current year; which authorize the Treasury " to issue and apply, from time to time, all such sums of money as shall be raised by exchequer bills, to such services as shall then have been voted by the commons in this present session of Parliament." By these enactments. Immediate effect is given to the votes of the commons; but there is still an irregularity in proroguing or dissolving Parliament before an Appropriation Act has been passed; singe, by such an event, all the votes of the commons are rendered void, and the sums require to be voted again in the next session, before a legal appropriation can be effected.

In the imposition and alteration of taxes, the effect given Duties altered ,. p,. p after votes of to a vote or the commons, in anticipation of the passing of the commons.

' This was shown on a remarkable occasion, not by those brandies of the legislature whose authority would be most slighted by an appropriation of money without their assent; but by the commons themselves, who protested against the principle of giving too much validity to their own votes. In 1784, when Mr. Pitt was in a minority in the House of Commons, and it was well known that he was only waiting for the supplies in order to dissolve tlie Parliament, the house resolved, "Tliat for any person or persons in his Jlajesty's Treasury, or in the Exchequer, or in the Bank of England, or for any person or persons whatsoever employed in the payment of public money, to pay, or direct or cause to be paid, any sum or sums of money, for or towards the support of services voted In the present session of Parliament, after the Parliament shall have been prorogued or dissolved, if it shall be prorogued or dissolved before any Act of Parliament shall have passed appropriating the supplies to such services, will be a high crime and misdemeanour, a daring breach of a public trust, derogatory to the fundamental privileges of Parliament, and subversive of the constitution of this country." 39 Com. J. 858. 2 ggg 13 yict, c. 3, s. 7, c.

Parliament was dissolved in April 1831, before any Appropriation Act had been passed. The new Parliament met on the 14th June, and all the grants were re-voted in the committee of supply. Before the dissolution of 1841 the supplies for six months were regularly appropriated.

a statute, is more remarkable than in the voting of sup-l)lies. It has been customary for the government to levy the new duties, instead of the duties authorised by law, immediately the resolutions for that purpose have been reported from a committee, and agreed to by the house; although legal effect cannot be given to them, by statute, for some weeks, and may ultimately be withheld by Parliament. It is obvious that this custom is not strictly legal; but the ultimate decision of Parliament is anticipated by the executive government, upon its own responsibility. If the house have resolved that a duty shall be reduced on and after a particular day, a treasury order is issued by which the officers for the collection of the revenue arc directed to collect the reduced duty from the time stated in the resolution. But before they permit the articles to be entered for consumption, they take a bond from the owners or importers by which the latter bind themselves to pay the higher rate of duty, in case Parliament should not, eventually, sanction the reduction. If, on the other hand, a duty has been increased by a resolution of the house, the revenue officers demand the increased duty, by virtue of a treasury order, and will not permit the articles to be entered for consumption until it has been paid, or security given for its payment. For these official acts there is no legal authority at the time; but when the Act is subsequently passed, it alters the duty from the day named in the resolution of the commons, however long a time may have since elapsed; and thus the duties which have been already collected since that day, become, ex post facto, the duties authorised by law.

Customs' Duties, 1842. Indian Corn, 1846, Sugar Duties, 1845 and 1848. In the latter instance the committee liad resolved that the new duties should commence on the 5th July; but as the resolution was not reported until the 11th, it was amended on the report by substituting 10th July. Alterations were afterwards made in the scale of duties sanctioned by that resolution.

84 Hans, Deb., M Series, 783.

=!)'J Hans. Deb.,;3d Series, 1314 (Sugar Duties.).

The legal right of the commons to originate grants Exclusion of cannot be more distinctly recognized than by these various aiterinrsu" "'" proceedings; and to this right alone their claim appears ' to have been confined for nearly 300 years. The lords were not originally precluded from amending bills of supply; for there are numerous cases in the Journals, in which lords' amendments to such bills were agreed to. But in 1671, the commons advanced their claim somewhat further by resolving, nem. con., "That in all aids given to the king by the commons, the rate or tax ought not to be altered;" and in 1678, their claim was urged so far as to exclude the lords from all power of amending bills of supply. On the 3d of July, in that year, they resolved,

"That all aids and supplies, and aids to his majesty in Parliament, are the sole gift of the commons; and all bills for the granting of any such aids and supplies ought to begin with the commons: and that it is the undoubted and sole right of the commons to direct, limit, and appoint in such bills the ends, purposes, considerations, conditions, limitations, and qualifications of such grants: which ought not to be changed or altered by the House of Lords."

It is upon this latter resolution that all proceedings between the two houses in matters of supply arc now founded. The principle is acquiesced in by the lords, and except in cases where it is difficult to determine whether a matter be strictly one of supply or not, no serious difference can well arise. The lords never attempt to make any but verbal alterations, in which the sense or intention is not affected; and even in regard to these, the commons have made special entries in their Journal, recording the character and object of the amendments, and their reasons for affreeinor to them.

In bills not confined to matters of aid or taxation, but in Rates and which pecuniary burthens are imposed upon the people, the bo'luereirby lords may make any amendments, provided they do not " lords.

' 9 Com. J. 235. 2 lb. 509.

75 Com. J. 251. 471; 81 lb. 388; 92 lb, Qo':), c. D D

Lords' aniend-meiits, wlien asreed to.

Pecuniary pe-luiltic and fees.

alter the intention of the commons Avith regard to the amount of the rate or cliarge; its duration, its mode of assessment, levy, collection, appropriation, or management; or tlie persons who shall pay, receive, manage, or control it; or the limits within which it is proposed to be levied. But all bills of this class must originate in the commons; as that house will not agree to any provisions which impose a charge ui)on the people, if sent down from the lords, but will order the bills containing them to be laid aside. Neither will they permit the lords to insert any provisions of that nature in bills sent up from the commons; but will disagree to the amendments, and insist in their disagreement, or lay the bills aside at once.

When the amendments of the lords, though not strictly regular, do not appear materially to infringe the privileges of the commons, it has been usual to agree to them, with special entries in. the Journal: as, that " they were only for the purpose of making the dates uniform in the bill;" that " they only filled up blanks which had not been filled with the sums which were agreed to by the house, on the report of a clause;" that "they were for the purpose of rectifying clerical errors;" that "they were in furtherance of the intention of the House of Commons;'"' that "they were rendered necessary by several Acts recently passed;" or, that " they were in furtherance of the practice of Parliament."

So strictly had the right of the commons been maintained in regard to the imposition of charges upon the people, that they denied to the lords the power of authorising the taking of fees,"' and imposing pecuniary penalties, or of varying the mode of suing for them, or of api lying them when recovered; though such provisions were neces- '
Doodands Abolition Bill, 184G, 101 Com. J. 724.
- See supra (Bili. s) 344. 361. 3 gg Com. J. 579.
"80 Com. J. 031. 5 75 J J 351; 79 Jb, 524; 86 lb. 684.
92 lb. 518; 104 lb. 420. 51)6, kc. 92 lb. 659.
90 Com. J. 375; 91 lb. 823. ' ' 8th March 1C92; 10 Com. J. 845.

saiy to give effect to the general enactments of a bill." A too strict enforcement of this rule, in regard to penalties, was found to be attended Avith unnecessary inconvenience; and, in 1831, the commons judiciously relaxed it;' and again on the 5tli February 1849, they introduced a further amendment of the rule, by the adoption of the following resolutions:

"That with respect to any bill brought to this house from the House of Lords, or re-turned by the House of Lords to this house, with amendments, whereby any pecuniary penalty, forfeiture, or fee, shall be authorized, imposed, appropriated, regulated, var-ied, or extinguished, this house will not insist on its ancient and undoubted privileges, in the following cases:

"1. When the object of such pecuniary penalty or forfeiture is to secure the execution of the Act, or the punishment or prevention of offences;

"2. Where such fees are imposed in respect of benefit taken, or service rendered, under the Act, and in order to the execution of the Act, and are not made payable into the treasury or exchequer, or in aid of the public revenue, and do not form the ground of public accounting by the parties receiving the same, either in respect of-deficit or surplus;

"3. When such bill shall be a private bill for a local or personal Act."

The principle of non-interference has even been pressed Financial in-so far by the commons, that when the lords have sent lords! ' messages for reports and papers relative to taxation, the commons have evaded sending them; and it has been doubted whether members should be allowed to be examined before a committee of the House of Lords upon matters involving taxation, although in practice they have been ' allowed to attend."

The constitutional power of the commons to grant sup- Tacks to bills plies, without any interference on the part of the lords, " " ' ' has occasionally been abused by tacking to bills of supply enactments which, in another bill, would be rejected by the lords; but which, being contained in a bill that their ' See supra, Cliapter XVIII, 344. gq Qq j 4-7 3 104 Com. J. 23.

Uurtlil'iis on Land Innuiry, lt!4G; Local Tiixatioii Imiuiry, Iboo.

lordships luive no right to amend, must either be suffered to pass unnoticed, or cause the rejection of a measure highly necessary for the public service. Such a proceeding is as great an infringement of the privileges of the lords, as the interference of their lordships in matters of supply is of the privileges of the commons, and has been resisted by protest, by conference, and by the rejection of the bills.

On the 9th December 1702, it was ordered and declared by the lords,

"That the annexing any clause or clauses to a bill of aid oi supply, the matter of which is foreign to, and different from, the matter of the said bill of aid or sujiply, is unparliamentary, and tends to the destruction of the constitution of this government."

There have been no recent occasions on which clauses have been irregularly tacked to bills of supply, in order to extort the consent of the lords; but, so lately as 1807, the above standing order was read in the lords, and a bill for abolishing fees in the Irish customs, rejected on the third reading. In that case the clause had been inadvertently allowed to form part of the bill, and it is extremely doubtful whether it was a tack within the intention of the standing order; as the bill was not one of supply for the current year, and the clause was not irrelevant to the other enactments of the bill.""' Constitutional The functions of tlie House of Lords, in matters of supply. " supply and taxation, being thus reduced to a simple assent or negative, it becomes necessary to examine the constitutional principle by which the other branches of the legislature are governed. The Crown, acting with the advice of its responsible ministers, being the executive power, is charged with the management of all the revenues of the state, and with all payments for the public service. The Crown, therefore, in the first instance, makes known to ' 16 Lords' J. 369. 13 Com. J. 320.

- 17 Lords' J. 18o. Lords' S. O., No. 30. 4(5 Lords' J. 342.

the commons the pecuniary necessities of tlie government, and the commons grant such aids or supplies as are required to satisfy these demands; and provide by taxes, and by the appropriation of other sources of the public income, the ways and means to meet the supplies which are granted by them. Thus the Crown demands money, the commons grant it, and the lords assent to the grant. But the commons do not vote money unless it be required by the Crown; nor impose or augment taxes, unless they be necessary for meeting the supplies which they have voted, or are about to vote, and for supplying general deficiencies in the revenue. The Crown has no concern in the nature or distribution of the taxes; but the foundation of all parliamentary taxation is, its necessity for the public service, as declared by the Crown through its constitutional advisers.

There is, however, a remarkable exception to this constitu- Militia Esti-tional rule, in the case of the charge for the disembodied militia. The commons there take the initiative; the estimate is prepared by a committee; and when its report is received it is referred to the Committee of Supply, and the Queen's recommendation is signified.

The principle of waiting for the suggestion and authority Recommcnja-01 the Crown for the votmg of public money, is extended Crown. further than to the annual grants. Thus, by a standing order, 11th December 1706, it was declared, "That this house will receive no petition for any sum of money relating to public service, but what is recommended from the Crown." And this rule is extended, by the uniform practice of the house, to all direct motions for grants, and to any motion which involves the expenditure of public money.

So strictly has this principle been enforced, that the house Reports rccom- I c 1,, n 1. iiiemlod by the riave even retuseci to receive a report from a select com- crown. mittee, suggesting an advance of money, because it had not been recommended by the Crown. On the 15th June 1837, ' loconi. J. 'ill.

Petitions for compoinidiiig Crowu debts.

Motions for grants.

notice was taken that a report on the petition of Messrs. Fourdrinier "contained a recommendation for public compensation for losses incurred by the patentees, and that the same has not been recommended by the Crown:"' and the report Avas recommitted in order to remove this informality.

Such an objection to a report was, apparently, premature, as no motion had been founded upon it, and none could have been made, unless recommended by the Crown; but it proceeded upon the same principle as that observed in regard to petitions, and is a good example of the strictness with which the rule is enforced.

On the same principle of imposing some check upon solicitations for money, and moderating the liberality of

Parliament, there is a standing order of the house,

"That this house will not receive any petition for cimpounding any sum of money owing to the Crown upon any branch of the revenue, without a certificate from the proper officer or officers annexed to the said petition, stating the debt, what prosecutions have been made for the recovery of such debt, and setting forth how much the petitioner and his security are able to satisfy thereof."

In addition to the necessity of a recommendation from the Crown, prior to a vote of money, the house have interposed another obstacle to hasty and inconsiderate votes, which involve any public expenditure.

On the 18th February 1667 it was resolved,

"That if any motion be made in the house for any public aid or cliarge upon the people, the consideration and debate thereof ought not presently to be entered upon, but adjourned till such further day as the house shall think fit to appoint; and then it ought to be referred to the committee of the whole house, and their opinions to be reported thereupon, before any resolution or vote of the house do pass therein."

A similar rule was made a standing order on the 29th March 1707, viz.,

"That this house will not proceed upon any petition, motion, or bill, for granting any money, or for releasing or compounding any 92 Com. J. 478.

sum of money owing to the Crown, but in a committee of the whole house." '

This order was renewed 14th April 1707, 7th February 1708, and 29th November 1710, and is constantly observed in the proceedings of the house.

In compliance Avith all these rules for receiving recommendations from the Crown for the grant of money; for deferring the consideration of motions for grants of money until another day; and for referring them to a committee of the whole house; the proceedings of Parliament, in the annual grants of money for the public service, are conducted in the following manner.

On the opening of Parliament, the Queen, in her speech Royal speecli. from the throne, addresses the commons; demands the annual provision for the public service; and acquaints them that she has directed the estimates to be laid before them.

Directly the house have agreed to the address in answer Supplygranted, to the Queen's speech, they order the speech to be taken into consideration on another day. When that day arrives, they proceed to take it into consideration, and so much of the speech as is addressed to the House of Commons is again read by INIr. Speaker. A motion is then made " that a supply be granted to her Majesty," and the house resolve that, on a future day, they will resolve themselves into a committee to consider of that motion. On the day appointed, the committee sit, the royal speech Is referred to them, and they agree to a resolution, " that a supply be granted to her Majesty;" which, being afterwards reported, is agreed to by the house, nemine contradicente.

The general question in favour of a supply being thus Committee of determined, the house appoint another day, on which they """" " will resolve themselves into a committee " to consider of the supply granted to her Majesty," or, as it is commonly called, " the committee of supply." As it is the duty of this committee to consider the estimates for the current 15 Com. J. 3G7. 15 lb. 386; IG lb. 9-t. 405.

Estimates, when pi'e-sented.

Annual grants described.

Committee of supply.

year, the next business of the house is to order the estimates for the army, navy, and ordnance, to be laid before them, and to address her Majesty to give directions to the proper officers for that purpose.

In order tliat tlie house may be informed, as early as possible, of the expenditure for which they will have to provide, the following resolution was agreed to, 19th February 1821, and has ever since been complied with:

"That this house considers it essentially useful to the exact performance of its duties, as guardians of the public purse, that during the continuance of the peace, whenever Parliament shall ue assembled before Christmas, the estimates for the navy, army, and ordnance departments should be presented before the 15th day of January then next following, if Parliament be then sitting; and that such estimates should be presented within ten days after the opening of the committee of supply, when Parliament shall not be assembled till after Christmas." '

The estimates for civil services, commonly known as the miscellaneous estimates, are usually presented somewhat later in the session, by command of her Majesty.

Before the proceedings of the committee of supply are entered upon, it should be understood that about three-fifths of the whole annual expenditure consist of payments out of the consolidated fund, secured by various Acts of Parliament. For these charges the commons had provided, in the first instance, before the passing of the Acts by which they are secured: but such payments no longer require the annual sanction of Parliament, as permanent statutes now authorise the application of the public income to the discharge of its legal liabihties. But for the remaining two-fifths of the expenditure the commons provide, annually, by specific grants, which authorise the payment of distinct sums of money, for particular services, as explained by estimates laid before thera upon the responsibility of the ministers of the Crown.

When these estimates have been presented, printed, and 76 Com. J. 87.

circulated amongst the members, the sittings of the committee of supply begin. The estimates and accounts which are necessary to guide the committee are referred, and the member of the Administration representing the department for which the supplies are required, first explains to the committee such matters as may satisfy them of the correctness and propriety of the estimates, and then proceeds to propose each grant in succession; which is put from the chair in these words, "That a sum not exceeding . be granted to her Majesty," for the object specified in the estimate.

At the beginning of a new Parliament the first business Chairman of . committees of of the committee of supply is to elect a chairman, who, supply and when chosen, continues to preside over that committee for gans?" the remainder of the Parliament. If any difference should arise in his election, the speaker resumes the chair, and it is determined by the house what member shall take the chair of the committee, in the manner already explained in reference to other committees of the whole house. This official chairman, who is designated the chairman of the committee of ways and means, also presides over the committee of ways and means, and other committees of the whole house; and executes various duties in connexion with private bills, which will be described in the proper place.""

When the first report of the committee of supply has Committee of been received by the house, and agreed to, a day is lueans. appointed for the house to resolve itself into a committee " to consider of ways and means for raising the supply granted to her Majesty;" or, as it is briefly denominated, " the committee of ways and means." The house will not appoint this committee, until they have voted a sum of money, as the foundation of its future proceedings; nor is the committee subsequently permitted to vote Avays and means in excess of the expenditure voted by the committee of supply.

' See p. 287. See Book III., Chapter XXVI.

Mutiny bills. When thc committee of supply has determined the number of men who shall be maintained, during the year, for the army and for the sea service respectively, and these resolutions have been agreed to by the house, the Mutiny Bill, and the Marine lutiny Bill, are immediately ordered to be brought in. The former provides for the discipline of the troops, and the latter for the regulation and discijjline of the royol marines while on shore, and subjects them to martial law. The discipline of the seamen, and of the royal marines while afloat, is secured by permanent statutes. By j assing the annual Mutiny Acts in this manner, the House of Commons have reserved to themselves the power of determining, not only the number of men and the sums which shall be appropriated, in each year, to their support; but whether there shall be any standing army at all. Without their annual sanction the maintenance of a standing army, in time of peace, would be illegal, and the army and marines on shore would be released from all martial discipline and subordination. This usage affords an additional security for the annual meeting of Parliament, which is otherwise ensured by the system of providing money for the public service by annual grants."

Sit on Monday, By a custom nearly as ancient as the committees of and Friday." U P J ways and means themselves, those committees have been appointed to sit every Monday, Wednesday, and Friday, and until recently were not permitted to sit on any other days. But since the 5th February 1849, it has been a sessional resolution that they may also be fixed " for any other day on which orders of the day shall have precedence of notices of motions, of which notice shall have been given on the preceding Friday."

Adjourned The effects of this rule upon the adjournment of debates upon financial questions, discussed in connexion with these committees, are liable to be misunderstood. If a debate ' 22 Geo. II. c. 33. 29 Geo. II. c. 27. 19 Geo. III. c. 17. lollvict. c. o9, 02. 2 See Preamble to annual Mutiny Act.

= See supra, p. 50. See 11 Com. J. 93. 501 (IGtli February 1693, c.) arising in the committee be not concluded in one night, it cannot be adjourned, but the chairman reports progress, and asks leave to sit again. The debate, therefore, cannot be resumed except on the next day upon which the house resolves itself into the committee. In that case it is clear that a debate must be interrupted by the intermediate days upon which it is not customary for these committees to sit. But if an amendment be proposed to the question for the speaker to leave the chair, the debate upon that amendment may be adjourned from day to day, without reference to the usual days for the sitting of the committees of supply and ways and means. If the debate, however, should be concluded on a Tuesday or Thursday, and the question upon the amendment be negatived, the house cannot resolve itself into the committee on that day, but must have the order of the day read and deferred, or negative the question for Ir. Speaker now leaving the chair, and resolve to go into committee on a future day.

As the committees of supply and ways and means Functions of continue to sit during the session, are presided over by the teerdistm-" same chairman, are both concerned in providing money g ished. for the public service, and are governed by the same rules and usage, it will be necessaiy to distinguish their peculiar functions, before a more detailed account is given of the forms of procedure which apply equally to both. The general resemblance between these committees has sometimes caused a confusion in regard to the proper functions of each; but the terms of their appointment define at once their distinctive duties. The committee of supply considers what specific grants of money shall be voted as supplies demanded by the Crown, for the service of the ' The debate on Lord Sandon's motion on the Sugar Duties, in 1841, continued for nine days, and was concluded on a Tuesday; and that on Lord G. Beutinck's motion, in July 1846, was concluded also on a Tuesday, and the order read, and another day named. The debate on education (Great Britain) continued from Monday 19th, to Friday 23d of April 1847.

Functions of the committee of supply.

Consolidated fund.

Functions of the committee of ways and means.

current year; as explained by the estimates and accounts prepared by the executive government, and referred by the house to the committee. The committee of v ays and means determines in what manner the necessary funds shall be raised to meet the grants which are voted by the committee of supply, and which are required for the public service. The former committee controls the public expenditure; the latter provides the public income: the one authorises the payment of money; the other sanctions the imposition of taxes, and the application of public revenues not otherwise applicable to the service of the year.

Their separate duties may be further explained by enumerating more particularly the matters considered by each. The committee of supply votes every sum which is granted annually for the public service the army, the navy, the ordnance, and the several civil departments. But the fact already explained should be constantly borne in mind, that in addition to these particular services, which are voted in detail, there are permanent charges upon the public revenue, secured by Acts of Parliament, which the treasury are bound to defray, as directed by law. In this class are included the interest of the national funded debt, the civil list of her Majesty, the annuities of the Royal Family, and the salaries and pensions of the judges and some other public officers. These are annual charges upon the consolidated fund; but the specific appropriation of the respective sums necessary to defray those charges having been permanently authoi'ised by statutes, is independent of annual grants, and is beyond the control of the committee of supply.

Parliament has already empowered the treasury to apply the consolidated fund to the payment of these statutory charges when they become due; but this fund cannot be applied generally to meet the supplies voted for the service of the year, without the annual authority of Parliament. For this purpose the committee of ways and means votes general grants from time to time out of the consolidated fund, " towards making good the supply granted to her Majesty: " and bills are founded upon these resolutions of the committee, by which the treasury receive authority ta issue the necessary amounts from the consohdated fund, for the service of the year.

The financial arrangements of this country require con- Exchequer siderable sums of money to be raised by exchequer bills, in anticipation of the annual revenue, and the committee of ways and means authorises them to be issued; while the committee of supply, from time to time, grants sums of money to pay off and discharge them. The precise distinction between the functions of the two committees cannot be better exemplified than in the proceedings of each in reference to exchequer bills. It is within the province of the committee of ways and means, as providing the revenue, to determine what sums shall be raised by exchequer bills; it is the business of the committee of supply, as authorising expenditure, to vote all sums which are required to pay off and discharge those bills when they become due.

One of the most important occasions for which the Annual budget, committee of ways and means is required to sit, is for receiving the financial statement for the year, from the chancellor of the exchequer. When that minister has had sufficient time to calculate the probable income and expenditure for the financial year, commencing on the 5th April, he is prepared to determine what taxes should be repealed, reduced, continued, or augmented, or what new taxes must be imposed. As it is the province of the committee of ways and means to originate all taxes for the service of the year, it is in that committee that the chancellor of the exchequer developes his views of the resources of the country, communicates his calculations ' Or sometimes the first lord of the treasury, if a member of the House of Commons.

Charges of collection.

Proceedings in committee.

Greater or lesser sum.

of the probable income and expenditure, and declares whether the burthens upon the people are to be increased or diminished. This statement is familiarly known as "the budget," and is regarded with greater interest, perhaps, than any other speech throughout the session. The chancellor of the exchequer concludes by proposing resolutions for the adoption of the committee; which, when afterwards reported to the house, form the groundwork of bills for accomplishing the financial objects proposed by the minister.

It may here be observed, that the charges of collecting the revenue are deducted by each department from the gross sums collected; and thus neither the whole produce of the taxes, nor the cost of collecting them, is within the immediate control of Parliament.

On the 30th May 1848, the house resolved, "That this house cannot be the effectual guardian of the revenues of the state, unless the whole amount of the taxes, and of various other sources of income received for the public account, be either paid in or accounted for to the exchequer;"' but this resolution is still unfruitful of any results.

The rules of proceeding in the committees of supply and ways and means are precisely similar to those observed in other committees of the whole house. It has been stated in other places, as an ancient order of the house, "That w here there comes a question between the greater and lesser sum, or the longer and shorter time, the least sum and longest time ought first to be put to the question." This rule is applicable to all committees where such questions arise, but is more frequently brought into operation in these committees, where money forms the only subject of discussion. The object of this rule is said to be, "that the charge may be made as easy upon the people as possible;"

103 Com. J. 580. See supra, pp. 289. 358.

3 88 Com. J. 325. Stamp Dutips Bill, 15t i April 1850; 105 Com. J. 224.

but how that desirable result can be secured by putting one question before the other, is not very apparent; for if the majority were in favour of the smaller sum, they would negative the greater when proposed. The practice, however is convenient, since it is not usual to dispose of the two propositions in committee by way of question and amendment. If the smaller sum be resolved in the affirmative, the point is settled at once, and no question is put upon the greater; if in the negative, the greater sum is generally agreed to without further opposition. A direct negative of the larger sum is, in this manner, avoided, when the majority of the committee are adverse to it; and it has been urged as one of the merits of the rule, that the discourtesy of refusing to grant a sum demanded by the Crown, is mitigated by this course of proceeding.

The questions of the longer or shorter time had reference Longer or to the ancient mode of granting subsidies, which were rendered a lighter burthen on the subject by being extended over a longer period; and the present system of grants does not, therefore, admit of the application of this part of the rule. But its principle is still regarded in the committee of ways and means, whenever the time at which a tax shall commence is under discussion; for the most distant time being favourable to the people, the question for that time is first put from the chair.

The same rule, however, does not extend to the proceedings of the house on the report from a committee, where amendments are proposed in the ordinary form.

The entire sums proposed to be granted for particular Votes on services are not always voted at the same time, but a certain sum is occasionally voted on account of such grants. Thus, for example, in 1841 one-half only of the estimates, as presented to the house, was voted, in anticipation of a speedy dissolution, and the remaining half was voted by the account.

3 Hats. Prec, 184 n. E E new parliament. In 1848 money was voted on account of the several grants, as two committees were sitting at the time upon the public expenditure. In 1850 money was also voted on account of several grants, before Easter, and the remainder was voted after Easter.

Report of sup. The resolutions of the committees of supply and ways and means. and means are reported on a day appointed by the house, but not on the same day as that on which they are agreed to by the committee. When the report is received, the resolutions are twice read and agreed to by the house; or may be disagreed to, amended, postponed, or recommitted.

If agreed to, bills are ordered to carry them into effect, whenever it is necessary. This is the course pursued upon resolutions from the committee of ways and means; but the greater part of the resolutions of the committee of supply are reserved for the Appropriation Act, at the end

Charge not to of the session. If it be proposed to amend a resolution on report. the report, the amendment can only effect a diminution of the proposed burthen, and not an increase. If the latter be desired, the proper course is to recommit the resolution; as an addition to the public burthens can only be made in committee.

Propositions It must always be borne in mind, that the house can for reducing.,.,., charges upon cutcrtam any motion tor dnumishing a tax or charge upon e peop e. j people; and bills are frequently brought in for that purpose, without the formality of a committee. Obstacles are opposed to the imposition of burthens, but not to their removal or alleviation; and this distinction has an influence upon many proceedings not immediately connected with supply. For instance, the blanks left in a bill for salaries, tolls, rates, penalties, c. are filled up in committee; but on the report, the house may reduce their amount. If, however, it be desired to increase them, the bill should be recommitted for that purpose. So, also, if a clause proposed to be added to a bill enact a penalty, which the house, on the report of the clause, desire to increase, the clause ought to be recommitted. Any boun- Drawiiacksand .,.- allowances.

ties, drawbacks, or allowances, involving payments out oi the revenue, have usually been proposed in committee; but if an allowance were merely in the form of a deduction from the amount of a proposed duty, it might be entertained by the house.

Doubts have been sometimes entertained whether on the Questions of report of resolutions from a committee by which duties are duties on reduced, it be regular to propose any amendment by which " P '"'-such reductions would be negatived, or the amount of reduction diminished. It has been contended that such an amendment would, in effect, increase a charge upon the people, which can be done in committee only; but it is clear that if the amendment were made, it would merely leave unchanged the duty, existing by law, or would reduce it; and that the charge upon the people would not be increased. It would, indeed, be an anomalous form to report such resolutions to the house at all, unless the house could disagree to or amend them, and there are numerous cases in which amendments of this character have been proposed, without objection, on the report. ' In the same manner it is competent for the committee when commit-on a bill for reducing taxes, to raise a tax beyond the increase a amount proposed by the bill and previously agreed upon charge. by a committee and by the house, provided the amount be not raised higher than the existing tax authorised by law. On the 19th March 1845, resolutions were reported from a committee on the Customs' Acts, by which the import duties on glass were reduced, and certain lower rates of duty imposed from and after the expiration of excise duties on British glass (proposed to be reduced in the present session), and until the 10th Oct. 1846, after which further ' See supra, p. 361.

Customs' Acts Report, 15th, 16th, and 17th March 1846; 101 Com. J. 323, 335. 349.

reductions were to take effect. An instruction was given to the gentlemen already appointed to bring in a Customs' Duties Bill, to make provision therein pursuant to these resolutions. In the committee on the bill it was proposed to postpone the period at which such reductions of duty were to take place; but it was questioned by some whether such an amendment was admissible, as it would have the effect of continuing a charge upon the people for a longer time than the committee had voted and the house had agreed to. It was decided, however (privately), by Mr. Speaker, after full consideration, that an amendment of that nature was perfectly regular. A bill for the reduction of taxes, as already stated, need not originate in a committee; but as Customs' Duties Bills affect trade, they have been, on that account, founded upon resolutions of committees, even when all the duties affected by them have been reduced. So long, therefore, as an existing tax is not increased, any modification of the proposed reduction may be introduced in the committee on the bill; being regarded as a question, not for increasing the charge upon the people, but for determining to what extent such charge shall be reduced. Distinction in But a clear distinction must always be observed between the case of a, r-i ' n i new tax. the case ot a tax tor the service of the year, and a pro- posed diminution of a tax or charge already existing. If a new tax were imposed or a temporary tax continued for the service of the year in the committee of ways and means, or other committee, and agreed to by the house, the committee on the bill would unquestionably have no right to increase it; but where a permanent tax is merely proposed to be diminished, a proposition in committee on the bill to modify that diminution, does not increase the charge upon the people. There can be no doubt that a committee is entitled to leave out of a bill ' Votes, 1845, p. 503.

portions of the resolutions upon which the bill is founded, and such an omission may leave a duty unchanged, and thus raise it above the amount previously agreed to by the committee of the whole house, and by the house itself. And it would seem difficult to maintain a distinction, in principle, between such a case as this, and an amendment which should merely modify the resolutions. It must be admitted, however, that the rule is not devoid of difficulties (more especially when the treasury have already given effect to the resolutions of the house), and though supported by precedent, it has not been uniformly approved by parliamentary authorities.

When the supplies for the service of the year have all Appropriation been granted, the committee of supply discontinues its sittings, but the financial arrangements are still to be completed by votes in the committee of ways and means. That committee authorises the application of money from the consolidated fund, the surplus of ways and means, and sums in the exchequer, to meet the several grants and services of the year; and a bill is ordered, to carry their resolutions into effect. This is known originally as the Consolidated Fund Bill, but after it has been committed, an instruction is given by the house to the committee, to receive a clause of appropriation, and it is then called in the Votes the " Consolidated Fund (Appropriation) Bill," but more generally the Appropriation Bill. It enumerates every grant that has been made during the whole session, and authorises the several sums, as voted by the committee of supply, to be issued and applied to each separate service. It also enacts, "That the said aids and supplies shall not be issued or applied to any use, intent or purpose, other than those bef(ire mentioned; or for the other payments directed to be satisfied by any Acts of Parliament, c. of this Session of Parliament."

12 13 Vict., c. 98, s. 26.

Expenditure not to exceed grants.

Boyal assent to

Appropriation

Act.

Grants voted otherwise than in committee of supply.

On the 30th March 1849, the House of Commons agreed to a resolution concurring in the opinion expressed by the lords of her Majesty's treasury, That " when a certain amount of expenditure for a particular service has been determined upon by Parliament, it is the bounden duty of the department which has that service under its charge and control, to take care that the expenditure does not exceed the amount placed at its disposal for that purpose." But by a clause in the annual Appropriation Act, the treasury may alter the proportionate amounts for each separate service in the array, navy, and ordnance grants, provided the total grant to each department be not exceeded.

When the Appropriation Bill has passed both houses, and is about to receive the royal assent, it is returned into the charge of the commons until that house are summoned to attend her Majesty or the lords commissioners, in the House of Peers, for the prorogation of Parliament: when it is carried by the speaker to the bar of the House of Peers, and there received by the assistant clerk of the Parliaments for the royal assent. When her Majesty is present in person, the speaker prefaces the delivery of the money bills with a short speech, concerning the principal measures of the session, in which he does not omit to mention the supplies granted by the commons. The money bills then receive the royal assent before any of the other bills awaiting the same ceremony, and the words In which it is pronounced acknowledge the free gift of the commons: "La reyne remercie ses bons sujets, accepte leur benevolence, et ainsi le veult."

Although every grant of money must be considered in a committee of the whole house, it is not usual to vote such grants in the committee of supply, as do not form part of the supplies for the current year. Any issue of ' 104 Com. J. 190, money out of the consolidated fund for salaries created by a bill, or other charges of whatever character, after the Queen's recommendation has been signified, is authorised by a committee of the whole house, to whom the matter is specially referred; and on their report a bill is ordered, or a clause is inserted, by instruction, in a bill already before the house.

Another mode of originating a grant of money without Addresses for the intervention of the committee of supply, is by an address to the Crown for the issue of a sum of money for particular purposes, with an assurance " that this house will make good the same." According to the strict rules of the house, this proceeding ought only to be resorted to when the committee of supply is closed, at the end of the session; for otherwise the more regular and constitutional practice is to vote the sum in that committee; but as this form of motion makes the royal recommendation unnecessary, it is often resorted to by members who desire grants which are not approved by the ministers of the Crown.

On the 22d February 1821, a resolution was agreed

"That this house will not proceed upon any motion for an address to the Crown, praying that any money may be issued, or that any expense may be incurred, but in a committee of the whole house, and that the same be declared a standing order of the house."" In compliance with this standing order, and with the resolution of the 18th February 1667, that the consideration and debate of motions for any public aid or charge should not be presently entered upon, the proper form to observe in proposing an address involving any outlay is to move, 1st, "That this house will on a future day resolve itself into a committee of the whole house, to consider of an address, c. c.;" and if that be carried, 2dly, To ' 83 Com. J. 716, c. 2 75 n, jiqi.

otherwise tliau in coin ways and means.

move tliat adtlress, in committee, on the day appointed by the house." If a motion for an address for public money were submitted to the house in any other manner, it would be irregular for the speaker to propose the question to the house. Taxes imposed As grants of money may be sanctioned by these methods, mitteeof otherwise than in committee of supply; so all taxes are not necessarily imposed in the committee of ways and means. The original intention of this committee was to vote all ways and means for the service of the year; and when taxes were ordinarily appropriated to specific services, its province was sufficiently defined; but since the practice has arisen of carrying the produce of all taxes to one general consolidated fund, the office of the committee of ways and means is not capable of so distinct a definition. All annual or temporary duties, and other taxes which are to take effect immediately, for purposes of revenue, are obviously subjects proper for the consideration of this committee; but the same rule is not always applicable to taxes of a more permanent and general nature.

The best illustration of this distinction will be found in the course adopted by the house, in reference to the sugar duties, which, until 1846, being annual duties, had always been voted in the committee of ways and means. In that year they were revised in the committee of ways and means; but were then made permanent instead of annual duties, in order to adjust gradually the discriminating duties upon foreign and colonial sugars. In 1848 a further revision of the duties was proposed in a committee of the whole house, and not in the committee of ways and means, as on former occasions; and it was stated, in debate, that this course was adopted, after full consideration, because the duties

Sugar dudes.

' Mirror of Pari. 1840, pp. 3244. 4179 (Church Extension). 98 Com. J. 415.

' 98 Com. J. 321 (Danish Claims;.

were now permanent." Every tax, indeed, whether it be permanent or not, is practically for the service of the current year so long as it continues to be levied; but it may be desirable to alter it for purposes unconnected with the actual condition of the revenue. This distinction is generally observed, and it is the prevailing custom to confine the deliberations of the committee of ways and means to such taxes as are more distinctly ai plicable to the immediate exigencies of the public income; and to consider, in other committees of the whole house, all fiscal regulations, and alterations of permanent duties, not having directly for their object the increase of revenue. Thus general alterations of the duties of customs, excise, stamps, and taxes, have been proposed in committees of the whole house; but additions to these duties, for the express purpose of supplying deficiencies in the annual revenue, have been considered in the committee of ways and means. This practice, though not without exceptions, has been sufficiently observed to establish a general rule, that, whenever the form of a motion points to taxation as an immediate source of revenue, it ought properly to be offered in the committee of ways and means.

' Question of Mr. M. Gibson, and Lord J. Russell's answer, 30tli June 1838; (not reported in Hansard).

"97 Com, J. 264; 92 lb. 499, 500. 3 95 lb. 351. 451.

criarxeR xxii.

ISSUE OF WRITS, AND TRIAL OF CONTROVERTED ELECTIONS BY THE HOUSE OF COMMONS.

Purport of this cliapter.

Issue of writs.

Vacancies during a session.

The law of elections, as declared by various statutes," and by the decisions of committees of the House of Commons, has become a distinct branch of the law of England. It is, in itself, of too comprehensive a character to admit of a concise analysis for the general purposes of this work, and it has already been collected and expounded, in all its details, by many valuable treatises. But as the issue of writs, and the trial of election petitions, form an important part of the functions of the House of Commons, an outline of these proceedings, apart from the general law in reference to elections, cannot be omitted.

Whenever vacancies occur in the House of Commons, from any legal cause, after the original issue of writs for a new Parliament by the Crown, all subsequent writs are issued out of chancery, by warrant from the speaker, and when the house is sitting, by order of the House of Commons. The most frequent causes of vacancy are, the death of members, their elevation to the peerage, the acceptance of offices under the Crown, and the determinations of election committees that elections or returns are void, upon any of the grounds which, by law, avoid them.

When the house is sitting, and the death of a member, his elevation to the peerage, or other cause of vacancy is ' There are upwards of 240 statutes, unrepealed, which relate to elections, exclusive of Acts for tlie trial of controverted elections. See Author's Pamphlet on the Consolidation of the Election Laws, 18.50.

"See 26 Hans. Deb., M Ser. 839, 11th March 1835; 2 Hats. G5 n., 393-397.

known, a writ Is moved by any member, and, on being seconded by another, Mr. Speaker is ordered by the house to issue his warrant for a new writ for the place represented by the member whose seat is thus vacated.

If a member becomes a peer by descent, a writ is usually Vacancy by moved, so soon as the death of his ancestor is known; ' though, occasionally, some delay occurs. If a n)ember be created a peer, it is often the practice to move the new writ when he has kissed hands; but sometimes not until the patent has been made out or the recepi indorsed. When it is advisable to issue the wa-it without delay, and it is doubtful whether the seat be yet legally vacated, the member accepts the Chiltern Hundreds.

A motion for a new writ ordinarily takes precedence of Precedence of ,1, J." D ' 1 0. 1 1 motion fur new other motions, as a question or privilege; but by a resolu- j.

tion of the 5tli April 1848, "in all cases where the seat of any member has been declared void by an election committee, on the grounds of bribery or treating, no motion for the issue of a new writ shall be made without previous notice being given in the Votes;" and if such a notice should be dropped, it must be renewed like other dropped notices.

K any doubt should arise concerning the fact of the vacancy, the oi'der for a new writ would be deferred until the house should be in possession of more certain infoitnation; and if, after the issue of a writ, it should be discovered that the house had acted upon false intelligence, the speaker will be ordered to issue a warrant for a supersedeas to the writ.

Thus, on the 29th April 1765, a new writ was ordered Supersedeas to for Devizes, in the room of Ir. Willey, deceased. On the " ' ' 74 Hans. Deb., 3d Ser. 108, (Lord Abinger 19th April 1844. Earl Powis, 103 Com. J. 162.

Lord Eddisbury sat until IStli May 1848, altliough his creation had appeared in the " Gazette " ou the 9th May. 103 Com. J. ol3.

' 103 Com. J. 4-23.

Sligo writ, 28th June 1848; 99 Hans. Deb,, 3d Ser., 1289.

Vacancies during the recess.

warrants.

30th it was doubted whether he was dead, and the messenger of the gi eat seal was ordered to forbear delivering the writ until further directions. Mr. Willey proved to be alive, and on the 6th May a supersedeas to the writ was ordered to be made out.". And in several more recent cases, when the house has been misinformed, or a writ has been issued through inadvertence, the error has been corrected by ordering the speaker to issue his warrant to the clerk of the Crown to make out a supersedeas to the writ." When vacancies occur by death, or elevation to the peerage, the law provides ibr the issue of writs during a recess, by prorogation or adjournment, without the immediate authority of the house, in order that a representative may be chosen without loss of time, by the place which is Speaker issues deprived of its member. By the 24 Geo. III., sess. 2, c. 26, on the receipt of a certificate, under the hands of two members, that any member has died, or that a writ of summons under the great seal has been issued to summon him to Parliament as a peer, either during the recess or previously thereto, the speaker is required to give notice forthwith in the London Gazette (which is to be acknowledged by the publisher); and after fourteen days from tlie insertion of such notice, to issue his warrant to the clerk of the Crown to make out a new writ.

But the speaker may not issue his warrant during the recess; 1, unless the return of the late member has been brought into the office of the clerk of the Crown fifteen days before the end of the last sitting of the house; nor, 2, unless the application is made so long before the next meeting of the house, for despatch of business, as that the writ may be issued before the day of meeting;" nor, 3, may ' See 2 Hats., 80 n.

2 64 Com. J. 48; 81 lb. 223; 8G lb. 134. 182. Votes, 5th February 1851; (Dungarvan writ).

See the form of the certificate in the Appendix.

That is to say, fourteen days must elapse after the insertion of the notice, and tlien the writ can only be issued before the meeting of the house.

he issue a warrant in respect ot" any seat tliat has been vacated by a member against whose election or return a petition was depending at the last prorogation or adjournment.

For any place in Great Britain, the speaker's warrant To wiiom wnr- ,., -(I 1 ritiits directed.

IS directed to the clerk ot tlie crown in Chancery; and for any place in Ireland, to the clerk of the crown in Ireland.

On the receipt of the speaker's warrant, the writ is Delivery of issued by the clerk of the crown and transmitted through the post-office, in pursuance of the provisions of the 53 Geo. III. c. 89. Neglect or delay in the delivery of the writ, or any other violation of tlie Act, is a misdemeanor; and in the event of any complaint being made, the house will also inquire into the circumstances.

At the beginning of each Parliament the speaker is Speaker's ap- ., poiutmeiit of required to appoint a certain number oi members, not members. exceeding seven, and not less than tliree in number, to execute his duties in reference to the issue of writs, in case of his own death, the vacation of his seat, or his absence from the realm. This appointment stands good for the entire Pa-liamcnt, unless the number should be reduced to less than three; in which case the speaker is required to make a new appointment in the same manner as before. This appointment is ordered to be entered in the Journals, and published in tlie London Gazette; and the instrument is to be preserved by the. clerk of the house, and a duplicate by the clerk of the Crown.

By the 52 Geo. III., c. 144, s. 3, similar powers are given Bankruptoy. to the speaker, and to the members appointed by him, for issuing warrants, in the event of a seat having become vacant by the bankruptcy of a member.

If any error should appear in the return to a writ, the Error in return.

' 103 Com. J. 195. ' Glasgow writ, 1837; 92 Com. J. 410. 418.

the Crowu.

434 OFFICES UNDER THE CROWN.

When no return clerk of til c Crown 13 ordered to attend and amend it; ' or 19 made. j j return be made to a writ, in due course, the clerk of the Crown is ordered to attend and explain the omission; when, if it should aj)pcar that the returning officer or any other person has been concerned in the delay, he will be sunimoned to attend the house; and such other proceedings will be adopted as the house may think fit. Offices under By the 26th scct. of the Act G Anne, c. 7, if any member

"shall accept of any office of profit from the Crown during such time as he shall continue a member, his election shall be and is hereby declared to be void, and a new writ shall issue for a new election, as if such person, so accepting, was naturally dead; provided, nevertheless, that such person shall be capable of being again elected," c.

By virtue of this provision, whenever a member accepts an office of profit from the Crown, a new writ is ordered, and it is the usual practice to move the new writ when the member has kissed hands, instead of waiting for the completion of the formal appointment. As the secretaries of the treasury, the under secretaries of state, the secretaries to the admiralty, to the board of control, and to the master-general of the ordnance, do not hold office by appointment from the Crown, their seats are not vacated; nor would the acceptance of any other offices, of which the appointment does not vest directly in the Crown, vacate a seat. But not more than one under secretary to each department would appear to be admissible to the House of Commons under the 15th Geo. II., c. 22, s. 3; and in practice there are only two under secretaries of state who hold seats in ' 86 Com. J. 578. Northampton county, 26th February 1846; 101 Cora. J. 207.

Waterford writ, 1806, 61 Com. J., 169. 175; 6 Hans. Deb., 536. 562. 751. Great Grimsby, 1832, 86 Com. J. 758. 762, c.; 72 Hans. Deb., N. S., 95. 159. 294. 400.

' The resumption of an office wliicli has been resigned, but to which no successor has been appointed, docs not vacate a seat.

2 Hats. 44.

that house at the same time J y the 41 Geo. III., e. 52, s. 9, it is declared that offices accepted immediately or directly from the Crown of the United Kingdom, or by the appointment and nomination, or by any other appointment. Or lord lieute-subject to the approbation of the lord lieutenant of Ireland, shall vacate seats in Parliament." But by the 6 Anne, c. 7, s. 28, the receipt of a new or other commission by a member who is in the army or navy, is excepted from the operation of the Act, and does not vacate his seat; and the same exception has been extended, by construction, to officers in the marines; and to the office of master-general or lieutenant-general in the ordnance, accepted by an officer in the army," It has always been held that the office of ambassador, or other foreign minister, does not disqualify, nor its acceptance vacate the seat of a member; but the acceptance of the office of consul or consul-general has been deemed to vacate a seat; though the member was considered to be re-eligible.

It is a settled principle of Parliamentary law, that a Chiltern iiun-member, after he is duly chosen, cannot relinquish his seat; and, in order to evade this restriction, a member who wishes to retire, accepts office under the Crown, which legally vacates his seat, and obliges the house to order a new writ. The offices usually selected for this purpose are those of steward or bailift' of her Majesty's three Chiltern Hundreds of Stoke, Desborough, and Bonenham, or of the manors of East Hendred and North-stead, which, though sometimes refused, are given by the treasury in ordinary cases' to any member who applies for 2 Hats. 63 n.

' The various offices which have licen liehl to vacate seats, may be collected from tlie several General Journal Indexes, tit. " Elections;" and from Rogers on Elections, p. 59.

2 Hats. 45 n. 22 June 1742.

2 Hats. 22. Votes, 5th February 1851; (Dungarvan writ).

2 Hats. 54 n. " 1 Com. J. 724, 2 lb. 201.

See letter of Mr. fjoulburn to Viscount Chelsea, Pari. Paper, 1842 (544).

them, and arc resigned again as soon as their purpose is effected. Accepted by a In the scssion of 1847-8, a member having had doubts member dis i i i i i t t t qualified. suggcstca whether he had not been disquahfaed at the tune of his election, as a contractor, thought it prudent not to take his seat in case of being sued for the penalties under the Act. He was, however, unwilling to admit his dis-quaufication, which was extremely doubtful, and he accordingly applied for the Chiltern Hundreds. Some doubts were raised as to the propriety of allowing him to vacate his seat by this method; but it was agreed that as the time had expired for questioning, by an election petition, the validity of his return, and as the House had no cognizance of his probable disqualification, there could be no objection to his accepting office, which solved all doubts, and at once obliged the house to issue a new Avrit.

Wiint of pro A singular method of vacating a seat was that of Mr.

tion'auuiitted. Southcy, in 1826, who had been elected for Downton, during his absence on the Continent. His return was not questioned, but he addressed a letter to the speaker, in which he stated that he had not the qualification of estate required by law. The house waited until after the expiration of the time limited for presenting election petitions,

Disqualifica- and then issued a new writ for the borough. A similar case occurred in 1847-8. Mr. Cowan, m. p. for Edinburgh, addressed a letter to the speaker on the 25th November 1847," stating that at the time of his election he had been disqualified as being a party to a contract then subsisting with her Majesty's stationery office. At the expiration of fourteen days, when his seat could no longer be claimed by any other candidate, his letter was read, and a new writ ordered."' ' MS. note. 82 Com, J. 28.

'8-2 Com. J. 108. M03Ib. 17.

8tb December, 1847; 103 Com. J. 102.

By the law of Parliament a member sitting for one Members va-place may not be elected for another, but must vacate his elected. seat by accepting the Chiltern Hundreds, or some other office under the Crown, in order to become a candidate.

At one time it was doubted whether a candidate claim- Petitioning -r-, T,. T! 1 i candidates mg a seat in 1 arliament by petition, was eligible tor eligible. another place before the determination of his claim; but it was resolved, on the 16th April 1728, "that a person petitioning, and thereby claiming a seat for one place, is capable of being elected and returned, pending such petition." In case the petitioner should, after his election, establish his claim to the disputed seat, the proper course would be to allow him to make his election for which place he would serve, in the same manner as If he had been returned for both places at a general election."

Another occasion for issuino; new writs is to c ive effect Trial of contm-to the determination of an election committee; and this jj Qg leads to the examination of the mode by which controverted elections are tried and determined by the House of Commons, according to law.

Before the year 1770 controverted elections were tried Formerly by and determined by the whole House of Commons, as mere house, party questions, upon which the strength of contending factions might be tested. Thus in 1741 Sir Kobert Wal-pole, after repeated attacks upon his government, resigned at last, in consequence of an adverse vote upon the Chippenham election petition.

"Instead of trusting to the merits of their respective causes," Grenville Act. said Mr. Grenville, in proposing the measure which has since borne his name, "the principal dependence of both parties is their private interest among us; and it is scandalously notorious that we are as earnestly canvassed to attend in favour of the opposite sides as if we were wholly self-elective, and not bound to act by the principles of justice, but by the discretionary impulse ' 21 Com. J. 136.

' Tliis point was considered in 18-19, when such a case seemed likely to nceur; but there have been uo precedeuts.

Constitiiti"!! of coiiiiiiittees under the Grenville Act.

of our own inclinations; nay, it is well known that in every contested election, many nicm'bers of this house, who are ultimately to judge in a kind of judicial cai)acity between the competitors, enlist themselves as parties in the contention, and take upon themselves the partial management of the very business upon which they should determine with the strictest impartiality."

In ortlcr tc prevent so notorious a perversion of justice, the house consented to submit the exercise of its privilege to a tribunal constituted by law; which, though composed of its own members, should be appointed so as to secure impartiality, and the administration of justice according to the laws of the land, and under the sanction of oaths. The object was praiseworthy, but the means adopted, compromised the privileges, and fettered the discretion of the commons; enacted many things by law, which would have been equally effectual, if directed by the authority of the house; and failed in securing that justice and impartiality which had been the price of these sacrifices. The principle of the Grenville Act," and of others which were passed at different times since 1770, was to select committees for the trial of election petitions by lot. By the last of these," thirty-three names were balloted from the members present at the time, and each of the parties to the election was entitled to strike off eleven names, and thus reduce the number of the committee to eleven. Whichever party attended on the day appointed for a ballot in the greatest force, was likely to have a preponderance in the committee; and the expedient of chance did not therefore operate as a sufficient check to party spirit in the appointment of election committees. Partiality and incompetence were very generally complained of in the constitution of committees appointed in this ' In 1773 the Grenville Act was made perpetual, but not without the expression of very strong opinions against the limitations imposed by it upon the privileges of the house. See 17 Purl. Hist., 1071; also. Lord Canij)l)eirs Chancellors, vol. vi., 98.

' D Geo. IV., c. 22.

manner; and in 1839 an Act was passed establishing a new system, upon different principles, increasing the responsibility of individual members, and leaving but little to the operation of chance.

This principle has since been maintained, with partial Present system, alterations of the means by which it is carried out, and all the proceedings on the trial of controverted elections are now conducted under the 11th and 12th Vict., c. 98. Without entering minutely into every detail, which will be best explained by the Act itself, or by general treatises upon the law of elections, a distinct view may be given of the resolutions, rules, and forms of the house, and of the provisions of the law.

At the commencement of each session the house order, Petitions, when to be presented. "That all persons who will question any returns of members to serve in Parliament, for any county, city, borough, or place in the

United Kingdom, do question the same within fourteen days next, and so within fourteen days next after any new return shall be brouglit in."

"That all persons who shall question any return of members to serve in the present Parliament, upon any allegation of bribery and corruption, and who shall in their petition specifically allege any payment of money or other reward to have been made by any member, or on his account, or with his privity, since the time of such election, in pursuance or in furtherance of such bribery or corruption, may question the same at any time within twenty-eight days after the date of such payment; or if this house be not sitting at the expiration of the said twenty-eight days, then within fourteen days after the day when the house shall next meet."

When the house has adjourned before the expiration of the When house fourteen days, or has not sat on the fourteenth day, election fourteeuth day. petitions have been received on the next sitting day;' and when Parliament has been prorogued within fourteen days after a return has been brouglit in, petitions complaining of such return have been received in the following session."' ' Rogers, 19, 1842-43.

xx. jttiiigham Petitions; 97 Com. J. 005 j 9? lb. 9.

Sitfng in Mil In regard to members whose scats may be affected by petitions, the following order is made, which divides itself into three parts, viz.

"1. That all members who are returned for two or more places ill any jiart of the United Kingdom do make their election for whicli of tlie places they will serve, within one week from and after the expiration of the fourteen days before limited for presenting jietitions, jirovided there be no question upon the return for that place; 2. And if anytiang shall come in question touching tlie return or election of any member, he is to withdraw during the time the matter is in debate; and, 3. That all members returned upon double returns do withdraw till their returns are determined."

Members re 1. The first part of the order regulates the manner of j)iaces. choosing for which place a member will sit, when he has been returned for more than one. When the time limited for presenting petitions against his return has expired, and no petition has been presented, he is required to make his election within a week, in order that his constituents may no longer be deprived of a representative. When a petition has been presented against his return for one place only, he cannot elect to serve for either. He cannot abandon the seat petitioned against, which may be proved to belong of right to another, and thus render void an election which may turn out to have been good in favour of some other candidate; neither can he abandon the other seat; because if it should be proved that he is only entitled to sit for one, he has no election to make, and cannot give up a seat without having incurred some legal disqualification, such as the acceptance of office or bankru)tcy. Upon this principle, on the 24th May 1842, Mr. O'Connell, who had been chosen for the counties of Cork and Meath, elected to sit for the former, directly after the report of the election committee, by which he Avas declared to have been duly elected for that county.

' 97 Com. J. 302, 2. The second part, of the order is in accordance with impmiwrs to the general rule of tlie house, which requires every member to withdraw, where matters are under discussion in which he is personally concerned.

3. When there is a double return, tliere are two inden- Double returns, tures, and both the names are entered in the return books.

Both members may therefore claim to be sworn, and to take their seats; but after the election of the speaker, neither of them can vote until the right to the scat has been detei mined; because both are of course precluded from voting where one only ought to vote; and neither of them has a better claim than the other. The practice of making such returns, though apparently prohibited in England by the 7 8 Will. III., c. 7, has been sanctioned by the law and practice of Parliament; and in Scotland it is directed by the Scotch Reform Act (s. 33). In Ireland, on the other hand, a double return is expressly prohibited.

The house, also, pass the following resolutions, in condemnation of irregular practices to influence the freedom of election:

"That no peer of this realm, except such peers of Ireland as Inlcrforencc of shall for the time being be actually elected, and shall not have P ers. declined to serve, for any county, city, or borough of Great Britain, hath any right to give his vote in the election of any member to serve in Parliament."

"That it is a high infringement of the liberties and privileges of the commons of the United Kingdom for any lord of Parliament, or other peer or prelate, not being a peer of Ireland at tlie time elected, and not having declined to serve for any county, city, or borough of Great Britain, to concern himself in the election of members to serve for the commons in Parliament, except only any peer of Ireland, at such elections in Great Britain respectively, where such peer shall appear as a candidate, or by himself, or any others, be proposed to be elected; or for any lord lieutenant or governor of any county to avail himself of any ' See supra, p. 2G4. 284.

Report, Oaths of Members, 1848, Q. 23-25.

' 35 Geo. HI,, c. 29, s. 13, and 4 Geo. IV., c. 55, s. 08.

authority ileriveil from his commission, to influence the election of any member to serve for the commons in Parliament."' Bribery. "Tiiat if it shall appear that any person hath been elected or returned a member of tliis house, or endeavoured so to be, by bribery, or any other corrupt practices, this house will proceed with the utmost severity against all such persons as shall have been wilfully concerned in such bribery or other corrupt practices."

Adniiiiistraiion Under the Act 11 12 Vict., c. 98, for the trial of law. election petitions, the House of Commons act as a court administering the statute law. Little discretion is left to them beyond that of interpreting the Act, and executing its provisions. Every enactment is positive and compulsory; the house, the committees, the speaker, the members, are all directed to execute particular parts of the Act; and, in short, it is not possible to conceive a legislative body more strictly bound by a public law, over which it has no control, and in administering which it has so little discretion."' The proceedings of the house, therefore, can only be described by following the several provisions of the law.

I'etitioii. An election can only be questioned by petition presented to the House of Commons, within the time limited by their sessional orders. All petitions are treated as election petitions, which complain 1. Of an undue election or return; 2. That no return has been made according to the requisition of a writ issued for the election of a member; 3. Or of the special matters contained in the return.

I5y wiiom to be Every election petition must be subscribed by some signed. 1 1 1 T 1 11' person (1) who voted or had a right to vote at the election to which the same relates; (2), or by some person claiming to have had a right to be returned or elected; (3), or

See Debate, 14th December 1847 (West Gloucester election); and precedents cited by the attorney-general in regard to proceedings of the house against peers who liave interfered in elections, 135 Hans. Deb., 3d Scr., 1077; and Debate, 19tli February 1846, 83 Hans. Deb., 3d Scr., 11G7. Stamford IJorough case, 1848,1)8 Hans. Deb., 3d Scr., 932. 970.

= Its helplessness was remarkably ilkistrated in the cases of disputed election rccoguizauces in tlie session of 1847-8.

alloi"inir liimsclf to have been a candidate at the election. K not subscribed in this manner, it will not be deemed an election petition.

This definition of the characteristics of an election pcti- Petitions not ,., 1 1 A 1 within the Act.

tion IS 01 great nnportance; bectiuse the Act has given no power to the house to apply its provisions to petitions Avhich merely contain general complaints against an election. The house, indeed, may appoint committees to inquire into the matters alleged in such petitions; but unless they complain of general bribery, for which special provision is made by statute," the inquiries can only be conducted according to the rules of that house, and without any sanction or powers from the law. The witnesses cannot be examined upon oath, nor can the election or return be legally aiffected by any decision of the house. If it be found after a petition has been presented, that it is not an election petition, within the terms of the Act, the orders for further proceedings are liable to be discharged, and the petition ordered to lie upon the table. Or the election committee, upon a preliminary objection, may subsequently refuse to entertain the petition.

Before any election petition is presented to the house, a Recognizances, recognizance is required to be entered into by one, two, three, or four persons as sureties for the person subscribing the petition for 1,000. in one sum, or in several sums of not less than 2501. each, for the payment of all costs and expenses arising out of the trial of the petition, and made payable by the Act. The recognizance is required to be in the fonii or to the effect set forth in the schedule to the Act. An officer called the examiner of recognizances, ai)pointed by the speaker, examines the recognizances; which may either be entered into before him, or before a justice of the peace, and afterwards delivered to him; and an option is allowed to petitioners, instead of finding sureties for the full amount, to pay any amount not less than tt: Com. J. 61. 7o. 70, c. = 5 G Vict., c. 102, s. 4.

Affidavits of sureties.

Certificate indorsed on petition.

Names of sureties.

Objections to sureties.

When to be made.

250. into the Bank of England, and to find sureties for so much only as the sum paid into the bank falls short of the 1,000.

Every person entering into a recognizance as surety for another is to testify upon oath in writing, to be sworn at the time of entering into the recognizance and before the same person by whom his recognizance is taken, that he is possessed of real or personal estate, or both, of the clear value of the sum for which he is bound; and every such affidavit is to be annexed to the recognizance; and in every recognizance is to be mentioned the name and usual place of residence of the sureties, with such other description of them as may be sufficient to identify them easily. No recognizance or affidavit requires to be stamped.

No petition can be received by the house, except it be indorsed by a certificate from the examiner, that the recognizance has been entered into, and received by him with the affidavit annexed; and, if not for the whole amount, that a bank receipt or certificate has been delivered for the remainder.

On or before the day on which the petition is presented, the names and descriptions of the sureties are entered in a book kept in the office of the examiner of recognizances; and the book, and also the recognizance, affidavits, and bank receipt, are open to the inspection of all parties concerned.

Any sitting member petitioned against, or any electors petitioning and admitted parties to defend the return, may object to any recognizance as being invalid, or not duly entered into or received by the examiner, or on the ground that the sureties are insufficient, or that a surety is dead or cannot be found, or that a person named in the recognizance has not duly acknowledged the same; provided the ground of objection be stated in writing, and delivered to the examiner within ten days, or not later than 12 o'clock of the 11th day after the presentation of the petition, if the surety objected to reside in England; or within 14 days, or not later than 12 o'clock of the l. Jth day, if the surety reside in Scotland or Ireland. When a statement of objection is received by the examiner, he is required to put up an acknowledgment thereof in some conspicuous part of his office, and to appoint a day for hearing such objections, not less than three nor more than five days from that on which he received the statement: and the petitioners or their agents may examine and take copies of the objections.

At the time appointed, the examiner of recognizances Objections inquires into the alleged objections, on the grounds stated eided. in the notice of objection, but not on any other ground. He is authorised to examine witnesses upon oath, and to receive in evidence affidavits sworn before himselfj a master in chancery, or a justice of the peace. He may adjourn the inquiry from time to time, until he has decided upon the validity of the objections; he may award costs to be paid by either party; and his decision is final and conclusive against all parties.

In case a surety should die, and his death should be Death of surclics stated as a ground of objection, before the end of the time allowed for objecting, the petitioner may pay into the Bank of England, on the account of the speaker and the examiner of recognizances, the sum for which the deceased surety was bound; and upon the delivery of the bank receipt within three days after the objection, the recognizance will be deemed unobjectionable, if no other ground of objection be stated thereto within the limited time.

When the examiner has decided, upon the objections, Suroiips re-that any recognizances are objectionable, he reports that decision to the speaker immediately; but when he has decided that the recognizances are unobjectionable, or has received no statement of objections, and the time for receiving objections has elapsed, he reports to the speaker that the recognizances are unobjectionable, and every such report is final and conclusive. The speaker acquaints the house, when he has received reports from the examiner; and a list of all the petitions, of which the recognizances ported.

Invalid recognizances.

Petitions withdrawn.

Proceedings when tlie seat becomes vacant, or tlie sitting member declines to defend his return.

are reported unobjectionable, is also kept in the office of the examiner, arranged and numbered in the order in which they are reported.

In 1848 petitions were presented complaining of the invalidity of the recognizances which had been entered into in the case of several election petitions then pending, and of which the sureties had been reported unobjectionable. After numerous discussions, and an inquiry by a committee, an Act was passed ' to enable the election committees of that session to decide upon any objections to the recognizances, which, under the provisions of the Act then in force, could not previously have been made by the sitting member, and in certain cases to amend the recognizance or permit another to be entered into. But by the 11 12 Vict., c, 98, 8. 17, the report of the examiner of recognizances upon the validity of a recognizance " is final and conclusive to all intents and puiposcs."

It is competent to a petitioner to withdraw his petition at any time after its presentation, upon giving notice in writing under his own hand, or that of his agent, to the speaker, and to the sitting member or his agent, and to any party admitted to oppose the petition, that it is not intended to proceed with the petition. In such case the petitioner is liable to the payment of the taxed costs and expenses incurred by the sitting member and others opposing the petition. When a petition is thus withdrawn, the order for referring it to the general committee of elections is discharged.

If, before the appointment of a select committee to try a petition, the seat of the member petitioned against should become vacant, or if the sitting member should decline to defend his return, by a declaration in writing, subscribed by him, and delivered to the speaker within fourteen days ' 11 1-2 Vict., c. 18. = 103 Com. J. 210, c.

' See form of notice to the sjicaker of tlie deatli of a member, 28tli Feb. 1848, 103 Com. J. 275.

after the presentation of the petition, notice is immediately sent by the speaker to the general committee of elections and to the chairman's panel, and also to the sheriff or re-tnrning officer, who is to affix a copy of such notice at the door of the county or town hall. The notice is also inserted, by order of the speaker, in one of the next two London Gazettes, and is communicated by him to the house.

Within fourteen days after the presentation of the peti- Voters may be-tion, or within twenty-one days after the insertion in the oppose the pe-Gazette of a notice that the seat is vacant, or that the ' i"-member will not defend his return, any person who voted or had a right to vote at the election may petition the house, praying to be admitted as a party to defend the return, or to oppose the prayer of the election petition, and will be admitted to defend the seat accordingly. If the time limited for receiving such petitions should expire during a prorogation or adjournment, the petition will be received on or before the second day on which the house shall afterwards meet.

Whenever the member whose return Is complained of J ienii)er not has given notice of his intention not to defend his seat, return nmy not he may not appear or act in any proceedings as a party ' ' ' ' against the petition; and he may not sit in the House of Commons, nor vote on any question, until the petition has been decided upon.

Where there is a double return, and the member whose Doumo rcium. return is complained of has declined to defend his return, and no party has been admitted to defend it; if the otlicr member has not been petitioned against, the petition complaining of the double return may be Avlthdrawn. The house Avill then order the clerk of the crown to attend and amend the return by taking off the file the indenture by which the member whose return had been complained of was returned."

' 11 12 Vict., c. 98, 9. 21; Montgomery election, 14tli Fehruaiy 1848, 103 Com. J. 218.

General committee of elections appointed.

Appointment (lisa)proved.

jvIembors ap-)oint('d for the session.

Vacancies.

Dissolution of committee.

Having tlius briefly stated tlic rules appointed by the liouse and by statute, in regard to the j etition, the recognizances and sureties, and the several parties to a controverted election; it is now proposed to describe the mode of appointing the tribunal to try the case.

At the beginning of every session, the speaker appoints, by warrant, six members of the house as " The General Committee of Elections." The members appointed must be willing to serve, their seats must be unquestioned by petition, and they must not themselves be petitioners against any election. The speaker's warrant is laid upon the table of the house, and if not disapproved of by the house, in the course of the three next sitting days, it takes effect, as the appointment of the committee.

If the house should disapprove the warrant, the speaker is required, within three days, to lay upon the table a new warrant. The disapproval of the warrant may either be general, in respect to the constitution of the whole committee, or sjiecial in respect of any member named in the warrant; and the speaker, in his new Avarrant, may name again those members who have not been specially disapproved.

After the appointment of the general committee, every member retains his appointment until the end of the session, unless, in the meanwhile, he ceases to be a member of the house, resigns his appointment, or is reported to be disabled, by continued sickness, from attending the committee. In case of a vacancy, the speaker makes it known to the house immediately, and all the proceedings of the committee are suspended until the vacancy is siip)licd. This is done by the speaker's warrant, which is subject to disapproval in the same manner as the original appointment.

The committee is liable to be dissolved at any time, from the following causes: 1. On the report of the committee, that they are unable to proceed in the discharge of their duties by reason of the absence of more than two of their members; 2. On their report that they are unable to proceed on account of irreconcilable disagreement of opinion; 3. Or the house may resolve, generally, that the committee be dissolved.

When from any of these causes the committee has been Reappoint- 1-1 ineiit.

dissolved, the speaker reappomts tlie committee by warrant; and may reappoint any of the former members if he pleases. The reappointment may be disapproved by the house, in the same manner as the original appointment.

To this committee, all election petitions are referred, Election i eti- ,.,.,. (1 1 n t " referred and it IS their duty to choose a committee tor the trial oi to general each petition in the manner appointed by the Act, which gj'ectjyi j' will presently be explained. The speaker communicates to the committee all reports concerning the recognizances, all notices of deaths or vacancies, and declarations of sitting members that they do not intend to defend their seats; and whenever a petition is withdrawn, or the recognizances are reported to be objectionable, the order for referring the petition to the general committee is discharged by the house. When notice of the death, or vacancy of the seat of a member, or that he declines to defend his seat, has been given, the committee suspend their proceedings upon the petition against him, for twenty-one days; unless a petition of persons claiming to defend the seat, be referred to them at an earlier period.

When more than one petition relating to the same Where more election have been referred to the general committee, they tjon suspend their proceedings ujjon all of them, until the report of the examiner of recognizances has been received upon each. Upon the receipt of the last of these reports the petitions are placed at the bottom of the list of election petitions; and are bracketed together, and afterwards treated as one petition.

The speaker appoints the time and place of the first First meeting meeting of the general committee; and before any member of pencralcom-

Quorum of general committee.

Members excused from serving on election committees, being above sixty.

List of excused members read.

of tlie committee Is qualified to serve upon it, he must have been svv orn at the table of the house, " truly and faithfully to perform the duties belonging to a member of the said committee, to the best of his judgment and ability, "without fear or favour."

No business can be transacted by the general committee unless four of the members be present; and no appointment of an election committee can be made by them, unless at least four out of the six agree in the appointment. Subject to these limitations, and to the several provisions of the Act, the general committee are empowered to make regulations for the order and manner of conducting the business transacted by them. The minutes of their proceedings are kept by the committee clerk in attendance upon them, in whatever form they may direct, and are to be laid before the house from time to time.

In case of the dissolution or suspension of the proceedings of the general committee, the speaker may adjourn any business that may be pending.

Every member who is upwards of sixty years old, is wholly excused from serving upon a committee for the trial of election petitions; but he must make his claim on that groimd, either in his place, or in writing under his hand, to be delivered to the clerk at the table. He is required to make his claim on or before the reading over the names of other members who have been excused; or afterwards, if he shall then become entitled to make that claim. But no member can be excused, unless he has made his claim before he is chosen to serve upon an election committee.

In the first session of a Parliament, on the next meeting of the house after the last day allowed for receiving election petitions, and in other sessions, on the next meeting after the speaker has laid on the table bis warrant for tha appointment of the general committee, the clerk of the house is required to read over all tiie names of the members who have claimed to be excused on account of age. At this Members tem-time other excuses may be made, and allowed by the house, cuseci! ' The substance of the allegations is taken down by the clerk, and the ground of excuse, and the opinion of the house, are entered in the Journals. Excuses of the high officers of state, that they could not attend election committees without material inconvenience to the public service, are generally made and admitted. The chairman of ways and means has also been excused, on the ground that the house had devolved upon him the duty of sitting as chairman of all committees upon unopposed private bills, and that he would be unable to perform that duty, if selected to serve on an election committee. All these excuses are only temporary, and are invariably limited by the house to the time during which the parties may hold their offices: they may be made at any time after the reading of the names of excused members; but in no case after a member has been chosen to serve upon an election committee.

Besides these excuses allowed in each case by the house. General excuses there are two other general grounds of excuse, which do not require a particular order: 1. Every member who has obtained leave of absence from the house, is excused from serving upon any election committee appointed, until his leave of absence has expired. 2. Every member who has served upon one election committee, and who, within seven days after its report, notifies to the clerk of the general committee his claim to be excused from serving again, is excused during the remainder of the session; unless the house, on the report of the general committee, resolve that the number of members who have not served is insufficient. But no member is entitled to claim exemption upon this ground, who, on account of inability or accident, has been 97 Com. J. 48. G G

Temporary disqualifications.

List of mem-liers printed with the Votes.

Correction of list.

Chairmen's panel

Vacancit's in chuirmeu's panel.

excused from attending an election committee throughout its proceedings.

Every member complaining of an undue election or return, who is a petitioner, or against whose return a petition is depending, is disqualified during the continuance of such ground of disqualification.

When all the usual excuses have been made, as above described, the clerk is required to prepare an alphabetical list of all the members of the house, omitting the names of those who have claimed to be wholly excused from serving. In this list, he distinguishes the name of every member who is for the time excused or disqualified; and notes the cause and duration of each excuse and disqualification. The list is printed and distributed with the Votes, and the names of all the members omitted are printed and distributed in the same manner. During three days after its distribution the list may be further corrected by leave of the speaker, if it should appear that any name has been improperly left in or struck out, or that there is any other error.

The list of members, when thus finally corrected, is referred to the general committee of elections. Their first duty is to select six, eight, ten, or twelve members to serve as chairmen of election committees, who are called " the chairmen's panel," and whose names are reported to the house. These members, unless sooner discharged by the house, are liable to serve as chairmen of election committees for the remainder of the session, whenever appointed to that ofllice; but they are exempted and disqualified from serving on election committees in any other capacity than that of chairman; and when they have served throughout upon one or more election committees, they may be excused from further service.

Whenever a member of the chairmen's panel ceases to be a member of the house, or is discharged from further service, the general committee immediately appoint another in his place; and if the number originally appointed should, at any timcj appear too small tor the number of committees about to sit, the general committee may select two, four, or six additional members; but in no case may the chairmen's panel consist of more than eighteen members, without the leave of the house.

The members of the chairmen's panel make regulations Rcgniationg of amongst themselves for the appointment of chairmen of panel, election committees, and for the equal distribution of their duties. The time and manner of appointing chairmen will be more particularly explained when the proceedings in the nomination of the committees have been described.

When the general committee have selected the chair- List divided men's panel, they divide all the members remaining upon "' ' " ' the list into five panels, in whatever manner may appear convenient; but each panel is required to contain, as nearly as may be, the same number of members. These panels are reported to the house, and the clerk decides by lot, at the table, the order in which they shall stand, and diijtinguishes each by a number. They are returned to the general committee, and the election committees are chosen from each panel, in succession, according to its number.

The general committee correct the panels, from time to Correction of time, by striking out the names of persons who have " ' ceased to be members, or who have been wholly excused from serving; and by adding new members. They continue to distinguish the names of members who are, for the time, excused or disqualified; and whenever they think fit, they report the corrected panels to the house, which are printed and distributed with the Votes, as before. When leave of absence has been granted to a member. Members ab-the general committee may transfer his name from one transferrettto panel to another subsequent in rotation, and from which t" " panels.

' See infra, p. 454. G G (ieiienil committee to determine when committees shall be chosen.

Notices.

When seat is vacant or not defended.

When time of choosing committees is altered.

SI cominittce will be chosen at a later period. By tliid arrangement, if election committees have been chosen from a member's panel, during his absence, he may find his name transferred to another on his return, and will be liable to serve as if he had been originally placed upon a later panel.

The general committee choose committees to try peti tions in the order in which they stand on the list, and determine how many committees shall be chosen in each week, and the days on which they will meet to choose them; and within two days after their first meeting, they appoint days on which to appoint committees to try petitions standing over from a previous session. Notice of the time and place at which every election committee will be chosen, is published with the Votes fourteen days before the committee is to be chosen; and when the conduct of the returning officer is complained of, a like notice is sent to him. Every notice directs all parties interested to attend the general committee, by themselves, or their agents, at the time and place appointed for choosing the election committee. Notice is also published with the Votes of the petitions appointed for each week, and of the panel from which each conmiittee will be chosen.

When notice has appeared in the Gazette that a member petitioned against is dead, that his seat is vacant, or that he declines to defend his return, and no party has been admitted to defend his return, if the conduct of the returning officer is not complained of, the general committee may meet to appoint the select committee at any time after the expiration of the time allowed for parties to come in to defend the return; but not less than one day's notice, of the time and place appointed for choosing the committee, must be given in the Votes.

After the general committee have appointed a time for choosing an election committee, they may change it whenever they think fit; but they must give notice in the Votes of the change, and must report it immediately to the house, with their reasons for the alteration.

Six days before the time appointed for choosing the Lists of voters committee (except in the case of undefended seats), the parties complaining of, or defending the election, are required to deliver to the clerk of the general committee, lists of the voters intended to be objected to, with the several heads of objection to each. They must be delivered not later than six o'clock on the sixth day before the choosing of the committee; and are afterwards open to the inspection of all parties concerned.

At the time appointed, the general committee choose Election com-four members from the panel in service; but no member may be chosen, 1, who has voted at the election; oi, 2, who is the party on whose behalf the seat is claimed; or, 3, who is related to the sitting member or party on whose behalf the seat is claimed, by kindred or affinity in the first or second degree according to the canon law. Each panel From what serves for a week, beginning with that first drawn, and not reckonincr those weeks in which no election committee is appointed to be chosen.

Unless four members, at least, of the general committee. Disagreement ., in the choice of agree m the choice of an election committee, they must a committee.

adjourn the choosing of that and every other committee remaining to be chosen on that day; and must meet on the following day, and from day to day, until they agree; and the parties are to be directed to attend on each day. If they do not agree at last, their disagreement being irreconcileable, will be reported to the house, and the general committee will be dissolved. The general committee may not proceed to choose a committee to try an election petition until they have chosen a committee to try every other petition standing higher on the list.

On the day appointed by the general committee for Parties io hear choosing an election committee, the chairmen's panel j."ot to disqna-appoint the chairman, and when the committee ie con- litied members

Disqualifica-tiou allowed.

Members chose n served with notice.

stituted, the parties in attendance are called in, and the names of the committee are read over to them. The parties then withdraw,, and the committee proceed with the choice of other committees ai)pointcd to be chosen on that day. Within half an hour, or after other parties have witli-drawn, the parties who have been consulting upon the names of the selected members, are again called in, in the same order in which they were directed to withdraw. The petitioners first, and after-. yards the sitting members, or parties defending the return, or their agents, may then object to all or any of the members chosen, or to the chairman, as being disqualified or excused from serving on tliat committee, for any of the reasons allowed by the Act, but not for any other reason.

If, at least, four members of the general committee be satisfied, on hearing the objections, that any member whom they have chosen is disqualified or excused, the parties are again directed to withdraw, and the committee proceed to the choice of another committee, from the same panel; or if such member be the chairman, another chairman is named by the chairmen's panel. The general committee may include in the second, or following committees, any of the menjbers first chosen to whom no objection has been substantiated; and no party may object to a member included in a subsequent committee who was not objected to when on the committee first chosen.

When four members and a chairman have been chosen, against whom no objection has been sustained, the clerk of the general committee gives notice, in writing, to each of the members, that he lias been appointed to serve upon the election committee. This notice points out every general and special ground of disqualification and excuse from serving, and names the time and i)lace at which the general committee will meet on the following day. In addition to this personal notice, the time and place of meeting are published with the Votes.

At the time thus appointed, any member who has been imen. i)ers may chosen may attend, and allege his disqualification. If he ficatiou. can prove to the satisfaction of, at least, four members of the genend committee that, for any of the proper reasons, he is disqualified, or excused i'rom serving on the committee to which he has been named; or if he can prove any circumstances, having regard, not to his own convenience, but solely to the impartial character of the tribunal, which render him ineligible; the general committee proceed to choose another committee, in the same manner as if the member had been objected to by the parties. If no member appear within a quarter of an hour, or if, on appearing, he fail to prove his disqualification or excuse, the constitution of the election committee is complete.

At the next meeting of the house, the general committee Election com- I 1 1 1 11 1 inittee re- rcport the names oi the committee, together with all the portedj petitions relating to the election, and the lists of voters; and this report is published with the Votes. On the next sitting day, at or before four o'clock, the members chosen are required to attend in their places, and before they leave the house to be sworn ' at the table by the clerk, " well and members and truly to try the matter of the petitions referred to " ""' them, and a true judgment to give, according to the evidence."

If any member should not attend within an hour after inlembers not four o'clock (if the house sit so long), or should leave the P" " " house before the committee is sworn (unless the committee be discharged, or the swearing adjourned), he is ordered into the custody of the serjeant-at-arms for his neglect of duty, and will be otherwise punished or censured, at the discretion of the house, unless it shall appear, by facts specially stated, and verified upon oath, that he was, by a sudden accident, or by necessity, prevented from attenduig ' If a Quaker, c., he will ho permitted solemnly to declare, 1U3 Com. J. oflg.- 100 Com J. Mo. oqo.

Swoarini jourued.

ail-

Comiuittco dis-c'liarged in certain cuses.

Meeting ofcom-niittee fixed by tlie house.

General caution to members.

the house. If the absent member should not be brought into the house within three hours after four o'clock, and if no sufficient cause can be shown for dispensing with his attendance, the swearing of the committee is adjourned luitil the next meeting of the house, when all the members of the committee must again be in attendance.

If, on the day to which the swearing is adjourned, all the members do not attend and be sworn within one hour after four o'clock, or if sufficient cause be shown on the day first appointed for the swearing, why the attendance of a member should be dispensed with, the committee is discharged. The general committee are then obliged to meet on the following day, or on the day to which the house stands adjourned, and choose a new committee from the same panel, and notice of their meeting is published with the Votes.

When all the members have been sworn, the house refers the petitions and lists of voters to the committee, and orders them to meet at a certain time, within twenty-four hours of their being sworn. Eleven o'clock on the following morning is the hour generally appointed, and they meet at that time in one of the committee rooms of the house.

Before the proceedings of an election committee are entered upon, it may prove useful to call the particular attention of members to the necessity of making themselves acquainted with the practice of the house in appointing svich committees, and with their own position and liabilities. If they neglect to attend at the proper time (as they too often do), they subject themselves to annoyance and expense, and may cause serious pecuniary damage to the parties. By a little attention to the course of proceedings, a member may always avoid being taken by surprise. He should first examine the panels which are printed and distributed with the Votes, and by observing the number of that in which his own name is inserted, he may judge how soon it is possible that he may be chosen. lie must bear in mind that a new panel is in the order of service for every week in which election connnittees are appointed; and if his absence should be unavoidable during the week in which committees will be chosen from his panel, he should apply to the house for leave of absence. He is acquainted also, every Saturday' morning, by a conspicuous notice in the Votes, what election committees will be chosen during the ensuing week, from what panel, and on what days; and if he be on that panel, he should be in readiness, in case he should be appointed on any one of the committees, and receive notice to attend and be sworn.

Every election committee must sit from day to day Committees to (with the exception of Sunday, Christmas-day, and Good Friday), and may not adjourn for a longer time than twenty-four hours, without obtaining leave from the house, upon motion, and assigning a special reason for a longer adjournment. If the house should be sitting at the time to which a committee has been adjourned, the business of the house will be stayed until a motion has been made for a further adjournment, for any time to be fixed by the house. When the house has been adjourned for more than twenty-four hours, and a committee have occasion to ap)ly or report to the house, they may adjourn to the day appointed for the next meeting of the house.

No member of an election conunittee may absent him- Member of self without leave obtained from the house, or an excuse to absent him-allowed by the house at its next sitting. If the excuse self, offered be on account of sickness, it must be verified upon the oath of his medical attendant; and if any other special cause be assigned, it must also be verified upon oath.

' When the house sits on Saturday, this notice may not appear until Monday morning, as the orders of the day, notices, and other business for the ensuing week, are not then printed with the Votes delivered on Saturday morning, hut are deferred till no further change can be made in them.

Whenever a member has leave to absent himself, or his excuse is allowed, he is discharged from further attendance, and is not entitled to sit and vote again in the committee. Committee not If, on the meeting of the committee, all the members uieet'

"' "' who are not excused should not be present, the committee cannot proceed to any business, but must wait for an hour; and if within that time the whole number have not arrived, the conuiiittee must adjourn, and the chairman is required to report the adjournment, and its cause, to the house, A member absenting himself without leave or excuse is directed to attend the house at its next sitting; and unless he can show by facts, verified upon oath, that his attendance had been prevented by sudden accident or necessity, he will be ordered into custody, and otherwise punished or censured at the discretion of the house. Committees In casc the number of members able to attend an elec- numbe'rv"wheu tion Committee should be reduced to less than three, and dissolved. should Continue so reduced for three sitting days, the com- mittee will be dissolved, their proceedings become void, and another committee will be appointed. But if all the parties consent, two, or even one member, may continue to act, and be the committee. Chairman of If the chairman should die, or be unable to attend, the

"' remaining members of the committee elect one of them-selves to be chairman; and in case of an equality of voices, the member whose name stands first in the list of the committee, as reported to the house, is entitled to a second or casting vote. Committees Evcry election committee is attended by a short-hand attended by. i i i i i r i i n i.

short-hand writer, appointed by the clerk of the house, and sworn by the chairman to take down the evidence faithfully and truly, and to write it down in words at length, for the use of the committee.

Witnesses It will have been remarked, that all the election pro- exammed upon ggc jpo; s in tlic housc are distinn-uished by the administra-oath. td J tion of oaths; and the evidence taken before election com- inittees is marked by the same solemnity. Every election conmiittee has power to send for persons, papers, and records; and the witnesses ai-e examined upon oath, wliioh the clerk of the committee is empowered to administer. Parties who have subscribed the petition may be examined, unless they appear to be interested witnesses. If any persons summoned by the committee, or by a speaker's warrant, disobey the summons; or if witnesses give false evidence, prevaricate, or misbehave themselves before the committee in giving, or refusing to give evidence, the chairman, by direction of the committee, reports the circumstance to the house." Thus far the practice, in dealing with ill-conducted witnesses, is the same as in other committees, where censure and punishment are reserved for the house to inflict; but in election committees, the chairman is, in the meantime, authorized to commit any witness (not being a peer of the realm, or lord of Parliament) to the custody of the serjeant-at-ainns, by a warrant under his hand, for any time not exceeding twenty-four hours, if the house be sitting; and if not, then for a time not exceeding twenty-four hours after the hour to which the house is adjourned. By this power, the escape of a witness may be prevented, and he is kept in safe custody until the house can censure or punish him for his oftxince.

A further diiference exists, in the case of elections, in False evijence the mode of punishing false testimony given before the pp"J'"'y. house or committees. In ordinary inquiries, as it has been shown elsewhere, the house can only regard false evidence as a breach of privilege and contempt;" but the Election Act, which confers upon it the power of administering oaths, attaches to false evidence the penalties of wilful and corrupt perjury. The power of the house to punish is not, however, superseded by the Act; and it may, there- ' See the several proceedings in regard to witnesses before an election committee, in the case of the Ipswich election in 18:3"), and 103 Com. J. 2."j8. See supra, p. 315.

fore, imprison witnesses, as in any other case, upon its own authority; and if it appear that a conviction at law can also be obtained, it is competent for the house to direct the attorney-general to prosecute the offending witnesses for perjury.

Lists of objec- As a general rule, the committee may admit any evidence which is offered, and which appears to them to be legally admissible; but in regard to tiie validity of votes, they are precluded by the Act from taking evidence upon any vote not previously contained in the lists of voters objected to, or upon any head of objection that had not been specified in the lists.

Majority de Every question is determined in the committee (when it consists of more than one member) by a majority of voices; and whenever the voices are equal, the chairman has a second or casting vote. Here the practice differs from that of other committees. The chairman does not wait to give his vote until the numbers are equal, but votes, in the first instance, like any other member; and if the numbers, inchiding his own vote, be equal, he decides the question by a second vote, in his capacity of chairman. Every member is obliged to vote upon each question, whenever a division arises; and the names of the members who vote in the affirmative or negative upon every question, are entered upon the minutes, and afterwards reported to the house.

Deliberate with Whenever the committee are about to deliberate upon c ose oors. question, in the course of their proceedings, as soon as they have heard the evidence and counsel on both sides, they may order the room to be cleared; and this practice is always observed, except when minor points arise, which may be settled without debate or division, by a brief conference between the members.

Witnesses It is a general rule that all witnesses who are to be examined before a committee are excluded from the room ' 75 Com. J. 332.

while other witnesses are under examination, and if, when called on, they prove to have been present, their evidence is not admitted. Agents and barristers are exceptions to this rule; and in special cases others have been allowed to be examined although they have been present." In order to give due notice of this rule to all the parties concerned, a paper is affixed to the door of every committee room, stating that " no witnesses are admitted;" but a more distinct explanation of the consequences might advantageously be given in a printed form, and in more conspicuous characters.

The counsel who opens a case before a committee, should Counsel. include in his statement the leading matters intended to be proved; or he may be afterwards precluded from adducing evidence in support of charges not previously alluded to. This rule is enforced with more or less strictness according to the view taken by the committee of the sufficiency of the general statement to embrace particular facts. The ordinary rules are observed in regard to the speeches and replies of counsel, and the examination, cross-examination, and re-examination of witnesses; and the committee determine every disputed point.

When the case, on behalf of all parties, is concluded, Decision of the room is cleared and the committee deliberate upon """' "" their final determination of the merits of the election. They are required to decide distinctly, 1. Whether the petitioners or the sitting members, or either of them, be duly returned or elected; or, 2. Whether the election be void; or, 3. Whether a new writ ought to issue. Their determination upon these points is final between the parties: and the house, on being informed of it, carries it into execution.

If the committee come to any resolution other than this Special reports. determination, they may report it to the house; but in that ' 2 Rogers, 98. Burroii and Austin, 58G, case It is not final; and the house may confirm or disagree with their resolution, or make whatever orders it thinks fit. The most frequent subject of a special report is the bribery or treating' proved to have been conunitted at the election. And here may be exemplified the distinction between those parts of the report which are final and those which are treated as matters of opinion only. An act of bribery disqualifies a member from serving in the House of Commons during the whole Parliament, for the county, city, or borough for which he had been returned, and if proved before a committee, is suflftcient to enable them to detei'mine, according to the Bribery Act, that his election was void. That determination alone is reported to the house in the first instance, and is final; but the committee add to their report a special resolution concerning the bribery. Special reports are also made concerning riots at elections, the conduct of returning officers, defects in the law, or any other circumstances which have been brought under their notice during the inquiry. Special reports It was formerly at the discretion of a committee to Agency!" ' report acts of bribery to the house, but a more distinct and stringent law has altered both the mode of inquiry and the character of the report, when bribery is alleged to have influenced an election. The obvious course in proving bribery not committed personally by the sitting member or candidate, is to establish the agency of parties who are alleged to have committed bribery on his behalf; and accordingly, until the agency was proved, it was usual for the committee to refuse to enter into general evidence of bribery; because if bribery were proved against persons not authorized by the candidate or sitting member to commit it, the merits of the election would not be affected. On this account notorious acts of bribery often failed in ' 7 Will. III., c. 4; 5 and C Will. III., c. 102. 522.

being proved, and of course the committee could not make a special report upon matters not establislied by the evidence. In order to expose acts of bribeiy more effectually, this practice has been materially altered.

By the Act 4 5 Vict. c. 57, it is enacted. Proof of agency. " That wherever a charge of bribery shall have been broiifjlit before any election committee of the House of Commons, the committee shall receive evidence upon the whole matter whereon it is alleged that bribery has been committed; neither shall it be necessary to prove agency, in the first instance, before giving evidence of those facts whereby the charge of bribery is to be sustained: and the committee, in their rejiort, shall separately and distinctly report upon the fact or facts of bribery which shall have been proved before them, and also whether or not it shall have been proved that such bribery was committed with the knowledge and consent of any sitting member or candidate at the election."

By this mode of inquiry, the discovery of acts of bribery Results of this is, undoubtedly, much facilitated; and in the course of the evidence, proofs or implications of agency may be elicited, which might not have arisen if the evidence had been confined, in the first instance, to the strict proof of agency. Since the passing of this Act the seats of several members have been avoided by the acts of their agents; and committees have reported that sitting members have been, by or through their agents, guilty of bribery; and, at the same time, that there was no evidence to show that any acts of bribery were committed with their knowledge and consent." Such determinations have been founded upon the principle that, so far as his seat in Parliament is concerned, a proof of general agency for the management of an election, is sufficient to make the principal civilly responsible for every unauthorized and illegal act committed by his agent, by which his own return had been secured. This principle, however, has been extended much further, and, in apparent 97 Com. J. 2G0. 279. Sfjl. Barron and Austin, 401. 453. 584. 009.

contratliction of the Bribery Act," lias been construed so as to attach the penalties of bribery to the principal, although such bribery has been committed by his agents, without his knowledge and consent. In 1842 the election of Mr. Harris for Newcastlc-undei-Lyne was avoided, by reason of bribery, but the Committee reported that " no evidence was given to show that these acts of bribery were committed with the knowledge and consent of Mr. Harris." Mr. Harris was re-elected, and petitioned against, and the Committee determined, "that Mr. Harris having been declared, by a Committee of the House of Commons, to have been guilty of bribery by his agents, at the previous election for the borough of Newcastle-under-Lyne, and that election having been avoided, was incapable of being elected at the election which took i lace in consequence of such avoidance."" And in later cases the same principle has been extended to unsuccessful candidates at a previous election. Writs SU3 When general and notorious bribery and corruption have pended.,.,. i i i i been proved to prevail in parliamentary boroughs, the iiouse have frequently suspended the issue of writs, Avith a view to further inquiry, and the ultimate disfranchisement of the corrupt constituency, by Act of Parliament.

' The words of the Act, 49 Geo. 3, c. 118, are, " and every such person so returned and so having given, or so having promised to give, or lowwing of and consenthuj to svich gifts or promises, upon any such engagement, contract, or agreement, shall be disabled and incapacitated to serve in that Parliament, for that county, c., and deemed and taken to be no member of Parliament, and as if he had never been returned or elected."

' Barron and Austin, p. 5G4.

2d Cheltenham petition, and 2d Horsham petition, 1848; 103 Com. J. 973. 1005.

Liverpool, 8G Cora. J. 458, 493. Warwick, 88 lb. Oil; 89 lb. 9. 579. Carrickfergus, 88 lb. 531. 599. Hertford, 88 lb. 578. G49. Stafford, 90 lb. 202, c. Sudbury, 97 lb. 188. 4G7, c., Act 7 8 Vict. c. 53. Ipswich, 97 Com. J. 221. 554. Yarmouth freemen, 103 lb. 213, 11 12 Vict. c. 24. Harwich, 103 Cum. J. 330. 702.

And by the 5 6 Vict. c. 102, if an election committee Election cnm-recommend further inquiry regarding bribery, the speaker "ssembicli'to is required to nominate an agent to)rosecute the investi- '"'lu're i"to ' bribery.

gation; and the committee are to re-assemble within fourteen days, and to inquire and report specially concerning the bribery, and the parties implicated. The committee, when re-assembled, possess all their original powers of inquiry. And by the same Act if charges of bribery be cimrfrcs of withdrawn, the committee are empowered to inquire into ",", ej " ""' and report the causes of their abandonment. Special Appointment powers are also given to the house, in certain cases, to othctcases. appoint election committees upon petitions complaining of bribery; and Avhen election petitions have been withdrawn. But no such committee, whether re-assembled or appointed to investigate the matter of a petition presented after the time limited for receiving election petitions, can affect the seat of any member, or the issue or restraining the issue of any writ.

Unlike the other proceedings of Parliament, the inqiii- committee not ries of election committees are not determined by a pro- ' ' o ' ". ' y ' i prorogation.

rogation. When an election petition is presented to the house before a prorogation, and a committee has not been appointed to try it, the general committee of elections in the ensuing session, within two days of their first meeting, appoint a day for choosing a committee, if, in the meantime, the recognizances have been reported unobjectionable. And when Parliament is prorogued after the appointment of an election committee, and before they have reported their determination, the committee are not dissolved, but only adjourn until 12 o'clock on the day following the meeting of Parliament for despatch of business. In the ensuing session they resume their sittings, as if there had been no prorogation: their former proceedings are valid, and they continue subject to the ordinary rules of election committees.

Costs, when iiiciirrod by jjetitioners; by parties opi)osiiig petitions, or not appcar-
Costs upon frivolous olyec-tions, and unfounded a leic; itions.
Costs, how ascertained.

Whenever an election committee report that a petition appeared to them frivolous or vexatious, the party or parties who appeared in opposition to it are entitled to recover from any of the persons who signed the petition, the full costs and expenses incurred in the opposition. In the same manner, parties opposing a petition frivolously or vexatiously, are liable to the payment of costs to the petitioners. When no party appears to defend an election or return, and the committee report it to have been vexatious or corrupt, the sitting member (unless he has given notice of his intention not to defend it), or the parties admitted to defend the return, are liable to the costs incurred by the petitioners In prosecuting their petition.

When any ground of objection Is stated to a voter. In the list of voters intended to be objected to, and the objection is reported by the committee to have been frivolous or vexatious, the opposite party may recover costs from the party by whom, or on whose behalf, the objection was made. And if either party should make, before an election committee, any specific allegation with regard to the conduct of the other party or his agents, and should either bring no evidence in support of It, or such evidence that the committee consider the allegation to have been made without any reasonable or probable ground, the committee may order the party who made It to pay all the costs and expenses incurred by the other party, by reason of the unfounded allegation.

All such costs and expenses adjudged by the connnlttee to be paid, whether incurred in prosecuting, or opposing, or preparing to oppose, election petitions, or payable to witnesses summoned before committees, are taxed in the following manner: Within three months after the conclusion of the proceedings, application may be made to the speaker to ascertain the costs and expenses incurred; and he directs them to be taxed by the examiner of recog-

COMimISSION TO EXAMINE WITNESSES IN ineLAND. 469 nizances, or by the taxing officer of the House of Commons. The examiner, or taxing officer, taxes them, and reports to the speaker the amount due, the names of the parties liable to pay and entitled to receive them; and the speaker, on being applied to, delivers to the parties a certificate of the costs allowed, which is conclusive evidence of the title of the parties to recover their claims.

The recovery of the costs, if not paid on demand, is by Recovery of costs.

an action of debt; in which a declaration, together with the speaker's certificate and an affidavit of demand, entitles the plaintiff to sign judgment as for want of pica by nil dicit, and take out execution for the sum and for the costs of the action; and the validity of the speaker's certificate cannot be called in question in any court. The plaintiff may sue any one of the parties who are jointly liable; and he, in his turn, may sue the others for their proportions.

The recognizances may be estreated if the petitioners Recognizances wicn cstrctcd neglect or refuse to pay a witness for seven days after any sum has been certified by the speaker to be due to him; or if, for six months after the speaker's certificate, they neglect or refuse to pay any party opposing the petition the sum certified to be due to him, such neglect or refusal being proved to the satisfaction of the speaker within one year after his certificate is granted. In case of such default, the speaker certifies the recognizance into the Court of Exchequer, which has the same effect as if the recognizance were estreated from a court of law.

In order to avoid the inconvenience and expense of Commission to examining witnesses from Ireland, a committee, appointed ncsses' n re-for the trial of a petition complaining of an election in ' "' Ireland, are empowered, on the application of any of the parties, to appoint a commission." This application may be made at any time during the proceedings, but notice 42 Geo. III. e. 106; 47 Geo. III. sess. l, c. 14, s. 5; GO Geo. III. c. 7. H II

Commissioners, bow appointed.

Chairnifin uj))uinted.

Wlirn parties ajine.

Wlierc more than two parties.

must be served on the opposite party as soon as the petition is presented. If the committee do not think it necessary to appoint a commission, they proceed as in other cases.

At the commencement of every session, the clerk of the Crown in Ireland is required to send to the speaker a list of barristers of six years' standing, who have consented to act as commissioners, and from this list the commissioners are selected in the following manner. On the next sitting of the committee, after an order has been made for the appointment of commissioners, each party delivers the names of three of the qualified barristers; and from the list of all the proposed names, each party, beginning with the petitioners, strikes off the name of one barrister, until the number has been redaced to two.

The 47 Geo. 3, stat,. 1, c. 14, s. 2, declares that no person shall be a commissioner who has voted at the election in question, or who has, or claims to have, any right to vote, without the consent of the parties; and (s. 3) that any objection to the appointment of a commissioner shall be made at the time of his appointment, or otherwise shall be of no effect.

Immediately after the appointment of these two commissioners, a third is appointed to act as chairman. If all the parties agree in the appointment of one of the barristers on the list, he is appointed the chairman; but if they cannot agree, the committee nominate as chairman a barrister on the list who has not been struck off by either of the parties."

If all the parties agree to nominate three barristers and deliver the names to the chairman, signed by the parties, they are appointed commissioners, without these formalities, and they choose one of themselves to be their chairman.

But where there are more than two parties upon distinct interests, and there appears to be no collusion between ' 42 Geo. III. c. loG, s. 8, 9.

them, none of the parties are permitted to deliver a list, but the committee appoint the commissioners and nominate Avhich of the three shall act as chairman.

When the commissioners are appointed, the chairman Warrant to or the committee issues a warrant cominandmg them to repair, on a certain day, to the place to which the petition relates; and addresses to their chairman a copy of the petition, and of the lists and disputed votes, and statements of the several parties, together with the order of the committee, specially assigning and limiting the facts and allegations concerning which they are to examine evidence, and all documents which the committee may think proper to refer.

The committee report these proceedings to the house, committee and ask permission to adjourn until they are re-assembled adiourir' by the speaker's warrant. They are also to state that they have gone through all the other parts of the petition, except those which have been specially referred to the commissioners.

The commissioners have the same powers as an election powers and committee to send for persons, papers, and records, and to "iss'ioners'"' examine witnesses upon oath; but they may not suffer counsel to plead before them. Within ten days after the Proceedings evidence is closed, or with all convenient despatch, assign- '"' "' '" "' ' ing reasons for the delay, the commissioners arc required to cause two copies of the minutes of proceedings and evidence to be made out, and to transmit one to the clerk of the Crown in Ireland, and the other to the speaker, who communicates it to the house.

If the commissioners object to any evidence offered Evidence oi)- 1 p 1 1., in JKCted to by before them, they are to state in writing the grounds of commissioners their objection, and the party tendering the evidence may separatdy!" require the commissioners to examine it. Evidence taken ' For the form of such a report, see!)3 Com. J. 583 (Wustmeath election).

GO Geo. III. c. 7; 94 Com. J. 7.

in this manner is transmitted separately, with the other proceedings, in the nature of a bill of exceptions to evidence; and if the committee should report that its production was frivolous or vexatious, the party who produced it is liable to costs.

Coinmittee Within two days after the receipt of the copy of the proceedings, the speaker is requn-ed to insert m the JUon-don Gazette a warrant directing the committee to meet ao; ain within a month: or if Parliament should not be sitting, within a month after the commencement of the next session, or of the meeting of the house after an adjournment."

Use of evidence "-pi Q committee when re-assembled may receive no further taken ui Ire ' land. evidence respecting any matter already examined by the commissioners, but determine from the written minutes. They may hear counsel, however, as to the effect of the evidence; and if the evidence appear incomplete, they may, at any time before their report, direct a warrant for re-assembling the commissioners. By the 47 Geo. III. c, 14, 8. 5, the committee are also empowered to send for any papers produced before the commissioners, without reassembling them; but they may not enter into any point that was not in issue before the commissioners.

Causes of delay jf jg commissioners have found it impracticable to in transmitting evidence. transmit the evidence taken before them, within ten days, and have given their reasons for the delay, as required by the 60 Geo. III., the committee are directed to investigate the reasons, and to report their opinion respecting them to tlie house.

' 42 Geo. III. c. 26; 60 Geo. III. c. 7; 94 Com. J. 7.

Impeachment by the commons, for high crimes and Rarity of im-misdemeanors beyond the reach of the law, or which no iuodvru"times" other authority in the state will prosecute, is a safeguard of public liberty well worthy of a free country, and of so noble an institution as a free Parliament. But, happily, in modern times, this extraordinary judicature is rarely called into activity. The times in which its exercise was needed were those in which the people were jealous of the Crown; when the Parliament had less control over prerogative; when courts of justice were impure; and when, instead of vindicating the law, the Crown and its officers resisted its execution, and screened political offenders from justice. But the limitations of prerogative the immediate responsibility of the ministers of the Crown to Parliament the vigilance and activity of that body in scrutinizing the actions of public men the settled administration of the law, and the direct influence of Parliament over courts of justice which are, at the same time, independent of the Crown " have prevented the consummation of those crimes ' For the number of impeachments at different times, see supra, p. 50.

By the Act 13 Will III. c."2, s. 3, the commissions of judges arc made quamdiu se bene gesscrint; their salaries are ascertained and established; but it may be lawful to remove them upon the address of both houses of Parliament.

Grounds of impeaclauont.

Peers and cora-1 1 1 oners.

wlilcli impeachments were designed to punish. The Crown is entrusted by the constitution with the prosecution of all offences; there are few which the law cannot punish; and if the executive officers of the Crown be negligent or corrupt, they are directly amenable to public opinion, and to the censure of Parliament.

From these causes, im)eachments are reserved for extraordinary crimes and extraordinary offenders; but by the law of Parliament, all persons, whether peers or commoners, may be impeached for any crimes whatever.

It was always allowed, that a peer might be impeached for any crime, whether it were cognizable by the ordinary tribunals or not; but doubts have been entertained upon the supposed authority of the case of Simon de Beresford, in the 4th Edward III., whether a commoner coidd be impeached for any capital offence.

Blackstone, relying upon this case, and overlooking later authorities, affirmed that " a commoner cannot be impeached before the lords for any capital offence; but only for high misdemeanors." And more recently Lord Campbell has expressed an opinion to the same effect." Simon de Beresford, however, was not impeached by the commons, but was charged before the lords at the suit of the Crown; and after they had given judgment against him they made a declaration, which by some has even been regarded as a statute, " that the aforesaid judgment be not drawn into example or consequence in time to come, whereby the said peers may be charged hereafter to judge others than their peers, contrary to the law of the land." Whatever weight may be attached to this declaration, it clearly applies to cases similar to that of de Beresford, and cannot be extended to impeachments by the commons. In subsequent cases, the ' See 2 Rot. Pari.53, 54; 4 Edw. III. Nos. 2 and G. 4 Conim. c. 10. ' 3 Lives of the Chaucellors, 357 n. 410 (3d Edit. 302). 14 Lords' J. 2G0.

lords violated their own declaration by trying commoners for capital offences at the suit of the Crown; and such trials were unquestionably contrary to jnIagna Charta " and to the common law. But an impeachment by the commons is a proceeding of a character wholly distinct; and its legality has been recognised by Selden Lord Hale, and otlier constitutional authorities,"' and established by numerous parliamentary precedents."

The only case in which it ajipears to have been ques- Caso of pitz-tioned by the lords was that of Fitzharris. On the 26th March 1681, Edward Fitzharris was impeached of high treason; but the House of Lords, on being informed by the attorney-general that he had been instructed to indict Fitzharris at common law, resolved that they would not proceed with the impcachment." The grounds of their decision were not stated; but from the protest entered in their Journals, from the resolution of the commons, and from the debates in both houses, it may be collected that the fact of his being a commoner had been mainly relied on. The commons protested against the resolution of the lords, as " a denial of justice, and a violation of the constitution of Parliaments;" and declared it to be their "undoubted right to impeach any peer or commoner for treason or any other crime or misdemeanor: " but tlie impeachment was at an end, and the trial at common law proceeded. On his prosecution by indictment, Fitz- ' Lord Hale, Jurisd. of II. of Lords, 92.

' " Nee super eum ibhmis uisi por legale judicium pariuin snoruui."

Judicature of rarliamcnt, 3 Seld. Works, Part II. 1589.

Jurisd. of tlie Lords, c. U5.

4 Hats. Prec. 60 n. 84. 21G n.; 2 Ilallara, Const. Hist. 144.

Sir R. Belknap and others, and Simon de Beverley and others, l."lg, 3 Rot. Pari. 238. 240; Judge Birkloy and other Judges, 1G40; 4 Hats. 163, c.; O'Neile, Jermyn, Piercy and others, 1641; 4 Hats. 187, c.

7 13 Lords' J. 755.

8 Howell's St. Tr. 231-239; 2 Burntt's Own Times, 280; 4 Hans. Pari. Hist., 1333.

Case of Sir Blair, and otliers.

Commence-ineut of proceedings.

Articles of impeachment.

haitis pleaded in abatement that an impeachment was then pending against him for the same offence, but his plea was ovei-ruled by the Court of King's Bench."

The authority of this single and exceptional case, however, is of little value; and has been superseded by later cases. An impeachment for high treason was depending at the very time against Chief Justice Scroggs, a commoner; and when, on the 26th June 1689, Sir Adam Blair, and four other commoners, were impeached of high treason, the lords, after receiving and considering a report of precedents, including that of Simon de Beresfbrd, and negativing a motion for requiring the opinion of the judges, resolved that the impeachment should proceed." And thus the right of the commons to impeach a commoner of high treason has been affirmed by the last adjudication of the House of Lords.

It rests, therefore, with the House of Commons to determine when an impeachment should be instituted. A member, in his place, first charges the accused of high treason, or of certain high crimes and misdemeanors, and after supporting his charge wnth proofs, moves that he be impeached. If the house deem the grounds of accusation sufficient, and agree to the motion, the member is ordered to go to the lords, " and at their bar, in the name of the House of Commons, and of all the commons of the United Kingdom, to impeach the accused; and to acquaint them that this house will, in due time, exhibit particular articles against him, and make good the same." The member accompanied by several others, proceeds to the bar of the House of Lords, and impeaches the accused accordingly.= In the case of Warren Hastings, articles of impeachment had been prepared before his formal impeachment at ' 8 Howell's St. Tr. 326.

See this report, 4 Hats. 428.

' 13 Lords' J. 752. ' 14 Lords'J. 2G0. 45 Lords' J. 350.

the bar of the House of Lords; but the usual course has been to prepare them afterwards. A committee is appointed to draw up the articles, and on their report, the articles are discussed, and, when agreed to, are ingrossed and delivered to the lords, with a saving clause, to provide that the commons shall be at liberty to exhibit further articles from time to time." The accused sends answers to each article, which, together with all writings delivered in by him, are communicated to the commons by the lords; and to these replications are returned if necessary.

If the accused be a peer, he is attached or retained in Accuseil taken custody by order of the House of Lords; " if a commoner, '" "' he is taken into custody by the serjeant-at-arms attending the commons, by whom he is delivered to the gentleman usher of the black rod, in whose custody he remains, unless he be admitted to bail by the House of Lords;' or be otherwise disposed of by their order.

The lords appoint a day for the trial, and in the mean- Manasers time the commons appoint managers to prepare evidence pp '-and conduct the proceedings, and desire the lords to sum- Witnesses summon all witnesses who are required to prove their charges. The accused may have summonses issued for the attendance of witnesses on his behalf, and is entitled to make his full defence by counsel.""

The trial has usually been held in Westminster Hall, The trial. which has been fitted up for that purpose. In the case of peers impeached of high treason, the House of Lords is presided over by the lord high steward, who is appointed by the Crown, on the address of their lordships; but, at other times, by the lord chancellor or lord speaker of the House of Lords. The commons attend the trial, as a 60 Com. J. 482, 483. 20 Lords' J. 297; 18 Com. J.391.

3 61 Com. J. 164. 20 Lords' J. 112; 27 lb. 19.

16 Com. J. 242; 42 lb. 793. 42 Com. J. 796.

7 37 Lords' J. 724. 61 Com. J. 169.

61 Com. J. 224. '" 20 Geo. IL c.-30; 45 Lords' J. 439.

Charges to be confined to the articles.

Lords determine if the accused be guilty.

Coinmons demand judg- committce of the whole house," when the managers make their eharges, and adduce evidence in support of them; but they are bound to confine themselves to charges contained in the articles of impeachment. Mr. Warren Hastings complained, by petition to the House of Commons, that matters of accusation had been added to those originally laid to his charge, and the house resolved that certain words ought not to have been spoken by IMr. Burke." AVhen the case has been completed by the managers, they are answered by the counsel for the accused, by whom witnesses are also examined, if necessary; and, in conclusion, the managers, as in other trials, have been allowed a right of reply.

When the case is thus concluded, the lords proceed to determine whether the accused be guilty of the crimes with which he has been charged. The lord high steward puts to each peer, beginning with the junior baron, the question upon the first article, whether the accused be guilty of the crimes charged therein. Each peer, in succession, rises in his place when the question is put, and standing uncovered, and laying his right hand upon his breast, answers " guilty," or " not guilty," as the case may be, " upon my honour." Each article is proceeded with separately in the same manner, the lord high steward giving his own opinion the last. The numbers are then cast up, and being ascertained, are declared by ihe lord high steward to the lords, and the accused is acquainted with the result."

If the accused be declared not guilty, the impeachment is dismissed; if guilty, it is for the commons, in the first place, to demand judgment of the lords against him; and they would protest against any judgment being pronounced until they had demanded it. On the 17th Mai-ch 1715, ' 45 Lorda' J. 519.

' Printed Trial of Lord Melville, p.-102.

- 44 Com. J. 20S. 320. lb. p. 413.

the commons resolved, iiciu. con., in the impeachment of the Earl of AVinton,

"That the managers for the commons be empowered, in case the House of Lords shall proceed to judgment hefore the same is demanded Ijy the commons, to insist upon it, tliat it is uot parliamentary for their lordships to give judgment, until the same be first demanded by this house." '

And a similar resolution was agreed to on the impeachment of Lord Lovat, in 1746.

When judgment is to be given, the lords send a mes- Tiiejmigment. sage to acquaint the commons that their lordships arc ready to proceed further upon the impeachment;

the managers attend; and the accused being called to the bar, is then permitted to offer matters in arrest of judgment. Judgment is afterwards demanded by the speaker, in the name of the commons, and pronounced by the lord high steward, the lord chancellor, or speaker of the House of Lords."

The necessity of demanding judgment gives to the commons the power of pardoning the accused, after he lias been found guilty by the lords; and in this manner an attempt was made, in 1725, to save the Earl of JMaccles-ficld from the consequences of an impcaclnnent, after he had been found guilty by the unanimous judgment of the House of Lords."

So important is an impeachment by the commons, that rrococdings not only does it continue from session to session, in spite jj ' 7oro'aiimi of prorogations, by which other parhamentary proceedinr'-s li solution. are determined; but it survives even a dissolution, by which the very existence of a Parliament is concluded. But as the preliminary proceedings of the House of ' 18 Com. J. 40o. 25 lb. 320.

3 22 Lords' J. 55G; 27 lb. 78. 22 Lords' J. 5G0, 22 Lords' J. 5o4, r, i b; 20 Com. J. 541 (27th May 1725); G ITowch's St. Tr. 7G2.

30 Lords' J. 191, and spc Rc iirt of Precedents, lb. 125; 4fi Coin. J. 13G.

Pardon not pleadable.

But may be given afterwards.

Crimes for wbicb peers are tried by their peers.

Commons would require to be revived in another session, Acts-svere passed in 1786 and in 1805, to provide that the proceedings depending in the House of Commons upon the articles of charge against "Warren Hastings and Lord lelville, should not be discontinued by any pro-roffation or dissolution of Parliament.

In the case of the Earl of Danby, in 1679, the commons protested against a royal pardon being pleaded in bar of an impeachment, by which an offender could be screened from the inquiry and justice of Parliament by the inten'ention of prerogative. Directly after the Revolution, the commons asserted the same principle, and within a few years it was declared by the Act of Settlement,"" " That no pardon under the great seal of England shall be pleadable to an impeachment by the commons in Parliament."

But, although the royal prerogative of pardon is not suffered to obstruct the course of justice, and to interfere with the exercise of parliamentary judicature; yet the prerogative itself is unimpaired in regard to all convictions whatever; and after the judgment of the lords has been pronounced, the Crown may reprieve or pardon the offender. This right was exercised in the case of three of the Scottish lords, who had been concerned in the rebellion of 1715, and who were reprieved by the Crown, and at length received the royal pardon.

Concerning the trial of peers, very few words will be necessary. At common law, the only crimes for which a peer is to be tried by his peers, are treason, felony, misprision of treason, and misprision of felony; and the statutes which give such trial have reference to the same offences, either at common law or created by statute. For misdemeanors, and in cases of praemunire, it has been held that ' 26 Geo. III. c. 96; 4-5 Geo. III. c. 123. M2 13 Will. III. c. 2.

peers are to be tried in the same way as commoners, by a jury."

Dm'ing the sitting of Parliament, they are tried by the In Parliammt, House of Peers; or, more properly, before the court of our lord'hio-h lady the Queen in Parliament, presided over by the lord '-high steward appointed by commission under the great seal; but at other times, they may be tried before the court of the lord high steward. This court was formerly constituted in so anomalous a manner, as scarcely to deserve the name of a court of justice. The lord high steward, himself nominated by the Crown, summoned to the trial, at his discretion, such peers as he selected, whose number was required to be not less than twelve; but was otherwise indefinite. The abuses arising out of this constitution of the court, however, were remedied by the 7 "Will. III. s. 3, which requires that, on the trial of a peer, all the peers shall be summoned.

By the 4 5 Vict., c. 22, it was enacted, "That every Indictments lord of Parliament, or peer of this realm, having place ' and voice in Parliament, against whom any indictment may be found, shall plead to such indictment, and shall, upon conviction, be liable to the same punishment as any other of Her Majesty's subjects."

Indictments are found in the usual manner against peers charged with treason or felony; but are certified into the House of Lords hy writs of ce-tiorari, when the proceedings are immediately taken up by that house. It is usual, in such cases, to appoint a committee to inspect the Journals upon former trials of peers, and to consider the proper methods of proceeding; and if the accused peer be not ' Rex i Lord Vaux, 1 Biilstr. 197.- Foster's Crown Law, 141, ' After the trial his grace breaks tlie wliite staff, and declares the commission dissolved. See published Trial of tlie Earl of Cardigan.

See 4 Bl. Comm. '260.

See Trial of Lord Dclamere, 11 Howell's St. Tr. 539; 2 Macaulay,-38.

Accused peers at the bar.

Trial of peers to be in full Parliament.

Declaration concerning appeals of murther, c.

Lord high steward.

already in custody, an order is forthwith made for the gentleman usher of the black rod to attach him, and bring him to the bar of the house.

Peers on trial before the lords for misdemeanors arc allowed a seat within the bar; but if tried for treason or felony they are placed outside the bar.

On the 14th January 1689, it was resolved by the lords, "That it is the ancient right of the peers of England to be tryed only in full Parliiiment for any capital offences:" but on the 17 th, it was declared that this order should not " be understood or construed to extend to any appeal of murther or other felonye, to be brought against any peer or peers.""

When a peer is tried in full Parliament, the lord high steward votes with the other peers; but when the trial is before the court of the lord high steward, he is only the judge to give direction in point of law; and the verdict is given by the lords-triers. Spiritual lords. In the trial of peers, the position of the bishops is at once anomalous and ill-defined. Not being themselves ennobled in blood, they are " not of trial by nobility,"" but would be tried for a capital offence by a jury, like other commoners. But though not entitled to a trial by the peers, they claim, and to a certain extent exercise, the right of sitting, as judges, upon the trial of peers in full Parliament. By the Act 7 Will. III. c. 3, it is enacted, "That upon the trial of any peer or peeress for high treason or misprision, all the peers who have a right to sit and vote in Parhament, shall be duly summoned tvrenty ' 99 Hans. Deb. 3d Ser. 1050 (23d June 1848); 80 Lords' J. 415.

' 4 Lord Campb. Lives of Chan., 538 n.

= Lords' S. O. No. 79. " Lords' S. O. No. G4.

3 Lord Campb. Lives of Chan., 557 n.

Lords' S. O. No. 79.

' 1st Inst. 31; 3d Inst. 30; Gibs. Cod. 133; Gilbert's Exch. 40; 1 Burn's Eccl. Law, 221 etseq.; Trials of Bishop Fislier and Arclibisliop Cranmcr, 1 Howell's St. Tr. 399. 771.

days at least before every such trial; and that every peer so summoned and appearing, shall vote in the trial." This Act, however, does not "extend to any impeachment, or other proceeding in Parliament, in any kind whatsoever." In other words, it relates solely to the trial of peers before the court of the lord high steward; and to this court no spiritual lord has ever been summoned, either before or since the passing of that Act. It expressly refers to " peers " only, and by a declai-ation of the House of Lords the "bishops are only lords of Parliament, and not peers." But, when a peer is to be tried in full Parliament, the bishops, as lords of Parliament, are entitled to take part in the proceedings of the House of Lords, of which they arc members, and they are always summoned to attend with the other peers. Here, however, they are restrained from the full exercise of their judicial functions by their ecclesiastical obligations. By the canons of the church, they are prohibited from voting in cases of blood; and by the Constitutions of Clarendon," it was declared, " that bishops, like other peers (or barons) ought to take part in trials in the King's court, or council, with the peers, until it comes to a question of the loss of life or limb."

It was declared by the lords, on the impeachment of Spiritual hn-ds the Earl of Danby, "That the loi'ds spiritual have a right to stay and sit in court in capital cases, till the court proceed to the vote of guilty or not guilty." And in accordance with this rule, the bishops are present during the trial of peers in Parliament, but ask leave to be absent from the judgment; which being agreed to, they withdraw, in compliance with the canons of the church, but enter a protestation, " saving to themselves and their '

73 Lords' J. 10; Foster's Crown Law, 247.

Gibson's Codex. 124,125; and see 2 Burnet's Own Time, 21G; and H Stil-lingfleet's Works, 820.

3 11 Hen. II., A. D. 11G4 J 1 Wilkins' Concilia, 435. 13 Lords' J. 571.

Bishops vote in bills of attainder.

Representative peers of Scotland, and Ireland.

Bills of attainder and of jiains and jienulties.

successors all such riglits in judicature as they have by law, and by right ought to have." ' In passing bills of attainder, the bishops would not be subjected to the same restraints as upon an impeachment. The proceedings, though judicial, are legislative in form, and as they consist of numerous stages, no particular vote would involve a conclusive judgment upon the accused. In the attainder of Sir John Fenwick, in

1696, the bishops voted in all the proceedings, and even upon the final question for the passing of the bill.

By the 23d article of the Act of Union with Scotland, it is declared, that the sixteen representative peers shall have the right of sitting upon the trials of peers; " and in case of the trial of any peer in time of adjournment or prorogation of Parliament, they shall be summoned in the same mannei', and have the same powers and privileges at such trial as any other peers of Great Britain;" and in case there shall be any trials of peers when there is no Parliament in being, the sixteen peers who sat in the last Parliament shall be summoned in the same manner. All peers of Scotland enjoy the privilege of being tried as peers of Great Britain.

By the 4th article of the Act of Union with Ireland, it was enacted, that " The (representative) lords spiritual and temporal respectively, on the part of Ireland, shall have the same rights in respect of their sitting and voting upon the trial of peers, as the lords spiritual and temporal respectively on the part of Great Britain;" and that all the peers of Ireland shall be sued and tried as peers, but shall not have the right of sitting on the trial of peers.

The proceedings of Parliament in passing bills of attainder, and of pains and penalties, do not vary from those adopted in regard to other bills. They may be introduced ' 27 Lords' J. 7G; 73 lb. 43 ' IG lb. 44. 48; 13 Howell's St. Tr. 750 et scq.

into either house; they pass tliruugh the same stages; and when agreed to by both houses, they receive the royal assent in the usual form. But the parties who are subjected to these proceedings are admitted to defend themselves by counsel and witnesses before both houses; and the solemnity of the proceedings would cause measures to be taken to enforce tlie attendance of members upon their service in Paruament.

In evil times, this summary power of Parliament to The iiiohest punish criminals by statute has been perverted and abused; meiitary'Tiid'i-" and in the best of times it should be regarded with jealousy; ""-but whenever a fitting occasion arises for its exercise, it is, undoubtedly, the highest form of parliamentary judicature. In impeachments the commons are but accusers, and advocates; while the lords alone are judges of the crime. On the other hand, in passing bills of attainder the commons commit themselves by no accusation, nor are their powers directed against the offender; but they are judges of equal jurisdiction and with the same responsibility as the lords; and the accused can only be condemned by the unanimous judgment of the Crown, the lords, and the commons.

See 35 Lords' J, 35. 364.

Definition of EveRY bill for the particular interest or benefit of any private bills. j. i. i-r t j. j.

person or persons, is treated, m Jr arliament, as a private bill. Whether it be for the interest of an individual, a public company or corporation, a parish, a city, a county, or other locality; it is equally distinguished from a measure of public policy, in which the whole community are interested. And this distinction is marked by the solicitation of private bills by the parties themselves whose interests are concerned. By the standing orders of both houses, all private bills are required to be brought in upon petition;" and the payment of fees by the promoters is an indispensable condition to their progress.

Origin of pri In treating of petitions, the orio-in of private bills has vate bills. i-, i been already glanced at; but it may be referred to again, in illustration of the distinctive character of such bills, and of the proceedings of Parliament in passing them. The separation of legislative and judicial functions is a refinement in the principles of political government and jurisprudence, which can only be the result of civilisation. In ' See infra, p. 582, and 2 Hats. 281-288. A bill for the benefit of three counties has been held to be a private bill. 1 Com. J. 388.

But see exceptions, i7ia, p. 514. Supra, p. 383.

the early constitution of Parliament tliese functions were confouncled; and special laws for the benefit of private parties and judicial decrees for the redress of private wrongs, being founded alike upon petitions, were not distinguished in principle or in form. When petitions sought obviously for remedies which the common law afforded, the parties were referred to the ordinary tribunals; but in other cases the Parliament exercised a remedial jurisdiction. Other remedies, of a more judicial character, and founded upon more settled principles, were at length supplied by the courts of equity; and from the reign of Henry TV., the petitions addressed to Parliament prayed, more distinctly, for peculiar powers beside the general law of the land, and for the special benefit of the petitioners. Wlienever these were granted, the orders of Parliament, in whatever form they may have been expressed, Avere in the nature of private acts; and after the mode of legislating by bill and statute had grown up in the reign of Henry VI., these special enactments were embodied in the form of distinct statutes.

Passinoj now to existing practice, the proceedings of Peculiarity of .-n 1 1 1 proceedings on

Parliament, in passing private bnls, are still marked by private bills. much peculiarity. A bill for the particular benefit of certain persons may be injurious to others; and to discriminate between the conflicting interests of different parties, involves the exercise of judicial inquiry and determination. This circumstance cavises important distinctions in the mode of passing public and private bills; and in the principles by which Parliament is guided.

In passing public bills. Parliament acts strictly In its Legislative .,,. n functions of legislative capacity; it originates the measures which ap- Parliament in pear for the public good; it conducts inquiries, when neces- Jfi gj" " " sary, for its own information, and enacts laws according to ' See supra, p. 343.

See Statutes of the Realm, by Record Commission, 9 lien. VI.

Its functions jjurtly jmliciiil in passing private bills.

Suitors restrained by injunction.

its own wisdom and jud ment. The forms In wlilch its deliberations are conducted are established for its own convenience; and all its proceedings are independent of individual parties; who may petition, indeed, and are sometimes heard by counsel; but who have no direct partlci)ation in the conduct of the business, nor immediate influence upon the judgment of Parliament.

In passing private bills, Parliament still exercises its legislative functions; but its proceedings partake also of a judicial character. The persons whose private Interests are to be promoted appear as suitors for the bill; while those who apprehend injiu-y are admitted as adverse parties in the suit. Many of the formalities of a court of justice are maintained; various conditions are required to be observed, and their observance to be strictly proved; and if the parties do not sustain the bill In its progress, by following every regulation and form prescribed, it is not for-Avarded by the house In which it is pending. If they abandon it, and no other parties undertake its support, the bill Is lost, however sensible the house may be of its value. The analogy which all these circumstances bear to the proceedings of a court of justice is further supported by the payment of fees, which is required of every party promoting or opposing a private bill, or petitioning for or opposing any particular provision. It may be added that the solicitation of a bill in Parliament has been regarded, by courts of equity, so completely in the same light as an ordinary suit, that the promoters have been restrained by injunction from proceeding with a bill, the object of which was held to be to set aside a covenant; and parties have been restrained, in the same manner, from appearing as ' The Manchester and Salford Improvement Bill in 1828 was abandoned, in committee, by its original promoters; when its opponents, having succeeded in introducing certain amendments, undertook to solicit its further progress.

' North Staffordshire Railway Company, 1850. The injunction was afterwards dissolved.

petitioners against a private bill, pending in the House of Lords. Such injunctions have been justified on the ground that they act upon the person of the suitor and not upon the jurisdiction of Parliament; which would clearly be otherwise in the case of a public bill.

This union of the judicial and legislative functions is Principles by not confined to the forms of procedure, but is an impoi'tant m nt ig guided, principle in the inquiries and decision of Parliament upon the merits of private bills. As a court, it inquires and adjudicates upon the interests of private parties; as a legislature, it is watchful over the interests of the public. The promoters of a bill may prove, beyond a doubt, that their own interest will be advanced by its success, and no one may complain of injury, or urge any specific objection; yet, if Parliament apprehend that it will be hurtful to the community, it is rejected as if it were a public measure, or qualified by restrictive enactments, not solicited by the parties. In order to increase the vigilance of Parliament, in protecting the public interests, the chairman of the lords' committees in the one house, and the chairman of ways and means in the other, are entrusted with the peculiar care of unopposed bills and with a general revision of all other private bills; while the agency of the Government Boards is also brought in aid of the legislature.

In pointing out this peculiarity in private bills, it must. Private bills however, be understood, that while they are examined and he saiiie" ' contested before committees and officers of the house like stages. private suits, and are subject to notices, forms, and intervals, unusual in other bills; yet in every separate stage, when they come before either house, they are treated precisely as if they were public bills. They are read as many times, and similar questions are put, except when any proceeding is

Hartlepool Junction Railway; 100 Haus. Deb., N. S., 783, See hij'ra, p. 527 et seq.

specially directed by the standing orders; and the same rules of debate and procedure are maintained throughout.

Proposed plan In ordcr to explain clearly all the forms and proceedings the progress of to be obscrvcd in passing private bills, it is proposed to private bills. gtate them, as nearly as possible, in the order in which they successively arise. It will be necessary, for this purpose, to begin with the House of Commons; because, by the privileges of that house, every bill which involves any pecuniary charge or burthen on the people, by way of tax, rate, toll or duty, ought to be first brought into that house.

It follows, from this rule, that by far the greater number of private bills are, from their chai'acter, necessarily passed first by the commons. Some others, also, which might originate in either house, are generally first solicited in the commons. It will be convenient, therefore, in the first place, to pursue this description of bills in their progress through the commons, and afterwards, to follow them in their passage through the lords. Those private bills which usually originate in the lords, as naturalization, name, estate, and divorce bills, will, for the same reasons, be more conveniently followed from the lords to the commons.

Private legisia- But before these classes of private bills are more par- by'puwic Acts, ticularly described, it will be necessary to advert to an important principle of modern legislation, by which special applications to Parliament for private acts have, in numerous cases, been superseded by general laws. A private act is an exception from the general law; and powers are sought by its promoters which cannot be otherwise exercised, and which no other authority is able to confer. It is obvious, however, that the public laws of a country should be as comprehensive as may be consistent with the rights of private property; and it has accordingly been the pohcy of the legislature to enable parties to avail themselves of the ' See siqmi, pp. 344. 361. 407 et scq.

provisions of)ubhc acts adiipted to different classes of objects, instead of requiring them to apply to Parliament for special powers in each particular case. The same principle may be still further extended hereafter; but in all cases in which any special legislation is sought for which is not within the scope of general laws, apphcation must still be made to Parliament.

The principal statutes relating to matters which have General Acts n ' r" T- T euumeratcd.

usually been the subjects oi private acts or Parhament may be briefly enumerated, in order to show the progress which has been made in this department of legislation.

The earliest attempt to provide, by a general law, for inclosures. the objects usually sought by the promoters of private bills, was that of the General Inclosure Act in 1801. By that act several provisions which had been usually inserted in each act of inclosure were consolidated, and the necessary proofs before Parliament were facilitated when such acts were applied for; but the necessity of applying for separate acts of inclosure was not superseded. In 1836 a general law was passed to facilitate the Inclosure of open and arable land; and, in 1845, the Inclosure Commissioners were constituted, to whom have been entrusted many of the powers previously exercised by Parliament. In some cases they have authority, under public acts, to complete inclosures, Avhile, in other cases, they make provisional orders for the inclosure of lands, to which legal eff'ect is given, from time to time, by public acts of Parliament. Except, therefore, in any extraordinary and exceptional case not provided for by the public acts, a private act of inclosure is now unnecessary.

' 41 Geo. III. c. 109. " 6 7 Will. IV. c. 115.

3 8 9 Vict. c. 118; 9 10 Vict. c. 70; 10 11 Vict. c. Ill j 11 12 Vict. c. 99; 12 13 Vict. c. 83.

See 9 10 Vict. c. 16. 117; 13 14 Vict. c. 8. GO, c.

For a return of the uumber of Inclosure Acts passed at different periods, and the acreage inclosed, see 8css. Paper, 1843 (32o.)

Drainage of lands.

Tithes.

Enfranchisement of copyholds.

Joint stock comjjanies.

Winding-up Acts.

Several general statutes have since been passed, to promote the drainage and improvement of land by which the agency of the Inclosure Commissioners and of other public boards and officers has been made available.

Applications to Parliament for the commutation of tithes and other similar pvirposes were frequent, until the passing of the General Tithe Commutation Act in 1836, and the constitution of commissioners, by whom that and other general laws for the commutation of tithes have been carried into execution. General Acts have also been passed to facilitate the enfi-anchisement of copyholds, and other manorial rights, the provisions of which have been carried out by the Tithe Commissioners.

By the Joint Stock Companies Registration Acts, various powers and privileges may be secured by companies, which had previously formed the subjects of applications to Parliament. They may be incorporated, and may sue and be sued in the name of the company; but the separate liability of the shareholders is not limited by such incorporation. So many powers, however, are still required by companies for special purposes, and particularly to obtain a limited liability, that applications to Parliament for incorporating and giving powers to companies are still frequent, independently of cases in which works are to be executed by public companies. For Avinding up the affairs of joint stock companies, unable to meet their pecuniary engagements, the extensive machinery of the Court of Chancery has been brought into ' 5 6 Vict. c. 89; 8 9 Vict. c. 69; 9 10 Vict. c. 4 j 10 11 Vict. c. 32 (Ireland). 9 10 Vict. c. 101; 10 11 Vict. c. 11; 11 12 Vict. c. 119; 11 12 Vict. c. 38 (113 Scotland). General Drainage Acts, 12 13 Vict, c. 100; 13 14 Vict. c. 31.

= 6 7 Will. IV. c. 71.

" 7 Will. IV. 1 Vict. c. 69; 1 2 Vict. c. 64; 2 3 Vict. c. 62; 3 4 Vict. c. 15; 5 6 Vict. c.54; 9 10 Vict. c. 73; 10 11 Vict. c. 104.

4 5 Vict. e. 35; 6 7 Vict. c. 23; 7 8 Vict. c. 55; 9 10 Vict. C.53; 10 11 Vict. c. 101.

' 7 8 Vict. c. 110; 10 11 Vict. c. 78.

operation by the "Winding-up Acts;" and similar provision has been made for winding up the affairs of joint stock companies in Ireland.

By the 9 10 Vict. c. 105, the Commissioners of Rail- Railway com-ways were constituted, to whom Avere transferred, by that P"""' " act, all the powers and duties which had previously been executed by the Board of Trade. The primary object of their appointment was to secure the general supervision of existing railways, and to assist Parliament in its railway legislation. But further powers have since been conferred upon them, by which applications to Parliament, in certain cases, have been rendered unnecessary. By the 11 12 Extension of Vict. c. 3, railway companies which had obtained par- chase of lands liamentary powers for the construction of railways, were ' enabled to obtain from the commissioners of railways, instead of from Parliament, an extension of the time limited by their acts for the purchase of lands and the completion of works. And by the 13 14 Vict. c. 83, Abandonment the agency of the commissioners was made available, in the same manner, to facilitate the abandonment of railways and the dissolution of railway companies.

Private acts of Parliament for the establishment of Local courts. small-debt courts, once very frequent, have been superseded, since 1846, by the establishment of county courts under the general act: And by the Poor Law Amend- Poor and poor ment Act of 1834, and subsequent acts for the general administration of the laws for the relief of the poor, private acts for all purposes connected with the poor and poor rates, have been rendered unnecessary.

Extensive provision for the lighting, watching, paving. Lighting, cleansing, improving, and sanitary regulation of towns, has licc ancuni-' also been made by means of public acts. In 1833 an act P vcraent of towns.

' 78 Vict. c. Ill; 9 10 Viet. c. 28; 11 12 Vict. c. 45; 12 13 Vict. c. 108. 2 8 9 Vict. c. 98.

M 2 Vict. c. 93; 3 4 Vict. c. 97; 5 G Vict, c. o5; 7 8 Vict, c. 85; 8 9 Vict, c 20. 33. 96.

9 10 Vict. c. 9.; 12 13 Vict. c. 101; 13; 14 Vict. c. GI.

General Board of Health.

Improvement of towns in Scotland.

County constabulary.

Entailed estates in Scotland.

was passed to enable the rate-payers to make arrangements for the hghtiug and watching of their parishes. In 1828, an important act was passed for the lighting, watching and cleansing of towns in Ireland, the provisions of which have been adopted by several towns. This act has since been amended, and a bill is now ' before Parliament for its further amendment. By the Public Health Act the general Board of Health was constituted, by whom are exercised important powers of local inquiry and provisional legislation, for the paving and sewerage of towns, the supply of water, and other local Improvements. In certain cases, the provisions of the Public Health Act may be applied, on the report of the Board of Health, by her Majesty in Council; and, in other cases, the provisional orders of the board are confirmed, from time to time, by Parliament, in public acts. " Provision by a general law is also made for regulating the police of towns and populous places in Scotland, and for paving, draining, cleansing, lighting and improving them. But, in the improvement of towns so many special powers become necessary in particular localities, which Parliament alone can confer, that applications for private acts, for that purpose, are still numerous, and form a veiy Important branch of private legislation.

The establishment of a police force, and police regulations. In English counties, has been provided for by the county constabulary acts.

By several acts affecting entailed estates in Scotland, numerous complicated estate acts have been rendered ' 3 4 Will. IV. c. 90 (a previous Act, 11 Geo. IV. c. 27, was thereby repealed).

3 6 7 Vict. c. 93. 11 12 Vict. c. 63. 13 14 Vict. c. 32. 90. 108.

C.3G 2 9 Geo. IV. c. 82.

"March 1851.

6 12 13 Vict. c. 94 ' 13 14 Vict. c. 33.

8 2 3 Vict. c. 93; 3 4 Vict. c. 88.

-' 10 Geo. III. c. 61; 5 Geo. IV. c. 87; 3 4 Vict. c. 48; II 12 Vict.

unnecessary, as the matters wliicli had been previously-provided for by private legislation are now within the operation of the general law. And by the acts to facili- incumbered tate the sale of incumbered estates in Ireland, the com- j nji. missioners for the sale of incumbered estates have been entrusted with powers which could not otherwise have been exercised without the authority of private acts of Parliament.

By the act 7 8 Vict. c. 66, aliens may obtain cer- Naturalization T. . 1 n 1 1 of aliens.

tmcates of naturalization from the secretary oi state, which confer the same privileges as those which were usually secured by special naturalization acts.

And, in conclusion, a hope may be expressed, that Divorce Acts. applications to Parliament for divorce acts may soon be superseded by an improvement of tlie general law relating to divorces.

CHAPTER XXV.

CONDITIONS TO BE OBSERVED BY PARTIES BEFORE PRIVATE BILLS ARE INTRODUCED INTO PARLIAMENT. PROOF OF COMPLIANCE WITH THE STANDING ORDERS IN THE HOUSE OF COMMONS.

For the purposes of the standing orders of both houses. The two classes all private bills to which the standing orders are applicable " P'"i ' te bills, are divided into the two following classes, according to the siibjects to which they respectively relate: 1st Class:

Burial-ground, making, maintaining or altering. 1st Class.

Charters and corporations, enlarging or altering jiowers of. Church or chapel, building, enlarging, repairing or maintaining.

11 12 Vict. c. 48; 12 13 Vict. c. 77. And see 10 11 Vict. c. 83 (Colonies).

City or town, paving, lighting, watching, cleansing or improving.

Company, incorporating or giving powers to.

County rate.

County or shire hall, court house.

Crown, church, or corporation property, or property held in trust for public or charitable purposes.

Ferry.

Fishery, making, maintaining, or improving.

Gaol or house of correction.

Land, inclosing, draining" or improving.

Letters patent, confirming, prolonging or transferring the term of.

Local court, constituting.

Market or market place, erecting, improving, repairing, maintaining, or regulating. Police.

Poor, maintaining or employing.

Poor rate.

Powers to sue and be sued, conferring.

Sewers and sewerage."

Stipendiary magistrate, or any public officer, payment of; and

Continuing or amending an Act passed for any of the purposes included in this or the second class, where no further work than such as was authorised by a former Act is proposed to be made.

2d Class: 2d Class. Making, maintaining, varying, extending or enlarging any

Aqueduct. Pier.

Archway. Port.

Bridge. Railway.

Canal. Reservoir.

Cut. Sewer.

Dock. Street.

Ferry, where any work is to be Tunnel.

executed. Turnpike or other public Harbour. carriage road.

Navigation. Waterwork.

"Making and maintaining any cut for drainage, being a new work, where it is not provided in the bill that the same shall not be of more than eleven feet width at the bottom.

' Standing Orders of the Lords. In the Commons, bills for general sewerage, where no specific work is to be constructed, are included in city or town improvements. Lords' S. O. only.

The requirements of the standing orders, which are to be Rpqumcments complied with by the jsromoters of such private bills, before "l-derl '"" '"" application is made to Parliament, were conveniently arranged by the commons in 1847 in the following oi'der; and a similar arrangement has since been adopted by the House of Lords:

"1. Notices by advertisement. 2. Notices and applications to owners, lessees, and occupiers of lands and houses. 3. Documents required to be deposited, and the times and places of deposit. 4. Form in which plans, books of reference, sections, and cross sections shall be prepared. 5. Estimates and subscription contracts, or declarations in lieu of subscription contracts, and deposit of monej' in certain cases."

The requirements of the two houses, under each of similarity of these divisions (except in a few particulars wliich will be pre- lonis ami com-sently noticed), are now almost identical. Their convenient " arrangement and general similarity render unnecessary their insertion in this work; and no version of them can, at any time, be safely relied upon by the i)romoters of bills, except the last authorised edition."

1. In regard to notices by advertisement, the standing Notices iiy ad-orders of both houses are alike, except in two points. In ertisement. the case of bills for burial grounds or cemeteries the lords require that " the notices shall set forth and specify tlie limits within which such cemetery or burial ground is Burial grouuds. intended to be erected or made." The commons, again. Letters patent.

have an order specially relating to the form of notice in the case of bills for confirming or prolonging the teitQS of letters patent, which is not amongst the orders of the lords.

2. In regard to notices and applications to owners, lessees Applications to and occupiers of lands and houses, the orders of both houses " "' ' ' ' The standing orders were printed at length in the first edition of this work, for the sake of improving their arrangement, and pointing out the numerous discrepancies between the orders of the two houses. No such object, however, would now be gained by printing them in the text; and tiiey have been omitted, after much consideration, in order that no parties may be misled by referring hereafter to obsolete orders. Ciieap editions are publislied annually, which contain the latest iilt(; rations.

are also alike with one exception. In the case of bills for the erection of works for the manufacture of gas the conunons require notice to be given, on or before the 15th December, to the owner and occupier of every dwelling-house situated within 300 yards of the boundary of the proposed gas-works." In the standing orders of the lords there is no such requirement. Deposits. 3. There are a few variations in the standing orders of the two houses, in regard to the documents required to be deposited, and the times and places of deposit, before the application is made to Parliament. The lords require Copy of Lords' that copics of SO much of their standing orders as relate ders. " to the deposit of plans, sections, books of reference, c.

with clerks of the peace, parish clerks and elsewhere, be delivered, together with the plans, c. so deposited. But with this exception the deposits required to be made on or before the 30th November, are the same by the orders of both houses. Deposit on or The commons require certain deposits to be made in the

December. offices of the house on or before the 31st December. These, of course, are peculiar to the commons; but the lords, in some cases, require a similar deposit at a later period, after the introduction of the bill into Parliament. These will be noticed, hereafter, in following the progress of a bill through that house. The only deposit required to be made elsewhere than in the House of Commons, on or before the 31st December, is that of a printed copy of every railway bill at the office of the commissioners of railways. The deposit of a railway bill, at this time, is required by the commons only, as it is then about to be considered in that house; but at subsequent periods the lords require similar deposits to be made.

' Com. S. O., No. 21 (1850).

See also Act 1 Vict. c. 83, for compelling clerks of the peace and other persons to take the custody of such documents.

4. As regards the fomis in which plans, books of" refer- Plans, sections, ence, sections and cross sections are required to be pre- rofereuce. pared, and the particulars they are to contain, there is no difference whatever in the orders of the two houses.

5. The orders of both houses are also alike in regard to Estimates and estimates and subscription contracts, or declarations in lieu contracts."" of subscription contracts; and the deposit of money.

In preparing their bills for deposit on the 31st December, Preparing bills. the promoters must be careful that no provisions be inserted which are not sufficiently alluded to in the notices, or which otherwise infringe the standing orders. If the bill be for Consolidation any of the purposes provided for by the Consolidation Acts, so much of those acts as may be applicable is to be incorporated; and the bill is otherwise to be drawn in general conformity with the model bills, by which the best forms are prescribed.

The promoters of certam classes of private bills are also Preliminary required by the Preliminary Inquiries Act to deliver, on '"i"""' or before the 30th November, to the Commissioners of Woods and Forests, or to the Admiralty, as the case may be, statements of the objects of their intended application, and such documents as are required by the standing orders of either House of Parliament, to be deposited at any public ' See also Act 9 Vict. c. 20, relative to the custody of such money. The date of such deposit (loth January), as required by the commons, is not specified in the orders of the lords.

"Companies' Clauses, Lands' Clauses, and Railways' Clauses Consolidation Acts, 184.5; Companies' Clauses and Lands' Clauses (Scotland) Acts, 1846; Markets and Fairs' Clauses, Gas Works' Clauses, Commissioners' Clauses Waterworks' Clauses, Harbours and Docks' Clauses, Towns' Improvement Clauses, Cemetery Clauses, and Police Clauses Consolidation Acts, 1847. These Acts, as stated in tlie preambles, were passed, " as well for avoidin"-the necessity of repeating such provisions in each of the several Acts relating to such undertakings, as for ensuring greater uniformity in the provisions themselves."

' 11 12 Vict. c. 129. Extensive amendments of this Act were recommended by a committee of the House of Commons in 1850, and will probably be carried into effect in the present session (1851).

Proof of compliance.

Examiners of petitions for private bills.

General list of petitions.

Memorialscom-plaiiiing of noncompliance.

office. This requirement is wholly independent of the standing orders of either house; but the proceedings under the act may come, at a later period, under the notice of Parliament'

Com liance with the standing orders is required to be separately proved, in the commons before the examiners of petitions for private bills, and in the lords before the standing order committee. Assuming that the bills to which these orders relate are to be first solicited in the commons, the proceedings in that house only will, for the present, be adverted to.

There ai'e two examiners of petitions, appointed by Mr. Speaker in pursuance of the standing orders, who, since the year 1846, have performed all the duties which were formerly executed by the sub-committees on petitions for private bills.

When all the petitions for private bills, with printed copies of the bills annexed, have been deposited, on or before the 31st December, in the Private Bill Office, the " General List of Petitions " is made out in the order of their deposit, according to the speaker's regulations, and each petition is numbered. The regulations by which that list is made out give every facility to the promoters of bills to select for themselves whatever position may be most convenient. If they secure an early number on the list their petitions will be heard by the examiners shortly after the commencement of their sittings. If, on the other hand, they desire their case to be heard at a later period, they may place their petition lower down in the list.

When the time has expired for depositing documents, and complying with other preliminary conditions, the par- ' See iwm, p. 528. 2 See infra, p. 559.

' See Mr. Speaker's printed regulations for the deposit of petitions in the Private Bill Office, and for determining the order in which they will be heard.

ties interested are enabled to judge whether the standing orders of the House of Commons have been complied with, and if it should appear to them that the promoters have neglected to comply with any of them, they may prepare memorials complaining of such non-compliance. These When to be memorials are to be deposited in the Private Bill Office, " ' according to the position of the bill to which they relate, in the general list.

"If the same relate to petitions for bills numbered in the general list of petitions;

From 1 to 100 1,,,,. r Jan. 17.

They shall be deposited on or) 101 to 200 S "-' '"""" " uci. usiitfu uii ur) 2 201 and upwards " 31.

And in the case of any petitions for bills which may be deposited by leave of the house after the.31st December, such memorials shall be deposited three clear days before the day first appointed for the examination of the petition."

All memorials are to be deposited before six o'clock on any day on which the house shall sit, and before two when the house shall not sit; and two copies are also to be deposited for the use of the examiners before twelve o'clock on the following day.

These memorials are addressed, "To the Examiner of How prepared. Petitions for Private Bills," and are prepared in the same form, and are subject to the same general rules as petitions to the house," as well as to other special rules, which will be noticed hereafter. When the time for depositing memo- opposed and rials has expired, the opposed and unopposed petitions are ""opposed .,. IT 1. petitions dis- distinguished in the general list; and the petitions are set distinguished. down for hearing before the examiners in the order in which they stand in the general list, precedence being given, whenever it may be necessary, to unopposed petitions.

' See sujjra, p. 384 et scq. K K

Sittings of tlic examiners.

Notice of examination.

Daily lists of petitions.

Petitions struck ofl' the list.

How to be re-inserted.

The public sittings of the examiners commence on the 25th of January, being generally a few days before the meeting of Parliament.

One of the examiners is required to give at least seven clear days' notice in the Private Bill Office of the day appointed for the examination of each petition; and, practically, a much longer notice has been given, as, for the convenience of all parties concerned, the examiners have usually given notices for the first hundred petitions on the 17th January, and for the second hundred on the 24th January, as soon as the memorials relating to such petitions have been deposited.

In order to facilitate the examination of unopposed petitions, the daily lists of cases set down for hearing before each of the examiners are divided into "unopposed" and "opposed" petitions; and the former are placed first on each day. By this arrangement all the cases are appointed to be heard according to their order in the " general list of petitions;" but precedence is given, on each day, to the unopposed petitions. These are disposed of, and the numerous agents and witnesses relieved from attendance during the subsequent hearing of opposed cases, which often occupy a considerable time.

In case the promoters shall not appear at the time when their petition comes on to be heard, the examiner is to strike the petition off the general list of petitions. The petition cannot afterwards be re-inserted on the list except by order of the house; and if the promoters should desire to proceed with the bill, it will be necessary to present a petition to the house, praying that the petition may be re-inserted, and explaining the circumstances under which it had been struck off. This petition will be referred to the standing orders committee, who will determine, upon the statement of the)arties, whether the promoters have forfeited their right to proceed or npt, and will rci)ort to the house accordingly.

If the petition for the bill should be re-inserted in the general list, the usual notice will be given by the examiner, and the case wul be heard at the appointed time.

When the case is called on, the agent soliciting the bill Statement of appears before the examiner with a written " statement of ' proofs," showing all the requirements of the standing orders, applicable to the bill, which have been complied with, and the name of every witness, opposite each proof, who is to prove the matters stated therein. K the bill be opposed on Appearances , T. n.1 1 i. 1 on memorials standmg orders, the agents tor the memorialists are required entered.

to enter their appearances' upon each memorial, at this time, in order to entitle them to be subsequently heard. In the meantime the " formal proofs," as they are termed, pro- Formal proofs.

ceed generally in the same manner, both in opposed and unopposed cases. Each witness is examined by the agent, and produces all affidavits and other necessary proofs, in the order in which they are set down in the statement; ' and in addition to the proofs comprised in the statement, the examiner requires such other explanations as he may think fit, to satisfy him that all the orders of the house have been complied with. Under the standing orders.

The examiner may admit affidavits in proof of the compliance Proof by affi-with the standing orders of the house, unless in any case he shall davit, require further evidence; and that such affidavit shall be sworn, if in England, before a justice of the peace; if in Scotland, before any sheriff depute or his substitute; and if in Ireland, before any judge or assistant barrister of that part of the United Kingdom.

In an unopposed case, if the standing orders have been Unopposed complied with, the examiner at once endorses the petition ' ' accordingly. If not, he certifies, by endorsement on the petition, that the standing orders have not been complied ' The appearance is a paper, which is previously obtained from the Private Bill Office, certifying that the agent has entered himself at that office, as a ent for the memorial. This appearance is given to the committee clerk. See also infra, p. 509.

One fair copy of such statement is required for the examiner, and another for the committee clerk.

In opposed cases.

Memorials complaining of iion-cuui-pliaiice.

Specific statements of noncompliance.

Preliminary objections.

with, and also reports to the house the facts upon which his decision is founded, and any special circumstances connected with the case. In an opposed case, when the formal proofs have been completed, the examiner proceeds to hear the memorialists. The agents for the latter, ordinarily, take no part in the proceedings upon the formal proofs; but if they desire that any of the promoters' witnesses, who have proved the deposit of documents, the service of notices, or other matters, should be detained for further examination, in reference to allegations of error contained in the memorials, the examiner directs them to be in attendance until their evidence shall be required. By the standing orders, any parties shall be entitled to appear and to be heard, by themselves, their agents and witnesses, upon a memorial addressed to the examiner, complaining of a non-compliance with the standing orders, provided the matter com-l)lained of be specifically stated in such memorial, and the party (if any) who may be specially affected by the non-comj)liance with the standing orders have signed such memorial, and shall riot have withdrawn his signature thereto, and such memorial have been duly deposited in the Private Bill Office.

Unless the matters complained of be specifically stated in the memorial, the memorialists are not entitled to be heard, and the utmost care is consequently required in drawing memorials. When a memorial complains of more than one breach of the standing orders, it is divided into distinct allegations. Each allegation should specifically allege a non-compliance with the standing orders, and should state the circumstances of such alleged non-compliance in clear and accurate lanffuase.

When the agent for a memorial rises to address the examiner, the agent for the bill may raise preliminary objections to his being heard upon the memorial, on any of the grounds referred to in the standing orders, or on account of violations of the rules and usage of Parliament, or other special circumstances. Such objections are distinct from any subsequent objections to particular allegations. It has been objected, for exam)le, that a memorial has not Memorials sub-been duly signed, so as to entitle the parties to be heard, jy gg as peti-No proof of the signatures, however, is required, in any case, " " ' unless there should be some prima facie reason for doubting their genuineness. The same rule is applied to the affixing of a corporate seal. On the 16th Febrviary 1846 an instruction was given to the select committee on petitions for private bills not to hear parties on any petition " which sliall not be prepared in strict conformity with the rules and oi'ders of this house." And as memorials addressed to the examiner have supplied the place of petitions to the house, complaining of non-compliance with the standing orders, the examiners have applied to them all the parliamentary rules applicable to petitions; and have otherwise followed the practice of the sub-committees on petitions for private bills.

If no preliminary objection be taken, or if it be over- Preliminary ruled, the agent proceed! to read the first allegation in his auegations." memorial. Preliminary objections may be raised to any allegation: as that it alleges no breach of the standing orders; that it is uncertain, or not sufficiently specific, or that the party specially affected has not signed the memorial, or has withdrawn his signature. In reference to the Parties spe-latter grounds of objection it may be explained that by numerous decisions of sub-committees and of the examiners, the signatures of parties specially affected are required iu reference to such allegations only as affect parties personally, and in which the public generally have no interest. Thus if it be alleged that the name of any owner, lessee or occupier of property has been omitted from the book of reference, or that he has received no notice, the examiner will not proceed with the allegation, unless the cially affected.

' 101 Com. J. 147.

Public objections.

Questions of merits excluded.

party affected has himself signed the memorial. But in the application of this rule considerable niceties often arise from the peculiar circumstances of each case.

There are numerous grounds of objection which relate to matters affecting the public, and do not therefore require the signatures of parties specially affected. Thus objections to the sufficiency of newspaper notices; to the accuracy of the plans, sections, and books of reference, where the errors alleged are patent upon such documents, or are separable from questions relating to property in lands and houses, have always been treated as public objections. The same principle has been applied to objections to the estimate, subscription contract or declaration; and to allegations that any documents have not been deposited in compliance with the standing orders. It is for public information and protection that all requirements of this character are to be complied with by the promoters of the bill, and any person is therefore entitled to complain of non-compliance, on behalf of the public, without proving any special or peculiar interest of his own.

Allegations are to be confined to breaches of the standing orders, and may not raise questions impugning the merits of the bill, which are afterwards to be investigated by Parliament and by committees of either house. It may be objected, for example, that a subscription contract is not valid, or that the subscribers do not bind themselves legally, for the payment of the money subscribed. But it may not be alleged that the subscribers are insolvent and will be unable to pay the money. It may be shown that an estimate is informal, and not such an estimate as is required by Parliament; but the insufficiency of the estimate is a question of merits over which the examiner has no jurisdiction. Again, in examining the accuracy of the section of a proposed railway, the examiner will inquire whether the surface of the ground be correctly shown, or the gradients correctly calculated; but he cannot entertain objections which relate to the construction of the work, its engineering advantages, its expense, or other similar matters Avhich will be afterwards considered by the committee on the bill.

The examiner decides upon each allegation, and, when- Decision ami ever it is necessary, explains the grounds of his decision, examiner. When all the memorials have been disposed of, he endorses the petition, and if the standing orders have not been complied with, he makes a report to the house, as already stated. In case he should feel doubts as to the due construction of any standing order, in its application to a particular case, he may make a special report of the facts to the house, without deciding whether the standing order has been complied with or not.

When the petition has been endorsed by the examiner Petition to be it is returned to the agent for the bill, who is to arrange for its presentation to the house by a member. All the proceedings preliminary to the application to Parhament being thus completed, the further progress of a private bill in the House of Commons is reserved for the next chapter.

Progress of private bills in the coimnoiis.

Parliamentary agents.

Personally responsible.

Declaration and registry.

The further progress of a private bill through the House of Commons will now be followed, step by step, precisely in the order in which particular rules are to be observed by the parties, or enforced by the house or its officers. But this statement of the various forms of procedure may be introduced by a few observations explanatory of the general conduct of private business in the House of Commons.

I. Every private bill or petition is solicited by an agent, upon whom various duties and responsibilities are imposed by the orders of the house. The rules laid down by the speaker, by authority of the house, in 1837, are to the following effect: 1. " Every agent conducting proceedings in Parliament before the House of Commons, shall be personally responsible to the house and to the speaker for the observance of the rules, orders, and practice of Parliament, and rules prescribed by the speaker, and also for the payment of all fees and charges."

2. " No person shall be allowed to act as an agent until he has subscribed a declaration before one of the clerks in the Private Bill Office, engaging to observe and obey all the rules of the house, and to pay all fees and charges when demanded. He shall also enter into a recognizance (if hereafter required) in 600 L, condi-tioned to observe this declaration. He shall then be registered in a book to be kept in the Private Bill Office, and shall be entitled to act as a parliamentary agent, without the payment of any fee upon the declaration, bond, or registry."

' But this recognizance has not been required.

3. " The declaration, c. shall be in such form as the speaker Form, may from tirae to time direct."

4. " No notice sliall be received in the Private Bill Office, for Appearance to any proceeding upon a petition for a bill, or upon a bill brought be c"tered upou from the lords (after such bill has been read a first time), until an appearance to act as the parliamentary agent upon the same shall have been entered in the Private Bill Office; in which appearance shall also be specified the name of the solicitor (if any) for such petition or bill."

5. " That before any party shall be allowed to appear or be Appearance on heard upon any petition against a bill, an appearance to act as the Petitions agent upon the same shall be entered in the Private Bill Office; in which appearance shall also be specified the name of the solicitor and of the counsel who appear in support of any such petition (if any be then engaged), and a certificate of such appearance shall be delivered to the parliamentary agent, to be produced to the committee clerk."

6. " In case the agent for any petition or bill shall be displaced Afresh appear-by the solicitor, or shall decline to act, his responsibility shall ance on cliangc cease upon a notice being given in the Private Bill Office; and a fresh appearance shall be entered upon such petition or bill."

7. " Any agent who shall wilfully act in violation of the rules Speaker may and practice of Parliament, or any rules to be prescribed by the prohibit an speaker, or who shall wilfully misconduct himself in prosecuting practising, any proceedings before Parliament, shall be liable to an absolute or temporary prohibition to practise as a parliamentary agent, at the pleasure of the speaker; provided that upon the application of such agent, the speaker shall state in writing the grounds for such prohibition."'

And by a speaker's order of the 25th April 1845:

"Every parliamentary agent and solicitor will be considered violation of personally responsible for any wilful violation of the sessional standing orders, orders or standing orders of the house of which he shall be guilty, in like manner and to the same extent as he has been, heretofore, responsible for any violation of the rules, orders, and practice of Parliament."

The name, description, and place of residence of the Registry of parliamentary agent in town, and of the agent in the country (if any) soliciting a bill, are entered in the " private ' Pari. Paper, No. 88, ofl837.

Members may not be asents.

Nor officers of the house.

Notices of private business, liow giveii.

Hours for giving notices.

If not duly givfu, proceedings void.

bin register," in the Private Bill Office, which is open to public inspection.

Besides these regulations, there are certain disqualifications for parliamentary agency. It was declared by a resolution of the house, 26th February 1830, nern. con.,

"Tliat it is contrary to the law and usage of Parliament that any member of this house should be permitted to engage, either by himself or any partner, in the management of private bills, before this or the other house of Parliament, for pecuniary reward."'

And in compliance with the recommendation of a select committee on House of Commons offices in 1835, no officer or clerk belonging to the establishment is allowed to transact private business before the house, for his emolument or advantage, either directly or indirectly.

II. It has been stated elsewhere, that the public business for each day is set down in the Order Book, either as notices of motions or orders of the day; but the notices in relation to private business are not given by a member, nor entered in the Order Book, except in the case of any special proceeding; but are required to be delivered at the Private Bill Office, at specified times, by the agents soliciting the bills. These notices will each be described in their proper places; but one rule applies to all of them alike: they must be delivered before six o'clock in the evening of any day on which the house shall sit, and before two o'clock on any day on which the house shall not sit; and after the house has adjourned beyond the following day, no notice may be given for the first day on which it shall sit again. If any stage of a bill be proceeded with when the notice has not been duly given, such proceeding will be null and void, and the stage must be repeated.

' 85 Coin. J. 107.

Pari. Rep. No. 648, of 1843, p. 9; No. 606, of 1835, pp. 17. 19.

3 Sui ra, pp. 210-215.)00 Com. J. 423 j 101 lb. 167.

All notices arc open to inspection in the Private Bill Notices ., ii' 1 published.

Office; but for the sake oi greater publicity and convenience, they are also printed with the Votes; and members and parties interested are thus as well acquainted with the private business set down for each sitting, as with the public notices and orders of the clay.

III. The time set apart for the consideration of all mat- Time for pri-ters relating to private bills, is between four and five in the afternoon, immediately after the meeting of the house. There is a " private business list" on the table of the house every afternoon, a quarter of an hour before the time appointed for ISIr. Speaker to take the chair; upon which members should have their names entered, if they desire to make any motion relative to private business; and their names will be called by Mr. Speaker, in the order in which they appear on the list.

But to entitle a motion to be heard at the time of private What to be business, it must relate to a private bill before the house, business. or strictly to private business in some other form. On the 3d April 1845, a member having given notice that he should, at the time of private business, make a motion for referring back a report, to the Board of Trade, for reconsideration: and having risen in his place for that purpose, was interrupted by Mr. Speaker, who stated, that, in his opinion, that motion ought not to be considered as private business, and ought not to be brought forward at that time; but, as this was a new case, he submitted it to the decision of the house. Whereupon a motion was made, and question put, "That the member be now heard in support of the motion intended to be made by him, and that the question be proposed to the house:" which the house decided in the negative. In this case the petition for the bill had been referred to the committee on petitions for private bills, but there was, in fact, no bill before the house. It was upon this ground that the motion was ruled not to relate to private business in such a way as to entitle it to be brought

Order of pro-ceeilin5s on private business.

Conduct of bills by members.

When special motions made.

on at that time. If the same motion had been offered after the commitment of the bill, when the house would have referred the report of the railway department to the committee, it would have been received as a question relating to a private bill then in progress, and would have been properly brought on at the time of private business.

As soon as the house is ready to proceed to private business the speaker desires the clerk at the table to read from the private business list the titles of the several bills set down for that day, in the following order: 1. Consideration of lords' amendments; 2. Third readings; 3. Con-deration of bills ordered to lie upon the table; and, 4. Second readings. If, upon the reading of any title, no motion be made relative to the bill, further proceedings are adjourned until the next sitting of the house.

Every form and proceeding, in the offices of the house, in conducting a bill is managed by a parliamentary agent (or by a solicitor who has entered his name as agent for the bill), or by officers of the house; but, in the house ilself no order can be obtained, except by a motion made by a member, and a question proposed and put (or supposed to be put) in the usual manner from the chair. Two members are generally requested by their constituents, or by the parties, to undertake the charge of a bill; they receive notice from the agents when they will be required to make particular motions of which the forms are prepared for them; and they attend in their places, at the proper time, for that purpose. In ordinary cases the different proceedings are prescribed by the standing orders, and the motion made by a member is a mere form, preliminary to the usual order of the house. But whenever any unusual proceeding becomes necessary, such as a special reference to the ' 100 Com. J. 191; 79 Hans. Deb., 3d N. S., 10.

' Tlie names of the members wlio are ordered to prepare and bring in the bill, are printed on the back of it.

examiner, or a committee, or a departure from tlic standing-orders or rules of the house, the member is I'equired, except in urgent cases, to give notice of his intended motion; and afterwards to make the motion in the usual manner.

IV. Every vote of the house upon a private bill is entered " Private bill in the " Votes and Proceedings," and Journals, and there "" is also kept In the Private Bill Office a register, in-which are recorded all the proceedings, from the petition to the passing of the bill. The entries In this register specify briefly each day's proceeding before the examiners, or in the house, or in any committee to which the bill may be referred. This book is open to public Inspection daily, between the hours of ten and six. As every proceeding Is entered under the name of the particular bill to whicli It refers, it can be immediately referred to, and the exact state of the bill discovered at a glance.

After these explanations, the proceedings in the house may be described without interruption, precisely In the order in which they usually occur.

When the petition for the bill has been endorsed by one Petition for bill of the examiners. It must be presented to the house, by a i ' ' " member, with a printed copy of the bill annexed, not later than three clear days after such endorsement; or if the house shall not be sitting, then not later than three clear days after the first sitting.

If the standing orders have been complied with, the bill when standing Is at once ordered to be brought In. If not complied with,, iiio, i uitii. the petition Is referred to the standing orders committee; and tiie report of the examiner, being laid upon the table, by the speaker, is also referred.

On the 7th March 1845, the South-Eastern Railway Petitions wlth-Company pe-titioned for leave to withdraw their original, J er"p"Htions petition for a bill, and to present petitions for seven presented, separate bills with reference to the olyects comprised in their original petition. Their petition was referred to

Private hills to he brought in upon petition.

Exceptions.

Petitions for additional provision.

the standing orders committee, who reported, on the 11th March, that if the house shall give leave to withdraw their original petition, the sessional order ought to be dispensed with, and that the parties be permitted to present petitions for seven separate bills. On the 14th March, the original petition was withdrawn, and leave given to present petitions for seven separate bills. In the same manner leave was given, on the 14th March 1845, that two London and Croydon Railway bill petitions be withdrawn, and that petitions might be presented for five different bills.

There is an express standing order, that no private bill shall be brought in otherwise than upon petition, signed by the parties, or some of them, who are suitors for the bill; and bills which have been proceeding as public bills, have sometimes been withdrawn, on notice being taken that they were private bills, and ought to have been brought in upon petition. But bius of a local character, to which the standing orders of the house are applicable, have occasionally been brought in, by order, as public bills, without the form of a petition. Their further progress, however, is subject to the proof of compliance with the standing orders before the examiner, and to the payment of fees. They have generally been bills for carrying out public works, or other objects in which the Government were concerned; as, for example, the Lagan Navigation Bills, in 1841 and 1842; the Knightsbridge and Kensington Openings Bill, in 1842; the Tralee Navigation and Harbour Bill, in 1844; the Fisher-lane (Greenwich) Luprovement Bill, in 1845; the Holyhead Harbour Bill, in 1847; the Caledonian Canal Bill and Windsor Castle Approaches Bill, in 1848; the Dublin Improvement (No."2) Bill, in 1849; the Portland Harbour and Breakwater Bill, in 1850; and the Smithfield Market Removal Bill, in 1851.

If, after the introduction of a private bill, any additional provision should be desired to be made in the bill, in respect 100 Com, J. 13G.

lb. 138.

80 lb. 488. 490, 491.

of matters to which the standing orders arc api)Iicablc, a petition for that purpose should be presented, with a copy of the proposed clauses annexed. The petition will be referred to the examiners of petitions for private bills, who are to give at least two clear days' notice of the day on which it will be examined. Memorials complaining of non-compliance with the standing orders, in respect of the petition, may be deposited in the Private Bill Office, together with two copies thereof, before 12 o'clock on the day preceding that appointed for the examination of the petition; and the examiner may entertain any memorial, although the party (if any) who may be specially affected by the non-com li-ance, shall not have signed it. After hearing the parties, in the same manner as in the case of the original petition for the bill, the examiner reports to the house whether the standing orders have been complied with or not, or whether any be applicable to the petition for additional provision.

It has occasionally happened that petitions for additional When such provision have sought for public legislation affecting the sidered in com-stamp duties or other branches of the revenue; which, """"' '=' t"' whole house.

according to the rules of the house," are required to originate in a committee of the whole house. In such cases the petition is presented, and the Queen's recommendation having been signified, the house resolves to go into committee on a future day. The matter is considered in committee on that day; and when the resolution is reported and agreed to, an instruction is given to the committee on the bill to make provision accordingly." If any such provision be included in the original bill it must be printed in italics; and before the sitting of the committee similar proceedings will be taken in the house.

' See supra, 411 et seq.

2 Rock Life Assurance Company Bill, 1849; 104 Com. J. 15G. 102. Universal Railway Casualty Compensation Company Bill, 1849; 104 Com. J. 139. 149. Guardian Assurance Company Bill, 1830; 103 Com. J. 158. 204. Clerical, Medical, c., and Licci'sed Victuallers' Assurance Companies Bills, 1830; 105 Com. J. 158. Law Property Assurance Ccnipany Bill, 18."1.

Standing orders committee.

When special report of examiner referred.

Other duties of standing orders committee.

Proceedings of standing orders committee.

The committee on standing orders consists of eleven members, who are nominated at the commencement of every session, of whom five are a quorum. To this committee are referred all the reports of the examiners in which they report that the standing orders have not been complied with; and it is their office to determine and report to the house whether such standing orders ought or ought not to be dispensed with; and whether, in their opinion, the parties should be permitted to proceed with their bill, or any portion of it; and under what conditions (if any): as, for example, after publishing advertisements, depositing plans, or amending estimates, when such conditions seem to be proper.

If any special report be made by the examiner as to the construction of a standing order it will also be referred to the standing orders committee. The committee, in such a case, are to determine, according to their construction of the standing order, and on the facts stated in the examiner's report, whether tlie standing orders have been complied with or not. If they determine that the standing orders have been complied with, they so report to the house; and if not complied with, they proceed to consider whether the standing orders ought to be dispensed with. To this committee are also referred all petitions praying that any of the sessional or standing orders of the house may be dispensed with; and they report their opinion upon such petitions to the house. Tlieir duties in reference to clauses and amendments and other matters, will be adverted to, in describing the proceedings to which they relate.

According to the usual practice of this committee, written statements ai-e prepared on one side by the agent for the bill, and on the other, by the agents for memorialists, who have been heard by the examiner. When these statements have been read by the committee, they determine whether the standing orders ought or ought not to be dispensed with, and whether "the parties should be permitted to proceed with their bill, and under what (if any) conditions." The parties arc called in and acquainted with the determination of the committee, Avhich is afterwards reported to the house. It is not usual to hear the parties, except for the explanation of any circumstances which are not sufficiently shown by the written statements. But in some inquiries of a special character which have been referred to the committee, they have heard agents and examined witnesses, before they have agreed to their report.

The committee, in their report to the house, do not Principles by ,., 1 n A '-I 1 1 which standing explain tlie grounds or their determination; but the orders commit-principles and general rules by which they are guided t ' governed. may be briefly stated. The report of the examiner being conclusive as to the facts, it is the province of the committee to consider equitably, with reference to public interests and private rights, whether the bill should be permitted to proceed. If the promoters appear to have attempted any fraud upon the house, or to be chargeable with gross or wilful negligence, they will have forfeited all claim to a favourable consideration. But assuming them to have taken reasonable care in endeavouring to comply with the orders of the house, and that their errors have been the result of accident or inadvertence, not amounting to laches, their case will be considered according to its particular circumstances. The committee will then estimate the importance of the orders which have been violated, the character and number of separate instances of non-compliance, the extent to which public and private interests may be affected by such non-compliance, the importance and pressing nature of the bill itself, the absence of opposition, or other special circumstances. And, according to the general view which ' Edinburgh and Perth Railway Bill, 1847; 102 Com. J. 226. 293; and evidence printed at the expense of the parties. Edinburgh and Northern Railway Bill, 1849; 104 Com. J. 37. 48. 70.

the committee may take of the whole of the circumstances, they will report that the standing orders ought or ought not to be dispensed with. Report. If the standing orders committee report that indulgence ceeii." ' " should be granted to the promoters of a bill, they are allowed to proceed with the bill or with the additional provision, either at once, or after complying with the necessary conditions, according to the report of the committee. To give effect to this permission, the proper form to be observed, is for a member to move that the report be read, and that leave be given to bring in the bill. In the case of a petition for additional provision, no further proceeding in the house is necessary, but the parties have leave to introduce the provision if the committee shall think fit. The compliance with the orders for giving notices, c. is generally required to be proved before the committee on the bill, but, in some Standingorders cases, before the examiners. If the committee report that pcnsecl witl " Standing orders ought not to be dispensed with, their decision is generally acquiesced in by the promoters, and is fatal to the bill. But in order to leave the question still open for consideration, the house agree to those reports only, which are favourable to the progress of bills, and pass no opinion upon the unfavourable reports, which are merely ordered to lie upon the table. Decision of In some few cases the decision of the standing orders st! in(liiij-orders.,,,., itiii couiinittceover- Committee has been distmctly overruled by the house, either upon the consideration of petitions from the promoters, or by a direct motion in the house, not founded upon any petition. But as the house have generally been disj)osed ' Dublin Improvement Bill, 1849; 104 Com. J. 76. Great Northern Railway Bill, 1849; 104 Com. J. 81.

2 Doncaster and Selby Road Bill, 1832; 87 Com. J. 150. 163. London Bridge Approaches Bill, 1834; 89 Com. J. 81. 122. London City Police Bill, 1839; 94 Com. J. 228. 234. London and Greenwich Railway Enlargement and Station Bill, 1840; 95 Coiti. J. 113.118.

3 Irish Great Western Railway Bill, 6th May 1845; 100 Com. J. 395. 80 Hans. Deb., N. S., 158. 175.

to support the committee, attempts to reverse or disturb its decisions have rarely been successful.

In one case the committee had decided that the standing Report referred orders ought not to be dispensed with; but by a clerical coiumuter error it was entered in the Votes that the standing orders ought to be dispensed with, and a bill was ordered to be brought in. The report was referred back to the committee, and the subsequent proceedings declared null and void. The committee again reported that the standing orders ought not to be dispensed with; but the promoters subsequently presented a petition for leave to present a petition for a bill, and their second bill ultimately received the royal assent.

If the promoters of the bill, without desiring to disturb Petitions for the decision of the standing orders committee, still entertain p'e Jtions'for' ' hopes that the house may be induced to relax the standing ' ""'-orders, or be willing to abandon portions of their bill; or if there be special circumstances, such as the consent of au parties, or the urgent necessity of the bill being passed in the present session, they should present a petition to the house, praying for leave to deposit a petition fur a bill, and stating fuuy the grounds of their application. The petition will be referred to the standing orders committee, who, after hearing the statements of the parties, will report to the house whether, In their opinion, the parties should have leave to deposit a petition for a bill. If leave be given, the petition is deposited In the Private Bill Office, and the case Is examined, and the petition certified by the examiner. In the same manner as if it had been originally deposited before the 31st December.

Birkenhead, Manchester, and Cheshire Junction Railway Bill, 25th April 1845; 100 Com. J. 338. Shrewsbury and Hereford Railway Bill, 1846; 101 Com. J. 486. 502.

West Riding Union Railway, 1846; 101 Com. J. 176. 223. 252.

3 Manchester and Southampton Railway Bill, 1847; 102 Com. J. 269, c.

'I'o (Ipposif jtt'ti-tioiis tor bills after time.

Bill presented.

Scliedules added.

Rates and tolls in italics.

First read in; If parties desire to solicit a bill during the cun'cnt session, who have not deposited a petition for the bill before the 31st December, they may present a petition, praying for leave to dei)Osit a petition for a bill, and explaining the circumstances under which they had been prevented from complying witli the orders of the house, as to the deposit of their petition at the proper time. Their petition will be referred to the standing orders committee, and if they succeed in making out a case for indulgence, leave will be given by the house, on the report of the committee, to deposit a petition for a bill, which will be proceeded with in the usual manner.

When leave has been obtained to bring in a private bill, it is required to be presented not later than three clear days after the presentation of the petition. It must be printed on paper of a folio size (as determined by the speaker), with a cover of jdarchment attached to it, upon which the title is written. The short title of the bill, as first entered in the Votes, is to correspond with that at the head of the advertisement, and may not be changed unless by special order of the house.

On the 20th February 1846, the solicitor and agent for a bill petitioned for leave to add schedules which had been accidentally omitted from the printed copies of the bill; and the house allowed the parties to make the alteration.

The proposed amount of all rates, tolls, fines, forfeitures, or penalties, or other matters which must be settled in committee, are ordered to be inserted in italics, in the printed bill. These were formerly left as blanks, and are still technically regarded by the house as blanks to be filled up by the committee on the bill; but it is more convenient that the particular amounts intended to be proposed, should be known at the same time as the other provisions of the bill.

The bill may be read a first time immediately after it is ' Soiitliport Iniprovenieut Bill, 20tli and 23d February 1846; 101 Com. J. 183. 185.

presented; but before tbe first reading of every private bill Copies of bill (except name bills) printed copies of the bill must be doorkoepers. delivered to the doorkeepers in the lobby of the house, for the use of members.

Between the first and second reading there may not be rrocecdings , before second less than three clear days nor more than ten, except by reading, special order of the house. The agent for the bill is required to give three clear days' notice in writing, at the Private Bill Office, of the day proposed for the second reading, and no such notice may be given until the day after that on which the bill has been read a first time. Meanwhile the bill is in the custody of the Private Bill Bill examined . in Private Bill

Office, where it is exammed, as to its conformity with tlie omce.

rules and standing orders of the house. If not in due form, the examining clerk specifies on the bill the nature of the irregularities, wherever they occur. If the bill be Withdrawn if

T 1 informal.

improperly drawn, or at variance with the stanumg orders, or the order of leave, the order for the second reading is discharged, the bill is withdrawn, and leave is given to present another. The bill so presented is distinguished from the first bill by being numbered (2), and, having been read a first time, is referred to the examiners of petitions for private bills. Two clear days' notice is given of the examination, and memorials may be deposited before twelve o'clock on the day preceding that appointed. The examiner inquires whether the standing orders, which have been already proved In respect of the first bill, have equally been complied with in respect of the bill No. 2, and reports accordingly to the house; when the biu proceeds in the ordinary course.

The House of Commons will not allow peers to be con- Peers' names, cerned in the levy of any charge upon the people; and If they be named In a private bill, for that purpose, their names are struck out. In particular cases such names ' 92 Com. J. 254. 425; 9U lb. 187. 211; 104 lb. 71 105 lb. 40,: c. c.

have escaped detection; but by the present practice,

"The clerks in tlie Private Bill Office are particularly directed to take care, that in tlie examination of all private bills, levying any rates, tolls, or duties on the subject, peers of Parliament, peers of Scotland, or peers of Ireland, are not to be inserted therein, either as trustees, commissioners, or proprietors of any company."

But if no tolls, rates or duties be proposed to be levied under the bill, a peer's name has been permitted to stand in the bill as a director."' If a violation of In 1845, Mr. Speaker called the attention of the house orders. to a bill which contained a clause giving compulsory power to take lands, of which no notice had been given, and without the proper plans, sections and estimates having been deposited according to the standing orders. The order for the second reading was discharged, and the bill referred to the committee on petitions for private bills. The committee reported that the standing orders had not been complied with; and were instructed to inquire by whom and under what circumstances the violation of the standing orders had been committed. Their report was referred to the standing orders committee, who determined that the standing orders ought not to be dispensed with, and the bill was not proceeded with. Second reading. The second reading is like the same stage in other bills, and in agreeing to it the house affirm the general principle and expediency of the measure. It is the first occasion on which it is brought before the house otherwise than pro forma, or in connexion with the standing orders; and if the bill be opposed, upon its principle, it is the proper time for attempting its defeat. K the second reading be deferred for three or six months, or the bill rejected, no new bill for the same object can be offered until the next

By speaker's order, 24th March 1840.

Farmers' Estate Society (Ireland) Bill, 1848.

3 Midland Railway Branches Bill, 1845; 100 Com. J. 219.

lb.:247. 5 lb. 2G2. 385. 419.

session. In order to avert surprises, if the second (or third) reading of a bill be opposed, its consideration is postponed until the next day's sitting.

Wlien a private bill has been read a second time, it is Commitment, immediately committed, and referred to the " committee Committee of of selection." This committee consists of the chairman of the standing orders committee, who is, ex-officio, cliairman thereof, and of four other members nominated by the house at the commencement of every session, of whom three are a quorum.

This committee classifies the bills, nominates the mem- its proceedings bers of every private bill committee, and otherwise arranges the private business of the session. Their several duties are distinctly prescribed in the standing orders, and a general outline of their proceedings is all that need be given in order to explain the progress of a private bill. The committee of selection having before them all the private bius of the session, which are laid before them at their first meeting, by the pi-omoters, forms into groups such private bills as may be conveniently submitted to the same committee; and names the bill or bills which shall be taken into consideration on the first day of the meeting of the committee.

Every railway bill committee consists of a chairman and Constitution of four members not locally or otherwise interested in the privatebtiu"" bill or bills referred to them. The constitution of committees on other private bills is somewhat different, the principle of local representation being still retained in a limited degree. Every unopposed private bill (and every unopposed unopposed railway bill which has not been included in a '" " group, or has been withdrawn from a group), is referred, by the committee of selection, to the chairman of the committee of ways and means and two other members, of whom one is to be a member who had been ordered to prc- ' See supra, p. "233.

pare and bring in the bill, and the other a member not Whenconsi- locally interested." No bill is considered as an opposed dercd as op- i-n i i posed. bill unless withm seven clear days after the second read- ing, a petition has been presented against it, in which the petitioners pray to be heard by themselves, their counsel or agents, or unless the chairman of ways and means reports to the house that a bill ought to be so treated.

Committees on Opposed private bills are referred to a chairman and four members not locally or otherwise interested, to whom

Local members are nddcd, in certain cases, members representing the county or borough to Avhich the bill or bills specially relate. The

But may not members who are added in respect of local representation, however, are merely entitled to attend and take part in the proceedings of the committee upon the bill, in respect of which they are added, but have no vote upon any question that may arise.

Notice given to The committee of selection give each member at least fourteen days' notice, by publication in the Votes, and by letter, of the week in which he is to be in attendance to serve as a member not locally interested, and they also give him sufficient notice of his appointment as the member of a committee, and transmit to every member not locally or otherwise interested, a blank form of declaration, which he is to return forthwith properly filled up and signed. If he neglect to return the declaration in due time, or do not send a sufficient excuse, the committee of selection will report his name to the house,"" and he will be ordered to attend the committee on the bill.

Members re If the committee of selection be dissatisfied with his fusing to at i 'n tend. excuse, they will require him to serve upon a committee; when his attendance will become obligatory, and if necessary will be enforced by the house. On the 5th May 1845, ' For bills originating in the lords, see infra, p. 577. " 103 Com. J. 500. 0:27; 105 lb. 287, c'.

r,9. r a member was reported absent from a group committee. lie stated to the house that a correspondenec had taken phicc between the committee of selection and himself, in which he had informed them that he was already serving on two public committees, and that his serving on the railway-group committee was incompatible with those duties. But the house ordered him to attend the railway committee.

In 1846 the committee of selection, not being satisfied with Case of Mr.,-.,, T-,., 1 1 1 Smith O'liiicn.

the excuses of Mr. bmith O linen, nominated hnn a member of a committee on a group of railway bills. He was reported absent from that committee, and was ordered by the house to attend it on the following day. He adhered, however, to his determination not to attend the committee, and was committed to the custody of the serjeant-at-arms for his contempt."

At any time before the meeting of the committee on One member. n 1 J. substituted for the bill, the committee oi selection may substitute one another. member for another whom they shall deem it proper to excuse. But after the committee has met, members can only be discharged from attendance, and other members added to the committee, by order of the house.

An interval of fourteen days is required to elapse between interval be- -,-,. n t Ml 1 1 ? twcpii second the second reading of every private bill and the hrst sitting leaiiing and of the committee, except in the case of divorce bills, where there are to be eight clear days, and of name bills and estate bills (not relating to either church or corporation property, c.), when there are to be three clear days between the second reading and the committee. Subject to this First sitting of . comniittee general order the committee of selection fix the time ior fixed, holding the first sitting of every private bill.

In all these matters the committee of selection ordinarily instructions to 1 1 T 1 1 committee of proceed in compliance with the standing orders; but where selection.

' 100 Com. J. 399; 80 Hans. Deb., N. S., IGG.

' See supra, Tp. 190. Special Rep. of Committee of Selection, '24fb April 184G; 101 Com. J. ogG. r,9-2. GO:. 85 Hans. Deb., 1071. IIM. 12'J-'. 1:300. 13. J1; 8G lb. 906. llts.

Chairman of ways and means, and counsel.

any departure from the standing orders or the usual practice of the committee is deemed advisable; or where, for any other reason, a particidar mode of dealing with any bills is desired by the house, special instructions have been given to the committee of selection. For example, the house have instructed the committee of selection to refer two or more bills to the same committee;' or to form all the bills of a certain class into one group; or to refer a bill to another committee;" or to remove a bill from a group, and refer it to a separate committee; or to withdraw a bill from one group and place it in another. Private bills connected with government works or crown property have been referred to a select committee nominated by the house, to whom five members were added by the committee of selection." And instruction shave been given to the committee of selection to appoint the first meeting of committees on an earlier day," or forthwith; or not to fix the sitting of committees upon certain classes of bills. until a later period. On the 18th February 1846 an instruction was given to the committee of selection that the committee on a bill be postponed for a fortnight, to give time for another bill, the petition for which was then before the sub-committee on petitions, to be brought forward, in order that both should be referred, as competing bills, to the same committee.""

Before the sitting of the committee on the bill, some important proceedings are necessary to be taken by the promoters. It is the duty of the chairman of Avays and means, with the assistance of the counsel to Mr. Speaker, 100 Com. J. 95. 224; 101 lb. 460. 104 lb. 248.

100 lb. 607. " 105 lb. 351. 105 lb. 418.

Fisher-lane (Greenwich) Improvement Bill; 100 Cora. J. 121. Spital-fields New Street Bill; 101 lb. 857. Brighton Pavilion Bill, 1849 j 104 lb. 478. Holyhead Harbour Bill, 1850; 105 lb. 634,-c.

7 100 Com. J. 730; 101 11). 475; 105 lb. 145.

103 lb. 700; 105 lb. 513, c.

105 lb. 72. 84. " Edinburgh Water Bill; 101 Com. J. 162.

to examine all private bills, whether opposed or unopposed, and to call the attention of the house, and also, if he think fit, of the chairman of the committee on every opposed private bill, to all points which may appear to him to require it. And in the case of unopposed bills he is also to report any special circumstances. To facilitate this exami- Copies of bin nation the agent is required to lay copies of the original them. " bill before the chairman and counsel, not later than the day after the examiner has endorsed the petition for the bill; and again, three clear days before the first meeting of the committee, the agent is required to lay before them copies of the bill, as proposed to be submitted to the committee, and signed by the agent. J3y the practice of the And before house of lords, copies of the bill as originally introduced, jo'r'Jis """

com- and also as proposed to be submitted to the committee '"ittces. on the bill, in the commons, are laid before the chairman of committees and his counsel; and a simidtaneous examination of the bill is consequently proceeding in both houses.

Amendments are suggested or required by the authorities Amondinents in both houses, which are either agreed to at once by the pro- eoinmittee. meters, or after discussion are insisted upon, varied, modified, or dispensed with. In the meantime the promoters endeavour, by proposing amendments of their own, to conciliate parties who are interested, and to avert opposition. They supervision by are frequently in communication with public boards or """"" " ' ' p "'-govei'nment departments, by whom amendments arc also proposed; and who, again, are in communication with the chairman of ways and means, or the chairman of the lords' committees. The Commissioners of Railways assist in the revision of railway bills, and suggest such amendments as they think necessary for the protection of the public, or for the saving of private rights. The Secretary of State for the ' Practically, this is done as soon as tlic bills are deposited in tlif Private Bill Office.

Home Department exercises a similar supervision over turnpike road bills. Where tidal lands are to be interfered with the Lords Commissioners of the Admiralty require protective clauses to be inserted; or may withhold the consent of the Crown to the execution of the proposed work. Where Crown property is affected, the Commissioners of Woods and Forests, who may give or Avithhold the consent of the Crown, have the bill submitted to them, and insist upon the insertion of protective clauses, or the omission of objectionable provisions. The Board of Trade offer suggestions in reference to bills affecting trade, patents, shipping, and other matters connected with the general business of that department. Bills for the improvement and sewerage of towns receive consideration by the Board of Health, by whom amendments are also suggested. And in case a bill should affect the public revenue, similar communications will be necessary with the Treasury and other rieiiniinary revenue departments. And where there have been local inquiries under the Preliminary Inquiries Act, amendments have been introduced, in compliance with the suggestions of the inspectors; or at a later period such suggestions have been enforced by reports from the Admiralty, or adopted by the committee on the bill.

Limits to such When the amendments consequent upon these various proceedings have been introduced, the printed bill, with all the proposed amendments and clauses Inserted, In manuscript, Is In a condition to be submitted to the committee. But care must be taken. In preparing these amendments, that they be within the order of leave, and Involve no Infraction of the standing orders. Where it was proposed to leave out the greater part of the clauses In the original bill, and to Insert other clauses, the chairman of ways and means has submitted to the house that the bill should be withdrawn.

Inquiries Act.

amendments.

' 11 12 Vict. c. 129; and see supra, p. 499.

= Bristol Parochial Hates Bill, 1845; 100 Com. J. 535.

By a regulation of the present session the committee of Committee not selection will not appoint a day for the first sitting of the,",", ui "hitl up- committee on the bill until the chairman of ways and means P""- has certified that the bill is so far approved of as to be ready for the consideration of the committee. The clerk to the committee of selection then gives seven clear days' notice of the meeting of tlie committee; and if it should be postponed he gives immediate notice of such postponement.

The agent is required to deposit in the Private Bill Filled up bill to. be deposited.

Office a fiued-up bill signed by himself, as proposed to be submitted to the committee, one clear day before the meeting of the committee: and all parties are entitled to obtain a copy of the filled-up bill, upon payment of the charges for making out the amendments. In 1845 certain committees upon bills reported that no filled-up bill had been deposited by the agent as required, and that the committee had therefore declined to proceed with the bill, and had instructed the chairman to report the circumstance to the house." In these cases the practice has been to revive the committees, and to give them leave to sit and proceed on a certain day, provided the filled-up bill shall have been duly deposited. The omission of the agents had arisen from the fact that the bills had undergone no alterations since they had been printed with the petition, and in such cases it had not been customaiy to deposit a filled-up bill, as required by this standing order.

Each member of a railway committee, and each member. Declaration of. in members not not locally or otherwise interested, of a committee on locally inte- opposed private bills, before he is entitled to attend and vote, is required to sign a declaration " that his constituents have no local interest, and that he has no personal interest" in the bill; " and that he will never vote on any question which may arise without having duly heard and attended to the evidence relating thereto." And no such 100 Com. J. 261. 302. ' lb. 302. 304.

rested.

Quorum to be always present.

Members not to absent themselves.

Proceedings suspended if quorum not present.

Members absent reported.

Excused, c.

If quorum cau' not attend.

committee can proceed to business until this declaration has been signed by each of the members. If a member who has signed this declaration should subsequently discover that he has a direct pecuniary interest in a bill or in a company who are petitioners against a bill, he will state the fact, and upon the motion of the chairman, will be discharged by the house from further attendance on the committee.

If three of the members not interested be present, the committee may proceed, but not with a less number, except by special leave of the house. And so soon after the expiration of ten minutes after the time appointed for the first sitting of a committee on an opposed bill (not being a railway bill), as three at least of such members are present, the chairman proceeds to take the chair. But no member of a railway committee, nor any of the five members, not locally or otherwise interested, of the committee on any other private bill, may absent himself, except in case of sickness, or by order of the house. If at any time a quorum of three should not be present, the chairman suspends the proceedings, and if at the expiration of an hour there should still be less than three members, the committee is adjourned to the next day on which the house shall sit. Members absenting themselves are reported to the house at its next sitting, when they are either directed to attend at the next sitting of the committee, or, if their absence has been occasioned by sickness, domestic affliction, or other sufficient cause, they are excused from further attendance.". If after a committee has been formed, a quorum of members cannot attend, the chairman reports the circumstance to the house, when the members still remaining will be enabled to proceed, or such orders will be made as the house may deem necessary.

100 Com. J. 386; 101 lb. 904; 104 lb. 357.

105 lb. 2-25.

101 lb. 56G. 575; 104 lb. 371, 391, c.; 105 lb. 426. 454, c.

All petitions in favour of or against private bills arc now Petitions for 111, ii 1 p and ajjaiiist pri- presented to the house, not m the usual way or presenting vate bills, how other petitions, but by depositing them in the Private Bill presented. Office, where they may be deposited by a member, party, or agent. Any petitioner may withdraw his petition, or Petitions with-his opposition, on a requisition to that effect being deposited in the Private Bill Office, signed by himself or by the agent who deposited the petition. Every petition Petitions against a private bill which has been deposited not later gfa d referred, than seven clear days after the second reading, stands referred to the committee on the bill, without any distinct reference from the house. And subject to the rules and orders of the house, the petitioners who have prayed to be heard by themselves, their counsel or agents, are to be heard upon their petition accordingly, if they think fit, and counsel heard in favour of the bill against such petition.

The agent for each petition must be prepared with a Appearances certificate from the Private Bill Office of his having ' " ' entered an appearance upon the petition. This document is delivered to the committee-clerk; and unless it be produced, the petition will be entered as not appeared upon.

On the 23d May 1848, a petition was presented, praying that a petitioner against a private bill be allowed to be heard upon his petition, notwithstanding he neglected to present a certificate from the Private Bill Office of his having entered an appearance upon his petition previous to the commencement of business by the committee. The petition was referred to the committee on the bill, without any further instruction."

Petitioners will not be heard before the committee unless Rules as to , 1.,. n hearing peti- their petition be prepared and signed in strict conlormity tioners, with the rules and orders of the house, and have been deposited within the time limited, except where the 103 Com. J. 562; and see Suppl, to Votes, 1848, p. 395. M M

Petitions depo- ited after time.

Special reference of a petition.

Grounds of objection to be specified.

When opposed bills to be treated as unopposed.

petitioners complain of any matter which may have arisen in committee, or which may be contained in the amendments as proposed in the filled-up bill.

If a petition be presented after the time limited, the only mode by which the petitioners can obtain a hearing, is by presenting a petition, praying that the standing orders be dispensed with in their case, and that they may be heard by the committee. The petition will be referred to the standing orders committee; and if the petitioners be able to show any special circumstances which entitle them to indulgence, and, particularly, that they have not been guilty of laches, the standing orders will be dispensed with. i

On the 17th May 1849, a petition from the attorney-general against a private bill was brought up, and read; and it being stated that it was essential to the public Interests that it should be referred to the committee on the bill, the standing order requiring all such petitions to be deposited in the Private Bill Office, was read, and suspended, and an instruction given to the committee to entertain the petition."

No petition will be considered which does not distinctly specify the grounds on which the petitioners object to any of the provisions of the bill. The petitioners can only be heard on the grounds so stated; and if not specified with sufficient accuracy, the committee may direct a more specific statement to be given, in writing, but limited to the grounds of objection which had been Inaccurately stated.

If no parties appear on the petitions against an opposed bill, or having appeared, withdraw their opposition before the evidence of the promoters is commenced, the committee is required to refer the bill back to the committee of ' See Votes, 14th and 18th March 1851, c. = 104 Com. J. 302.

selection, who deal with it as an unopposed bill. And in the case of a railway bill, the committee may refer the bill back to the committee of selection, under the same circumstances, if they think fit, but otherwise may consider the bill, though unopposed. And, on the other hand, if the When unop-chairman oi ways and means report that any unopposed be treated as bill should, in his opinion, be treated as opposed, it is again P referred to the committee of selection, and dealt with accordingly.

The committee on each group of bills is to take first Order in which into consideration the bill or bills named by the committee ered by the ' of selection; and is to appoint the day for considering committee, each of the other bills on that day parties promoting and opposing are to enter appearances; and the committee clerk is to give at least two days' notice of such appointment, and of any subsequent postponement, in the Private Bill Oflfice. Before this ai-rangement was made, in 1849, all the parties concerned in the various bills, comprised in the same group, were required to enter appearances on the first sitting of the connnittee; and although the bills were wholly unconnected in regard to locality or interest, the parties promoting and opposing one bill were detained, at enormous expense, while other bills were under consideration. Copies of the bill as proposed to be submitted Copies of the to the committee, and signed by the agent, are to be laid before mem-before each member, at the r meeting of the committee. " '

All questions before committees on private bills are Questions de-decided by a majority of voices, including the voice of the forily. chairman; and whenever the voices are equal, the chairman has a second or casting vote. In applying this rule, it must When chairman always be recollected, that none but selected members are entitled to vote. If the chairman be absent, the member next in rotation on the list of members, not locally or otherwise interested, who is present, acts as chairman.

' See supra, p. 524. M M

Provisions to be inserted in bills.

Committees on unopposed bills.

Special orders and rules.

Filled-upbillto be delivered.

Duties of the committee.

It is the duty ol' every committee to take care that the several provisions required by the standing orders of the house to be inserted in Private Bills, are included in them, wherever they are applicable. Some of these provisions rehite to private bills generally, and others to particular classes of bills. Of the former are clauses for compelling the payment of subscriptions; for the safe custody of monies, and audit of accounts in bills authorising the levy of fees, tolls, or other rate or charge; and for defining the level of roads, and otherwise protecting them, when altered by the construction of any public work.

The constitution of committees on unopposed bills has already been described; but a short reference to their functions will be convenient in this place, to avoid any interruption in stating such orders of the house as apply equally to both classes of committees. The chairman of ways and means, and one of the two other members of the committee, are a quorum; and unless they be of opinion that the bill referred to them should be treated as an opposed bill, they proceed to consider the preamble and all the provisions of the bill, and take care that they are conformable to the standing orders. The chief responsibility is imposed upon the chairman, who, being an officer of the house as well as a member, is entrusted, as already stated, with the special duty of examining, with the assistance of Mr. Speaker's counsel, every private bill whether opposed or unopposed. A copy of the bill, signed by the agent, as proposed to be submitted to the committee, is ordered to be laid before each member of the committee at their first meeting; and similar copies have already been laid before the chairman and Mr. Speaker's counsel three clear days before such meeting.

As there are no opponents of the bill before the committee, the promoters have only to prove the preamble, and satisfy the chau-man and the other members, of the propriety of the ' For the other duties of Chairman of Ways and Means, see supra, p.526e seq.

several provisions; that all the clauses required by the standing orders are inserted in the bill; and that such standing orders as must be proved before the committee, have been complied with. But if extensive alterations are proposed to be made in the original bill annexed to the petition, it is liable to be withdrawn by order of the house, on the report of the chaii-man. If it should appear that the bill, from its character or other circumstances, ought to be treated as an opposed bill by a more public tribunal, the chairman reports his opinion to the house, and the bill is referred to the committee of selection, who deal with the bill accordingly."

There are various orders of the house which are binding Orders relating upon all committees on private bills, and others which on bills" relate only to particular classes or descriptions of bills. It wl'ether op-,, posed or un- is proposed to state these in their order; and afterwards opposed, to describe the ordinary forms observed in the hearing of parties, their counsel or agents, the settlement of the clauses, and the making of amendments.

The names of the members attending each committee Names of mem-are entered by the committee clerk in the minutes; and nutesr " when a division takes place, the clerk takes down the names of the members, distinguishing on which side of the question they respectively vote; and such lists are to be given in, with the report, to the house.

The committee are precluded from examining into the what standing compliance with such standino- orders as are directed to be?"" P ". ' ' " inquired into.

proved before the examiners of petitions for private bills, unless they have received an instruction from the house to that effect. Such an order is only given when the house, on the report of the standing orders committee, allow parties to proceed with their bill, on complying with certain standing orders which they had previously neglected. In such cases it has been customary for the committee on 98 Com. J. 120; 99 lb. 411; see also supra 528.

' Waterford and Limerick Railway Bill, 1850; South Eastern Railway (3 and 4 Shares) Bill; 165 Com. J. 133. 281.

the bill to inquire whether the orders of the house have been complied with, instead of referring that matter to the examiner of petitions; but when any special inquiry in reference to the standing orders has been necessary, the matter has been referred to the examiner instead of to the committee;' and his certificate has been produced before the committee.

Proof of com- Compliance with such orders may be proved before the davil! ' ' committee by affidavits sworn in the same manner as affidavits produced before the examiners. The committee may also admit proof of the consents of parties concerned in interest in any private bill, by affidavits sworn in the same manner, or by the certificate in writing of such parties, Avhose signatures are to be proved by one or more witnesses, unless the committee require further evidence.

Railway bills. Eailway bills have been the most important class of private bills, in modern times, and there are numerous standing orders applicable to them to which the particular attention of the committee on every railway bill, and of the promoters and opponents of such bills, should be directed. By these standing orders, 1, particular matters for the investigation of the committee are pointed out; 2, certain fixed principles of legislation are laid down, from which the committee, except in special cases, will not be justified in departing; and 3, particular clauses are required to be inserted.

Special reports. 1 Whether the bill be opposed or unopposed, the promoters, in proving the preamble of a railway bill, must be prepared with sufficient evidence to satisfy the committee and enable them to report to the house the matters specially

Subscription referred to their consideration. Wherever there is a subscription contract, the committee are to make a special inquiry into its bona fide character, and the sufficiency of the subscribers; and are to report their opinion to the house.

' Dublin Improvement and Great Northern Railway Bills, 1849; 104 Com. J- 76. 81. a lb. 84. 3 See mpra, p. 503.

contract.

The committee are to inquire and report specially as to seventeen special mat inquiry.

the proposed capital and loans of the company; the amount matters o of shares subscribed for and deposits paid; the directors and different classes of shareholders; if any report from the railway commissioners have been referred, and whether its recommendations have been adopted or rejected; the various engineering particulars of the line; and the assents, dissents, and neuters. The committee are also to report the name of each engineer examined in support of the bill and in opposition to it; the main allegations of every petition in opposition to the preamble of the bill, or to any of its clauses; and whether the allegations have been considered, and why any have not been considered. The committee are also to Engineering report generally as to the fitness, in an engineering point of view, of the projected line of railway, and any circumstances which, in their opinion, the house should be informed of.

Many of these orders for a special inquiry and report When the are often inapplicable; and in such cases the committee jq jj apply, state in their report their reasons for considering that any of them do not apply to the bill, and report upon the others. All such reports should be carefully prepared by the promoters of the bill, and submitted for the approval of the committee, before the conclusion of their sittings.

2. The principles of legislation to be observed by the committee on a railway bill are as follow. No company is Restriction to be authorised to raise by loan or mortgage, a lai-ger ' sum than one-third of their capital; and until fifty per cent, on the whole of the capital has been paid up, they are not to raise any money by loan or mortgage. Where Ascent of the level of any road is to be altered in making a railway, '"" " the ascent of a turnpike road is not to be more than one foot in thirty; and of a public carriage road not more than one in twenty; unless a report from an ofiicer of the com-
' Every report from the railway commissioners relating to a railway bill which is laid before the house, is referred to the committee on the bill.

Fence to bridges.

Level crossings.

Railway company not to acquire docks, c.

Committee to fix tolls and charges.

Preference dividends not to be altered.

No powers of sale in bill for construction of a railway.

Matters to be proved before railway commissioners.

When application is construed to be made to Parliament.

missioners of railways shall be laid before the committee, recommending that steeper ascents may be allowed, with the reasons and facts upon which his opinion is founded, and the committee report in favour of the recommendation. A sufficient fence of four feet, at least, is to be made on each side of every bridge which shall be erected. No railway is to be made across any turnpike road, or other public carriage road on the level, unless the committee report that such a restriction ougiit not to be enforced, with the reasons and facts upon which their opinion is founded.

No railway company is to be authorised to construct or acquire any dock, pier, harbour, or ferry, or to acquire and use any steam-vessels for the conveyance of goods and passengers, or to apply any portion of their capital or revenue to other objects, distinct from the undertaking of a railway company, unless the committee report that such a restriction ought not to be enforced, with the reasons and facts vipon which their opinion is founded.

The committee are to fix the tolls and determine the maximum rates of charge for the conveyance of goods and passengers; or are to make a special report, with their report of the bill, explanatory of the grounds of their omitting to determine such maximum.

No railway company is to be authorised to alter the terms of any preference or priority of interest or dividend, unless the committee report that such alterations ought to be allowed, with the reasons on which their opinion is founded-

No powers of purchase, sale, lease, or amalgamation, are to be contained in any bill for the construction of a railway. And no powers of purchase, sale, lease, or amalgamation are to be given to railway companies, unless previously to the application to Parliament certain matters connected with the capital of such companies be proved to the satisfaction of the railway commissioners. And it has been held that application is made to Parliament by presenting the petition for the bill to the house, and not by depositing it ill the Private Bill Office, or proving compliance with the standing orders.

No railway company is to be authorised, except for the Company not execution of its original lines sanctioned by Parliament, dividend miti to guarantee interest on any shares which it may issue for completion of creating additional capital, or to guarantee any rent or dividend to any other railway company, until such first mentioned company have completed and opened for traffic its original Hnes. In bills for the amalgamation of railway Limitation of companies, the amount of capital created by such amalga- anfaigamation. mation is, in no case, to exceed the sum of the capitals of the companies so amalgamated.

In bills for empowering a railway company to purchase Additional any other railway, no addition is to be made to the capital chasing a rail-of the purchasing company, beyond the capital of the y railway purchased; and in case such railway is to be purchased at a premium, no addition on account of such premium is to be made to the capital of the purchasing company. It is the duty of the committee to take care that Dutyofcom-the provisions of the bill are in conformity with these prin- rards these ciples and regulations; but no special form of enactment is provisions, prescribed for carrying the intentions of Parliament into effect. Some of these orders are not obligatory upon the committee, provided they report to the house their reasons for not enforcing them in any particular case. In other cases the house has not entrusted the committee with discretionary powers; but committees have occasionally exercised a discretion, (subject to the approval of the house,) and have made special reports."

3. There are also special clauses which are to be inserted in every railway bill to which they are applicable. Where Clause protcct-it is proposed to authorise the company to grant any pre- p ffej'ence ference or priority in the payment of interest or dividends harea.

' York and North Midland Railway, 1850; Suppl. to Votes, p. 59. Eastern Union Railway, 1850; Suppl. to Votes, p. 113. Manchester, Sheffield and Lincolnshire Railway Bill, 1850; Suppl. to Votes, p. 151.

on any shares or stock, a clause is required to be inserted providing that the granting of such preference shall not prejudice or affect any preference or priority in the payment of interest or dividends on any other shares or stock already lawfully subsisting; unless the committee report that such provision ought not to be required, with the reasons on which their opinion is founded." Interest or A clause is to be inserted in every railway bill, pro- be pahioucaiis! bibiting the payment of interest or dividend in respect of calls under such bill (except the interest by way of discount on subscriptions prepaid, agreeably to act 8 Vict. c. 16, s. 24), out of any capital which they have been authorised to raise, either by means of calls, or of any power of borrowing. Deposits not to And another clause is to be inserted prohibiting a rail-capital. ' " ' y company from paying, out of the capital which they have been authorised to raise for the purposes of any existing act, the deposits required by the standing orders to be made for the purposes of any application to Parliament for Railway not to a bill for the Construction of another railway. And, lastly, Gener 'Acts. clause is to be inserted providing that the railway shall not be exempted from the provisions of any general acts, or from any future revision and alteration, under the authority of Parliament, of the maximum rates of fares and charges previously authorised. Letters patent The committee on a bill for confirming letters patent are to see, in compliance with the standing orders, " that there be a true copy of the letters patent annexed to the bill." This copy should be attached to the bill when first brought into the house; and if its omission were noticed in the house, at any time before the bill was in committee, the bill might be ordered to be withdrawn, inclosiire and There are several standing orders relating specially to bills for the inclosure and drainage of lands, compliance with which is to be examined and enforced by the committee ' S. O. No. 128, as amended 31st March 1851.

on the bill. These are relative to the proof of notices and of the allegations in the preamble of the bill; the consent bill, signed by the lord of the manor and the owners of property; a statement of the property of owners, assenting, dissenting, and neuter; and the names, qualification, and pay of the commissioners. On a report from the committee that the lord of the manor had declined to sign the bill, but did not oppose it, and desired to remain neuter, the pai't of the order relating: the consent of the lord of the manor has been dispensed with."

In the ease of drainage bills, the assents of the occupiers Drainage bills, as well as owners of land are to be proved, but not that of the lord of the manor.

It is ordered that in every bill for inclosing lands, pro- Inclosure bills.

vision be made for leaving an open space sufficient for jea nt p n purposes of exercise and recreation of the neighbouring P o"" """-, o o jjjgg J recrea- population, and for its fencing and maintenance. tion.

The committee on a turnpike road bill relating to Ireland Turnpike roads . (Ireland). are to insert a clause providing for the qualification of commissioners.

If the committee should report any bill to the house in Committee which proper provision had not been made in conformity clmirman o with these standing orders, it is the duty of the chairman ' ' ",. o ' means, and by of ways and means to inform the house of the fact, or to the house, signify it in writing to the speaker, on or before the consideration of the bill; when the house will make such orders as it shall think fit.

Having adverted to the several orders which are to be General pro-observed by committees, in reference to the proof of com- ceedmgs of ' committees on pliance with the standing orders, and the peculiar provisions opposed bills.

required to be inserted in particular bills, the general proceedings of committees upon opposed private bills may be briefly explained. These are partly regulated by the usage of Parliament, and partly by standing orders of the house.

When counsel are addressing the committee, or while wit- Room, whea open, ' Thetford Inclosure, 1st April 1844; 99 Com. J. 182.

Cleared.

Parties appear before the committee.

When there is no appearance.

Case opened.

Proof of preamble.

nesses are under examination, the committee-room is an open court; but when the committee are about to deliberate all the counsel, agents, witnesses, and strangers are ordered to withdraw, and the committee sit with closed doors. When they have decided any question, the doors are again opened, and the chairman acquaints the parties with the determination of the committee, if it concern them.

The first proceeding of a committee on an opposed bill, when duly constituted, is to call in all the parties. The counsel in support of the bill appear before the committee; the petitions against the bill, in which the petitioners pray to be heard, are read by the committee clerk; appearances are entered upon each petition with which the parties intend to proceed, and the counsel or agents appear in support of them. And it is usual, at this time, to intimate that objections will be raised to the hearing of petitioners.

If no parties, counsel, or agents appear when a petition is read, the opposition on the part of the petitioners is held to be abandoned.

In the case of a committee on a group of bills, as already stated, the committee take the bill or bills first into consideration which have been named by the committee of selection; and unless a bill comprised in the group be set down for the first day, it wul not be necessary for the promoters and opponents to enter their appearances on that day in respect of such bill.

When the parties are before the committee, the senior counsel for the bill opens the case for the promoters. Unlike the practice in regard to public bills, the preamble of a private bill is first considered; and if the preamble be opposed, the counsel addresses the committee more particularly upon ' By a standing order, 3d January 1701, it was ordered, "That it be an instruction to the committee of privileges and elections, that they do admit only two counsel of a side in any cause before them." 13 Com. J. 648. This order has been understood to apply to all committees (62 Hans. Deb., N. S., p. 311); but by its words it would appear to be limited to a committee which is no longer in existence, and in practice it is certainly not observed. See Suppl. to Votes 1845, p. 1538.

the general expediency of the bill, and then calls witnesses to prove every matter which will establish the truth of the allegations contained in the preamble. In a railway bill, this is the proper occasion for producing evidence to satisfy the committee upon the most material of the points which, by the standing orders, they are obliged to report to the house. The witnesses may be cross-examined by the counsel who appear in support of petitions against the preamble, but not, as to the general case, by the counsel of parties who object only to certain provisions in the bill. After the cross-examination, each witness may be re-examined by the counsel in support of the bill. When all the witnesses in support of the preamble have been examined, the case for the promoters is closed, unless the right to an opening speech have been waived by the counsel for the bill.

All the petitions against a bill which have been deposited When petition-within the time limited, stand referred to the committee; q heard. but no petitioners are entitled to be heard unless they have prayed to be heard by themselves, their counsel or agents, nor unless they have a locus standi, according to the mles and usage of Parliament; nor unless their petition and the proceedings thereupon be otherwise in conformity with the rules and orders of the house.

Some petitions pray to be heard against the preamble Petitions and clauses of the bill; some against certain clauses only; pfg bie." and others pray for the insertion of protective clauses, or for compensation for damage which will arise under the bill. Unless the petitioners pray to be heard against the preamble, they will not be entitled to be heard, nor to cross-examine any of the witnesses of the promoters upon the general case, nor otherwise to appear in the proceedings of the committee until the preamble has been disposed of. Nor will a general prayer against the preamble entitle the petitioner to be heard against it, if his interest be merely ' See supra, p. 537. The formal matters required to be reported, are generally proved at a later period.

affected by certain clauses of the bill." The proper time for urging objections to parties being heard against the preamble is when their counsel or agent first rises to put a question to a witness, or to address any observations to the committee. This is also the proper time for objecting that petitioners are not entitled to be heard on any other grounds.

Locus standi. Petitioners are said to have no locus standi before a com- mittee, when their property or interests are not directly and specially affected by the bill, or when, for other reasons, they are precluded from opposing it. The committee will determine, according to the circumstances of each case, whether petitioners have such an interest as to entitle them to be heard; and such circumstances will necessarily vary according to the special relations of the petitioners, and the nature and objects of the bill itself.

Competition. It has been held generally, as a parliamentary rule, that competition does not confer a locuss tandi; but, of late years, this rule has been considerably relaxed, and numerous exceptions have, in practice, been admitted. The proprietors of an existing railway have no right to be heard upon their petition against another line, on the ground that the profits of their undertaking will be diminished. But if it be proposed to take the least portion of land belonging to

Landowners. the company, their locus standi immediately becomes unquestionable. The result of this rule has been, that most of the great parliamentary contests between railway companies have been conducted in the names of landowners. Each company have obtained the signatures of landowners to petitions against the rival scheme; have instructed counsel to appear upon them; and have defrayed all the costs of the nominal petitioners. A variation of the practice, however, has been introduced as regards competing schemes referred to the same committee; and, in 1848, the rule was further relaxed in favour of the proprietors of

Suppl. to Votes. 1843, p. 131; 1850, p. 45. 199, c. lb. 1850, 45. 99. 104. 127. 156. 175. 181.

canals or navigations. An existing water or gas company has been held to have no locus standi against a new company proposing to supply the same district, unless their property be taken or interfered with; but in recent cases this rule has not been enforced."

Another important ground of objection to the locus standi siiareiioiders. of petitioners Is, that they are shareholders or members of some corporate body by whom the bill is promoted, and that being legally bound by the acts of the majority, they are precluded from being heard as individual petitioners. This objection was argued at great length In the Cases cited, case of the Birmingham and Oxford Junction Railway Bill, in 1847, when the committee decided that shareholders In the company were not entitled to be heard. Again, In the London, Brighton, and South Coast Kallway Bill, in 1848," determined " that the general rule, that in the case of a joint-stock company the decision of the majority Is binding on the minority, ought to be observed, and that the minority of the shareholders in this case had no locus standi before the committee." In the Queensferry Passage Bill, in 1848, It was decided that Individual trustees of the Queensferry Passage could not be heard against the bill promoted by the general body of the trustees. On the other hand, in the Manchester Cemetery Bill, in 1848, objection was taken to the locus standi of certain petitioners, being trustees and proprietors of shares in the cemetery, on the ground that they were a minority of a corpoi'ate body, In respect of Interest in which body, they opposed the bill; but the committee determined that they were entitled to be hcard. In 1850, the committees on the Shrewsbury and Hereford, the Shropshire Union, c., and the Water- ' 103 Com. J. 309; and see Suppl. to Votes, 1850, p. 147, 148.

Great Central Gas Consumers' Company Bill, 1850; Minutes. Mr. Goulburn, chairman; Suppl. to Votes, 7th May 1847.

Sir R. Peel, chairman; Suppl. to Votes, 1848, p. 309.

Minutes of Committee, 14tli April 1848. Minutes of Committee.

Preference shareholders.

Informalities ill petitions.

Common seal.

When petitions not specific.

ford and Kilkenny Railway Bills' determined that dissentient shareholders could not be heard. With very few exceptions, indeed, it has been the rule, in the commons, not to hear dissentient shareholders, unless they have any interest diffei'ent from that of the general body of shareholders. In the lords a different rule has prevailed; and shareholders Avho have dissented to the bill at the meeting called in pursuance of Lord harncliffe's order,"' are expressly peraiitted to be heard, and have even been heard without such dissent."' In the case of preference shareholders, the commons have been obliged to depart from tlieir usual practice. The proprietor of preference shares has a special interest often opposed to that of the general body of shareholders, and justice requires that he should not be excluded from a hearing.

Objection may also be taken that a petition is informal, according to the rules and orders of the house applicable to petitions generally,"' or as specially applicable to petitions against private bills. In the Glasgow Gas Bill, 1843, an objection was taken, that the seal attached to a petition was not the corporate seal of a company; and when this Avas proved to be the case, all the evidence in support of the petition was ordered to be expunged.

On the 7th May 1847, a motion was made that it be an instruction to the committee on the Great Northern Railway bill, that they do entertain a petition, signed by the chairman of a company, as the petition of that company, although it does not bear the corporate seal of the company, but negatived."

It may also be objected that petitions do not distinctly ' Suppl. to Votes, 1850, p. 41. 75. 43. 182. See infra, p. 5G0.

3 Caledonian Railway, c., Bill; by order, 17tli July 1850,

South Eastern (3 and 4 shares), 1850; Suppl. to Votes, p. 165. 195. South Devon Railway Bill, lb. 33, Shropshire Union, c. Bill, lb. p. 72, 73. York, Newcastle and Berwick Bill, lb. p. 102.

See supra, p. 384, 385. e Minutes of Committee. ' 102 Com. J. 490.

specify the grounds on which tlie petitioners object to the bill. An objection of this nature may be fatal to the petition; as, for example, if the committee determine that the grounds there stated do not amount to an objection to the preamble of the bill. The committee, however, may direct a more specific statement of objections to be given in, limited to the grounds of objection which had been inaccurately stated. The counsel who objects to a party being Objections heard, explains and supports his olyection, and is answered by the counsel claiming to be heard, to whom he may reply. Sometimes the committee have decided without having heard counsel, and have been afterwards induced to hear them upon that decision, with a view to its reconsideration.

When counsel ai e allowed to be heard against the pre- Proceedings on amble, one of them either opens the case of the petitioners, or reserves his speech until after the evidence. Witnesses may be called and examined, in support of the petition, cross-examined by the counsel for the bill, and re-examined by the counsel for the petitioners. When the evidence against the preamble is concluded, the case of the petitioners is closed, unless an opening speech have been waived; and the senior counsel for the bill replies on the whole case. If the petitioners do not examine witnesses, the counsel for the bill has no right to a reply; but in some special cases where new mattei's have been introduced by the opposing counsel (as, for exany:)le. Acts of Parliament, or precedents,) a reply, strictly confined to such matters, has been permitted. AVhere there are numerous parties appearing on separate interests, the committee will make such arrangements as they think fit, for hearing the different counsel.

When the arguments and evidence upon the preamble Question upon have been heard, the room is cleared, and a question is put, "That the preamble has been proved," which is resolved in the affirmative or negative, as the case may be.

' See Supp. to Votes, 1843, p. 131.

Preamble not proved.

Alterations in preaiul)le.

If affirmed, tlie committee call in the parties, and go through the bill clause by clause, and fill up the blanks; and when petitions have been presented against a clause, or proposing amendments, the parties are heard in support of their objections or amendments as they arise: but clauses may be postponed and considered at a later period in the proceedings, if the committee think fit. When all the clauses of the bill have been agreed upon, new clauses may be offered either by members of the committee or by the parties. It must be borne in mind, however, that the committee may not admit clauses or amendments which are not within the order of leave; or which are not authorised by a i)revious compliance with the standing orders applicable to them, unless the parties have received permission from the house to introduce certain provisions in compliance with petitions for additional provision.

If the proof of the preamble be negatived, the committee report at once to the house, "That the preamble has not been proved to their satisfaction." This is the only report required to be made; and although the house had affirmed the principle of the bill on the second reading, no reasons are given by the committee for thus practically reversing the judgment of the house. The want of such information is obvious; and in 1836 the committee on the Durham (South West) Railway Bill, were ordered to re-assemble, " for the purpose of reporting specially the preamble, and the evidence and reasons, in detail, on which they came to the resolution that the preamble had not been proved." '

No alterations were formerly admissible in the preamble of a private bill; but since 1843 they have been allowed; subject to the same restriction as in the case of other amendments, that nothing be introduced inconsistent with the order of leave, or with the standing orders of the house applicable to the bill." Such amendments, however, are to be specially reported.

91 Com. J. 396.

See Report on Revision of Standing Orders, 1843, p. iii.

SPECIAL RKPORTS ON PRIVATK luLLS."49

There are particular duties of the chairman and of tlie committee on a private bill, in recording the proceedings of the committee, and reporting them to the house, which remain to be noticed. These are distinctly explained in the standing orders, and are as follow:

"That everj'plan, and book of reference thereto, which shall Plan,: c. fo be produced in evidence before the committee upon any private,."S'" '! "y

Giitilriiirn bill (whether the same shall have been previously lodged in the Private Bill Office or not), shall be signed by the chairman of such committee, with his name at length; and he shall also mark, with the initials of his name every alteration of such plan and book of reference which shall be agreed upon by the said committee; and every such plan and book of reference shall thereafter be deposited in the Private Bill Office."

"That the chairman of the committee do sign, with his name Committee bill at length, a printed copy of the bill (to be called the committee and clauses to bill), ou which the amendments are to be fairly written; and also (. hairnian sign, with the initials of his name, the several clauses added in the committee."

"That the chairman of the committee upon every private bill Chairman to shall report to the house that the allegations of the bill have been report on alle-examined, and whether the parties concerned have given their g ' consent (where such consent is required by the standing orders) to the satisfaction of the committee."

"That the chairman of the committee shall report the bill to the Committee to house, whether the committee shall or shall not have agreed to ' "Po"' bill m the preamble, or gone through the several clauses, or any of them; or where the parties shall have acquainted the committee that it is not their intention to proceed with the bill; and when any alteration shall have been made in the preamble of the bill, such alteration, together with the ground of making it, shall be specially stated in the report."

"That the minutes of the committee on every private bill be Minutes of brought up and laid on the table of the house, with the report committee, of the bill."

If matters should arise in the committee apart from the Special reports, immediate consideration of the bill referred to them, which they desire to report to the house; the chairman should move that leave be given to the committee to make a special report. The house may also instruct the committee to make a special report. A case of a very unusual cha- Brighton rail- way competing ractcr occurred in 1837, winch deserves particular notice, uucs.

The bills for making four distinct lines of railway to Brighton had been referred to the same committee: when an unprecedented contest arose among the promoters of the rival lines, and at length it was apprehended that the preamble of each bill would be negatived, in succession, by the combination of three out of the four parties against each of the lines in which the three were not interested, and on which the committee would have to determine separately. This result was prevented by an instruction to the committee " to make a special report of the engineering particulars of each of the lines, to enable the house to determine which to send back for the purpose of having the landowners heard and the clauses settled. This special report was made accordingly; but the house being unable to decide upon the merits of the competing lines, agreed to address the Crown to refer the several statenients of engineering particulars to a military engineer. On the report of the engineer appointed, In answer to this address, the house Instructed the committee to hear the case of the landowners upon the direct llne. Witnesses, bow It has been explained in another part of this work," that to be sum. i-n i i i i nioned. Committees upon private bills are not entrusted by the house with the power usually given to other select committees, of sending for persons, papers, and records. The parties are generally able to secure the attendance of their own witnesses, without any summons or other process. A large proportion of all the witnesses examined, attend professionally; and local Interest in the bill, or liberal payments for loss of time, rarely fail in attracting abundance of voluntary testimony. But when it becomes necessary to compel the attendance of an adverse or unwilling witness, or of any official person who would otherwise be unable to absent himself from his duties, application is made to the committee, who, when satisfied that due diligence has been ' 92 Com. J. 350. lb. 417.

' lb. 519. 4 See svpni, p. 308.

iised, that the evidence of the witness is essential to the inquiry, and that his attendance cannot be secured witliout the intervention of the house, direct a report to be made to the house; upon whicli an order is made for the witness to attend and give evidence before the committee

Besides making the prescribed form of report, or special Evidence 1 1 1 1 reported, reports in particular cases, committees have had leave given to report the minutes of evidence taken before them; which have been ordered to be printed, at the expense of the parties, if they think fit, and even, in special cases, at the expense of the house;" or have been referred to the committee on another bill.

If parties acquaint the committee that they do not desire Reports that to proceed further with the bill, that fact is reported to the l house, and the bill will be ordered to be withdrawn."' On one occasion, a report was made, that from the protracted examination of witnesses, the promoters desired leave to withdraw their bill, and that the committee had instructed the chairman to move for leave to lay the minutes of evidence on the table of the house." In another case, the committee reported " That the consideration of two bills should be suspended, in order to afford opportunity for the introduction of another bill;" and they recommended " That every facility, consistent with the forms of the house, should be given to such a bill during the present session.""

It is the duty of every committee to report to the house AW bills to be reported.

the bill that has been committed to them, and not by long-adjournments, or by an informal discontinuance of their sittings, to withhold from the house the result of their proceedings. If any attempt of this nature be made to ') Com. J. 152, 153. 174. 279. 288; 105 lb. 2G2, c. 2 81 lb. 343,; 91 lb. 338; 98 lb. 324.

' Clan; nce Railway, 1843; Siipp. to Votes, 5th May, p. 83. O. vford, Worcester, and Wolverl)ami)ton Railway, fee, 1845; 100 Com. J. 56G.

Northumberlaikl (Atmospheric) Railway, 1845; 100 lb. 536.

104 lb. 510. 79 lb. 445. 7 Edinburgh Water Bills, 1840; 101 lb. 732.

Adjournment of committees.

Committees revived.

Report.

Amended bill to be printed; and delivered.

defeat a bill, tlie house will interfere to prevent it. Thus, ill 1825, the coraniittee on a private bill having adjourned for a month, was " ordered to meet to-morrow and proceed on the bill;'" and again, on the 23d March 1836, the house being informed that a committee had adjourned till the 16th May, ordered them "to meet to-morrow and proceed on the bill.""

Whenever a committee adjourns, the committee clerk is required to give notice in writing to the clerks in the Private Bill Office, of the day and hour to which the committee is adjourned.

If a committee adjourn, without naming another day for resuming their sittings; or if, from the absence of a quorum, the committee be unable to proceed to business, or to adjourn to a future day; they have no power of re-assem-blino; without an order from the house; and the committee is said to be revived, when this intervention of the house is resorted to. The form in which the order is usually made is, "That the committee be revived, and that leave be given to sit and proceed on a certain day." To avoid an irregularity in the adjournment, care should be taken to appoint a day, before the proceedings of the committee are interrupted by the serjeant-at-arms giving notice that the speaker is at prayers.

When the report has been made out and agreed to by the committee, the committee clerk delivers in to the Private Bill Office "the committee bill," being a printed copy of the bill, with the written amendments made by the committee; and with every clause added by the committee, regularly marked in those parts of the bill in which they are to be inserted. In strict conformity with this authenticated copy, the bill, as amended by the committee, is required by the standing orders to be printed at the expense of the parties. When printed, they must be delivered to the doorkeepers.

80 Com. J. 474, ' 91 lb. 195.

3 105 lb. 201.

three clear clays at least before the consideration of the bill; but it may not be delivered before the report of the bill has been made to the house; and agents, when they give notice at the Private Bill Office of the day for the consideration of the bill, must produce a certificate from the doorkeeper, of the delivery of the amended printed bill on the proper day.

In some cases the alterations made by the committee Bills with-have been so numerous and important, as almost to con- fe'i. m"to' e! m-stitute the bill a different measure from that originally mi"er after ' report.

brought before the house. In such cases the house has sometimes required the bill to be withdrawn, and another bill presented, which has been referred to the examiners. Thus, on the 21st May 1849, on the report of the Holme Reservoirs Bill, notice being taken that almost the whole of the bill as brought in had been omitted, and a new set of clauses introduced, the bill was ordered to be withdrawn." But, unless the case be one of great irregularity, the later and better practice has been to refer the bill, as amended, " to the examiners, to inquire whether the amendments involve any infraction of the standing orders."" If the examiner report that there is no infraction of the standing orders, the bill proceeds, without further interruption; but if he report that there has been such an infraction, his report, together with the bill, will be referred to the standing orders committee.

The report of the bill, when first made to the house by Report to lie the chairman, is ordered to lie upon the table, together with "?"" " ' the bill (if a railway bill or a bill amended in committee); but if not amended in committee, the bill is ordered to be read a tliird time. The bill reported to the house is a ' Order of the clerk of the house, 30th March 1844.

104 Com. J. 320.

' River Dee Conservancy, and Belfast Iniprovenicnt, Bills, 1 oo; Lee River Trust; loJ Com. J. 446. 481. 485.

duplicate copy of the committee bill, including all the amendments and clauses as agreed to by the committee. Interval be Jn the case of railway bills, seven clear days, and in the tween report . mi i i t i i i and eonsidera- casc 01 othcr private bills Ordered to lie upon the table, three clear days are required to intervene between the report and the consideration of the bill; and the house will proceed on Tuesday and Thursday to consider the reports

Billasamendtd on railway bills of the second class. And three clear days, fore chairman at least, before the consideration of the bill, a copy of the of ways and q amended in committee (except where the committee means. ' have reported the amendments to be merely verbal or literal) is to be laid by the agent before the chairman of ways and means, and the counsel to the speaker. Who is to state On or before the consideration of the bill the chairman of if it conform to, i i ii i.

standing orders, ways and means IS also to mtorm the liouse, or sigmty in writing to Mr. Speaker, whether the bill contain the several provisions recpiired by the standing orders; and until he has done so tlie bill will not be considered.

Notice of re One clear day's notice in writing is required to be given port, and fur ii-ii ii-i-r-' ther eonsidera- by the agent for the bill to the clerks m the Private Bill repor. Qff f le day proposed for the consideration of every private bill ordered to lie upon the table. Consideration When it is intended to bring up any clause, or to of bill, and.,.,.,, third reading; propose any amendment on the consideration oi any bill ameudm ents. I' ercd to lie upon the table, or on the third reading, notice is to be given, in the Private Bill Office, one

When referred clear day previously. No clause or amendment may then orders com- be offered, unless the chairman of ways and means have mittee. informed the house, or signified in writing to Mr. Speaker, whether, in his opinion, it be such as ought (or ought not) to be entertained by the house, Avithout referring it to the

Clauses or standing orders committee. And the clause or amendment amendments to.,., be printed. IS to DC printed at the expense of the parties; and when any clause is proposed to be amended, it is to be printed in extenso, with every addition or substitution in different type, and the omissions therefrom in brackets and underlined. And on the day on which notice is given, the clause or amendment is to be laid before the chairman of ways and means and the counsel to Mr. Speaker.

If a clause or amendment be referred to the standing Report of orders committee, there can be no further proceeding until cominiuecr their report has been brought up. When the clause or amendment has been offered on the consideration of the bill, they report whether it should be adopted by the house or not, or whether the bill should be recommitted. If offered on the third reading, they merely report whether it ought (or ought not) to be adopted by the house at that stage; as it is then too late to recommit the bill.

On the consideration of the bill, the house may agree or Clauses and ,. 1 1 araendmenls.

disagree to the amendments of the committee, and, subject to the preliminary proceedings already described, may introduce new clauses or amendments, or the bill may be recommitted, or ordered to be considered on a future day.

When bills are recommitted, they are referred to the Recommit- 1 1 1 ment.

former committee; and no member can then sit, unless he had been duly qualified to serve upon the original committee on the bill or be added by the house. Unless the bill be recommitted by the house, with express reference to particular provisions, the whole bill is open to reconsideration in committee.

Three clear days' notice is to be given by the agent. Notice of com- n 1 ' 1 i? n 1 1 Ml iiiittetj.

of the meeting of the committee; and a filled-up bill, as proposed to be submitted to the committee, on recommittal, is to be deposited by the agent in the Private Bill Office one clear day before the meeting of the committee.

When amendments are made by the house on the con- Entry of .-I. 1-n 1 1 1 T 11 ameudincnrs on sideration of a bill, or on the third reading, and wlien report or third lords' amendments have been agreed to, they are entered ords'amend-by one of the clerks in the Private Bill Office, upon the ents. printed copy of the bill, as amended in committee. That copy is signed by the clerk, as amended, and preserved in the office.

Notice of third reading.

Third reading.

Certificate of examination.

No bill to pass through more than one stage in a day.

When standing orders to be dispensed with.

Lords' amendments.

One clear days' notice, in writing, is required to be given by the agent for the l)ill, to the clerks in the Private Bill Office, of the day proposed for the third reading; and this notice may not be given until the day after the bill has been ordered to be read a third time.

On the third reading, clauses may be offered, and amendments proposed, subject to the rules already stated in regard to the report or further consideration of the bill as amended. In other respects, this stage is the same as in public bills; the house finally approves of the entire bill, with all the alterations made since the second reading, and pre)aratory to its being passed and sent up to the House of Lords."

No private bill is permitted to be sent up to the House of Lords until a certificate is endorsed on the fair printed bill, and signed by the proper officers, declaring that such printed bill has been examined, and agrees with the bill as read a third time.

Every stage of a private bill, in its passage through the commons, has now been descnbed, and the several standing orders and proceedings applicable to each. In conclusion, it may be added L "That no private bill may pass through two stages on one and the same day without the special leave of the house;" and, 2. "That (except in cases of urgent and pressing necessity) no motion may be made to dispense with any sessional or standing order of the house, without due notice thereof."

If the bill be subsequently returned from the lords Avith amendments, notice is to be given in the Private Bill Office one clear day before they are to be considered, and if any amendments be proposed thereto, a copy of such amendments is to be deposited;

and no such notice may be given until the day after that on which the bill has been returned from the lords. A copy of such amendments is also to be laid before the chairman of ways and means and the counsel to Mr. Speaker, before two o'clock on the day ' See supra, p. 364 et seq.

previous to that on which they arc to be considered. And as the lords' amendments may relate to matters which miglit be construed to involve an infringement of the privileges of the commons, and the amendments proposed may be in the nature of consequential amendments the speaker's sanction should be obtained before they are proceeded with. Before lords' amendments are taken into consideration they are printed at the expense of the parties, and circulated with the Votes; and where a clause has been amended or a lords' amendment is proposed to be amended, it is printed in extenso, with every addition or substitution in different type, and omissions included in brackets and underlined.

In case a bill should not be proceeded with in the lords, Committee to in consequence of amendments having been made which j gi rnais' ' infringe the privileges of the commons, the same proceedings are adopted as in the case of a public bill. A committee is appointed to search the lords' journals, of which notice is to be given by the agent, in the committee clerks' office; and on the report of the conmiittcc, another bill (No. 2) will be ordered, including the amendments made by the lords.

CHAPTER XXVir.

COURSE OF PROCEEDINGS IN THE LORDS, UPON PRIVATE BILLS SENT UP FROM THE COMMONS.

Some few of the private bills included in the first class Private bills IT.-, t., orij'inatini' iu already enumerated,"' may occasionally origmate in the the commons. lords, because rates, tolls, or duties are not essential to their operation; but all bills in the second class must be brought in to the commons on petition, and the others are, with very rare exceptions, also commenced in the same house. The private bills which are first brought into the ' See supra, p. 367. ' Supra, p. 237. = Supra, p. 495.

Tiie two lords arc estate, naturalization name and divorce bills, and such as relate to the peerage. In tracing the progress of private bills through this house, it will be convenient to assume that the two classes of bills have been sent up from the commons, and that the last bills only are brought in upon petition. As the progress of the former has been alread ' followed through the commons, it is now proposed, in the first place, to pursue them through their various stages in the lords.

Bills submitted It may here be observed that the progress of a bill c 'whiltbill through the lords, after it has passed the commons, is much pending in facilitated by the practice of layino; the bill before the commons. j l. o chairman of the lords' committees and his counsel and giving effect to their observations during the progress of the bill through the commons. The amendments suggested in the lords are thus embodied Avith the other amendments, before the bill has passed the commons; and unless the bill be opj)Osed, its progress through the lords is at once easy and expeditious. Another advantage of this mode of amending the bill, as it were, by anticipation, is that numerous amendments may then be conveniently introduced which could not be made by the lords without infringing the privileges of the commons. Bills in the Whenever a private bill, in the nature of an estate bill, bills referred to brought up from the commons, it is read a first time; tiie judges. copy of the bill, signed by the clerk, is referred to two of the judges in rotation, not being lords of Parliament, who are to report their opinion, whether, presuming the allegations of the preamble to be satisfactorily established, it is reasonable that the bill do pass; and whether the provisions are proper for carrying its purposes into effect, and what alterations or amendments are necessary. In the event of their approving the bill, they are to sign the ' Since the passing of the Naturalization Acts, 7 Sc 8 Vint. c. GG, and 9 10 Vict. c. 83, there have been very few applications to Parliament for acts of naturalization.

- See supra, p. r'27.

same. But except in special cases, no other commons' bills are referred to the judges.

The standing order committee is appointed at the com- Standinp: orders mencement of every session, which consists of forty lords, besides the chairman of the lords committees, who is always chairman of the standing order committee; and three lords, including the chairman, are a quorum.

Before the second reading of any private bill in either of Private iiiiisro- 1 I 1 1 Ml 1 1 T 1 ferrcd to tliain.

the two classes, the bill is reterred to the standing order committee, before whom compliance with the several standing orders applicable to such bills are required to be proved. Three clear days' notice is to be nyen of the meetino: of Notice of meet-this committee on any bill.

Any parties are " at liberty to appear and to be heard Petitions com- ,,, 1. T. plaining of non- by themselves, their agents, and witnesses, upon any peti- compliance tion which may be referred to this committee, complaining ordjj. ' " '"

of non-compliance with the standing orders, provided the matter complained of be specifically stated in such petition, and that it be presented," if the bill be brought from the commons, " on or before the second sitting day after the introduction of the bill."

It is ordered, ' That such committee shall report whether the standing orders What matters have been complied with; and if it shall appear to the committee ' ' '-' rc'l'orted. that they have not been complied with, they shall state the facts upon which their decision is founded, and any special circumstances connected with the case, and also their opinion as to the propriety of dispensing with any of the standing orders in such case."

Thus, the standing order committee in the House of Lords combines the functions of the examiners of petitions and of tlie standing orders committee in the House of Commons, which are there kept distinct.

Statements of proofs are prepared, in the same form as Proceedings ,.,,. T iii-i before standing in the commons, and copies are deuvered to the lord m the order committee.

See supra, p. 497 ct scq. Lords' S. O., No. 178.

Witnesses sworn.

What standing orders proved.

Estimates, Sec. deposited.

Standing orders peculiar to the lords.

Bill to be submitted to a meeting of piojirietors in incorporated companies in certain cases.

chair and the committee clerk. The main diflperence in the proofs offered to the lords is that no affidavits are received, and that all the witnesses are required to have been previously sworn at the bar of the house.

The several standing orders required by both houses to be complied with, before application is made to Parliament for a bill, have already been referred to, and distinguished according to each class or description of bill." These it will be unnecessary to repeat, as the slight variations between the orders of the two houses were there pointed out. It may be noticed, however, that the estimates, declarations, and lists of owners, lessees and occupiers, which are deposited at the House of Commons on or before the 31st December, are to be deposited in the House of Lords on or before the first reading of the bill; and printed copies of the estimates, subscription contracts and declarations before the second reading. There are other orders peculiar to the House of Lords, compliance with which must be proved at the same time, before the standing order committee. They relate to particular classes or descriptions of bills, and shall be stated as they respectively apply to each.

It is directed by an order conunonly known as " Lord Wharncliffe's order,"

1. That no bill to empower any company already constituted by act of Parliament to execute, undertake, or contribute towards any work other than for which it was originally established, or to sell or lease their undertaking or any part thereof, or to amalgamate the same or any part thereof with any other undertaking, or to abandon their undertaking or any part thereof, or to dissolve the said company, shall be allowed to proceed unless the committee on standing orders shall have reported, 1st. That the bill as proposed to be introduced into this house was submitted to a meeting of the proprietors of such company at a meeting held specially for that purpose.

' The agent usually waits upon the latter the day before the sitting of the committee, and goes over the proofs with him in order to ensure accuracy. Chapter XXV. p. 490.

2d. That such meeting was called by advertisement inserted for two consecutive weeks in a morning newspaper published in London, Edinburgh, or Dublin, as the case may be, and in a newspaper of the county or counties in which the principal office or offices of the company is or are situate; and also by a circular addressed to each proprietor at his last known or usual address, and sent by post or delivered at such address not less than ten days before the holding of such meeting.

3d. That such meeting was held on a period not earlier than seven days after the last insertion of such advertisement.

4th. That at such meeting the said bill was submitted to the proprietors aforesaid then present, and was approved of by at least four iifths of such proprietors."

It is ordered,

"That in case any proprietor of any company who, by himself Proprietordis-or any person authorised to act for him in that behalf, have dis- petition Tctbe sented at any meeting called in pursuance of the first section of heard, the aforesaid standing order, such proprietor shall be permitted, on petitioning the house, to be heard by the committee on standing orders on the compliance with the standing orders, by himself, his agents and witnesses, or by the committee on the proposed bill, by himself, his counsel or agents, and witnesses."

It is further ordered.

That when in any bill to be hereafter introduced into this Consent of house for the purpose of establishing a company for carrying on directors, c.

any work or undertaking, the name of any person or persons shall?, '! named,.,, 1.,. in a bill, to be be introduced as manager, director, proprietor, or otherwise con-proved.

cerned in carrying such bill into effect, proof shall be required before the standing order committee that the said person or persons have subscribed their names to the petition for the said bill, or to a printed copy of the said bill, as brought up or introduced into the house.

There is another important order which requires that Notices to be whenever any alteration has been made or is desired by the deposits made parties to be made in any work of the second class, after w'lere work is the introduction of the bill into Parliament, plans and liament. sections of such alterations are to be deposited with the clerks of the peace, c. one month before the introduction of the bill into that house; and notices are to be published, and application made to the owners, lessees, and occupiers of the lands through which the alteration is intended to be

Lords' S. 0., No. 185. Lords' S. O., No. 190.

Deposit of plans of alterations in the House of Lords.

Deposit of statement as to lands of owners who have not consented.

Railway bills.

Private bills to made, and their consent proved before the standing order committee.

It is also ordered, in reference to alterations of plans, "That previous to any bill for making any work, included in the second class, being brought to this house from the commons, in which any alteration has been made in its progress through Parliament, a map or plan, and section of such work, showing anj" variation, extension, or enlargement which is intended to be made in consequence of such alteration, shall be deposited in the office of the clerk of the Parliaments; and that such map or plan, and section, shall be on the same scale, and contain the same particulars as the original map or plan, and section of the said work."

That after any road, or canal, or railway, or dock bill shall be read a first time, and before anj further proceeding thereupon, there be deposited in the office of the clerk of the Parliaments a statement of the length and breadth of the space which is intended or sought to be taken for the proposed works, and to give up which the consent of the owners of the land has not been obtained, together with the names of such owners, and the heights above the surface of all proposed works on the ground of each such owner; and also, in the case of railway bills, that a return shall be presented at the same time of the names of the owners or rate-paying occupiers of any houses situated within three hundred yards of the proposed works, who shall, before the 31st day of December prior to the introduction of the bill into Parliament, have sent to the promoters of the railway their dissent, or any written objections to the railway.

A copy of every railway bill as brought into the House of Lords is to be deposited with the commissioners of railways one day at least before the bill is considered in the standing order committee; and afterwards a copy of the bill, as amended in committee, is to be deposited three days before the third reading.

These are the several standing orders of the lords, peculiar to that house, which must be proved before the standing order committee. Others will presently be added, in describing the further stages of bills.

Private bills of every description are subject to the following standing order:

"That for the future no private bill shall be read in this house ' Lords' S. O., No. 182 (13).

lb. No. 182 (14).

a second time until printed copies thereof be left with the clerk of be printeil bo- the Parliaments, for the perusal of the lords; and that one of the f' e spcond said copies shall be delivered to every person that shall be con- ' ';'"'S' ""J J 1–J L-n l r. p, dtlivercd to cerned in the said bill, beiore the meeting of the committee upon parties before such bill; and in case of infancy, to be delivered to the guardian meeting of com- or next relation of full age, not concerned in interest or in the '""

passing of the said bill.""

By another standing order, when any cause shall be Not to be rend appointed to be heard in this house, no private bill whatso ino-ofcauses!!" " ever shall be read that day before the hearing of the cause."'

No petition praying to be heard upon the merits against Petitions 1 Ml 1 1 1 I 1 against liills, any bill brought irom the commons, in either oi the two wiien to be classes, will be received by the house unless it be presented P"" " on or before the second day on which the house sits after the bill has been reported from the standing order committee.

No bill for the regulation of any trade, or the extension Bills for regu-of the term of a patent, is to be read a second time until extending a select committee has reported upon the expediency of p ""'-taking it into further consideration. And bills for incor- Bills respecting porating, or giving powers to, joint-stock companies (except companies, for executing public works, and some other purposes), are not to be read a second time until a select committee has reported " that three-fourths of the capital intended to form the joint-stock of the company is deposited in the Bank of England, or vested in exchequer bills, or in the public funds, in the name of trustees;" ' and if the company have been previously constituted by royal charter, it is to be proved to a committee, before the second reading, that three-fourths of the capital have been paid up by the individual proprietors."

No bill included in cither of the two classes is to be read When bills may a second time before the third day on which the house sits second time, after the bill has been reported from the standing order committee.

Lords' S. O., No. 145. lb. No. 146.

lb. No. 176. lb. No. 176, lb. No. 177.

Second reading and commitment.

Unopposed bills referred to open committees.

Counsel to chairman of oommittees.

Unopposed bills when treated as opposed.

Committees on opposed bills.

The second reading, as in the commons, affirms the principle of the bill, and is immediately followed by the commitment. Unopposed private bills are referred to " all the lords present this day," who are presided over by the chairman of the lords' committees, assisted by his counsel. These open committees are attended by any of the lords who had been present; but the business is practically transacted by the chairman of committees, and the responsibility is vested in him by the house. Every private bill has been previously examined by the chairman and his counsel; but at this period the chairman exercises the authority of his own office, combined with that of a committee of the house. This supervision of private bills, by responsible officers, originated in the House of Lords; and for many years the House of Commons, relying upon the aid which its legislation received from the other house, did not adopt any similar arrangement of its own. But, as private business increased in importance, the house gradually entrusted to the chairman of ways and means many duties analogous to those performed by the chairman of committees in the House of Lords. And with the assistance of the counsel to Mr. Speaker, he has recently been charged with the supervision of all private bills.

The chairman of committees may, in any case, report his opinion to the house, that an unopposed bill ought to be proceeded with as an opposed bill; in which case it will be referred to another committee, as if it had been treated as an opposed biu in the first instance.

Every opposed private biu is referred to a select committee of five lords, who choose their own chairman. Every lord appointed on the committee is ordered to attend during the whole continuance of the inquiry; and no lord who is not one of the five, is permitted to take any part in the proceedings. Lords are exempted from serving on the ' Lords'S. O., No. 178.

committee on any bill in wiiich they are interested, and may be excused from serving for any special reasons, to be approved of in each case by the house.

These committees are appointed in a manner very similar Committee of sgicc tioti.

to that adopted in the commons, by a committee resembling the committee of selection. A committee is named by the house every session, consisting of the chairman of committees and four other lords, who select and propose to the house the names of the five lords who are to form a select committee for the consideration of each opposed private bill.

The attendance of the lords upon such committees is Sittings of com- . 1 . 1 mi raittees on billt.

very strictly eniorced. ihe committee is to

"Meet not later than eleven o'clock every morning, and sit till four, and shall not adjourn at an earlier hour without specially reporting the cause of such adjournment to the house at its next meeting; nor adjourn over any days excejit Saturday and Sunday, Christmas Day, and Good Friday, without leave of the house."

"If any member is prevented from continuing his attendance, the committee shall adjourn, and report t! ie cause of such member absenting himself to the house at its next meeting, and shall not resume its sittings without leave of the house." '

The committee on the bill, whether opposed or not, per- proceedings of ,, 1 i.1 rri committeei on form the same duties as in the commons, iney examine j jug the provisions of the bill, make amendments, add clauses, and, in particular cases, inquire into the compliance with such standing orders as are to be proved before them. No committee on a bill, however, may examine into the compliance with such standing orders as are required to be proved before the standing order committee."

The proceedings of a lords' committee differ in no ma- Witnesseg on terial point from those of a committee in the commons, except that witnesses are examined upon oath, previously administered at the bar of the house. When petitions ' See debates on the absence of Lord Gardner, 24th and 26th June 1845; 81 Hans. Deb., N. S., 1104. 1190; and supra, p. 190. 3 Lords' S. O., No. 178 (7).

LOiuW' CO. MMITTEES

Petitioner heard.

Special stand-inir orders to be proved or enforced.

Payment of purchase-money into the bank, c.

Inclosure and drainage bills.

against the bill are I'eferred, the parties are heard by themselves, their counsel, agents, and witnesses, in the same manner, and subject to nearly the same rules, as in the commons. Some are heard upon the preamble, and others against particular clauses, or in support of new clauses or amendments; but the committee require both parties to state all the amendments which they intend to propose, before the room is cleared for the purpose of deliberating upon the preamble. The bill is gone through, clause by clause, and after all amendments have been made, it is reported, with the amendments, to the house.

The proceedings of lords' committees upon private bills differ also, in some cases, from a committee in the commons, in regard to particular matters, which, by special standing orders, are required to be proved or enforced there, either in relation to all bills, or to bills of particular classes or descriptiuns. These orders may now be enumerated.

The first relates to the payment of the purchase-money of lands, c. into the bank, and applies to private bills generally, in which powers are given for the purchase or exchange of lands, where sums are to be laid out in the purchase of lands, but is more particularly applicable to estate bills. It is ordered, that in all such bills provision shall be made for the payment of the purchase-money into the Bank of England, or into one of the banks of Scotland established by Act or royal charter, or into the Bank of Ireland; with special conditions particularly laid down in the standing orders. And certain powers, in reference to the purchase-money so deposited, are required to be given to commissioners in inclosure or drainage bills, when they find any difficulty in obtaining a purchase in land of equal value, or when the purchase is otherwise disadvantageous."

' Lords' S. O., No. 186.

lb. No. 186 (2).

In all bills, the committees on which are to receive proof of consents, it is ordered,

"That no notice shall be taken by the committee of the consent Consents to of any person, except trustees for a charity, to any private bill, P"v t "" to unless such person appear before such committee, or proof be made proof of dis'ubi-to such committee, by two credible witnesses, that such person is Hty. not able to attend, and doth consent to the said bill."'

"That the consent of all trustees for charitable purposes may be How consent of given to any private bill by which the estate, revenues, manage- '""-". or ment, or regulation of the charity may be affected, by each of such poses to be sio–trustees signifying his assent to such bill by signing a printed copy nified. of the said bill, in the presence of one credible witness, who shall attest such signature."

Compliance with the following standing orders specially Letters patent ,.,.,,-,.,, bills, special relatmg to bills tor extendnig the terms oi letters patent, orders. is to be proved before the committee on the bill: 1. " That no bill for extending the term of any letters patent for any invention or discovery granted under the great seal of England, Scotland, or Ireland, shall be read a third time in this house unless it shall appear that the letters patent, the term of which it is intended by such bill to extend, will expire within two years from the commencement of the session of Parliament in which the application for such bill shall be made."

2. " That no such bill shall be read a third time unless it shall appear that the application to Parliament for extending the terra of the letters patent is made by the person, or by the representatives of the person who himself originally discovered the invention for which such letters patent were granted by his majesty; and that the knowledge of such invention was not acquired by such person as aforesaid, by purchase or otherwise, from the inventor or owner of the same, or by information that such invention was known and pursued in any foreign country."

The following order respecting a cemetery or burial ground is to be proved before the committee on the bill:

"That no bill for erecting or making any cemetery or burial Cemetery or ground shall be read a third time unless the committee on such burial ground. bill shall report that such bill contains a provision whereby the company, or persons or person intended to be authorised by such bill to make or erect such cemetery or burial ground, are restricted ' Lords' S. O., No. 148. lb. No. 149.

Levels of roails.

Time limited for completing works.

Provisions required to be inserted in railway bills.

Election of directors in railway companies.

from erecting or making the same, or any part thereof, within 300 yards of any house of the annual value of 50., or having a plantation or ornamental garden or pleasure ground occupied therewith, except-with the consent of the owner, lessee, and occupier thereof, in writing."'

With regard to bills of the second class, the committee on the bill are to make the same provision, as in the commons, as to the level of roads, when altered by making any-work, and as to the height of the fences; and that unless the work be completed within a limited time, the powers of the Act are to cease, except in regard to so much of the work as shall have been completed."

But the first of these orders being also enforced by the commons, a provision is made in that house to effect the proposed object, if omitted in the original bill: and a clause embodying the purport of the second, is always inserted in bills of the second class, when first introduced into the commons.

In the case of railway bills, in addition to the general inquiries conducted by the committee, they are ordered to observe that particular provisions be inserted for restricting loans or mortgages; for maintaining the levels of roads; and for restraining the crossing of roads on a level. They are also required to observe the same rules, and introduce the same clauses and provisions, as in the commons, relative to the non-payment of interest on calls or deposits out of capital, and the financial arrangements of companies in cases of purchase and amalgamation. " All these provisions, however, being included in the bill when it leaves the commons, need not be more particularly mentioned here.

A clause is also required to be inserted in every railway bill:

"That the directors appointed by this Act shall continue in office until the first ordinary meeting to be held after the passing of the Act, and at such meeting the shareholders present, personally or ' Lords' S. O., No. 188. lb. No. 189. =' See supra, p. 534.

Lords' S. O., No. 189; and see sii jra, p. 537, cl seq.

by proxy, may either continue in office the directors appointed by this Act, or any number of them, or may elect a new body of directors, or directors to supply the places of those not continued in office, the directors appointed by this Act being eligible as members of such new body."

Notice is required to be given of a motion to recommit Recommittal of a private bill, which may not be proposed before the third day on which the house sits after the notice has been given.

It is further ordered, that all private bills in which any Amended bills amendments have been made in the committee, shall be reprinted as amended, previously to the third reading, unless the chairman of the committee shall certify that the reprinting of such bill is unnecessary.

No amendment may be moved to any bill on the report Amendment or third reading, unless it have been submitted to the chairman of committees, and printed copies deposited with the clerk of the Parliaments one clear day, at least, prior to such report or third reading.

When a private bill has been read a third time and Proceedings . after tliird passed, it is either returned to the commons, with amend- reading. ments, or a message is sent to acquaint the commons that it has been agreed to without any amendment. The ordinary proceedings in the commons upon amendments made to such bills were described in the last chapter. In the event of any disagreement between tlie houses in reference to amendments, the same forms are observed as in the case of public bills."

Lords' S. O., No. 190. See supruy p. 566.

See supra, p. 366.

Private bills originatin the lords.

Petitions for bills.

Bills for restitution of honours and in blood.

Petitions for estate bills referred to two of tlie judges.

RULES, ORDERS, AND COURSE OF PROCEEDINGS IN THE LORDS UPON PRIVATE BILLS BROUGHT INTO THAT HOUSE UPON PETITION; AND PROCEEDINGS OF THE COMMONS UPON PRIVATE BILLS BROUGHT FROM THE LORDS. LOCAL AND PERSONAL, AND PRIVATE ACTS OF PARLIAMENT.

Having traced the progress of private bius received from the coininons, through every stage in the House of Lords, until they are returned to the house in which they originated, it is time to advert to the proceedings peculiar to those bills which are first solicited in the lords.

It Is ordered,

"That for the future no private bill shall bo brought into this house until the house be informed of the matters therein contained, by petition to this house for leave to bring in such bill;" ' and, " that all parties concerned in the consequences of any private i. e. estate bill shall sign the petition that desires leave to bring such private bill into this house.""

To this rule, however, there is a remarkable exception. Bills for reversing attainders; for the restoration of honours and lands; and for restitution in blood, are first signed by the sovereign, and are presented by a lord to the House of Peers, by command of the Crown; after which they pass through the ordinary stages in both houses, and receive the royal assent in the usual form.

The lords having power to consult the judges In matters of law, order,

"That when a petition for a private i e. estate bill shall be offered to this house, it shall be referred to two of the judges, who, after perusing the bill, without requiring any proof of the allegations therein contained, are to report to the house their opinion

Lords' S. O., No. 139. = Jb. No. 140.

3 56 Lords' J. 260. 425; and Report of Precedents, lb. 286. Maxwell's Restitution Bill, 1848; 80 Lords' J. 270. 365.

thereon, under their hands; and wliether, presuming the allegations contained in the preamble to be)roved to the satisfaction of the lords spiritual and temporal in Parliament assembled, it i reasonable that such bill do pass into a law, and whether the provisions thereof are proper for carrying its purposes into effect, and what alterations or amendments, if any, are necessary in the same: and in the event of their approving the said bill, they are to sign the same."'

But where an estate bill has been settled by a master in wiiere settled ,. 11 1 1 1 1 " chancery.

chancery, as is usually the case with charity estates, the petition is not referred to the judges. '

At the commencement of every session, an order Is made Time limited that no petitions for private bills shall be received after a ' i" ' " certain day; nor any report from the judges thereon, after another day more distant;' but this order, like the preceding, refers to estate bills alone. All further proceedings upon such bills are suspended until the report of the judges fudges' report, is received, as it is ordered,

"That no private bill, the petition for which shall be referred to two of her Majesty's judges, shall be read a first time until a copy of the said petition, and of the report of the judges thereupon, shall be delivered, by the party or parties concerned, to the lord appointed by this liouse to take the chair in all committees." '

When this has been done, the bills may proceed through their several stages. But before the proceedings of the house are entered upon, it will be necessary to cite several special standing orders relating to particular bills.

In the case of private bills concerning estates in land Estatebills.

I'll 1 'Oil'. 1 11 Petitions for or heritable subjects in Scotland, it is ordered, that when Scotch estate the petition is offered to the house,

"It shall be referred to two of the judges of the Court of Session, who are forthwith to summon all parties before them who may be concerned in the bill; and after hearing all the parties, and perusing the bill, are to report to the house the state of the case, and their opinion thereupon, under their hands, and are to sign the bill."

The same method is ordered to be adopted before the second reading of Scotch estate bills sent up from the ' Lords' S. O., No. 141. Lords' Minutes, 1851; 151. 160. 181.

' ' The order is not enforced wlirre a peer is the petitioner, or if jiroceedings be pending in chancery. Lords" S. O., No. 142. 'lb. No. 140.

bills.

Consents to Scotch estate bills.

Estate bills, generally.

Concerning bills for selling lands and purchasing others ill Scotland.

Irish estate buls.

Consents.

commons; but in practice, nearly all bills of this nature are first solicited in the lords, whose proceedings are greatly facilitated by their power of delegating inquiries to the judges. There are other orders for regulating the consents to Scotch estate bills, and the mode of proving such consents; the consent of heirs of entail; and the proportion of consents necessary."

In reference to estate bills generally, there are several orders in force respecting consents 1. Where a petitioner is tenant for life, and another tenant in tail;' 2. Where women have an interest; 3. Where children have an interest; ' 4. Trustees to consent in person in certain cases; 5. That the appointment of new trustees is to be with the approbation of the Court of Chancery; 6. Notice to be given to mortgagees when the petition for the bill is presented; 7. That bills for exchanging or selling settled estates are to have schedules of their value annexed.

In bills for selling lands, and purchasing or settling others in Scotland, the committee on the bill are to take care that the values be fully made out, and to provide other securities for the fulfilment of the agreement; which are particularly described in the standing orders.

The standing orders in relation to Irish estate bills are similar to those concerning estates in Scotland, being referred to two judges of the Court of Queen's Bench, Common Pleas, or Exchequer, in Ireland, who inquire and report and receive consents in the same manner.""

And the same instruction is given to the judges as in the case of Scotland, to require the personal presence of persons consenting, except in certain cases."

lb. No. 151.

lb. No. 154.

' Lords' S. O., Nos. 161, 162. 164.

3 lb. No. 152. lb. No. 153.

lb. No. 155. 7 lb. No. 156.

Lords' S. O. No. 157. All these orders are printed at length in the published collection of the standing orders of the lords relative to private bills (1850), p. 8-11.

' Lords' 8. O., No. 163. lo Jb. No. 165, 166.

"lb. No. 167, In regard to bills for selling lands, and purchasing or settling others in Ireland, an order, similar to that in relation to Scotch bills, mutatis mutandis, is binding upon the committee upon the bill.

In regard to divorce bills, it is ordered that no petition Divonce for a bill shall be presented unless there be delivered an, '.".

' Petition tor official copy of the proceedings, and of a definitive sentence I'iii to be pre-

T 7-1 1 1 seated witli 01 divorce, a mensa et tkoro, in the ecclesiastical court, at copy of the the suit of the party desirous of presenting such petition; fn'thtecdesiat- and that no bill to dissolve a marriao; e on the ground of court.

'='., No divorce bill, adultery be received, without a clause prohibiting the to be received offending parties from marrying. But this clause is struck clause proiiibit-out in committee, or on the report, except in very peculiar! JJ the offend-

Cases." from marryii! g.

UM 111 1. o " struck out

VV here there has been a trial at nisi prius, or a writ ot in committee inquiry, a report of the proceedings is to be transmitted; proceedings and the bill will not be read a second time until such report " " ' has been laid upon the table of the house. The petitioner Petitioner to for the bill is required to attend the house on the second second reading, reading, in order to be examined at the bar, if the house ' examined " ' as to collusion.

think fit, as to any collusion between the parties in reference to the divorce bill or other proceedings."

It is ordered, " that no bill for naturalizing any person Naturaliza- bom in any foreign territory shall be read a second time, ",,-. No bill to be until the petitioner shall produce a certificate from one of read a second his majesty's principal secretaries of state respecting his certificate, conduct." But certificates of naturalization being now granted by the secretary of state, under the 7 and 8 Vict., c. 66, this order is almost obsolete, as naturalization acts are no longer applied for except in a few exceptional cases.

' Lords' S. O., No. 168. lb. No. 171.

' lb. No. 173.

In 1800 a bill was passed by the House of Lords containing a clause to prohibit the marriage of a divorced woman with her paramour; but it was not agreed to by the commons. 35 Hans. Pari. Hist. 237. 27G.

Lords' S. O., No. 174. lb. No, 172.

' lb. No. 170. Bishop of Jerusalem, 1846; Mr. Tufton, 1849.

When judges' When the reports from the judges upon petitions for on estate bills, estate bills have been delivei ed to the chairman of committees, the bills may be presented and read a first time. If, however, a report of the judges should be adverse to an entire bill, it would not be offered to the house at all; and if the report should object to particidar provisions or suffgest others, the bill would be altered before its presentation. Second reading No particular interval is enforced between the first and second readings, and if printed copies of the bill have been delivered, and the bill be unopposed, it may be read a second time on any future day. K it be opposed upon its principle, this is the proper stage for taking the decision of the house upon it.

Petitions j Jg not usual for petitions to be presented, praying to against second,, i! reading. be heard against any private bills on the second readmg, except divorce and peerage bills; and in those cases, whether there are opposing petitions or not, counsel are heard and witnesses examined at the bar in support of the bill on the second reading,

Divorce bills; Noticc of the sccond reading of a divorce bill, with an reading. ' attested copy of the bill, signed by the clerk assistant, is required to be served upon the wife, or the husband if the bul be prosecuted by the wife; which service must be proved on the second reading; but if the party cannot be found, or is in a distant part of the world, service will be allowed upon his or her agent, upon a petition from the agent of the promoter of the bill, stating the facts, and after the proof thereof on oath at the bar.

Evidence re In divorce bills, the proceedings of the ecclesiastical ' court, the sentence of divorce, and the proceedings in trials at nisi prius, are before the house, but are not admitted as evidence to establish the fact of adultery. Of that fact, already twice proved, their lordships must be satisfied by ' 82 Lor. is' J., 146. Lords' S. O., No. 174.

other testimony offered at the bar; and if that should fail, even when the application is unopposed, the bill will not be read a second time. And, as shown above, the petitioner is required to be in attendance to be examined as to collusion if the house think fit, unless a special order has been obtained to dispense with his attendance."

The only occasion upon which the lords will receive Depositions in evidence in support of a divorce bill, taken before other courts, is when the adultery is alleged to have been committed in India; in which case depositions taken before the judges in India are admitted as evidence. By the Act 1 Geo. IV., c. 101, when any person petitioning either house of Parliament for a divorce bill, states that the witnesses necessary to substantiate the allegations of the bill are resident in India, the speaker of such liouse may issue his warrant or warrants to the judges of the supreme courts of Calcutta, Madras, or Ceylon, or the recorder of Bombay, for the examination of witnesses; and the evidence taken before them, accompanied by a declaration that the examinations have been fairly conducted, is admissible in either House of Parliament. The proceedings upon a divorce bill, when a warrant has been issued under this Act, are not discontinued by any prorogation or dissolution of Parliament, until the examination shall have been returned; but " such proceedings may be resumed and proceeded upon In a subsequent session, or in a subsequent Parliament, in either House of Parliament, in like manner and to all intents and purposes, as they might have been in the course of one and the same session."

When a petitioner prays tliat evidence may be taken In AVarrant for

T T 1 r 1 r taking dcposi- India, by virtue or this Act, it is rererrecl to a committee tions, how upon whose report the orders are made for issuing the ' necessary warrants, and the bill is read a first time. No further proceeding can then take place, until the depositions ' 80 Lords' J. 100.; 82 lb. 120, c. 1 Geo. IV. c. 101, a. 4.

Commitment.

Divorce bills to a committee of the whole house.

Report. Third reading, c.

Lords' private bills in the commons.

have been returned from India; and, unless they are received in time to proceed while Paruament is sitting, the bill is not read a second time until the following session. If the proceedings of ecclesiastical and other courts have been laid before the house, upon a divorce bill, in the preceding session, the agent may petition the house to dispense with a second copy.

All the ordinary private bills for estates, naturalization, names, and other matters, are referred to an open committee, being, as already explained, the lords then present; who inquire whether all the standing orders have been complied with, and take care that the proper provisions are inserted. The committee on an estate bill may not sit until ten days after the second reading." It is a standing order of the house,

"That the lord who shall be in the chair of a committee to whom any private bill shall be committed, shall state to the house, when the report of such committee is made, how far the orders of the house, in relation to such private bill, have or have not been duly complied with."

Unlike other private bills, divorce bills Instead of being committed to an open committee, or to a selected committee, are committed, like public bills, to a committee of the whole house.

When a private bill is reported from a committee, and any amendments that may have been made are agreed to by the house, the bill is ordered to be read a third time on a future day, when it is read a third time, passed and sent to the House of Commons in the usual form.

The bills sent down to the commons pass through the same stages, and are subject to nearly the same rules as other private bills, except that name bills need not be printed.

The bills when received from the lords are read a first time and, unless they be name or divorce bills, are referred 78 Lords' J. 104,3.

Supra, p. 564. lb. No. 158.

3 Lords' S. O., No. 147.

to the examiners of petitions for private bills. Two clear Rofprrcri to days' notice is given of the examination of every bill brouglit from the lords, and memorials complaining of non-compliance with the standing orders may be deposited before twelve o'clock on the day preceding that appointed by the examiner. If the examiner report that the standing orders have been complied with, or that no standing orders are applicable, the bills are read a second time. Not less than three clear days nor more than ten are required to elapse between the first and second reading. Three clear days' Second notice of the second reading is to be given, but not until commitnient. the day after the first reading. After the second reading every such bill except a divorce bill, is referred to the committee of selection, by whom they are committed to the chairman of ways and means and two other members; of w hom one at least is not to be locally or otherwise interested in the bill. There must be three clear days between the second? "t"- "' ' intervals.

reading of a name or ordinary estate bill and the sitting of the committee; and fourteen days if the estate bill relate to crown, church or corporation property, or property held in trust for public or charitable purposes. One clear day's notice is given, by the clerk to the committee of selection, of the sitting of the committee. But many of these bills are standing orders received by the commons at so late a period of the session, "P ' that it becomes necessary to suspend the standing orders and to permit them to proceed without the usual intervals and notices.

The manner of dealing with divorce bills is peculiar, and differs from the mode of proceeding upon other bills.

At the commencement of each session a committee is Divorce bills in , T. p l c a l the coiuniona.

nominated, consisting oi nine members, oi wliom three are a quorum, and is denominated " The Select Committee on Divorce Bills." To this committee all divorce bills are committed after the second reading. Eight days are required to elapse between the second reading and the sitting of the committee, and the agent is to give seven clear days' notice

What evidence to be given in divorce cases.

When petitioner for bill to attend committee.

Committee to report bill in all cases.

Service of orders and notice.

of the committee. An instruction is given to the committee " that they do hear counsel, and examine witnesses for the bill; and also that they do hear counsel, and examine witnesses against the bill, if the parties concerned think fit to be heard by counsel, or produce witnesses." A message is sent to the lords, to request their lordships to communicate a copy of the minutes of evidence taken before them upon the bill, or for the depositions transmitted from India. When these arc communicated, they are referred to the committee on the bill. It must be noticed that from the words of the instruction, the promoter is bound to examine witnesses, or otherwise to substantiate the allegations of the bill, and that the last part of the instruction only is permissive, in regard to parties opposing the bill. Besides this general instruction, the committee are desired by the standing order,

"To require evidence to be given before them that an action for damages has been brought in one of her Majesty's courts of record at Westminster, or in one of her IMajesty's courts of record in Dublin, or in one of her Majesty's supreme courts of judicature of the presidencies of Calcutta, Madras, Bombay, or the island of Ceylon respectively, against the persons supposed to have been guilty of adultery, and judgment for the plaintiff had thereupon; or sufficient cause to be shown, to the satisfaction of the said committee, why such action was not brought, or such judgment was not obtained."

It is also ordered,

"That the committee shall, in all cases in which the petitioner for the bill has attended the House of Lords upon the second reading of the bill, require him to attend before them to answer any questions they may think fit that he should answer; " and,

"That the committee shall report every such bill to the house, whether such committee shall or shall not have agreed to the preamble, or gone through the several clauses, or any of them."

The party oj)posing a divorce biu may appear before the committee without presenting a petition to the house against the bill; and the promoter of the bill or his agent loSCom. J. 481, c.

is required to serve (him or) her with tlic orders of the house, and a copy of the bill. In ease he should not be able to effect this service, in consequence of the absence of the party from the United Kingdom, or for any other sufficient cause, his agent should present a petition to the house, stating the circumstances, and praying that service of the orders and notice upon the agent of the party may be deemed an effectual notice and service upon the party herself. On the appearance of the opponent's agent, at the bar, and his consent being given to accept the service of the orders, and a copy of the bill for his client, the house make the necessary order in compliance w ith the prayer of the petition. In conformity with the instruction and stand- Report of ing orders of the house, the committee make the necessary inquiries, and report,

"That they have examined the allegations of the bill as to the marriage of the parties, the adultery charged as the ground for dissolving the marriage, the verdict at law, and the sentence of divorce in the ecclesiastical court; and upon evidence satisfactory to the committee, found the same and other allegations to be true."

In the case of Chiijpendall's Divorce Bill in 1850, the Special reports, committee made a special report recommending the remission of the fees on account of the poverty of the promoter; and their report was agreed to by the house."

Nothing need be added concerning the progress of lords' Lords' bills subject to tlie private bills through the commons, ihey are subject to same intervals the same rules, and pass through the same stages, and with the same intervals and notices, as those which have already been detailed, in reference to private bills, originating in the commons; but if received at the close of a session, more indulgence is usually shown in dispensing with the orders of the house, and in permitting them to pass with less delays.

' 104 Com. J. 144. 105 lb. 66t; and see injwi, p. 583.

and statce.".

Divisions of private bills.

Local and personal Acts.

All private bills, during their progress in the commons are known by the general denomination of private bills; but in the lords the term " private " is applied technically to estate bills only, all other bills being distinguished as local" or " personal," although in the standing orders no such distinction is expressed. After they have received the royal assent, private bills are divided into three classes: 1. Local and personal, declared public; 2. Private, printed by the Queen's printers; and 3. Private, not printed.

1. Every local and personal Act passed before the year 1851 has contained a clause, declaring that it "shall be a public act, and shall be judicially taken notice of as such;"

and such acts receive the royal assent as public acts. But by Lord Brougham's Act of 1850, for shortening the language of acts of Parliament, it is enacted that every act " shall be deemed and taken to be a public act, and shall be judicially taken notice of as such, unless the contrary be expressly provided and declared by such act," and the " public clause" will consequently be omitted from all future local and personal acts. The practice of declaiing particular acts of a private nature to be "public acts," commenced in the reign of William and Mary, and was soon extended to nearly all private acts, by which felonies were created, penalties inflicted, or tolls imposed." Such acts were printed with the other statutes of the year, and were not distinguishable from public acts, except by the character of their enactments; but since 1798 they have been printed in a separate collection, and are known as local and personal acts. With the exception of inclosure, or inclosure and drainage acts, all the bills of the two classes so often referred to, are included in this category, and have contained the public clause. In some special cases where local and per- ' 13 Vict. c. 21. s. 7. A bill for repealing this act is now before Parliament (29 March ISil). ' Preface to Spiller's Index to tlie Statutes.

In the I)lack letter edition of the Public General Acts.

sonal acts have been of an unusually public cliaractcr, they have not only contained the ordinary public clause, but have been printed amongst the public general acts.

2. From 1798 to 1815, the private Acts, not declared Private Acta public, were not printed by the Queen's printers, and could "' only be given in evidence by obtaining authenticated copies from the statute rolls in the Parliament Office; but since 1815 the greater part of the private acts have been printed by the Queen's printers, and have contained a clause declaring that a copy so printed ' shall be admitted as evidence thereof by all judges, justices and others." These consist, almost exclusively, of inclosure, or inclosure and drainage and estate acts.

3. The last class of acts are those which still remain Private Acts unprinted: they consist of name, naturalization, divorce, " and other strictly personal acts, of which a list is always printed by the Queen's printers, after the titles of the other private acts.

A local and personal act, declared public, may be used Legal distinc-for all purposes, as a public general statute. It may be given in evidence upon the general issue, and will be judicially noticed, without being formally set forth. Nor is it necessary to show that it was printed by the Queen's printers, as the words of the public clause do not require it, and the printed copy of a public act is supposed to be used merely ibr the purpose of refreshing the memory of the judge, who has already been acquainted with its enactments. A private act, on the contrary, whether printed or not, must be specially pleaded, and given in evidence like any other record. If printed, the copy printed by the Queen's printers is received as an examined copy of the record; If not printed, an authenticated copy is produced from the statute rolls In the Parliament Office."' Since ' Manchester Stiptndiary Magistrate Acts, 53 Geo. III. c. 72; 7 8 Viet, c. 30. Maiichiislcr Warelvnising Act, 7 8 Vict. c. 31. 2 Phillipiib Amos, Gil.

Lord Brougham's act, however, tliis distinction between public and pi'ivate acts Avill be no longer maintained, as every act will be judicially noticed, unless the contrary be expressly declared; and the usual evidence clause will consecpiently be omitted from future private acts. Queen's By the Act 8 9 Vict., c. 113, s. 3, it is enacted " that printers' copies. j c pj jg f private and local and personal Acts of Parliament not public acts, if purporting to be printed by the Queen's printers " " shall be admitted as evidence thereof by all courts, judges, justices, and others, without any proof being given that such copies were so printed."

CHAPTER XXIX.

FEES PAYABLE BY THE PARTIES PROMOTING OR OPPOSING PRIVATE BILLS. TAXATION OF COSTS OF PARLIAMENTARY AGENTS, SOLICITORS, AND OTHERS.

Fees payable on The fecs which are chargeable upon the various stages private bills. private bills, and are payable by the several parties promoting or opposing such bills, have been settled in both houses. The tables of fees are well known to parliamentary agents; they are published in the standing-orders of the commons, and in the House of Lords they are separately printed and are readily accessible to parties interested.

It is declared by the commons, "That every bill for the particular interest or benefit of any person or persons, whether the same be brought in upon petition or motion, or report from a committee, or brought from the lords, hath been and ought to be deemed a private bill within the meaning of the table of fees;" and that "the fees shall be charged, paid, and received at such times, in such manner, and under such regulations, as the speaker shall from time to time direct' In both houses there are officers whose special duty it is How collected, to take care that the fees are properly paid by the agents, who are responsible for the payment of them."" If a parliamentary agent or a solicitor acting as agent for any bill or petition be reported as a defaulter in the payment of the fees of the house, the speaker orders that he shall not be permitted to enter himself as a parliamentary agent in any future proceeding until further directions have been given. In the House of Commons the whole of the fees were formerly collected and carried to a fee fund, whence the salaries and expenses of the establishment Avere and applied, partly defrayed; the balance being supplied from the consolidated fund. But by the 12 13 Vict. c. 72, all monies arisino; from the fees of the house are carried to the conso-lidated fund; and the officers are paid from the public revenues. In the House of Lords a considerable portion of the fees is appropriated to a general fee fund; but a part is still reserved for the particular use of officers, whose emoluments ai'e derived from that source.

In the case of Chippendall's Divorce Bill in 1850, the Divorce bill promoter petitioned to be allowed to prosecute the bill in!; er ' forma pauperis, and in both houses this privilege was conceded to him, on proof of his inability to pay the fees. The committee on the bill in the commons, to whom his petition had been referred, distinguished his case from that of the suitor for any other kind of bill, and considered that the remission of the fees would not afford a precedent in other parliamentary proceedings.

The last matter which need be mentioned in connexion Taxation of C06t9.

' Table of Fees. See supra, p. 508.

' See Report, 2oth July 1850; 105 Com. J. 663. In 1604 counsel was assigned to a party, in a private bill, in formd pcatpcris, he " being a very poor man." 1 Com. J. 241.

with the passhig of private bills, is the taxation of the costs incurred by the promoters, opponents, and other parties. Prior to 1825 no provision had been made by either house, as in other courts, for the taxation of costs incurred by suitors in Parliament. In 1825 an Act was passed to establish such a taxation in the commons; and in 1827 another Act was passed, to effect the same object in the lords. Both these Acts, however, were very defective, and have since been repealed. By the present " House of Commons" and " House of Lords Costs Taxation Acts," a regular system of taxation has been established in both houses, and every facility is afforded for ascertaining the reasonable and proper costs arising out of every application to Parliament.

Taxing officers. lu each liouse there is a taxing officer, having all the necessary powers of examining the parties and witnesses on oath, and of calling for the production of books or writings in the hands of either party to the taxation.

Lists of Lists of charges have been prepared, in pursuance of these

Acts, in both houses, defining the charges which Parliamentary agents and solicitors will be allowed to charge for the various services usually rendered by them.

Applications Any person upon whom a demand is made by a parlia- I'or taxation. ' i r i ' mentary agent or solicitor, lor any costs incurred in respect of any proceedings in the house, or in complying with its standing orders, may apply to the taxing officer for the taxation of such costs. And any parliamentary agent or solicitor who may be aggrieved by the nonpayment of his costs, may apply, in the same manner, to have his costs To he within taxed, preparatory to the enforcement of his claim. The six niontlis i i i i i after delivery Client, howcvcr, IS required by the Act to make this application within six months after the delivery of the bill. But the speaker in the commons, or the clerk of the of bill.

' 6 Geo. IV. c. 69. 7 8 Geo. IV, c. 64.

10 11 Vict. c. 69; 12 13 Vict. c. 78.

These lists are printed for distribution to all persons wlio may apply for them.

parliaments in the lords, on receiving a report of special circumstances from the taxing officer, may direct costs to be taxed after the expiration of the six months.

The taxing officer of either house is enabled to tax the Costs of both whole of a bill b! t)ught before him for taxation, whether '"g t' 'er' """' the costs relate to the proceedings of that house only, or to the proceedings of both houses; and also other general costs incurred in reference to the private bill or petition. And each taxing officer may request the other, or the proper officer of any other court, to assist him in taxing any portion of a bill of costs. And the proper officers of other courts may, in the same manner, request their assistance in the taxation of parliamentary costs.

In the commons the taxing officer reports his taxation Certificate to to the speaker, and in the lords to the clerk of the parlia- of rvvarrajfr ments. If no objection be made within twenty-one days, confess judgment.

either party may obtain from the speaker or clerk of the parliaments, as the case may be, a certificate of the costs allowed, which in any action brought for the recovery of the amount so certified, will have the effect of a warrant of attorney to confess judgment, unless the defendant shall have pleaded that he is not liable to the payment of the costs.

The Oath of Fidelity.

I, A. B. do sincerely promise and swear, that I will be faithful, and bear true allegiance, to Her Majesty Queen Victoria. So helj? me God.

The Oath of Supbemacy.

I, A. B, do swear, that I do from my heart abhor, detest, and abjure, as impious and heretical, that damnable doctrine and position, that princes excommunicated or deprived by the Po2)e, or any authority of the see of Rome, may be deposed or murthered by their subjects, or any other whatsoever.

And I do declare, that no foreign prince, person, prelate, state, or potentate, hath, or ought to have, any jurisdiction, power, superiority, pre-eminence, or authority, ecclesiastical or spiritual, within this realm. So help me God.

The Oath of Abjuration.

I, A. B. do truly and sincerely acknowledge, profess, testify, and declare, in my conscience, before God and the world, that our sovereign lady Queen Victoria is lawful and rightful Queen of this realm, and all other her Majesty's dominions and countries thereunto belonging.

And I do solemnly and sincerely declare, that I do believe in my conscience, that not any of the descendants of the person who pretended to be Prince of Wales during the life of the late King James the Second, and since his decease pretended to be, and took upon himself the style and title of King of England, by the name of James the Third, or of Scotland, by the name of James the

Eightli, or the style and title of King of Great Britain, hatli any right or title-whatsoever to the crown of this realm, or any other the dominions thereunto belonging; and I do renounce, refuse, and abjure any allegiance or obedience to any of them.

And I do swear, that I will bear faith and true allegiance to her Majesty Queen Victoria, and her will defend to the utmost of my power against all traitorous conspiracies and attempts whatsoever which shall be made against her person, crown or dignity.

And I will do my utmost endeavour to disclose and make known to her Majesty and her successors, all treasons and traitorous conspiracies which 1 shall know to be against her or any of them.

And I do faithfully promise, to the utmost of my power, to support, maintain, and defend the succession of the crown against the descendants of the said James, and against all other persons whatsoever; which succession, by an Act intituled, "An Act for the further Limitation of the Crown, and better securing the Rights and Liberties of the Subject," is and stands limited to the Princess Sophia, Electoress and Duchess Dowager of Hanover, and the heirs of her body, being Protestants.

And all these things I do plainly and sincerely acknowledge and swear, according to these express words by me spoken, and according to the plain common sense and understanding of the same words, without any equivocation, mental evasion, or secret reservation whatsoever. And I do make this recognition, acknowledgment, abjuration, renunciation, and promise, heartily, willingly, and truly, upon the true faith of a Christian. So help me God.

The Oath to be taken by Roman Catholics. I, A. B. do sincerely promise and swear, that I will be faithful and bear true allegiance to her Majesty Queen Victoria, and will defend her to the utmost of my power against all conspiracies and attempts whatever, which shall be made against her person, crown, or dignity; and I will do my utmost endeavour to disclose and make known to her Majesty, her heirs, and successors, all treasons and traitorous conspiracies which may be formed against her or them; and I do faithfully promise to maintain, support, and defend, to the utmost of my power, the succession of the Crown, which succession, by an Act, intituled, ' An Act for the further Limitation of the Crown, and better securing the Rights and Liberties of the Subject," is and stands limited to the Princess Sophia, Electress of Hanover, and the heirs of her body, being Protestants; hereby utterlj" renouncing and abjuring any obedience or allegiance unto any other person claiming or pretending a right to the crown of this realm: and I do further declare, that it is not an article of my faith, and that I do renounce, reject, and abjure the opinion, that princes excommunicated or deprived by the Poi)e, or any other authority of the see of Rome, may be deposed or murdered by their subjects, or by any person whatsoever; and I do declare, that I do not believe that the Pope of Rome, or any other foreign prince, prelate, person, state, or potentate, hath or ought to have any temporal or civil jurisdiction,)Ower, superiority, or pre-eminence, directly or indirectly, within tliis realm. I do swear, that I will defend to the utmost of my power the settlement of property within this realm as established by the laws; and I do hereby disclaim, disavow, and solemnly abjure any intention to subvert the present Church Establishment as settled by law within this realm; and I do solemnly swear, that I never will exercise any privilege to which I am or may become entitled, to disturb or weaken the Protestant religion or Protestant government in the United Kingdom: and I do solemnly, in the presence of God, jjrofess, testify, and declare, that I do make this declaration, and every part thereof, in the plain and ordinary sense of the words of this oath, without any evasion, equivocation, or mental reservation whatsoever. So help me God.

2.   THE DECLARATION OF QUALIFICATION, BY MEMBERS OF THE HOUSE OF COMMONS.

I, A. B. do solemnly and sincerely declare, that I am, to the best of my knowledge and belief, duly qualified to be elected a member of the House of Commons, according to the true intent and meaning of the Act passed in the second year of the reign of Queen Victoria, intituled, "An Act to amend the Laws relating to the Qualification of Members to serve in Parliament;" and that my qualification to be so elected is as set forth in the paper signed by me, and now delivered to the clerk of the House of Commons.

3. FORM OF CERTIFICATE TO AUTHORIZE THE SPEAKER TO ISSUE A WARRANT FOR A NEW WRIT DURING A RECESS.

Schedule of 24 Geo. III. sess. 2, c. 26.

We whose names are underwritten, being two members of the House of Commons, do hereby certify, that M. P., late a member of the said house, serving as one of the knights of the shire for the county of or as the case may be died upon the t" y oi'j is become a peer of Great Britain, and that a writ of summons liath been issued under the great seal of Great Britain to summon him to Parliament as the case may be, and we give you this notice, to the intent that you may issue your warrant to the clerk of the Crown, to make out a new writ for the election of a knight to serve in Parliament for the said county of or as the case may be in the rooiu of the said il7. P. Given under our hands this day of

of his limited authority, upon the conduct of debates, 241. 263. Appoints tellers on a division, 271. Votes on every question, but does not leave the vroolsack, ib.

Form in which he receives messages from the commons, 321. Reads messages under the royal sign manual, 332. Reads joint addresses of both houses, 340. The speaker of the House of Commons on his left hand, ib.

II. Of the House of Commons; 1. Generally:

Earliest mention of the office, 23. May have existed long before, ib. His rank, above all commoners, 196. When accompanied by the mace, can commit without previous order of the house, 86. Never adjourns the house but upon question; except for want of 40 members, 193. And on Wednesdays at 6 o'clock, 211.

2. Choice of Speaker:

Commons desired to choose a speaker, at the commencement of a new Parliament, and to present him for royal approbation, 168. Election of a speaker described, 170, 171. Royal approbation of the speaker elect, 171. Lays claim to the privileges of the commons,.56. 172. Retains the office for the whole Parliament, 172. Forms observed in the election of a speaker, on a vacancy occurring during a session, ib. Exceptions to the forms observed in electing a speaker, 173. Royal approbation refused, ib. First takes the oaths required bv law. 174.

3. His Duties and Authority: Form of a speaker's warrant for taking persons into custody, 65. No case until 1810 of its legal consequences being explained and recognised by a court of law, ih. Orders a person into custody who had assaulted a member, 85. Persons committed to custody by the speaker, 86, 87. Reads prayers in the absence of the chaplain, 174,. Formerly wrote letters to sheriffs to summon members to attend on calls of the house, 189. Counts the house after prayers, 191. Again counts it at four o'clock, ib. Adjourns the house without question first put, 192. Tells the house if notice taken, or it appears on division that 40 members are not present, ib. General view of his duties, 195. No provision for supplying his place when absent, 196. House adjourns, ib. Another speaker elected, ib. Effect of the different character of the office of speaker in the two houses upon their sittings, 196,197.

Votes of the house perused and signed by him, 200. Presents supply billsfor-royalassent with a speech, 208. 372. 426. Without any speech when Parliament prorogued by commission, 208. Does not attend at further prorogations, 209 and n. Adjourns house on Wednesdays at six o'clock without question put, 210. Orders members to take their places, 260. Restores silence, 261. Directs members to bring up bills, 351. Ancient practice in regard to speaker reading breviates of bills and sometimes the bill itself, 352. Reads so much of the royal speech as relates to the commons on the house proceeding to the consideration of supply, 413. Demands judgment on impeachments, 479.

Questions; proposed by him, 216. Put by him, after the close of a debate, 218. 223. But this act intercepted by the previous question being negatived, 218. Mode of putting questions, 223, 224; and collecting voices, 224. Questions again stated by, ib. Rules that a member's voice determines his vote, 225. Mode of stating amendments to questions, 227.

LONDON: PRINTED BY HENRY HANSARD, NEAR LINCOLN'S INN FIELDS.
PUBLISHED BY

Messrs. BUTTERWORTH,

LAW BOOKSELLERS AND PUBLISHERS,

PUBLISHERS TO THE PUBLIC RECORD DEPARTMENT.

8vo., 21s, cloth.

A PRACTICAL TREATISE on the LAW, PRIVILEGES, PROCEEDINGS and USAGE of PARLIAMENT. By Thomas Erskine May, Esq., of the Middle Temple, Barrister at Law, one of the Examiners of Petitions for Private Bills, and Taxing Officer of the House of Commons. Second Edition, enlarged and improved.

Book I. contains The Constitution, Powers and Privileges of Parliament.

Book II. Practice and Proceedings in Parliament; including the several Forms of Procedure in the conduct of Public Business, c. c.

Book III. The Manner of Passing Private Bills; showing the Practice in both Houses, according to the latest Standing Orders and the most recent Precedents.

tout's tm nf Cnr mrntinii3 h mral

Royal 8vo., 2Gs. boards.

A PRACTICAL TREATISE on THE LAW of CORPORATIONS in GENERAL, as well Aggregate as Sole.

INCLUDING

Municipal Corporations,

Railway, Banking, Canal, and other

Joint-Stock and Trading Bodies,

Dean and Chaj ters, Universities, Colleges, Schools, Hospitals, with

Quasi Corporations aggregate, as Guardians of the Poor, Churcli-wardens, Church-wardensand Overseers, etc., and also

Corporations sole, as Bishops, Deans, Canons, Archdeacons, Parsons, etc.

By James Grant, Esq., of the Middle Temple, Barrister at Law.

"The object has evidently been to render the work practically useful to persons in any way, as Officers or Members, connected with any Corporation; and we think that object is eminently answered. Vast research and diligence are displayed in the execution." The Times,

"We think the arrangement happy. Another feature in Mr. Grant's work is the honesty with which it has been compiled." Laio Magazine.

"A valuable Treatise on an important subject, ably and carefully executed." Legal Observer.

"In itself, and as a lawbook, Mr. Grant's work is unexceptionable." Lawtimes.

"The task has been admirably executed by Mr. Grant, whose Work will be henceforward cited as the Text Book of Corporation Law." Morning Herald.

LAW BOOKS PUBLISHED BY 8vo., One Guinea, cloth.

The MAGISTERIAL SYNOPSIS: comprising Summary Convictions and Indictable Offences, with their Penalties, Punishment, c., and the Stages of Procedure, tubularly arranged: together with all other Proceedings before Justices out of Sessions: adapted practically throughout to the provisions of Sir John Jervis's Acts; with Forms, Cases, Copious Notes and Observations, c. Third Edition, enlarged and improved. By George C. Oke, Assistant Clerk to the Newmarket Bench of Justices, Author of

The Magisterial Formulist."

In this edition the Statutes and Cases, c., are brought down to the close of the last Session, and references made in all cases to its Companion, "Oke's Magisterial Formulist," for the Forms to be used.

(Dkf H lllegistrrifil nrmiilist.

8vo., 21s. cloth.

The MAGISTERIAL FORMULIST, being a Complete Collection of Magisterial Forms and Precedents for practical use in all Matters out of Quarter Sessions, adapted to the Outlines of Forms in Jervis's Acts, 11 12 Vict. cc. 42, 43, with an Introduction, Explanatory Directions, Variations and Notes. By George C. Oke, Author of " The Magisterial Synopsis." The above Work is intended as a Companion to " Oke's Magisterial Synopsis," and maybe used with that or other Boolis of Magisterial Practice.

"Another of Mr. Oke's laborious productions which have recommended themselves by their practical character. A very copious Index gives ready access to whatever may be sought for." Law Times.

"The same care pervades the present elaborate Work as characterized the Author's earlier labours, and the utter uselessness of old forms since the passing of Jervis's Acts, render it of paramount utility." Britannia.

Mmnl m tljb lligjits tn Iji Ira Ijinrth.

8vo. 7s. boards.

A DISSERTATION on the RIGHTS to the SEA SHORES and to the SOIL and BED of TIDAL HARBOURS and NAVIGABLE

RIVERS, with especial Reference to Mr. Serjeant Merewether's published Speech upon the same subject. By James Jerwood, Esq., of St. John's College, Cambridge, M. A., and of the Middle Temple, Barrister at Law.

Svo., 5s. cloth,

AN IMPROVED SYSTEM of SOLICITORS' BOOKKEEPING, practically exemplified by a Year's supposed Business, with Directions for Posting, Balancing, Checking, c. Adapted to small, moderate and large Offices; to Partnership and sole Concerns. By George C. Oke, Author of " The Magisterial Synopsis" and " The Magisterial Formulist."

"Mr. Oke has rendered great service lo the profession in compiling the above admirably arranged work. The value and necessiiy of such a work as this to Solicitors is obvious, and we predict for it a speedy sale." Lav) Magazine.

"rhis is a very clever and extremely useful treatise. Such a work is of the highest value to Solicitors." Morning Herald,

"To the Practitioner we would recommend its purchase, and if he will follow out its instructions, he will, we are sure, always consider that the tritiing cost of the book was the best money he ever laid out." Legal Practitioner.

Sets of SOLICITORS' ACCOUNT BOOKS, prepared upon Mr. Oke's Plan, with the proper Headings, c., and of various degrees of thickness, may be obtained at the Publishers.

MESSRS. BUTTERWORTH, 7, FLEET STREET. i 3Kr. ix unt ltr ilirtt'0 lim Cnmmnitnnrij. Irrnnli drmtinii.

Four Vols. 8vo., Four Guineas, cloth, (dedicated, by permission, to iter majesty the qdeen.)

NEW COMMENTARIES on the LAWS OF ENGLAND, ill which are interwoven, under a now and original arrangement of the general subject, all such parts of the work of BLACKSTONE as are applicable to the present times; together with full but compendious expositions of the modern improvements of the law; the original and adopted materials being throughout the work typographically distinguished from each other. By HENRY JOHN STEPHEN, Serjeant at Law. Second Edition. Prepared for the Press by James Stephen, Esq., Barrister at Law.

"The correction of the Work in reference to the new Statutes and Cases and the revision q' the press in general, have been confided by the Author to his Son; his oivn retirement from professional practice, and the transfer of his attention to official duties, rendering him less competent than formerly to labours of' that description. But the sheets have been invariably laid before him during the progress of the printing, and he feels himself able to vouch for their accuracy." Extract from the Author's Advertisement to the present Edition.

"Taking the book" (Stephen) " as a whole it is the best commentary on a great subject we ever read. Whatever in the former book" (Blackstone) " was important is fully retained and further explained, what was immaterial is passed by, what was confused and intricate is made plain, what was illogical is reduced to reason, and what was chaotic to order. The student will reap a rich harvest of knowledge from these volumes; we recommend every member of the profession, be he young or old in it, to read them." Law Magazine.

"This work, now that it has been carried out to the fullest extent, and all the volumes been siniultaneo isly put forth to the world in one entire edition (itself considerably altered by correction and revision from the first), challenges comparison not only with what may be termed ' other editions of Blackstone," but with Blackstone itself." The Times.

"We must frankly say, preferring upon the whole Serjeant Stephen's writing to Blackstone's, that we think the book before us a somewhat better book than Blackstone's would have been, could that learned judge have survived, with his likings and dislikings, to write in our day. It is a monument of conscientious labour, of diligent and scrupulous care, and of acute professional learning, with a wider scope and range than is common in Westminster Hall." Tlie Eiamiuer.

"We are proud to recognize the merits of a performance which we think will redound to the credit of the authoi's, while it is eminently calculated to accomplish a destiny which has been hitherto denied to all new ' Blackstones' tliat, namely, oi superseding the old one." The Morning Chronicle.

"The attempt, we repeat, has been eminently and deservedly successful: for Serjeant Stephen has produced a work which need not fear any comparison which can be made between it and its predecessor (Blackstone's Commentaries), cither with respect to style, learning, or general accuracy; whilst, we are bound to say, in the philosophical arrangement of the general subject it is decidedly superior." The Morning Post.

(tmilm u r. frrjrnnt ltr ilini'3 Mm C niiimnitarirh.

8vo., 10s. 6d. cloth.

QUESTIONS for LAW STUDENTS on the SECOND EDITION of Mr. SERJEANT STEPHEN'S NEW COMMENTARIES on the LAWS of ENGLAND. By James Stephen, Esq., of the Middle Temple, Barrister at Law.

"We have already strongly recommended Mr. Serjeant Stephen's Commentaries. To students who have an earnest desire of reaping the store of learning to he found there, these Questions, which are neatly put and very carefully framed, will be invaluable." Law Magazine.

LAW BOOKS PUBLISHED BY 2 thick vols, royal 8vo. 3 boards. A COMPLETE SERIES of PRECEDENTS IN CONVEYANCING and of COMMON and COMMEKCIAL FORMS, in

Alphabetical Order, adapted to the Present State of the Law and Practice of Conveyancing, with copious Prefaces, Observations, and Practical Notes on the several Deeds. To which are added the late Real Property Acts, with Notes, and the Decisions thereon. The Third Edition, revised and greatly enlarged. By George Crabb, Esq. of the Inner Temple, Barrister at Law.

This Work, which embraces both the Principles and Practice of Conveyancing, contains likewise evert description of Instrument wanted for Commercial p lrposes. " Crabb's Precedents are already well known to the profession. Two editions have been exhausted in a very short period, a decisive proof of the estimation in which they are held, and how useful and satisfactory they have bt en found in practice. The Third Edition, just published, presents a multitude of improvements, giving to it almost the value of a new work. The original design has been largely extended both in number of precedents and prefatory matter. The Transfer of Property Act has received due attention, and it has been enriched with ample and learned notes. The work thus improved, is indeed something more than a mere collection of precedents: it is an able treatise on the Law of Real Property, illustrated by examples; and as such may be read with advantage by the student, as well as consulted by the practitioner." Law Times.

ItrhbE nil Cnjuijinte. nnrtji Mm, hq Italmiiii.

2 vols, royal 8vo. 2: 10s. boards.

A TREATISE on COPYHOLD, CUSTOMARY FREEHOLD, and ANCIENT DEMESNE TENURE; with the Jurisdiction of Courts Baron and Courts Leet; also an Appendix containing Rules for holding Customary Courts, Courts Baron and Courts Leet, Forms of Court Rolls, Deputations, and Copyhold Assurances, and Extracts from the relative Acts of Parliament. By John Scriven, Serjeant at Law. The Fourth Edition, embracing all the authorities to the present period, by Henry Stalman, Esq. of the Inner Temple, Barrister at Law.

"This Treatise is one of great practical utility, not a little enhanced by the care, industry and ability with which the present Editor, Mr. Stalman, has enriched and enlarged the original work." Law Magazine.

"This is a careful revision of a very valuable standard work." Legal Observer.

"Mr. Stalman, the editor of the present edition, has effected considerable improvements by the application of great industry guided by sound judgment." Law Times.

fotmm u 5lrtinti3 at jcaiii.

8vo. ICs. boards.

A PRACTICAL TREATISE on ACTIONS AT LAW; embracing the subjects of Notice of Action; Limitation of Actions; necessary Parties to and proper Forms of Action, the consequence of mistake therein; and the Law of Costs with reference to Damages. By Rowland Jay Browne, Esq. of Lincoln's Inn, Special Pleader.

"The most copious and most recent information is furnished upon every subject of which he proposes to treat, and the work, which is eminently useful to Common Law practitioners in all situations, is indispensable at Nisi Prius." Times.

MESSRS. BUTTERWORTH, 7, FLEET STREET. 5 ! lqrlvliniirn'0 S'lrm fjiaiirpni rnrtirr. (J"liirlr drmtinii.

12mo., l(js. boards,

THE NEW CHANCERY PRACTICE; comprisinrr all the Alterations effected by the RECENT ORDERS AND STATUTES; with Practical Directions, a Copious Selection of Modern Cases, and an APPENDIX OF FORMS. By Hubert Ayckbouhn. Third Edition, enlarged and carefully revised. By Thomas H. Ayckbourn, Esq. of the Middle Temple, Barrister at Law, and Hubert Ayckbourn.

"That which Archbold is to Common Law Practice Ayckbourn is to that of Chancery. The one work is quite as indispensable as the other. The present edition of Ayckbourn is a decided improvement on the former one." Law Magazine.

"In the new edition, which has almost doubled its original size, Mr. Ayckbourn has collected the decisions upon the New Orders with his accustomed care, and the work is now the completest Handbook of Chancery Practice which the profession possesses." Law Times.

(lutirstinns nn 2i rkhdttrii'H Cjianttrt l rattirf.

12mo., 6s. boards,

QUESTIONS for LAW STUDENTS on the THIRD EDITION of AYCKBOURN'S NEW CHANCERY PRACTICE. By John Swithinbank, Solicitor in Chancery.

Sngnb'3 de qiiittf Digrst ml 3iiki.

Royal 8vo. Vols. L and II. 2: '2s. boards (to be completed in Three Volumes).

An INDEX to the EQUITY CASES, not overruled or obsolete, reported in the House of Lords, Privy Council, and Courts of Equity in England and Ireland, from the earliest period down to the present time. By John Jagoe, Esq., Barrister at Law.

The First Volume contains a digest of all the decisions during the periods when Lords Lyndhurst and Cottenham were Chancellors of England, and Lord Plunkett and Sir Edward Sugden Chancellors of Ireland. This Volume separately, 1: Us. 6d. boards.

The Second Volume gives the Pleading and Practice Cases, and the Rules, Orders and Statutes, including those of the last Session of Parliament, and the Rules founded on them, with the table of Cases for both volumes, forming a complete Equity Practice: So the First and Second Volumes are, in themselves, a perfect work, invaluable to Equity Practitioners, and to those who have Chitty's Equity Lidex, as they continue that work to 1850. This Vol. separately, 1: Is. bds.

The Third Volume, containing the early decisions which relate to the Principles of Equity, not overruled or obsolete, will be ready for delivery during Easter Term.

"This is a most valuable book, both to the Practitioner and the Student. If Mr. Jagoe completes the work according to his design, of which his First Volume is a favourable example, he will confer great benefit on the Profession." Legal Observer.

"The Lawyer and Student have been without means of reference to that mass of later cases which has grown up in the interval out of the two additional Vice-Chancellors, and the revision of their decisions by tlie Lord Chancellors Lyndhurst and Cottenham. These cases contain much that is wholly new, as well as a searching investigation of the authorities that preceded them; and the Index of Mr. Jagoe will be found an acceptable work at a seasonable time. We safely recommend it as a successful accomplishment." Morning Chronicle.

"This arduous task has been most ably fulfilled. A nice discrimination has been evinced in dividing the cases and classifying them under their most appropriate heads. On the whole, we can earnestly commend the work to all practitioners in equity." The Sun.

"Mr. Jagoe's work is favourably distinguished from those of others who appear to think that the more cases that can be crammed into a law book the more valuable it becomes. The most useful law book is a compendium of cases, but they must be cases of authority." The Standard.

"A large amount of praise must be conceded to the learned compiler of this production for the care, the discretion, and the clearness with which he has digested the cases." The Observer.

LAW BOOKS PUBLISHED BY jbnntngtt nii! r xwn locttto it ITniu. Ikda imm, 2 closely printed volumes, 8vo.,

MONTAGU and AYRTON'S LAW and PRACTICE in BANKRUPTCY, as altered by the Recent Statutes, Orders, and Decisions; containing Forms, Precedents, and Practical Directions in Bankruptcy, with New Tables of Costs, c. c. The Second Edition. By John Herbert Koe, Esq. one of Her Majesty's Counsel, and Samuel Miller, Esq. Barrister at Law.

"We are glad to find that a New Edition has heen confided to the able pens and careful superintendence of Mr. Koe and Mr. Miller. They have produced a complete, accurate, and comprehensive statement, both of the Law and Practice, and great pains and labour have evidently been bestowed." Legal Observer.

A SUPPLEMENT to the above Work is in preparation, including the New Bankruptcy Consolidation Act, 1849, the New Orders, and all the Alterations to the latest period.

iunis's iijwa Cntirts (i nihurt 12mo. 8s. boards. A MANUAL of the LAW of EVIDENCE on the TRIAL of ACTIONS and OTHER PROCEEDINGS in the NEW

COUNTY COURTS. By James Edward Davis, Esq., of the Middle Temple, Barrister at Law.

"It appears to be a useful and well-aitanged manual." haw Magazine.

"A volume like the present appeared to be requisite in lieu of the ponderous works of Selwyn, Starkie, and Phillips. In this ' Hand-Book for the County Courts' the materials have been well-arranged and concisely stated, and we doubt not it will be found a very useful book for the practitioner." Legal Observer.

"We have examined the work and can speak of it in terms of approval; every page of it testifies that the author has industriously applied himself to compress, within a small compass, as much information as possible." County Courts Chronicle.

Sniiit Itntk Cnmpmra EBgibtrntinu M, ISmo. 3s. 6d. boards. An ACT (7 8 Vict. c. 110,) for the REGISTRATION, INCORPORATION and REGULATION of JOINT STOCK COMPANIES; with Preface and Index, by James Burchell, Esq. and an Analysis, by Charles Rann Kennedy, Esq. Barrister at Law.

vigil's Mm piim, 2 vols. 8vo. 2: 8s. boards.

An ABRIDGMENT of the LAW of NISI PRIUS. By

P. B. Leigh, Esq. Barrister at Law. Author of " A Treatise on the Poor Laws," c.

"It enters with a very laborious minuteness into the details of those branches of the law of which it treats, and deserves great praise for the industry with which the cases are collected, and the accuracy evinced in the absti-act of them. The cases on the New Rules, and on the modern law in general, are very carefully collected, and the Work altogether is a very practical and a very useful Book." Jurist,

MESSRS. BUTTERWORTH, 7, FLEET STREET.

intrigntt nii Binrint Snsurniitrb. I'l 3. l rrrbitjj.

Royal 8vo., 30. s. boards,

A TREATISE on the LAW of MARINE INSURANCES.

By Balthazard Marie Emerigon. Translated from the French, with an Introduction and Notes. By Samuel Meredith, Esq.

"This Treatise on Insurances by Einerigon is not merely a book on French Law, but a Code of universal law recognized iu every civilized comnuxnity. The Translation is admirably done, and reflects great credit upon Mr. Meredith." Law Times.

"We think the profession is much indebted to Mr. Meredith for his able translation of that eminent author (Emerigon)." Legal Observer.

"The publisher and translator are both entitled to praise for having provided the profession with a most useful authority in the most convenient form. No insurance lawyer will neglect to become possessor of this edition of Emerigon." Standard., (innuing u nlls.

8vo. 9s. boards.

A PRACTICAL TREATISE on the LAW of TOLLS; and tlierein of Tolls Thorough and Traverse; Fair and Market Tolls; Canal, Ferry, Port and Harbour Tolls; Turnpike Tolls; Rateability of Tolls; Exemption from Tolls; Remedies and Evidence in Actions for Tolls. By Frederick Gunning, Esq. of Lincoln's Inn, Barrister at Law.

2 vols, royal 8vo. 2: 5s. boards.

A TREATISE on POWERS, with SUPPLEMENT, containing the New Enactments and Cases down to 1841. By Henry Chance, Esq. Barrister at Law.

The Supplement may be had separately, price Gs. boards.

lit Ott ntt i tm nf tjjt Itnrlt cl itjinngl 12mo., 8s. cloth,

The LAW relating to TRANSACTIONS on the STOCK EXCHANGE. By Henry Keyser, Esq., of the Middle Temple, Barrister at Law.

8vo. IGs. boards. A TREATISE upon the LAW and PRACTICE of the COURT for RELIEF of INSOLVENT DEBTORS; with an Appendix, contain-ino- all the Acts of Parliament, Rules of Court, Forms, Tables of Costs, c. The Second Edition, much enlarged. By Edward Cooke, Esq. Barrister at Law.

ijnlc'H Cnniinnii Xnui.

Royal 8vo. 1: los. boards.

The HISTORY of the COMMON LAW of ENGLAND, and an Analysis of the Civil Part of the Law; by Sir Matthew Hale. The Sixth Edition, with Additional Notes and References, and some Account of the Life of the Author. By Charles Runnington, Serjeant at Law.

LAW BOOKS PUBLISHED BY l ills nil Cirtumstntitinl fnteua. fljirii (!? Mtrnii.

8vo., 9s. boards,

An ESSAY on the PRINCIPLES of CIRCUMSTANTIAL EVIDENCE, illustrated by Numerous Cases. Third Edition. By William Wills, Esq.

"I have read this Essay thoroughly and with great satisfaction. It is written clearly, strongly and elegantly, with conclusive evidence of much research and profound reflection." The late Chancellor Kent.

"The popularity which we ventured to prophesy for it has been achieved. The Third Edition is before us; and we heartily congratulate Mr. Wills on the reputation he has so worthily won." Law Times.

uwb u mm m knxwn, 1 thick vol. 8vo. II. 8s. boards.

The PRACTICE of the ECCLESIASTICAL COURTS, with Forms and Tables of Costs. By Henry Charles Coote, Proctor in Doctors' Commons, c.

"Ecclesiastical Practice is now for the first time made the subject of a formal and elaborate treatise, and it has remained for Mr. Coote, by a combination of industry and experience, to give to the profession a work which has long been wanted, but which so few are competent to supply." Law Times.

8vo. IBs. boards.

The COMMON LAW of KENT; or the CUSTOMS of GAVELKIND. With an Appendix concerning Borough English. By T. Robinson, Esq. The Third Edition, with Notes and References to modern Authorities, by John Wilson, Esq. Barrister at Law.

Sioiiiiilirftgi m 3Biiirs ml Sinrrnls.

8vo. 16s. boards. A PRACTICAL TREATISE on the LAW of MINES and MINERALS; comprising a detailed Account of the respective Rights, Interests, Duties, Liabilities, and Remedies of Landowners, Adventurers, Agents, and Workmen; and of the Local Customs of Derbyshire, Cornwall, and Devon. With an Appendix of Legal Forms, relating to Grants, Leases, Transfers, Partnerships, and Criminal Proceedings. By William Bain-bridge, Esq. Barrister at Law.

lib MM C krk's Slssistnnt.

12mo. 6s. cloth.

The ARTICLED CLERK'S ASSISTANT; or, GUIDE to the EXAMINATION: containing a Series of Questions and Answers relative to Real Property, and the Theory and Practice of Conveyancing. By William Gardnor, Esq., and revised by the late Charles Barton, Esq.

i n ttpm Slnglirnnnrimi.

Royal 8vo. 1: 4s. boards.

A DIGEST of PRINCIPLES of ENGLISH LAW; arranged in the order of the Code Napoleon, with an Historical Introduction. By George Blaxland, Esq.

MESSRS. BUTTERWORTH, 7, FLEET STREET. 9 fiuu'n jcigigrn ijiirnl Cjinrt nf lavkl: Jrn irrtt.

On a large sheet, 6s. coloured.

A LEGIGRAPHICAL CHART of LANDED PROPERTY in ENGLAND from the time of the Saxons to the present ra, displaying at one view the Tenures, Mode of Descent, Power and Alienation of Lands in England at all times during the same period. By Charles Fearne, Esq. of the Inner Temple, Barrister at Law.

ICnm ltttkttt'3 ibAh 12mo. 6s. boards. The LAW STUDENT'S GUIDE; containing an Historical Treatise on each of the Inns of Court, with their Rules and Customs respecting Admission, Keeping Terms, Call to the Bar, Chambers, c., Remarks on the Jurisdiction of the Benchers, Observations on the Study of the Law, and other useful Information. By P. B. Leigh, Esq. of Gray's Inn. Barrister at Law.

nmn's nrnih nf ddrigiiml loill 2s. 6d. boards.

The COMMON FORMS and RULES for Drawing an ORIGINAL BILL in CHANCERY, as directed by the New Orders of Court, and Reported Cases. Carefully collected by G. Farren, Jun. Esq. Chancery Barrister.

"The work has been very carefully compiled, and displays the industry, research, and skill in arrangement, for which Mr. Farren is distinguished." Legal Obierver.

Cljittij's Cnmmtrrinl tm, 4 vols, royal 8vo. 6: 6s. boards. A TREATISE on the LAW of COMMERCE and MANUFACTURES, and the Contracts relating thereto; with an Appendix of Treaties, Statutes, and Precedents. By Joseph Chitty, Esq. Barrister at Law.

This work embraces the whole Law of Foreign Commerce and Internal Trade, from the most general and extensive provisions to the minutest details of private contracts, together with the Forms and Precedents of every kind of legal instrument in use or required within the ample range of this department of British jurisprudence; and will be found a valuable acquisition to the learned profession, and an important addition to the library of the statesman, the merchant, and the manufacturer.

lurfsbt's C nitimtrrinl mlm.

Vols. 1 to 7, 8vo. 6: 15s. boards. A Complete Collection of the TREATIES and CONVENTIONS, and RECIPROCAL REGULATIONS, at present subsisting between GREAT BRITAIN and FOREIGN POWERS, and of the Laws, Decrees, and Orders in Council concerning the same, so far as they relate to Commerce and Navigation, to the Repression and Abolition of the Slave Trade, and to the Privileges and Interests of the Subjects of the High Contracting Parties; compiled from Authentic Documents. By Lewis Hertslet, Esq. Librarian and Keeper of the Papers, Foreign Office.

LAW BOOKS PUBLISHED BY Irant 's Hubs nf 51tiimiig. 'Brniilr deWtinn.

12mo. 12s. boards.

A TREATISE on the NEW RULES of PLEADING. By Charles Rann Kennedy, Esq. Barrister at Law. Second Edition, with great Additions.

flbl u Drnming Xcgnl Snstrumbnts.

8vo. 10s. cloth.

A PRACTICAL TREATISE on the ANALOGY between LEGAL and GENERAL COMPOSITION, intended as an Introduction to the drawing of Legal Instruments, Puwic and Private. By S. H. Gael, Esq. Barrister at Law.

12nio. 7s. boards. A PRACTICAL TREATISE on LIFE ASSURANCE; in which the Statutes and Judicial Decisions affecting unincorporated Joint Stock Companies are briefly considered and explained; including Remarks on the different Systems of Life Assurance Institutions; the Premiums charo-ed, and the increased Expectations of Human Life. To which is added, a comparative View of the various Systems and Practices of Assurance Offices; with useful and interesting Tables, c. c-c. Second Edition. By Frederick Blatney, Esq. Author of "A Treatise on Life Annuities."

8vo. 1: Is. boards.

A TREATISE on the LAW of SHERIFF, with Practical Forms and Precedents. By Richard Clarke Sewell, Esq. D. C. L. Barrister at Law, Fellow of Magdalen College, Oxford.

3f5iilling'0 tm nf meutilt Ittnimts.

12mo. 9s. boards.

A PRACTICAL COMPENDIUM of the LAW and USAGE of MERCANTILE ACCOUNTS: describing the various Rules of Law affecting them, the ordinary Mode in which they are entered in Account Books, and the various Forms of Proceeding, and Rules of Pleading, and Evidence for their Investigation, at Common Law, in Equity, Bankruptcy and Insolvency, or by Arbitration. With a SUPPLEMENT, containing the Law of Joint Stock Companies' Accounts, and the Legal Regulations for their Adjustment under the Winding-up Acts of 1848 and 1849. By Alexander Pulling, Esq. of the Inner Temple, Barrister at Law.

12nio. 4s. boards.

A REPORT of the BREAD STREET WARD SCRUTINY; with Introductory Observations, a Copy of the Poll, and a Digest of the Evidence, Arguments, and Decisions in each Case. By W. T. Haly, Esq.

MESSRS. BUTTERWORTH, 7, FLEET STREET.

8vo. 14s. boards.

A PRACTICAL TREATISE on the LAW of ADVOW-

SONS. By John Mirehouse, Esq. of Lincoln's Inn, Barrister at Law.

: iilliiig u tjit tm nf Xnnkn. Irrnia imm, 1 vol. 8vo. 18s. boards.

A PRACTICAL TREATISE on the- LAWS, CUSTOMS, USAGES and REGU-LATIONS of the CITY and PORT of LONDON, with Notes of the various Charters, By-Laws, Statutes, and Judicial Decisions by which they are established. Second Edition, with considerable Additions, and a SUPPLEMENT containing the LON-DON CORPORATION REFORM ACT, 1849, and the City Election Act, 1725; with Introductory Comments, Explanatory Notes, and the Statutes verbatim. By Alexander

Pulling, Esq. of the Inner Temple, Barrister at Law. The SUPPLEMENT may be had separately, price Is. 6d. sewed.

Itrirfs (S.) Cnjitijinlh ((JEfrnnrliiiitinrtit Slrl 12mo. 6s. 6d. boards.

The COPYHOLD and CUSTOMARY TENURE ACT, 4 5 Victoria, c. 85, with Analytical Notes and Index; also the Forms of Agreement as settled by the Commissioners, c. By John Scriven, Esq. Barrister at Law.

Svo. 18s. extra boards.

A REPORT of the PROCEEDINGS of the HOUSE of LORDS, on the CLAIMS of the BARONY of GARDNER: with an Appendix, containing a Collection of Cases illustrative of the Law of Leo-i-timacy. By Denis Le Marchant, Esq. Barrister at Law.

This Work contains the only authentic and detailed Beport of the celebrated Banbury Case which has yet been published.

Xiim nf (fuming, 23nrbT-rnring; Ijnrsrs, ki.

12mo. 5s. cloth.

A Treatise on the LAW of GAMING, HORSE-RACING, and WAGERS; with a Full Collection of the Statutes in force in reference to those subjects; together with Practical Forms of Pleadings and Indictments, adapted for the General or Professional Reader. By Frederic Edwards, Esq. Barrister at Law.

12mo. 5s. boards,

The HORSEMAN'S MANUAL; being a Treatise on Soundness, the Law of Warranty, and generally the Laws relating to Horses. By R. S. Surtees, Esq.

LAW BOOKS PUBLISHED BY 3 iillrag's tm nf Mni Itnrlt (Tnmiiniibb' 5lrtntittth.

12mo., 3s.6d. boards,

The LAW of JOINT STOCK COMPANIES' ACCOUNTS, and the Regulations for their Adjustment in Proceediugs at Common Law, in Equity and Bankruptcy, and under the Winding-up Acts of 1848 and 1849, intended as an Accompaniment to the "Law of Mercantile Accounts." By Alexander Pulling, Esq., of the Inner Temple, Barrister at Law. " A correct analysis of the complex law it simplifies and explains." Law Mag.

um u tjR 3Knrriiigt ml llrgihtrittidtt 5lrts.

2mo. 6s. 6d. boards.

The MARRIAGE and REGISTRATION ACTS, 67 Will.4, caps. 85, 86; with Instructions, Forms, and Practical Directions for the Use of Officiating INIinisters, Superintendent Registrars, Registrars. Also a Supplement containing the Acts of 1837, viz. 7 Will. 4, c. 1, and 1 Vict, c. 22, with Notes and Observations, showing the Alterations made in the original Acts, with the New Rules of the Registrar General, up to the 11th of July, 1837; and a full Index. By John Sotjtherden Burn, Esq. Secretary to the Commission. Author of " The History of Parish Registers," " The Fleet Registers," c.

"This work will be found to contain numerous useful Forms not provided by the Act, and such directions as cannot fail to ensure a due observance of the provisions of these Acts. To such parties, in particular, it will prove a valuable Vade Mecum." Times.

SGrnmn'B (Djinnrtrti Ctisrh lit 36dt.

4 vols, royal 8vo. 4: 16s. boards. REPORTS of CASES in the HIGH COURT of CHANCERY, during the Times of Lord Chancellor Thurlow and the several Lords Commissioners of the Great Seal, and Lord Chancellor Loughborough, from 1778 to 1794, by William Brown, Esq. Barrister at Law. The Fifth Edition, with important Corrections and Additions from the Registrar's Books; from the Author's MS. Notes in his own Copy, intended for a further Edition; from various MS. Notes of the highest authority, by eminent contemporary and dignified Members of the Profession; together with Observations from the subsequent Reports on the Cases reported by Mr. Brown, and Decisions on the Points of Law to the present Time. By Robert Belt, Esq. Barrister at Law.

12mo. 2s. cloth, gratis lo Parchaseis,

A GENERAL CATALOGUE of LAW BOOKS, including all the Reports; intended as a Guide to Purchasers. By Messrs. Butterworth. ' Per ardua, Deojavente"

SCOTT'S NEW REPORTS in the COURT of COMMON PLEAS and in the EXCHEQUER CHAMBER, from Easter Term 1810 to Michaelmas Term 18H. 8 vols, royal Svo.

(These Reports are regularly continued by Messrs. Mannirig, Granger and Scott.)

FONBIiaNQUE'S

Mm Erprts in tjir Cmnnubsinnrrs' Cnurts nf 33iitiltrti itq.

This day is published, in royal Svo., 6s. sewed, Vol. I. Part I. of

REPORTS of CASES adjudicated in the SEVERAL COURTS of the COMMIS-SIONERS in BANKRUPTCY, under the Bankrupt Law Consolidation Act, 1849. Byj. W. M. Fonblanque, Esq., of the Middle Temple, Barrister at Law.

The original jurisdiction in Bankruptcy having, under the " Bankrupt Law Con-solidation Act," been transferred from the Courts of Chancery to those of the Com-missioners in Bankruptcy, these Reports have been commenced, as a collection of decisions under that statute. It is intended they shall consist of selected cases involv-ing important points of Law and Practice. Each number will contain a copious and thoroughly Practical Index of matters, and it is hoped the publication will prove a useful companion to all works on the Law and Practice in Bankruptcy.

IU inrt3 itt Dttttltrnjitn;.

ROSE'S REPORTS of CASES in BANKRUPTCY, 1810 to 1815. 2 vols. roy. Svo. BUCK'S, from 1816 to 1820. Royal Svo. GLYN and JAMESON'S, from 1820 to 1828. 2 vols. Svo. MONTAGU and MACARTHUR'S, from 1828 to 1830. Royal Svo. MONTAGU'S, from 1831 to 1832. Royal Svo. MONTAGU and BLIGH'S, from 1832 to 1833. Royal Svo. MONTAGU and AYRTON'S, from 1S33 to 1838. 3 vols, royal Svo. MONTAGU and CHITTY'S, from 1838 to 1840. Royal Svo.

MONTAGU, DEACON and DE GEX'S, in 1840, 1841, 1842, 1843, and 1844. 3 vols, royal Svo.

(These Reports are regularly continued by Mr. De Gex.)

Dr. llnhittbtttt's Mm Ikiirnltii lujinrts.

REPORTS of CASES argued and determined in the HIGH COURT of ADMI-RALTY, commencing with the Judgments of the Right Honourable Stephen Lushing-ton, D. C. L. By William Robinson, D. C. L. Advocate.

Vols. I. and II., and Vol. III. Part I., containing Cases decided from Michaelmas Term 1833 to Hilary Vacation 1850. 3: 16s. sewed.

(These Reports are in immediate continuation of Dr. Haggard's, and will be regularly continued.)

Sntrsf nf mm k tjjj (Jtrrlrsinstirnl ml M xiiim mb.

This Work contains carefully digested Reports of all Cases of importance in the Arches Court of Canterbury, the High Court of Admiralty, the Prerogative Court of Canterbury, the Court of Peculiars of Canterbury, the Consistorial Courts of London and other Dioceses, the Court of Surrogates, the Dean and Chapter and Archidiaconal Courts, the Admiralty Court of the Cinque Ports, the Court of the Master of the Faculties, c., together with the Decisions of the Judicial Committee of the Privy Council on Appeal from the Superior Courts of both Provinces, and from the Court of Admiralty.

Now complete in Seven Volumes, including all the Cases decided in the several above-named Courts from Easter Term, 1841, to Trinity Term, 1850. 14: 15s. sewed.

Any of the Volumes or Parts may be purchased separately.)

Slncicnt Haius antr Ifngttttitfjg of 3Englan"0; coniprii tng Eatosi enacted under the Anglo-Saxon Kings from thelbert to Cnut, with an English Translation of the Saxon; the Laws called Edward the Confessor's; the Laws of William the Conqueror, and those ascribed to Henry the First; also, Monumenta Ecclesiastica Anglicana, from the Seventh to the Tenth Century; and the Ancient Latin Version of the Anglo-Saxon Laws. With a compendious Glossary, c. Fol., 21.; or in 2 vols, royal 8vo. 1. 10s.

Ancient Haii) mti Biigtituteg o! Winlts; fompri ing Haluis isup posed to be enacted by Howel the Good, modified by subsequent Regulations under the Native Princes prior to the Conquest by Edward the First; and Anomalous Laws, consisting principally of Institutions which by the Statute of Ruddlan were admitted to continue in Force: with an English Translation of the Welsh Text. To which are added a few Latin Transcripts, containing Digests of the Welsh Laws, principally of the Dimetian Code. With Indexes and Glossary. Folio, 21. 4s.; or in 2 vols, royal 8vo. 1. 16s.

(Dedicated, by permission, to the Queen's most Excellent Majesty.

JHoniinunta? listovica JSi-itanmca, ov ibatcrialg for t)t 1 t! Stor) of Britain from the earliest period. Vol. I., extending to the Norman Conquest. Prepared and illustrated with notes by the late Henry Petrie, Esq., F. S. A., Keeper of the Records in the Tower of London, assisted by the Rev. John Sharpe, B. A., Rector of Castle Eaton, Wilts. Finally completed for publication, and with an Introduction, by Thomas Duffus Hardy, Assistant Keeper of Records. (Printed by command of Her Majesty.) Folio, Two Guineas.

"Sir Robert Inglis remarked, that this Work had been pronounced by one of our most competent collegiate authorities to be the finest Work published in Europe." Proceedings in Parliament, March Uth, 1850.

i tovv of t)c (Sobcrnment (Rccs. f otc of ilitatenalis for tl; c

History of Public Departments. Demy folio, 10s.

"It is remarkable that there should not exist in the language any complete account of the different Public Offices, the heads of which compose the Executive Government of the country." Companion to the British Almanac for 1847.

Cigcriptibc Catalogue of 3 ccortf Morfeg, pubiid; ctj unttct i)z

Authority of the Commissioners upon the Public Records, now on Sale by Messrs. Butterworth, Publishers to the Public Record Department. 8vo. M. sewed.

(Dedicated by permission to Lord Langdale.) 9 Catalogue of ti; e Eortjis Cijaucelloig, H tcperis of tl; e (xt? ii cal,

Masters of the Rolls, and principal Officers of the High Court of Chancery; with Notes and References to the Authorities. By Thomas Duffus Hardy, Assistant Keeper of Records. Roy. Svo. 20s. Only 250 copies printed.)

"The use of this volume will be obvious to all inquirers into the History of the Court of Chancer)', and it will be most helpful in general investigations, aifording the means of identifying dates with great precision." Law Magazine.

PREPARING FOR PUBLICATION. '

A SUPPLEMENT to JERVIS'S, andalso to SEWELL'S, Practical Treatises on the OFFICE and DUTIES of CORONERS; being a Compendium of the Recent Cases, Statutes, c., atfecting the Office of Coroner, practically arranged. By William Baker, Esq., Coroner for Middlesex.

An INDEX to the UNREPEALED STATUTES connected with the Administration of the Law in England and Wales, commencing with the Reign of William the Fourth, and continued up to the close of the Session 1850. By Thomas Archer, Esq.

The THIRD VOLUME of JAGOE's EQUITY DIGEST and INDEX.

A SUPPLEMENT to the THIRD EDITION of AYCKBOURN'S NEW CHANCERY PRACTICE, embodying the New Orders and Statutes of 1850, and the Cases upon them to the date of publication.

The LAW and PRACTICE of BANKRUPTCY as settled by the BANKRUPT LAW CONSOLIDATION ACT, 1849; with all the New Rules and Orders, and a Copious Index. By Samuel Miller and E. Vansittart Neale, Esqrs., Barristers at Law.

This work will be so framed that it maybe used either as a continuation or Supplement to the Second Edition of Montagu and Ayrton's Bankrupt Law, or as a separate and complete work CD the Law and Practice in Bankruptcy as at present existing.

A TREATISE on the RIGHT to the SEASHORE, and the SHORES of PORTS, HAVENS, and ARMS of the SEA, and of NAVIGABLE RIVERS, where the TIDE Ebbs and Flows. By Henry Alworth Merewether, Serjeant at Law.

The PRACTICE of the COMMON LAW COURTS, with Forms.

By James Stephen, Esq., of the Middle Temple, Barrister at Law.

jt This Work, which has been in active preparation for a considerable period, and which will form a condensed but comprehensive Book of Practice for Students and Practitioners of the Common Law, will be published uniformly with " Mr. Serjeant Stephen's New Commentaries," and " Stephen's Questions."

A MANUAL of the PRACTICE of the CRIMINAL COURTS. By R. Marshall Straight, of the Middle Temple, Esq.

The EIGHTH VOLUME of HERTSLET'S Complete Collection of Commercial Treaties and Conventions, c. between Great Britain and Foreign Powers.

The THIRD EDITION or SHELFORD'S LAW of RAILWAYS.

ROBINSON'S NEW ADMIRALTY REPORTS, Vol. III. Part IL

The SECOND PART of FONBLANQUE'S NEW REPORTS of CASES adjudicated in the Several COURTS of the COMMISSIONERS in BANKRUPTCY, under the Bankrupt Law Consolidation Act, 1849. These Reports uitl be regularly continued.)

The LAW MAGAZINE, or QUARTERLY REVIEW of JURISPRUDENCE, for May, No. 91, O. S., No. 27, N. S.

The Statutes, Law Reports, including the Lmv Journal, and Periodicals supplied, and the nsual Discnunl ntloived.

LAW LIBRARIES TURCIIASED OR VALUED.

A LARGE STOCK OF SECOND-HAND REPORTS IN LAW AND EQUITY, AT A CONSIDERABLE REDUCTION IN PRICE,

CONSTANTLY ON SALE.

Copies of Scarce Private Acts furnished from, a very Complete Series.

MESSRS. BUTTERWORTH, 7, FLEET STREET.

QUARTERLY REVIEW OF JURISPRUDENCE,

Commenced in 1828,

AND REGULARLY PUBLISHED ON THE FIRST OF THE MONTHS OF FEBRUARY, MAY, AUGUST, AND NOVEMBER, IN EACH YEAR,

AT SIX SHILLINGS A NUMBER.

This well-established Law Periodical is recommended to the Profession by 1. Articles on all subjects of prominent interest and practical usefulness to Practitioners. Among the Contributors are Judges, and many Lawyers of eminence.

2. Notes of all Leading Cases, explaining their practical effect.

3. A Quarterly Alphabetical Digest of all Cases in all Superior Courts of Law and Equity, c. carefully classed and indexed.

4. Statutes useful to the Profession, carefully abstracted and noted.

5. Reviews, or Short Notes of New Law Books of value, and List of all New Law Publications.

6. Events of the Quarter, comprising Rules of Court, Calls, Promotions, Obituary, c.

7. Parliamentary Papers of value, abstracted.

The Law Magazine thus affords a mass of information essential to the Practitioner at a cost of 24s. per annum, which can be obtained from no other publication at less than double that price.

The Number for February, No. 90 Old

CON L The New Code of Procedure of New York. IL The Office of Woods and Forests, Land Revenues, c. in. The Offices of the Lord Chancellor. Second Article." IV. On the Term Hereditament. V. Codes of Merchant Law. VI. Scotch Consistorial Law. Lord Broughams. The Scotch Judges and Bar.

Series, No. 26 New Series, is just published. tents:

VII. Sea Shore Rights. VIII. On Parties to Actions of Covenant. IX. The Law Amendment Society. X. The Papal Aggression. Short Notes of New Books. Notes of Leading Cases. Events of the Quarter. List of New Publications. Digest of Cases, c.

LONDON:

Butterworths, Law Booksellers and Publishers, 7, Fleet Street.

By whom Subscribers' Names will be received, and by all Booksellers.

An Annual Subscription of 24., if paid in advance to the Publishers, will ensure the delivery of the Law Magazine on the day of publication, postage free, for one year, in any part of the United Kingdom.

Lightning Source UK Ltd.
Milton Keynes UK
10 November 2010

162652UK00001B/141/P